ANCIENT EUROPE

from the beginnings of Agriculture
to Classical Antiquity

Hilary E. Flenley
April 1986

Ancient Europe

from the beginnings of Agriculture to Classical Antiquity

A SURVEY

BY STUART

PIGGOTT

FBA

EDINBURGH

at the University Press

EDINBURGH UNIVERSITY PRESS
22 George Square, Edinburgh
Printed in Great Britain
at The Pitman Press, Bath
First paperback edition, *1973*
ISBN 0 85224 252 2

Contents

Preface, page vii

List of Line Illustrations, page x

List of Plates page xix

1
BACKGROUND OF THE ENQUIRY
page 1

2
THE EARLIEST AGRICULTURALISTS
page 24

3
TRADE, METAL-WORKING AND CONSOLIDATION
page 71

4
CLIMAX AND CHANGE
page 113

5
NEW TECHNIQUES AND PEOPLES
page 168

6
THE CELTIC WORLD AND ITS AFTERMATH
page 215

Bibliography, page 267

Index, page 307

To my pupils, past and present

Preface

THIS BOOK is, in its present form, based on the Rhind Lectures in Archaeology given at the invitation of the Society of Antiquaries of Scotland in November 1962; behind these again lies my teaching of later European prehistory to Honours Students in Archaeology in the University of Edinburgh since 1946. The book does not pretend to be an outline prehistory of Europe within its stated limits of time and space, but is a personal estimate of certain factors which, I am persuaded, contributed to the eventual character of the ancient world which lay behind early historical Europe.

The necessity of ruthless selection and compression may at times have lead to an unfortunate but unintentional appearance of dogmatism, when space has not admitted of the use of constant qualifications, or of the definition of degrees of probability. I am, as was the grave Glanvill, well aware of the Vanity of Dogmatizing, and I trust that readers will mentally insert appropriate grades of dubiety where these are not overtly stated.

I have organised the book in a manner which I hope will permit of its being read on two levels. For the general non-specialist reader, the text and illustrations should give a sufficient idea of the nature of the theme and of the evidence, and of the development of the barbarian cultures side-by-side with the civilizations of antiquity, as their precursors and their subsequent counterparts. In conjunction, these formed the cultural pattern of the Ancient Europe of my title.

For the archaeological student however I have documented the text with rather full references and notes at the end of each chapter, and a select bibliography which should facilitate access to the original sources. I have naturally given preference to those in English, but the international nature of the subject results in a high proportion of entries in other European languages; here German or French sources have been selected where possible. Russian titles are given in translation. The book represents published and unpublished material known and accessible to me up to the end of June 1964.

The illustrations have been planned as a visual counterpart to the text so far as this is possible. I have deliberately stressed such evidence as that of house and settlement plans, not always presented to the general reader, and minimised other aspects, such as pottery typology, significant only to the specialist. While of necessity much that is familiar is re-illustrated, I have also taken the opportunity of including little-known but important material where possible. Dates have been given in all instances, but it must be remembered that these in many instances represent an approximation and at best are, in the nature of things, imprecise. It seemed desirable however to enable the reader to place the illustrated material quickly within some sort of a chronological framework. I have endeavoured to preserve a geographical balance of representation across the European continent, within the limits set by the intrinsic significance of the evidence, and by the varying standards of archaeological investigation in the different countries concerned.

I have been fortunate in securing the co-operation of my former pupil, Mrs D. D. A. Simpson, in the preparation of the line drawings, and of Mr I. G. Scott for the maps.

For help in obtaining photographs and for permission to publish, I am grateful to the following individuals and institutions: Mr C. Aldred and the Service des Antiquités, Cairo; Dr W. Angeli and the Naturhistorisches Museum, Vienna; Mr R. D. Barnett; Dr H. Behrens and the Landesmuseum, Halle; Mr I. M. Blake; Mr J. Brailsford and the British Museum; Mr M. B. Cookson and the Institute of Archaeology, London University; Dr G. E. Daniel; the Detroit Institute of Arts; Professor J. Filip and the Archeologiský Ústav, Prague; the Gloucester Museum; Mr D. W. Harding; the Hermitage, Leningrad; Dr H-J. Hundt and the Römisch-Germanische Zentralmuseum, Mainz; Institutul de Archeologie, Bucharest; Professors K. Jażdżewski and Z. Rajewski and the Muzeum Archeologiczne, Warsaw; M. R. Joffroy; Dr K. Kenyon and the Jericho Excavation Fund; Professor O. Klindt-Jensen and the Jysk Archaeologisk Selskab; the Magyar Nemzeti Museum, Budapest; Dr S. Marstrander and the Universitets Oldsaksamling, Oslo; Professor V. Mikov; Dr P. Modderman and the Rijksdienst voor het Oudheidkundig Bodemonderzoek; Dr W. Modrijan and the Landesmuseum Johanneum, Graz; Mr Malcolm Murray; the Musée des antiquités nationales, St Germain-en-Laye; the Narodni Musej, Ljubljana; Mr W. Neurath and Messrs Thames and Hudson; Dr J. Neustupný and the Narodni Muzeum, Prague; Nationalmuseet, Copenhagen; the National Museum of Malta; Dr A. Rieth and the Staatliche Amt für Denkmalpflege, Tübingen; Dr H. Savory and the National Museum of Wales; Dr M. Schröder and the Württemburgisches Landesmuseum, Stuttgart; Dr. H. K. St Joseph; Dr C. Strohm and the Bernisches Historisches Museum; Miss R. Tringham; Dr R. von Uslar and the Landesmuseum, Bonn; Dr D. van der Waals and the Rijksuniversiteit, Groningen; and Mr Cary Welch.

For the benefit of the general reader, radiocarbon dates have been given in the text as 'c. 2500 B.C.' rather than with the standard deviation, e.g. '2500 ± 110 B.C.'. In each case however a reference is given to the original publication of the date, where the margin of error and laboratory number will be found. Earlier dates from the Groningen Laboratory have been corrected in terms of the Suess effect, and the half life of 5570 ± 30 years accepted throughout, with one stated exception.

It is difficult to express thanks adequately and individually when so many scholars, all over the world, have indirectly or directly helped me at one time or another. But I owe particular gratitude to Professor R. J. C. Atkinson, Dr J. M. Coles, Mr J. D. Cowen, Dr G. E. Daniel, Dr M. Gimbutas, Mr J. V. S. Megaw, Mr T. G. E. Powell, Dr Anne Ross, Miss N. K. Sandars, and Dr A. M. Snodgrass. Successive generations of students have stimulated me with their questions and conversation, as I hope they will continue to do.

STUART PIGGOTT
University of Edinburgh

List of Line Illustrations

1. Middle Palaeolithic tent stance, c. 40,000 B.C., Molodova, South Russia. *29*
2. Upper Palaeolithic structure in cave, c. 30,000 B.C. Arcy-sur-Cure, France. *30*
3. Upper Palaeolithic settlement, c. 20,000 B.C., Avdeevo, South Russia. *31*
4. Mesolithic settlement, c. 5,000 B.C., Moita do Sebastião, Muge, Portugal. *32*
5. Mesolithic cave-painting of hunting scene, between 12,000 and 3,000 B.C. Cueva Remigia, Spain. *33*
6. Mesolithic cave-painting of bowmen, between 12,000 and 3,000 B.C., Cueva Remigia, Spain. *34*
7. Mesolithic cave-painting of bowmen, between 12,000 and 3,000 B.C., Cueva Remigia, Spain. *34*
8. Generalised distribution of a, wild goat; b, sheep; c, pig and d, cattle. *37*
9. Generalised distribution of 1, wild barley (*Hordeum spontaneum*); 2, wheat (*Triticum aegilopoides*); 3, wheat (*Triticum dicoccoides*). *38*
10. Mesolithic houses of the Natufian Culture, c. 9,000 B.C. 'Eynan, Palestine. *41*
11. Flint-bladed bone tools; 1, harpoon-head, Mesolithic, Denmark; 2–4, knives, Mesolithic, Lake Baikal; 5, reaping-knive, Natufian; 6–9, reaping-knives, Neolithic, Iran; 10, reaping-knife, Neolithic, Egypt; 11, Sickle, Neolithic, Karanovo, Bulgaria; 12, sickle, Bronze Age, Spain. *42*
12. Distribution of the earliest agricultural communities in East Europe (Starčevo-Körös and related cultures), c. 5,000 B.C. *43*
13. 1-2, single-room houses, perhaps sixth-seventh millennium B.C., Jeitun, Turkmenia; 3, agglomerated rooms, perhaps sixth millennium B.C., Tal-i-Bakun, Iran. *45*
14. Mud-walled houses, sixth-fifth millennium B.C., 1, Otzaki-Magula, Thessaly; 2, Karanovo I, Bulgaria; 3, Tsangli, Thessaly. *45*
15. Pottery model of house, log-built with gabled roof, fourth millennium B.C., Strelice, Moravia. *46*
16. Wattled and mud-walled houses at Karanovo, Bulgaria, from sixth to third millennium B.C.: 1, Period I; 2, Period II; 3, Period V; 4, Period VI. *47*
17. Pottery figurines, 1–4, and 'stamp-seals', 5-7, Starčevo-Körös culture, sixth-fifth millennium B.C., Hungary. *48*
18. Anthropomorphic pot, Tisza culture, fourth millennium B.C., Tüsköves, Hungary. *49*

19. Pottery figure of seated man, Tisza culture, fourth millennium B.C., Tüsköves, Hungary. *50*

20. Distribution of Linear Pottery settlements and finds, fifth millennium B.C. *51*

21. Excavated area of Linear Pottery settlement with post-holes and bedding-trenches of timber-built houses, ditches, pits, etc., fifth millennium B.C., at Sittard, Netherlands. *53*

22. Defended promontory settlement of Tripolye culture, fourth millennium B.C., at Habașești, Rumania. *54*

23. Settlement of Tripolye culture, fourth millennium B.C., at Kolomiishchina, Ukraine, U.S.S.R. *55*

24. Clay-rendered gable-end of house, Tripolye Culture, fourth millennium B.C., from Ariușd, Rumania. *55*

25. Clay anthropomorphic 'altar' (restored) of Tripolye culture, fourth millennium B.C., from Trușești, Rumania. *56*

26. Generalised distribution of agricultural communities in Europe, fifth millennium B.C.: 1, Starčevo and allied cultures; 2, Linear Pottery culture; 3, Impressed pottery cultures. *57*

27. Distribution of main sites of 1, Impressed Ware cultures, from fifth millennium B.C. onwards; 2, Chassey-Cortaillod cultures, fourth-third millennium B.C.; 3, Windmill Hill and allied cultures, late fourth-early second millennium B.C. *58*

28. Generalised distribution of agricultural communities in Europe, late fourth-early third millennium B.C.: 1, 'Western' cultures; 2, South Italian-Sicilian cultures; 3, TRB cultures; 4, Tripolye culture; 5, Boian, etc., cultures; 6, Area of settlement from fifth millennium B.C. *59*

29. Generalised distribution of megalithic chambered tombs in Western Europe. *61*

30. Megalithic chambered tomb, mid third millennium B.C., at West Kennet, Wiltshire, England. *62*

31. Generalised distribution of 1, Earliest TRB finds; 2, later settlement area; 3, Tripolye culture sites. *63*

32. Earlier forms of copper shaft-hole axes and axe-adzes, third millennium B.C., from Slovakia. *74*

33. Distribution of the earliest Transylvanian copper industry, third millennium B.C.: 1, shaft-hole axes and adzes; 2, copper ore sources. *75*

34. Distribution of metal pins with double-spiral heads, from late third millennium B.C.: 1, single find; 2, many finds. *75*

35. Distribution of earliest copper-working 'colonies' in Iberia, third millennium B.C.: 1, settlement; 2, cemetery; 3, settlement and cemetery. *76*

36. Bastioned town walls at 1, Los Millares, Spain; 2, Chalandriani, Syros; third millennium B.C. *77*

37. Objects from the Maikop barrow, South Russia, late third millennium B.C.: 1, 2, Silver vessel with animal frieze; 3, gold lion appliqué; 4, 6, gold bulls; 5, 7, copper adze and axe-adze. *82*

38. Burial with wheels of three carts, end of third millennium B.C., Tri Brata barrows, South Russia. *83*

39. Objects from burial at Bleckendorf, East Germany, end of third millennium B.C.: 1, Corded beaker; 2, bone hammer-headed pin; 3, copper awl; 4, copper tanged knife-dagger. *84*

40. Distribution of 1, Hammer headed pins; 2, Derivative forms; end of third millennium B.C. *85*

41. Generalised distribution of 1, Globular Amphorae-Single Grave-Corded Ware cultures; 2, Early Pit-Grave culture. *86*

42. Palisades of successively enlarged cattle kraal, Single Grave culture, end of third millennium B.C., at Anlo, Netherlands. *87*

43. Mortuary house under barrow, Corded Ware culture, end of third millennium B.C., at Sarmenstorf, Switzerland. *87*

44. Mortuary house under barrow, Corded Ware culture, end of third millennium B.C., at Seifartsdorf, East Germany. *88*

45. Mortuary house under barrow with burials in tree-trunk coffins, mid second millennium B.C., at Grünhof-Tesperheide, Schleswig-Holstein. *88*

46. House plans, late third millennium B.C.: 1, Dullenried, 2, 3, Goldberg, South Germany. *90*

47. Decorated plaster-work from gable-end of house, Tisza culture, fourth millennium B.C., Kökenydomb, Hungary. *90*

48. Pottery models of wagons (wheels restored except in 1): 1, Budakalász, Hungary, beginning of second millennium B.C.; 2–5, Transylvania, mid second millennium B.C. *93*

49. Distribution of early solid-wheeled vehicles in Europe: 1, Vehicles in burials, late third millennium B.C.; 2, Wooden wheels, c. 2000 B.C.; 3, Models of vehicles and wheels, late third-early second millennium B.C.; 4, Models, mid second millennium B.C. *94*

50. Bone cheek-piece of horse bridle, South Russian Timber Grave culture, early second millennium B.C., from barrow at Komarovka, middle Volga. *96*

51. Plans of temples, third millennium B.C., at Ggigantija, Malta. *98*

52. Objects from Bell-Beaker grave, beginning of second millennium B.C., at Prague, Czechoslovakia: 1, Beaker; 2, silver ear-rings; 3, copper tanged knife-dagger. *99*

53. Objects from Bell-Beaker grave, beginning of second millennium B.C., at Roundway, Wiltshire, England: 1, Beaker, 2, flint arrow-head; 3, archer's wrist-guard; 4, copper pin; 5, copper tanged knife-dagger. *99*

54. Generalised distribution and movements of Bell-Beaker cultures, end of third to beginning of second millennium B.C.: 1, 'Maritime' Group; 2, Eastern

and Central Groups; 3, Netherlands, Rhenish and Austrian Groups and Reflux derivatives; 4, Other Reflux derivatives. *101*

55. Objects from Bell-Beaker grave, beginning of second millennium B.C., from Radley, Oxon., England: 1, Beaker; 2, gold ear-rings; 3, flint arrow-heads. *101*

56. Copper beads, pins, rings, riveted knives and ingot-torcs, early second millennium B.C., from graves at Straubing, South Germany. *103*

57. Jet buttons with V-perforation, early second millennium B.C.: 1, Rudstone, E.R. Yorks, England; 2 and 4, Butterwick, E.R. Yorks; 3, Crawford Moor, Lanarks., Scotland. *104*

58. Burials of women, mid second millennium B.C., showing position of dress-pins and other ornaments. 1, Mühltal; 2, Wixhausen; 3, Asenkofen, South Germany. *105*

59. Limestone and alabaster figurines and clay model of woman on couch, third millennium B.C., from Hagar Qim and Hal Saflieni temples, Malta. *114*

60. Relief carvings of stylised female figures, one with hafted stone axe, in chalk-cut tomb of early second millennium B.C., Courjeonnet, Marne, France. *115*

61. Ground plan of ritual building or temple, mid third millennium B.C., at Tustrup, Jutland, Denmark. *116*

62. Circular Henge Monuments, Long Mortuary Enclosure and part of the ditches of a Cursus, end of third millennium B.C., at Dorchester-on-Thames, Oxon., England. *117*

63. House-plans, with post-holes for timber-framed buildings, earlier second millennium B.C., at 1, 2, Postoloprty, Czechoslovakia and 3, Crestaulta, Switzerland. *119*

64. Houses, stone and mud, of megaron plan: 1, third millennium B.C., at Dimini, Thessaly; 2, Middle Helladic culture, early second millennium B.C.; 3, Late Helladic culture, later second millennium B.C., both at Korakou, Greece. *122*

65. Objects of gold and silver, sixteenth century B.C., from the 'A' group of Shaft Graves, Mycenae, Greece: 1, silver vessel in the form of a Red Deer; 2, gold pendant; 3, 4, gold beads; 5, gold animal-headed pin. *124*

66. Bronze metal-hilted dagger and metal-shafted halberd, Únětice culture, mid second millennium B.C., from Lustenitz, Stubbendorf, East Germany. *125*

67. Wooden mortuary house under barrow, Únětice culture, mid second millennium B.C., at Leubingen, East Germany. *127*

68. Objects from male burial, Wessex culture, sixteenth century B.C., in Bush Barrow, Wilts., England: 1, 2, copper and bronze daggers; 3, bronze rivets, perhaps from helmet (twice scale); 4, bone mountings of sceptre; 5, gold belt-hook; 6, gold plate; 7, bronze axe-blade; 8, gold plate from clothing; 9, stone mace-head. *128*

69. Part of hoard, mid second millennium B.C., from Borodino, South Russia: 1, silver pin; 2–4, silver spear-heads with gold ornament; 5, alabaster mace-head; 6–9, jadeite battle-axes. *131*

70. Antler cheek-pieces for horse-bits, Füszesabony culture, second half of second millennium B.C.: 1, 2, Tószeg; 3, Pákozdvár; 4, Köröstarcsa, Hungary. *132*

71. Burial with solid-wheeled wagons, second half of second millennium B.C., at Lchashen, Lake Sevan, Armenian S.S.R. *133*

72. Decorated antler and bone objects, second half of second millennium B.C. 1–3, Alalakh, Turkey; 4, Cezavy; 5, Věteřov, Czechoslovakia; 6, 7, Vattina, Rumania; 8, Surčin, Jugoslavia; 9, Tiszafüred, Hungary; 10, Nitrianski Hradok, Czechoslovakia; 11, Vinča, Jugoslavia; 12, Kakovatos; 13, Asine, Greece. *135*

73. Distribution of Mycenaean objects and influences beyond the Aegean (hatched rectangle): 1, Pottery; 2, Metal-work; 3, Decorated bone-work; 4, Faience beads. *136*

74. Amber space-plate beads with complex perforations, sixteenth to fifteenth centuries B.C.: 1–4, 'B' group of shaft Graves, Mycenae; 5, Kakovatos, Greece; 6–9, Lake, Wilts., England; 10, Upton Lovell, Wilts., England; 11, Hundersingen-Weidenhang; 12, Mehrstetten, South Germany. *137*

75. 1, Main routes of trade and exchange in amber, mid second millennium B.C.; 2, complex-bored space-plates. *138*

76. Distribution of Late Mycenaean bronzes: 1, shaft-hole double-axes; 2, square-shouldered short swords, thirteenth-twelfth centuries B.C. *139*

77. Rock-carvings of chariots or carts, horses and wheels, late second-early first millennium B.C., at Frännarp, Sweden. *143*

78. Engraving of boat on sword-blade, mid second millennium B.C., from Rørby, Kalundborg, Denmark. *144*

79. Generalised map showing expansion of Urnfield cultures: 1, Thirteenth century B.C.; 2, Twelfth-tenth century; 3, Tenth-eighth century. *146*

80. Fighting with sword, dagger and spear. Impression from engraved gold ring, sixteenth century B.C., from the 'A' group of Shaft Graves, Mycenae, Greece. *147*

81. Distribution of bronze flange-hilted swords of 'Naue II' type, earlier Urnfield culture, late thirteenth-early twelfth century B.C. *148*

82. Timber-built settlement on island, Urnfield culture, twelfth-ninth century B.C., at the Wasserburg, Federsee, Buchau, South Germany. Earlier houses stippled, later in outline. *149*

83. Log-built house of second settlement, Urnfield culture, tenth-ninth century B.C., the Wasserburg, Federsee, Buchau, South Germany. *149*

84. Settlement with post-holes of timber-built houses, Urnfield culture, early first millennium B.C., at Perleberg, East Germany. *151*

85. Part of settlement with stone-built houses of three periods, Capo Graziano to Ausonian II cultures, early second to early first millennium B.C., Acropolis of Lipari, Aeolian Islands. *152*
86. Settlement with post-holes of timber-built houses, Deverel-Rimbury culture, twelfth-eleventh century B.C., at Itford Hill, Sussex, England. *152*
87. Part of settlement with post-holes of timber-built houses, Deverel-Rimbury culture, twelfth-eleventh century B.C., at Thorny Down, Wilts., England. *153*
88. Distribution of beaten bronze vessels, earlier Urnfield cultures, thirteenth-twelfth century B.C.: 1, Situlae; 2, Drinking cups; 3, Strainers. *154*
89. Stone-built settlement of the Nuraghic culture; three periods from fifteenth century (black) to sixth century B.C. (outline), at Su Nuraxi, Barumini, Sardinia. *156*
90. Stone-built towers, second half of second millennium B.C.: 1, 2, *nuraghi* at Muràrtu and Sa Còa Filigosa, Sardinia; 3, 4, *torri* at Foce and Balestra, Corsica. *157*
91. Pottery female figurines showing details of dress, second half of second millennium B.C.: 1, 2, Cîrna, Rumania; 3, Kličevac, Jugoslavia. *158*
92. Distribution of Urnfield culture bronze helmets, twelfth-eighth century B.C.: 1, Cap-helmets; 2, Bell-helmets; 3, Crest-helmets. *169*
93. Distribution of decorated bronze-work in the 'Situla' style, sixth-fifth century B.C.: 1, earlier; 2, later examples. *170*
94. Distribution of sites of Hallstatt salt production, seventh-fifth century B.C.: 1, certain; 2, probable sites. *170*
95. Distribution of Celtic place-names in *-briga*: 1, Classical; 2, post-Classical source. *172*
96. Distribution of Celtic place-names in *-dunum*: 1, Classical; 2, post-Classical source. *173*
97. Distribution of Celtic place-names in *-magus*: 1, Classical; 2, post-Classical source. *174*
98. Distribution of 1, 'Thraco-Cimmerian' horse-bits and harness mountings, eighth-seventh century B.C.; 2, Timber-grave cultures. *178*
99. Horse-bits and harness-mountings of 'Thraco-Cimmerian' and derivative types as probably worn, eighth-seventh century B.C., from Court-St-Étienne, Belgium. *179*
100. Distribution of 1, Hallstatt culture, seventh-fifth century B.C.; 2, Wagon-graves of Hallstatt C; 3, Wagon-graves of Hallstatt D; 4, Wagon-graves, C or D. *180*
101. Wagon-grave in plank-built chamber, showing remains of wagon, position of male and female burials, grave-goods, etc., Hallstatt D culture, sixth century B.C., Grave VI, the Hohmichele barrow, Heuneburg, South Germany. *183*
102. Wagon-grave in plank-built chamber, showing dismantled wagon, female

burial, imported Greek bronze crater and other objects, Hallstatt D culture, sixth century B.C., at Vix, Chatillon-sur-Seine, France. *184*

103. Constructional details of plank-built burial chamber, Hallstatt D culture, sixth century B.C., central grave of the Hohmichele barrow, Heuneburg, South Germany. *186*

104. Restoration of boat with 'sewn' planks, eighth century B.C., from River Humber at North Ferriby, E.R. Yorks., England. *187*

105. Distribution of Hallstatt imports and luxuries: 1, Imported Greek etc., bronzes, seventh century B.C.; 2, Imported bronzes and gold, sixth century B.C.; 3, Imported Greek pottery, seventh-sixth centuries B.C.; 4, Massaliote amphorae, seventh-sixth centuries B.C.; 5, Hallstatt C and D gold objects; M, Massalia; H, the Heuneburg; V, Vix. *188*

106. 1, Hill-forts with evidence of Scythian attack; 2, Stray Scythian finds, mainly arrow-heads; 3, Scythian settlement areas. *190*

107. Bronze crested helmet and corselet, Geometric Period, eighth century B.C., from male grave at Argos, Greece. *191*

108. Pair of iron fire-dogs in the form of stylised ships, Geometric Period, eighth century B.C., from male grave at Argos, Greece. *191*

109. Distribution of circular shields, eighth-seventh century B.C.: 1, V-notched 2, U-notched; 3, British and northern types. *194*

110. Representations of men and women fighting, Hallstatt culture, sixth century, incised on pottery from Sopron, Hungary. *197*

111. Representations of women, Hallstatt culture, sixth century B.C., incised on pottery from Sopron, Hungary: 1, spinning; 2, weaving on upright loom; 3, playing the lyre; 4, dancing; 5, riding on horse-back. *198*

112. Settlement with post-holes of timber houses and other buildings, Hallstatt culture, seventh-sixth century B.C., at the Goldberg, South Germany. *200*

113. Settlement with post-holes of timber houses and enclosing palisades, seventh century B.C., at Staple Howe, N.R. Yorks., England. facing p. *201*

114. Burnt traces of timber-built house in palisaded enclosure, Hallstatt D culture, sixth century B.C., below Tumulus IV, the Heuneburg, South Germany. *201*

115. Timber-framed rampart of hill-fort, late Urnfield culture, ninth-eighth century B.C., at Montlingerberg, Oberreit, Switzerland. *203*

116. The Heuneburg hill fort, South Germany, with bastioned stone and clay-brick wall, Hallstatt D culture, sixth century B.C. *205*

117. 'Inturned' gateways: 1, Stabian Gate, Pompeii, Italy, third century B.C.; Hill-forts, third-first century B.C., at 2, Nitrianski Hradok, Czechoslovakia; 3, Finsterlohr, Germany; 4, Fécamp, France; 5, Hembury, Devon, England; 6, The Trundle, Sussex, England; 7, St Catherine's Hill, Winchester, England; 8, The Wrekin, Shropshire, England. *206*

118. Distribution of early La Tène culture: 1, Imported bronze wine-flagons, fifth century B.C.; 2, chariot-burials. *208*

119. Timber-framed wall of hill-fort, middle La Tène culture, second century B.C., at Preist, Trier, Germany. *217*

120. Timber-framed wall of hill-fort, of *murus gallicus* type with iron nails, late La Tène culture, first century B.C., at Le Camp d'Artus, Huelgoat, France. *217*

121. Hill-forts of *oppida* status, late La Tène culture, probably first century B.C. in final constructional phase, at 1, Steinburg, Römhild; 2, Heidentränk-Talenge; 3, Donnersberg; 4, Dürnsberg: all Germany. *218*

122. *Oppidum*, late La Tène culture, probably first century B.C. in final constructional phase, at Zavist, Czechoslovakia. *219*

123. Post-holes of timber-framed buildings, late La Tène culture, second-first century B.C., in the *oppidum* of Manching, South Germany. *219*

124. Remains of burnt buildings with squared timbers, late La Tène culture, first century B.C., in the *oppidum* of Bibracte (Mont Beuvray), Autun, France. *221*

125. Stone-walled *oppidum*, middle La Tène culture, second century B.C., at Entremont, Aix-en-Provence, France. *222*

126. Stone-walled hill-fort and settlement, probably second-first century B.C., at Citania, Guimarães, Portugal. *224*

127. Painted designs on pots, Iberian culture, third century B.C., from south-east Spain. *225*

128. Painted frieze of warriors on pot, Iberian culture, third century B.C., San Miguel de Liria, Spain. *225*

129. Objects from middle La Tène grave, second century B.C., at Obermenzingen, South Germany: 1, sword in scabbard; 2, shield-boss; 3, spear-head; 4, surgeon's probe; 5, retractor; 6, trephining saw. (All iron: 4-6 twice scale of weapons). *228*

130. Section of ritual shaft with upright wooden stake; late La Tène culture, first century B.C., in the *viereckshanze* at Holzhausen, South Germany. *231*

131. Square sanctuaries and cemeteries, with post-holes of timber structures and enclosing ditches, La Tène culture, third-first century B.C., at 1, Heath Row (London Airport), England; 2, Écury-le-Repos; 3, Fin d'Écury; both Marne, France. *233*

132. Long ditch-enclosed sanctuary sites: 1, Urnfield culture, eleventh-tenth century B.C., at Aulnay-aux-Planches, Marne, France; 2, final Hallstatt culture, third century B.C., at Libenice, Czechoslovakia. *234*

133. Circular house plans in Britain, timber and timber-and-stone, third century B.C. to first century A.D., at 1, Little Woodbury, Wilts.; 1, Kestor, Devon; 3, Scotstarvit, Fife; 4, West Plean, Stirlingshire. *237*

134. Distribution of mature La Tène culture; 1, La Tène culture and influences; 2, Sword scabbards in Swiss style; 3, British derivatives; 4, Many scabbards. *239*

135. Engraved decoration on bronze wine-flagon, early La Tène culture, end of fourth century B.C., from near Besançon, France. *242*

136. Decorated pots, early La Tène culture, fourth century B.C.: 1, incised, from St Pol-de-Léon, Brittany; 2, painted, from Prunay, Marne, France. *242*

137. Constructional details of wooden chariot-wheel with single-piece felloe, iron tyre and nave-bushes, first century A.D., from Newstead, Scotland. *245*

138. Distribution of double-pointed iron ingots, late La Tène culture, second-first century B.C. *246*

139. Distribution of iron fire-dogs, late La Tène culture, first century B.C. *248*

140. Distribution of sites of La Tène salt production, fifth-first century B.C.; 1, certain; 2, probable sites. *249*

141. Ancient field-systems at 1, Plumpton Plain, Sussex, England, twelfth century B.C.; 2, Nordse Veld, Zeyen, Netherlands; 3, Figheldean Down, Wilts., England; Skøbaek Hede, Jutland, Denmark; all probably second-first century B.C., to first century A.D. *251*

142. Distribution of Roman wine amphorae imported into the late La Tène world. 1, Pre-Caesarian; 2, Caesarian-Augustan. *254*

143. Distribution of Roman bronze wine-flagons and pans imported into the late la Tène world, first century B.C.-first century A.D.: 1, flagons; 2, pans. *255*

List of Plates

I. Naturalistic plaster modelling over human skull, seventh millennium B.C., from Jericho, Palestine. (*Photo. Jericho Excavation Fund*) *op. p. 46*

II. (a) Square wattle-and-mud-walled houses, Starčevo-Körös culture, sixth millennium B.C. lowest level of 'tell' of Karanovo, Bulgaria. (*Photo. Mikov*)
(b) Section through 'tell', sixth-second millennium B.C., at Karanovo, Bulgaria. (*Photo. author*) *op. p. 47*

III. Houses of Linear Pottery culture, showing as post-holes and bedding-trenches under excavation, fifth millennium B.C., at (a) and (b), Bylany, Czechoslovakia (*Photos. Ruth Tringham*); (c), Elsloo, Netherlands. (*Photo. Rijksdienst voor het Oudheidkundig Bodemonderzoek*) *op. p. 50*

IV. Pottery figures of man and woman, fourth millennium B.C., from grave at Cernavoda, Rumania. (*Photo. Institutul de Arheologie, Bucharest*) *op. p. 51*

V. (a) Air view of stone alignments, early second millennium B.C., at Carnac, Brittany, France. (*Photo. Lapie*) *op. p. 62*
(b) Megalithic chambered tomb, second millennium B.C., at Essé, Brittany, France. (*Photo. Daniel*) *op. p. 62*

VI. Carving of stylised female figure at entrance to chalk-cut chambered tomb, early second millennium B.C., at Coizard, Marne, France. (*Photo. Louis*) *op. p. 63*

VII. Carving of designs including stylised stone axe-blades, on upright stone of megalithic chambered tomb, early second millennium B.C., at Gav'r Inis, Brittany, France. (*Photo. Le Rouzic*) *op. p. 70*

VIII. Stag and bull in copper, gold and silver, late third millennium B.C., Alaca Hüyük Royal Tombs, Turkey. (*Photos. Hirmer*) *op. p. 71*

IX. (a) Single-piece wooden wheel, c. 2000 B.C., from De Eese, Overyssel, Netherlands. (*Photo. Centrale Photodienst, Rijksuniversiteit Groningen*) *op. p. 96*
(b) Timber corduroy roadway in bog, c. 2000 B.C., at Nieuw Dordrecht, Drenthe, Netherlands. (*Photo. Biologisch-Archaeologisch Instituut, Groningen*) *op. p. 96*

X. (a) Pottery model of solid-wheeled wagon, Baden culture, late third millennium B.C., from grave at Budakalàsz, Hungary. (*Photo. Magyar Nemzeti Museum*) *op. p. 97*
(b) Rectangular wattled-and-mud-walled houses, Gumelniţa culture, mid fourth millennium B.C.; Phase VI of the 'tell' of Karanovo, Bulgaria. (*Photo. Mikov*) *op. p. 97*

XI. (a) Interior façade in rock-cut temple, third millennium B.C., the Hypogeum, Hal Saflieni, Malta. *following p. 112*

(b) Stone carving in temple, third millennium B.C., at Hal Tarxien, Malta. (*Both photos. National Museum of Malta*) *following p. 112*

XII. (a) Pottery Bell-Beaker, beginning of second millennium B.C., from West Kennet Long Barrow, Wilts., England. (*Photo. Malcolm Murray*)
(b) Wattled-and-mud-walled house, rectangular with apsidal end, end of third millennium B.C., Phase VII of the 'tell' of Karanovo, Bulgaria. (*Photo. Mikov*) *following p. 112*

XIII. (a) Henge Monument with fallen stones, early second millennium B.C., Arbor Low, Derbyshire, England. (*Photo. H. K. St Joseph*)
(b) Excavated Henge Monument showing ditches and ritual pits, late third millennium B.C., Site 1, Dorchester-on-Thames, Oxon., England. (*Photo. Institute of Archaeology, London University*) *following p. 112*

XIV. Gold mask of bearded man, profile view, Mycenaean culture, sixteenth century B.C., from Shaft-Grave V, Mycenae, Greece. (*Photo. Hirmer*) *following p. 112*

XV. Stone stela with relief carvings including chariot scene, Mycenaean culture, sixteenth century B.C., from Shaft Grave V, Mycenae, Greece. (*Photo. Hirmer*) *op. p. 128*

XVI. (a) Fragment of gold dagger, mid second millennium B.C., from Persinari-Ploești, Rumania. (*Photo. Institutul de Arheologie, Bucharest*) *op. p. 129*
(b) Gold armlet, pins, ear-rings and bead, Únětice culture, mid second millennium B.C., from grave at Leubingen, East Germany. (*Photo. Landesmuseum, Halle*) *op. p. 129*

XVII. (a) Two views of gold cup, mid second millennium B.C., from Fritzdorf, Bonn, Germany. (*Photo. Landesmuseum Bonn*) *op. p. 134*
(b) Two views of gold cup, mid second millennium B.C., from grave at Rillaton, Cornwall, England. (*Photo. British Museum*) *op. p. 134*

XVIII. (a) Necklace of faience and shale beads, second half of second millennium B.C., from grave at Upton Lovell, Wilts., England. (*Photo. Malcolm Murray*) *op. p. 135*
(b) Decorated bone cylindrical mounting, second half of second millennium B.C., from Blučina, Czechoslovakia. (*Photo. Narodni Museum, Prague*) *op. p. 135*

XIX. (a) Oval wooden bowl, decorated with gold foil and in the form of a stylised boat, late second-early first millennium B.C., from Caergwrle, Wales. (*Photo. National Museum of Wales*) *op. p. 144*
(b) Carvings of stylised boats on rock surface, second millennium B.C., at Ostfold, Norway. (*Photo. Universitets Oldsaksamling, Oslo*) *op. p. 144*

XX. (a) Excavated settlement with oval stone-built houses, mid second millennium B.C., on Capo Graziano, Filicudi, Aeolian Islands. (*Photo. author*) *op. p. 145*
(b) Excavated surface of cross-ploughed field, later second millennium B.C., at Gwithian, Cornwall, England. (*Photo. Malcolm Murray*) *op. p. 145*

XXI. (a) Ruined *nuraghe* or defensive tower-house, thirteenth-seventh century B.C., at Santa Barbara, Sardinia. *op. p. 154*
(b) Stone-built circular houses, eighth-sixth century B.C., around *nuraghe* of Su Nuraxi, Barumini, Sardinia. (*Both photos. Bromofoto, Milan*) *op. p. 154*

XXII. (a) Male bronze figure, Nuraghic culture, early first millennium B.C., from Sardinia. *op. p. 155*
(b) Bronze figure of seated woman and child, Nuraghic culture, early first millennium B.C., from Sardinia. (*Both photos. Edwin Smith*) *op. p. 155*

XXIII. Replica of woman's dress, in natural brown wool, second half of second millennium B.C., Egtved, Denmark. (*Photo. Nationalmuseet, Copenhagen*) *op. p. 160*

XXIV. Bronze situla or bucket, with relief decoration, early fifth century B.C., from Vače, Jugoslavia. (*Photo. Narodni Musej, Ljubljana*) *op. p. 161*

XXV. (a) Wooden cheek-piece of horse-bit, carved in the form of a deer, East Scythian, fourth-third century B.C., from Barrow I, Pazyryk, Altai Mountains. *op. p. 176*
(b) Bridle ornament of carved wood and felt in the form of a fabulous bird, fourth-third century B.C., from Barrow I, Pazyryk, Altai Mountains. (*Both photos. Hermitage, Leningrad*) *op. p. 176*

XXVI. (a) Bronze mounting in the form of a curled feline, Scythian, sixth century B.C. (*Private Collection*) *op. p. 177*
(b) Bronze ritual vehicle with human and animal figures, Hallstatt culture, sixth century B.C., from grave at Strettweg, Graz, Austria. (*Photo. Fürbock, Graz*) *op. p. 177*

XXVII. (a) Leather cap, Hallstatt culture, sixth century B.C., from the Kilbwerk salt mine, Hallstatt, Austria.
(b), (c) Two views of leather, wood-framed, rucksack, Hallstatt culture, sixth century B.C., from the Appold-werk salt mine, Hallstatt, Austria. (*Both photos. Naturhistorisches Museum, Vienna*) *following p. 192*

XXVIII. (a) Bronze vessel engraved with animal figures, Hallstatt culture, sixth century B.C., from Grave 682, Hallstatt, Austria.
(b) Bronze bowl with figures of cow and calf, Hallstatt culture, sixth century, from Grave 671, Hallstatt, Austria. (*Both photos. Naturhistorisches Museum, Vienna*) *following p. 192*

XXIX. (a) Gold bowl, Hallstatt culture, sixth century B.C., from wagon-burial at Bad-Cannstadt, South Germany.
(b) Gold neck-ring, Hallstatt culture, sixth century B.C., from wagon-burial at Bad-Cannstadt, South Germany. (*Both photos. Württemburgisches Landesmuseum, Stuttgart*) *following p. 192*

XXX. (a) Imported bronze cauldron on tripod, Greek, sixth century B.C., from grave of Hallstatt culture at Ste Colombe, Côte d'Or, France. (*Photo. Chambon, Chatillon-sur-Seine*) *following p. 192*

(b) Bronze cauldron on tripod, Urartian, eighth century B.C., from Altin Tepe, Turkey. (*Photo. R. D. Barnett*) *following p. 192*

XXXI. Bronze figure of mounted warrior with helmet, spear and shield, Hallstatt culture, sixth century B.C., from the Strettweg ritual vehicle (*Pl.* XXVI *b*), Graz, Austria. (*Photo. Landesmuseum Johanneum, Graz*) *following p. 200*

XXXII. (a) Upper part of imported bronze hydria, Greek, sixth century B.C., from grave of Hallstatt culture at Grächwil, Switzerland. (*Photo. Historisches Museum, Bern*) *following p. 200*

(b) One of a pair of Pegasus figures on the gold 'diadem' or neck-ring from grave of Hallstatt culture, sixth century B.C., at Vix, Côte d'Or, France. (*Photo. Ina Bandy*) *following p. 200*

XXXIII. Neck-pad of wooden yoke for two horses, with decorative bronze studding, Hallstatt culture, seventh century B.C., from wagon-grave at Lovosice, Czechoslovakia. (*Photo. Archeologický Ústav, Prague*) *following p. 200*

XXXIV. Air view of excavation, showing timber houses, corduroy streets, and timber-framed fortifications, Urnfield culture, sixth century B.C., at Biskupin, Poland. (*Photo. Muzeum Archeologiczne, Warsaw*) *op. p. 208*

XXXV. Timber-framed defences, corduroy street and houses, Urnfield culture, sixth century B.C., at Biskupin, Poland. (*Photo. Muzeum Archeologiczne, Warsaw*) *op. p. 209*

XXXVI. (a) Stone footings of bastion, with clay brick walling above, Hallstatt culture, sixth century B.C., at the Heuneburg hill-fort, South Germany. *op. p. 214*

(b) Excavated footings of bastion in hill-fort rampart, Hallstatt culture, sixth century B.C., at the Heuneburg, South Germany. (*Both photos. Staatliche Amt für Denkmalpflege, Tübingen*) *op. p. 214*

XXXVII. Bronze flagon with paste inlay, one of a pair, early La Tène culture, fourth century B.C., from Basse-Yutz, Lorraine, France. (*Photo. British Museum*) *op. p. 215*

XXXVIII. (a) Bastion of fort wall, middle La Tène culture, second century B.C., at Entremont, Aix-en-Provence, France. *op. p. 218*

(b) Stone pillar with carvings of severed human heads, re-used as threshold, middle La Tène culture, second century B.C., at Entremont, Aix-en-Provence France. (*Both photos author*) *op. p. 218*

XXXIX. Silver cauldron with decorative panels in relief, middle La Tène culture, first-second century B.C., votive deposit in bog at Gundestrup, Jutland, Denmark. (a) General view; (b) detail of internal panel. (*Photos. Nationalmuseet, Copenhagen*) *op. p. 219*

XL. (a) Gold helmet with relief ornament, Dacian, third-second century B.C., from Poiana-Coțofenști, Rumania. (*Photo. Institutul de Arheologie, Bucharest*) *op. p. 224*

(b) Silver helmet with relief ornament, Dacian, third-second century B.C., from River Danube at the Iron Gates, Rumania. (*Photo. Detroit Institute of Arts*) *op. p. 224*

XLI. (a) Stone-built circular house during excavation, second century A.D., at Sollas, North Uist, Scotland. (*Photo. Malcolm Murray*) *op. p. 225*

(b) Excavated post-holes of circular timber-framed house, third century B.C., at Pimperne, Dorset, England. (*Photo. I.M.Blake & D.W.Harding*) *op.p.225*

XLII. Tattooed design on right arm of East Scythian man, fourth-third century B.C., from Barrow 2, Pazyryk, Altai Mountains.
(*Photo. Hermitage, Leningrad*) *following p. 240*

XLIII. Shields, La Tène culture, third century B.C.-early first century A.D.
(a) stone sculpture, Augustan, from Montdragon, Vaucluse, France;
(b) wood, from the Fayum, Egypt; (c) bronze, from River Witham, Lincs., England.
(*Photos. Musée Calvet, Avignon ; Services des Antiquités, Cairo ; British Museum following p. 240*

XLIV. Replica of bronze flagon with engraved ornament, La Tène culture, early fourth century B.C., from a woman's grave at Reinheim, Saarbrücken, Germany. (*Photo. Römisch-Germanische Zentralmuseum, Mainz*) *following p. 240*

XLV. (a) Gilt bronze helmet, La Tène culture, fourth-third century B.C., from Amfreville, Eure, France. (*Photo. Musée des antiquités nationales, St Germain-en-Laye*) *following p. 240*

(b) Bronze mounting in the form of a fantastic bird, La Tène culture, third century B.C., from Malomerice, Czechoslovakia. (*Photo. Kleibl*) *following p. 240*

XLVI. Engraved back of bronze mirror, early first century A.D., from a woman's grave at Birdlip, Glos., England. (*Photo. Gloucester Museum*) *op. p. 244*

XLVII. Bronze mountings from cauldron, La Tène culture, third century B.C., from Brå, Jutland, Denmark. (a) Owl-head handle-attachment; (*b*) bull-head ornament. (*Photos. Jysk Archaeologisk Selskab*) *op. p. 245*

XLVIII. Iron fire-dogs, late La Tène culture, first century B.C.-first century A.D. (a) Fire-dog from Niederurssel, Mainz, Germany (*Photo. Stadtmuseum, Frankfurt-am-Main*); (b) Detail of fire-dog, Capel Garmon, Wales. (*Photo. National Museum of Wales*) *op. p. 252*

XLIX. Stone relief showing captive Dacians, Roman, first century A.D., on Trajan's Trophy at Adamklissi, Rumania. (*Photo. Institutul de Arheologie, Bucharest*) *op. p. 253*

L. Defeated Britons: stone relief on distance-slab from Bridgeness on the Antonine Wall, Scotland, mid second century A.D. (*Photo. National Museum of Antiquities of Scotland*) *op. p. 256*

LI. Part of silver dish, Byzantine, representing barbarian members of the Imperial Bodyguard of Theodosius I, 388 A.D., from Almendralejo, Spain. (*Photo. Römisch-Germanische Zentralmuseum, Mainz*) *op. p. 257*

Publisher's Note

Notes and references are printed at the end of each chapter. To assist the reader, the page on which the notes appear is given, in square brackets, on the headline to each text page. Thus

[22] BACKGROUND OF THE ENQUIRY 7

indicates that the notes to page 7 will be found on page 22.

1

Background of the Enquiry

WHEN I had the honour to be invited by the Society of Antiquaries of Scotland in 1962 to deliver the Rhind Lectures on which this book is based, I had to decide, it seemed to me, between two alternatives. I might offer a rigorous and technical course, addressed only to my fellow prehistorians and dealing with those archaeological minutiae which have formed the subject of much of my research over the past years. On the other hand, I might take a risk, and offer instead a broad synthesis of material widely distributed in time and space, necessarily lacking in profundity, but presenting some general observations on the wider problems of prehistory. This would be appropriate to put before an audience not wholly of archaeologists, but of scholars in other disciplines, and those with a general interest in human antiquity.

I say 'take a risk', for I knew that if I chose to navigate on such wide and inevitably shallow waters of learning, I should obviously lay myself open to a charge of superficiality and a lack of comprehension of the complexities involved. Indeed, I might lose any reputation I might have had for being a 'sound scholar': here, however, we may recall the famous definition of this phrase, as 'a term of praise applied to one another by learned men who have no reputation outside the university, and a rather queer one inside it'.[1] At all events, I decided to make a general survey which would take the form of a broad enquiry into the ancient origins of historical Europe; of the last five or six thousand years of the prehistoric past which culminated in the barbarian world as known to classical antiquity.

I think that I should make it clear at this point that I am not making an attempt to write a prehistory of Europe from the time of the first agricultural communities. Though the recent advances in prehistoric studies are bringing such a task at least within the realms of ultimate possibility, it would necessarily have to be conceived on a scale and according to methods commensurate with its magnitude and complexity. Here I can offer nothing more than an individual prehistorian's view of what seem to him the salient and significant factors of the period and area under review, and his estimation of components which were to make up later barbarian Europe and to be transmitted to part of our own heritage. It is a sketch, an essay in interpretation, and should not be judged as more than that; with Professor Rhys Carpenter I realise 'the dangers of discoursing easily on difficult matters and offering concise conclusions from inevident evidence'.[2]

As my title indicates, I am going to make a broad enquiry into ancient Europe: the contribution of those peoples in the past who are classified as 'prehistoric'. It will be necessary to spend some time in discussing what is involved by this classification, so that we can get a clearer idea of what in fact we are studying. We can then make some examination of the means whereby we have knowledge of prehistoric communities, and how we should handle the evidence once we have recognised it for what it is. In the latter part of this chapter we may concern ourselves with some general observations about the type of communities involved in prehistory, and their peculiar interest to us, so that in the second chapter we can start off with the main theme of our survey.

It is perhaps worth reminding those who are not archaeologists that we are dealing with a discipline which is constantly and rapidly developing, which is dynamic and not static, and which continuously enforces on the research worker the necessity of keeping abreast of the new material or changed viewpoints circulating in conversation, correspondence or in publications, and of the assimilation of these within the existing framework of knowledge. This is a situation familiar enough to those who work in scientific disciplines, but is perhaps less apparent to those in other fields of learning where the tempo of discovery is slower, and sources a generation or more old may still be valid documents. A recent review in a scientific journal stigmatised a new book as 'middle-aged', on the grounds that certain chapters had been written two years previously: if we have not reached this alarming state of affairs in prehistory, a glance at the bibliography of this book will show how very few sources more than ten or fifteen years old have been included, and will emphasise the dangers in wait for the non-specialist who inadvertently uses out-of-date material.

The enquiry before us constitutes an attempt to examine the main streams of European, prehistoric, barbarian, antiquity from a date somewhat before 6000 B.C. to the emergence of the classical civilisations of the Mediterranean, and the eventual incorporation of much of the barbarian world within the Roman Empire. It is necessarily dependent on the work of numerous scholars of almost every nationality, who have laid the foundations of European prehistory by their field-work and excavations, their comparative studies, and their works of synthesis and interpretation. My debt to these archaeologists and prehistorians is obvious, and my task has been one of selection from the mass of available evidence—often confused and ambiguous, sometimes admittedly conflicting—and following selection, that of interpretation with I believe honesty, and I hope clarity.

The content of the human past as a whole can be broadly called *history*, but convention (perhaps since Daniel Wilson, who invented the word) separates a prehistoric from an historic past. While this separation is normally made, both in technical and colloquial usage, the definition of prehistory is often left rather vague. The logical French say that *la préhistoire* stops with the first written document: stops everywhere, in the New World as in the Old, from the moment signs are scratched on clay in late fourth millennium Sumer; English technical usage, less logical but surely more reasonable, ends prehistory locally at different dates, determined by the first use of an historical record of some kind in each area. And colloquially the word 'prehistoric' is used in several senses, all very imprecise, ranging from 'very ancient', and uncritically conflating dinosaurs and mammoths, cave-men and lake-dwellers, Ancient Britons and Ancient Egyptians, to a vague label applied to any 'barbarian' or 'uncivilised' peoples in antiquity.

How then can we make a meaningful distinction between 'prehistoric' and 'historic' peoples, and could such a distinction be equated with one between 'barbarians' and the civilised world? I think it does not help to use the French concept of 'absolutely before all history', and I am a little uneasy for instance when 'prehistory' or 'prehistoric' is used in a world-wide context: I am not sure what is really regarded as the significant factor uniting the various communities so described. I would suggest that what really distinguishes our historic from our prehistoric communities is just what these words say: one group is historic, because the evidence for its existence is essentially based on written documents, studied by historians; and the other group, wherever encountered, is before the local invention or adoption of writing, and is therefore studied by prehistorians, using non-documentary sources. What we are really dealing with is *literate* and *non-literate* societies in antiquity. Could then this division be more appropriate? I think so. This distinction in the nature of the evidence is of paramount importance.[3]

We cannot necessarily, by thinking in terms of literate and non-literate, distinguish civilisation from barbarism, or rather complex urbanism from simple peasantry; we shall see that in the Near East large urban communities existed which were formally illiterate. But literate and non-literate make sense in terms of the evidence that each provides for the reconstruction of the human past. The evidence for the existence of non-literate societies in antiquity is that of surviving material culture, but no documents, and is the subject-matter of archaeology. Literate societies have also their material culture (including architecture and the arts on occasion), the province once again of the archaeologist and of the art-historian, but essentially such societies are documented in the main by written records, the affair of the historian. It follows, therefore, that as the type of evidence is different in the two classes of society, the type of reconstruction we can make is also going to be different. A prehistorian, in the sense of the student of non-literate societies in the past, does not and cannot write history as the historian does. The view of the past is wholly conditioned by the evidence available for its existence.

This apparently seems hard doctrine to some people, but only because, I feel, they have never thought about the nature of our knowledge of the past. Many persons, I believe, feel that it only needs enough people working hard enough for long enough to accumulate all the available 'facts' about the human past, and that these when arranged in the right order will tell us 'the truth': that these 'facts' are a sort of 'truth' in themselves. Certainly this was what was thought by historians and prehistorians in the first flush of enthusiasm for their new techniques in the 1890s. Lord Acton's comment of 1896 is well known: 'Ultimate history we cannot have in this generation, but we can dispose of conventional history, and show the point we have reached on the road from one to the other, now that all information is within reach, and every problem has become capable of solution.'[4]

Less known is Robert Munro's credo of the prehistorian of a year earlier: 'Under the application of the scientific methods of modern archaeology, no past civilisation, however far its limits may lie beyond those of history, is likely to escape detection sooner or later; and however meagre the traces of that civilisation may be, they often disclose a story of humanity more reliable than could be constructed from written records. The materials with which the archaeologist deals are absolutely free from the bias and ignorance which so frequently distort the statements of the historian.'[5] The fascinating holier-than-thou attitude of the prehistorian here expressed even now sometimes makes an appearance, but only I think by archaeologists who have thought little about the nature of their own discipline, and less about that of the historian.

But can we for a moment entertain such views today? We have lost the confidence of the nineteenth century, and are children of an age of doubt. But it is not that alone that has caused us to revise our view of the nature of historical investigation, nor any facile assumption that we must necessarily know better than our forefathers. Our thought has been permeated with the concepts of the scientist, and we are not shocked by relativity in other spheres than Einstein's. 'Facts', a scientist writing of his own discipline has recently said, 'are particular observational data relating to the past or the present' and, he goes on, 'starting from a collection of facts we can often infer several possible theories, all of which cannot be true as some may be mutually incompatible; indeed none of them may be true'.[6] Collingwood said in effect the same thing for historical and archaeological investigation in the 1930s; there is a past-in-itself which we can never grasp, as each historian can only perceive a past-as-known to him as an individual, conditioned also by the nature of the actual evidence available.[7] And recently a distinguished historian, Mr E. H. Carr, declared roundly that 'the belief in a hard core of historical facts existing objectively, and independently of the historian, is a preposterous fallacy, but one which is very hard to eradicate'.[8]

This is not of course to take up a position of extreme subjectivity in which there is a private view of the past for each historian and prehistorian. But we must recognise that in archaeology, just as Carr has pungently said of history, there are no facts other than those which are, as Beveridge said of the scientific field, 'observational data'. As for Munro's absolute freedom from bias and ignorance, the observational data of prehistory seem to me in almost every way to be more ambiguous, and more capable of varied interpretations, than the normal run of material available to historians. What we have at our disposal, as prehistorians, is the accidentally surviving durable remnants of material culture, which we interpret as best we may, and inevitably the peculiar quality of this evidence dictates the sort of information we can obtain from it. Furthermore, we interpret the evidence in terms of our own intellectual make-up, conditioned as it is by the period and culture within which we were brought up, our social and religious background, our current assumptions and presuppositions, and our age and status. Few have faced this with the honesty of Mr Osbert Lancaster, who prefaced a book with the words: 'My criteria, political, architectural and scenic, remain firmly Anglo-Saxon, and the standards of judgement are always those of an Anglican graduate of Oxford with a taste for architecture, turned cartoonist, approaching middle age and living in Kensington.'[9] Similar acts of self-revelation would contribute greatly to our understanding of works of historical scholarship.

We cannot recognise our evidence for what it is, nor make our observations of so-called facts, unless we know what to regard as meaningful and significant. This can only be done conceptually in terms of some working hypothesis, or in scientific language, a model of the past. Henri Frankfort had this in mind when he talked of 'a viewpoint whence many seemingly unrelated facts are seen to acquire meaning and coherence is likely to represent an historical reality':[10] this I would call a valid model. The concept is applicable to all fields of historical research, as Mr R. W. K. Hinton showed when discussing the Whig interpretation of recent English history in just these terms.[11] Models of the more ancient past have been numerous—theological and teleological, moral and aesthetic, racial and cyclical.

Archaeological evidence has for over a century been viewed in terms of a technological and evolutionary model put forward by Christian Thomsen in 1836: the Three Ages of Stone, Bronze and Iron.[12] It was a very good model, and still holds valid in many contexts, now co-existing with alternative schemes, rather as in another field Newtonian physics still retains its own place. We have for instance an alternative model based on the subsistence-economics of prehistoric communities which is in many ways more useful than the purely technological one, though it does not wholly supersede it. But we must always remember that we are using the models in question with their limitations and our limitations too. 'The Bronze Age' is an intellectual construct to accommodate data viewed within the framework of the technological model of prehistory. Childe's book, *What Happened in History*, is necessarily what Childe thought happened; the 'Ancient Europe' of my title is a synthesis of what I have thought to be relevant and significant factors.

Any attempt to interpret the past must be carried out in terms of valid models, constructed with strict reference to the nature of the evidence used. A technological and an economic model can each have validity, and not be mutually exclusive, because both use the same archaeological evidence. They can therefore both be used, side by side. But I would say here that I think writers such as Teilhard de Chardin and Arnold Toynbee have not helped towards an understanding of the past, but have introduced a mass of misleading concepts into the problem, because among many other errors of methodology they have tried to use simultaneously two or more incompatible models, one based on theology, and the others on archaeological and historical observations. The model based on the evidence used by the Christian apologist or mystic cannot meaningfully be combined with that based on the evidence of the scientist; each has its respective validity, but any attempt to use them in conjunction can only produce nonsense.

I think this discussion has been necessary to understand the content of this book, and the nature of the information on extinct non-literate communities that can be obtained from archaeological evidence alone.

However much we might wish to the contrary, we have to recognise, as Professor Atkinson has recently said, that 'the raw material of prehistory is not men, but things'.[13] As prehistorians we move in a world of anonymous societies, defined by their distinctive traditions in the style and manufacture of everyday objects. 'We find', wrote Gordon Childe in a now famous definition, 'certain types of remains—pots, implements, burial rites, house forms—constantly recurring together. Such a complex of regularly associated traits we shall term a "cultural group" or a "culture". We assume that such a complex is the material expression of what today would be called a people.'[14] We assume, in fact, that recurrent assemblages of types and styles in the manufacture and use of everyday objects, or in belief and ritual as expressed in burial rites or temples, have a significance in human terms. They will not occur by accident or chance, for this is not the nature of human activity. We use in effect the art-historian's maxim proposed by Wölfflin, that 'not everything is possible at every time'.

Our archaeological cultures, defined in time and space, constitute for the prehistorian the peoples known by name to the historian: the equivalent of Sumerians or Greeks, Anglo-Saxons or Scythians. In default of such valid nomenclature, we have to invent our own labels; often grotesque enough, and formed unsystematically over the years, so that we can have a culture named after pots, like that of the Bell Beakers, or from a place, like that of Hallstatt, or from a tomb-type, like the south Russian Timber Graves. We may deplore these inconsistencies and curiosities, but they have become an established technical shorthand virtually impossible to replace.

Archaeological evidence is then based on the accidentally durable remnants of material culture surviving to the present day. To convert these remnants to evidence, or archaeological 'facts', they must be recognised and interpreted within one or more conceptual models of the past. Inference from the evidence must then proceed in terms of questions posed in such a manner that they respect the nature of the evidence, and do not violate it. In other words, the nature of the archaeological evidence, or of other evidence about the past, conditions and limits the nature of the information it can provide. A bronze axe blade will not in itself tell you what language its maker spoke, nor how he observed his harvest festival, but it will tell you a good deal about the technology of metal-founding at the time of its manufacture, and probably something of the circumstances of fashions in armament, trade and exchange. The archaeologist's view of the past is inevitably a technological and materialistic one, simply because it is based on the products of ancient technology, and not because this viewpoint has any particular intrinsic validity.

The viewpoint can be extended to cover the field of subsistence-economics by co-operation with the natural sciences, notably zoology and botany, but beyond this point inference from archaeological evidence alone can inform us of only the broadest aspects of social structure or religious belief, and that often in a very tentative way.[15] We shall see that by a judicious use of analogy from historical situations, or from our knowledge of recent primitive peoples, inferences of a second order can be made, and for Europe in later prehistory we can sometimes use the documents of literate societies to illuminate the non-literate; but this is not using archaeological evidence by itself alone. Using archaeological and historical evidence side by side, one discipline can check the other, since we can claim for neither that objectivity and infallibility that Acton and Munro thought they could achieve seventy years ago.

I would like to say a word about the way archaeologists can make an interdisciplinary attack on problems of prehistory with the help of botanists and zoologists,[16] because this joint approach has enabled us to make some of our most significant advances in recent years. We have been able to work towards an understanding of man's relation to his environment, how he has exploited it and how his own culture has been affected by his habitat. As a result we have been able to make new classifications and, as I have suggested, new conceptual models, notably that based on the variations in the types of subsistence-economics of various prehistoric peoples.

In the north of Europe and the British Isles, one of the most important developments has been the co-operation of archaeologists and botanists, particularly those studying the changes in the natural plant cover by means of the resistant and identifiable pollen-grains that survive in peat and mud deposits. Half a century's work, starting in Scandinavia, has enabled a long sequence to be built up, from glacial into post-glacial times, showing the changes in forest history caused by climatic variations. In post-glacial times, the pollen percentages in stratified deposits show how, with the retreating ice-sheet, tundra conditions are replaced by woodland, first with birch dominant, then pine, then mixed oak forest. Archaeological material, such as stray finds lost overboard in a lake and so incorporated in the peat, or a settlement site itself, can be tied into this natural sequence, and an approximate relative position in time established; by the radiocarbon dating method which I will describe later, this can be translated into an age in actual years.

But man is not always a passive agent in the landscape. With agriculture comes the need for clearing woodland for cultivation, or lopping the leaves of trees for cattle fodder. Both these activities can show themselves in the tell-tale pollen percentages: tree pollens drop in frequency, and then the pollen of cereals and of weeds of cultivation may appear. In the whole field of the earliest agriculture, as we shall realise in the second chapter, the co-operation of the botanist with the archaeologist is essential, identifying grains and seeds, and even recognising them from casts left in ancient pottery or clay hearths where accidentally included grains have burnt out in firing.

Zoological co-operation can help us either with hunting or with agricultural peoples. From the proportions of age groups shown by bones from food refuse, in relation to the known breeding cycle of reindeer or red deer, it can be shown for instance that some hunters' camps in northern Europe were occupied in summer, some in winter. Again, in the study of the beginnings of agriculture the zoological evidence is obviously of cardinal importance, both in the identification of the relevant species, and in the more difficult task of assessing the genetic effect of domestication on the skeleton. Similarly, the choice of animals and even of certain joints for consumption can contribute to our knowledge of the basic economic structure of the societies we are studying in the prehistoric past.

When the existence of prehistoric man was first being recognised in the nineteenth century, much play was made with comparisons taken from recent primitive societies: Sollas's *Ancient Hunters and their Modern Representatives* of 1911 is a classic title in this context. Similarly, approaching less remote human antiquity, Sir Arthur Mitchell's famous *The Past in the Present* (1880), still remains a model of inspired but controlled interpretation. Unfortunately, however, the comparative ethnographical approach was more often applied uncritically, and fell into deserved disrepute. In our own day, Professor Grahame Clark, among others, has re-established the validity of the method when properly applied, and shown its potentialities in his *Prehistoric Europe: The Economic Basis* of 1952. I have used this approach from time to time and I hope judiciously: so used, I think it can be very illuminating.

It is because of the imperfection of archaeological evidence that prehistorians have necessarily to be much involved in techniques scientific or semi-scientific in character. The necessity of extracting the maximum from the fragmentary evidence at our disposal has led to a number of ingenious and elegant procedures being invented or adopted to do no more than make the best of a bad job. This attitude of dissatisfaction with the available evidence I believe to be salutary, and the determination of archaeologists to use every available technique for the investigation of the past helps to keep the subject alive and moving—even if it makes for difficulties in teaching it at undergraduate level! The nature of the evidence has forced archaeology, and especially the archaeology of non-literate peoples, into taking a position which, as we have just seen, is essentially inter-disciplinary. On the one hand it depends on co-operation with historians, philologists and sociologists, as well as with architects and art historians, and the executants of the visual arts and crafts, no less than with the practical farmer and fisherman. On the other, it works in collaboration with the geographer, the geologist, the zoologist, the botanist and other natural scientists; the anatomist and the geneticist, the physicists and the statisticians.[17] Later in this chapter I shall say why I think that the study of non-literate societies in antiquity has a peculiar value in itself, but parenthetically I would say here how important I regard a discipline that comprises, and demands a knowledge of the principles of, such a range of enquiry within the humanities, the sciences, and the arts. This does not make for ease of comprehension nor for simplicity of execution, but it does afford the opportunity of a practical participation in diverse intellectual disciplines which to so many people seem wholly disparate and unconnected. The possibility of meaningful synthesis from so complex a series of sources is itself a mental stimulus of no mean order, and perhaps archaeologists are among those least likely to feel that they find any essential dichotomy between Snow's *Two Cultures*.

A word on techniques is necessary since they, in relation to the evidence they are designed to elucidate, contribute to condition the nature of our knowledge of prehistory, and hence the subject-matter of this book. One major technique, or rather group of techniques, is that of archaeological excavation. To many, this is virtually the whole content of archaeology, and bookshop shelves are alarmingly full of little volumes for beginners and amateurs with the recurrent theme of 'What Fun to Go on a Dig'. Excavation, in fact, is an excruciatingly responsible operation, an unrepeatable experiment which destroys its own evidence as it goes. Its results, in published form, are archaeological 'facts' in the sense we have already discussed; the record of the observations and interpretations made by the excavator. Upon their reliability, and therefore upon the competence and standards of the excavator, depend their validity as data for further interpretation and synthesis. Partial control only can be exercised over the results: the unique qualities of human actions result in no two sets of circumstances being quite the same, and thus a new excavation of a comparable site can only yield evidence broadly similar to, but not identical with, that of the first. Cumulative credibility can be established by the examination of a sufficiently large number of comparable sites in certain circumstances, but this principle cannot be applied indiscriminately. Furthermore, apart from rescue operations, excavations must be directed to the solution of specific problems formulated within the framework of the current state of knowledge, and frequently rescue digs must be directed in these terms too. If the question-and-answer process, so brilliantly conceived by Collingwood, is ignorantly or improperly applied, or even not applied at all, the results may be misleading or nugatory.

Excavation, with its observation and record of stratified sequences and associated assemblages of artifacts, has contributed important evidence for the construction of relative time-scales for non-literate communities. It is here that the prehistorian encounters some of his greatest difficulties; the defining of chronology in relative terms, or worse still, in absolute terms of calendar years. For certain areas of the Old World after the inception of historical records elsewhere—for instance, in Mesopotamia and Egypt in the third millennium B.C.—it is possible to construct chains of connection between the non-literate and literate societies in greater or lesser degrees of closeness and probability. Here trade exchanges whereby the product of a recognisable non-literate culture are found in historically dated contexts in a literate civilisation, or vice versa, when datable products from the latter appear in barbarian contexts, form an invaluable source of evidence. But these are at best scanty, and often ambiguous, and the circumstances do not apply to the vast periods of antiquity before written history began, nor to areas wholly remote from ancient literate civilisations, such as the New World or the Antipodes before European contact.

Until ten or twelve years ago we had in fact two kinds of dates in human antiquity. One set was historical, derived from written records and in the ancient world of varying degrees of precision, but nevertheless usually established within reasonable limits of accuracy. Side by side with these historical dates went archaeological dates, worked out with a wide range from high probability to remote possibility for periods within that of written records—from soon after 3000 B.C., as we have seen. Some of these dates, like those of the later Minoan and Mycenaean periods, based on Egyptian chronology, could be taken as representing a fairly high order of validity; others, like those for Neolithic Britain or China before the Shang Dynasty, came nearer to reasoned estimates, or just plain guesses.

As a by-product of atomic physics in the late 1940s however, the possibility of using a radio-active isotope of carbon, C^{14}, for a form of dating for certain organic materials surviving from antiquity, was realised.[18] I cannot here describe in detail the process, theoretically not difficult to understand and indeed now fairly widely appreciated. All living matter absorbs radio-active carbon from the atmosphere, directly or indirectly, and maintains its content at a stable level until death, when no further absorption takes place. Like all radio-active substances, C^{14} disintegrates at a steady and measurable rate, expressed as its 'half-life', which is the number of years by which half the radio-carbon has disintegrated and become nitrogen: this has been calculated at 5570 ± 30 years. The point in its radio-active decay of a sample of, say, wood charcoal from an ancient site can be measured in relation to this half-life. As this is done by counting a random series of radio-active emissions it can only be expressed in statistical terms, normally of a single standard deviation, or a two-to-one chance of the real date lying between two figures with a separation, in most recent determinations, of 200 to 300 years.

The recognition of this process immediately gave potentialities for a time-scale independent of human activity or frailty in the past, and extending back to possible dates around 30,000 (or exceptionally 50,000) years ago. There are still uncertainties in the process, and the general tendency, in the period under review in this book, has been to give a higher antiquity to many European cultures in the fourth and third millennia B.C. than we had estimated by archaeological means. Nevertheless the general pattern emerging seems to me sound, and I shall make use of radiocarbon dates throughout. We therefore have now three kinds of dates available for the Old World. From 50,000 years or so ago the radiocarbon method can give statements of statistical probabilities for absolute dates, as we have seen; from the early third millennium B.C. historical dates become available for certain cultures, and from these again archaeological dates can be extrapolated with varying degrees of probability. Where more than one method of dating can be employed, one checking the other, our chronologies can of course be more sure.

I have been at pains to stress the difficulties inherent in the archaeological approach to the past, because these difficulties are so often ignored or brushed aside. The result has been that certain popular expositions have tended to give the impression that we have achieved a certainty of knowledge which would fulfil Munro's hopes of 1895. But while our knowledge is unhappily incomplete at almost every point, it would be idle to deny that one of the most remarkable intellectual achievements in the wider field of human history over the past three-quarters of a century has been the recognition and recovery of prehistory. The appreciation of the extended perspective of the antiquity of man has become an almost unconscious part of our general knowledge, and we forget how revolutionary it seemed to our fathers. In this book I hope to demonstrate the reality of this knowledge for ancient Europe, and to indicate something of the achievement of international scholarship in this field.

I am of course not the first in this country to attempt a general survey of a limited period of European prehistory. A most interesting and now almost forgotten pioneer essay was Christopher Dawson's *Age of the Gods* of 1928; he was mainly concerned with barbarian Europe but necessarily discussed the beginnings of civilisation in the Near East and covered the period from the Lower Palaeolithic to the Etruscans, writing, so far as the evidence permitted, as an historian. What is perhaps Gordon Childe's most famous book, *The Dawn of European Civilisation*, had appeared in its first edition in 1925; in the author's words 'as a pioneer attempt at a comprehensive survey of European prehistory', but in fact it only covered the period from the later Mesolithic down to the middle of the second millennium B.C., and was an archaeology rather than a prehistory from the first. The later 1920s and the 1930s saw the publication of the successive volumes of Peake's and Fleure's *Corridors of Time*, an Old World prehistory and ancient history in which Europe necessarily played an important role. Christopher Hawkes's *Prehistoric Foundations of Europe: To the Mycenaean Age* of 1940 declared its chronological limits in its title; ten years later Childe in his *Prehistoric Migrations in Europe* produced a survey concentrating on folk movements in prehistory, and ending effectually in the eighth century B.C. Both these books I would again regard rather as archaeologies than as prehistories, enumerating and classifying numerous cultures and their artifacts. An entirely novel approach was represented by Grahame Clark's *Prehistoric Europe: The Economic Basis* (1952), a study of material culture over the total range of European prehistory. Childe's posthumous *Prehistory of European Society* (1958) set out to describe 'how and why the prehistoric barbarian societies of Europe behaved in a distinctively European way', but again ended at 1500 B.C.; Grahame Clark's *World Prehistory* (1961) of course includes Europe in its wide survey. But there still seems room for the modest essay in interpretation I now offer.

With these preliminaries, let us turn to the main theme; the preliminaries have been necessary, I think, to explain some of the peculiarities of the view of the past which can be inferred from archaeological evidence alone. I shall not of course use this evidence in isolation, except where I have to: elsewhere I shall take every opportunity of using, not only the contributions from the natural sciences or of contemporative ethnography such as I have mentioned, but the evidence of history itself. As Professor Ian Richmond has said, 'while indeed there are many ages for whose cultures archaeological material is the sole evidence, this is no ideal state of affairs. The archaeologist must count himself the luckier when literature can inform him of standards contemporary with his material.'[19]

We begin our enquiries in a deeply pre-literate antiquity, some ten thousand years and more ago, but here already man himself is ancient. As a recognisable species he had emerged perhaps two million years before, and one of his outstanding peculiarities, distinguishing him from other species, was that to the usual 'biological methods of transmission and evolution' his brain had so developed that 'it endowed him with a second method of heredity based on the transmission of experience, and launched him on a new phase of evolution based on ideas and knowledge'. These are Sir Julian Huxley's words; he goes on to point out that this utilisation by the brain of 'the raw material of its subjective experience' results in the 'psycho-social' evolution which has rendered us 'capable of many things that no other animal is capable of: conscious reflection, the idea of self, death and of the future in general; we have the capacity of framing conscious purposes which can be translated into action . . .'.[20] The surviving material products of this purposive action form the subject-matter of the archaeologist.

While in our survey we will be mainly, and rightly, concerned with achievement, and mastery over environment and technical problems, there is inevitably much that, in Baudelaire's phrase, 'bears witness to the eternal and incorrigible barbarity of man'. Driven by circumstances to change from foraging as a vegetarian in the forest, to hunting in the open, the earliest hominids, even if they did develop (as has been suggested) unselfishness and altruism as a result of the necessary food-sharing and limitation of sexual appetites,[21] contributed less endearing features to our eventual make-up.

There seems a prevalent reluctance to admit that many characteristics of man which conflict with our current views of good and bad behaviour may well be as indelibly a part of his natural make-up as those we regard as desirable. The myth of the Noble Savage is restated in different terms—violence and hatred, cruelty and the enjoyment of killing, aggression and brutality, for instance, are not on the whole approved qualities in modern civilised societies, and when exhibited are often regarded as unfortunate deviations from an assumed norm of socially acceptable (and therefore 'good') behaviour, natural to man when not exposed to corrupting forces. The problem of course has produced a fascinating series of philosophical, religious, and ideological speculations; some have found it necessary to assume a Fall from original goodness, while others depend on optimistic views of the natural nobility of man as a basis for doctrines of ultimate perfectibility within appropriate political systems.

Here we may merely note that so far as inference can reasonably be made from archaeological evidence there is nothing to suggest that the desire for domination by force and if necessary killing is not as deeply seated a human emotion and urge as any other. In the period of antiquity reviewed in this book, 'warfare, the brutal suppression of man by man, of class by class, of sex by sex, of age group by age group, of one tribe by another, are as inseparable from the life of prehistoric village civilisation as they are implied by the organisation of even very humanised town civilisations up to the present day'.[22] Behind this again, though the evidence is inevitably slighter and more ambiguous, there seems to me a case for regarding man, from his first emergence as a species, as essentially 'a predator whose natural instinct is to kill with a weapon', a primate with 'instincts demanding the maintenance and defence of territories' in a manner familiar in many other animals. The formation of human communities and social units, from the simplest hunting band to the most complex civilisation, is a process of restraint and the canalisation of natural instincts within the framework of the social structure considered desirable in each instance, and in the majority of societies aggression and warfare have played a greater or less part. The basic theme of prehistory and history recurs as 'the instinct to dominate one's fellows, to defend what one deems one's own, to mate, to eat and avoid being eaten'.[23] In the intervals between these essential and absorbing activities, man has exercised his emotions, his imagination, and less frequently his intellect. Some of the products of these complex human forces form the evidence on which this book is based.

In the modern scene of international affairs an insistent problem is presented to us in terms of the unequal status of the so-called developed and under-developed regions of the world. The situation is brought to our attention in a variety of ways, some menacing and almost all based on emotion and prejudice rather than anything approaching dispassionate thought. Two simplistic explanations for the state of affairs are sometimes given. One (not so often overtly expressed) is that poor countries are poor because of the inherent inferiority in capability and energy of their people. Another, favoured by the Marxist model of the past, is that the under-developed countries have been systematically robbed by the richer nations. Both seem the product of subconscious guilt rather than an understanding of history.[24]

'Man', as Julian Huxley has recently put it, 'is the most variable of all organisms—anatomically and physiologically, intellectually and temperamentally',[25] and this situation of unequal development in material culture is hardly a new thing, as a moment's consideration will show. We should remember that we are dealing with material culture in this context: the under-developed country is not given its low status in terms of its philosophers, its saints and its artists, but of its technology, susceptible in the past to archaeological perception. And from the time when pebbles were roughly bashed into tools in what is now the Olduvai Gorge perhaps two million years ago, we are confronted throughout antiquity with the phenomenon of developed and under-developed communities, the essential subject-matter of prehistorians, and later of historians as well. While the circumstances of inequality present continuous and fascinating problems, their survival into the present world is hardly surprising. It is merely the expression of a long-standing pattern which may well be as ancient as the hominids themselves, and a demonstration of the wide range of individuality which characterises our species.

For much of the period under review in this book, which is roughly from soon after 10,000 B.C. to the Christian era, we are confronted in the Old World by the antithesis which in classical antiquity was recognised as that between the civilised and the barbarian peoples of the then known world; a distinction which was also broadly between literate and non-literate societies. The later classical world saw the antithesis in precisely these terms: 'If anyone extinguishes our literature, we are put on a level with the barbarians', wrote Libanius in A.D. 358 and later the sentiment is echoed by Sidonius.[26] In modern terms the situation resolves itself into the phenomenon of developed and under-developed peoples, in which formal literacy is, however, no longer the sole criterion of distinction. Instead, since the Industrial Revolution, the disparity has been in terms of applied technology (which of course includes literacy as well). In classical antiquity, apart from a very few special cases, such as the use of water power for milling, and of brick and masonry for building, there was virtual technological parity between barbarian and civilised communities, apart from literacy. The real distinction lay in polity and social structure, between stability and the complex intellectual and moral attitudes involved in the conduct of the affairs of a state on the one hand, and the impermanence and emotion-charged unpredictability of the clan or tribe on the other. It was this psychological antinomy that produced what Alföldi called the 'moral barrier' between the two worlds, to which I will return in the last chapter.[27] It is a recurrent frontier problem, in Asia as in Europe, and indeed one of the most illuminating studies of the question is that of Owen Lattimore in respect of China and Mongolia.[28]

As we move back in time beyond the classical world the phenomenon of disparity, though constantly with us, changes in character. The differences, so far as we can perceive them from evidence which becomes increasingly that of archaeology rather than of history, are those of degree rather than of kind. The element of permanence and stability, made possible by relatively advanced agricultural methods intelligently administered, characterises the ancient civilisations of the Near East, while the steppe and forest of Eurasia is populated by agricultural or pastoral societies at a sensibly lower level of technological competence, or even by surviving communities whose economy is still that of the hunter and food-gatherer. Literacy distinguishes the higher cultures, but not universally, for we encounter the phenomenon of what are obviously, from the archaeological evidence, cultures whose technological achievement equals that of the literate civilisations, but which are themselves without writing. We will return to this point in the next chapter, but I would just give two instances. Round about or before 6000 B.C., in a context of stone- and copper-using agriculturalists, a town of 32 acres in extent was flourishing at Çatal Hüyük in Anatolia; Jericho at the same time enclosed about 10 acres within its town wall. These communities represent a command over environment and a capacity for social organisation not unequal to literate early Dynastic Sumer some 3,000 years later. And the other side of the picture is the situation of Palestine in the third and early second millennium B.C., surrounded by literate states but itself apparently without the craft of writing, yet with towns such as Megiddo, Lachish or Shechem, of from 15 to 25 acres in extent: Turkmenia gives us a comparable state of affairs at this time.

So we have a curious situation in which 'prehistoric' (because non-literate) communities exist contemporaneously with 'historic' (because literate) societies, yet with no perceptible technological disparity save in this one respect, the capacity or the incapacity to make a permanent verbal record. While we do not, and cannot know from archaeological evidence alone, the nature of the social organisation in these non-literate communities, yet the establishment and maintenance of such large urban units argues for something beyond the simple administrative skills of the village headman. But it was among the literate peoples of antiquity that what we generally agree to call civilisation first developed, and in such societies it was maintained and transmitted. What we can perceive, even in remote antiquity, is a broad classification between *innovating* and *conserving* societies. In the one group, technological developments in the arts of peace and war must have been socially acceptable and therefore encouraged; in the other, once a satisfactory *modus vivendi* for the community within its natural surroundings had been achieved, there seems to have been no urgent need felt to alter the situation. Or again, the cultural pattern devised might be too delicately adjusted to the circumstances, and too rigidly conceived, to be susceptible of modification by technological innovation: the steppe pastoralists after the domestication of the horse would be a case in point. 'Technical practices are significant only when they suit the needs of a society', Lattimore remarked in this very context, but it is a principle of widespread application.[29] 'We must imagine', as Ruth Benedict put it in a well-known passage, 'a great arc on which are ranged the possible interests provided either by the human age-cycle or by the environment, or by man's various activities.' The identity of a culture 'depends upon the selection of some segments of this arc'. 'In one society technology is unbelievably slighted even in those aspects of life which seem necessary to ensure survival; in another, equally simple, technological achievements are complex, and fitted with admirable nicety to the situation.' 'Every human society everywhere has made such selection in its cultural institutions. Each from the point of view of the other ignores fundamentals and exploits irrelevancies.'[30]

The assumptions and beliefs of innovating societies are familiar to us, for however much of their doctrines we may from time to time reject, we are their product. But we have not got to look far, even in the British Isles, for communities of conservators, where differentiation of behaviour, if it is associated with ideas not sanctioned by long tradition within the group, is difficult and dangerous. Nothing can recompense the alienation of the individual from his group: if his new ideas prosper he will be envied; if they fail he will be ridiculed. The economy of the community may be well adapted to its environment, and the risk of disturbing a delicate balance between man and nature, valid and important and complex even if apparently simple to the outsider, is a real one. But even if the symbiosis has broken down, and is no longer working as well as it once did, the tradition of a conserving society is to abide by tradition, even at the risk of prolonging an archaic and ineffective economy, or allowing itself to be superseded by an alien culture, at whose door at least all blame can then be laid.

The point of view of Western historiography from its beginnings has been that of the innovating societies in which such enquiry, naturally enough, was first formulated. The barbarian or non-literate peoples of antiquity have been ignored, or at best recognised rather uneasily, only to be relegated quickly to a marginal position of unimportance. An implicit thesis has been that a development from barbarism to civilisation is, or rather should have been, the norm, and that those societies that did not adopt the path of continued technological innovation have failed to achieve a mystic destiny towards which they should have striven. This view, still not infrequently held, was emphatically stated by Herbert Spencer in 1850. 'Progress is not an accident but a necessity', he wrote. 'It is a part of nature. . . . Evil tends perpetually to disappear. . . . Civilisation, instead of being artificial, is a part of nature; all of a piece with the development of the embryo or the unfolding of a flower.'[31] It is an attitude of mind which characterises the cyclical model of the past constructed by Arnold Toynbee, and to me it is a view which in part ignores significant evidence, and in part is the product of an unfortunate confusion between historical enquiry and the making of *a priori* moral judgments.

In the first place, as Collingwood and Frankfort both pointed out, the historian must strive to assess a civilisation or a barbarian community only on its own terms; each is 'a form of life having its own problems, to be judged by its success in solving those problems and no others'. He must not assume, in Collingwood's telling phrases, 'that the two different ways of life were attempts to do one and the same thing', nor ask 'whether the second did it better than the first. Bach was not trying to write like Beethoven and failing; Athens was not a relatively unsuccessful attempt to produce Rome.'[32]

In the second place, we must guard against hasty value-judgments in which, because we rate civilisation as praiseworthy and desirable, we therefore place all the qualities inherent in non-civilised peoples at a lower and a derogatory level. The process of making value-judgments about human societies often follows a familiar pattern. Out of the whole potential range of man's behaviour and action, certain characteristics are selected which, within the framework of the habits of thought of those making the judgment, are regarded as essential and praiseworthy. These behaviour-patterns, emotional or mental attitudes, or conventions of apprehension, may be those of frequent occurrence in many types of societies, or they may be rarely displayed: for instance one community may laud the solidarity of the group and the use of warfare for achieving the domination of a chosen religious or political creed, another stress the unique value of the solitary and contemplative individual eschewing force. Once selected, however, the assemblage of chosen culture-traits is proclaimed as the real content of civilisation, against which other assemblages are then compared, usually to their detriment. In certain contexts of thought the validity of the selected and approved states of mind and courses of action is enhanced by the assumption that these represent imperfect attempts to realise theoretical absolute qualities, supposed to exist independently of their human expression.

There then arises, as a corollary, the view that features which a nominally civilised community has in common with nominally barbarous societies have to be regarded as regrettable, and not in themselves an essential part of that civilisation, or indeed of civilisation as an abstract concept. We select the qualities we regard as desirable in terms of our own moral and ethical presuppositions of the moment, and constitute civilisation out of them alone. Moses Finley made this point with regard to slavery in ancient Greece: 'We condemn slavery, and we are embarrassed for the Greeks, whom we admire so much; therefore we tend either to underestimate its role in their life, or we ignore it altogether, hoping that somehow it will quietly go away.'[33]

I do not propose to allow the barbarians to quietly go away merely because they may be felt to be embarrassing. Far from thinking civilisation a normal development, and accepting the idea often held that 'a civilisation could grow up almost anywhere or at any time, given the right climate', all my study of the past persuades me that the emergence of what we call civilisation is a most abnormal and unpredictable event, perhaps in all its Old World manifestations ultimately due to a single set of unique circumstances in a restricted area of western Asia some 5,000 years ago. It has been neatly put by one of the scientific directors of the Rockefeller Foundation in that context of the under-developed countries we have already touched on: 'It is not only rather graceless . . .' he writes, 'but rather pointless . . . to ask why Africa or the Americas never developed a written language and all the other technologies. . . . The wonder is that such things occurred at all.'[34] It is, I would rather suggest, the non-civilised societies of antiquity that were the norm, and their contribution to the technologically innovating societies cannot be evaded or dismissed.

Much of our thinking on these matters has inevitably been coloured by the wish to see a pattern of progress in man's history, whereby a continuous elimination of his less pleasant attributes over the ages would prepare the way to an ultimate and inevitable state of ordered well-being. I have already indicated that I do not find myself sympathetic to these ideals, nurtured in eighteenth-century optimism, which found expression alike in the American Declaration of Independence and the Communist Manifesto. To me, the study of the non-literate societies of antiquity has a value not only for an estimate of their contribution to past and present civilisations, but because we are their heirs as well as those of more reputable peoples. As I have said in another context: 'We inherit a complex mass of unapprehended mental attitudes which go back not only to Greece and Rome, not only to Ur and Memphis, but back beyond this to the hunters and fishers of the Ice Ages. What we like to call our thinking may be as much conditioned by the fears and prejudices of the mammoth-hunter or the Neolithic peasant as by the religious aspirations of the early Semites or the speculative thought of the Greeks. . . . Our ancestry not only includes Plato and the New Testament, but the sweaty blood-stained ritual of Stone Age magic, and the irrational terrors of the world of shaman and seer.'[35]

I propose in this book to take a limited geographical area, that of Europe, and sketch, in such manner as the evidence permits, our knowledge of the non-literate societies of antiquity in that and in significantly adjacent areas. We may remind ourselves, incidentally, that Europe marches with Asia on the Ural Mountains and the Caspian Sea, and the East is as important to our enquiry as the West; and often more so. I shall begin with the economic and social dislocation brought about by the first invention, and subsequent adoption, of agriculture as a basis of livelihood rather than hunting and gathering. On this all subsequent development is based, including the rise of the first European civilisations in the Mediterranean. With ultimately Oriental roots themselves, shared by the non-literate inhabitants of the remainder of the continent, they formed distinctive versions of urban social organisation which were not developed elsewhere, despite common ancestry of tradition and equal advantages of soil and climate.

Indeed the content of much of the later part of this book is the relation of barbarian to classical Europe—first that of the Greeks, and later the Roman Empire. To my mind, neither aspect of the ancient world can be studied in isolation, for each form interdependent parts of a whole. In the history of the study of European antiquity there has been—with a few fortunate exceptions—a regrettable tendency for the two groups of scholars, classical archaeologists and ancient historians on the one hand, prehistorians on the other, to work independently, even in antagonism. From Robert Munro in 1895 declaring (as we saw) that 'the materials with which the archaeologist deals are absolutely free from the bias and ignorance' of historical evidence, to Professor Grahame Clark in 1943 writing 'To the peoples of the world generally. . . . I venture to think that Palaeolithic Man has more meaning than the Greeks',[36] the prehistorians have shown a touching faith in the validity and content of their discipline. On the other side, to quote Professor Rhys Carpenter again, 'the bimillennial superiority of the Hellenist will leave him loath to admit that any illumination won by his more barbarous colleagues from northern lands . . . can bring him enlightenment'.[37]

In this book I have endeavoured to place barbarian Europe in what I conceive to be its rightful place, as the necessary precursor and subsequent contemporary of the ancient civilised world. Some at least of the writers of classical antiquity realised their debt to their barbarous ancestors. Cicero, for instance, praising the heroes of the past, goes on: 'All these were great men; earlier still the men who first discovered the fruits of the earth, clothing, houses, an ordered way of life and protection against wild beasts—men under whose civilising influence we have gradually passed on from the basic crafts to the finer arts.'[38] In Cicero's time, before it, and for some time to come, the two groups of cultures, literate innovators and non-literate conservators, are found side-by-side in the Europe of the Roman Empire and beyond. It would surely be surprising if the subsequent Europe were the product of only one type of culture: our final task will be to pose this question again.

Notes

1. F. M. Cornford, *Microcosmographia Academica* (1953 edn.), 11.
2. Carpenter 1958, 184.
3. Cf. discussion in Piggott 1959c, 1-23; Daniel 1943, 1962, Atkinson 1960b; Hawkes 1951.
4. Quoted for instance in Carr 1961, 1.
5. R. Munro, *Rambles and Studies in Bosnia-Herzegovina and Dalmatia* (1895 edn.).
6. Beveridge, 1961, 87, 85.
7. Collingwood 1939, 1946; cf. Slotkin 1948.
8. *Op. cit.* 6.
9. O. Lancaster, *Classical Landscape with Figures* (1947), 11.
10. Frankfort 1951, 21.
11. *The Listener*, 6 February 1958, 233.
12. Cf. Daniel 1943.
13. Atkinson 1960b, 8.
14. Childe 1929, v-vi.
15. For these progressive difficulties in inference, cf. Hawkes 1954; for limitations of inference, M. A. Smith 1955.
16. A comprehensive and documented review is in Brothwell and Higgs 1963.
17. For the relationship of archaeological techniques to humanistic and scientific disciplines, cf. Hawkes 1957b.
18. For a convenient description of the method, see Willis 1963.
19. Richmond 1950, 5.
20. J. Huxley, *Journal of Neuropsychiatry* III, Supplement 1, 1962.
21. Cf. Hill 1957, 102-3.
22. Heichelheim 1958, 93.
23. Quotations from Ardrey 1961. His thesis, though put forward in an unfortunate and irritatingly journalistic manner, doesnot seem to have received the serious attention I feel it deserves. He may well have overstated his case for weapon-wielding Australopithicenes, but this does not invalidate his main contentions.

24. Cf. the discussion of this problem by R. S. Morison, *Daedalus* (Amer. Acad, Arts and Sciences), 1962, 319-40.
25. J. Huxley, *Nature* 197, January 1963, 8-13.
26. Quoted in Thompson 1948, 19.
27. Alföldi 1952.
28. Lattimore 1962.
29. Lattimore 1962, 65.
30. Benedict 1959, Chapter II.
31. Quoted in Daniel 1950a, 117.
32. Collingwood 1946, 329.
33. Finley *et al.* 1960, 160.
34. Quoting again R. S. Morison (cf. note 24).
35. Piggott 1961c, 15, 387.
36. Clark 1943, 118.
37. Carpenter 1958, 185.
38. Tusc. 1. 25.

2

The Earliest Agriculturalists

WE are now in a position to begin our general enquiry, but first let us return for a moment to the question of models of the past. In the old technological model, going back to Thomsen, and in this country Lubbock, there was a Stone Age, defined by the use of flint and stone for edge-tools. These had a good survival-value, so that entire cultures were represented almost wholly by stone artifacts. Of the other elements of material culture, a certain amount of bone and antler and ivory objects could also be put into this Stone Age, and a very few of such perishable substances as wood or fibre. Geological considerations showed, from an early stage in the enquiry, that this Stone Age was of long duration, and lay partly in periods of such antiquity that man and his implements were contemporary with extinct animals, themselves indicative of very different climatic conditions, and in a geography antecedent to that of today. Lubbock therefore took a bold step, and split the Stone Age into two unequal parts—an Old Stone Age or Palaeolithic period, and a New Stone Age, or Neolithic period. The criteria for differentiating the latter were primarily technological: the technique of grinding or polishing the surfaces of stone or flint axe-blades, and the making of pottery. In addition, there were geological overtones, for the Neolithic was seen to lie in the Holocene or Recent period of geological time, the Palaeolithic in the Pleistocene.[1]

With the material available and the field techniques employed in the nineteenth century it would have been difficult or impossible to work within an alternative model, though the possibility had in fact been glimpsed by certain French archaeologists. They suggested a broad classification within what we would now call the Middle and Upper Palaeolithic in terms not only of human artifacts, but of the large mammals on which depended the subsistence of the hunting communities of that time—a Mammoth Age and a Reindeer Age, which could be defined by zoologists classifying the discarded food bones in the various layers of ancient settlement-debris excavated by the archaeologists. This was really a step towards an interdisciplinary approach combining archaeology and the natural sciences, and during the nineteenth century this interest in the ecological setting of prehistoric man was maintained, and applied to later sites, such as the so-called 'lake dwellings' of Switzerland and kitchen-middens of Denmark. And by the beginning of the present century we have the work of Pitt-Rivers on the domestic animal remains from his Dorset sites, and in the Near East, the pioneering efforts of Pumpelly and his team at Anau in Turkmenia.[2]

In these investigations we had in fact the foundations laid for the construction of a new model, which would classify the societies of antiquity in terms of their subsistence-economics; as to whether the basic economy of the community was, for instance, that of hunters, fishers, and food-gatherers, or whether it was that of agricultural food-producers, domesticating animals and growing grain. But, although there was such a promising beginning, interest in this approach lapsed for a generation or so, to be taken up again only in the nineteen-thirties. In the meantime, much irreparable loss had been occasioned, especially on oriental and classical excavations, where the material evidence for ecological interpretation—animal bones, plant or seed remains and so on—was ignored or thrown away. Even today the dominance of the old tradition in these fields, based on art-history rather than archaeology, and the acquisition of museum specimens rather than of knowledge, gravely hampers ecological research. Our information is then incomplete and patchy, but work in the last decade has amassed a great deal of new information, especially on the earliest animal domestication.

When the Stone Age, in its original nineteenth-century form, is looked at in terms of the subsistence-economics model, we find the distinction between the Old and New, the Palaeolithic and the Neolithic, is more or less restated in different terms: the Neolithic cultures are differentiated by being those of agriculturalists. But only more or less: an intermediate group of Mesolithic cultures had already been defined many years ago, continuing the traditions of the Advanced Palaeolithic societies into a temperate and modern environment; traditions not only of a hunting (and increasingly a fishing) economy, but also in the technologies of working in stone, bone and antler. Furthermore, it had long been apparent that agricultural economies ('Neolithic' in the newer sense) did not appear and develop all over the Old World as the natural outcome of local Final Mesolithic traditions, but originated in a restricted area centred on western Asia, spreading thence by complex processes of transmission that we can only guess at. Any ideas of a series of local self-contained evolutionary sequences from Palaeolithic, through Mesolithic, to Neolithic had to be abandoned. The time was ripe for Childe to issue his manifesto of the Neolithic Revolution and its consequences.[3]

It looked at one time as if some of the criteria of the technological model could be embodied in the re-defined economic one. But grinding or polishing stone was soon seen to be meaningless as a distinctive feature of the Neolithic economies, since it was a technique used in Mesolithic and even late Palaeolithic contexts. The making of pottery for long seemed significant, but in recent years the status of this criterion of agricultural economies has been seriously eroded. First we discovered communities in what we had, clumsily, to call a 'pre-pottery Neolithic' state of culture in a desperate attempt to retain something of the old technological model.[4] Such communities had domestic animals, grain, permanent settlements, stone implements of so-called Neolithic type, like axe-blades, but no use of pottery, only stone vessels. The identification of such cultures from Jericho to Thessaly started us re-thinking this whole problem, and then we found we had also to consider another group of cultures, whose stone and flint equipment was that of late Mesolithic hunters and fishers, but in whose occupation debris were the remains of domesticated sheep or goats. We will discuss these problems shortly. I just mention them here to show that, with whatever conceptual model one is working, the definition between the Mesolithic and the Neolithic, the food-gathering and the food-producing economies, is not clear-cut and obvious. So far as possible, I try to avoid using the old Thomsen-Lubbock nomenclature, though it still has its uses. We should note in passing that the use of the terms 'Palaeolithic', 'Mesolithic', and 'Neolithic' in reference to subsistence-economics of communities, is a Western usage not shared by Russian archaeologists, who still work within the framework of the old technological model, and use the presence of polished stone tools, pottery, etc., as the criterion for denoting a culture 'Neolithic'. The term 'Mesolithic' is rarely used; cultures which we would group under this head tend to be called 'Early Neolithic'.[5] It is important to remember that a move from a hunting and gathering economy to one involved in animal husbandry or crop-growing will only take place when it is to the economic advantage of the community concerned, and when the ancestors of domestic species—suitable wild mammals or plants—exist in natural conditions. Agriculture is irrelevant to a well-functioning hunting community and its adoption involves profound shifts of psychological habit; it is significant that in northern Europe at least only the dog was domesticated by Mesolithic communities, and as an adjunct to more efficient hunting, not a modification of the existing economy.

As a necessary background for the beginnings of agriculture we must first look briefly at the general characteristics of the final hunting and food-gathering peoples in certain areas of Europe and west Asia. The two continents are indivisible for our immediate purposes: we shall see shortly how the natural factors of zoology and botany enforce this on us. Again, we shall only deal with certain regions, important to us either as European (and so the direct subject of our enquiry) or as those of agricultural origins. We must remember that the temporal overlap of agricultural and hunting economies has to be reckoned in millennia; the survival of the latter groups, whether in the Circumpolar Zone or in central Asia, forms a classic instance of the conserving type of society to which I referred in the first chapter.

We must first consider the question of chronology. Using radiocarbon (or C^{14}) dates (which with their imperfections are the best we have), we may place the beginning of the Upper Palaeolithic phase, and with it an early stage of the last (Würm) glaciation, at between *c.* 40,000 and *c.* 30,000 years ago.[6] So far as western Europe is concerned, we are in a world in which *Homo sapiens*—modern man, as handsome and as wise as us—was colonising the west from origins that seem to lie in the Near East, bringing with him a set of new techniques for manufacturing flint implements, and consequently new types of tools and weapons. These latter were essentially related to hunting techniques dictated by the changing mammalian fauna with which these little communities had to deal to obtain their basic protein diet: by the end of the glacial period the reindeer was the main quarry, as those nineteenth-century French archaeologists saw when they talked of L'Âge du Renne. And in terms of dates, the final retreat of the glaciers from Europe, and so the end of the late Glacial period and the beginning of modern climatic conditions, came around 8,500 years ago.[7]

This means that the Advanced Palaeolithic hunting communities of Europe with their varying techniques of tool making (often no doubt reflecting changing hunting modes) and their remarkable naturalistic art on cave walls or carved in stone or bone, have to be spread over a time-span of some 25,000 or 30,000 years. During this staggering period of time, so great as to be almost meaningless to most of us, there appears, from the archaeological evidence, to have been little re-adjustment of the human societies to the natural conditions, once a satisfactory mode of livelihood had been created. That it must have been satisfactory, the very survival of the peoples concerned, over the long millennia, is demonstration: again, the fact that no profound modification was made in the material equipment of daily life implies that the basic needs of the food quest were satisfied by the use of gear modified only in detail over the vast period of time involved. This does not necessarily mean that the hunting tactics of these peoples were very efficient, or that the human population by any means exploited to the full the natural resources of, for instance, animal meat. 'The population of the primary hunting and collecting culture is not limited by the potential amount of food, but by man's ability to get it during the leanest season.'[8] We shall see shortly that we can make approximate calculations to test this in another context of hunting and gathering.

Estimates of population in antiquity are notoriously tricky things: historians are not very happy when questioned even on the population of England at the time of the Domesday survey, and that of Roman Britain is still more contentious. However, provided we remember we are embarking on no more than reasoned guesses, it should not be impossible to make demographic estimates, even if our evidence is less secure than for historical periods: we may now begin by enquiring into the hunting population of Late Glacial Europe. We can of course only use analogies from recent primitive peoples, such as the Australian aborigines or the Caribou Eskimos, the average of which would be three persons per 100 square miles. Again on analogy, we may suppose that hunting bands would more likely number twenty or twenty-five people than larger totals: fifty would be the limit. Grahame Clark once reckoned the known cave-shelters which could be inhabited by such groups in Late Glacial England, south of the limit of permanent ice, and added a percentage of assumed undiscovered sites, with the result that he suggested a population of 250 persons for the area. A few bus-loads in a traffic jam, as he remarked, but though he favoured this minimum figure he pointed out that higher figures, up to the order of 2,000 were possible.[9]

By the closing phase of the Glacial Period, from about 11,000 B.C. we can see in north and west Europe such a tiny and migratory population engaged essentially in reindeer-hunting. In the south-west, we know them from their winter cave-shelters, one of which, that of La Madeleine in the Dordogne, has given its name to this Magdalenian culture. They have elaborate and finely made tools and weapons, including barbed bone or antler spear-points,[10] and their art marks the culmination, in modelled polychrome technique, of the long traditions of the Franco-Cantabrian area: Altamira and Font-de-Gaume belong to this phase, with the finest work at Lascaux rather earlier (occupation in the cave is dated to 15,000 years ago).[11]

In northern Germany, the counterparts of these reindeer-hunters are known from summer lake-side camping-places near Hamburg, as for instance at Meiendorf and later at Stellmoor, where sacrificed reindeer had been lashed to stones and thrown into the pool in some rite of hunting magic; at the later site, there seem to have been three sacred poles set up, one schematically carved into a human head and shoulders.[12]

At both sites too the remains of wooden arrows survived, showing that bows as well as spears were used in hunting;[13] remains of wood spears have been found in earlier Palaeolithic contexts; one, nearly 8 feet long, was found between the ribs of a mammoth at Lehringen near Hanover, and the tip of another at Clacton on the Essex coast.[14]

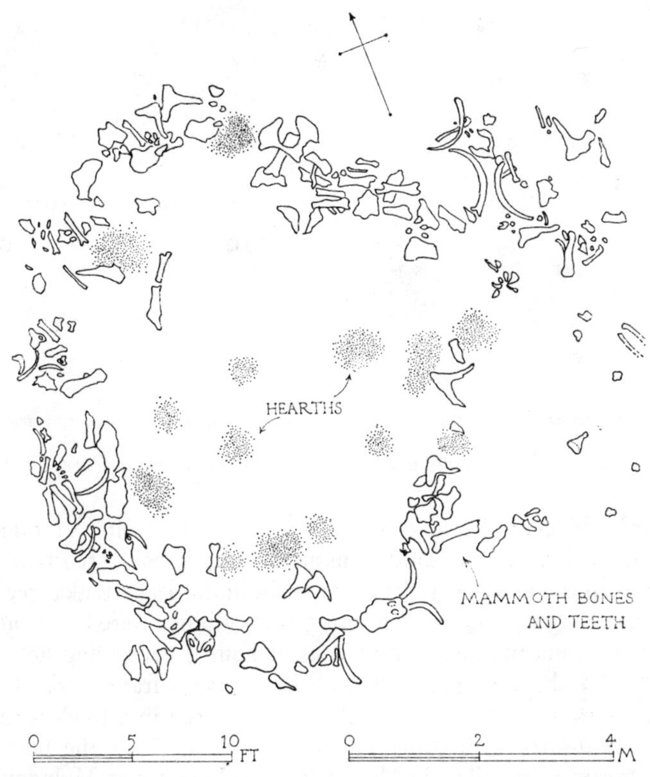

1. *Middle Palaeolithic tent-stance, c. 40,000* B.C., *Molodova, South Russia.*

Perhaps the earliest evidence for a humanly-constructed shelter or hut so far known are the tent-standings marked by a ring of mammoth bones, and dating the Middle Palaeolithic Mousterian phase, at Molodova in south Russia, and perhaps before 40,000 B.C. In the mouth of the cave known as the Grotte du Renne at Arcy-sur-Cure in the Yonne valley in France, 'post-holes' set in a rough oval enclose hearths and occupational debris: the 'posts' seem to have been mammoths' tusks, and a radio-carbon date of a little over 30,000 years has been obtained for the structure; representations of such huts are known in later Paleolithic art.

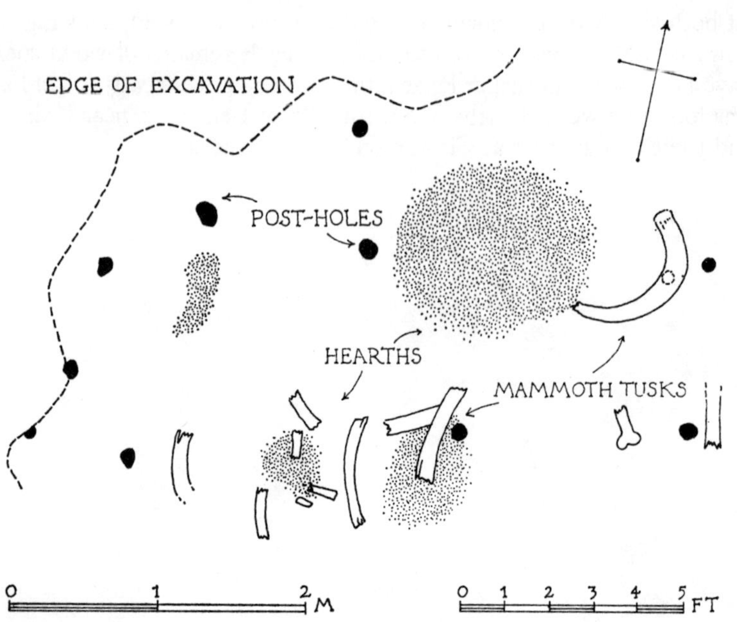

2. *Upper Palaeolithic structure in cave, c.30,000* B.C., *Arcy-sur-Cure, France.*

Eastwards, in central and eastern Europe (as at Dolní Věstonice in Czechoslovakia), and in south Russia at such sites as Kostienki and Gagarino on the Don, at Avdeevo, or again in the Lake Baikal region at Malta and Buryet, mammoth-hunting communities were living, at least seasonally, in encampments or villages of houses partly dug down into the subsoil and roofed probably with skins over a framework of mammoth's bones or tusks, for want of better material in a treeless tundra. Circular tent-sites with stones or bones to hold down the tent or to secure its guy-ropes, like the Middle Palaeolithic sites at Molodova just mentioned, are known from Mezin in the Ukraine and at sites near Hamburg such as Ahrensburg; these last date from the final glacial phase, about 8500 B.C.[15] (Figs. 1–3)

The English Channel had not yet been formed; the Thames is the abbreviated headwaters of a river tributary to a greater Rhine, flowing through low-lying land now submerged in the southern part of the North Sea. Britain was a peninsula of the European continent, and there was a coming and going of hunting peoples, their movements dictated by that of the herds of larger mammals on which they depended for their livelihood, over the whole northern seaboard from the Pyrenees to the White Sea.[16] The climatic conditions were changing; by 8000 B.C. the last of the

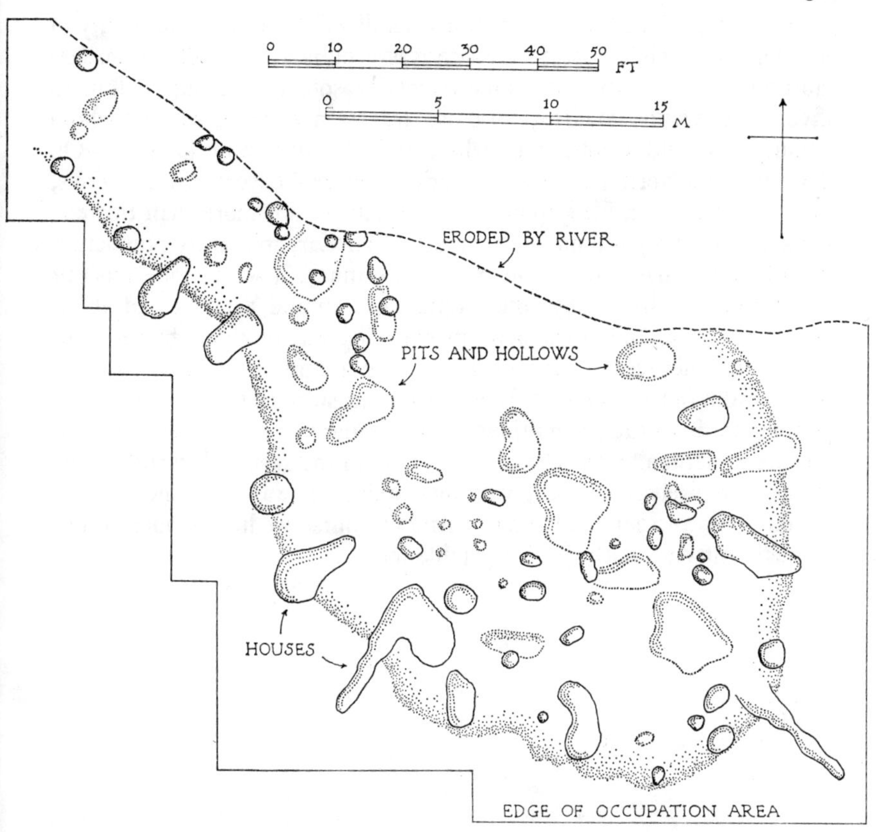

3. *Upper Palaeolithic settlement*, *c.* 20,000 B.C., *Avdeevo*, *South Russia.*

final glacial phases is over. With the retreat of the ice the vegetation changed accordingly. The botanical climax—the maximum number of plant species that can successfully survive—shifts from the stunted sub-arctic flora of the tundra to the beginnings of woodlands and grasslands, with the hardy birch as the dominant tree. The day of the reindeer, in what was becoming temperate Europe, was over, and in its place the red deer and the elk (in natural conditions animals of the woodlands), were establishing themselves as the main source of meat, together with wild cattle. Hunters of red deer take the place of those who speared the reindeer in northern Spain and south-western France;[17] and again in Britain, Scandinavia, and on the north European plain we can identify, by the eighth millennium B.C., variant groups of hunting communities; less certainly, we can perceive them elsewhere in Europe at the same time. In

Yorkshire, the Star Carr excavations enable us to study a community of hunters in detail.[18] A lake-side site was occupied repeatedly from late autumn to early spring for some twenty seasons by a group of four to five family groups, totalling not more than twenty-five persons, of whom about five would be adult men who could effectively hunt big game. On analogy from North American conditions before the European invasions, one can asssume a likely population density of not more than thirteen persons to 100 square miles, so that the Star Carr migratory population would have ranged over some 200 square miles: if we average this out for Britain we arrive at a total population, around 7500 B.C., of about 10,000 persons. Now their main protein diet was provided by red deer meat, and they could have obtained their minimum necessary calorie intake from the venison of fifty beasts a year, so since the likely red deer population in natural conditions would amount to about 3,400 deer to the 200 square miles we have allotted our hunting group, they could have gorged themselves on meat without coming anyway near the full exploitation of the game potential.[19] And of course we have ignored other animals and said nothing of vegetable food.

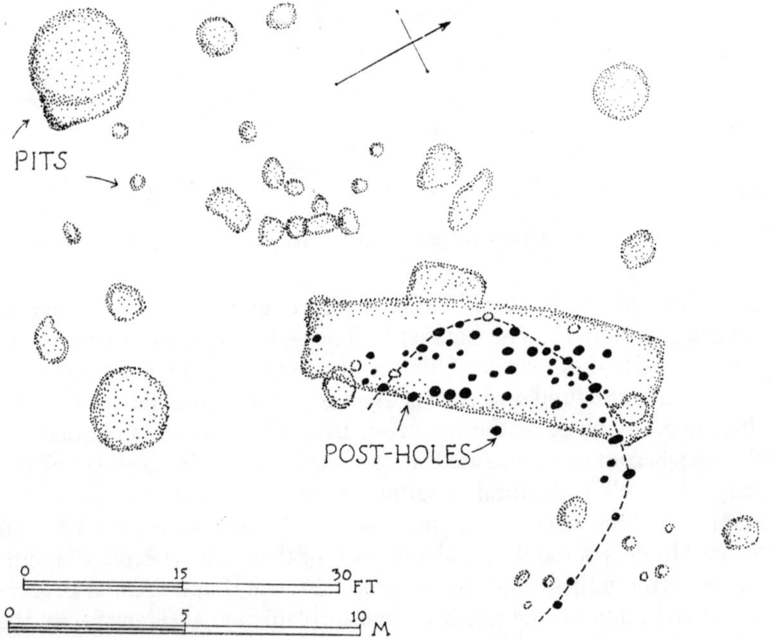

4. *Mesolithic settlement, c.5,000* B.C., *Moita do Sebastião, Muge, Portugal.*

5. *Mesolithic cave-painting of hunting scene, between 12,000 and 3,000* B.C., *Cueva Remigia, Spain.*

Settlements of these post-glacial groups of hunting and fishing peoples are known from several localities in Europe, with huts marked by roughly oval hollows, as at Tannstock on the Federsee in south Germany, at Schötz in Switzerland, and Farnham in England. Circular or horse-shoe shaped setting of posts for huts or windbreaks are also known, for instance in Portugal at Moita do Sebastião (*c*. 5400 B.C.: Fig. 4), in north Germany as at Hörste and other sites, or on Oransay in the Hebrides; and other settings of less certain plan as at Downton in Wiltshire. Tent stances with stones in the manner of the earlier sites in the Hamburg region are also known in later contexts, in both instances reminiscent of North American Indian 'tipi rings' of similar function.[20] Paintings on the walls of rock-shelters in south-east Spain, broadly Mesolithic in date, show vivid scenes of hunting and warfare with bows and arrows, (Figs. 5–7) as well as domestic affairs such as gathering wild honey.[21]

One animal was domesticated, at least by the eighth millennium B.C., and that was the dog. As I have said, domestication in this instance does not involve any change in the basic economy, it merely intensifies and

6. *Mesolithic cave-painting of bowmen, between 12,000 and 3,000* B.C. *Cueva Remigia, Spain.*

7. *Mesolithic cave-painting of bowmen, between 12,000 and 3,000* B.C., *Cueva Remigia, Spain.*

renders more efficient the techniques of hunting, like inventing a new type of trap or an improved fish-hook. And indeed, in recent discussions, it has been asked whether perhaps the initial taming of the species had not in fact taken place in contemporary agricultural societies, even if at geographically long remove, or that Mesolithic peoples had acquired the idea of domesticating animals as a borrowed cultural trait. So far, however, the north European domestic dogs are the earliest known, those claimed for the Mesolithic Near East being in fact wolves.[22]

The basic traditions of these eighth millennium hunting and fishing communities were continued until at least the second millennium B.C. in various conservative areas of northern Europe and Asia where agriculture was not adopted.[23] A series of cemeteries, from the Baltic to south Siberia, represent such peoples, with a basically hunting, and perhaps even more significantly, a fishing economy, which may permit of permanent settlement in one place, as with the Indians of British Columbia up to recent times.[24] Within the circumpolar zone there was a notable survival of conserving hunter-fisher communities.[25] The skills of these Palaeolithic and Mesolithic peoples were not negligible: to them we owe not only the all basic crafts of the hunter with spear, bow and arrow and the fisherman with line, net or trap, but also the invention of the first boats, cut from the solid or skin-covered; sledges and skis, probably whistles and even pan-pipes.[26] Even in our modern western world the hunting of the seas plays its important role, and Neolithic and Mesolithic economies are concisely enshrined today in the title of the Ministry of Agriculture and Fisheries.

We noted in passing that agriculture, whether involving taming animals or domesticating plants, could necessarily only be conceived as a technique of subsistence in regions where the wild ancestors of the cultivated types appeared in abundant and demonstrative form. It is theoretically possible, for instance (though there is no evidence for it) for reindeer to have been tamed or half-tamed among Advanced Palaeolithic societies as with the Lapps of today;[27] if Mesolithic societies did in fact initiate dog-breeding, it would have been (as the skeletal evidence indeed implies) based on the taming of local wolves; elsewhere the wild ancestor would have been the dingo or pariah type. Basically, of course, the ancestors of the Old World domestic animals go back to the Pleistocene, but by the beginning of modern climatic conditions around 10,000 B.C. the distribution of the key species was sporadic and by no means universal. The wild ox, which was by no means the earliest animal to be domesticated, had in fact a wide range in Eurasia, from Britain to North Africa in the west in a broad band extending north of the Himalayas to the Pacific coast; the pig too was wild over most of Europe, and in extensive tracts of southern Asia. But what we are now perceiving from the archaeological evidence to be the critical species in earliest domestication, sheep and goats, have in their wild state a very limited distribution indeed.[28] With exceptions in Mediterranean coasts and islands and perhaps in east Rumania,[29] they did not occur wild in Europe in post-glacial times, so that whatever the date and context of their original domestication, it is more likely to have taken place within those west or central Asiatic regions where the wild species commonly occur. It should be noted in passing that wild sheep show no more obvious wool than wild goats, and domestication for fleeces would be a secondary development:[30] woollen textiles have however been found at Çatal Hüyük in Anatolia in a context probably before 6000 B.C.[31] The natural circumstances of geography and zoology combined to limit the likely areas of initial domestication to a quite restricted region, and, as we shall see, the same applies to cereal cultivation. (Figs. 8–9)

Within this area we must visualise hunting and food-gathering communities in climatic conditions approaching those of today: open dry grass-lands or park-lands on the lower flanks of the hills with a fauna including not only deer but wild sheep and goats. The hunting of small ruminants by driving them into traps or enclosures for immediate slaughter could easily be modified to herding them within corrals, with the intention of pursuing a longer-term policy, and we would have the situation implied by the archaeological evidence, in which the first animal domestication was in fact herding. The domestication of the dog would have helped in this process: its initial association with man, as wolf-cub or dingo pup, would have been that of the scavenger and camp-follower. With the cultivation of plant crops, a secondary relationship between man and animals was set up—not only scavenging by pigs, but crop-robbing by them and by wild cattle. Human settlements could offer their first attraction to animals by their refuse and offal; to this was now added green crops, as irresistible as were Mr Macgregor's lettuces to Peter Rabbit. The essential conditions for the domestication of all the main farm stock would now have been achieved, and the theoretical basis for either pastoralism or settled mixed farming established. Domestication not for flesh and milk and hides alone, but for transport, was a later development, largely dependent on the recognition of castration as a means of subduing the uncomfortably potent bull. The taming of the horse was an altogether separate achievement of later prehistory, to be discussed in a later chapter.

Archaeological evidence shows us the same story with the earliest cereal crops, those of barley and wheat.[32] Here the wild ancestors—the so-called noble grasses—have a most restricted distribution, between the

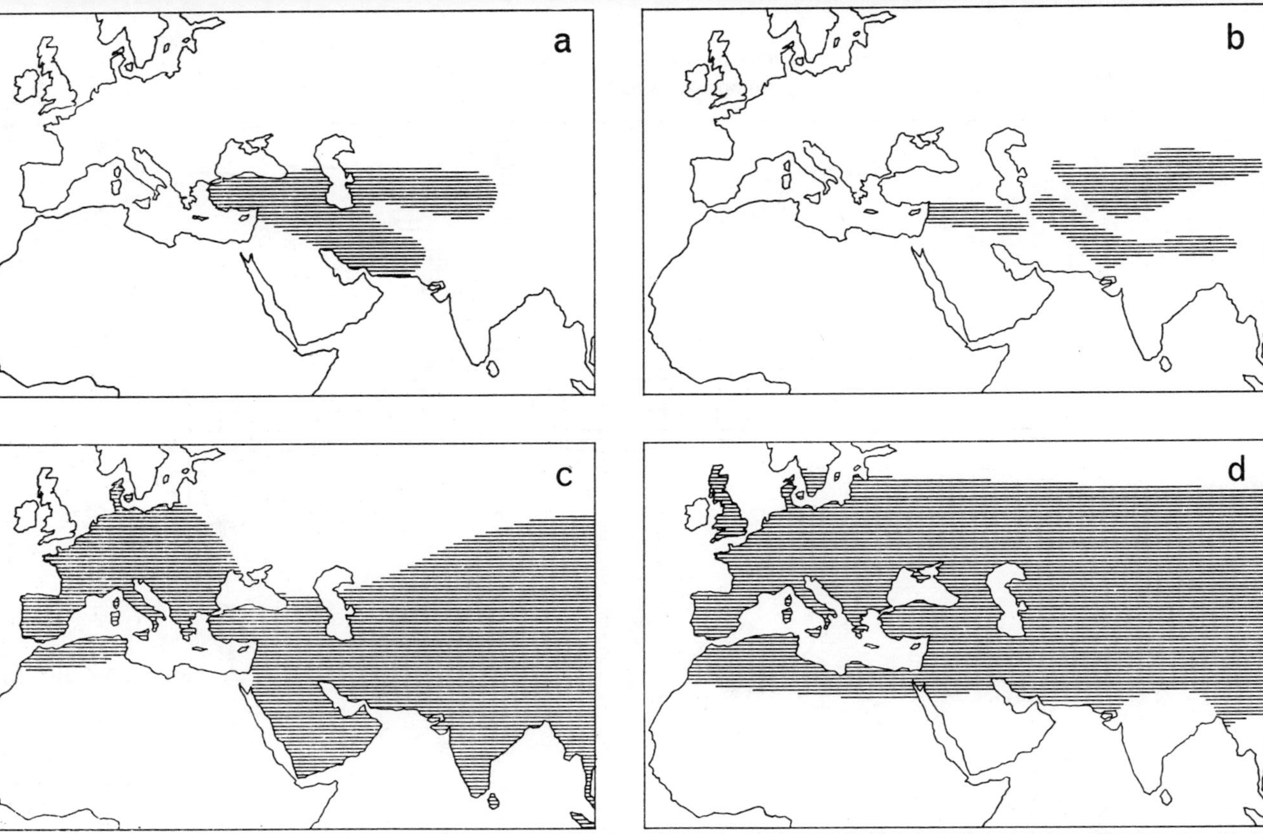

8. *Generalised distribution of a, wild goat; b, sheep; c, pig and d, cattle.*

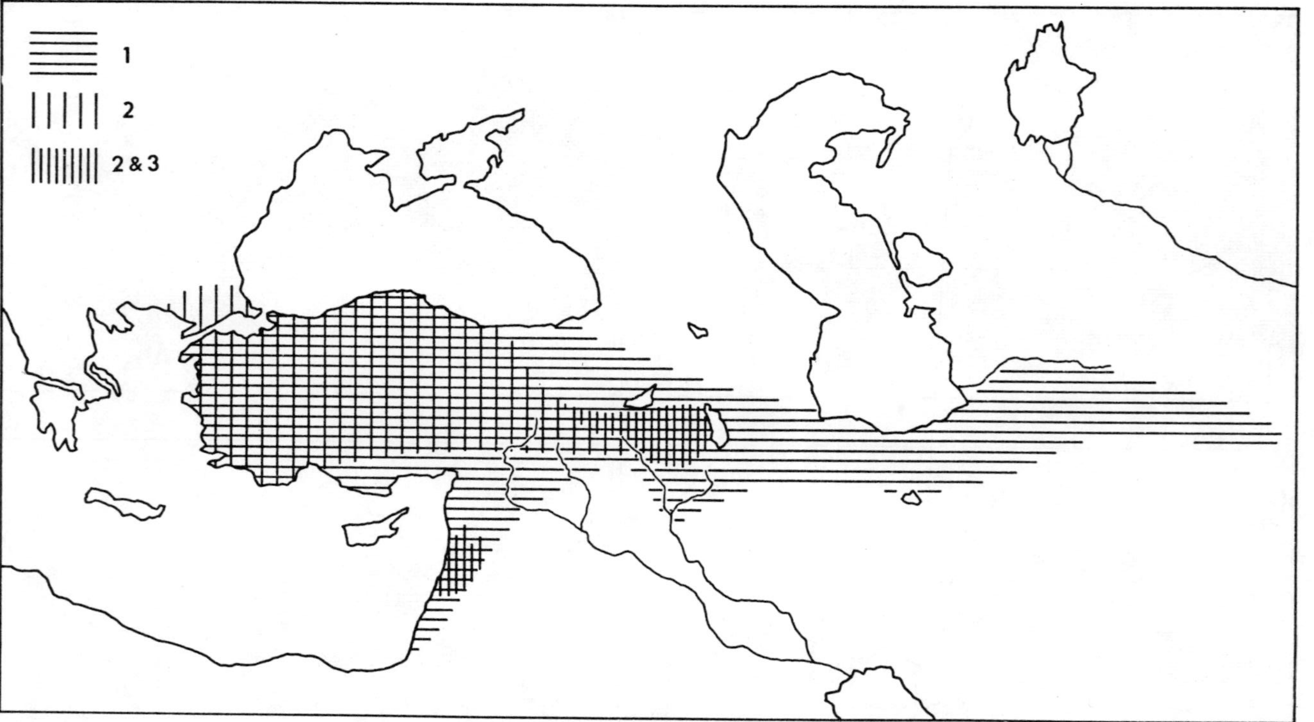

9. *Generalised distribution of* 1, *wild barley* (Hordeum spontaneum); 2, *wheat* (Triticum aegilopoides); 3, *wheat* (Triticum dicoccoides).

Adriatic and the Caspian Sea; in just this area we have evidence of their first cultivation. The carbohydrate content of a balanced diet was thus added to the protein of the hunters and herdsmen, and as in antiquity a pure crop was hardly ever grown, we can see only an alternative domination of wheat or barley in the grain yield. But on these two all primary cereal cultivation was based, utilising a variety of forms including at least three wheats and two barleys. As agriculture in Europe was pushed further and further beyond the bounds of the natural habitat of the original grasses, forms resistant to the deteriorated conditions of damp and cold were developed, and types of grasses originally present as weeds of cultivation in wheat and barley crops became established in their own right as rye and oats. These are secondary cereal crops, characteristic of later prehistory. Millet was cultivated in Neolithic Europe but not apparently in the Near East: one form has a wild ancestor in the Mediterranean area, and we may here have a specifically European domestication. (Fig. 9)

The leguminous plants, of the type of peas, beans, vetches, and lentils, were again cultivated in primary contexts: whereas cereal crops exhaust the soil of nitrogen, these plants replace it, and crop rotation may have been appreciated as a technique for continuous cropping at an early age. A simple system of rotation involving a period of fallow is inherently likely to have been developed at an early stage, and the use of some form of manure appreciated. The scatter of potsherds, food-bone fragments and so on found on British prehistoric field-surfaces from the later second millennium B.C. onwards testifies to the use of household and farmyard muck for such purposes.[33] Flax was evidently grown for its nutritive oily seeds before the fibres of its stems were used for textiles,[34] and although their story is obscure, many of the cultivated fruits must be of high antiquity: small apples were cultivated in Switzerland and Britain around 3000 B.C.[35] And before we leave these generalities, let us remember that man does not live by bread alone, and all the cereals and most fruits can form the basis of fermented drinks, as can honey.[36]

If we now turn to the Near East, we can review the evidence for the initial local domestication of animals and the cultivation of plants. As I have said, herding of sheep or goats seems, on present showing, the earliest step away from a purely hunting and gathering economy. In northern Iraq, a settlement site at Zawi Chemi Shanidar, with traces of oval or circular semi-permanent huts implying perhaps intermittent and transient occupation, and a flint and stone industry including heavy ground stone axe-blades, is of great importance. Although earlier cave deposits near by show wild goats to be three times as common as sheep, the animal bones on the site included only a few wild goats, but large quantities of those of sheep, 60 per cent of them yearlings: this implies selective herding and killing off the greater part of each year's young for food and skins before the end of the year. The radiocarbon date for this site is *c.* 9000 B.C., and this so far is our earliest date for any form of animal domestication, around 11,000 years ago.[37] A similar situation seems to have existed on the Black Sea coast of Rumania in the La Adam cave in the Dobrogea. Here there is a long series of stratified deposits going back to the beginning of the last glaciation, and in these Pleistocene levels are wild sheep. In the post-glacial deposits, in a Mesolithic context, one finds the percentage of sheep to other animals greatly increases, and young animals predominate, as in the Iraqi site.[38] Unfortunately there is no direct evidence of date, and the same applies to sites in southern and western France, where a similar association of sheep or goat with post-glacial cultures of late Mesolithic type has been recorded.[39]

In the Near East we next have, at a radiocarbon date around 8850 B.C.[40] communities in Palestine who although they did not domesticate animals but had their economy based on gazelle-hunting, nevertheless used flint-bladed reaping knives or straight sickles for cutting some crop that is likely to have been a wild or cultivated cereal. These Natufian people lived in cave shelters or (as at 'Eynan or Naḥal Oren) in open settlements of oval or circular houses up to about 25 feet diameter, partly sunk in the ground with walls of polished red-painted plaster.[41] (Fig. 10) In the famous site of Jericho a settlement and probable shrine of these people formed the first occupation of the place, followed by a long series of subsequent phases, with mud brick oval, single-roomed, huts and later rectangular many-roomed houses: the oval houses have contemporary counterparts at Naḥal Oren. The material equipment of the builders included stone and flint tools, stone bowls and platters, querns and sickles, but no pottery. Goats were domesticated in the later phases and a cereal crop grown, and at a date before 7000 B.C. the settlement, estimated at 10 acres in extent, was surrounded by a town wall with defensive towers up to 30 feet high. A most remarkable feature was the modelling in clay of the features of the living on human skulls; the earliest individual human portraiture. This, the first 'pre-pottery Neolithic' culture to be described in detail, continued to at least 6000 B.C. on the Jericho site.[42] Comparable cultures are represented in Iraq, as at Jarmo, and in other areas such as Anatolia and Cyprus, and must form the basis of the development of the subsequent peasant (and later urban) economies of the Fertile Crescent.[43] (Pl. 1, page 46; Fig. 11)

But Europe also came into the ambit of these earliest farming communities who were not making pottery. At Argissa, near Larissa in

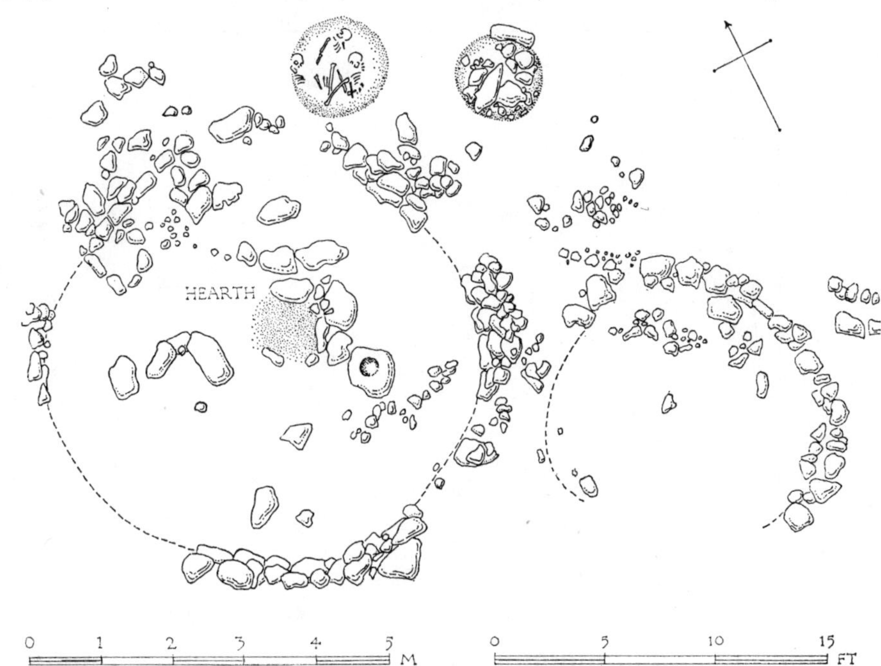

10. *Mesolithic houses of the Natufian Culture, c. 9,000* B.C. *'Eynan, Palestine.*

Thessaly, the lowest occupation in a prehistoric 'tell' settlement was that of people growing wheat and barley, flax and probably millet, and with sheep forming 84 per cent of their domesticated animals, followed by 10 per cent of pig and 5 per cent of cattle; the dog was also tamed. There was a flint, obsidian, and stone equipment, and houses were probably timber-framed and mud-walled, but no pottery was made. The site can hardly be unique, and northern Greece and the Balkans must evidently now be regarded as the westward fringe of these early agricultural settlements. Radiocarbon dates are unfortunately not yet available from Argissa, but those from other sites suggest that it should certainly lie before 6000 B.C. The Nea Nikomedeia site in Macedonia, of an archaeological stage (with pottery) subsequent to that of Argissa, has a radiocarbon date of *c*. 6220 B.C.[44]

In Mesopotamia, the earliest evidence we have of domesticated cattle is in contexts of about 5000 B.C., but those need not be the earliest. By this time we have, from Anatolia and the Levant eastwards to Persia and Turkmenia, a well-established pattern of peasant communities, with villages and small towns of mud-walled or mud-brick buildings forming

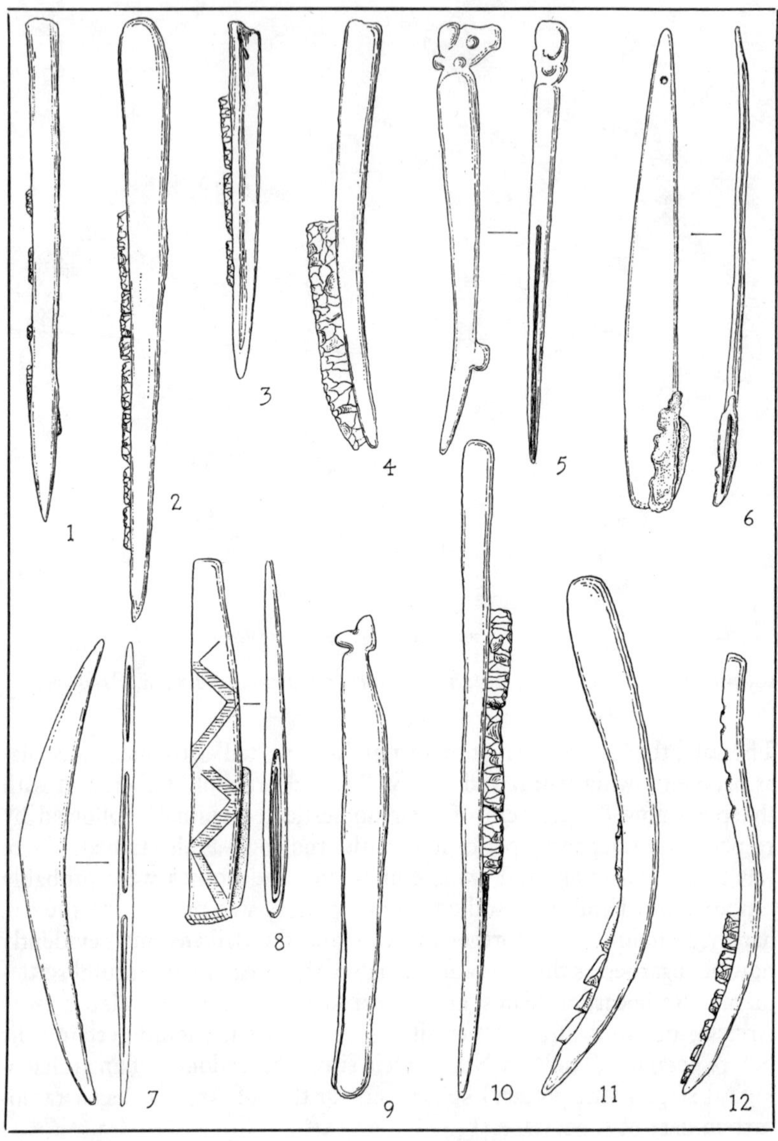

11. *Flint-bladed bone tools: 1, harpoon-head, Mesolithic, Denmark; 2–4, knives, Mesolithic, Lake Baikal; 5, reaping-knife, Natufian; 6–9, reaping-knives, Neolithic, Iran; 10, reaping-knife, Neolithic, Egypt; 11, Sickle, Neolithic, Karanovo, Bulgaria; 12, sickle, Bronze Age, Spain.*

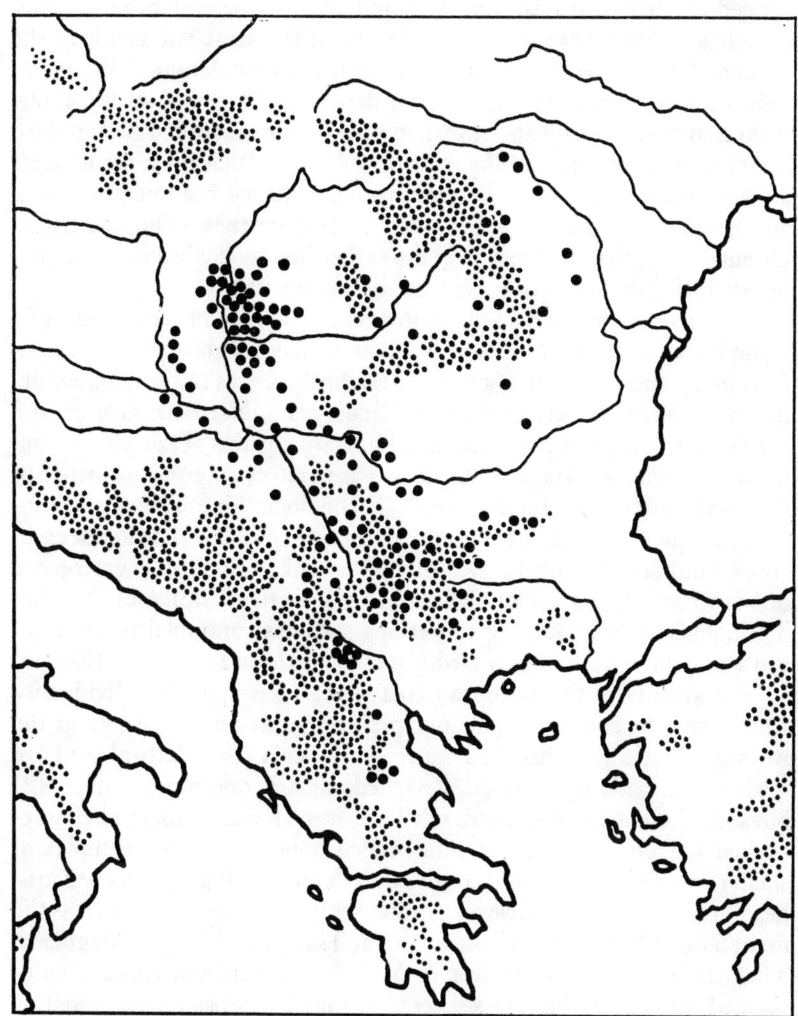

12. *Distribution of the earliest agricultural communities in East Europe (Starčevo-Körös and related cultures), c.5,000* B.C.

permanent settlements supported by a farming system sufficiently advanced to obviate any shifting of population, owing to temporary land exhaustion. Successive occupation levels on the same site result in the familiar 'tell' formations resulting from the accumulation of mud-wall debris and on occasion wind-blown deposits. There are strong hints, from traditions already ancient when they became recorded by the third millennium in Sumer and the second in Anatolia, that these settlements are the outcome of a social system involving elected headmen or rulers, an Assembly of elders, and a body of free citizens. The pattern of Oriental despotism familiar from the earlier literate civilisations may not be original, but a comparatively late development.[45]

The archaeological evidence shows that this type of settlement, of a stone-using agricultural peasantry, was widely established in eastern Europe by about 5000 B.C. and once established, was to form an enduring and consistent pattern for some 3000 years. Northern Greece and the Balkans, the great Danubian and Hungarian plains, Transylvania and northwards to Slovakia; this vast area was in effect a western province of the Near Eastern peasant cultures.[46] Technological innovation in Mesopotamia, including the invention of writing and the development of copper and bronze metallurgy, formed the background to the emergence of Sumerian and Akkadian civilisation, but on the peripheries, whether Turkmenia or Bulgaria, the conserving societies continued in their set ways, still illiterate, and only tardily moving to the use of copper. (Fig. 12)

But already in the European area we can see signs of individuality which were to endure throughout prehistory. At an early stage in the western Asiatic sequence, at least in Turkmenia (as at Jeitun) we have settlements made up of small, detached, square, one-roomed houses,[47] but soon the settlement-pattern of village or town was (as today) a closely-packed warren of contiguous mud-walled buildings, each a complex of small rectangular rooms and courts, with flat roofs. (Fig. 13) In the European 'tell' settlements, however, the houses in the earlier sites, such as the first phase of Karanovo in Bulgaria, or at Tsangli and Otzaki-Magula in Thessaly, or Nea Nikomedeia in Macedonia, were individual single-roomed structures, loosely scattered within the village area, and this form of planning was never given up. Furthermore, the house construction involves not only baked mud, but a light framing of poles and wattles; we know also from numerous house-models, that the roofs were gabled or pitched, not flat.[48] (Figs. 14, 15) What we are seeing is in part a modification in architectural modes in response to changed climatic conditions. Effective mud-wall construction and maintenance demands hot summers and dry winters, and just as agriculture itself was extended beyond the original natural habitat of the wild cereals, with the consequent

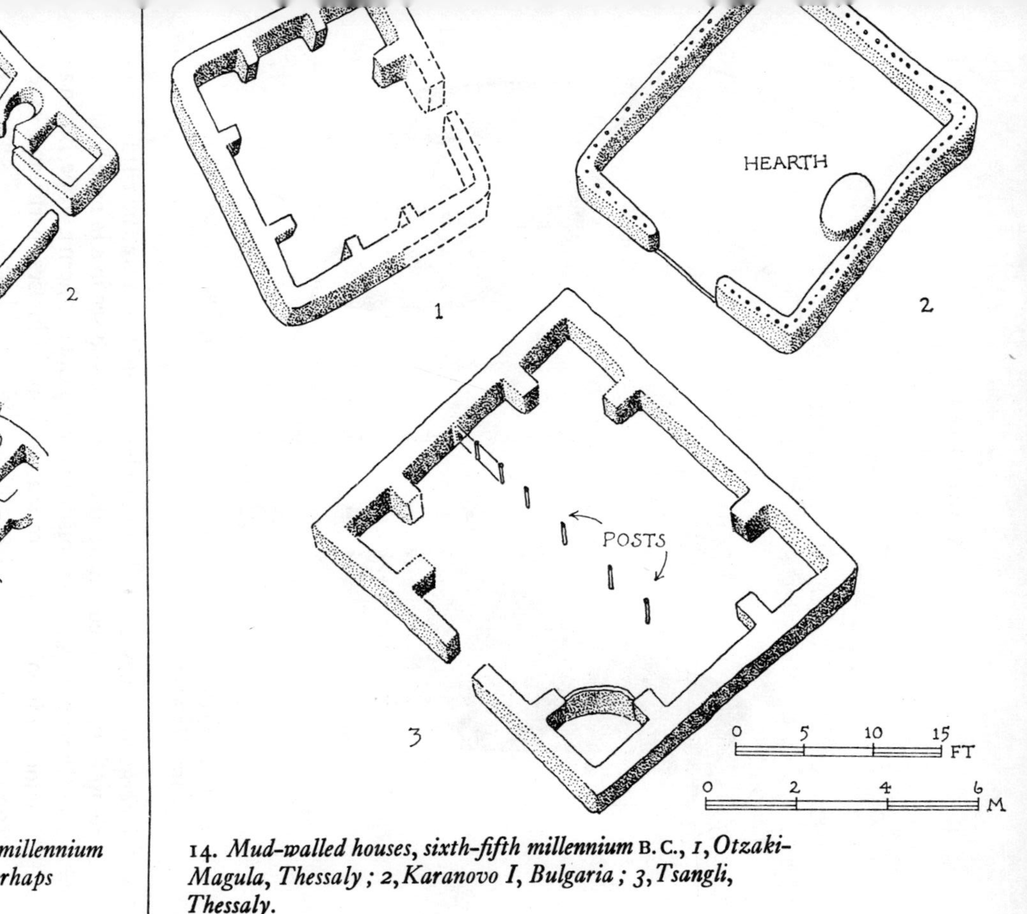

13. *1–2, single-room houses, perhaps sixth–seventh millennium* B.C., *Jeitun, Turkmenia; 3, agglomerated rooms, perhaps sixth millennium* B.C., *Tal-i-Bakun, Iran.*

14. *Mud-walled houses, sixth–fifth millennium* B.C., *1, Otzaki-Magula, Thessaly; 2, Karanovo I, Bulgaria; 3, Tsangli, Thessaly.*

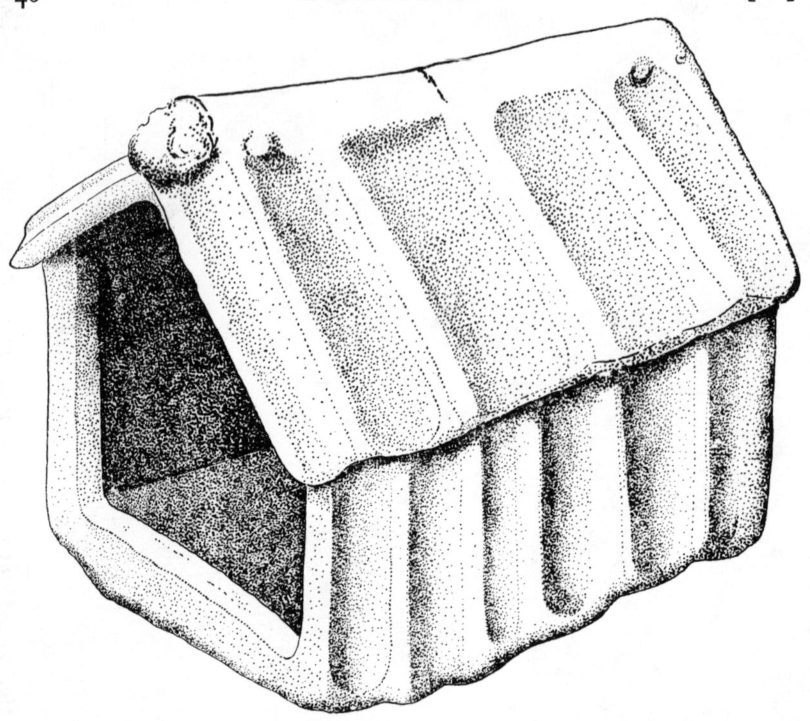

15. *Pottery model of house, log-built with gabled roof, fourth millennium* B.C., *Strelice, Moravia.*

emergence of new hardy forms, so house-building was changed in character to fit the less clement weather. And we will see in a minute how even more drastic changes were made in central and northern Europe. But in all instances the village plan of scattered single houses, barns and byres, contrasting as it still does with the Oriental, close-packed settlement unit, seems to go back to the earliest farming cultures of Europe.

A good well-excavated example of an east European 'tell' settlement is that of Karanovo, near Stara Zagora in Bulgaria.[49] (Pl. II; Fig. 16) There are seven main phases of occupation, the debris of which forms a mound over 40 feet high. In the sixth phase a few copper objects, probably imports, appear. The primary settlement on the site is probably of the sixth or early fifth millennium B.C., the sixth ends about 2000 B.C. or a little earlier. As we saw, the single-roomed houses are square in the earliest phase, but oblong and with a porch in the later phases, mud-walled with a wattle core, and with wall-plaster gaily painted in white and maroon bands and S-curves: coloured wall-plaster, with red and white zigzags on a yellow ground, is known from Neolithic huts elsewhere

1. *Naturalistic plaster modelling over human skull, seventh millennium* B.C., *from Jericho, Palestine.* (Photo. Jericho Excavation Fund)

II (*caption on facing page*)

a

b

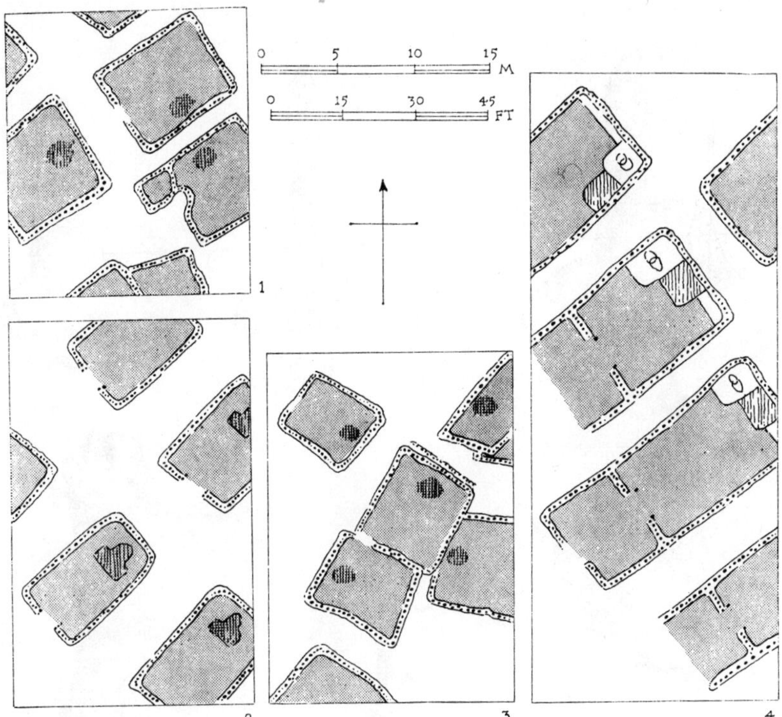

16. *Wattled and mud-walled houses at Karanovo, Bulgaria, from sixth-third millennium* B.C.: *1, Period* I; *2, Period* II; *3, Period* V; *4, Period* VI.

as at Grossgartach in Germany, probably of the fourth millenium B.C.[50] At another Bulgarian site of the same period as Karanovo clay models of chairs, benches and couches give a hint as to household furniture.[51] The houses are of a size appropriate to a natural or nuclear family of say five persons, and throughout the history of the site there were about 50 to 60 at any one time, so the population would have been about 300. Now we can make approximate calculations, based on corn yield per acre in primitive conditions, with deductions for fallow land and seed corn, which indicate an annual consumption-yield of about 7 bushels. In classical times, the annual grain consumption per head of the population

II. (*a*) *Square wattle-and-mud-walled houses, Starčevo-Körös culture, sixth millennium* B.C., *lowest level of 'tell' of Karanovo, Bulgaria.* (Photo. Mikov)

II. (*b*) *Section through 'tell', sixth–second millennium* B.C., *at Karanovo, Bulgaria.* (Photo. author)

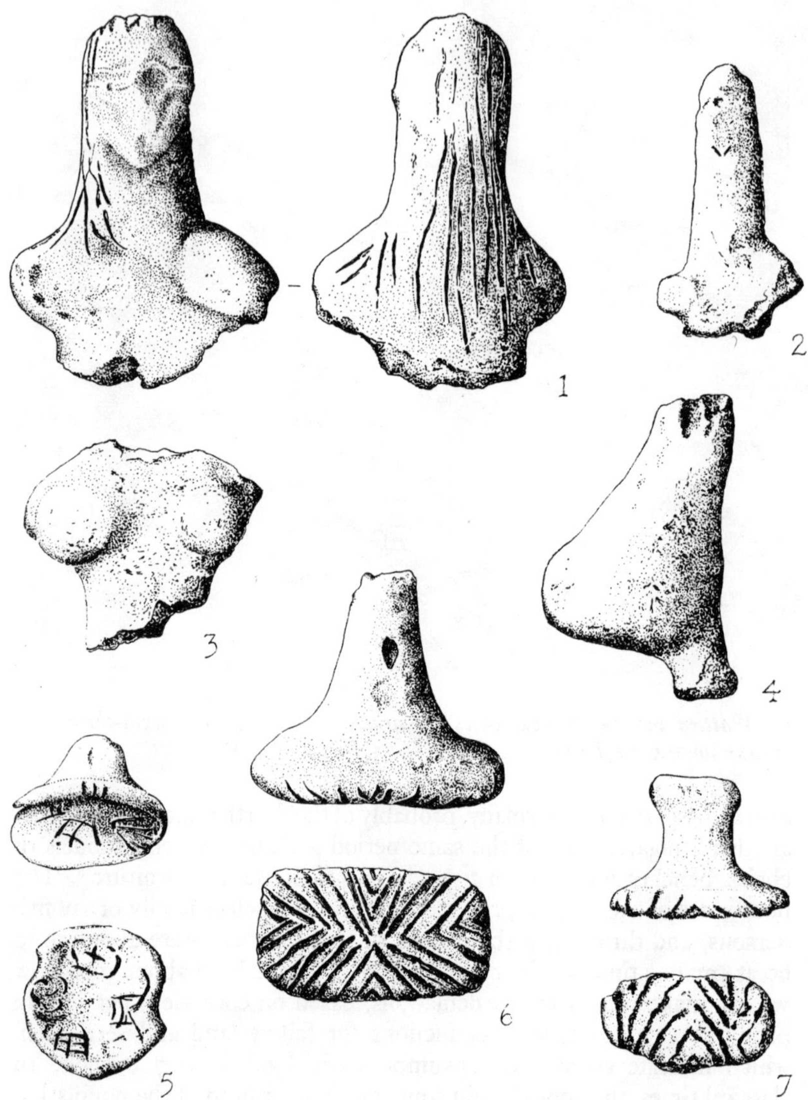

17. *Pottery figurines*, 1–4, *and 'stamp-seals'*, 5–7, *Starčevo-Körös culture, sixth–fifth millennium* B.C., *Hungary*.

was reckoned at a value approximating to about 10 bushels a year so that if these factors were taken as valid, the Karanovo village would need the annual consumption-crop off some 430 acres, or about 7 acres per family.[52] The houses in the middle phase are of the hall-and-porch or *megaron* type, which I shall refer to again. (Fig. 16; Pls. X, XII)

18. *Anthropomorphic pot, Tisza culture, fourth millennium* B.C., *Tüsköves, Hungary.*

So far we have dealt with that part of Europe which was virtually an extension of the Near Eastern province of simple peasant communities: links between the two areas also include some common traditions in pottery styles, the use of little amulets in the form of Oriental stamp-seals in Europe, and the presence in both areas of figurines of human beings (usually female), and sometimes of animals, which may relate to religious cults. (Figs. 17–19; Pl. IV) Mud-brick architecture and the developed techniques of agriculture together result in permanent settlements, each successive phase building on the ruins of the earlier and forming a 'tell'. With these characteristics, agriculture had been carried into central Europe up the Danube to the region of Budapest, perhaps initially before 5000 B.C. and certainly during the fifth millennium.

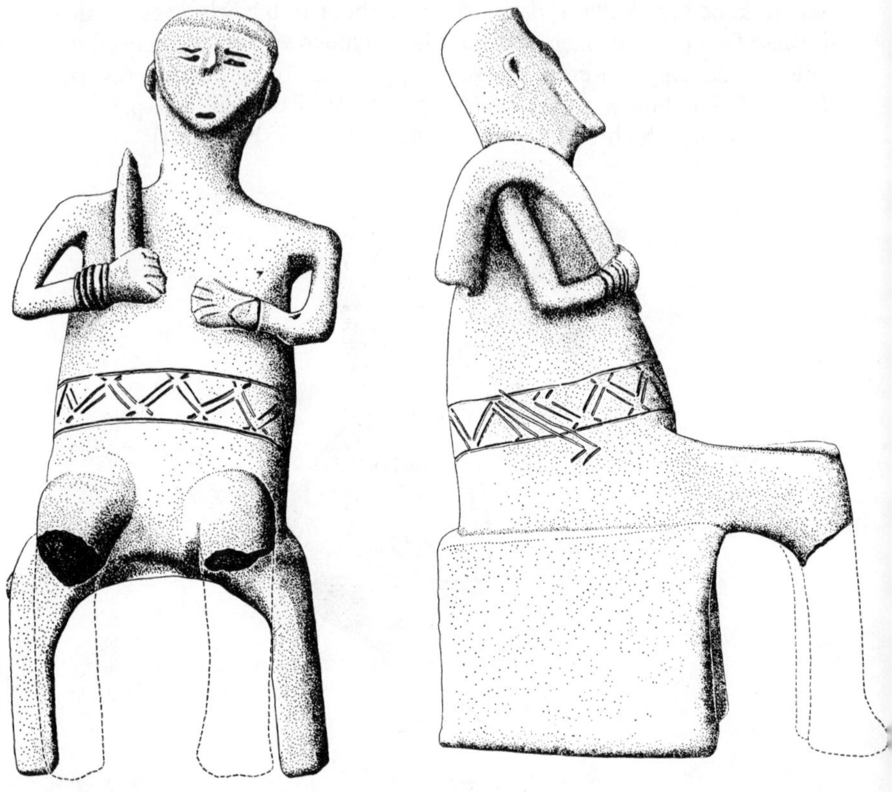

19. *Pottery figure of seated man, Tisza culture, fourth millennium* B.C., *Tüsköves, Hungary.*

Beyond this area of colonisation and acculturation we find in the fifth millennium evidence of a still further spread of farming communities into central and north-western Europe. From Belgrade to Brussels and from the Rhine to the Vistula and the Dniestr there stretch a great series of settlements of agriculturalists tilling the loess soils of central Europe, and reaching Czechoslovakia, Germany and the southern Netherlands by 4500 B.C. or soon after, and all remarkably uniform in house plans and other elements of material culture, including distinctive 'Linear'

III. *Houses of Linear Pottery culture, showing as post-holes and bedding-trenches under excavation, fifth millennium* B.C., *at* (*a*) *and* (*b*), *Bylany, Czechoslovakia* (Photos. Ruth Tringham); (*c*), *Elsloo, Netherlands* (Photo. Rijksdienst voor het Oudheidkundig Bodemonderzoek)

III (*caption on facing page*)

a

b

c

IV. *Pottery figures of man and woman, fourth millennium* B.C., *from grave at Cernavoda, Rumania*. (Photo. Institutul de Arheologie, Bucharest)

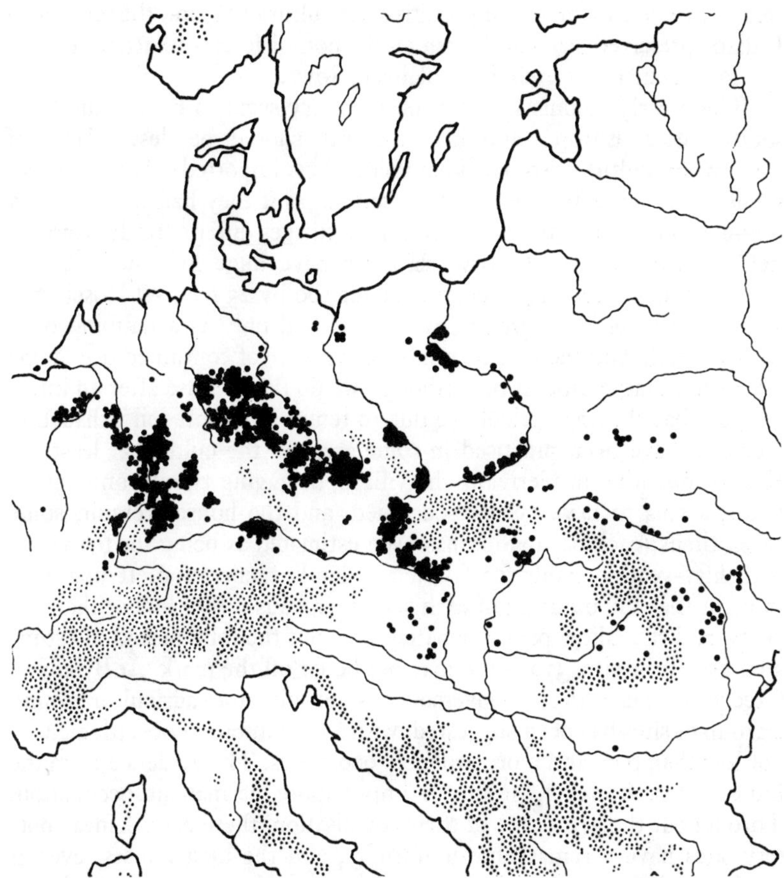

20. *Distribution of Linear Pottery settlements and finds, fifth millennium* B.C.

pottery. (Fig. 20) The regions these early Danubian people colonised must have been forested (as pollen-analysis shows us in the Netherlands) even if the loess soil is light and well suited to cultivation, and although some areas of East Europe, such as the Hungarian and Thracian plains, may have been park-land or open steppe grasslands, here again some forest clearance would have been necessary.[53] The most likely procedure would be that of the so-called slash-and-burn cultivation; burning down woodland and cultivating with hoes or digging sticks in the ash-enriched soil between the charred stumps: such a manner of forest clearance is of course incompatible with plough agriculture. The evidence suggests that the basic economy was that of growing grain in areas cleared of woodland, with cattle-grazing at a minimum. The tough grass cover of the open steppe can be a deterrent to primitive agriculturalists, and the American Indians preferred slash-and-burn cultivation of forests to attempting to till, for instance, the rich grass plains of Iowa.[54]

These early colonists with Linear pottery seem to have come from south-eastern Europe, and in some way should be descendants of the earlier cultures so far identified: they imported Mediterranean shells for ornaments wherever they settled, as if they had never lost an original contact with that sea.[55] But their villages differ entirely from the 'tell' settlements. In the first place we have huge long houses with massive timber framing, averaging about 100 by 25 feet, set loosely but sometimes in ordered groups, with clay used only as a daubing on a wooden wall. And then we do not have evidence of continued use of one site over a long period of time (though we do have re-use after an interval), so that shifting agriculture due to temporary local soil exhaustion seems to have been practised in some areas of the culture at least. At Köln-Lindenthal in Germany the village, averaging twenty-one households, seems to have been re-occupied, and the houses rebuilt, some seven times; each occupation has been estimated as being for ten years, with fifty-year intervals for fallow and land regeneration. It might be thought that the duration of each settlement was rather longer than ten years, and the fallow proportionately less, but the total period of estimated use of the site, 370 years, may not be far off the mark. At Bylany in Czechoslovakia, a 'cyclic' movement of semi-migratory agriculture round a group of sites has been suggested, with a total duration of settlement of not less than 600, and more probably 900, years. The evidence from the Dutch sites, however, seems to imply more permanent occupation. Throughout the great area of their colonisation, these early Linear pottery sites have a remarkable uniformity, and the long houses, even if partly used for byres or crop storage, can only reasonably be interpreted as housing members of an undivided or extended family, which might well involve up to four or five units with a total of twenty or so persons. In the New World, the Iroquois Indians formed a classic instance of such an arrangement in long houses under a matriarchal system; the Nootka and Kwakiutl of British Columbia, with their highly developed fishing and hunting culture, though not matriarchal in structure, also had huge communal houses with up to 100 occupants on occasion.[56] Linear Pottery villages of twenty or more houses are known, which could imply population groups of about 400, cropping 600 acres per year. Whatever the detailed interpretation may be, the contrast between small and large house-type in the 'tell' settlements and these Danubian villages must represent some fundamental difference in social structure. (Fig. 21; Pl. III)

. *Excavated area of Linear Pottery settlement with post-holes and bedding-trenches of timber-built houses,*
ches, pits, etc., fifth millennium B.C., *at Sittard, Netherlands.*

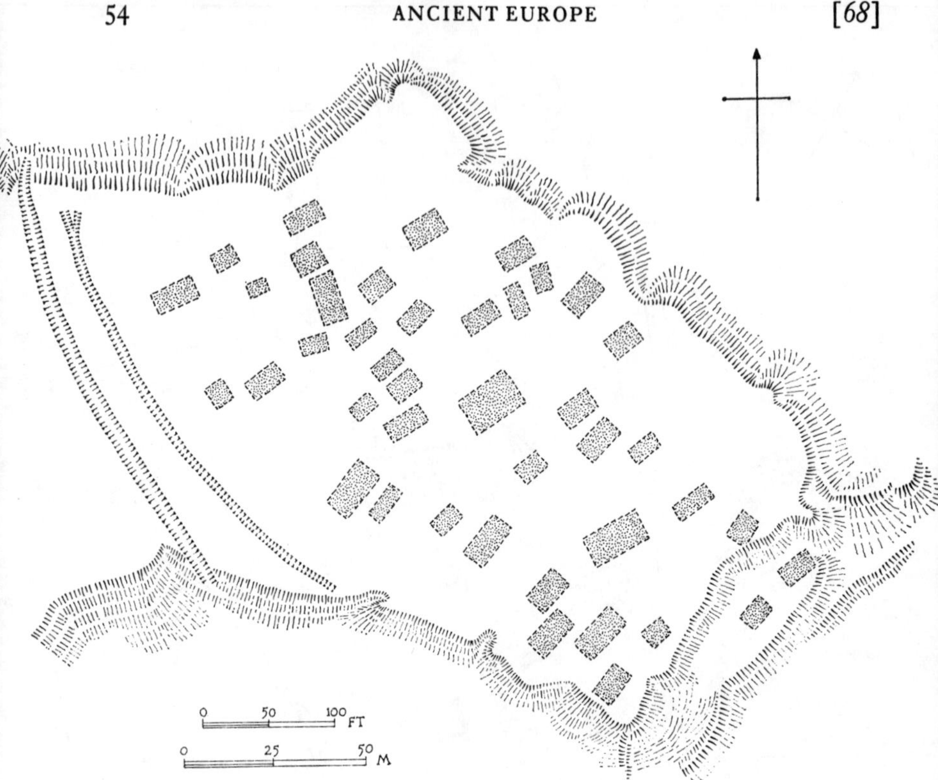

22. *Defended promontory settlement of Tripolye culture, fourth millennium* B.C., *at Habaşeşti, Rumania.*

Eastwards of the 'tell' cultures in the forest-steppe zone of the Ukraine we have, about 3000 B.C. or earlier, another group of long-house settlements, those of the Tripolye culture.[57] The material equipment of these people shows no connection with that of the Linear pottery culture but rather more contacts with the ultimately Oriental traditions expressed for instance in female figurines in some abundance; but the big long-houses on baked clay standings, sometimes with internal subdivisions emphasising the several family units, seem to show us that once again we may be dealing with social units of extended families. The villages run to from thirty to fifty houses, not always so long and narrow as the Early Danubian plan, but sufficiently large to house families of some twelve to twenty persons. Their area of distribution extends into Transylvania, with settlements on promontories defended by earthworks, and in the Ukraine the lay-out of the houses is sometimes on a circular or oval

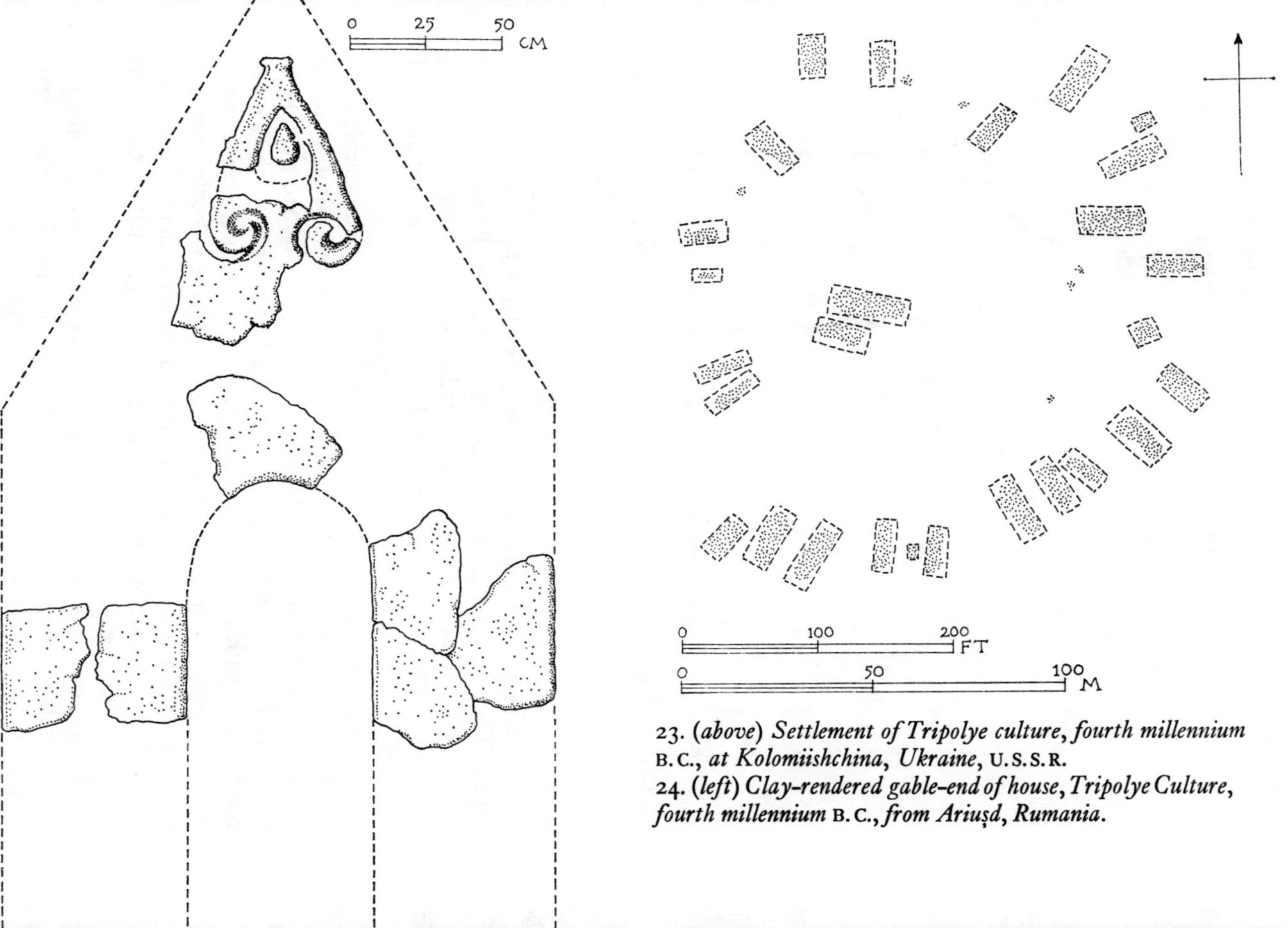

23. (*above*) *Settlement of Tripolye culture, fourth millennium* B.C., *at Kolomiishchina, Ukraine,* U.S.S.R.
24. (*left*) *Clay-rendered gable-end of house, Tripolye Culture, fourth millennium* B.C., *from Ariușd, Rumania.*

25. *Clay anthropomorphic 'altar' (restored) of Tripolye culture, fourth millennium* B.C., *from Truşeşti, Rumania.*

plan: at Kolomiishchina about twenty houses are set radially in a rough circle over 100 metres in diameter, with two large buildings near the centre. The remains of the clay rendering of a gable-wall from a building at Ariuşd in Rumania show a round-headed doorway surmounted by a double-spiral motif in relief, and very large anthropomorphic 'altars' of baked clay occur at several sites. (Figs. 22–25)

So we seem to have, in the early stages of European agriculture, a nuclear area in east Europe closely linked in material culture (and by inference, social structure) with the Near East, and beyond this, up to the Rhine in one direction and away to the Dniepr in the other, other communities with a different and distinctive social structure reflected in their house-plans. In the nuclear area the 'tell' type of settlement, and by inference the social structure and agricultural system of which it was the tangible outcome, was to continue until the second half of the second millennium B.C. (Fig. 26)

To the west, the Mediterranean sea-ways served to transmit the first agricultural techniques by colonisation or adoption, from the Aegean to Iberia. Common pottery traditions link a widely-scattered series of sites, each locally at the beginning of the Neolithic sequence from south Italy and Sicily to the Spanish Levant, with dates in the fifth millennium B.C.[58] Around 3000 B.C. or so, we can trace the spread of the first agriculturalists from the Mediterranean littoral inland to France, Switzerland and the north Italian lake district.[59] As with their coastal predecessors, we have little information on house types or settlement plans, but in Switzerland we have in these peoples the earliest builders of timber-framed villages on the edge of the lakes. The 'Swiss Lake-Dwellings' have had a long history in archaeological investigation, and were originally conceived as settlements on platforms supported by wooden piles over the open water. Now it can be shown that they were in fact sited on the damp ground between the lake reed-bed and the scrub cover of the main valley bottom. House-plans from the first (as at Egolzwil) seem to have been rectangular but no larger than would

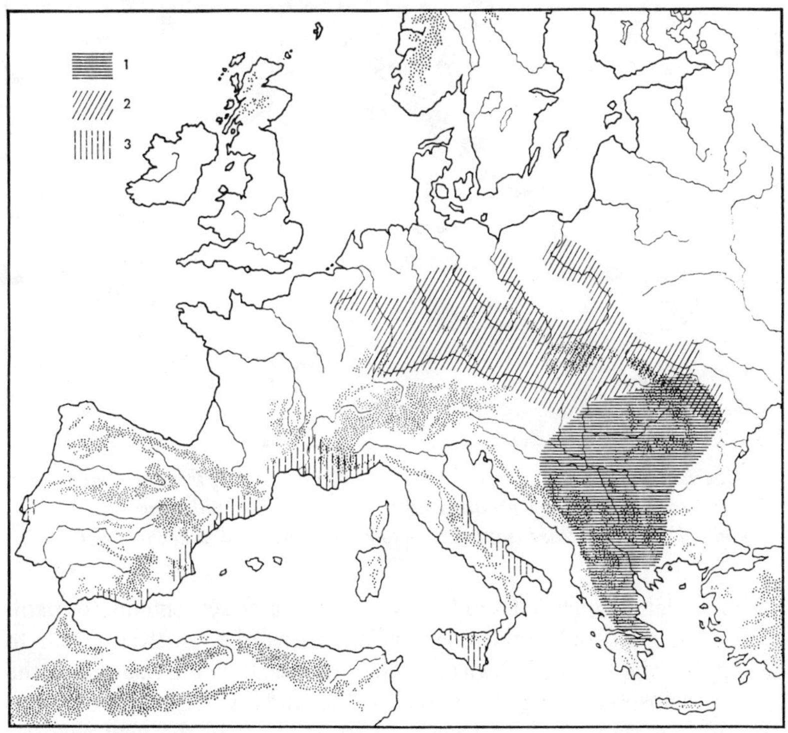

26. *Generalised distribution of agricultural communities in Europe, fifth millennium* B.C.: *1, Starčevo and allied cultures; 2, Linear Pottery culture; 3, Impressed pottery cultures.*

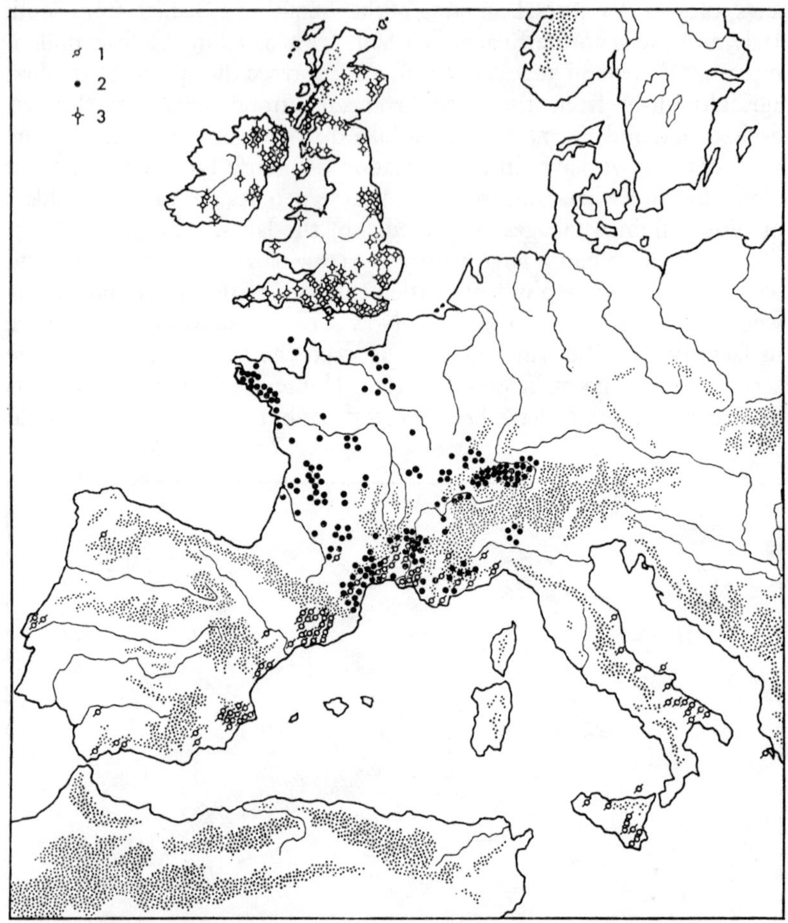

27. *Distribution of main sites of* 1, *Impressed Ware cultures, from fifth millennium* B.C. *onwards*; 2, *Chassey-Cortaillod cultures, fourth–third millennium* B.C.; 3, *Windmill Hill and allied cultures, late fourth–early second millennium* B.C.

accommodate a nuclear family; in somewhat later settlements (but still within the third millennium B.C.) village plans of from twenty-four to seventy-five houses are known (as in the Federsee sites and elsewhere), the houses themselves being about 20 by 10 feet and divided into two rooms, and often with a porch:[60] I shall return to these in the next chapter. Populations of from 120 to 370 or so are therefore implied in these villages, comparable with those estimated for the earlier 'tell' settlements of the Balkans. In passing we may note that these figures imply agregations

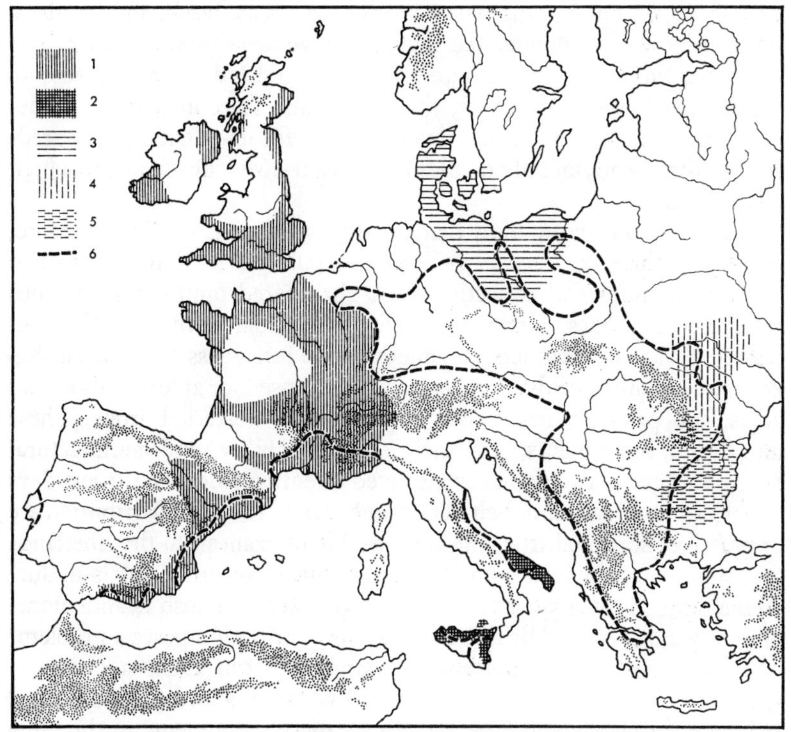

28. *Generalised distribution of agricultural communities in Europe, late fourth-early third millennium* B.C.: *1,'Western' cultures; 2,South Italian-Sicilian cultures; 3, TRB cultures; 4,Tripolye culture; 5,Boian, etc., cultures; 6,Area of settlement from fifth millennium* B.C.

of population well beyond the average of the English village at the time of the Domesday survey, where a unit of thirty or so households was exceptionally large.[61] (Figs. 27–28)

In south Italy ditch-enclosed settlements may go back (as at Stentinello in Sicily) to the earliest agricultural colonists; rather later are the remarkable Apulian sites, with multiple enclosing ditch-systems that may involve areas of up to 500 by 800 yards overall, containing circular or penannular ditched 'compounds' usually from 40 to 70 feet across.[62] Here we are seeing early examples of house and settlement planning using basically circular or curved, rather than rectangular, units; a tradition long to endure in western Europe and above all in the British Isles.

The economy of these third millennium farming settlements was initially based on growing wheat and barley, peas, beans and lentils; a small apple was also cultivated and may have been used for cider. The domesticated cattle were tethered or stalled and fed in part at least on the leaves of trees, particularly the elm, as also in contemporary settlements in Denmark. Flax was also cultivated for its nutritious oily seeds and its fibres, and not only textiles but basketry were developed to a high pitch of skill.[63]

Radio-carbon dates imply that as early as 3000 B.C. or slightly before, peoples of these or allied early Neolithic cultures in France were also building monumental collective stone-chambered tombs.[64] In various architectural modes, tombs embodying the ritual setting for the successive burials of members of something we can guess to be a kinship group, be it family or dynasty, were built and used for at least a thousand years, and probably more, over large areas of western Europe. These megalithic monuments, by their size, durability and architectural qualities, have not unnaturally attracted attention from the earliest days of field archaeology, and their very numbers and range of distribution are impressive; scattered from the western Mediterranean to the Shetlands and south Scandinavia, with such approximate recorded totals of surviving tombs as over 5,000 for France, 3,500 on the Danish Islands alone, or nearly 2,000 for the British Isles. Their distribution poses a problem: what likely set of circumstances in antiquity can cause a group of specialised ritual structures to be built over such a sweep of territory? It is not, I think, inapposite to consider these monuments in the same terms as one would the churches of Christendom or the mosques of Islam, had the religions to which these afford architectural witness wholly vanished from our knowledge. The collective chambered tombs of third and second millennium western Europe are in their way monuments to a lost faith, the adoption or propagation of which must have preceded the construction of the monuments themselves. Creeds and beliefs can be transmitted in many ways; conquest or evangelism, fanaticism or fashion, by saints or by merchants. Some or all these, and other possibilities, may well have operated to bring about an eventual situation in which precise details of architectural modes and ritual planning recur from one end of the western Megalithic world to the other. (Figs. 29–30; Pl. v)

These tombs raise many problems. An eastern Mediterranean origin seems inherently likely, but is difficult to document with any precision. The corbelled or false-vaulted burial chamber, recurrent in the west from perhaps the beginning and certainly the middle of the third millennium B.C., first appears in this fully stone-vaulted form in the Aegean around 1600 B.C., where it is usually thought to be derived from earlier circular, but not unambiguously stone-vaulted, tombs. In the western chambered

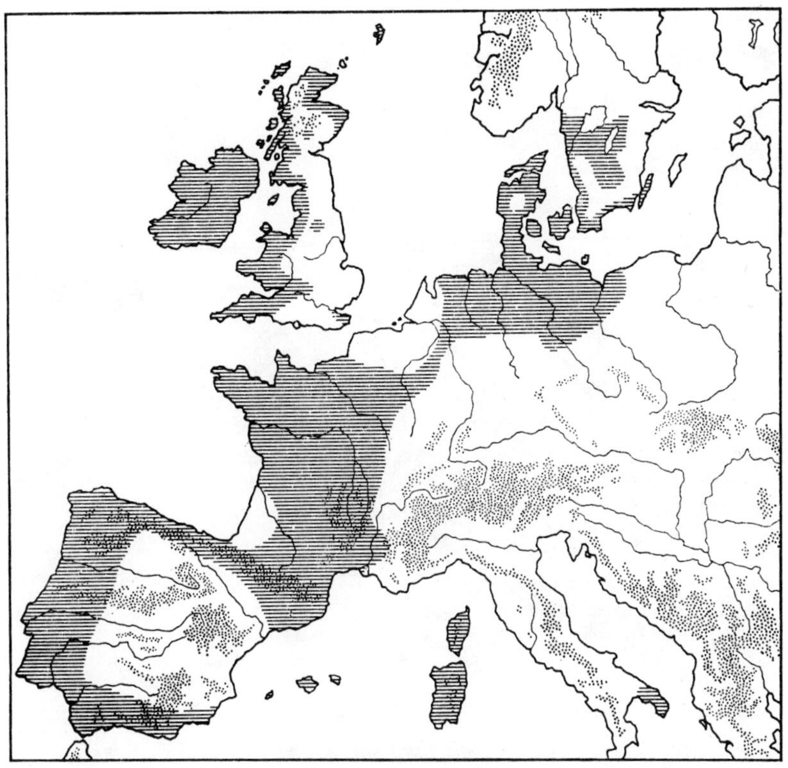

29. *Generalised distribution of megalithic chambered tombs in Western Europe.*

tombs a variety of plans can be recognised, but ultimately these seem to be versions of one or other of two main architectural themes—Passage Graves with an approach passage leading to a circular or polygonal burial chamber, or Gallery Graves, with no structurally separate passage but on occasion an elaborated entrance, giving access to a basically oblong burial chamber. In varied forms, collective chambered tombs continued to be used, and indeed in some regions to be built, up to and perhaps beyond the mid second millennium B.C. Some of these tombs constitute notable architectural monuments, such as Romeral or Maturabilla in Spain; Kercado or Gav'r Inis in Brittany, and the great Gallery Graves here or in the Loire basin; New Grange in Ireland, Maes Howe in Orkney, and West Kennet in Wiltshire continue the story to these islands. (Fig. 30)

In certain areas the tombs are decorated with incised, carved, or painted designs, some employing abstract forms including spiral and

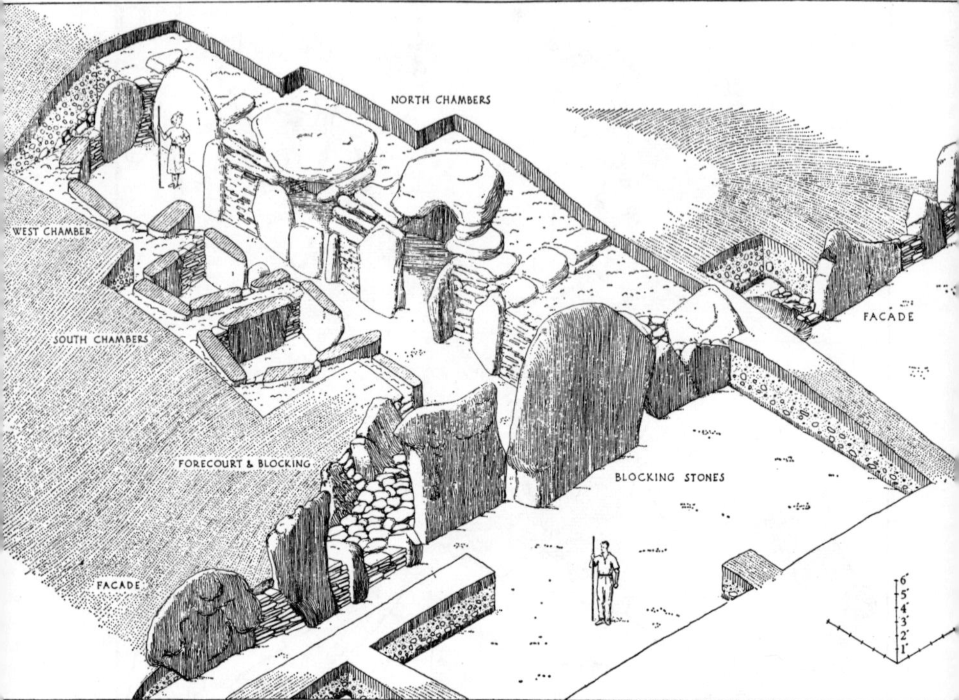

30. *Megalithic chambered tomb, mid third millennium* B.C., *at West Kennet, Wiltshire, England.*

curvilinear patterns as well as rectilinear motifs—Gav'r Inis and New Grange are famous examples of such decorated tombs. Elsewhere (as in Brittany and the Marne chalk-cut tombs) we find symbolical representations of a female, either stylised with face, necklet and breasts, or reduced to pairs of breasts alone. With these too go representations of axes or their blades, and the 'Goddess' representations link on directly to the 'statue-menhirs' noted in Chapter IV.[65] (Pls. VI–VIII)

On the north European plain and in south Scandinavia farming communities were establishing themselves around 3000 B.C., perhaps as the result of the adoption of the new economy from the Danubian peasantry by the hunting and fishing peoples on their northward boundaries. The pollen diagrams show a disturbance in the natural forest growth, notably a sharp decrease in elm, which has been associated with the use of elm branches for fodder, as in Switzerland at this time. The pollen of cereals and of weeds of cultivation may also appear; in Scandinavia the traces of land-clearance by burning have also been

a

b

V. (*a*) *Air view of stone alignments, early second millennium* B.C., *at Carnac, Brittany, France.* (Photo. Lapie)
V. (*b*) *Megalithic chambered tomb, second millennium* B.C., *at Essé, Brittany, France.* (Photo. Daniel)

VI. *Carving of stylised female figure at entrance to chalk-cut chambered tomb, early second millennium* B.C., *at Coizard, Marne, France*. (Photo. Louis)

recognised in the peat stratigraphy. Settlements, burials and votive offerings in bogs—food or drink in pots—combine to give us a picture now familiar, of another group of stone-using agriculturalists, a Neolithic peasant economy, with communities of up to fifty or so households in rectangular houses, as at Barkaer in Jutland. Burial sites included the construction of elongated earthern mounds and of massive stone cists; later in the third millennium B.C. collective chambered tombs of 'Atlantic' type were being built.[66] (Fig.31)

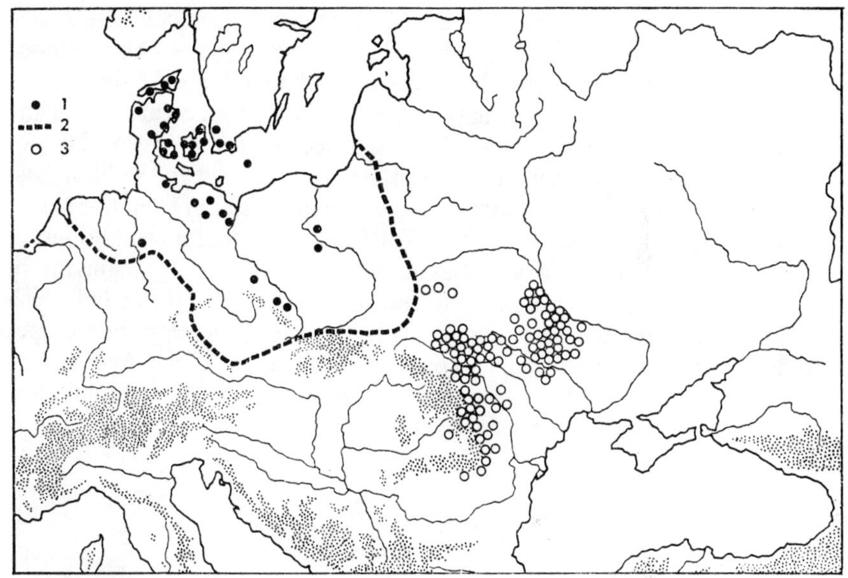

31. *Generalised distribution of 1, Earliest TRB finds; 2, later settlement area; 3, Tripolye culture sites.*

The British Isles stood at the cross-roads of Neolithic north-western Europe. The first agriculturalists in Britain were establishing themselves before 3000 B.C., and may well have come in part from Western and northern France, in part from the north European plain: our earthen unchambered long barrows may reflect this latter area of contact. The impetus for the building of collective chambered tombs affected the British Isles in complex and confusing form, giving rise to numerous local variations on the basic theme. We know distressingly little of the settlements of our first agriculturalists, though in Ireland as at Lough Gur, Wales (Clegyr Boia) and south-west England (Haldon) we have rectangular houses, not apparently grouped into regular villages, but sited as individual homesteads for small families, and circular huts or storage buildings are also known. Late in the third millennium Orcadian settlements such as Skara Brae show architectural modes of planning and construction reflecting the ancient Circumpolar world and still surviving into recent times among Eskimo and allied peoples. As elsewhere in contemporary Europe, both igneous rocks and flint were being actively exploited for axe-blades; flint was mined in Britain as in France, Belgium, Poland and Denmark, and stone axes were widely traded from their centres of manufacture.[67]

By 2500 B.C. or so, stone-using peasant economies had been established over the whole of Europe, side-by-side with those peoples who continued to gain a livelihood by the ancient skills of the hunter and fisherman. A dual pattern of life must have persisted for many centuries in many regions, but with a give-and-take of techniques between the two economies: this is clear in Denmark for instance. But in the Near East the middle of the third millennium marks not a phase of primitive stone-using peasant communities, but of literate and complex civilisations, at least in Mesopotamia and Egypt, technologically fully cognisant of working in copper, bronze, gold, and silver. Already in the early Danish Neolithic sites there are copper tools imported from eastern Europe; here metallurgy had early become established, as in the Aegean and Iberia, before 2500 B.C. Change and an advance in technology is in the air.

Notes

1. The situation has been discussed many times; cf. Daniel 1943, 1950a, 1962.
2. Rütimeyer was publishing detailed reports on the fauna of the Swiss sites as early as 1862, while Neuwiler's studies of the plant remains run from 1905 onwards. The combination of archaeological, zoological and geological techniques as applied to the Danish Mesolithic sites goes back to the pioneer work of Worsaae, Steenstrup and Forchhammer in 1850, and Sarauw was identifying seed remains from impressions in potsherds at the end of the last century. Pitt-Rivers published full details of the animal bones from his Wessex excavations from 1887 onwards, and Duerst's reports on the Anau fauna were published in the excavation volumes of 1904.
3. The classic statement is in Childe 1936.
4. The phrase seems first to have been used in describing the culture-sequence at Jericho; Kenyon 1956 ff.
5. Cf. Häusler's remarks on this (1962, 1176).

6. A convenient chronological summary based on radiocarbon dates is in Movius 1960; cf. also Brandtner 1961 and table in Leroi-Gourhan 1960. There seems to be a widespread acceptance of this chronology as against for instance that of Zeuner (1958, 110-306).
7. There is no up-to-date comprehensive treatment of the Old World or European Palaeolithic, and perhaps the best (though very short) statement is that in McBurney 1950, Chapter 1. A more general account is in Clark 1961, Chapters 2 and 3.
8. Braidwood and Reed 1957, 25.
9. Clark 1939, 178; 1960, 242.
10. For a distribution-map showing the extent of the Magdalenian and other reindeer-hunting cultures in Late Glacial Europe see Clark 1952, Fig. 6.
11. The literature of Upper Palaeolithic art is large, but accessible: recent studies include Maringer and Bandi 1953; Laming 1959; Graziosi 1960; McBurney 1961.
12. Rust 1937, with English summary, Clark 1938; Rust 1943, 1951.
13. Cf. Clark 1952, 32-41 for Advanced Palaeolithic bows and arrows.
14. Movius 1950; Behn 1962, Pl. 12a; Oakley 1950, 14, Fig. 5.
15. Representations of huts in Upper Palaeolithic art are in Graziosi 1960, 185-6, Pl. 270; Molodova, Kernd'l 1963; Arcy, Leroi-Gourhan 1961; Dolní Věstonice, Klima 1954, 1962; south Russia and Siberia, Childe 1950a; Rogachev 1956; Quitta 1957; Mezin, Behn 1962, Pl. 11; Ahrensburg, Rust 1958b.
16. The North European Mesolithic cultures are described by Clark 1936; since then, cf. Clark 1950, 1954, 1958, 1962b; Mathiassen 1943; Schwabedissen 1944; Schuldt 1961; Rust 1958a, b; Barrière 1954.
17. Discussed in Thompson 1954.
18. Full publication in Clark 1954.
19. Clark 1954; Braidwood and Reed 1957.
20. For early European house-plans in general, Childe 1949b; Clark 1952, 134-5, Schlette 1958; Tannstock, Reinerth 1929, 44-57; Schötz, Bodmer-Gessner 1950; Farnham and comparable sites, Clark and Rankine 1939; Moita do Sebastião, Roche 1960; Oransay, Bishop 1914; Downton, Higgs 1959; Hamburg sites, Rust 1958a, b; north Germany, Bodmer-Gessner 1950; Schwabedissen 1944; tipi rings, Kehoe 1961.
21. Maringer and Bandi 1953, 114-42; Pijoan 1953, 132-44; Kühn 1952, 59-80, Pls. 35-48.
22. On domesticated dogs in general, Zeuner 1963, Chapter 4; Herre 1963; Mesolithic dogs, Degerbøl 1961; Near Eastern, Clutton-Brock 1962, 1963.
23. Interaction between these surviving hunter-fisher traditions and the incoming agriculturalists led to mixed economies which have been classed as 'Secondary Neolithic'; Piggott 1954, 277-8; Gabel 1957, 1958.

24. For these cemeteries and the cultures they represent, see Häusler 1962; Michael 1958; Okladnikov 1959; Piggott 1962b; Bastian and Schuldt, 1961.
25. The original study is that of Gjessing (1944, cf. *ibid.* 1953); see also Larsen (ed.) 1960; Rudenko 1961.
26. Bows and arrows generally are discussed in Clark 1952, 32-41; for finds since that date, cf. Troels-Smith 1959 (Mesolithic, Denmark); Clark 1963; Michael 1958, 49, 57; Okladnikov 1959, 13, 71; Häusler 1962, 1153 (Sub-Mesolithic, Siberia). For fishing in prehistoric Europe, Clark 1948; 1952, 84-90; nets, traps, etc., Clark 1952, Chapters 2 and 3; boats in general, *ibid.* 282-92; Hornell 1938 (coracles and curraghs). The earliest dated evidence for Mesolithic boats is the paddle from Star Carr of *c.* 7500 B.C. (Clark 1954, 177) and the earliest dug-out canoe in northern Europe that from Pesse, Holland (De Laet 1958, 55, Pl. 7) of *c.* 6000 B.C. Sledges and skis, Clark 1952, 293-301; Berg 1935, Berg *et al.* 1950. Whistles, Megaw 1960, 1963b; Häusler 1960; pan-pipes from south Russia and Siberia, Michael 1958, 70, Fig. 66; Häusler 1960, 329.
27. For reindeer domestication, see Zeuner 1963, Chapter 5; Herre 1963.
28. For the beginnings of animal domestication in the Near East and Europe, there are summary accounts in Zeuner 1963; Cole 1959; Reed 1960, 1961; Herre 1963.
29. As suggested by the evidence from the La Adam Cave in the Dobrogea further discussed below (Radulesco and Samson 1962).
30. Reed 1960, 137.
31. Textiles described in Helbaek 1963a. For the site, see above p. 17.
32. There is no large-scale treatment of early plant cultivation in Asia and Europe; general discussion, however, in Zeuner 1954; Cole 1959; Helbaek 1960, 1963c; La Baume 1961. For the British Isles there are the detailed studies of Jessen and Helbaek 1944; Helbaek 1952a.
33. Megaw *et al.* 1961; Bowen 1962.
34. For a general study of the earliest cultivated flax, see Helbaek 1959.
35. Apples in northern Europe, Helbaek 1952a, 200 (English Neolithic); 1952b (Switzerland etc.).
36. Braidwood *et al.* 1953 discuss early contexts for beer; Clark 1942, 1952, 128 stresses the importance of bees and honey in prehistory. Wine (Forbes 1954a, 275-85) was made from grapes from Early Dynastic times in Egypt and probably from Middle Minoan times in Crete (Hutchinson 1962, 244); grapes in Cyprus in late thirteenth century B.C., Helbaek 1963b. In Italy the evidence suggests that the cultivated grape may be an Etruscan importation (Helbaek 1956, 292), though there was little Roman wine production before the early second century B.C. (Forbes, 1956, 133). For wine north of the Alps, see below, Chapters V and VI.
37. Reed 1961, 34; Solecki 1963a,b. The flint-bladed, bone-hafted knives from

Shanidar may be reaping knives similar to those of the Natufian culture in Palestine (see below); the type also occurs in the Siberian sub-Mesolithic cultures (Michael 1958, 43, 49, 65).

38. Radulesco and Samson 1962.
39. Clark 1958; cf. sheep, goat and cattle bones in the Mesolithic Final Tardenoisian (pre-pottery) phase at Châteauneuf-les-Martigues (Escalon de Fonton 1956, 43, 107) and the evidence for agriculture (with pottery) with a Tardenoisian industry at Belloy-sur-Somme (Salomonsson 1960).
40. Using here the re-calculated radiocarbon date for the Natufian at Jericho, Zeuner 1963, 30-31. Other Jericho dates cited below are again the recently re-calculated values.
41. General survey of the Natufian culture in Garrod 1957; Natufian at Jericho, Kenyon 1960, Chapter 2; 'Eynan, Perrot 1957, 1960. The Tepe Asiab site in Persian Kurdistan, with sunk oval or circular houses, seems comparable with 'Eynan: here again there was a hunting and gathering economy represented (Braidwood 1960).
42. Kenyon 1960, summarising earlier papers, with re-calculated radiocarbon dates in Zeuner 1963, 30-31; Naḥal Oren, Stekelis and Yizraely 1963.
43. General discussion of earliest agricultural settlements in Braidwood, Howe *et al.* 1960; Braidwood and Reed 1957; ecology and land use, Whyte 1961, Solecki 1963a. Jarmo is described in Braidwood, Howe *et al.* 1960; aceramic levels at Hacilar in Anatolia, Mellaart 1961, 70-73 (earlier than *c.* 5500 B.C.); the Khirokitia site in Cyprus in Dikaios 1953, but note radiocarbon date of *c.* 5600 B.C. obtained since that publication (Östlund and Engstrend 1960, 144).
44. Argissa, Milojčić *et al.* 1962; Nea Nikomediea, Rodden 1962.
45. The Mesopotamian evidence is discussed by Jacobsen (1943) and that from Anatolia by Gurney (1952, 63, 68-69).
46. In Greece itself we now have an early Neolithic phase at Elateia in Phocis with a radiocarbon date of *c.* 5500 B.C. (Weinberg 1962; Vogel and Waterbolk 1963); in Macedonia and Thessaly we have the Nea Nikomedeia date of *c.* 6220 B.C. already quoted for Neolithic settlements with painted pottery in the Sesklo tradition, preceded however at least in some sites by impressed and finger-nail ornamented pottery (Milojčić 1954). In the Lower Danube the earliest Neolithic cultures appear to be those of the Starčevo-Körös-Criș group (Childe 1957, 85 and Map I; Milojčić 1951, 115, fig. 3) with radiocarbon dates of *c.* 4900 and *c.* 4700 B.C. from Serbian sites (Mellaart 1960a, with long chronology based on radiocarbon dates; controverted by Garašanin (1961); Vogel and Waterbolk 1963. I have used the long chronology here.)
47. Masson 1961, 1962.
48. House-models mainly from later Neolithic contexts; cf. Childe 1957, Fig.

55 (Bulgaria); Gimbutas 1956a, Fig. 56 (Ukraine); Neustupný 1961, Fig. 10 (Czechoslovakia).

49. The phases I to V of the site as outlined by Mikov (1959) and adopted by others (e.g. Piggott 1960) have been re-defined as I to VII by Georgiev (1961), by numbering Mikov's Ia and Ib as I and II, and intercalating a short Phase IV after Mikov's II (III in Georgiev's scheme). I now follow the later numeration.
50. Schliz 1901.
51. From Yassa-Tepe, Plovdiv: Detev 1959, Figs. 80-82.
52. These very rough calculations have been based on an assumed corn-yield of about 10 bushels per acre, a yield supported by the statements of Roman agronomists such as Columella, as well as by figures from medieval England. Approximately one-third has been deducted as seed corn, giving an annual consumption-harvest of 7 bushels per acre in convenient round figures. Modern corn consumption per head of the British population is 4½ bushels per year, but the figures for the military grain ration in the Greek and Roman armies (*choenix* and *modius*) work out at about 11 bushels per annum. This is here taken as 10 bushels for convenience, and is more likely to be applicable to prehistoric conditions than the modern reduced consumption. Calculations of this type, involving corn yield and consumption, seem first to have been applied to archaeological problems by Bersu when assessing the likely acreage of arable for the Little Woodbury Iron Age farm (Bersu 1940), and I used them in the context of British corn production at the time of the Roman Conquest (Piggott 1958). But we both used the modern figure of about 5 bushels per head, certainly an underestimate, and this factor should reasonably be doubled, as it is here.
53. English usage following Childe has preferred the use of 'Danubian I' or 'Early Danubian', but continental terminology has been based on the distinctive pottery styles (Bandkeramik, Linearbandkeramik, Poterie rubané). Summary accounts in Childe 1957, 105-10; Buttler 1938. Origins and dating (radiocarbon dates ranging from *c.* 4580 to *c.* 3890 B.C.), Quitta 1960; houses and settlements, Stieren 1951; Sangmeister 1951 (Germany); De Laet 1958, Fig. 18; Modderman *et al.* 1959 (Netherlands); Soudsky 1962 (Czechoslovakia); cemeteries, Kahlke 1954; eastern contacts, Milojčić 1951; Passek 1962; Chernych 1962; in France, Arnal and Burnez 1957; Arnal *et al.* 1960.
54. Driver and Massey 1957, 225.
55. The shells are those of *Spondylus Gaederopus*: map in Clark 1952, Fig. 132.
56. Driver and Massey 1957, 299, 297.
57. Material summarised to date in Gimbutas 1956a, 99-108; Rumanian sites, Dumitrescu 1945, 1954; Petrescu-Dimbovița 1957; Vulpe 1957; Piggott 1960; Berciu 1961. There are radiocarbon dates of *c.* 3380 and *c.* 3000 B.C.

for the Rumanian Cucuteni A and B phases respectively (Vogel and Waterbolk 1963, 185).

58. These are sites with 'impressed' or 'cardial' wares; maps in Brea 1950 (Italy, Sicily, etc.); Arnal *et al.* 1950 (France); Almagro 1958 (Iberia); radiocarbon dates of *c.* 4600 and *c.* 4280 B.C. in Italy (Ferrara *et al.* 1961, 100).
59. These constitute the Chassey-Cortaillod-Lagozza group of cultures: Piggott 1953-54; Arnal and Burnez 1957; Arnal *et al.* 1960 (France); von Gonzenbach 1949; Vogt 1951; Guyan *et al.* 1955; Sauter 1959 (Switzerland etc.) Radiocarbon dates for the French Chassey culture range from *c.* 3200 to *c.* 2180 B.C. (Coursaget *et al.* 1960, 1961); the recalculated Swiss figure for early Cortaillod at Egolzwil is *c.* 2940 (Tauber 1960), and later phases of Cortaillod have dates of *c.* 2790 (St Léonard) and *c.* 2830 and *c.* 2670 at Burgäschisee Sud I (Gfeller *et al.* 1961). Dates for the comparable Lagozza culture in Italy are *c.* 2800 B.C. (Ferrara *et al.* 1961).
60. Childe 1957, 282.
61. Cf. Darby 1936, 208.
62. Bradford 1949, 1957, 95-103; Bradford and Williams-Hunt 1946.
63. Evidence for stalled cattle at Weiher (Thayngen) (with radiocarbon dates of *c.* 2800-2500 B.C.); Guyan *et al.* 1955; Troels-Smith 1959, 1960. For Neolithic basketry and textiles, cf. Vogt 1937.
64. The Île Carn chambered tomb in Brittany has a radiocarbon date of *c.* 3280 B.C. (Giot *et al.* 1960; Vogel and Waterbolk 1963, 186, with recalculated date.)
65. The literature of the chambered tombs is very large: recent surveys, however, in Daniel 1958 (general); 1960 (France); Daniel 1950b; Piggott 1954; Henshall 1963 (British Isles); Leisner and Leisner 1943, 1956, 1959; Leisner *et al.* 1961; Pericot 1950; Almagro and Arribas 1963 (Iberia); Evans 1959; Trump 1961 (Malta); Sprockhoff 1938; Brøndsted 1900 (north Europe and Denmark); Kaelas 1955, 1962 (Holland, Sweden); Powell 1960 (central Europe); Hood 1960 (Aegean).
66. These cultures are variants of that of the Funnel Beakers (TRB culture): earliest settlements, Childe 1949a, Becker 1948, 1955a; radiocarbon dates for early phase in northern Germany of *c.* 3190 and *c.* 3070 B.C. (Scollar 1959, 109), in Denmark of *c.* 2820 (Tauber 1960) and in Poland of *c.* 2720 (Jażdżewski 1961). Evidence for agriculture and forest-clearance, Troels-Smith 1959, 1960; Iversen 1941, 1949, 1960; Heybroek 1963. Relationship of TRB culture to Mesolithic (Ertebølle) cultures, etc. Troels-Smith 1953; Becker 1954; Hinsch 1953. Barkaer and other settlements, Glob 1949; Bibby 1957, 296-301, Pl. XIX; Schlette 1958, Pls. 59-65. Long barrows and cists (dolmens), Chmielewski 1952; Becker 1948; Piggott 1955, 1961, 564; later tombs, etc., Becker 1955b.

67. The British material was summarised to date in Piggott 1954, but with too low a chronology in the absence of radiocarbon dates at that time. These now place the earliest Neolithic cultures in the British Isles from *c.* 3200 B.C. (Clark and Godwin 1962; Watts 1960). The likely connections with North Europe are discussed in Piggott 1955, 1961a; Case 1962; important new excavations of unchambered long barrows include Nutbane (Morgan 1959; radiocarbon date of *c.* 2720 B.C., Vatcher 1959) and Fussell's Lodge (Ashbee 1958: unpublished radiocarbon date of *c.* 3230 B.C.). For chambered tombs, cf. note 65; also Powell and Daniel 1956; Hartnett 1957; de Valera 1960; Corcoran 1960; Piggott 1962a. New work on settlements include Lough Gur (O Ríordáin 1954) Hurst Fen (Clark *et al.* 1960); and Windmill Hill (I. Smith, 1959, 1960: earliest occupation *c.* 2950 B.C.). Artificial trackways in the Somerset fens, Godwin 1960; stone axe manufacture and dispersal in Britain, Evens *et al.* 1962; flint mines, Grimes Graves radiocarbon dates in Clark and Godwin 1962; mines in Scandinavia, Becker 1958, 1959, 1961; Althin 1951; in Poland, Hensel and Gieysztor 1958, 12; older information in Clark and Piggott 1933.

VII. *Carving of designs including stylised stone axe-blades, on upright stone of megalithic chambered tomb, early second millennium* B.C., *at Gav'r Inis, Brittany, France.* (Photo. Le Rouzic)

VIII. *Stag and bull in copper, gold and silver, late third millennium* B.C., *Alaca Hüyük Royal Tombs, Turkey*. (Photos. Hirmer)

3

Trade, Metal-Working and Consolidation

ONE of the most important stages in man's mastery of natural resources was the discovery of the nature and use of metals. This demanded an entirely novel complex of technological innovations, and involved the development of new skills and new habits of thought on the part of those who had previously worked only in natural substances in their raw state. Working in stone or flint to make edge-tools calls for no more than locating and selecting the appropriate rock, and then knocking or flaking or grinding it into the required shape; the same goes for tool-making in bone or ivory or wood. The skills of ancient man while technologically in a Stone Age were therefore limited, however competently or indeed brilliantly employed. The making of pottery, which involves heating clay to a temperature sufficient to remove the water of constitution, is the first step towards producing an artificial product that does not occur in nature in that particular form, and a technical relationship between kiln-fired pottery and the earliest smelted metal seems inevitable.

Copper, the first metal to be recognised and used, occurs naturally in its pure metallic state only in very small quantities in the Old World. The use of such native copper by simply hammering fragments into the shape of pins or other small objects, and treating it as a queer sort of malleable stone, seems to have been known in such areas as Persia before 5000 B.C. and in Anatolia perhaps a millennium earlier. This use of copper, however, does not mean the beginnings of true metallurgy, any more than in aboriginal north America, where the Indians utilised the large deposits of native copper on the southern shore of Lake Superior, and smaller supplies elsewhere, but only by cold-hammering it into shape. Similarly, the Polar Eskimos treated locally available meteoric iron in the same way, but in neither instance can we regard this as metal-working in the true sense.[1] But the recognition of the fact that metallic copper could be artificially produced from an ore which in no way resembled the end product, crucial to real metallurgy, involved an increase in man's understanding of nature. It meant a realisation that a sort of transmutation of one natural substance into another was within man's power, a step in understanding beyond the simpler process of fire-hardening clay into pottery. With this enlargement in human comprehension, this first step on the road to chemistry and our own world of synthetic substances, there followed another hardly less significant. Copper is not a common metal; tin, soon used to make the harder alloy of bronze, is rare. A stone-using community can be near to self-sufficiency (though long-distance trade in flint, obsidian, and other stones did in fact occur on a rather remarkable scale), but a metal-using one is wholly dependent on its relatively scarce raw materials. Prospectors and miners, traders and middlemen, the organisation of shipments or caravans, concessions and treaties, the concept of alien peoples and customs in distant lands—all these and more are involved in the enlargement of social comprehension demanded by the technological step of entering, in the older archaeological terminology, a 'Bronze Age'.[2]

This step was taken by certain innovating societies of western Asia at an early date. In Anatolia at Çatal Hüyük there is evidence for cold-worked native copper in the seventh millennium B.C., and by the earlier third millennium copper smelting and casting was a technological commonplace in, for instance, Early Dynastic Sumer or Egypt.

Initially, the potentiality of bronze, the copper-tin alloy, was not realised, though it seems to have been appreciated at an early stage that copper ores with a significant proportion of arsenic as an impurity gave a harder metal, and one more easy to cast. Pure copper is difficult to cast in a closed mould owing to the presence of free oxygen bubbles; the addition of up to 10 per cent of tin not only hardens the metal but minimises this release of gas, and so makes complex castings possible. Remarkable castings in copper were, however, achieved in quite remote antiquity, such as the large figures of stags and cattle in the Alaca Hüyük Royal Tombs of the late third millennium B.C.,[3] probably cast by the *cire perdue* method in a closed mould of clay, the internal cavity of which is formed by melting out an enveloped wax original, which is replaced by the molten metal. (Pl. VIII) The earliest certain *cire perdue* casting (of copper) in the ancient Orient appears to be the elaborate model of a chariot drawn by four onagers from Tell Agrab, of Early Dynastic II date, in the earlier third millennium B.C.[4] As with the beginnings of agriculture, the origins of non-ferrous metallurgy seem to lie within a restricted region of the Near East, but not in this instance because of the lack of sources of raw material outside this area, but by reason of the temper and tradition of the innovating societies of that part of the Old World—indeed Egypt, which quickly developed an elaborate copper-working industry from the late fourth millennium onwards, was always without resources of raw material nearer than the Eastern Desert and Sinai, and Mesopotamia too had to import its ore. So far as ready supplies of raw material were concerned, our Old World metallurgy could well have started in Ireland or Iberia, save for the fact that the stone-using peasantry of those parts lacked the precocity in technological innovation that characterised the otherwise largely comparable societies of western Asia. The circumstances involving the beginnings of metallurgy in the Old World form a striking exemplification of the difference between innovating and conserving societies to which I drew attention in the first chapter.

By the early third millennium B.C. copper working was practised not only in Anatolia but the Aegean: the first settlement of Troy, or those of Thermi on Lesbos or Poliochni on Lemnos are examples of such early metal-working communities. On the Greek mainland copper imports at least go back to 3000 B.C. or so; by the Early Helladic phase (with radiocarbon dates of *c.* 2670 B.C. at Lerna), metal-working was well established. Crete hardly became cognisant of copper metallurgy before the Early Minoan II period, in the second half of the millennium, when, as we shall see, not only was craft widespread in the east Mediterranean, but political circumstances among the higher powers resulted in disturbed conditions and there were movements of peoples over wide areas.[5] Beyond the Aegean, there were two centres of early copper-working established in Europe well before 2000 B.C., one in eastern Europe centred on the Transylvanian ore deposits, and the other in Iberia, exploiting the copper resources of that peninsula. In both instances the impetus to develop this novel technology must have come from outside, and in the contemporary circumstances a broadly Anatolian or Aegean origin is almost inevitable and has archaeological support. Furthermore, the impetus must have been received from prospectors and metal-smiths in search of raw materials for home workshops. Once the demand for copper (and soon after, tin) was an insistent item in the economy of the innovating societies of the east Mediterranean, there would be inevitable competition in the discovery and exploitation of new sources of ore: the prospectors would look west and north-west not only for the utilitarian metals, but for the gold they were to find in the Transylvanian hills and, perhaps as early as this, the silver of Spain.[6]

In Hungary, Rumania, and Slovakia it seems as though individual schools of copper metallurgy were operating before 2500 B.C., contemporary with the Early Helladic I phase of mainland Greece, and utilising the copper deposits of the Carpathians. Among their most characteristic products were massive shaft-hole axes, a type probably of Anatolian ancestry; in later phases we have also axe-adzes, both

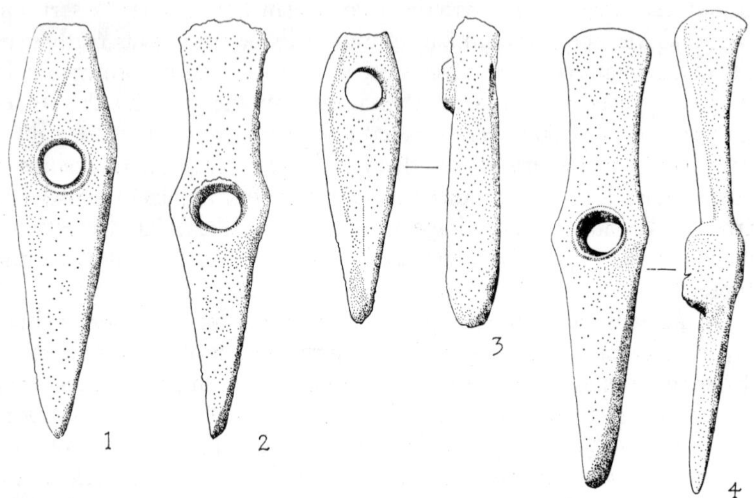

32. *Earlier forms of copper shaft-hole axes and axe-adzes, third millennium* B.C., *from Slovakia.*

suggesting large-scale tree-felling and woodworking. (Fig. 32) Ornaments such as spiral arm-rings, spiral wire beads, and bossed discs of copper, and flat copper axe blades, were traded north-westwards as far as Poland and even Denmark, where they were acquired, as we have seen, by members of the local stone-using communities who had themselves not so long before adopted an agricultural economy.[7] By the closing centuries of the third millennium B.C. we find types of copper ornaments, such as the dress-pin with double-spiral head, common not only to the Lower Danube and Anatolia, but scattered as far afield as the Caucasus, Persia, and even the Indus Valley, showing how trade and fashion linked a great stretch of Eurasia north of the centres of higher civilisation in Mesopotamia and Elam.[8] Indeed, the shaft-hole axes and axe-adzes of the earlier Transylvanian tradition are again ultimately members of a group with a somewhat similar distribution, stretching eastward not only to India again, but to Samarkand and the Karakorum.[9] South Russia and the Caucasus were also, in the second half of the third millennium, beginning to establish centres of copper-working.[10] (Figs. 33–34)

For these early centres of copper metallurgy in east Europe we have hardly more evidence than the metal objects themselves, but when we turn to the west we have more extensive information. It has recently come to be recognised that in Spain and Portugal there is a group of half-a-dozen settlement sites and cemeteries of copper-using communities

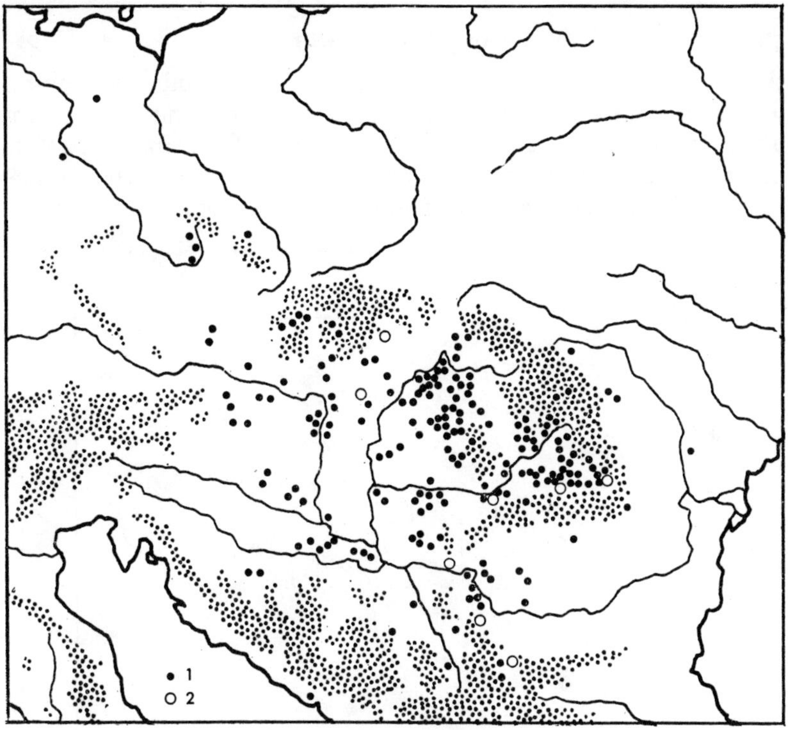

33. *Distribution of the earliest Transylvanian copper industry, third millennium* B.C.: *1, shaft-hole axes and adzes; 2, copper ore sources.*

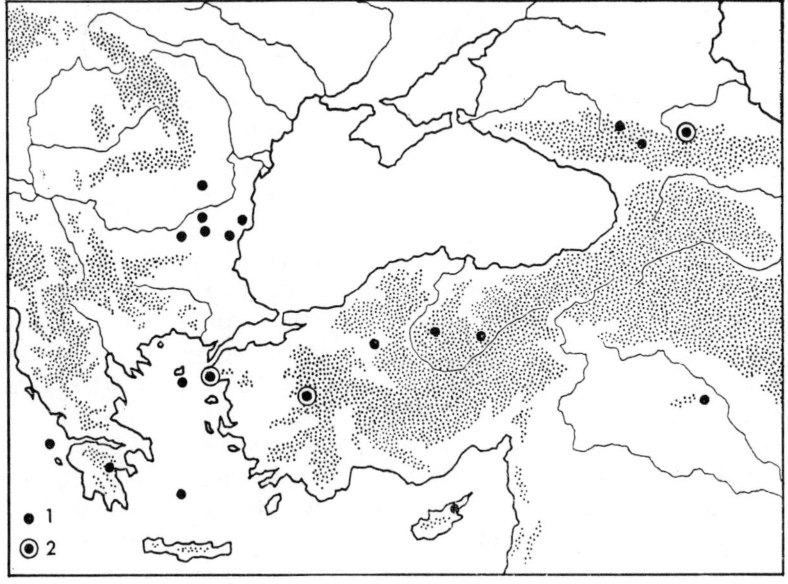

34. *Distribution of metal pins with double-spiral heads, from late third millennium* B.C.: *1, single find; 2, many finds.*

that have no perceptible local antecedents; but a number of features link them to the east Mediterranean world of the mid third millennium B.C. (Fig. 35) These have been called 'colonies' on the assumption that their origin lies in deliberate settlement from the Aegean, presumably in connection with a trade in copper; still more recently it appears that similar

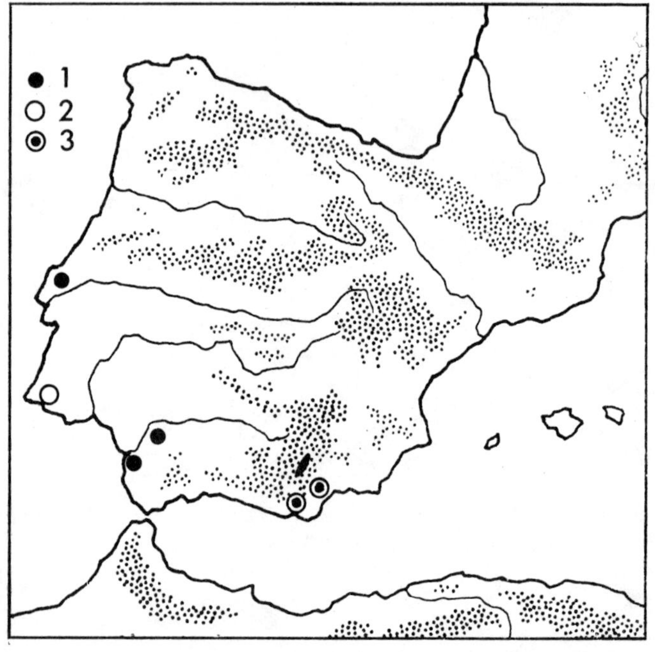

35. *Distribution of earliest copper-working 'colonies' in Iberia, third millennium* B.C.*: 1, Settlement; 2, Cemetery; 3, Settlement and cemetery.*

sites exist in the south of France, as at Lébous near Montpellier.[11] At Los Millares in southern Spain the settlement is defended by a stone wall having a series of semi-circular bastions or half-towers, and an outlying fort is similarly defended; at Vila Nova de São Pedro not far north of Lisbon is another small structure, a chieftain's castle, with bastioned walls again. Such defences are unknown outside the Aegean at the early date demanded—a mature phase of Los Millares has a radiocarbon date *c.* 2340 B.C.—but the bastioned defences of Chalandriani on Syros form an exact counterpart, and there are similar bastions at Lerna, of Early Helladic I date. (Fig. 36) Other elements of material culture, such as pottery types and decorative techniques, pin-types and tool forms, again link the Iberian 'colonies' with the Aegean and especially the Cycladic Islands,

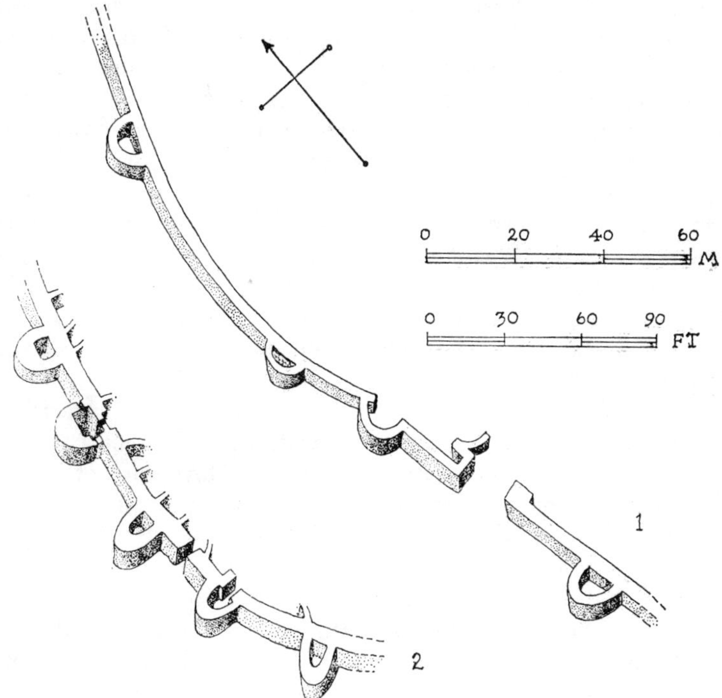

36. *Bastioned town walls at 1, Los Millares, Spain; 2, Chalandriani, Syros; third millennium* B.C.

at a date around 2500 B.C. Outside the Los Millares settlements is a cemetery of collective chambered tombs of the general type already mentioned in Chapter II, in part belonging to the period of the bastioned township; and here again east Mediterranean connections may be implicit, as with the whole chambered tomb tradition. So far as metallurgy is concerned, these Iberian colonists smelted and worked copper with assurance, casting it in closed moulds, as did their contemporaries in east Europe, and as had Oriental smiths for centuries—a skill however temporarily to be lost in barbarian western Europe after these precocious intrusions from an outside world.[12]

The last centuries of the third millennium B.C. were times of stress and trouble for the two great powers of Sumer and Egypt. In Mesopotamia, the Semitic-speaking kingdom of Akkad had been created under Sargon from about 2370 B.C. and consolidated by his son Naram-sin. But on the latter's death around 2250 there was a break-up, with the invasions of hill-tribes from the Zagros and elsewhere and the temporary establishment of a kingdom by one such tribe, the Guti, 'the stinging serpent of the hills'. 'Who was king, who was not king?' wrote a worried chronicler at this time. Within a century or so the barbarous Amurru, the Biblical Amorites, were raiding Mesopotamia in force—'the Amorite who knows not grain'; 'a host whose onslaught was like a hurricane, a people who had never known a city'.[13] In Egypt, on the death of Pepi II in about 2265 B.C., there was a similar break-up of the central authority, with the result that Asiatic raiders successfully set up their own petty kingdom in the Delta. Here again the scribes are eloquent—'Behold it has come to a point where the land is robbed of kingship by a few irresponsible men . . . no office at all is in its place, like a stampeded herd without its herdsman.'[14]

The records of the literate civilisations give colour and precision to these historical events; elsewhere the evidence of archaeology presents a picture of widespread sack and pillage. The townships of Palestine fell before the Amorites around 2000 B.C., and in Anatolia some 300 sites show evidence of destruction and burning about the same time; the second city of Troy had fallen probably about 2300 B.C.[15] In Greece, at least half-a-dozen towns, including Tiryns, Asine, Zygouries, and Lerna, were sacked and burnt at the end of the Early Helladic II period (rather than at the end of Early Helladic III, as has previously been thought), at a radiocarbon date of *c.* 2100 B.C.; Eutresis seems to have survived another century or so before it too was burnt, at the end of Early Helladic III.[16]

It is clear that the Near East and Aegean, by a series of related circumstances whereby barbarian movements were temporarily favoured by the weakened power of the great states, were jolted into an uneasy condition of change and conflict. Such conditions, with the forcible disruption of town and village life, can bring about a movement of craftsmen, losing their patrons by civil disruption, escaping from impending violence or carried by capture into alien service, and it can hardly be coincidence that the end of the third millennium B.C. and the beginning of the second should see the establishment of copper and bronze working in so many European localities. Trading or manufacturing centres set up in barbarian lands by civilised authorities can also in such circumstances find themselves cut off from their original homeland and forced to develop on their own. But apart from these factors, we can infer from the archaeological evidence that widespread movements of peoples were affecting Europe beyond the Aegean shores, and that some at least of the events of the late third millennium B.C. were connected with peoples speaking languages of the Indo-European language group.

This is not the place to discuss the philological reasoning which leads to the necessary hypothesis that the relationship of the ancient languages within the Indo-European group can best be explained by assuming an original central area from which subsequent dispersal took place. Within this hypothetical area a basic single language or group of closely related dialects would have been ancestral to all the primary Indo-European tongues—Greek, Latin, Sanskrit, Celtic, for instance—and their dispersal and subsequent differentiations would be the result of their transmission by movements of peoples.[17] For our enquiry we are concerned with four main problems. First, there is the likely date of the assumed linguistic unity, and secondly the likely geographical area as indicated by a common vocabulary for natural features, flora or fauna. Thirdly, the common vocabulary should also indicate something of the material culture of the speakers before dispersal, leading us to the fourth problem, that of identifying one or more linguistic groups in terms of their archaeology—an extremely difficult task.

The first question, however, can be answered up to a point. After the time of troubles in Mesopotamia, recovery was made under the kingdoms of Babylon and Assyria, and by soon after 2000 B.C. the latter had established an elaborate system of trade with countries as far afield as Anatolia. Here trading colonies of Assyrian merchants, dealing largely in metals, were established, and part of the records of their chamber of commerce at Kanesh, in the territory of the Hatti, survive. In these fascinating documents appear the names not only of indigenous Hatti, who spoke a language of unknown affinities and certainly not Indo-European, but of other persons the etymological structure of whose names indicates that they must be Indo-European and belong to one or more of the groups of languages later known to have been spoken by the Hittites, who were shortly to conquer the Hatti and to make themselves one of the great powers of antiquity. In other words, an intrusive group of Indo-European speakers were already on the Anatolian plateau by 2000 B.C.; the dispersal was already taking place.[18] With the coming of the Hittites has been associated the archaeological evidence for the destruction of towns in the last centuries of the third millennium, already mentioned. Can we not see in the contemporary events at the end of Early Helladic II the coming of peoples 'bringing an Indo-European idiom which, after influence by the surviving indigenous peoples, emerged as Greek'? This, it would seem, is a preferable way of stating the likely circumstances, rather than the older view that the Greek language was originally developed outside Greece, and thence introduced in separate immigrant movements corresponding to the three main dialects of later Greek antiquity.[19]

Chronologically then we must look for our undivided Indo-European homeland in the third millennium B.C., before these movements were taking place. As to its likely location, despite a minority favouring the north European plain,[20] philologists on the whole agree that an area west of the Urals and north of the Black Sea between the Carpathians and the Caucasus would best suit the evidence of common words for trees such as birch, beech, oak and willow; or animals such as bear, wolf, goose, pig, wasp; and salmon, or a similar large river fish; there is other linguistic evidence in support of this same general region. Our third point, material culture, can again be illuminated linguistically, the evidence demanding agriculturalists domesticating cattle, pigs and probably sheep; knowing the horse, wild or tamed, and growing grain. A metal which is either copper or bronze was known, as were wheeled vehicles denoted by common words for wheels, axles, hubs and yokes, but not for the spokes of a wheel.

In view of the sometimes uncritical interest it has aroused, we must take notice of another suggested criterion, virtually imperceptible by archaeological means alone, which is that of common institutional patterns. This involves the social organisation of elected ruler, a Council of Elders and an Assembly of freemen, and of a graded series of obligations in society for which the word 'feudal' has been used with perhaps less respect for its strict definition than a medieval historian would hope for: 'nowhere do the exotic feudalisms which so irritated Marc Bloch grow more luxuriantly and in less appropriate surroundings.'[21] Furthermore, the forms of land tenure and allocation implied by the Greek documents in the Linear B script have been claimed as another essential Indo-European characteristic.

The basic form of Indo-European society has been reconstructed, on this hypothesis, as 'divided into three castes, presided over by a god-king elected from a royal family. The warriors formed a feudal hierarchy with fiefs of "individual land". The totality of the fighting men comprised the sovereign assembly—the **teuta*. The third caste of free men comprised the producers organized in village "collectives" with land possibly cultivated on the open-field system.'[22] Most of these conditions would be impossible to substantiate directly by purely archaeological means, without some sort of written documents, but the demands implicit in this theory for advanced agricultural and social systems have influenced some philologists and archaeologists in considering the area of the likely Indo-European homeland. It has been felt that the early Balkan or Danubian Neolithic cultures would be the only possible claimants for the possession of this complex hypothetical agrarian system, even if the nature of archaeological evidence precludes its actual demonstration in such contexts, and evidence for a warrior-aristocracy is completely absent, though apparent in other and later cultures, as we shall shortly see. Now these are points of some interest and I shall say more about them in a later chapter: here I would point out that the social system of ruler, council, and assembly is attested earliest in Sumer, and its manifestation in Anatolia is as likely to be Hattic as Hittite—in neither area Indo-European. But the palace bureaucracies of Pylos or Knossos in the later second millennium B.C. are of the Orient: complex and sophisticated, ancient and tortuous, and it would surely be unwise to extrapolate from these to the simple societies among whom the Indo-European languages must have arisen at least a thousand years earlier.[23]

We are left with our final task: the attempt to correlate linguistic groups with archaeological evidence, either before or after the diaspora. Speakers of Hittite languages had reached Anatolia by 2000 B.C. or so; the speakers of the Indo-European dialect which lies behind Greek may have sacked Lerna and Asine, Tiryns and Zygouries, rather earlier, as we have seen. The Aryans were not to reach India for a half-millennium or more; with or before their dispersal may have gone the Indo-European rulers of the Mitanni in north Syria, but the Kassite dynasty of Mesopotamia (with Indo-European names) was established early in the second millennium B.C.[24] But what of Europe beyond the Aegean? What of those related language groups, Celtic, Germanic, and Italic on the one hand, Balto-Slav on the other?

If we look at the archaeological evidence from what we can broadly call the south Russian region in the middle third millennium B.C. we do in fact find communities of copper-using agriculturalists who would perfectly well fit the philological necessities so far as they go. Settlement sites, such as that of Mikhailovka in the Lower Dneipr area, provide evidence of copper-using agriculturalists, reaping and grinding a presumptively cereal crop, domesticating cattle, sheep, goats, and pigs, and either hunting or taming horses, and living in villages of rectangular timber-built thatched houses. Precise dating is lacking, but the earliest phases of the complex of cultures represented must date around 2500 B.C.[25] Their graves are known in some detail, and are those of individual burials under a tumulus or barrow, or kurgan: the cultures involved have indeed been broadly contained within a Kurgan Culture. Features of construction and of funerary ritual, notably the burial of the hides or fleeces of sacrificed cattle or sheep, attested by skulls and foot-bones, link such tombs with the Royal Tombs of Alaca Hüyük in Anatolia, of the late third millennium, and constructionally even with the Mycenae shaft-graves of the middle of the second.[26] At Maikop in the northern

37. *Objects from the Maikop barrow, South Russia, late third millennium* B.C.: *1,2, Silver vessel with animal frieze; 3, gold lion appliqué; 4,6, gold bulls; 5,7, copper adze and axe-adze.*

Caucasus and elsewhere we have wooden (exceptionally stone-built) mortuary houses under the kurgan to contain the dead—the Maikop tomb itself was richly furnished with copper, gold and silver objects, turquoise and carnelian, and elaborately woven fabrics were found here and elsewhere.[27] So too were solid-wheeled wooden carts or wagons and models of others, again in tombs, and the mortuary house under the barrow or cairn is a constantly recurring feature.[28] (Figs. 37, 38)

There seems to me to be a good case for suggesting an equation between the linguistic evidence for an assumed Indo-European homeland between the Carpathians and the Caucasus, and the archaeological evidence for people whose material culture and chronological position would fit the philological requirements in that area. And when we turn to Europe west and north of this region we find, in the last few centuries of the third millennium, widespread evidence usually interpreted as implying the spread of new peoples whose affiliations are broadly with the

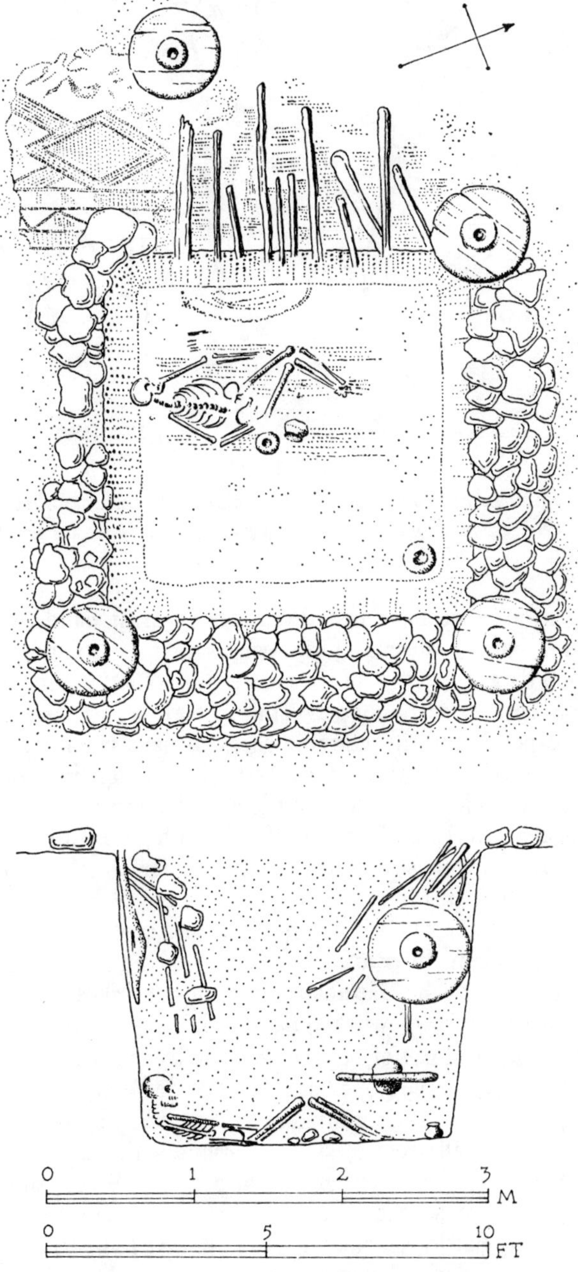

38. *Burial with wheels of three carts, end of third millennium* B.C., *from Tri Brata barrows, South Russia.*

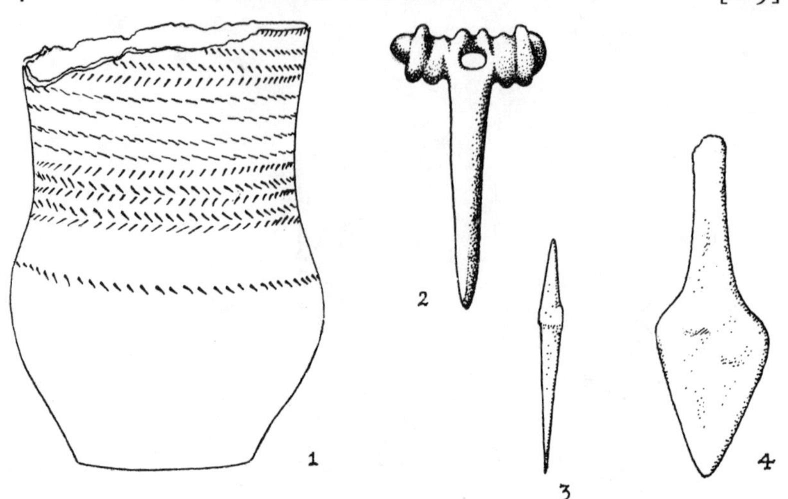

39. *Objects from burial at Bleckendorf, East Germany, end of third millennium* B.C.*: 1, Corded beaker; 2, bone hammer-headed pin; 3, copper awl; 4, copper tanged knife-dagger.*

south Russian area we have just discussed. Near at hand, we find in east Rumania barrow-burials of the ochre-grave or steppe type with a radiocarbon date of *c.* 2580 B.C., appearing as something intrusive into the local sequence of early copper-using cultures;[29] settlements of the late Tripolye peoples in the Ukraine seem to have been destroyed by other groups of cognate origin. Specific indications of trade or contact with the Pontic region are peculiar types of hammer-headed clothes- or hair-pins characteristic of certain of the south Russian early copper-using communities, but scattered not only as far as Alaca Hüyük in Anatolia and Lerna in Greece, but in north-central Europe and even Denmark.[30] (Figs. 39, 40) Over much of east and central Europe, on the north European plain, in Scandinavia and Holland, we have, cutting across the traditions of the Danubian long-house villages and their successors, the appearance of what appear to be new peoples whose pot forms, with a plentiful use of ornament made by impressing cords into the surface, their shaft-hole stone battle-axes buried with their warriors as weapons of prestige, and their individual burials under barrows and often in mortuary houses, all seem to show relations with the regions north of the Black Sea; fortified settlements also appear.[31] Archaeologically the new-comers represent a complex of cultures—Globular Amphorae, Corded Ware, Battle-Axe people, Single-Grave folk—and some have regarded them as derived from local and late Neolithic groups.

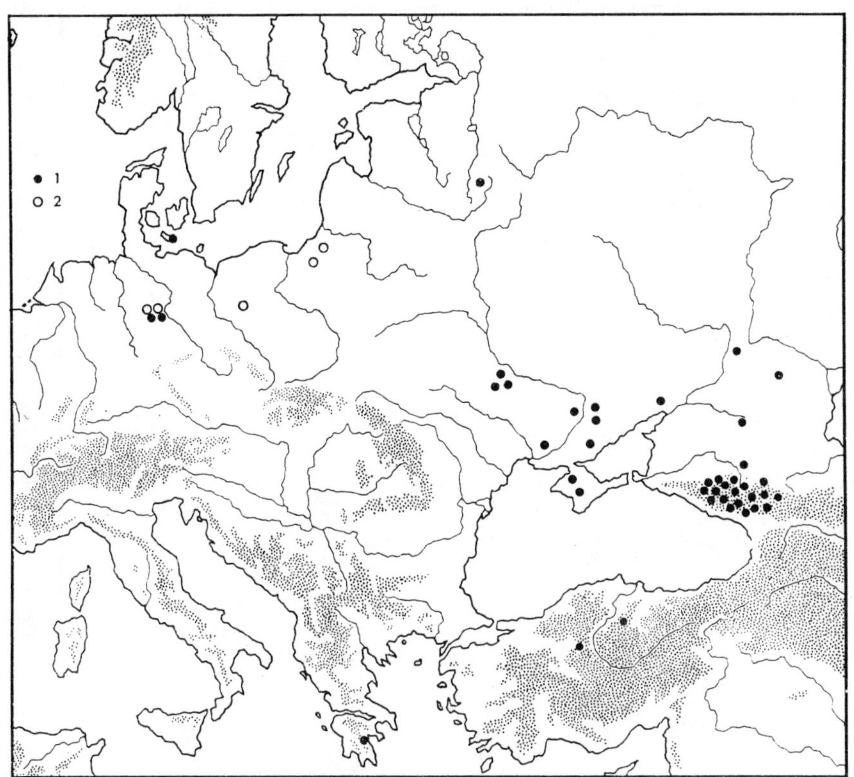

40. *Distribution of 1, Hammer-headed pins; 2, Derivative forms; end of third millennium* B.C.

But the general opinion is that in essentials they seem to represent a diffuse and perhaps rapid movement of inter-related peoples from the south Russian steppe, north-westwards at least to the Rhine and the Low countries, where radiocarbon dates show that makers of corded ware and battle-axes had arrived by *c.* 2500 B.C.[32] Did they speak an Indo-European language? This is a question difficult to answer, and we must temporarily postpone asking it. (Fig. 41)

There is some evidence, not wholly conclusive, that would imply that these barrow-burying peoples had an economy in which pastoralism, perhaps partly nomadic, may have played an important part; a palisaded cattle-kraal at Anlo in Holland of *c.* 2300 B.C. may be significant in this regard.[33] (Fig. 42) But at all events their advent in central and north-western Europe marks a complete break in the long-established Danubian tradition, with its long houses of presumptively undivided families in

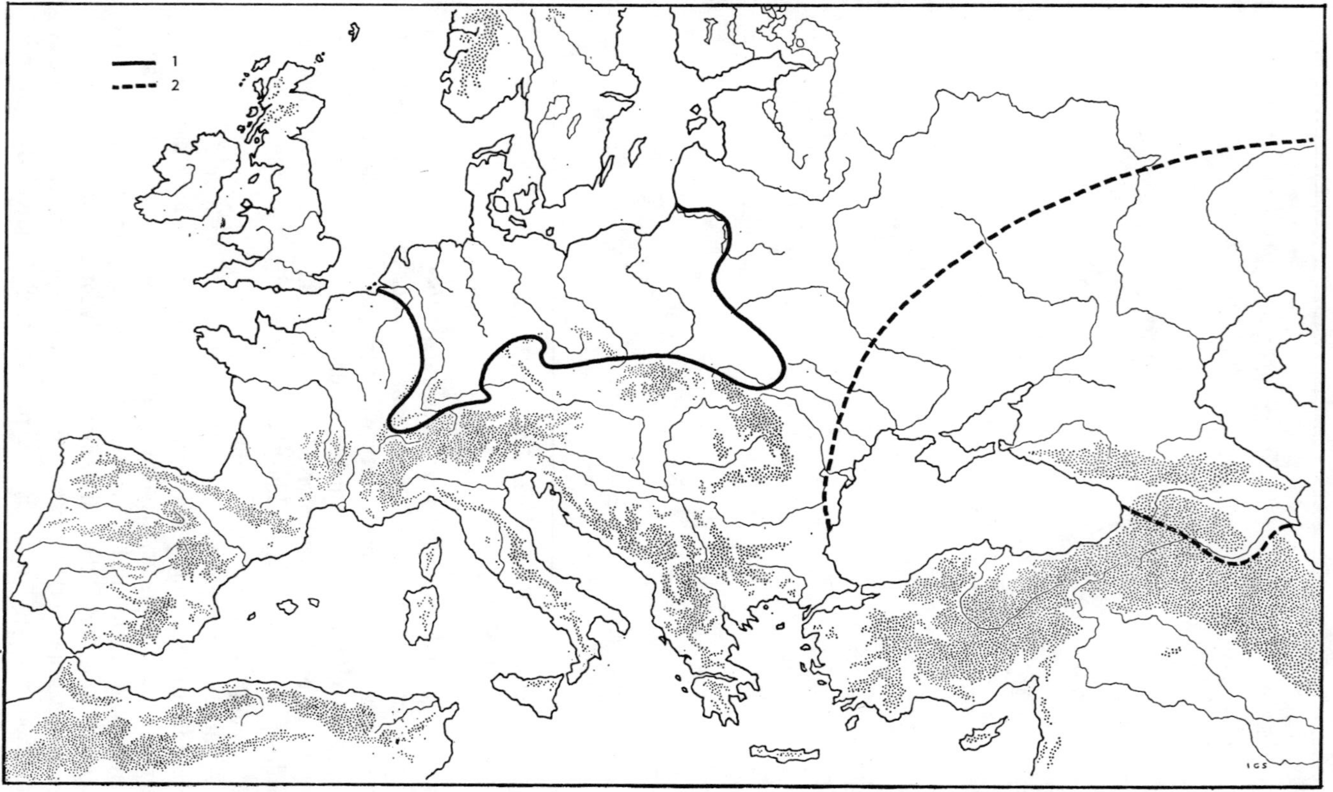

41. *Generalised distribution of* 1, *Globular Amphorae–Single Grave–Corded Ware cultures;* 2, *Early Pit-Grave culture.*

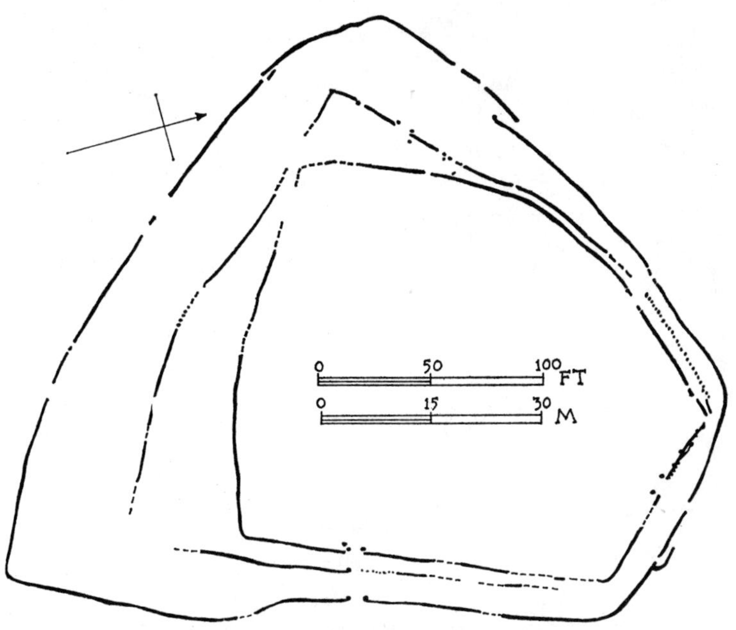

42. *Palisades of successively enlarged cattle kraal, Single Grave culture, end of third millennium* B.C., *at Anlo, Netherlands.*

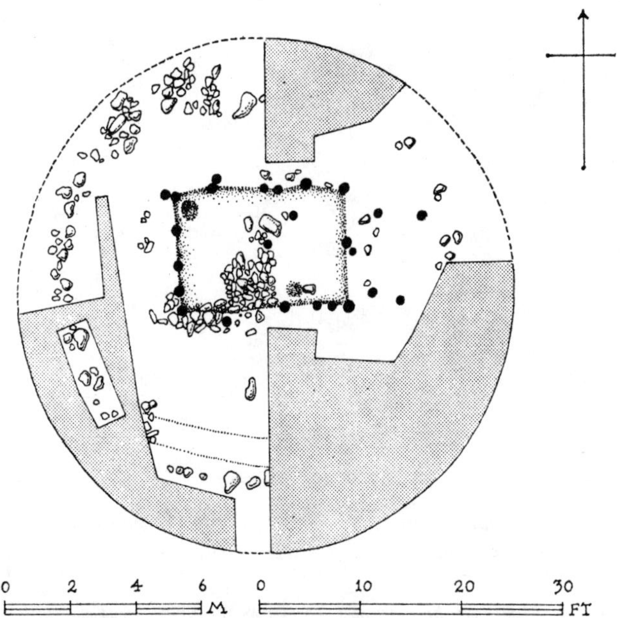

43. *Mortuary house under barrow, Corded Ware culture, end of third millennium* B.C., *at Sarmenstorf, Switzerland.*

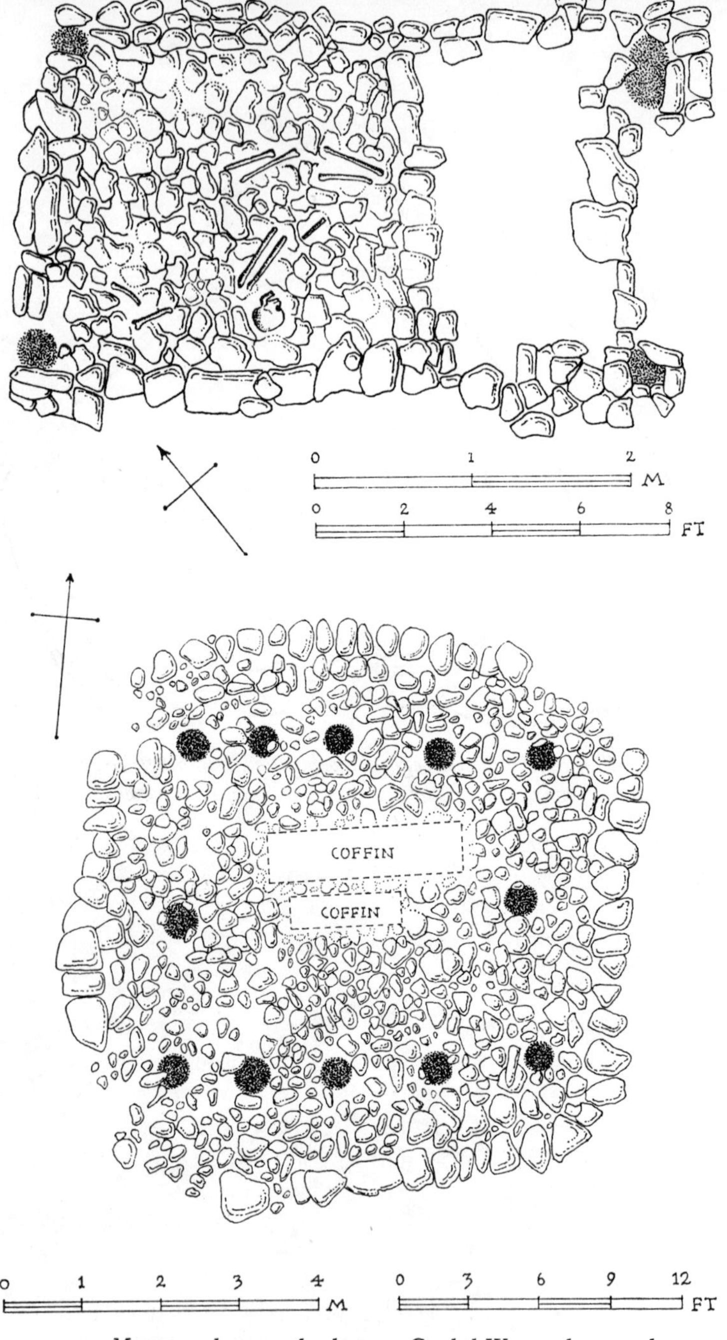

44. *Mortuary house under barrow, Corded Ware culture, end of third millennium* B.C., *at Seifartsdorf, East Germany.*

45. *Mortuary house under barrow with burials in tree-trunk coffins, mid second millennium* B.C., at *Grünhof-Tesperheide, Schleswig-Holstein.*

large villages. The house-type represented by the mortuary structures under the barrows is that of a simple single-roomed cabin for a nuclear family, sometimes with a porch and belonging to a widespread group of houses of the *megaron* plan, ancient in Anatolia and later to be well-known in Greece. (Figs. 43–45; Pl. x b) We saw that villages of houses of this type appear in Bulgaria in the early third millennium (as at Karanovo in Phase VI), and in Germany, towards the end of the third millennium or early in the second, there are villages such as that of Aichbühl or Riedschachen on the Federsee in Württemburg, the former with twenty-two houses. Contemporary or later settlements such as Dullenried, or the Altheim phase of the Goldberg, have small, unsophisticated and flimsy huts only 12 to 15 feet square, contrasting very strikingly with the massive carpentry of the great early Danubian long-houses.[34] Settlements too are smaller: at Homolka in Czechoslovakia, there were only six houses in the first phase and ten in the second—a population of from thirty to fifty. A certain amount of sophistication can be observed on occasion, however, notably in the external gable-end pargetting, with incised and coloured geometric patterning, in some of the Hungarian houses of about this time, as at Kökénydomb.[35] (Figs. 45–47)

A new set of traditions had become established as a result of these folk-movements from the steppe, breaking with those of the Danubian peasants but containing much which was to survive as distinctive of successive culture-patterns almost throughout the prehistory of these regions of central and northern Europe. The warriors buried with their finely-made stone shaft-hole battle-axes foreshadow the dominance, in the prehistory and early history which is to follow, of an heroic aristocracy and a warrior caste; if indeed an element of pastoralism was present it would be ancestral to that which certainly becomes perceptible at the end of prehistoric times. Tumulus-burial, with the timber mortuary house beneath the mound, was again to continue sporadically in central Europe, and continuously on the steppe, where the Scythian tombs we will discuss later on are the counterparts of the Celtic burials of Vix or Hradenin of the sixth and seventh centuries B.C. Indeed the Viking barrow-burials carried on the tradition, but less long in northern Europe than among the peoples of the Asiatic steppe whose burial customs were recorded later in the Middle Ages by William of Rubruck or Carpini.[36]

What then of that deferred question: are these newcomers into central and northern Europe before and around 2000 B.C. speakers of Indo-European dialects? I would stress again that it seems to have been these peoples who made a break with what had gone before but laid discernible foundations for what was to follow. We shall see later that the introduction and development of copper and bronze working in central

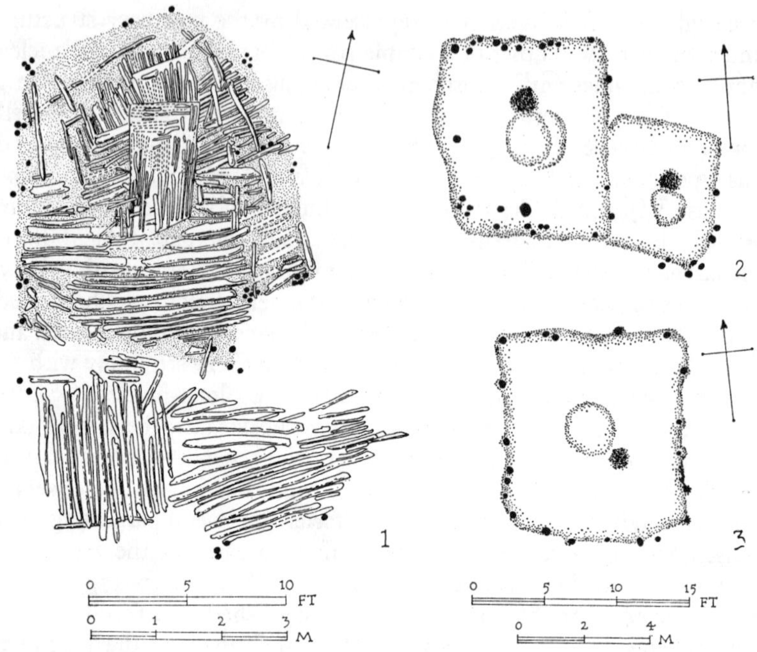

46. *House plans, late third millennium* B.C.*: 1, Dullenried, 2,3, Goldberg, South Germany.*

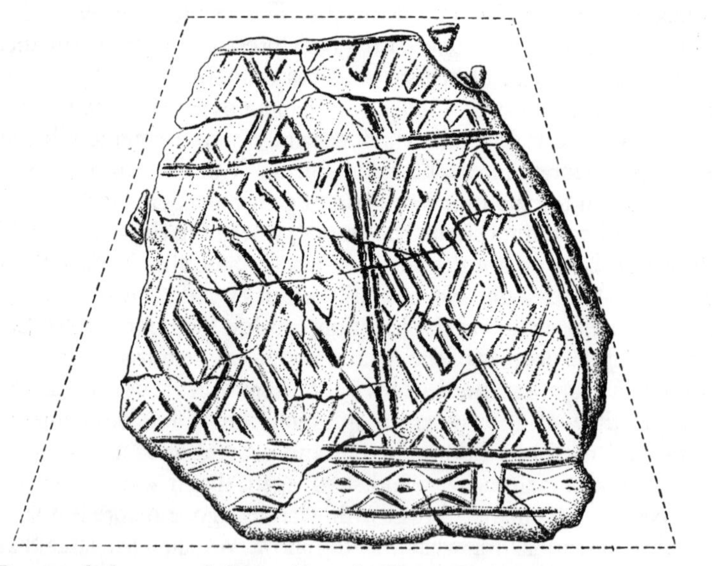

47. *Decorated plaster-work from gable-end of house, Tisza culture, fourth millennium* B.C., *Kökénydomb, Hungary.*

Europe was a technological modification which does not seem to have involved new drafts of population, other than those we must shortly consider, coming from the west, and who appear to have been themselves submerged by the cultural traditions of the Corded Ware or Single Grave peoples. From the beginning of the second millennium B.C. we move without a substantial break into a central Europe that, by early in the first, can hardly be other than Celtic and perhaps Germanic-speaking. I would not say that our late third millennium immigrants from the south Russian steppes spoke Celtic, or Italic or Germanic or any other known Indo-European language of central or west Europe. But the likelihood that they did speak one or more dialects within the Indo-European group seems to me a very strong one. They need not have survived; many languages must have been lost without trace in the absence of even conditional literacy—without the chance, for instance, of being discovered anew, like Tocharian, or even the Hittite group. If the views of Krahe and the Tübingen school of philologists are given weight, an early Indo-European, non-Celtic language may lurk in their 'Old European' river-names: the thesis has not however won universal acceptance and the archaeologist must be proportionately cautious.[37]

We have just noted the impact of the new peoples from the steppe upon some of the European neolithic cultures, notably that of Tripolye in the forest-steppe zone of the Ukraine, and the Danubian culture centred on that great river basin but extending from the Rhine to the Vistula. What we must now return to is that area of eastern Europe in which we saw that what was virtually a western extension of the Near Eastern peasant communities was established before 5000 B.C. This is the area of the 'tell' settlements with their implications of relatively advanced agriculture and social systems which could have approximated to the more ancient Oriental scheme of Council and Assembly. I have already mentioned the Bulgarian tell of Karanovo as a typical example of these settlements, and throughout the fourth and third millennia it flourished, with successive rebuildings but a basic continuity of culture during its long sixth period. Copper and rare gold objects were acquired by the inhabitants of this and other villages in the Thracian plain;[38] the double-spiral-headed pins mentioned above are a case in point. Karanovo itself seems to have been deserted perhaps about 2000 B.C. and was re-settled by new people; elsewhere, around the same time, the end of the tell settlements in east Europe sometimes came with violence. Sporadic resettlement took place, but on the whole the cultures responsible for these village communities, south and east of their northern boundary on the Danube, around its tributary the Tisza, come to an end, and we encounter other alien cultures, the warriors of some of which used stone battle-axes.

But beyond the Tisza, on the Hungarian plain and northwards to Slovakia, the story is different. Here the settlements of the early copper-using peoples come to an end in the now familiar circumstances of the end of the third millennium, again marked by the incursions of peoples, this time of the Baden culture,[39] for whom Indo-European affinities have often been claimed; but thereafter we seem to be observing the phenomenon of the transference of the tell type of settlement, with its implications of advanced agriculture, from those regions where it had flourished since the sixth millennium, to a new territory. Here it was to continue into the thirteenth century B.C., when it in turn was to collapse under the incursions of warrior bands, this time coming from the west.[40]

A technological development of some importance that we may consider at this point is that of the wheel and wheeled draught-vehicles. All the evidence suggests that the use of the wheel, so far as the Old World was concerned (and it was never invented in the New) originated among the early peasant communities of Mesopotamia at some date well before 3000 B.C., and that its use was disseminated thence among the barbarian communities of Europe and Asia.[41] I would make a couple of general points here. The first is that wheeled vehicles have a limited use to communities occupying such broken or hilly country that pack or sledge transport is more suitable—wheeled transport was introduced into hilly but by no means remote areas of Britain practically within living memory; a classic instance of the contrast between innovating and conserving traditions. The other point is that there are two basic forms of simple wheeled vehicles—the cart with two wheels and the wagon with four.[42] (Eccentricities can of course occur, as in the three-wheeled vehicle, of the early first millennium B.C., from a grave in Russian Armenia).[43] And at the beginning of the history of the wheel we are dealing with solid one-piece or plank-built discs; spokes are a later development, almost certainly invented in response to improved woodworkers' tools such as saws, and to the need of a light cart as a war chariot, a phenomenon we will encounter later on.[44] One may note that the word for 'spoke' used in Akkadian (*tirtitu*) is a loan-word, thought to be probably of Kassite origin, and therefore suggestive of the invention of the spoked wheel outside the Mesopotamian world.[45]

Both in Sumerian and in the later Akkadian language heavy, presumptively four-wheeled, working wagons are distinguished from lighter two-wheeled carts or battle-cars; the Akkadian word for the latter (*narkabtu*) was later used of undoubted two-wheeled war chariots.[46] Representations and surviving remains of actual vehicles confirm the

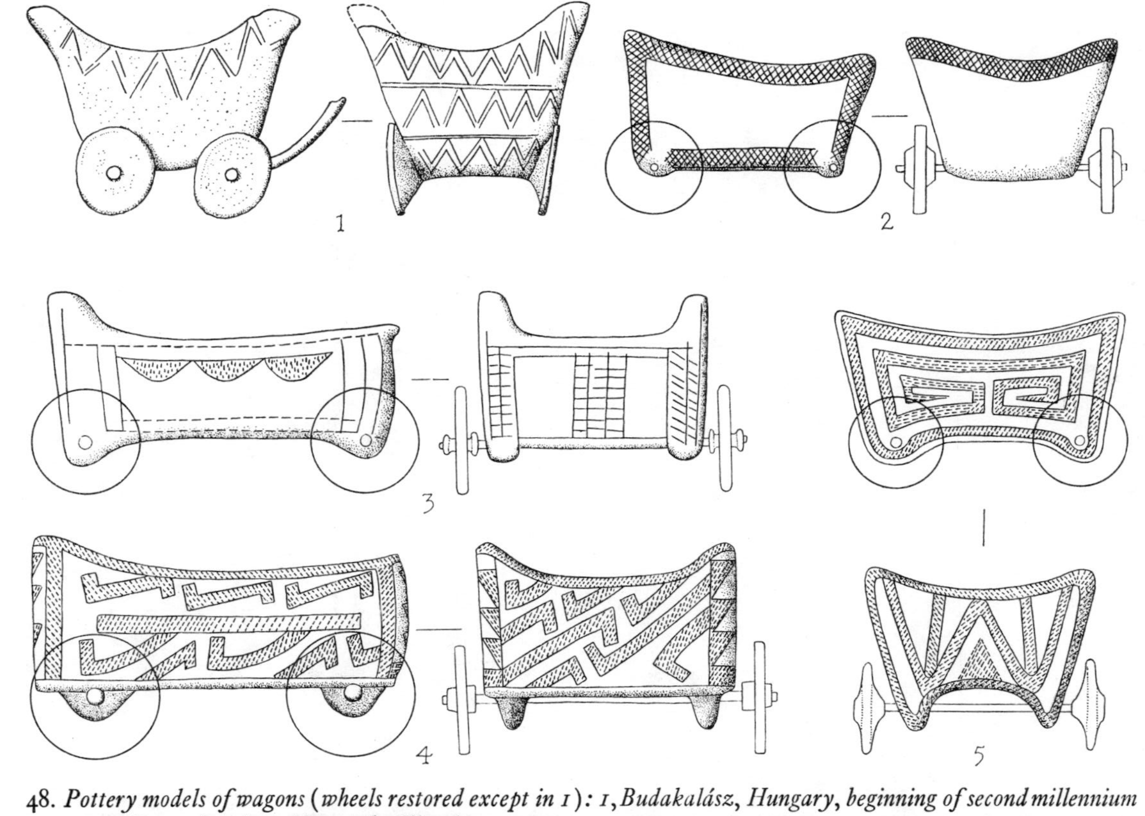

48. *Pottery models of wagons (wheels restored except in* 1): 1, *Budakalász, Hungary, beginning of second millennium* B.C.; 2–5, *Transylvania, mid second millennium* B.C.

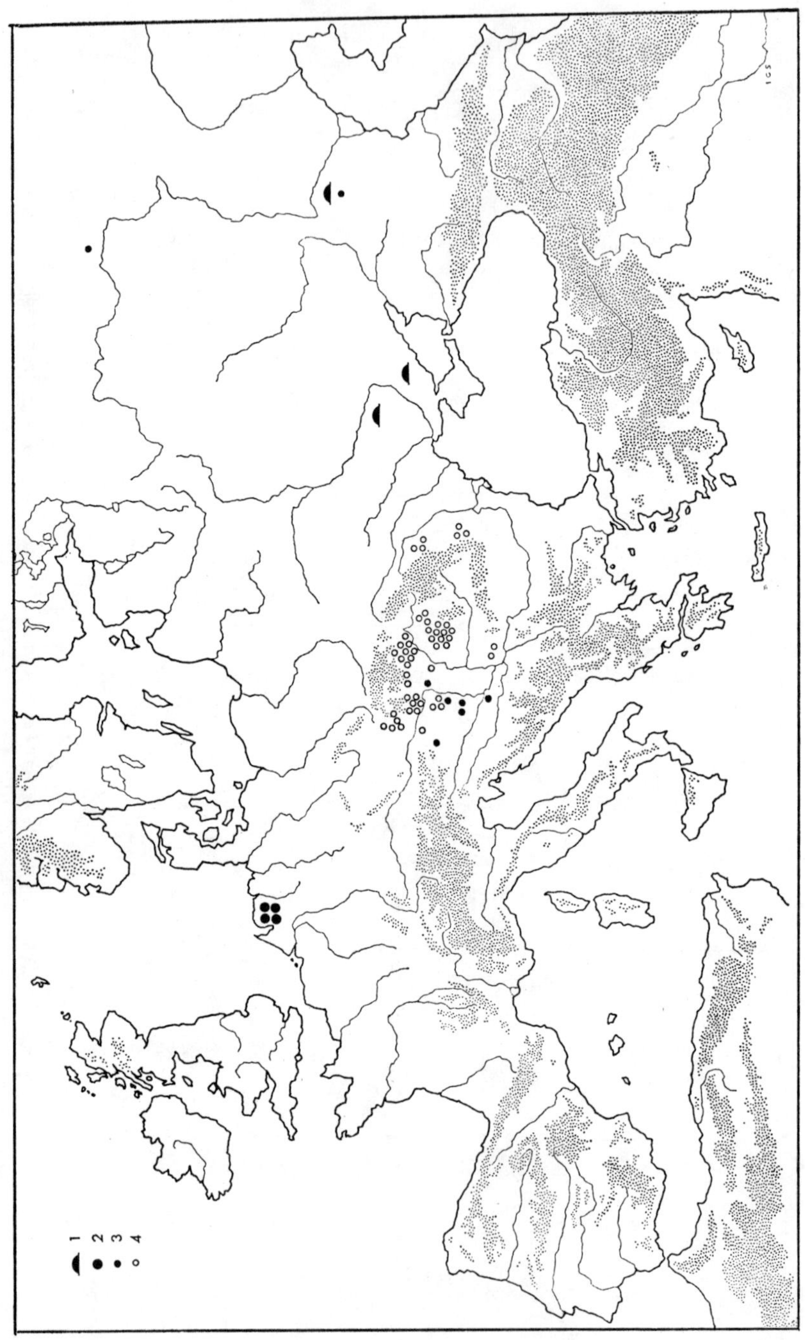
1
2
3
4

existence of carts and wagons from the beginning, and outside the civilizations of the Ancient Orient we have models and surviving traces of carts with solid disc wheels, and perhaps of wagons, in the probably late third millennium B.C. South Russian graves of the type that we have already noted. In northern Holland several solid wheels have been found, one near a corduroy road in the peat, evidently designed for wheeled traffic; these are all closely dated as contemporary, between 2100 and 2000 B.C. on radiocarbon readings, and similar tracks in the Somerset fens may be contemporary or probably earlier.[47] On the Hungarian plain a fine model wagon of the period of the folk movements around or before 2000 B.C. shows us a type which further models indicate continued in use for some five centuries at least,[48] and we may here be seeing something of the prehistory of the modern distribution of carts and wagons in Europe, with the great mid-continental wagon zone and (of interest in connection with the prehistoric south Russian finds) carts in the Crimea and the Caucasus.[49] In all, the dispersal of carts and wagons around 2000 B.C. seems likely to be connected in some way with the movements of peoples we have seen some reason to connect with the speakers of Indo-European languages. And at this point we must say something about the domestication of the horse as a traction and riding animal. (Figs. 48, 49; Pls. IX; Xa)

Wild horses, ultimately descendants of Pleistocene forms, fall into two main groups. The first comprises the steppe ponies, represented by the Tarpan and Przewalski's Horse, both now extinct in their wild form, though small numbers of the latter survive in zoos. The other group has been the subject of much discussion, but there seems to have been a European wild forest-zone type, with a large and a small form.[50] The steppe horses seem to have been the first to be domesticated, and bones are certainly present in third millennium sites in south Russia, and Przewalski's Horse is represented on a silver vase from the Maikop tomb of before 2000 B.C. (Fig. 37) It is difficult to prove domestication from a bare record of the occurrence of bones, though it is inherently likely; our first definite evidence comes in the first half of the second millennium B.C., with the pairs of horse skeletons found with the bone cheek-pieces of their bridles in the tombs of the Timber Grave culture centred on the Lower Volga.[51] In Hungary horse bones appear in the Baden culture (before or around 2000 B.C.) but evidence of bits or bridles does not occur before about 1500 B.C. at the earliest.[52] (Figs. 50, 70)

49. *Distribution of early solid-wheeled vehicles in Europe: 1, Vehicles in burials, late third millennium* B.C.*; 2, Wooden wheels, c.2,000* B.C.*; 3, Models of vehicles and wheels, late third-early second millennium* B.C.*; 4, Models, mid second millennium* B.C.

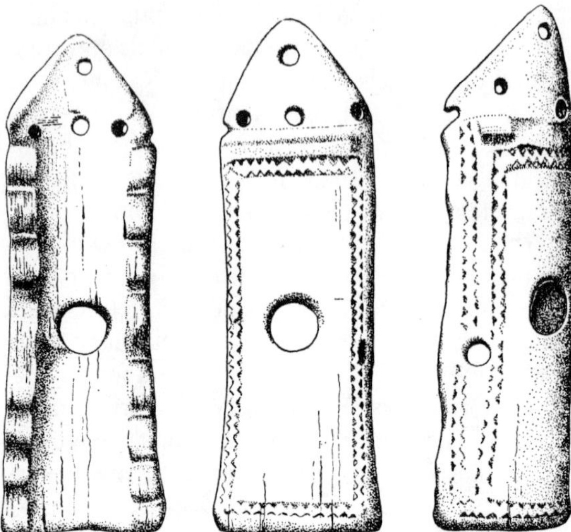

50. *Bone cheek-piece of horse bridle, South Russian Timber Grave culture, early second millennium* B.C., *from barrow at Komarovka, middle Volga.*

It appears that domestication of the north European indigenous horse was also taking place at least by the beginning of the second millennium B.C. in Sweden and could have taken place elsewhere (e.g. in Spain and in Britain, where horse bones (presumably of wild animals) occur in contexts of the third millennium B.C.).[53] There are a few finds in northern Europe associating horse bones with late Neolithic cultures including Corded Ware and comparable contexts, but the evidence is in fact less secure than has sometimes been claimed.[54] On the whole, however, the evidence suggests an initial domestication of horses of the Tarpan and Przewalski type in the south Russian steppe area, and probably on that westward extension of the steppe constituting the Great Hungarian Plain, before 2000 B.C.; then a subsequent spread of the notion of domestication into north and west Europe, with the sporadic local taming of the indigenous Forest types of horse.[55] Such a dissemination it would be reasonable to associate with the movements of peoples northwards and westwards into Europe implied by the archaeological evidence we have just discussed. Both the tamed horse, and the solid-wheeled vehicles whether drawn by them, or by onagers or by oxen,

---

IX. (*a*) *Single-piece wooden wheel, c.2000* B.C., *from De Eese, Overyssel, Netherlands.* (Photo. Centrale Photodienst, Rijksuniversiteit Groningen)
IX. (*b*) *Timber corduroy roadway in bog, c.2000* B.C., *at Nieuw Dordrecht, Drenthe, Netherlands.* (Photo. Biologisch-Archaeologisch Instituut, Groningen)

IX (*caption on facing page*)

a

b

x (*caption on facing page*)

a

b

would of course be consonant with the linguistic evidence in the common Indo-European vocabulary.

By the end of the third millennium B.C. we have then a situation over large areas of eastern, central and northern Europe in which the earlier agricultural economies had been disrupted and their place taken by new settlers, themselves of course farmers, but perhaps more pastoral in their mode of life. There seems to have been insecurity and perhaps raiding; earthwork or stone wall defences round settlements become not infrequent. In one or two areas, notably Transylvania and Iberia, precocious copper-working had begun, but the basic economy remained formally Neolithic in areas where agriculture had long been established. But there still remained even more conservative peoples, still wholly or in large part dependent on hunting and fishing for their livelihood. We can trace them on the Baltic shores and on the River Elbe, and suspect them in northern Britain; eastwards we find them represented by settlements and cemeteries from the White Sea and Lake Onega, into south Siberia. Many of these communities seem to have subsisted mainly on fishing, an economy which can give a marked degree of stability and even wealth to a non-agricultural society, as the Indians of British Columbia showed in recent times.[56]

We must now turn to western Europe, which lay beyond the range of the folk-movements we have been considering. In the east Mediterranean, the end of the third millennium saw also the end of the Early Minoan II period. In the centre and west, we have at this time the development of stone-using agricultural colonies, at best importing a few scanty objects of copper; in Malta elaborating rock-cut tombs to huge stone-built temples in their curious island cult, in the Lipari Islands profiting from the trade in obsidian, that volcanic glass that provides sharp but easily broken flakes, most likely to have had their main use as razor blades, in consonance with the long-established fashion of shaving in the Mediterranean world, in contrast to the bearded barbarians of continental Europe. Despite much recent work, Malta is still somewhat of an enigma. There now seems no recognisable prototype for the sophisticated trefoil-plan temples (as at Ggantija, of a phase with a radiocarbon date of *c.* 2700 B.C.) which are the earliest in the architectural and

---

X. (*a*) *Pottery model of solid-wheeled wagon, Baden culture, late third millennium* B.C., *from grave at Budakalàsz, Hungary.* (Photo. Magyar Nemzeti Museum)

X. (*b*) *Rectangular wattled-and-mud-walled houses, Gumelniţa culture, mid fourth millennium* B.C.; *Phase* VI *of the 'tell' of Karanovo, Bulgaria.* (Photo. Mikov)

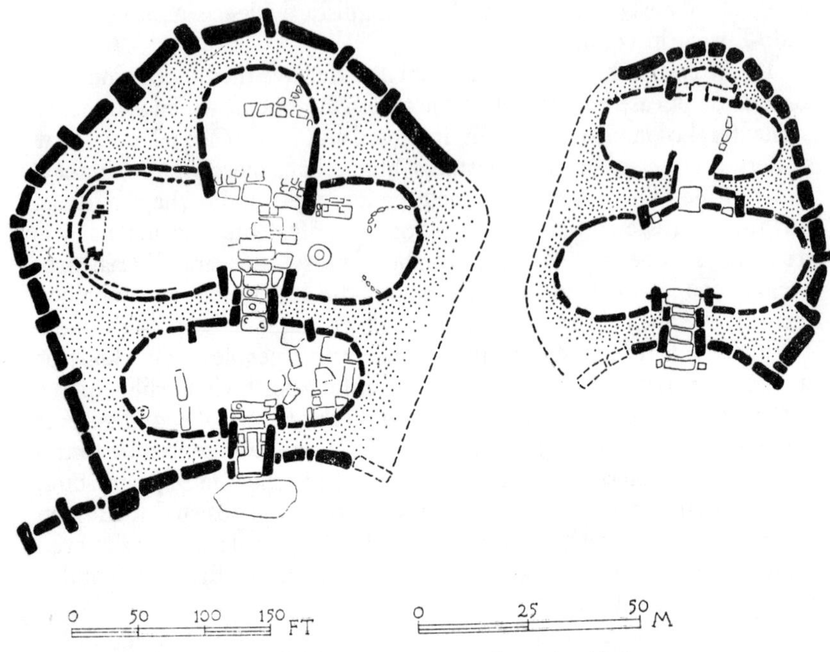

51. *Plans of temples, third millennium* B.C., *at Ggantija, Malta.*

stratigraphic sequence. The later phases, with spiral relief carvings (as at Tarxien) must lie just before 2,000 B.C.[57] (Fig. 51; Pl. XI) In Spain and Portugal, as we saw earlier, what seem to be colonies of east Mediterranean, perhaps mainly Cycladic, inspiration, were working copper in their bastioned trading-posts. But shortly before 2000 B.C. these came to an end—a violent end, at Vila Nova de São Pedro; and here the site was re-occupied by a people whose pottery styles, notably cups or beakers probably copying esparto-grass baskets, suggest that they may have been descendants of indigenous inhabitants making 'impressed' wares before the arrival of the 'colonists'. From them, however, they appear to have acquired the knowledge of copper-working, but at a lower technological level in that they did not use the closed or valve mould for casting, only the simple open type. (Pl. XII a)

---

52. *Objects from Bell-Beaker grave, beginning of second millennium* B.C., *at Prague, Czechoslovakia: 1, Beaker; 2, silver ear-rings; 3, copper tanged knife-dagger.*
53. *Objects from Bell-Beaker grave, beginning of second millennium* B.C., *at Roundway, Wiltshire, England: 1, Beaker; 2, flint arrow-head; 3, archer's wrist-guard; 4, copper pin; 5, copper tanged knife-dagger.*

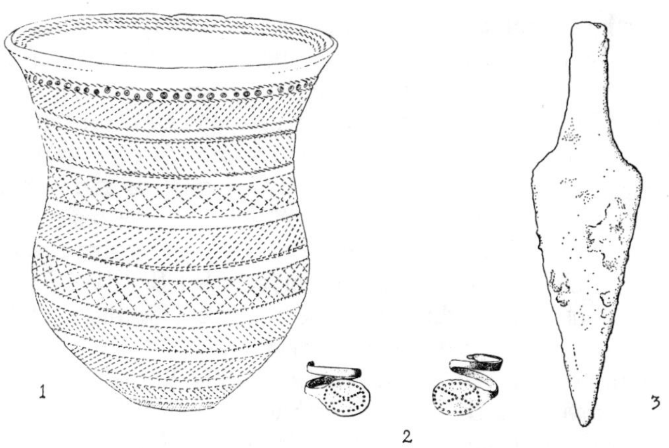

52

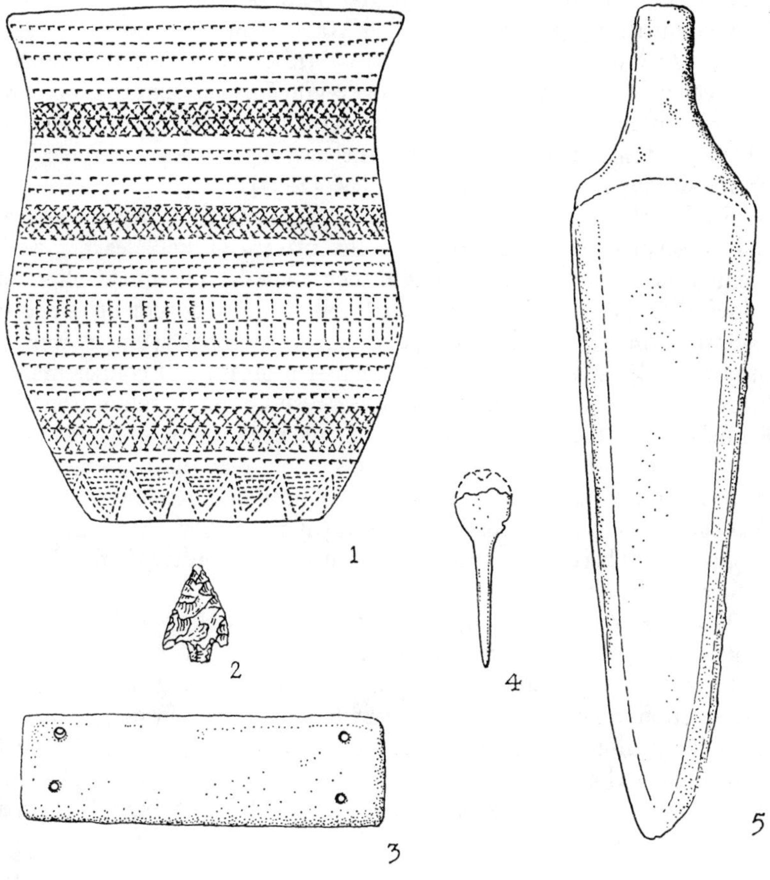

1

2

4

3

5

53

Nevertheless, these makers of Bell-Beaker pottery were to spread the knowledge of simple copper and gold metallurgy over many regions of Europe as yet ignorant of the metal-smith's craft and still essentially stone-using.[58] From their original coastal settlements in central Portugal, around the Tagus estuary, they undertook, at a date somewhat before 2000 B.C., a series of remarkable journeys westwards and northwards, taking with them not only their metallurgical knowledge, but the tradition of making their highly standardised pottery. The fact that the pot style remained so close to its Iberian prototypes that Bell-Beakers made in Britain or Bohemia might almost be mistaken for those of Spanish manufacture suggests that the movement was rapid. By sea routes up the Atlantic coasts they reached Brittany and the Rhine mouth, possibly also the British Isles. By routes we cannot give precision to, they made quite massive settlement in Czechoslovakia, and even got as far as Budapest and the River Vistula. Once established in central Europe, they evidently mixed to no small degree with local communities; in the Low countries these were of Corded Ware or Single Grave folk, and their pottery was there modified into hybrid form; so too their burial rite became consistently that of a single-grave usually under a barrow. Their menfolk were archers, buried with their appropriate equipment of which the flint arrow-tips and the finely wrought stone wristguard or bracer survive from many graves. (Figs. 52–55)

Radiocarbon dates from Holland and Germany show that the arrival and subsequent cultural mixing of the makers of Bell-Beakers were events centred on 2000 B.C.[59] There then comes a subsequent phase of colonisation which has been called the Reflux Movement, since it affected France, Sardinia, Sicily, and even Spain once again, as well as the British Isles, which received their first intimation of copper metallurgy in the early second millennium as a result of immigration from the Rhineland and the Low countries, as Lord Abercromby first perceived in essence half-a-century ago. We now know that the movements of trade and immigration involved must have been infinitely more complex than he was prepared to think, but let us pay a tribute to his acumen and percipience. There are two radiocarbon dates so far available for British beakers, both of *c.* 1800 B.C.[60]

Wherever they colonised, the makers of Bell-Beakers, either in their primary moves or their secondary diaspora, are seen to be concerned with the local exploitation of copper and gold; and as I have said, the introduction of non-ferrous metallurgy to many areas of western Europe must be attributed to these remarkable people, recognisable not only from their archaeological remains, but from their distinctive physical type, at least in the Reflux phase, round-headed and strongly built in a

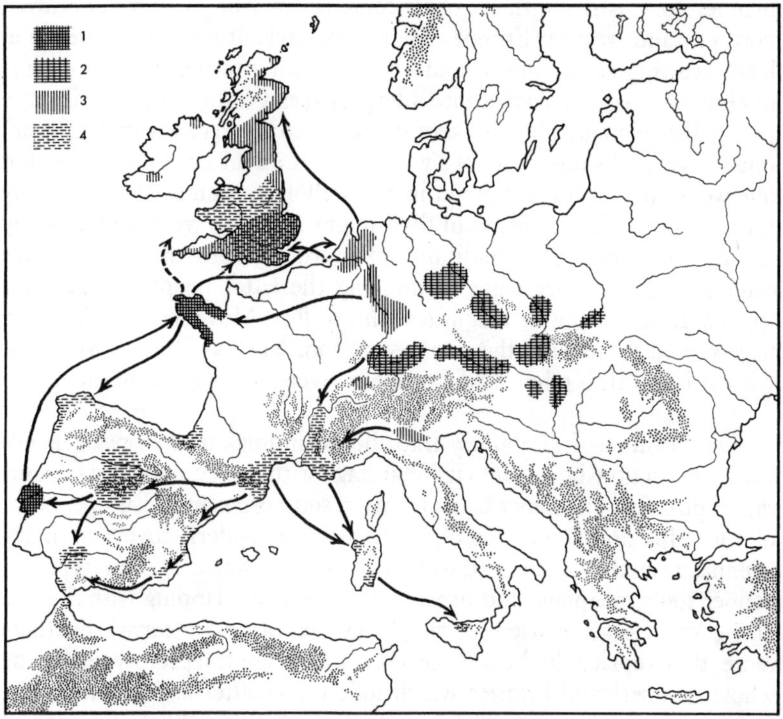

54. *Generalised distribution and movements of Bell-Beaker cultures, end of third to beginning of second millennium* B.C.: *1, 'Maritime' Group; 2, Eastern and Central Groups; 3, Netherlands, Rhenish and Austrian Groups, and Reflux derivatives; 4, Other Reflux derivatives.*

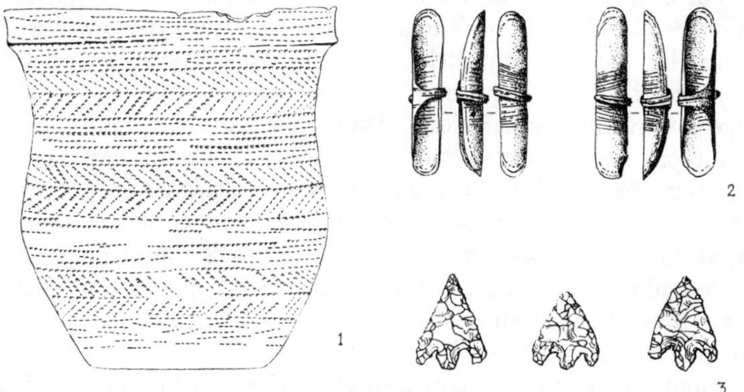

55. *Objects from Bell-Beaker grave, beginning of second millennium* B.C., *from Radley, Oxon., England: 1, Beaker; 2, gold ear-rings; 3, flint arrow-heads.*

manner contrasting with the other contemporary populations of central, northern and western Europe. They were agriculturalists, in Britain at least, growing barley and flax and domesticating cattle, sheep and pigs; in Holland a palisaded enclosure interpreted as a cattle-kraal may imply a pastoralist element. Their beakers, deposited so invariably with their dead, must have held some drink of significance: it might have been milk, but one would like to think it might just as well have been beer or mead. By the time of the Reflux phase of their migrations they were in part clearly much permeated with traditions of Corded Ware or Single-Grave origins, and if we are right in thinking the latter peoples could have spoken Indo-European languages, the Reflux Movement could again have served to transmit these to new regions, such as Britain, where for what it is worth Krahe's Old European river-names again occur.

Our technological enquiry into the beginnings of European metal-working can now be taken to its final stage with the examination of some rather puzzling phenomena. In an area of southern central Europe, north of the Alps and lying roughly between the modern towns of Bern, Vienna, Frankfurt, and Dresden, a consistent series of new types of copper tools, weapons, and ornaments appear overlapping with the end of the Bell-Beaker phase, but not themselves of beaker forms. Furthermore, they replace the beaker metal types and are the prototypes for the whole rich series of bronzes which follow thereafter and dominate the greater part of Europe. The new features include the techniques of riveting a dagger-blade into its haft instead of using a tang as in the beaker tradition; the use of ornaments including spiral wire pendants and ingot-torcs (necklets with returned ends that could also be used as units of copper); and the use of garments fastened by pins instead of buttons.[61] I will come back to this interesting sartorial question in a minute, but for the moment let us consider these novel copper types. They owe nothing to anything which goes before in Europe, but riveted daggers were the normal Near Eastern type, and the ingot-torcs and specific pin forms do in fact occur in several Near Eastern sites, but especially those in Syria such as Byblos and Ugarit, during a limited period of time around 2000–1800 B.C.[62] Furthermore, the grave-finds in central Europe show a swing-over in the warrior's equipment from the beaker tradition of bow and arrow, to that of the dagger and axe: this change in weapons means a change in tactics to one also current in contemporary Syria. (Fig. 56)

It looks therefore as if shortly after 2000 B.C. contact was established between the metal-smiths and merchants of Syria and the peoples and copper ores of south-central Europe; spectrographic analysis shows that

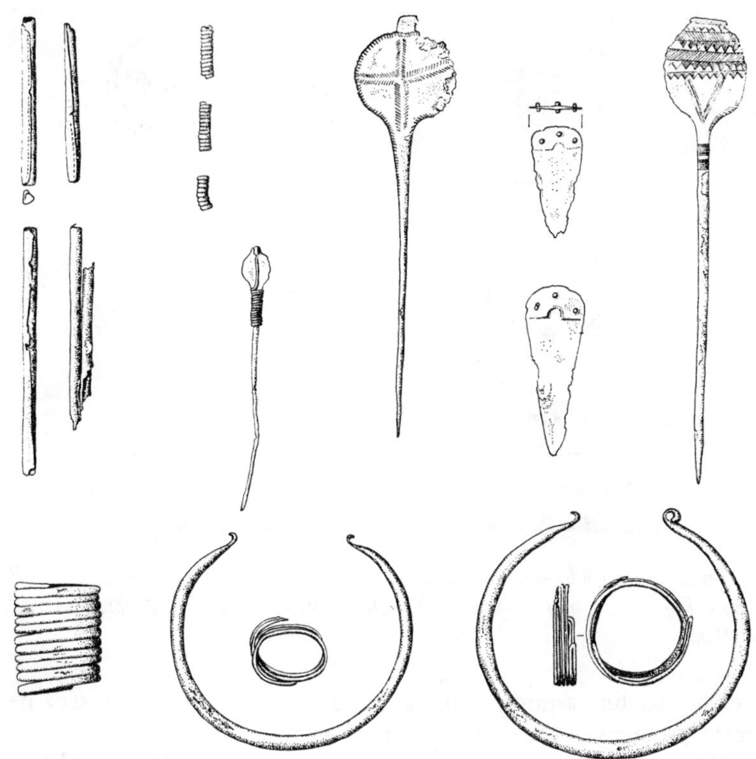

56. *Copper beads, pins, rings, riveted knives and ingot-torcs, early second millennium* B.C., *from graves at Straubing, South Germany.*

the metal deposits of the Tyrol and elsewhere in central Europe were now being worked. But by what route could such contact be made? The distribution in Europe of the types in question shows that while some are found as far east as the River Tisza, they do not occur further east, and the majority are not found further down the Danube than just beyond Vienna. A route up the Danube from the east to south-central Europe seems then unlikely, and we must consider the possibility of trade from the head of the Adriatic over a 200 mile-long route probably crossing the Alps by the St Gothard Pass. Mediterranean shells (*Columbella rustica*) were used for ornaments by our metalworkers, so some contacts with that sea existed. And if we look for occasions which might prompt such merchant venturing from the Levant, the disturbed conditions precipitated by the Amorite and other raids at the beginning of the second millennium might well play their part, with the dislocation of

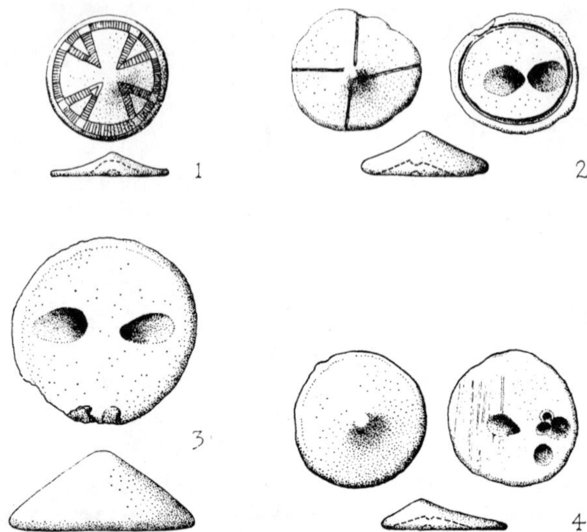

57. *Jet buttons with* V-*perforation, early second millennium* B.C.: *1, Rudstone, E.R. Yorks, England; 2 and 4, Butterwick, E.R. Yorks; 3, Crawford Moor, Lanarks., Scotland.*

previous trading arrangements, and a consequent impetus to seek new metal resources in the outer barbarian world.

Whatever the precise circumstances of its origin, the new phase in central Europe, following that of the Corded Ware and Bell-Beaker cultures, seems to have involved more than an accelerated metal-working technology. Weapons, tools, and ornaments are produced in novel forms to satisfy novel demands: for the warrior who is no longer trained as a bowman, but who knows the tactics of in-fighting with dagger and axe; for men and women whose clothes are no longer of styles fastened with buttons or toggles, but with dress-pins. And here we must return to the question of prehistoric European clothing as we know it from this time.

In the broadest terms there are two basic types of clothing in the Old World, the tailored garments normally consisting of trousers and coat, and the single-piece wrapped style.[63] The former, which we ourselves inherit, derives from skin prototypes and is an invention of Advanced Palaeolithic or Mesolithic peoples, surviving in prototype form among the Eskimos today. The single-piece garment—toga or chiton, burnous or phillimore—is a simple product of textile-weaving; the bath-towel one hastily dons at the demands of an exigent telephone. Skin or fur clothes are best fastened by toggles or buttons, but the one-piece cloth

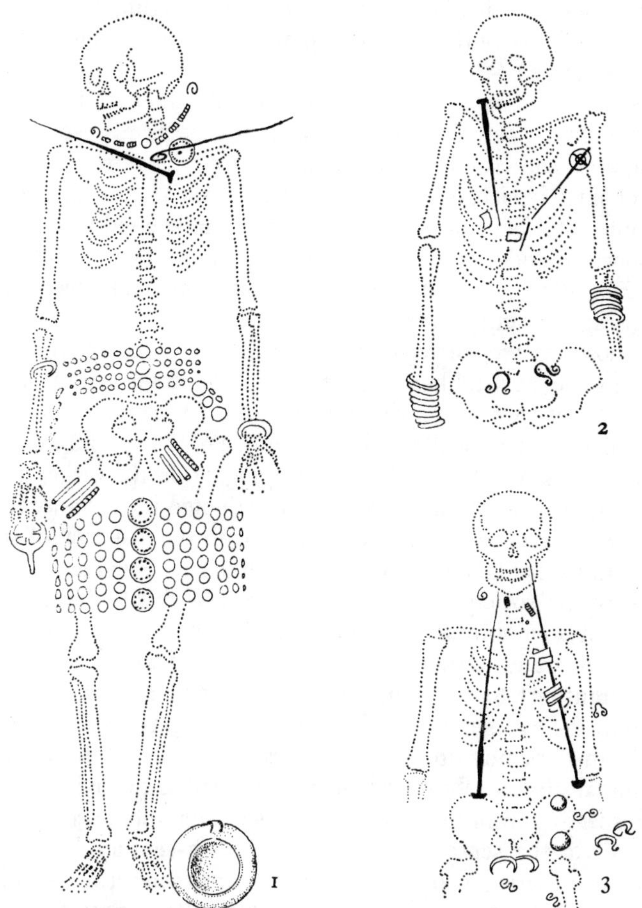

58. *Burials of women, mid second millennium* B.C., *showing position of dress-pins and other ornaments: 1, Mühltal; 2, Wixhausen; 3, Asenkofen, South Germany.*

garment, especially the looser weaves of antiquity, can better be pinned into place. Archaeologically it is the fastenings that usually survive, but they are significant indexes of changing fashion in the clothes to which they belonged. Buttoned garments were used by Corded Ware and Bell-Beaker peoples,[64] and now, at this point, with other evidence of innovations from the Levant, comes the new style in dress implied by the elaborate series of metal pins—worn, as we know from slightly later graves, by women in the manner of those on classical Greek *peploi*.[65] The style was to endure over most of second and first millennium Europe, though it was never adopted in conservative Britain, which seems to have retained the buttoned garment well into the second millennium B.C. (Figs. 57–58)

And so, at the beginning of the second millennium B.C., we stand on the threshold of a new Europe. Over the past 3000 years or so agricultural communities had established themselves, however widely scattered and however small in size, over the greater part of the Continent. The population must still have been tiny, with wide uninhabited tracts of marsh and moorland and mountain; the forests no more than nibbled into by clearings and assarts. But the villages and homesteads were those of metal-using peasantry differing in degree rather than in kind from those whose mastery of techniques had included that of iron-working and were to be the neighbours of the Greeks and Romans in the centuries to come. Indeed we are moving into a world not far removed from that of Hesiod and, as we shall see, by the middle of the second millennium, recognisably akin to that of Homer. Impinging on the earlier substrate population of stone-using farmers we have noted immigrants from the steppes who have reason to be associated with the dispersal of speakers of Indo-European languages and who seem to have provided a dominant element in the society which was to follow. With the development of copper and soon bronze metallurgy, and that of gold, we have the necessity for trade relations to make possible the winning of the metal and its transport to the centre of manufacture, a network of routes attested by the widespread distribution of common types of weapons and tools. In this opening up of the European continent we have, probably as the initial stimulus for the whole development, the activities of traders and prospectors from the centres of higher civilisation, setting up their 'factories' (in the sense of those of eighteenth-century India), in the Carpathians, Iberia, or the Tyrol, and perhaps themselves escaping the time of troubles in their own lands to seek employment in the courts of barbarian chieftains.

What we have been calling technological advances in metallurgy are of course ultimately the first stammering words in the long history of competitive armaments. The arms race had been on from at least the fourth millennium B.C. in the Ancient Orient and there is no sign that the European barbarians showed any reluctance in learning the new arts of war made possible by improved weapons. More and more the archaeological evidence begins to reflect the existence, over most of Europe, of a warrior aristocracy of a type familiar to us from heroic and epic literature ranging from the Iliad to the Sagas; from the Rig-Veda to the Taín Bó Cuailnge. If we look for an early context for the structure of society already ancient in early historical Europe, the tripartite social grading in its various forms; the government by king, elders, and assembly; the importance of the warrior class—it fits readily within the framework of what we can infer from the archaeological evidence from the early second millennium B.C. onwards. This appears to be something different from what we can infer from the archaeology of the peasantries of the east European plains or of the Russian Steppe, or the Danube basin of an earlier date; these belong to an archaic world, not recognisable in anything we encounter at the dawn of European history. But now, out of this curious amalgam of traditions and techniques, of peoples and ideas, we come to what I would like to call the High Barbarian phase of Ancient Europe. Antecedent to what was to become in the main a Celtic, Germanic, and Slavic world north of the Alps, and perhaps already containing the elements from which these linguistic entities were to develop, the second millennium B.C. must be regarded as one of Europe's formative periods. It is a phase full of interest, as the centres of higher civilisation shift to include the Aegean, for part of our story is the beginning of Greece. To this and other events we will turn in the next chapter.

Notes

1. Driver and Massey 1957, 345.
2. For the beginnings of copper and bronze metallurgy and technology, see Forbes 1950, 1954b; Coghlan 1951, 1954; Maryon 1954; Tylecote 1962.
3. Best illustrations in Akurgal and Hirmer 1962, Pls. I, II, 1-6, but erroneously described as of bronze.
4. The earliest (probably cold-hammered) copper in Anatolia is from Çatal Hüyük IX (before 6500 B.C.; Mellaart *in litt.* September 1963); rather later finds include objects in Hacilar II (Mellaart 1960b) in Mersin XXIII (Garstang 1953) and Beycesultan XXXIV (Stronach 1959), the latter assigned to the second half of the fifth millennium B.C. The copper macehead from Can Hasan, assigned to the early fifth millennium, is presumably from smelted and cast metal (French 1962). The Tell Agrab chariot group is illustrated in Frankfort 1954, Pl. 20, and my knowledge of its technology is due to Professor Seton Lloyd, quoting Mr Herbert Maryon.
5. Troy, Lloyd 1956, 85-88; Mellaart 1959, 1962; Blegen 1961; Thermi, Lamb 1936; Poliochni, Brea 1955, 1957b; Greek Mainland, imports in Dimini phase, Childe 1957, 64; Dow 1960; Lerna radiocarbon dates, Kohler and Ralph 1961 (I have used their dates calculated on the 'new half-life' of 5,800 years); Crete, Hutchinson 1962.
6. For map of Aegean copper, cf. Forbes 1950, Fig. 61; for tin, Wainwright 1944. It is probable that expeditions from Mesopotamia were making contact with Anatolian and Aegean tin sources as early as the time of Sargon

of Akkad, from about 2370 B.C., and possibly metal resources further west were involved, suggesting that competition had begun early (Gadd 1963, 11, 15). By the twentieth century B.C. the Assyrian trade in Anatolian metals was well organised (Lloyd 1956, Chapter VII; Gurney 1952, 18).

7. General account in Patay 1938; Piggott 1960; Kutzián 1963; distribution maps, Driehaus 1955; gold, Patay 1958a; pottery relationships, Kutzián 1958; Slovakia, Patay 1958b. Bossed copper discs, etc. Driehaus 1960, 165: Dumitrescu *et al.* 1454, 435-41 (Rumania); Becker 1948, 253-5; Gimbutas 1956a, 118-19 (Denmark and Poland); Forssander 1936, Pl. I; Kersten 1938, Pl. I; Sylvest and Sylvest 1960 (copper hoards).
8. Piggott 1948a, with map.
9. Deshayes 1960 (unreliable for east Europe); Piggott 1961b.
10. Gimbutas 1956a, 56 ff.
11. Arnal and Martin-Granel, 1961; Arnal and Sangmeister 1963.
12. Blance 1961; do Paço and Sangmeister 1956; Arribas 1959, 1960; Almagro and Arribas 1963.
13. Gadd 1963.
14. For the First Intermediate Period in Egypt, Drioton and Vandier 1952, 213-17; Wilson in Frankfort *et al.* 1949, 111-12, with quotations from texts.
15. For Palestine, Kenyon 1960, 159; Anatolia, Mellaart 1958, 1962.
16. I follow here the argument for a break at the end of E.H. II, rather than after E.H. III, set out in Caskey 1960; radiocarbon date from Ralph and Kohler 1961.
17. The literature is enormous, but a recent documented summary of the linguistic position is in Crossland 1957. Archaeological correlations in Childe 1926; Hencken 1955; Mellaart 1958; Gimbutas 1963.
18. Gurney 1952, 17-21, 117-31; Lloyd 1956, 112-26; Mellaart 1962.
19. Following Chadwick 1963.
20. The main protagonist of this view is Thieme (1954).
21. Finley 1957, 141.
22. Palmer 1955, 18-19.
23. Cf. Finley 1957.
24. Piggott 1950, Chapters VI and VII. The date of about 1500 B.C. for the Aryan invasion of India there suggested is almost certainly too high, and the thirteenth or even the twelfth century B.C. may be more appropriate. A late movement of Indo-Iranian eastwards is cautiously favoured by Crossland (1957, 32, 37). For the Mitannian rulers of the Hurri from the late fifteenth century B.C., see Kupper 1963, 38; for the Kassite Dynasty in Mesopotamia (with Indo-European names: from about 1750 B.C.), Delaporte 1948, 152.
25. Gimbutas 1956a, 72. The presence of pig is important, in view of Beneviste's recognition that words for 'pig' are part of the common Indo-European

vocabulary (Crossland 1957, 22-23). In view of the recognition by Lundholm and others of wild horses at this time in northern Europe, the linguistic value of the 'horse' words in Indo-European languages as a geographical determinant is lessened (see below, p. 179).

26. Gimbutas 1956a, 70-89; 1961a; Merpert 1961: I have followed the former's chronology. For links in ritual, etc., with Alaca Hüyük, cf. Piggott 1962c.
27. Gimbutas 1956a, 58.
28. Wheeled vehicles are discussed below, p. 141, but for disc-wheeled carts in Kurgan Culture graves as at Tri Brata, Storozhova Mogila and Akkermen, cf. Childe 1951, 1954; Gimbutas 1956a, 78; Merpert 1961. Mortuary houses and timber roofing of graves in the Kurgan cultures, Gimbutas 1956a, 70-89; in Fatyanovo Culture, etc., Briussov 1962; Ozols 1962.
29. Berciu 1961, 124. The date (Hamangia 2) is now recalculated to 2580±65. (Vogel and Waterbolk 1963, 184).
30. Gimbutas 1956a, 75-83; 1963 (south Russia); Milojčić 1955a (Alaca Hüyük); Caskey 1956, 160 (Lerna); Redlich 1935 (north and central Europe). The grave-group from Bleckendorf, Stassfurt (Behrens 1952) comprises a hammer-head pin, a Corded Ware beaker, a copper awl of metal presumptively of Iberian origin, and a tanged dagger of presumptively east European copper, implying that contacts with the Bell-Beaker cultures from the west were already made (Junghans *et al.* 1950, 190, 189), cf. p. 100.
31. Fortifications in Late Neolithic central Europe are discussed in Neustupný 1950; Neustupný and Neustupný 1961, 55; cf. also the Altheim site, Driehaus 1960 and Maier 1962.
32. Childe 1957, Chapter IX; Gimbutas 1960; 1963; most recent survey in Malmer 1962; Dutch radiocarbon dates for 'protruding foot' Corded Ware beakers, ranging from *c.* 2505 and 2470 to 2265: Waterbolk 1959, 1960, 1961a, with dates corrected for Suess effect as in Vogel and Waterbolk 1963; also Anlo recalculated date, *ibid.* 180. Arguments against a south Russian origin have been set out by Malmer (1962) and Häusler (1963a,b).
33. Waterbolk 1961a.
34. Georgiev 1961 (Karanovo); Clark 1952, 146-9 (Federsee and Altheim).
35. Neustupný and Neustupný 1961, 73 (Homolka);
36. For Vix and Hradenin see Chapter V; medieval burials on the steppes, recorded among the Comans by John of Plano Carpini and William of Rubruck between 1245 and 1253, translated and edited in Dawson 1955, 12-13 and 105.
37. Krahe 1954; Nicolaisen 1957 (British river-names). I am indebted to Dr W. Nicolaisen for drawing my attention to this linguistic evidence.
38. Childe 1957, 98-104; Georgiev 1961, 74-75.
39. Childe 1957, 124-7.
40. Piggott 1960.

41. Demonstrated by Childe 1951a and 1954.
42. Jenkins 1961, 1-46.
43. Hančar 1956, 173, Pl. VI.
44. Childe 1951, 1954; Salonen 1950, 1951, 1955 (Mesopotamia); Piggott 1950, 273-81 (chariot origins).
45. Salonen 1951, 120.
46. Salonen 1951, 28, 1956, 208.
47. Wheels from Dertienhuizen, De Eese and Gasseller Boerveen, Vogel and Waterbolk 1963, 180-1; Nieuwe Dordrecht trackway and wheel, de Laet and Glasbergen 1959, 17, Pl. 14. Somerset trackways, Godwin 1960.
48. For Budakalász and other Hungarian cart models, see Bona 1960.
49. Jenkins 1961, 43-46, with map, Fig. 10.
50. Zeuner 1963, Chapter 12; Hančar 1956.
51. Gimbutas 1961b, with illustrations of bridle cheek-pieces belonging to the 'Classical' phase of the Timber-Grave culture, its beginning dated by her to about 1700 B.C.
52. There has been much discussion on this point but it now seems clear that although horse bones are known in Hungary from Baden times onward, and there is evidence of domestication from the beginning of the Bronze Age (Bronze I, or the Nagyrév Phase), the characteristic curved side-pieces of antler do not appear with certainty until Bronze III (the Füzesabony Phase). The earlier horses are of steppe type, but forest zone types are also domesticated in Bronze III (Piggott 1960; Mozsolics 1954, 1960).
53. Lundholm 1949; the well-known phalange idols in theLos Millares culture in Spain include those of horses (Leisner and Leisner 1943; Maier 1962), and additions to the British evidence as given by Lundholm are in Piggott 1954.
54. For a critical commentary on these see Behrens 1962.
55. Simultaneously the ancient Near East was becoming acquainted with the horse from about 2000 B.C. (mention in the Sulgi Hymn), and increasingly later, perhaps through the trading contacts with Anatolia. The standard Akkadian words for 'horse' (*sisu*) and 'chariot' (*narkabtu*) first appear in the Cappodocian texts which represent the business correspondence of this trade, from about 1900 to the early eighteenth century B.C. (Salonen 1951, 45; 1956, 21; Kammenhüber 1961, 9-11).
56. For these Sub-Mesolithic groups, see above p. 35.
57. The Neolithic and earlier Bronze Age sequence in the Lipari Islands is described in Brea 1952; Brea and Cavalier 1956, 1957, 1958, 1960. The Malta sequence as set out in Evans 1959 has been modified by later excavations, notably at Skorba, with results summarized by Trump 1961, and by the new series of radio carbon dates (Trump 1963).
58. The most comprehensive survey of the Bell-Beaker culture is still that of Castillo (1928), but his views of origin and dispersal were criticised by

Smith (1953) and by Blance (unpublished Ph.D. thesis, Edinburgh University Library; cf. Blance 1961). The fundamental re-orientation in thought and the concept of the Reflux Movement is due to Sangmeister (1957, and in Junghans *et al.* 1960; fullest published treatment, 1963). For Czechoslovakian beakers, cf. Hájek 1962; Holland, van der Waals and Glasbergen 1955; Britain, Piggott 1962d, 73-85; 1963.

59. Relevant dates range from *c.* 2190 (cord-zoned beaker at Anlo) to *c.* 1960–*c.* 1900 (maritime beaker at Vlaardingen) and *c.* 1930 (zigzag beaker in Drenthe). Waterbolk 1959, 1960, 1961a; Vogel and Waterbolk 1963, with corrections for Suess effect.
60. Barker and Mackey 1960, 28; unpublished information.
61. This is equivalent to Reinecke's phase A of the south German Bronze Age; cf. Holste 1953; Junghans *et al.* 1954, 1960; Hundt 1958, 1961; Torbrügge 1959a; Switzerland, Vogt 1948; France, Sandars 1957, 12-31; British relationships, Piggott 1963.
62. The thesis of the derivation of some European Early Bronze Age types, notably 'ingot-torques' and 'swollen-neck-perforated' pins, from the Levant has been much discussed. It was treated on more than one occasion by Childe, notably in Childe 1939. It was then stated dogmatically by Schaeffer (1949), but unfortunately from the first he ignored the relative dating of the relevant types in Europe. The ingot-torques (of copper) belong to the early (Reinecke A) south German Bronze Age, but the swollen-neck pins do not appear until the fully developed Middle Bronze Age of Reinecke B. (Junghans *et al.* 1954; Holste 1953a; Hundt 1961). Nevertheless, 'plate-headed' pins of Reinecke Ai forms also occur in Syria: e.g. Byblos (Schaeffer 1948, Fig. 68, 32) and Tell As (*ibid.* Fig. 104, 19; 105, 17-18); they are themselves ultimately of Sumerian derivation, and the 'Cypriot' or 'knot-headed' pin has long been recognised as a West Asiatic type recurring in Europe. It is clear that the long survival of some of the types in the Near East makes it impossible to use the material for a very precise chronology, as Childe demonstrated, but I find the evidence broadly convincing: my acceptance of it here in general terms is strengthened by a preliminary re-investigation of the problem in an unpublished paper by Mr Ralph Rowlette submitted to my graduate seminar in Harvard University in 1961.
63. There is no comprehensive treatment of ancient clothing in Europe and west Asia, but cf. Hald 1950 for northern Europe; 1961 for trousers.
64. Cf. Hájek 1957; Guyan 1950, 181-4; Sangmeister 1963.
65. Cf. the arrangement of pins in German Bronze Age burials at, e.g. Asenkofen (Bavaria), Wixhausen (Middle Rhine) and Schwarza (Thuringia) (Hachmann 1957b, Figs 3, 4; Feustel 1958, Pl. IX) with the illustrations from Greek vase paintings in Jacobsthal 1956, 332-8. But cf. Lorimer 1950, 394-405 for some of the Greek puzzles involved.

Facing

XI. (*a*) *Interior façade in rock-cut temple, third Millennium* B.C., *the Hypogeum, Hal Saflieni, Malta.*
XI. (*b*) *Stone carving in temple, third millennium* B.C., *at Hal Tarxien, Malta* (Both photos. National Museum of Malta)

Overleaf

XII. (*a*) *Pottery Bell-Beaker, beginning of second millennium* B.C., *from West Kennet Long Barrow, Wilts., England.* (Photo. Malcolm Murray)
XII. (*b*) *Wattled-and-mud-walled house, rectangular with apsidal end, end of third millennium* B.C., *Phase* VII *of the 'tell' of Karanovo, Bulgaria.* (Photo. Mikov)

XIII. (*a*) *Henge Monument with fallen stones, early second millennium* B.C., *Arbor Low, Derbyshire, England.* (Photo. H. K. St Joseph)
XIII. (*b*) *Excavated Henge Monument showing ditches and ritual pits, late third millennium* B.C., *Site* I, *Dorchester-on-Thames, Oxon., England.* (Photo. Institute of Archaeology, London University)

a

b

XII (*caption on p. 112*)

a

b

XIII (*caption on p. 112*)

a

b

XIV. *Gold mask of bearded man, profile view, Mycenaean culture, sixteenth century* B.C., *from Shaft-Grave* V, *Mycenae, Greece*. (Photo. Hirmer)

4

Climax and Change

At the end of the last chapter we reached what I tried to demonstrate was a very important turning-point in European prehistory, conveniently marked by the opening years of the second millennium B.C. It may be convenient to recapitulate some of the more significant points. We are looking at a Europe which, with the exception of a few communities in the north still clinging to a hunting and fishing economy, is a continent of agriculturalists, who are in the main still using stone for edge-tools—in other words, a Neolithic Europe. At least three main cultural provinces are perceptible: in eastern Europe, in the Balkans and Carpathians, and in northern Greece, we have the later phases of what is ultimately a westward extension of the earlier peasant economies of the Near East, with settlements of 'tell' type. Beyond this province, in the Ukraine and on the Danube and Rhine as far north-west as Belgium, and on the north European plain, variants of a different settlement-pattern, with shifting agriculture and long houses implying social units of the undivided or great family type, can be uniformly traced. West of the Rhine (already curiously enough a cultural boundary) and in the central and western Mediterranean lands other forms of agricultural economies less easy to define but with fair-sized settlements are recognisable; the British Isles partake mainly of the nature of this western world, but may yet have links with northern Europe. In a few centres—Iberia, Transylvania—Aegean-derived copper-working is established as a technological increment to the older skills, while in the adjacent lands of western Asia—Anatolia, the Levant, Mesopotamia, and Egypt—urban cultures of some complexity have developed, and the two latter indeed have achieved literacy and the political status of the kingdoms of Sumer and Akkad in the land of the Twin Rivers, the Egyptian Old Kingdom on the Nile.

While the east European communities at least reflect much that is Oriental in origin, yet even here there is nothing in the archaeological evidence to suggest the existence of any structures within the village settlement that can be interpreted as temples or communal shrines forming

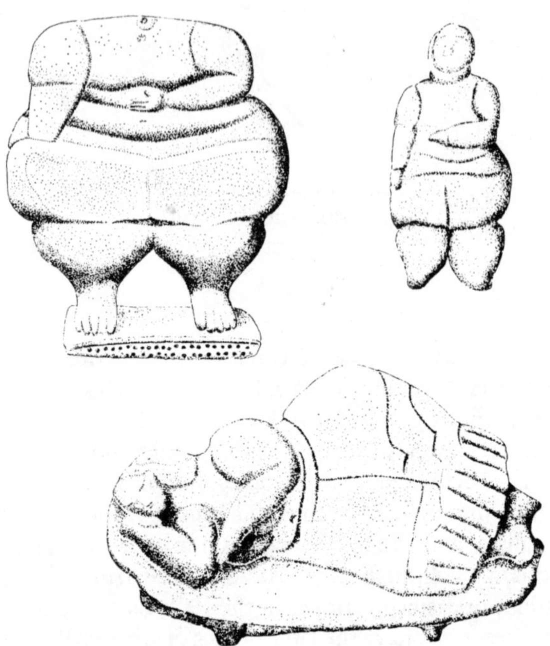

59. *Limestone and alabaster figurines and clay model of woman on couch, third millennium* B.C., *from Hagar Qim and Hal Saflieni temples, Malta.*

a focal point or integral part of the layout: there are in fact no structures in the known plans that are differentiated by size or character from the usual run of houses or storage buildings. The evidence of clay figurines of animals or of women, sometimes confidently interpreted in terms of a mother-goddess cult, is, in the European scene at least, ambiguous; dolls and toys are hardly to be distinguished by their intrinsic physical characteristics from idols or votive simulacra.[1] Even if in part or as a whole they do indicate such a cult, it would be one of the home or the humble shrine, not of temples; some are very remarkable objects in their own right, and as works of art. When we move into the Danubian area of the long-house settlements the same absence of differentiated buildings is apparent, and here the cult-figures (or domestic toys) are virtually absent. In the west Mediterranean and beyond, the megalithic and rock-cut tombs were clearly the centres of elaborate ritual for which they provided the architectural setting; ritual which may have been more far-reaching than that wholly dedicated to the burial of the dead, but in Malta alone do we find monumental structures which can fairly be called temples. Here too are the presumed cult-figures of obese women, and elsewhere the carved or more rarely painted designs in chambered tombs include representations of a female 'divinity', represented again in free-standing form in some areas of western Europe, and constituting there the earliest examples of relief sculpture, beyond those of the Upper Palaeolithic societies.[2] (Pl. IV; Figs. 17-19; 24; 59-60; Pl. V)

In northern Europe we do have some evidence of ritual but non-sepulchral buildings: in Denmark two small rectangular 'temples' of the third millennium B.C. have been excavated, probably associated with the funeral rituals of the collective chambered tombs.[3] (Fig. 61) In the British Isles, circular embanked enclosures, sometimes containing rings of upright stones or wooden posts, can only be interpreted as open-air temples or sanctuaries, comparable to the embanked circles and rings of carved wooden posts of the North American Indians. (Pl. XIII; Fig. 62) One such site in England, at Arminghall in Norfolk (with timber uprights), has a radiocarbon date of *c.* 2500 B.C., and another constitutes the first phase of Stonehenge, and contains pits of non-utilitarian and presumed ritual function.[4] Similarly (and on occasion connected with the circular 'henge monuments'), another British speciality in ritual monuments is represented by the long, embanked, parallel-sided enclosures of the 'cursus' type[5]; in the form of circles and parallel alignments of standing stones:

60. *Relief carvings of stylised female figures, one with hafted stone axe, in chalk-cut tomb of early second millennium* B.C., *Courjeonnet, Marne, France.*

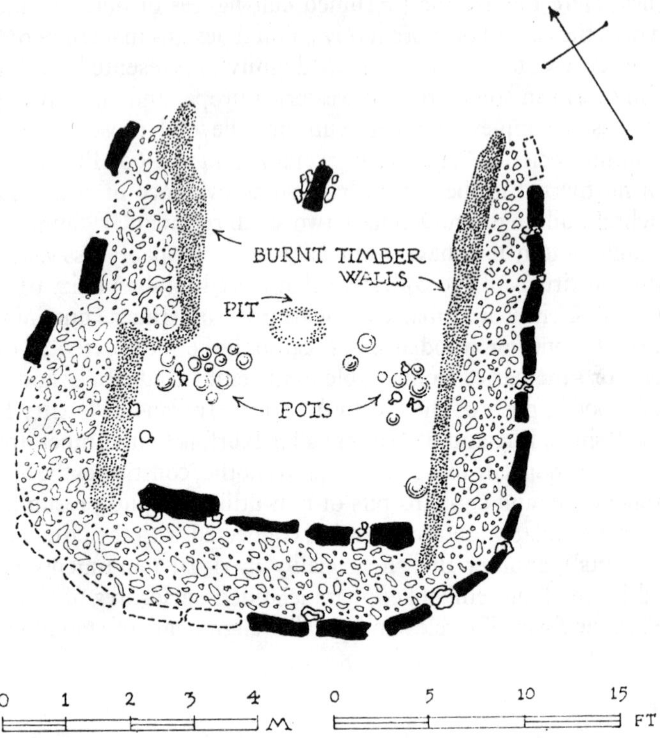

61. *Ground plan of ritual building or temple, mid third millennium* B.C., *at Tustrup, Jutland, Denmark.*

these basic ritual forms appear not only in Britain in the second millennium B.C. but in a restricted area of Brittany, probably through cross-Channel contacts implicit in other phenomena of the same period. (Fig. 62; Pl. va) And in the final phase of Stonehenge, we have the idea of the circular sanctuary transmuted into a monumental temple of dressed stone under the unique circumstances of Aegean contacts around the sixteenth century B.C. Yet, since we are dealing with non-literate societies, we have no information on the beliefs which prompted the construction of these sacred places, nor of the rites performed within them: the nature of purely archaeological evidence is such that it cannot, within the bounds of permissible inference, inform us of such aspects of prehistoric peoples.

In the closing years of the third millennium, however, even the two civilised powers are temporarily weakened and disrupted, and barbarians are raiding into their territories, as into the still illiterate Levant. In

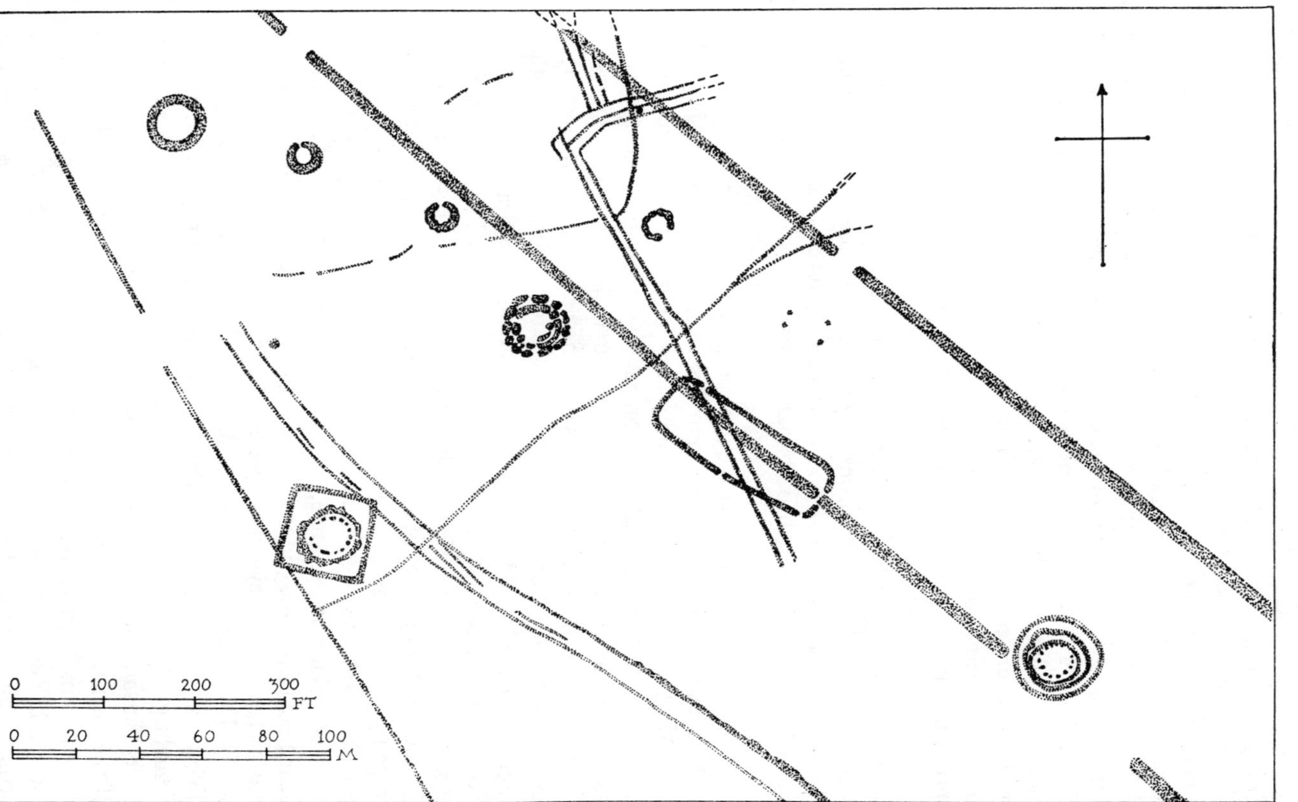

62. *Circular Henge Monuments, Long Mortuary Enclosure and part of the ditches of a Cursus, end of third millennium* B.C., *at Dorchester-on-Thames, Oxon., England.*

Anatolia, the speakers of the Hittite group of languages of the Indo-European family are establishing themselves by around 2000 B.C.; in Greece rather earlier, the sack and burning of old established settlements betoken other newcomers, likely to be ancestors of those who were to be Greek-speaking. In Europe beyond the Aegean we can trace the movement of peoples from the south Russian Steppe westwards and northwards, soon to be met by the early beaker-using metallurgists from Iberia. Over a large area of central Europe there is change and adjustment. The older agricultural communities with their long-houses vanish; settlements are now in smaller units, with houses for nuclear families, and often fortifications. Copper, and soon bronze, is coming into widespread use, increasingly for weapons; the disparity in the grave deposits show us the emergence of a stratified society with a warrior-aristocracy, perhaps speaking Indo-European languages. The innocuous archaeological phrase 'The Early Bronze Age' in reality indicates the opening of a new epoch, the foundation of what I ventured to call in the last chapter the period of High Barbarian Europe.

The nature of the archaeological evidence for second millennium Europe changes in character to some degree from that previously available. Most of our evidence is from graves, or from the bronze objects themselves, lost or hoarded, and comparatively few settlement sites or houses are known from the first half of the millennium; Postoloprty in Czechoslovakia and Crestaulta in Switzerland belong here, with rectangular houses ranging from about 20 by 12 to 30 by 15 feet.[6] (Fig. 63) Rather later are the Middle Bronze Age levels of the east European 'tells' such as Tószeg in Hungary, or the Monteoru settlement in Rumania,[7] or that of Barca in Slovakia,[8] with similar types of houses. We saw that one of the inevitable outcomes of a metal-using economy is the development of trade in raw materials and finished products: this network of routes, by sea, river and land, gives an international character to much of the bronze-working at this time, and we find techniques and styles widely distributed from one end of Europe to the other. The dominating power, the archaeological evidence suggests, becomes a nameless people in central Europe, who have access not only to copper resources, as in the Tyrol for instance, but to the Czechoslovakian tin deposits in the Erzgebirge. In the arc of the Carpathians another important centre of craftsmanship and, one infers, political prestige, grew up on the basis of the ancient 'tell' tradition, now implanted on the Great Hungarian Plain and in Transylvania, mixed with incoming steppe traditions. On the south Russian Steppes themselves one can trace the emergence of peoples ancestral to the later Scythians and Cimmerians. The east

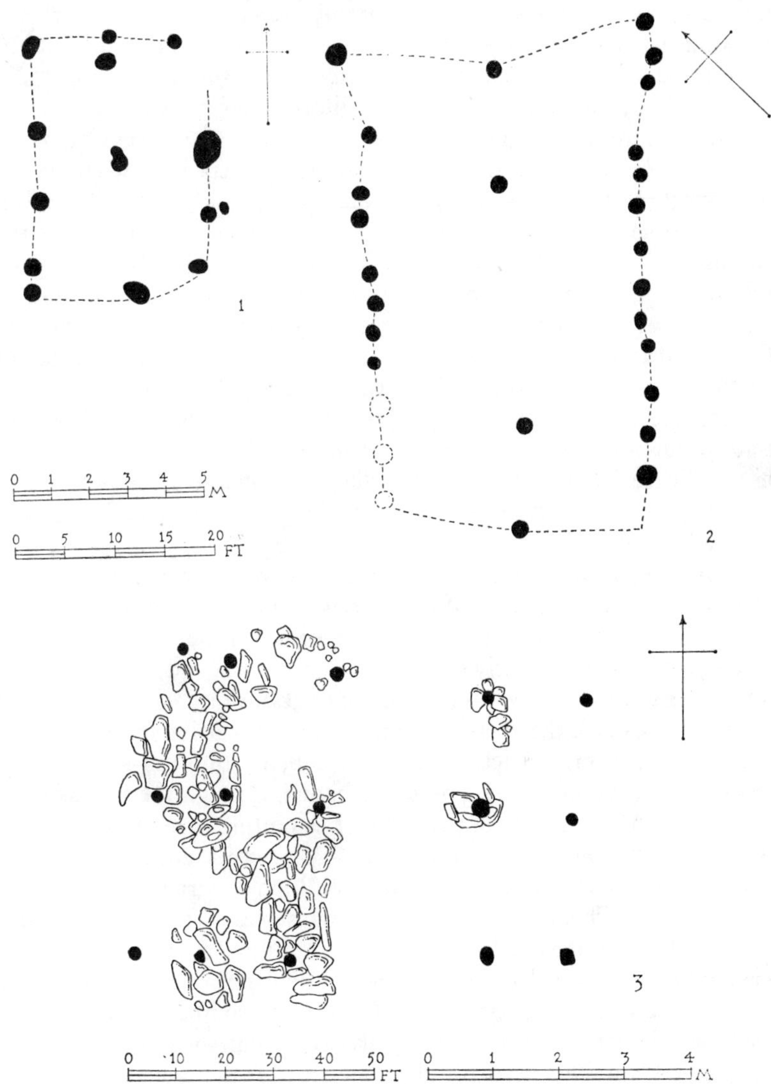

63. *House-plans, with post-holes for timber-framed buildings, earlier second millennium* B.C., *at 1, 2, Postoloprty, Czechoslovakia and 3, Crestaulta, Switzerland*

Mediterranean sees the growth of Minoan and later Mycenaean power; the western end of the sea now temporarily loses the leadership of metal-working it had in the days of the 'colonists', and, technologically impoverished owing to a lack of tin supplies or access to them, supports in Iberia only a provincial copper-using culture, itself indeed almost surely of central European origin. In west France and southern England, trade contacts with, once again, the central European powers, by now looking for new metal resources, develop locally brilliant societies in Wessex and in Brittany, their wealth derived from the copper and tin and gold from the Breton, Cornish, Irish and Welsh hills. Scandinavia, without any metal resources of its own, is in the early second millennium an underdeveloped area, importing its bronzes mainly from Britain, but also from the central and even the eastern European powers, in exchange no doubt partly for furs and skins but also, demonstrably, for amber.

Outside the close mesh of the Aegean sea-ways, the main European trade routes follow fairly well defined courses in the earlier second millennium. There is coming and going along the Steppe grasslands which stretch from central Asia to end in the Hungarian plain, and there is a great axis of trade which links Transylvania to Denmark, on an approximate line (in modern terms) through Bratislava, Prague, Dresden, and Hamburg.[9] From the head of the Adriatic, the routes over the Alpine passes run either to join the Transylvanian-Danish route around Prague, or to go by a more westerly course through Bavaria and the Rhineland; by these routes amber was traded to the Aegean world, as we shall see.[10] Further westward, the Iberian peninsula was now being by-passed, and the Lusitanian and Galician coasts avoided, by the well-known ways leading from the Gulf of Lions at Narbonne, through the Carcassonne Gap, and so to the mouth of the Loire, thus putting Brittany and Britain in easier touch with the Mediterranean. The chalk downs of Wessex, good farming land with by now a long tradition of agricultural development over a millennium and a half, lie themselves on a trans-peninsular route from the English Channel (and so from the Rhineland or Saxony) via the Bristol Channel and west Wales to the copper and gold of Ireland and down the Devon coast to the all-important sources of tin in Cornwall; small wonder that powerful dynasties enriched themselves on Salisbury Plain. Nor need all the tin needed for the flourishing bronze industries of the British Isles have come from Cornwall; for east Scotland, for instance, in the van of this technological progress, tin from Bohemia could have been obtained at the Rhine mouth by a shorter sea-route than that to Land's End.[11]

We must return to this European Common Market shortly, but it is time to review the situation in the Aegean, for this in its turn was necessarily to affect continental Europe. The beginning of the Middle Minoan period in Crete, from *c.* 1900 B.C., marks the inception of the great palace-building phase and the first flowering of the highest achievement of that civilisation.[12] We saw how at the end of the Early Helladic II period on the Greek mainland the sacking and burning of a number of towns denotes the forcible entry of newcomers about 2100 B.C. and how such disturbances continued for perhaps a century. But by 2000 B.C. or so the intrusive peoples, archaeologically constituting the Middle Helladic phase and in human terms likely to be the first people we can reasonably call Greeks, are established. At Malthi in Messenia a fortified settlement of this period, rather larger than the second city of Troy, has been completely excavated; it had an inner citadel with metalsmiths' and other workshops around it, and the small town houses backed on to the five-gated walls in a rough ring.[13] We have already noted in passing a feature of prehistoric Greek architecture that has been much discussed, the house of *megaron* or hall-and-porch plan. This we now know to be an early Anatolian type going back in Asia Minor to the fourth millennium B.C. at least, and in Troy II, before 2300 B.C., it has taken on the specialised form of a public hall for audiences and ceremony as a part of a palace; a role it was to play in Mycenaean Greece, as at Pylos and elsewhere. In Greece itself the *megaron* appears in contexts of at least the third millennium B.C. at, for instance, Sesklo and Dimini—the latter indeed a little rustic Troy in layout, with more than one phase of fortification; at Thermi and Poliochni *megara* are adapted to form town houses.[14] The type does not appear to be known in the Early Helladic period, curiously enough, but appears again in Middle Helladic times (as at Korakou, and Lerna[15] but not incidentally at Malthi) and, as I have said, it was a regular feature of Mycenaean palaces. Houses of *megaron* plan appear built in timber or timber-and-clay in third millennium Europe beyond the Aegean, from Karanovo in Bulgaria to Aichbühl on the Federsee in south Germany; in the final phase of Karanovo, in the settlement of peoples associated with the barrow-burying, battle-axe-wielding traditions of the late third millennium, such houses have a curved, apsidal end very like the Korakou and Lerna examples.[16] Ultimately Anatolian, the *megaron* house in its varying forms must have become a general east and central European phenomenon in the third millennium, but in Greece alone it was later developed into a monumental and stylised Great Hall for the palace of a ruler. (Figs. 16, 64; Pls. xb; xiib)

It may be salutary to remind ourselves at this point of a few facts with regards to scale and size. The use in, for instance, Aegean archaeology of words such as 'palace' and 'city' has unfortunately resulted in their

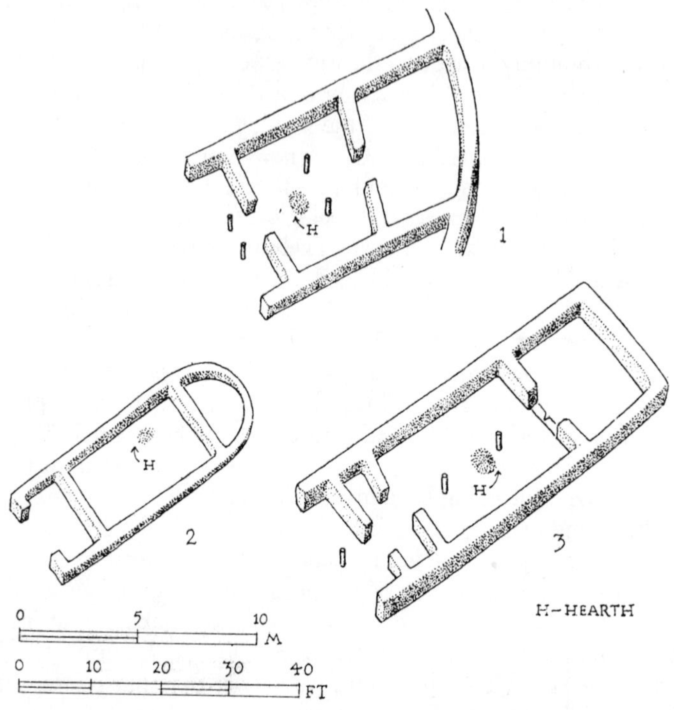

64. *Houses, stone and mud, of megaron plan : 1, third millennium* B.C. *at Dimini, Thessaly ; 2, Middle Helladic culture, early second millennium* B.C. *; 3, Late Helladic culture, later second millennium* B.C., *both at Korakou, Greece.*

acquiring an emotive quality and an illusion of grandeur incommensurate with the sites they describe. The second city of Troy would fit inside the earthwork circle of the first phase of Stonehenge; the Middle Minoan palace of Mallia in Crete is just about the same size as the Roman villa at Woodchester in Gloucestershire; in Troy VI (and so in the Homeric city) 'you could still saunter from side to side in less than two minutes; and a moderate sprinter could cover the ground in twenty-five seconds'[17]; the built-up area of a central European village of the fourth or fifth millennium B.C. could be about equal to that of Knossos, and the Iron Age settlement at Glastonbury in Somerset is roughly double the area of the excavated palace of Pylos. This is not to belittle the Aegean achievement of the second millennium B.C. and earlier, but to stress that size alone is no criterion of importance in such a context.

The Middle Helladic period comes to an end with the appearance at Mycenae, probably in the late seventeenth century B.C., of a new dynasty; the rulers and their successors were to be buried in the two groups of Shaft-Graves, and with their arrival begins the great age of Mycenaean Greece, the first civilisation of mainland Europe, profoundly influenced by Minoan art and architecture at least, but with its own individual, more barbaric qualities. Greek legend held that some of the founders of their first heroic age were immigrants—from Syria, like Cadmus, or from Egypt, like Danaus—and the traditional chronology set the beginnings of the heroic age of Athens in the fifteen-eighties; Danaus at the same time.[18] Archaeologically, although there is a great element of continuity from Middle to late Helladic times in the Shaft-Graves and their contents, there is much that is new. This has of course been commented upon on many occasions—the trimmed beard and moustache of the famous gold death-mask, a style alien to the clean-shaven Minoan world; the gold and silver ornaments linked stylistically to a province which includes the Caucasus and Iran; the northern amber ornaments. The representations of horse-drawn chariots on the stelae are the first monumental and representational stone-carvings in Greece,[19] and also mark the first appearance of this engine of war in Europe: the sculptor, by the way, seems to have been more familiar with carving bulls than horses.[20] So too the Shaft-Graves themselves, stone-lined with flat timber roofs over the burials, recall the earlier royal tombs of Alaca Hüyük in Anatolia and contemporary Hut- and Timber-Graves in south Russia where again a curious burial posture with outbent knees is found, as at Mycenae.[21] The bronze rapiers or swords, which occurred in such fantastic numbers in the Shaft-Graves (forty-six in one grave with five bodies; ninety in another with only three persons!) seem partly Minoan, partly Levantine in derivation, and may be partial evidence for direct Asiatic contacts on the part of the Mainlanders.[22] (Fig. 65; Pls. xiv, xv)

The martial quality of the Shaft-Grave dynasties is not in doubt, and wherever the founders came from it must have been from outside the Minoan world. And whether before their arrival at Mycenae or very soon after it, they made contacts with both the world of continental Europe and that of the Eurasiatic Steppe.[23] By the time the Shaft-Grave dynasties were in power, the central European barbarians were consolidating their own kingdoms.

Centred on Czechoslovakia, but with controlling interests beyond, highly competent schools of bronze metallurgy were flourishing before 1500 B.C., and archaeologically denoted by the Únětice and related cultures.[24] The wide dispersal of their products can be traced on distribution maps: their daggers especially were in demand, and they probably

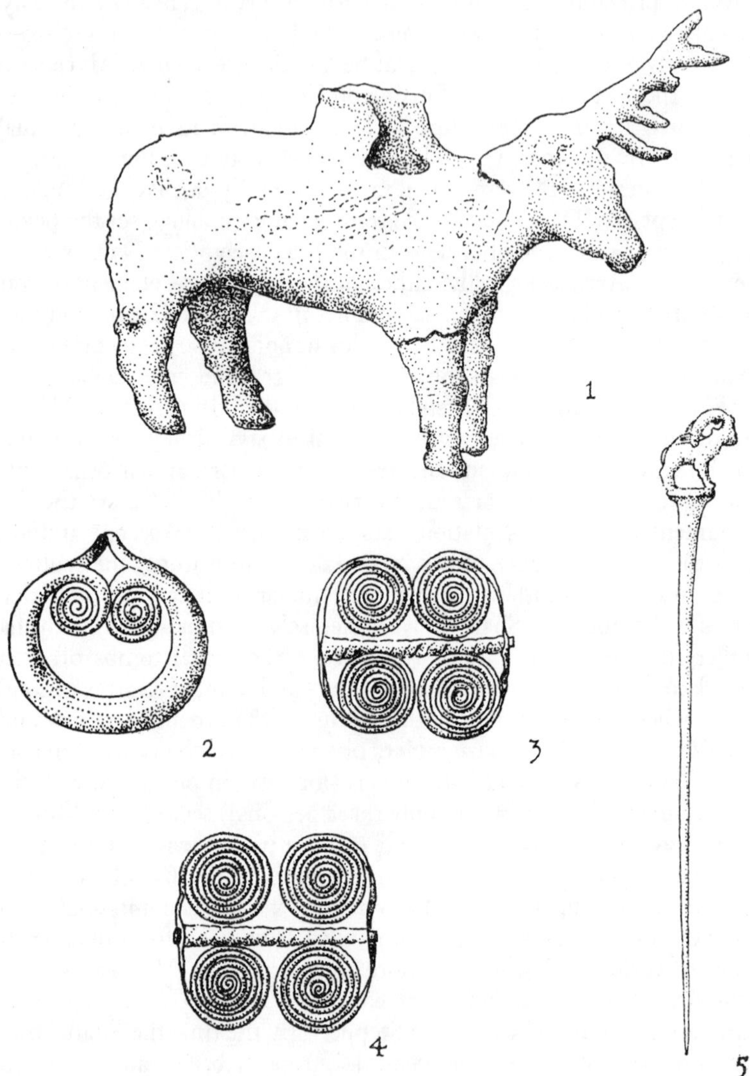

65. *Objects of gold and silver, sixteenth century* B.C., *from the* 'A' *group of Shaft Graves, Mycenae, Greece:* 1, *silver vessel in the form of a Red Deer;* 2, *gold pendant;* 3, 4, *gold beads;* 5, *gold animal-headed pin.*

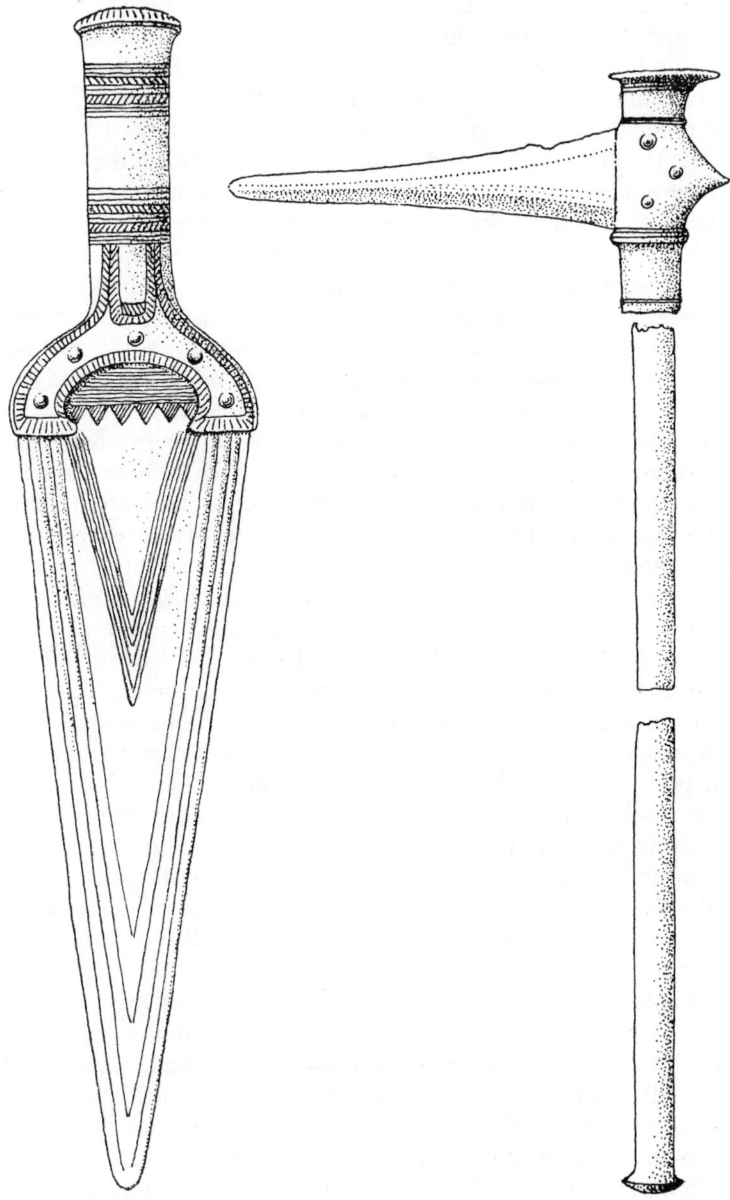

66. *Bronze metal-hilted dagger and metal-shafted halberd, Únětice culture, mid second millennium* B.C., *from Lustenitz, Stubbendorf, East Germany.*

invented, certainly developed and disseminated, the bronze halberd.[25] (Fig. 66) Behind this and similar patterns of trade at this time must lie the social and political factors necessary for the support of skilled craftsmen, the assurance of supplies of raw material, and the subsequent disposal of their products in some sort of trade arrangements. Indeed for Childe this was the decisive phase of barbarian Europe, in which the craftsmen in metal achieved a potential independence which could enable them to 'shake off the bonds of allegiance to an overlord or the more rigid fetters of tribal custom' in a manner impossible in the contemporary ancient Orient, and so found a European tradition which was to endure through classical antiquity and into the Middle Ages.[26] Unfortunately this technological emancipation is no more than an assumption, in its very nature impossible to document in archaeological terms. While we should be on our guard against over-rating the degree of sophistication achieved, we should equally beware of placing too wide a gulf between the early Mycenaean world, before literacy and bureaucracy had been acquired from Crete, and the contemporary societies in central or eastern Europe. Technological disparities existed, largely due to Mycenae's proximity to the centres of higher civilisation in the Levant, Crete, and Egypt, but the pattern of society, so far as we can infer it, differed in degree rather than in kind between one community and another. True, there is in one sense an antithetical relation between civilisation and barbarism beginning to develop, but it is not the antithesis between incompatible systems of thought or political organisation. The world of Homer, however composite, reflects almost wholly a situation as non-Minoan as it is in another sense post-Minoan[27]; the nobility of the hexameters should not deceive us into thinking that the *Iliad* and the *Odyssey* are other than the poems of a largely barbarian Bronze Age or Early Iron Age Europe. 'There is no Minoan or Asianic blood in the veins of the Grecian muses . . . they dwell remote from the Cretan-Mycenaean world and in touch with the *European* elements of Greek speech and culture', Rhys Carpenter remarked; 'behind Mycenaean Greece . . . lies Europe'.[28]

I would like to return to the heroic world shortly; archaeologically we find it represented over much of Europe at this time in the form of graves which, with their lavish provision for the dead warrior or his womenfolk, show us that we are dealing with a stratified society, with an aristocracy at once the patrons of the arts and crafts, and the potential cause of their disruption by internecine wars. We have no settlement plans that show us a structure that could be interpreted as a chieftain's house or palace however; at Barca in Slovakia, for instance, the twenty-three surviving houses of the partly eroded fortified site show no differentiation of such a kind in their close-planned layout.[29]

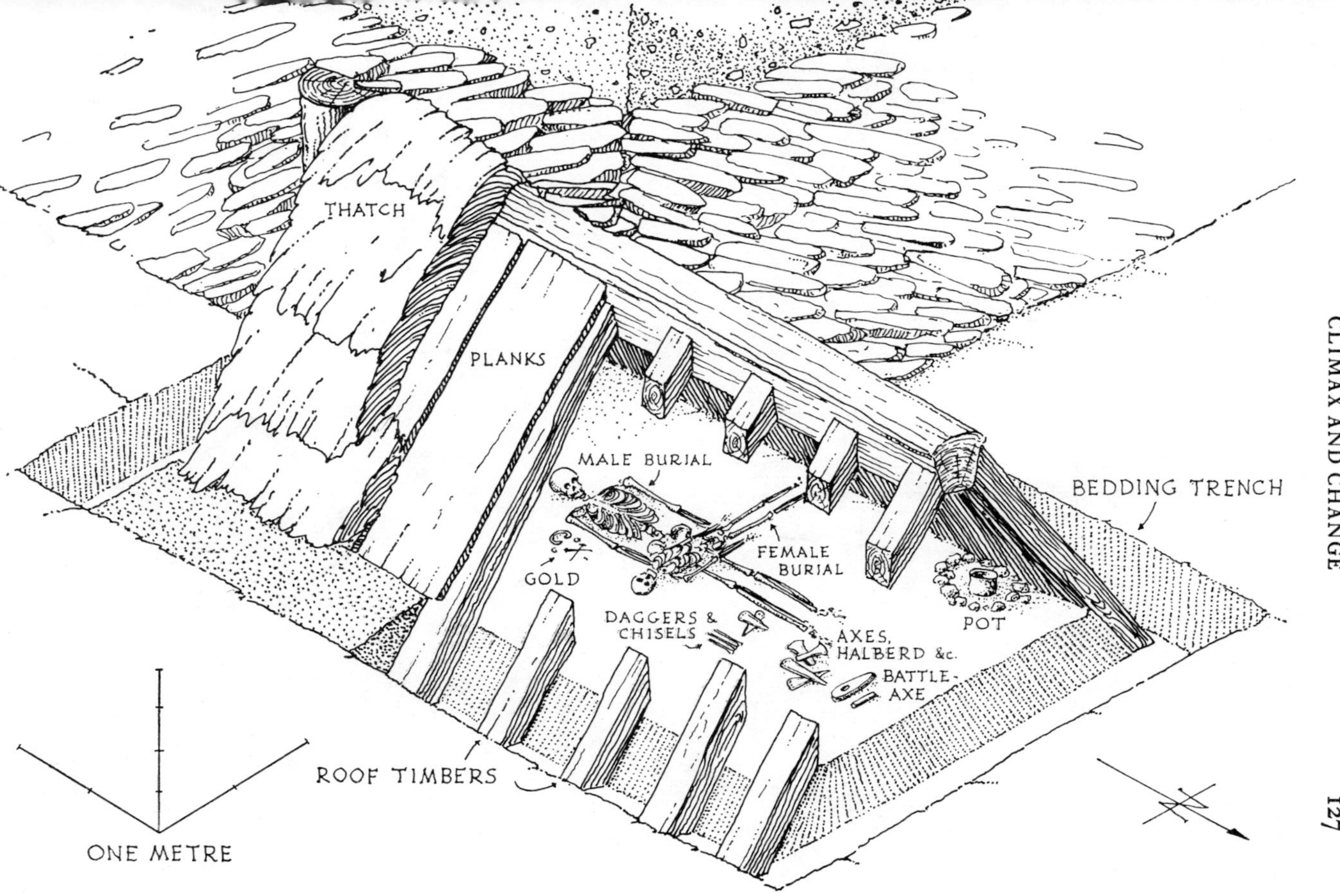

67. *Wooden mortuary house under barrow, Únětice culture, mid second millennium* B.C., *at Leubingen, East Germany.*

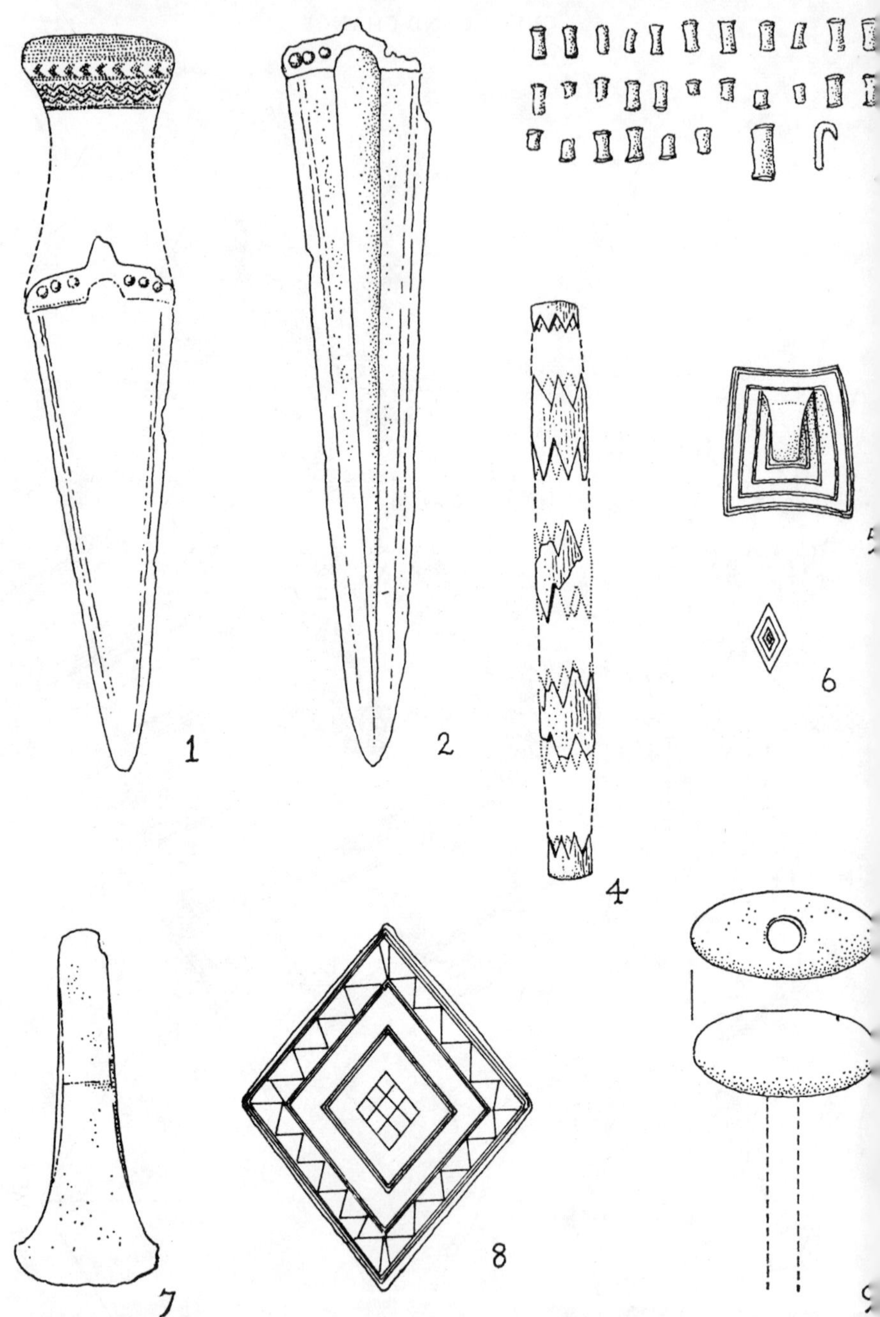

68. *Objects from male burial, Wessex culture, sixteenth century* B.C., *in Bush Barrow, Wilts., England: 1, 2, copper and bronze daggers; 3, bronze rivets, perhaps from helmet (twice scale); 4, bone mountings of sceptre; 5, gold belt-hook; 6, gold plate; 7, bronze axe-blade; 8, gold plate from clothing; 9, stone mace-head.*

XVI (*caption on facing page*)

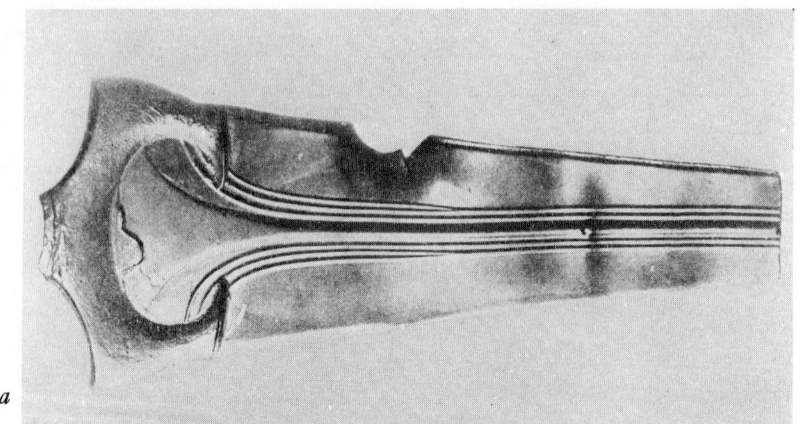

a

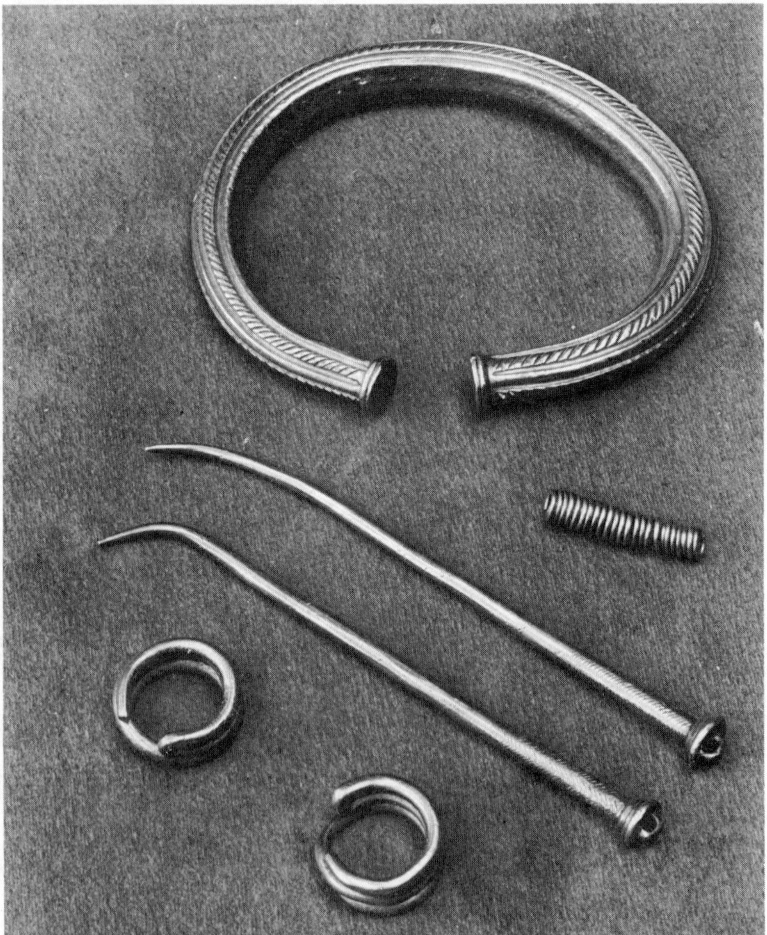

b

From archaeological evidence alone, too, we cannot directly perceive what social structure or structures lay behind the material products we study, though by inference one in which graded obligations within the society, from chieftain through a warrior élite to freeman and commoners, would be appropriate. However organized, the central European powers, as reflected in the trade relationships which can be perceived by archaeology, were in contact with the west as far as Spain (in the Argar culture, probably an eventual outcome of the Beaker Reflux Movement), again with the culture of the Tumulus graves in Brittany, and the Wessex culture of Britain; with north Italy and the Terremare settlements of the Po Basin; with their neighbours in east Europe, and with Scandinavia and the Baltic countries.[30] The timber mortuary house under a barrow, a legacy from the steppes, recurs, especially for chieftains' graves such as those of Leubingen and Helmsdorf in Saxony, with gold and silver ornaments as well as bronze weapons and tools laid with the dead,[31] and similar tombs appear in Brittany and Britain. The tombs of the British Wessex Culture contain such rich offerings as cups of gold or amber; gold hilted bronze daggers; beads of imported Oriental faience; and sceptres or maces of fine stone, gold and jet. (Figs. 67, 68; Pls. XVI-XVIII)

In Brittany the equipment of the warrior-graves almost reminds us of the Shaft-Graves in the excessive provision of weapons—in this instance of bronze daggers: up to six or seven to one grave is not uncommon, with usually a couple of bronze axe-blades, ceremonial whetstones, and arrows with finely worked flint tips. We shall see the wider significance of some of these barrow-burials shortly. 'They are assuredly, the single sepulchres of kings and great personages, buried during a considerable space of time, and that in peace', wrote William Stukeley in the eighteenth century of the barrows on Salisbury Plain, and he was right.[32]

If the tombs of the princes have not as yet been found in east Europe, some of their panoply has, not only in the form of magnificent bronze weapons, but ceremonial silver battle-axes, or the great golden dagger of Perşinari in Rumania, incomplete but still weighing 3 lb avoirdupois of 21 carat gold! From Borodino, north-west of the Black Sea, was a hoard of treasure containing not only silver spears, but weapons of prestige

---

XVI. (*a*) *Fragment of gold dagger, mid second millennium* B.C., *from Perşinari-Ploeşti, Rumania.* (Photo. Institutul de Arheologie, Bucharest)
XVI. (*b*) *Gold armlet, pins, ear-rings, and bead, Únětice culture, mid second millennium* B.C., *from grave at Leubingen, East Germany.* (Photo. Landesmuseum, Halle)

in the form of superb battle-axes of semi-precious jadeite (in a tradition going back to the 'Treasures' of Troy II) and maceheads of alabaster: the hoard is probably of the fifteenth century B.C.[33] In south Russia the tradition of the timber-chambered barrow for burial, established in the third millennium B.C., now continues, and from these Timber-Graves came (as we noted) the first indications of the domestication of the horse in the form of bone cheek-pieces for bridles buried on the animals; these date from about 1700 B.C. onwards,[34] and a little later cheek-pieces (of a different type) appear with horse-bones in the settlements of the Hungarian Plain such as Tószeg and in Rumania as at Monteoru.[35] It is probably chance that so far no princely burials of the Timber-Grave culture have been found in south Russia—not far distant, in the Trialeti region of the Caucasus and again round Lake Sevan in Armenia, richly furnished wood-chambered tombs have been found, of the second half of the second millennium, and sometimes containing solid-wheeled wagons or spoked-wheel chariots.[36] (Pl. XVIa; Figs. 69-72)

In the south Russian Timber-Graves and in the Lake Sevan graves just mentioned we find a continuance of ritual practice from the earlier Kurgan cultures, in which hides and fleeces of cattle, sheep and horses (archaeologically represented by skulls and the bones of the lower limbs alone) were deposited with the dead. Such ceremonial survived on the steppe throughout prehistory, and is found in northern Europe in the early centuries A.D. in contexts related to contacts with the Eastern world; the Scythian horse sacrifices represent another aspect of the same cult. Such sacrifices, with the animal's skin impaled on a pole, were recorded among the steppe people by European travellers in the Middle Ages, and persisted until recent times in Siberia and the Altai. Perhaps we may see reflections of these cults in a Hittite context, not only in the horse and donkey bones in the Osmankayasi cemetery, but in the final episode of the Telepinus myth, when 'a pole was erected before Telepinus and from this pole the fleece of a sheep was suspended. It signifies fat of the sheep, it signifies grains of corn and wine, it signifies cattle and sheep, it signifies long years and progeny.' The Golden Fleece in Pontic Colchis may not be unconnected, nor the Amazons' horse-sacrifices on the Island of Ares.[37]

There are excellent reasons for regarding the makers of the Timber-Graves as the ancestors of the Scythians of historic antiquity, to whom we will return in a later chapter: they may indeed be Homer's 'proud mare-milkers'.[38] They lived on the northern edge of the Caucasian province of metal-working, which during the later second millennium was working in a fantastic animal-art style, with affinities to that of Luristan and Amlash further east, with roots in the tradition of the Alaca Hüyük

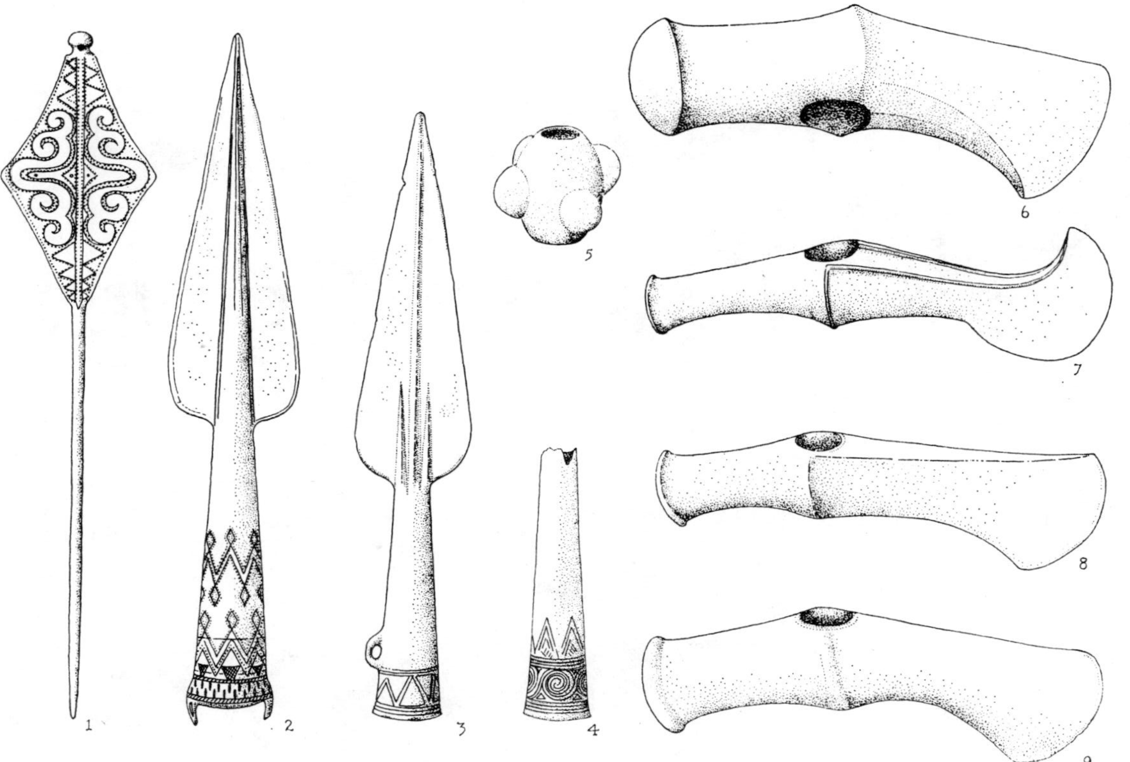

69. *Part of hoard, mid second millennium* B.C., *from Borodino, South Russia:* 1, *silver pin;* 2–4, *silver spear-heads with gold ornament;* 5, *alabaster mace-head;* 6–9, *jadeite battle-axes.*

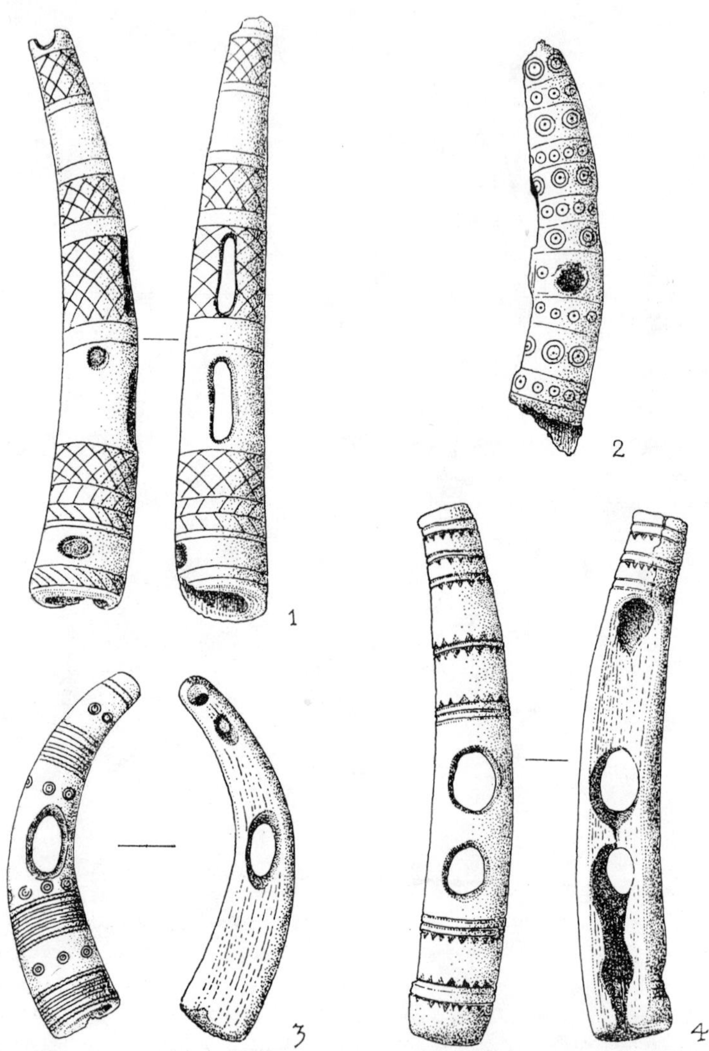

70. *Antler cheek-pieces for horse-bits, Füszesabony culture, second half of second millennium* B.C.*: 1, 2, Tószeg; 3, Pákozdvár; 4, Köröstarcsa, Hungary.*

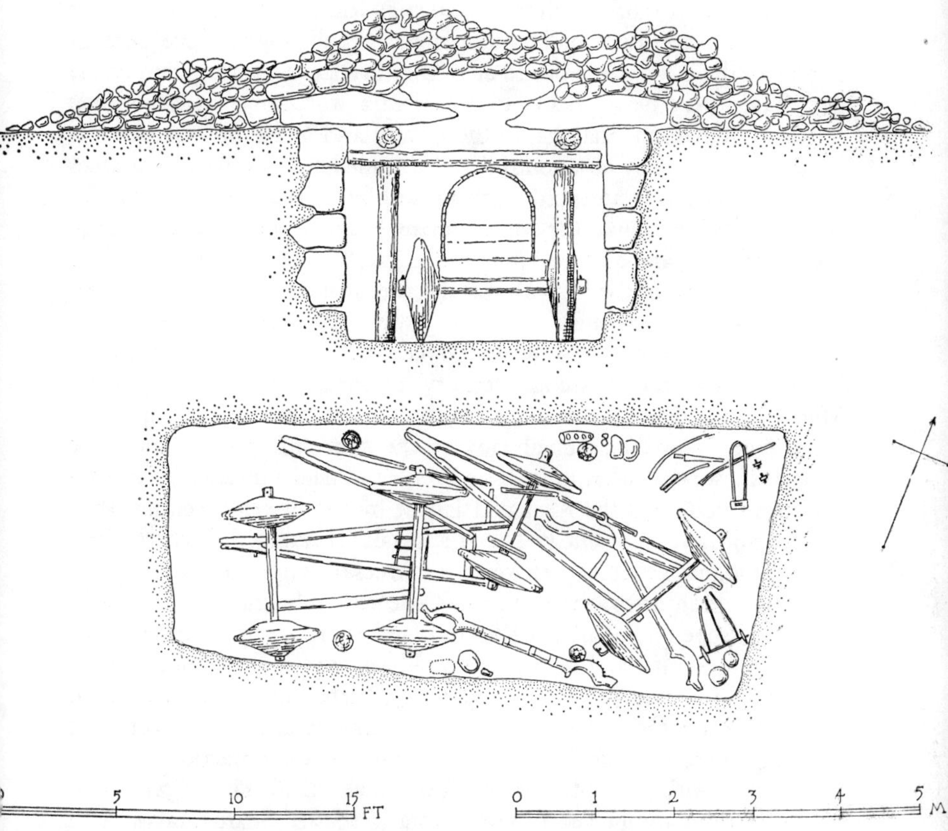

71. *Burial with solid-wheeled wagons, second half of second millennium* B.C., at *Lchashen, Lake Sevan, Armenian* S.S.R.

Royal Tombs, perceptible in some Hittite stone sculpture, and represented (as Evans saw many years ago) in some objects from the Mycenaean Shaft-Graves. This 'Caucasian' element seems likely to be among the roots of Scythian art, together with more ancient animal style, ultimately of Mesolithic origins, and appearing among the last remnants of the hunting and fishing peoples in the Urals and Siberia; here too is involved, though outside our province, the animal-art of China.[39]

The new dynasties of Mycenae were clearly in a position, from the very start, to command considerable resources of wealth, the tangible expression of which is the astonishingly rich contents of the two groups of Shaft-Graves. Whether gold and bronze and silver was initially acquired by conquest and loot, or by means which we (unlike the ancients) would regard as more meritorious, such as legitimate trade, we cannot tell; but the necessity for constant metal supplies must have been as urgent to the Mycenaeans as to any other bronze-using kingdom of the day. They were newly rising to power in a world of long-established states—in Crete, in Anatolia, in the Levant and in Egypt—whose mercantile operations by now controlled the immediately available resources of copper, tin, silver, and gold. Early in the fifteenth century, it is true, the Mycenaeans seem, like the Macedonians later, to have 'struck against their civilisers', and assumed power in Crete,[40] but even if this obtained for them control of the Minoan metal trade, armaments are ever a costly business and new supplies of bronze always in demand. It is in such a context that the contacts of the Mycenaean world with continental Europe, from the sixteenth century onwards, are best explained. Mycenaean colonies were soon to be founded in the Aegean, especially from about 1400 B.C., but already in the sixteenth century imported pottery shows that what must have been Mycenaean trading-posts were set up in Sicily and the Aeolian Islands; by the fifteenth century they existed not only here but in Ischia and near Taranto.[41] Such trading-posts could make contact with western sources of copper and tin. (Fig. 73)

In these centuries around 1500 B.C. we suddenly find that notably in central Europe and southern England, and sporadically elsewhere, objects, ideas, motifs, and techniques of Mycenaean origin appear among the High Barbarian cultures; reciprocally, barbarian objects are traded to the Aegean. On present showing the earliest datable contact is in Wessex, where in Bush Barrow on Salisbury Plain a warrior-chieftain was buried with a sceptre or wand of office inlaid with zigzag bone mounts exactly duplicated in Grave Iota of the 'B' Shaft-Graves, with late Middle Helladic pottery, and so a date near 1600 B.C. A pottery cup from Nienhagen in Saxony has a handle crudely copying a Mycenaean metal form (as on the famous Vapheio cups) and could be of the late sixteenth century, certainly about 1500 B.C. A bronze helmet from Beitzsch in Brandenburg is closely comparable with one from a warrior's grave at Knossos of the second half of the fifteenth century, and this Mycenaean model seems to have inspired the subsequent development of helmets in northern Europe: we shall see that body-armour was also developed in central Europe before the end of the second millennium B.C. Mycenaean metal-working techniques were however now influencing craftsmen in the far north-west; the gold cups from Fritzdorf near Bonn and Rillaton in Cornwall are instances of this, the latter with corrugated sides as in a pair from the Shaft-Graves, and other gold-work from the barrow-burials of the Wessex Culture[42] shows similar contacts. (Fig. 68; Pl. XVII)

XVII. (*a*) *Two views of gold cup, mid second millennium* B.C., *from Fritzdorf, Bonn, Germany*. (Photo. Landesmuseum Bonn)
XVII. (*b*) *Two views of gold cup, mid second millennium* B.C., *from grave at Rillaton, Cornwall, England*. (Photo. British Museum)

XVIII (*caption on facing page*)

a

b

72. *Decorated antler and bone objects, second half of second millennium* B.C. *1–3, Alalakh, Turkey; 4, Cezavy; 5, Větěrov, Czechoslovakia; 6, 7, Vattina, Rumania; 8, Surčin, Jugoslavia; 9, Tiszafüred, Hungary; 10, Nitrianski Hradok, Czechoslovakia; 11, Vinča, Jugoslavia; 12, Kakovatos; 13, Asine, Greece.*

XVIII. (*a*) *Necklace of faience and shale beads, second half of second millennium* B.C., *from grave at Upton Lovell, Wilts., England.* (Photo. Malcolm Murray)
XVIII. (*b*) *Decorated bone cylindrical mounting, second half of second millennium* B.C., *from Blučina, Czechoslovakia.* (Photo. Narodni Museum, Prague)

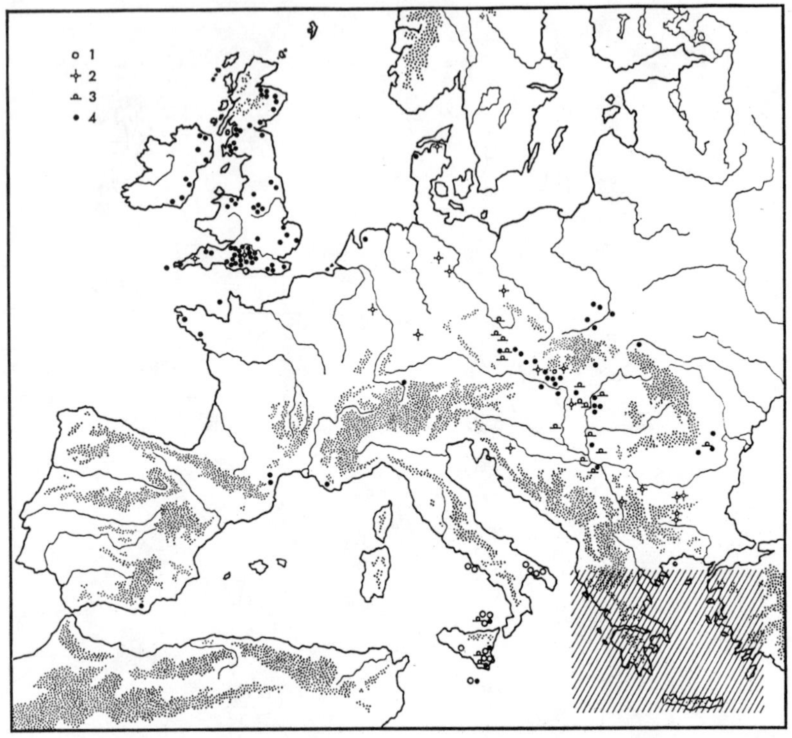

73. *Distribution of Mycenaean objects and influences beyond the Aegean (hatched rectangle): 1, Pottery; 2, Metal-work; 3, Decorated bone-work; 4, Faience beads.*

These are isolated examples of contact, but more significant are two groups of finds which occur in some numbers; objects decorated with specifically Mycenaean motifs, and beads and ornaments of faience, the artificial substance with a glass base much used in the ancient Orient and the Aegean. The decorated bone or antler objects—bridle cheek-pieces, ferrules of staffs, discs—occur, over a dozen of them, in the Danube and Tisza plain of Hungary, in the Carpathians, and finally in Czechoslovakia, and their archaeological context suggests a fifteenth or even fourteenth century date; here again we may suspect an interest in the ores of Transylvania and the Erzgebirge. (Fig. 72; Pl. XVIIb) In these regions we find beads of blue faience, of Oriental or Aegean origin, of restricted types; westwards, in Sicily and the Aeolian Islands, others again, with a scatter in France leading to a concentration in Britain. Glass beads, again of Egyptian or Aegean origin, also occur sporadically in both the central

European and the western areas. We have, it appears, two spheres of Mycenaean influence in High Barbarian Europe—one, connected with the western Mediterranean trading-posts and operating via the Narbonne-Carcassonne-Loire route to the British Isles, and the other an eastern and central European connection. In both areas copper, tin and gold can be obtained, and must, to a great extent, be the motivating force behind these not inconsiderable merchant ventures.[43] But at least one other substance was involved—amber. (Pl. XVIII a; Fig. 73)

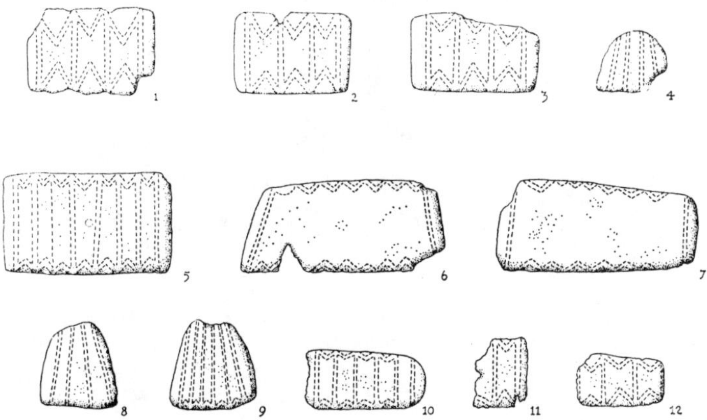

74. *Amber space-plate beads with complex perforations, sixteenth to fifteenth centuries* B.C.: *1–4, 'B' group of shaft Graves, Mycenae; 5, Kakovatos, Greece; 6–9, Lake, Wilts., England; 10, Upton Lovell, Wilts., England; 11, Hundersingen-Weidenhang; 12, Mehrstetten, South Germany.*

I have already mentioned the routes whereby amber was brought down from the Jutland coast to the head of the Adriatic; passing as they did through the richest areas of central European power at the time, the trade must either have been organised and controlled by this power, or a considerable toll levied *en route*. Amber, obtained almost certainly through central European middlemen, was being imported into Britain and worked into elaborate multi-strand necklaces with the strings separated by space-beads with complex perforations; similar space-beads in amber appear in the Shaft-Graves, others in later fifteenth century contexts, and simple amber beads continued to be imported into Greece in the late Helladic period, the trade rising to a peak in the fourteenth century.[44] (Figs. 74, 75)

The circumstances whereby Britain was connected with so remote a centre of civilisation as Mycenae in the middle second millennium

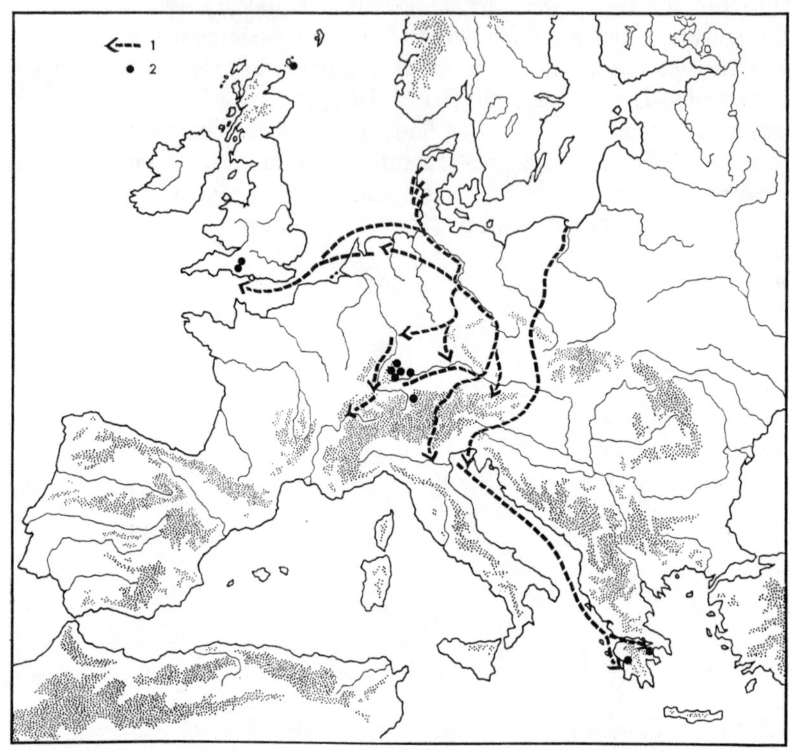

75. *1, Main routes of trade and exchange in amber, mid second millennium* B.C.; *2, Complex-bored space-plates.*

seems then not so strange when the general picture of European trade at this time is seen as a whole. The connection was incidentally to continue sporadically for centuries, the four Mycenaean bronze double axes from Ireland and England, and the short-sword from a Cornish burial at Pelynt, being all datable to the end of the thirteenth century, just before the Aegean collapse. (Fig. 76) And in the same context, or in that of the piratical raids of a century or so later which we will touch on again at the end of this chapter, Cypriot styles of twisted ear-rings, and Egyptian penannular hair-rings, were traded west to influence the fashion in Irish gold jewellery.[45] But of course the most remarkable connection, if only inferential, is afforded by the sophisticated construction in dressed stone, and the architectural competence, and indeed refinement, of the final monument of Stonehenge, without parallel in Europe beyond the Mediterranean at its date—probably the sixteenth century B.C. Whether

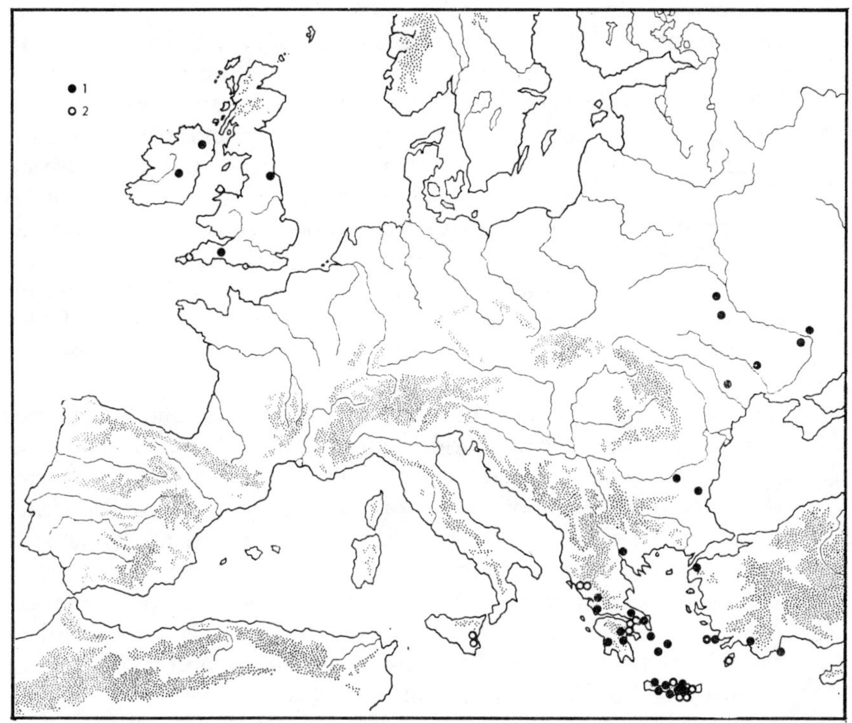

76. *Distribution of Late Mycenaean bronzes: 1, shaft-hole double-axes; 2, square-shouldered short swords, thirteenth-twelfth centuries* B.C.

or not the famous dagger-carving is that of a Mycenaean weapon the other features of the monument demand interpretation in terms of the momentary introduction of superior skills and techniques from an area of higher culture, and in the context we have just been discussing, this can hardly be other than that of the Aegean, and of Mycenae.

Stonehenge raises an interesting point with regard to the likely social organisation in Britain in the mid second millennium B.C. and earlier. The command of labour and craftsmanship involved in bringing huge blocks of stone to the site from far afield, and in the third constructional phase dressing these accurately to predetermined sizes and proportions, poses problems even before one considers their final erection. The monument bespeaks unified and indeed personal authority, not only in concept and realisation as an architectural entity, but in the prestige and power that could draw on the actual labour force and technical skills required, if only for relatively short or seasonal occasions, over many years: the continuity of building and rebuilding on the site over probably five centuries argues for a similar continuity of tradition and authority. We can hardly imagine these qualities within the framework of inchoate barbarism, but they could well exist within the the structure of graded obligations in a society of chieftainship, aristocracy, and freemen, such as we know in later prehistoric or early historic Europe. If, however, we are tempted to compare the Stonehenge situation too closely with that of the contemporary Aegean, it may be well (in both instances) to remember that quite monumental stone structures can be achieved under relatively barbaric conditions, as under the early Bantu chieftains of the fourteenth or fifteenth centuries A.D. in southern Rhodesia, when Zimbabwe, Dhlo-Dhlo or Mapungubwe were built.

I said earlier on that the world of second millennium barbarian Europe was essentially the world of the *Iliad*, the *Odyssey*—I would add, and of the Argonauts,—just as, in the later first millennium, it becomes recognisably the world of the heroes of the old Irish tales of the Ulster Cycle. Homer's Aegean and Anatolian world of course has its wall-girt towns and ashlar palaces, rather than the palisaded timber-built villages of the woodlands north of the Alps, and the expedition to Colchis was perhaps on a scale beyond that of one mounted in Wessex or at the mouth of the Elbe; but the heroes of the stories, for all the poet's skill, remain obstinately of an alien world, primitive and barbaric. Perhaps not enough stress is laid on the features of Homer's world that are common to those of the Irish hero-tales, Beowulf or the Sagas, and must have been a commonplace of the lost oral literature of the whole of ancient barbarian Europe. 'The noblest behave like savages in battle'; emotionally unstable, 'the manliest warriors weep copiously and publicly', seeking women is 'an avowed aim and approved prize of war', as are sacking cities and killing or enslaving the men and children, and dragging the girls into concubinage. 'Piracy, raiding at large for human and other booty, is an honourable trade' (as it was to Thucydides), and 'successful theft and perjury are admired'.[46] Agamemnon systematically strips his victims of their equipment as he smites them to the earth with as little compunction as the legendary Indian brave dealt with a Paleface cowboy biting the dust; indeed, the atmosphere of the *Iliad* is often distressingly like that of a Western: or perhaps one should say, a European north-western.

It is within such a world that we must set the anonymous peoples of prehistoric Europe in the second millennium. Coalitions, confederacies, petty nations and little kingdoms must lie behind the variations in material culture defined by archaeologists. On a secure basis of an agricultural peasantry, we have the structure of a stratified, class-conscious society, with a ruler—sometimes dignified with the title of a king when enshrined in the literary tradition, sometimes a nameless rustic princeling—and a warrior class, themselves a nobility as well as a fighting force: 'knights' is perhaps as good a word as any for them. On analogy, craftsmen (including poets and bards in the oral tradition) would be honoured and free, and the aristocracy would be at once their protectors and best customers; a merchant class could even have emerged in some places. It is a familiar pattern, and one which was to endure in Europe for many centuries, centred on a court (and in the Mediterranean a palace-complex) rather than a city, and with the personal chain of allegiance and of the obligations of society that gave it a rude coherence. In the Mediterranean the pattern was changed, largely as a result of contact with the Asiatic traditions of city and city-state, and versions of urban civilisation were produced; but north of the Alps the older order endured, up to and beyond the beginnings of recorded history.

Since warfare was an essential element in the heroic age we are discussing (as it always has been, and still is, in one less heroic), we must now turn to some aspects of attack and defence. Two factors had combined, in the second millennium, to revolutionise the art of war in western Asia, and, from the time of the Shaft-Grave dynasties, in the Aegean as well. We have already seen that the evidence implied that solid-wheeled carts and wagons were first invented in Sumer in the fourth or third millennium B.C. and were quickly adopted by the peoples of the south Russian Steppe. Again we recall that the steppe is the homeland of the wild horse, and it must have been first tamed in the third millennium, by these same people, so that a vehicle formerly drawn by slow oxen or uncertain onagers could now be adapted for horse traction. And at the same time the advancing bronze technology was producing tools which rendered more intricate carpentry possible, and so the invention of the light spoked wheel. The fast horse and the light cart in conjunction produced that revolutionary engine of war, the chariot. The archaeological and historical evidence points to a likely origin for the chariot in some area within the general region of Upper Mesopotamia, Syria and Anatolia; it has been argued that the character of the terrain east of the Orontes, with its grass-grown alluvial plains, would favour development there.[47]

As we saw in Chapter III, the Sumerians had used heavy solid-wheeled battle-cars in warfare, drawn by onagers; by 2000 B.C. they were beginning to know of a novel animal—an 'ass from foreign parts' as the original name goes—'a fast horse, with a waving tail' as a hymn of this date describes him.[48] By the early eighteenth century we find horses mentioned, significantly enough (as we saw in Chapter III) in the business correspondence of the Assyrian merchants in Anatolia, and so too vehicles called by the name thereafter always used for a war-chariot. Connection with the Hittites or allied peoples seems inevitable, and before long horse-drawn chariots, with the necessary tactics involved, are a part of Assyrian as well as Hittite warfare. From 1720 or so Egypt had been taken over by foreign rulers, the so-called Hyksos, probably mainly Semitic in origin, and about this time the first horses, and probably chariots, came to the Nile Valley. The earliest horse known there was given an honoured burial about 1750 B.C. at Buhen; chariot warfare is first specifically mentioned two centuries later, by the King Kamose who finally ended the Hyksos domination, and the first pictorial representations appear under Amenophis I, about 1549-1529 B.C.[49]

As we saw, it was just about this time that the first evidence for European chariotry appears, in the scenes carved on the grave-slabs at Mycenae. (Pl. xv) The Mycenaeans like their contemporaries in the Aegean and West Asiatic world bred horses, on the Argive plain and elsewhere, using the chariot as a light mechanised arm of their services; in Homer its use is obsolete except to bring the warrior to the front line where he fights on foot, and only Nestor remembers the older tactics. But a passage in the *Iliad* records that chariot-wheels were made with a single-piece felloe from a poplar tree. 'A chariot-maker fells it with a gleaming [axe of] iron, so that he may bend a felloe for a splendid carriage'; so too a simile in the Sanskrit *Rig-Veda* of the second millennium runs, 'I bend myself before [Indra] with song, as a carpenter his felloe of good wood', for the chariots of the Aryan warriors.[50] Precisely this form of wheel-construction continued to be used in European chariots, among the Celts at the time of the Roman conquest of Britain, and examples of such single-felloe chariot wheels survive in Britain. The technique appears to have been employed in the later second millennium B.C. for spoked-wheel chariots or carts in the Lake Sevan region of Armenia, and again in the fifth/fourth century B.C. in Scythian contexts in the Altai Mountains; it is still used in Turkestan and in Turkey, where I was delighted to record it for myself a few years ago.[51] In later second millennium Europe there is some evidence of the use of chariots outside the Mycenaean world, afforded by rock-carvings in south Sweden, and model spoked wheels and model spoked-wheeled ritual 'vehicles' are known in central Europe and Scandinavia from the thirteenth century B.C., a date appropriate also for the earlier rock-engravings.[52] We meet the chariot again in a Celtic context from the fifth century onwards, frequently buried with the dead warrior,

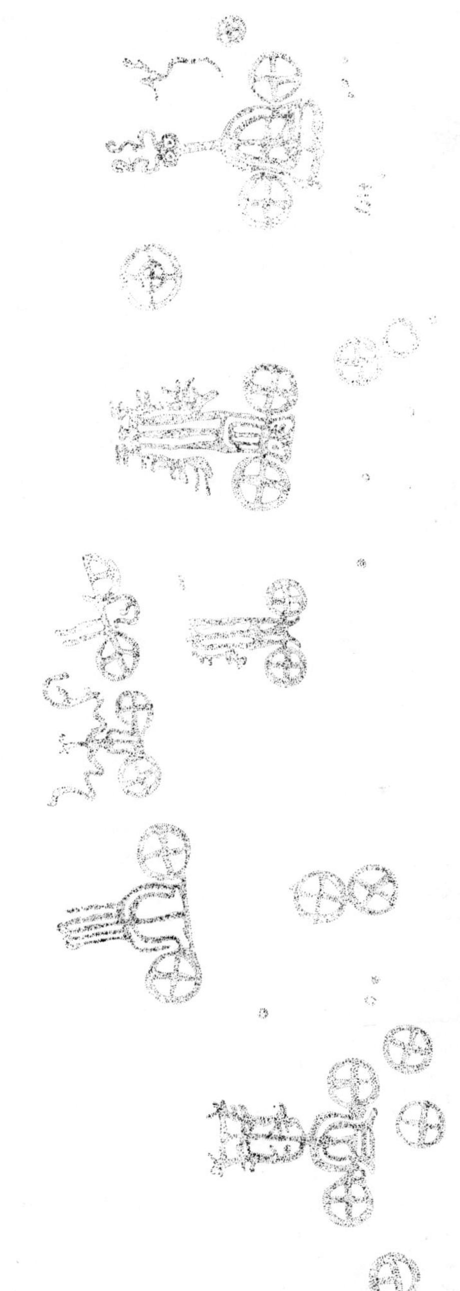

77. *Rock-carvings of chariots or carts, horses and wheels, late second–early first millennium* B.C., *at Frännarp, Sweden.*

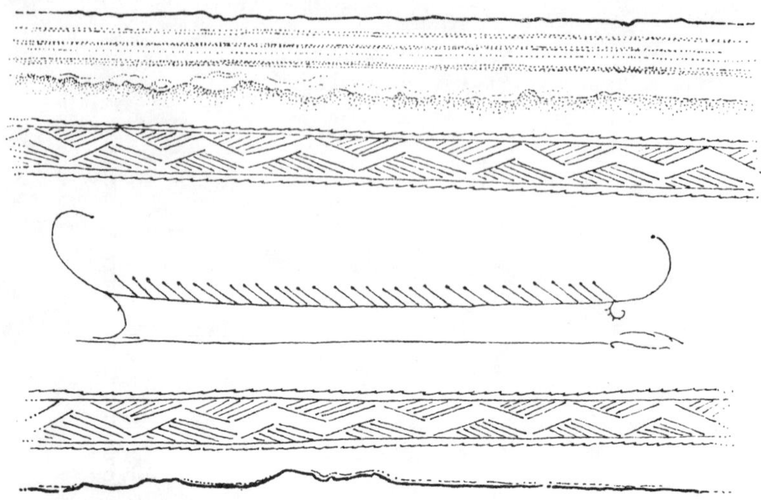

78. *Engraving of boat on sword-blade, mid second millennium* B.C., *from Rørby, Kalundborg, Denmark.*

as perhaps in a Mycenaean tomb near Marathon with a pair of horses, and certainly in the seventh century at Old Paphos and Salamis in Cyprus, where Mycenaean tradition lingered to so late a date.[53] Representations of chariots appear on the decorated bronze buckets or *situlae* found around the head of the Adriatic and dating from the sixth to the fourth centuries B.C.[54] (Fig. 77)

We saw how boats, of simple skin-covered or dug-out types, had been used in northern Europe since the eighth millennium B.C. at least. In the eastern Mediterranean big rowing-boats of up to thirty oars were in use from the third millennium B.C. at least, and in northern Europe we not only have numerous rock-carvings of what are clearly large sea-going craft of comparable size, but engravings of similar ships on a bronze sword from Denmark enable us to date the type to the middle of the second millennium B.C. The schematic indications of the 'crew' of these boats suggest that, as in the Aegean, we are dealing with ships of triaconter status. The vast majority of the rock-engravings show

---

XIX. (*a, above*) *Oval wooden bowl, decorated with gold foil and in the form of a stylised boat, late second-early first millennium* B.C., *from Caergwrle, Wales.* (Photo. National Museum of Wales)

XIX. (*b, below*) *Carvings of stylised boats on rock surface, second millennium* B.C., *at Ostfold, Norway.* (Photo. Universitets Oldsaksamling, Oslo)

XIX (*caption on facing page*)

a

b

XX (*caption on facing page*)

a

b

rowing boats, and the few with sails cannot be dated, and may be later. An oval wooden bowl inlaid in gold, and representing a boat with 'oculi' at the prow and a row of round shields hung along the gunwales in the manner of Viking ships, comes from Caergwrle in north Wales and could be as early as the very end of the second millennium B.C., but if the shields are to be taken as representing metal originals, it can hardly be before the eighth century B.C., when these became current in north-west Europe. Here the schematised 'oars' would imply a crew of over forty.[55] (Pl. xix; Fig. 78)

In central and eastern Europe there is continuous development from the middle of the millennium; tumulus-burial, once thought to characterise this secondary phase, can now be seen to have existed from the first. In the thirteenth century the culture of the Hungarian tells is brought to an end perhaps partly by central European raiders, now able to control Transylvanian metal resources. About the same time burial rites in central Europe begin to change from inhumation under a barrow to cremation in an open cemetery, but there seems no need to invoke newcomers from outside Europe for this change. Cremation was always an alternative rite to inhumation, and in east Europe occurs not infrequently from the beginning of the second millennium in such cemeteries as those of the Kisapostag group in Hungary, or at Cîrna in Transylvania. In Britain a comparable change took place in the fifteenth century B.C. without the slightest evidence of any outside stimulus (and here again cremation as an alternative rite goes back to 2000 B.C. or earlier), and in the Roman world of the early centuries A.D. inhumation replaced cremation as a wholly internal affair. The so-called Urnfield Peoples, by now a recognisable archaeological entity, did however expand in the early first millennium as we shall see, and introduced their novel burial rite to other areas, but its origins seem an entirely central European phenomenon.[56] (Fig. 79)

In the Aegean, fighting tactics had rather rapidly changed from the use of the dagger to that of the rapier or sword, supported by spears and with shields or body-armour as a defence. (Fig. 80) In continental Europe we can see the same trend, with the early daggers becoming the rapiers and short-swords of the middle and the long-swords of the end, of the second millennium. Perhaps Mycenaean influence may be at work here,

---

XX. (*a*) *Excavated settlement with oval stone-built houses, mid second millennium* B.C., *on Capo Graziano, Filicudi, Aeolian Islands.* (Photo. author)
XX. (*b*) *Excavated surface of cross-ploughed field, later second millennium* B.C., *at Gwithian, Cornwall, England.* (Photo. Malcolm Murray)

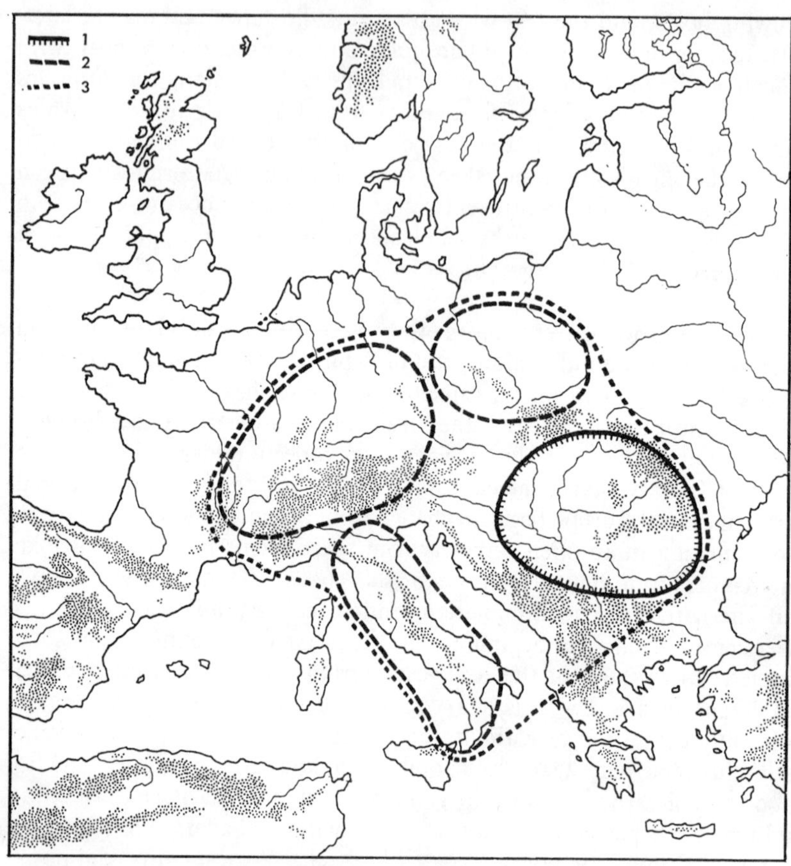

79. *Generalised map showing expansion of Urnfield cultures: 1, Thirteenth century* B.C.; 2, *Twelfth–tenth century*; 3, *Tenth–eighth century.*

and apart from traders we must always reckon with adventurers and mercenaries returning from foreign service with new notions of armament. In east central Europe there developed, from the fifteenth century, a new type of slashing sword unknown at that time in the Mediterranean world; heavy, and with its hilt securely fastened by a flanged tang. It became immensely popular, particularly in the north, and then, between 1250 and 1200, such swords, or copies of them, suddenly appear in the Aegean world. We shall shortly see in what circumstances of piracy and raiding, on the eve of the break-up of Mycenaean power, the presence of European barbarians and their weapons would be not only likely, but almost inevitable.[57] (Fig. 81)

80. *Fighting with sword, dagger and spear. Impression from engraved gold ring, sixteenth century* B.C., *from the* 'A' *group of Shaft Graves, Mycenae, Greece.*

Towards the end of the second millennium we have a few settlement sites to augment our knowledge. In Holland, at Elp, a group of long rectangular houses of the Middle Bronze Age has been found, and on the Federsee in south Germany an island settlement (the 'Wasserburg') defended by palisades, had in its first phase thirty-eight small rectangular, almost square houses, and one larger, perhaps that of a chief; in its second building period they were replaced by nine big houses with a plan of hall and lateral wings, and other rectangular barns or byres. The largest of the big houses had six rooms, five with hearths, and the main hall was something over 30 by 15 feet—the whole building has much the size and proportions, and indeed layout, as an average smallish English medieval house with hall and lateral wings. (Figs. 82, 83) But settlements are noticeably smaller than the big Neolithic villages of the Danube valley three millennia before; at Perleberg in north-east Germany for instance, a rather later village consisted of five *megaron* type houses with hearths and another eleven rectangular buildings without; there was a communal baking-oven near the centre of the settlement. Internal wall-plaster painted red and white has come from other north German house-sites of this period.[58] In Britain the dominant house-form is now circular, though oval or subrectangular plans also existed, as in the western Mediterranean. (Figs. 84, 86; Pl. XX a)

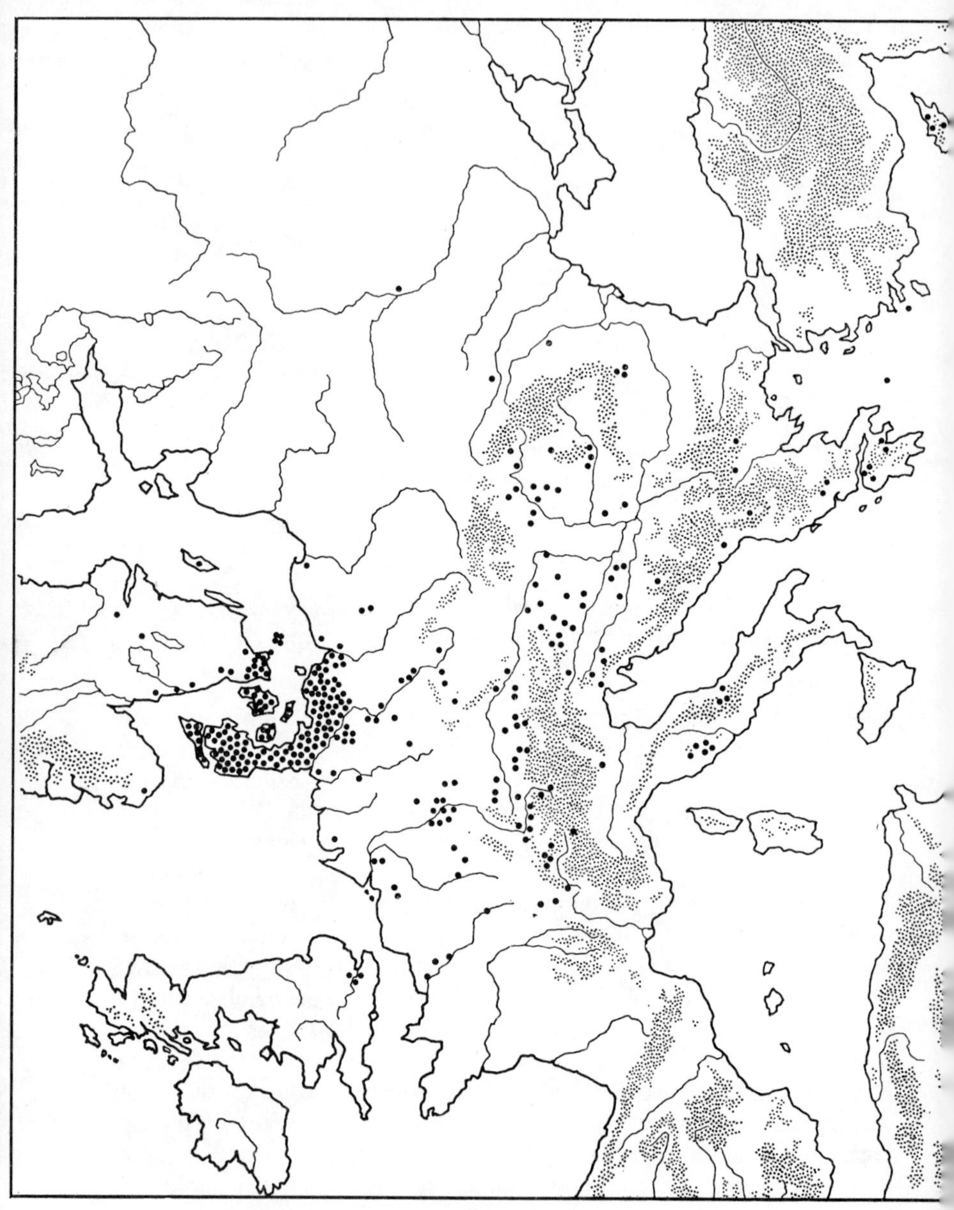

81. *Distribution of bronze flange-hilted swords of 'Naue* II' *type, earlier Urnfield culture, late thirteenth–early twelfth century* B.C.

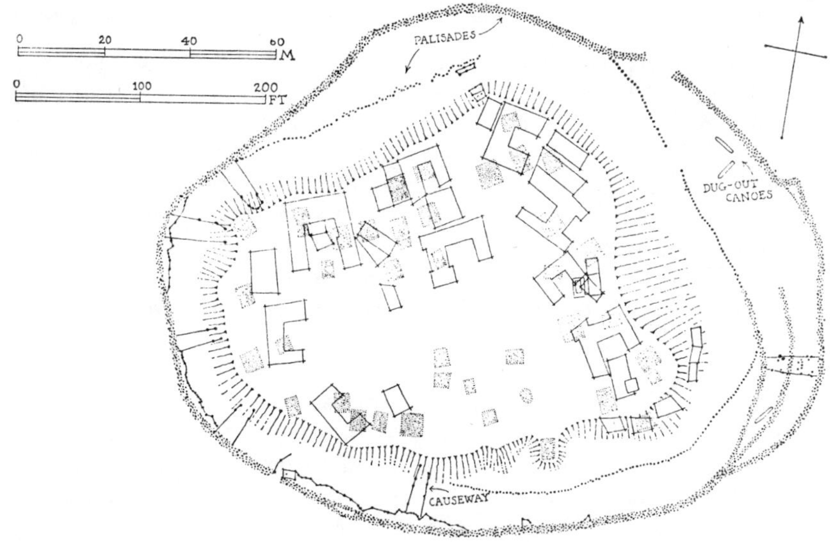

82. *Timber-built settlement on island, Urnfield culture, twelfth–ninth century* B.C., *at the Wasserburg, Federsee, Buchau, South Germany. Earlier houses stippled, later in outline.*

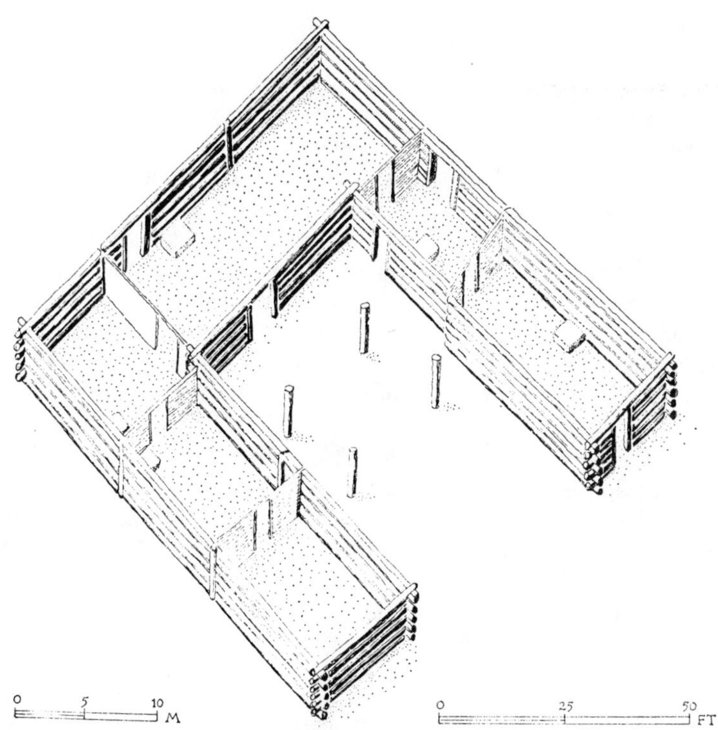

83. *Log-built house of second settlement, Urnfield culture, tenth–ninth century* B.C., *the Wasserburg.*

Circular huts or houses, timber framed or stone-walled, appear to go back to Neolithic antecedents in the British Isles, as at Lough Gur, and they are certainly established as the standard type by early in the second millennium B.C. Rectangular or sub-rectangular houses are however known somewhat later, as at Gwithian in Cornwall, where a house 28 by 12 feet can be dated to about 1200–1000 B.C. At other sites in Wessex and Sussex of the same date, sub-rectangular houses do occur (as at Thorny Down in Wiltshire, where a building 28 by 15 feet, has a porched entrance on one side), but circular buildings were more common (as at Itford Hill in Sussex, a settlement with about a dozen circular timber-framed houses each about 20 feet in diameter). Here we are presumably dealing with a small village, but other sites seem to have been those of isolated farms or steadings.[59] In many instances such sites are associated with earthwork enclosures and systems of small, more or less rectangular, arable fields, their form presupposing plough agriculture with the light 'ard'; at Gwithian, furrows show cross ploughing from a date early in the second millennium B.C. (Figs. 86–87; Pl. xx b) This raises the question of the beginnings of plough agriculture in prehistoric Europe. It is usually assumed that hoes and digging-sticks were used by the earlier Neolithic cultures of east and central Europe, but claims have been made for the use of certain perforated stone 'axe-heads' as shares for ploughs of the light 'ard' type.[60] The acceptance of this theory would take the use of the traction-plough back to at least the fourth millennium B.C. in Europe; actual traces of cross-ploughed fields as at Gwithian, preserved under the mounds of barrows in northern Europe, date to the first half of the second millennium B.C., and in Mesopotamia the use of the plough was well established by about 3000 B.C. and could have been in use at a much earlier date.[61] The well known rock engravings of ploughing scenes, as at Val Camonica in the Italian Alps and in south Sweden, are extremely difficult to date, but some at least must go back to the second millennium B.C.[62] Though one assumes an increasing population and advances in agricultural technique, the social units have clearly become smaller; in the first phase of the Federsee, it is true, cropping some 285 acres, but the Perleberg village may have housed no more persons than a single long-house of Danubian type, and have drawn its corn supplies from no more than 35 to 40 acres of arable. Some sites were fortified, with defences having timber-faced and timber-braced ramparts, but these are more conveniently dealt with in the next chapter, when we consider the long history of Celtic fortification.

An important technique in bronze-working, early discovered in the Near East, is the process of annealing, or periodic re-heating to enable

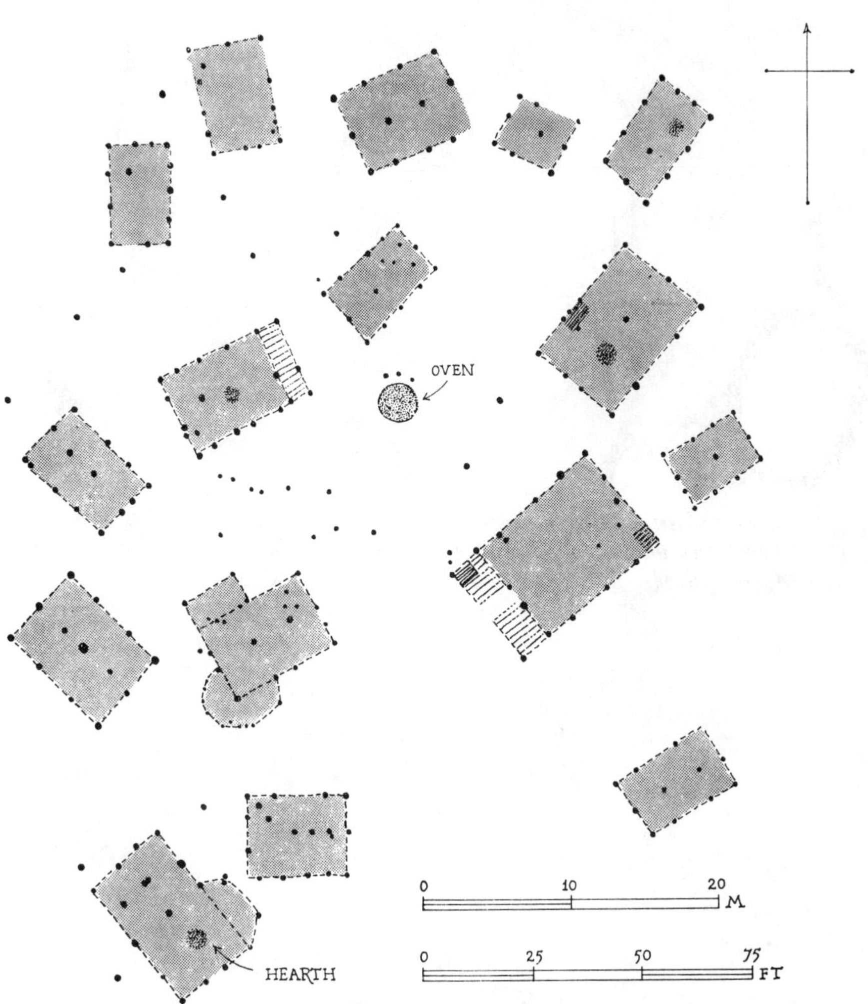

84. *Settlement with post-holes of timber-built houses, Urnfield culture, early first millennium* B.C., *at Perleberg, East Germany.*

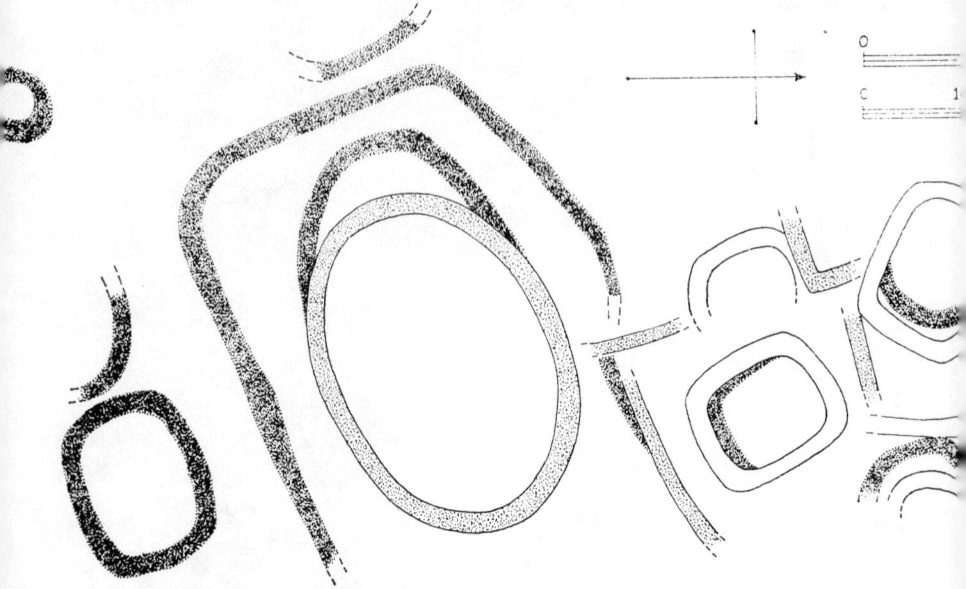

85. *Part of settlement with stone-built houses of three periods,* Capo Graziano *to* Ausonian II *cultures, early second to early first millennium* B.C., *Acropolis of Lipari, Aeolian Islands.*

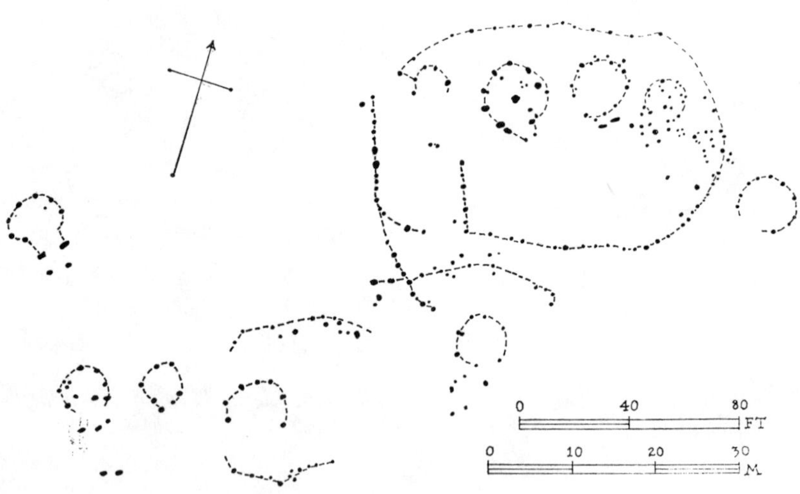

86. *Settlement with post-holes of timber-built houses,* Deverel-Rimbury *culture, twelfth–eleventh century* B.C., *at Itford Hill, Sussex, England.*

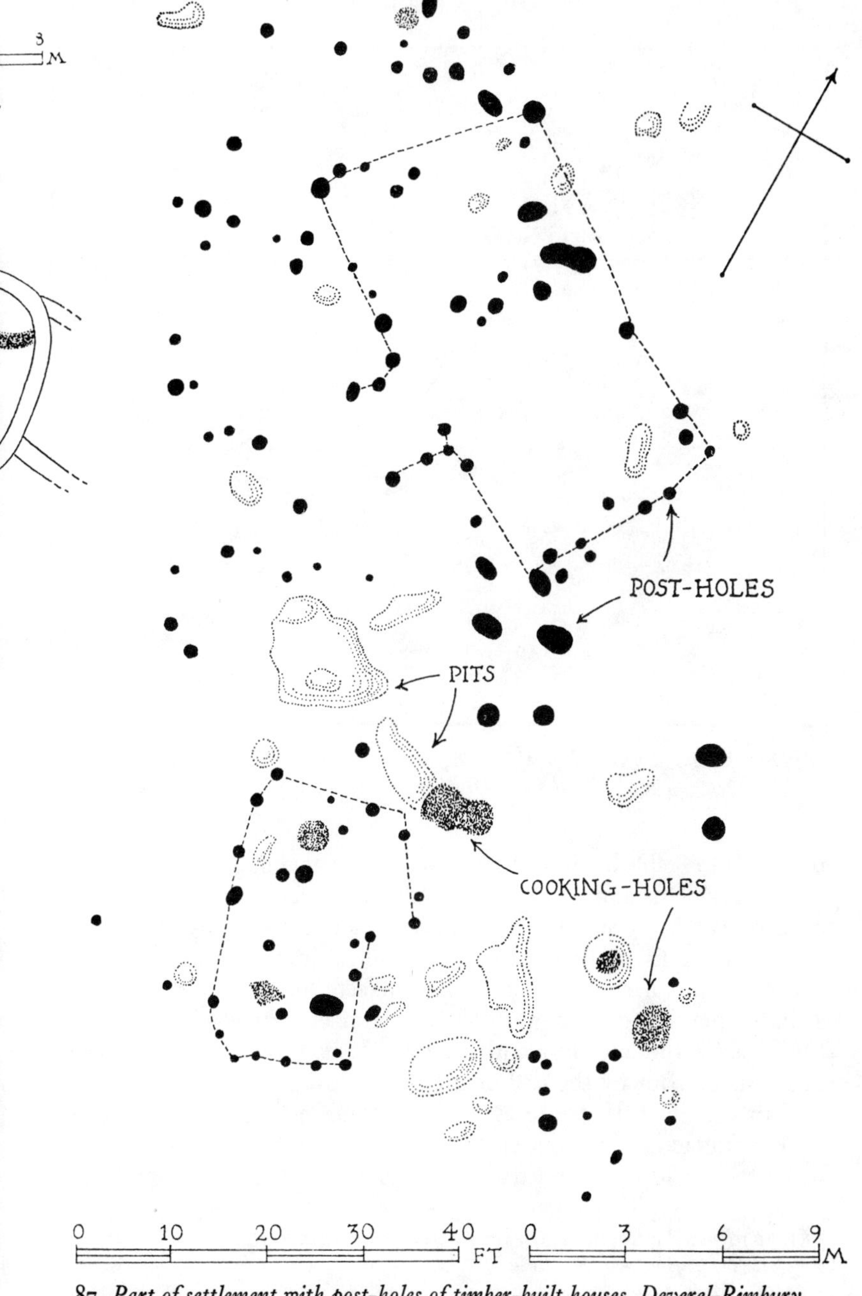

87. *Part of settlement with post-holes of timber-built houses, Deverel-Rimbury culture, twelfth-eleventh century* B.C., *at Thorny Down, Wilts., England.*

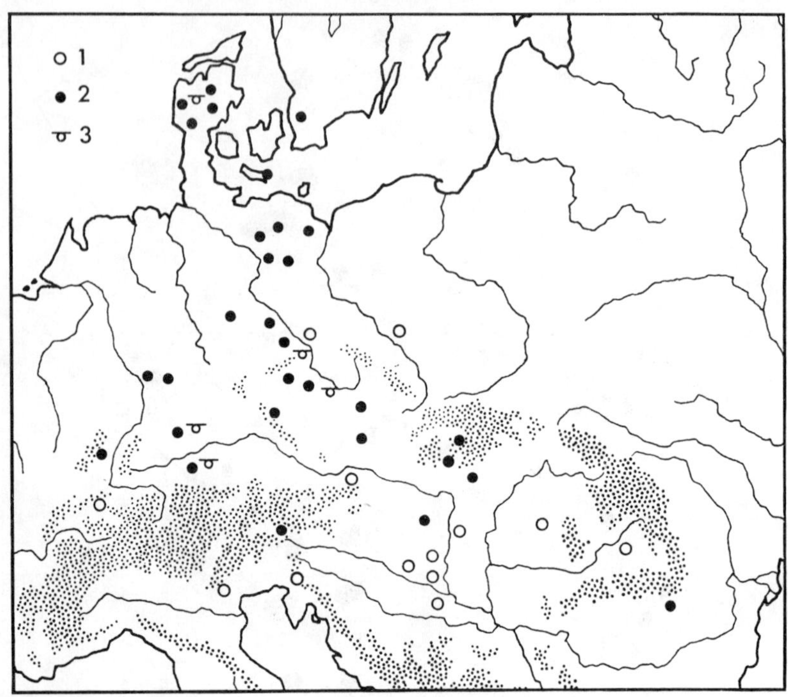

88. *Distribution of beaten bronze vessels, earlier Urnfield cultures, thirteenth-twelfth century* B.C.: *1, Situlae; 2, Drinking cups; 3, Strainers.*

the metal to be beaten into sheet form, and so enabling vessels, helmets, corselets, shields and so on to be made. The secret of efficient bronze-beating was however more or less confined to western Asia and the Aegean until the end of the second millennium, and in continental Europe it was hardly known, though objects like the Beitzsch helmet already mentioned, and a two-piece bronze corselet from Čaka in Slovakia (of the late thirteenth century)[63] show that some knowledge of it existed. But by the end of the thirteenth, and increasingly in the twelfth and eleventh centuries, a whole group of beaten bronze vessels were manufactured in central Europe, and in north Italy in areas later to be the nucleus of the Etruscan kingdom.[64] Three main types were

XXI. (*a*) *Ruined* nuraghe *or defensive tower-house, thirteenth-seventh century* B.C., *at Santa Barbara, Sardinia.*
XXI. (*b*) *Stone-built circular houses, eighth-sixth century* B.C., *around* nuraghe *of Su Nuraxi, Barumini, Sardinia.* (Both photos. Bromofoto, Milan)

XXI (*caption on facing page*)

XXII (*caption on facing page*)

produced; a bucket or *situla*, a handled cup, and a cup-shaped strainer. Now these in combination call for comparison with the equipment for serving wine known in the later classical world, the *situla* taking the place of a *stamnos* or *crater*, and the strainer necessary for wine that had suffered the indignities of mixture with other substances, as Mediterranean tradition so curiously demanded. Are we seeing in this group of bronzes not only the expression of a new technology, that of beaten bronze-work, but also of a new conviviality made possible by the importation of Mediterranean wine, and perhaps its production in southern central Europe?[65] (Fig. 88)

By this time viticulture was already ancient in the Near East and the Aegean, grapes being used either crushed as the basis for wine, or dried as raisins to be eaten direct or used as a sweetening agent in food. We shall see later how a wine trade from the Mediterranean to central Europe can certainly be perceived from the sixth century B.C. onwards, with once again the use of the right equipment for its serving and consumption. A new, expensive, upper-class drink needed the equivalent of the modern decanter and glasses; or indeed the teapot and cups imported from China as a necessary accompaniment of the first tea-drinking in the West.

In the western Mediterranean imported Mycenaean pottery continues to show Aegean contacts in Sicily and the Lipari Islands up to late in the thirteenth century, and here, as in north Italy, vigorous schools of bronze-working existed.[66] In the Tyrol, elaborate deep-mining for copper, with timbered adits cut into the mountain-side, had taken the place of the less productive open-cast working, and perhaps this implies technical aid introduced from the Aegean.[67] In Sardinia the local copper resources were exploited and the metal probably exported, while from the second half of the second millennium the tower-like chieftains' castles or *nuraghi* developed as a peculiar architectural feature and have provincial counterparts in the *torri* of Corsica; later, Sardinia developed its series of bronze figures of men, women and animals, and schematised carved stone monuments were executed in Corsica.[68] (Figs. 89–90; Pls. XXI, XXII) Of Iberia and west France we know little at this time; the British Isles developed in comparative isolation except for the stimulus of the international bronze trade, effecting contacts between Britain and the north European world; Scandinavia again built up its own localised

---

XXII. (*a*) *Male bronze figure, Nuraghic culture, early first millennium* B.C., *from Sardinia.*

XXII. (*b*) *Bronze figure of seated woman and child, Nuraghic culture, early first millennium* B.C., *from Sardinia.* (Both photos. Edwin Smith)

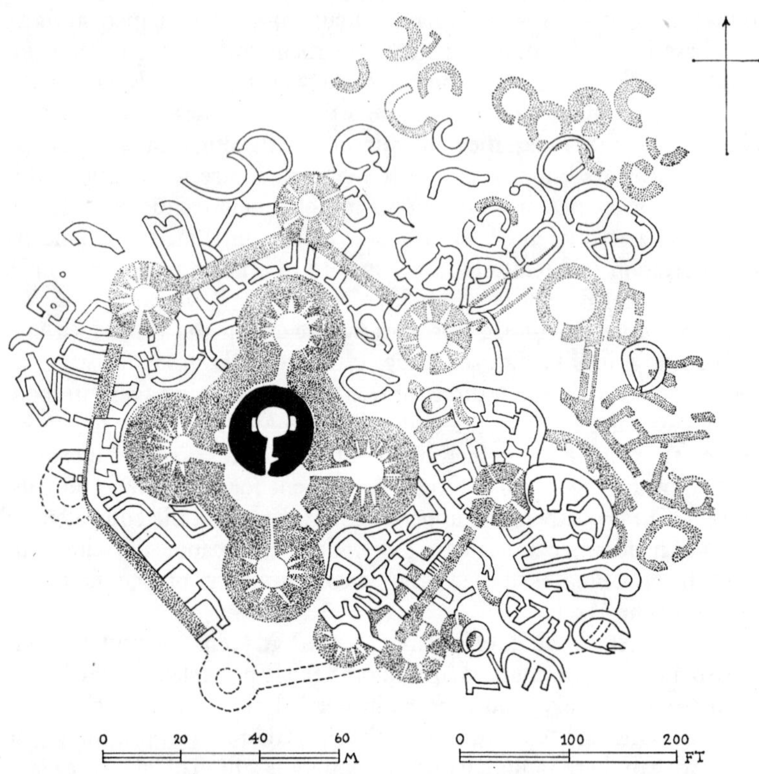

89. *Stone-built settlement of the Nuraghic culture; three periods from fifteenth century (black) to sixth century* B.C. *(outline), at Su Nuraxi, Barumini, Sardinia.*

traditions, now importing and working bronze in quantity, and to a high degree of excellence; this is the period of the well-known finds of men's and women's woollen garments in barrow-burials. (Pl. XXIII)

We have already touched on the evidence for prehistoric European clothing, and the garments in question are peculiarly interesting. Neither pins nor buttons were used, and the men's clothing comprised a simple wrap-around kilt, sometimes reaching from the armpits to the knees, with shoulder-straps, sometimes only from the waist, and in both instances with a leather belt. A long oval cloak was worn over this, and close-fitting round caps were also in use. The women wore a short-sleeved jerkin and a short corded skirt with a woven tasselled belt, and hair-nets and false hair were used in their elaborate coiffures. The curious standard pattern to which the jerkins had been cut shows clearly its derivation from skin originals, its shape and size being

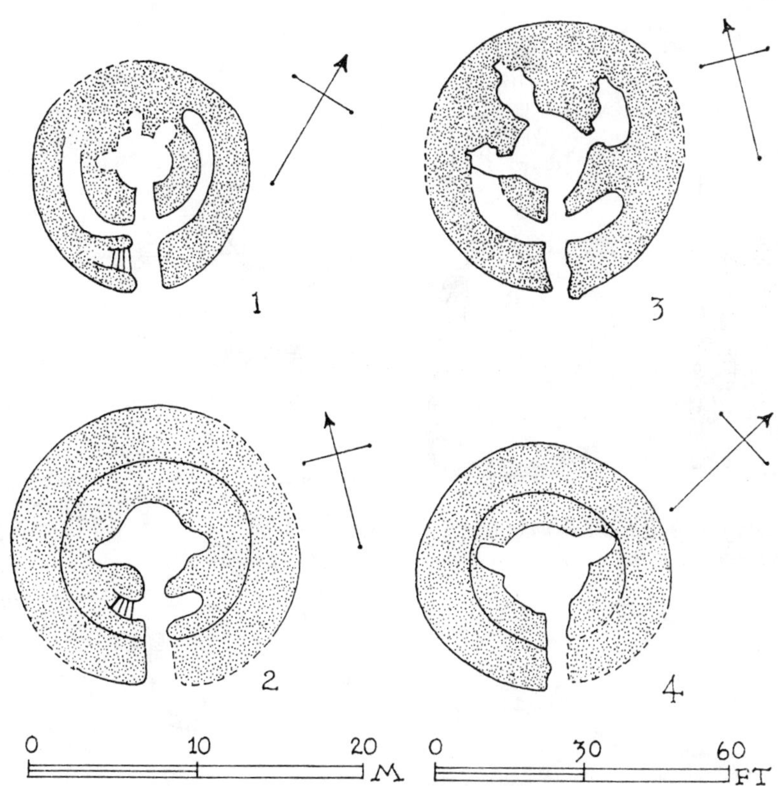

90. *Stone-built towers, second half of second millennium* B.C.: *1, 2,* nuraghi *at Muràrtu and Sa Còa Filigosa, Sardinia; 3, 4,* torri *at Foce and Balestra, Corsica.*

determined by those of a deer's half-hide.[69] North German graves of this time show us the women there were wearing caps and shoulder-capes of cloth or leather decorated with rows of little bronze studs or bosses, and a magnificent princely version of such a shoulder-cape in sheet gold was found in a man's grave in North Wales.[70] Some of the elaborate figurines of around the middle or second half of the second millennium B.C. in central Europe show schematised details of dress, such as on the well-known Kličevac figure from Jugoslavia, or the women in full bell-shaped skirts, with perhaps embroidered aprons over this, from the Cîrna cemetery in Rumania.[71] (Fig. 91)

We have a picture of prosperity and of increasing technological development, but also of improvements in the art of war. More and more barbarian Europe must have been aware of the rich civilisations

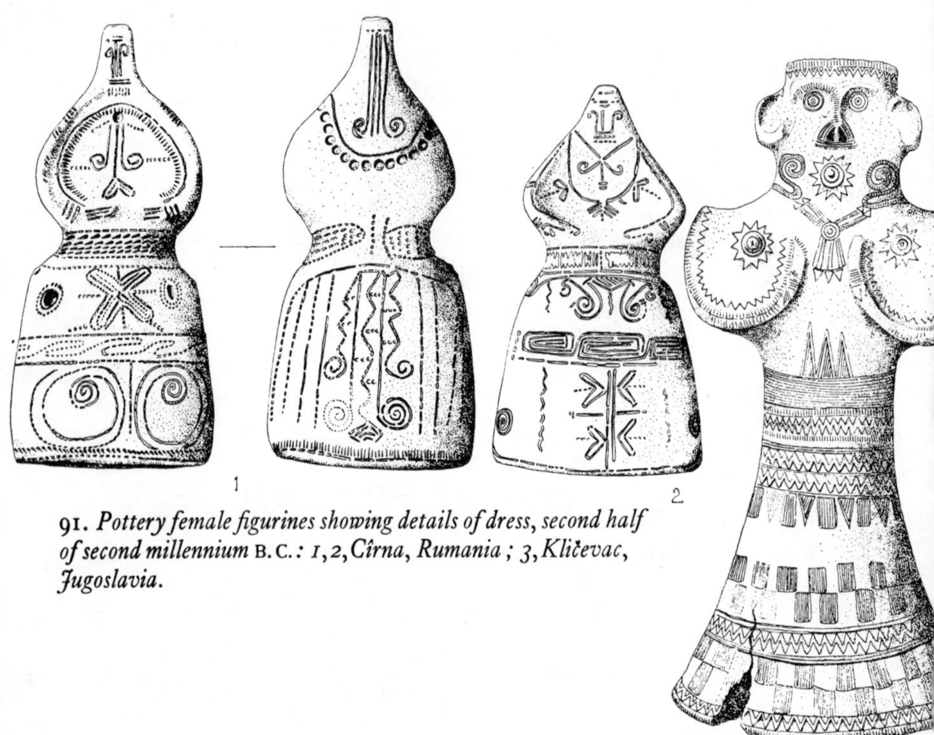

91. *Pottery female figurines showing details of dress, second half of second millennium* B.C.: *1, 2, Cîrna, Rumania; 3, Kličevac, Jugoslavia.*

of the Aegean and the Orient as the coming and going of trade increased. From trade to piracy was ever an easy step in antiquity, and perhaps many made no fine distinctions between the one and the other, but by the fourteenth century pirates were becoming a sufficiently serious menace in Aegean and Levantine waters for their raids to be mentioned in official quarters. The king of Alasiya (probably Cyprus) complains to Akhenaton that his territory is being raided about 1350 B.C. by barbarians called Luka; soon they are marauding in the Delta. A century or so later, the Luka are heard of again, in a more serious situation. About 1230 B.C. the pharaoh Merenptah of the XIX Dynasty met a concerted attack from the Western Desert of a mixed force of Libyans and what are described as the 'Sea People'—'all peoples of the north, coming from every country' Merenptah's scribes go on to say, naming among them the Luka, the Meshwesh, the Sheklesh, the Sherden, the Akawasha, and the Tursha. They were defeated, and the booty was said to include 9,000 swords. The identity of the Sea People has been much discussed, but they may be Lycians, Manyes, Sicilians,

Sardinians, Achaeans and Tyrrhenians; as we shall see, archaeology suggests that there were others among them; they were to come again, and in greater force.[72]

The crash came in the later twelfth century. In about 1170 B.C. Ramesses III had won a great sea-battle, and the commemorative inscription at Medinet Habu recorded the circumstances, with vivid low-relief scenes of the naval engagement: 'The foreign countries made a conspiracy in their islands. All at once the lands were removed, and scattered in the fray. No land could stand before their arms, from Hatti, Kode, Carchemish, Arzawa and Alasiya. . . . They were coming forward towards Egypt while the flame was prepared before them. . . . They laid their hands upon the lands as far as the circuit of the earth, their hearts confident and trusting: "Our plans will succeed." '[73] In the confederacy were Sheklesh and Sherden again, Peleset or Philistines, the Danuna from Cilicia, and the unknown Weshesh. Archaeology confirms and extends the historical record; Mycenaean power has fallen, with the burning of cities and palaces: the charcoal of burnt Pylos gave radiocarbon dates of *c.* 1180–1190 B.C.[74] The siege of Troy can hardly have been (did it ever take place?) at the Greek traditional date of 1183 B.C. but rather, as others have argued, in the general context of the Sea Raids, around 1240–30[75]; indeed a recent review of the Mycenaean pottery of the site has caused one scholar to suggest that it was Troy VI and not VIIa, that was Priam's city; barbarians using pottery of central or east European types squatted there in VIIb.[76]

The Hittite Empire from 1250 onwards, under Tudhaliyas IV and his successor Arnuwandas IV, was being attacked by its western neighbours in mainland Anatolia, and perhaps the King of Ahhiyawa, one of the trouble-makers, was an Achaean ruler. At all events the western threats developed, with the added menace of the people later known as Phrygians, now settling in Anatolia about the Sangarios river; legendary history brought them from Thrace, and, as we know from the excavations of the great tumuli at Gordion, of the eighth century B.C., they buried their royal dead in wooden mortuary houses under huge barrows in the manner of the Steppe, and sometimes their horses in like fashion. With the added force of the sea-raiders, the long story of Hittite power was brought to an end around 1200 B.C., almost simultaneously it would seem with that of Mycenae. We have already noted the development in central Europe from the fourteenth century onwards of the highly efficient slashing sword with flanged hilt-grip, and we can study its spread and adoption among the barbarians in the successive stages of its development. In the Aegean area, swords of this type, some imported and some copied, appear suddenly soon after

1250, the first time that the general European distribution comes so far to the south-east. Here we must have central and western European adventurers and mercenaries forming part of the raiding bands along with the Luka and the rest. If Tyrrhenians, Sardinians, and Sicilians did indeed take part in these raids, some may have joined in west and central Mediterranean waters with people from the islands in the midst of the sea; others again may have come through Thrace and Macedonia.

And so at the end of the second millennium we reach another period of crisis and change, curiously similar to that of just about a thousand years earlier. The middle phase of barbarian Europe is over, the phase too of the power of the Indo-European Hittites and Mycenaean Greeks. We move towards a temporary Dark Ages in the Aegean—or in other words the Aegean is for a time on a level of culture no higher than that of the rest of Europe. Then comes recovery and a wholly new beginning in Greece, and the development of Etruscan culture in Italy. Northwards, we are now in a Europe predominantly Celtic, and the rest of our story is largely centred in that world.

XXIII. (*facing page*) *Replica of woman's dress, in natural brown wool, second half of second millennium* B.C., *Egtved, Denmark.*
(Photo. Nationalmuseet, Copenhagen)

XXIV. *Bronze situla or bucket, with relief decoration, early fifth century* B.C., *from Vače, Jugoslavia.* (Photo. Narodni Musej, Ljubljana)

Notes

1. I have here taken a viewpoint which some might regard as too cautious, but cf. Ucko 1962 for the difficulties inherent in any interpretation of these figurines.
2. For Malta, Evans 1959; for the free-standing statue-menhirs, etc., Octobon 1931; carvings in Brittany, Péquart and Le Rouzic 1927; south French paintings in rock-shelters, Glory 1948; Marne tombs, etc., best illustrations in Pijoan 1953, Figs. 282-97; anthropomorphic 'idols' in Iberian chambered tombs, Leisner and Leisner 1943, 1951. Useful illustrations in Kühn 1952 and Crawford 1957, but uncritical texts.
3. Kjaerum 1955; Marseen 1960.
4. General account of 'henge monuments' (a jocular back-formation from 'Stonehenge' originated by T. D. Kendrick: Kendrick and Hawkes 1932, 83), in Atkinson *et al.* 1951. Cf. Piggott 1940, with Amerindian examples. Arminghall radiocarbon date of 2490±150 B.C. (BM-129, Barker and Mackey 1963); Stonehenge, Atkinson 1960.
5. Stone 1948; Atkinson 1955.
6. Postoloprty, Soudský 1953; Crestaulta, Burkart 1946; Drack 1959, Pl. 4, 11.
7. Tószeg, Piggott 1960; Csalog, Mozsolics *et al.* 1952; Banner *et al.* 1957; Monteoru, Piggott 1960 and personal information from the excavator, Professor Ion Nestor. Cf. also Powell 1963b.
8. Neustupný and Neustupný 1961, 99, Fig. 26; Hájek 1961.
9. Already foreshadowed by the early copper objects of east European derivation in the north (above p. 84) and demonstrated for the mid-second millennium B.C. by Hachmann 1957a; Lomborg 1960.
10. The amber routes were first demonstrated by de Navarro (1925); map in Clark 1952, Fig. 142; Childe 1957, Map IV and many other sources.
11. As originally pointed out to me by Mr Dennis Britton.
12. Hutchinson 1962, 161.
13. Valmin 1938; Dow 1960, 7.
14. Discussed by Mellaart (1959). The Dimini plan has often been reproduced (e.g. Wace and Thompson 1912, Fig. 38; Childe 1957, Fig. 33) but it does not seem to have been pointed out that the arrangements of the concentric walls and their gateways are in places mutually contradictory, and we must be dealing with a site with several periods of fortification, not a single unit. Childe has indeed suggested that it is possible that the fortifications and megara at both Dimini and Sesklo are not earlier than Middle Helladic (1957, 63).
15. Plan of Korakou house conveniently in Wace and Stubbings 1962, Fig. 9; Lerna, Caskey 1955, 1957.

16. Karanovo, Georgiev 1961; Aichbühl, Clark 1952, 147; Childe 1949b. Cf. also Vučedol (Schmidt 1945).
17. Page 1959a, 54.
18. The question as to whether the Shaft-Grave dynasties represent intrusive elements has been much discussed, and opinion seems in general favourable to the view. Miss Lorimer after cautious evaluation of the evidence then available (before the discovery of Grave Circle B) felt that 'the advent of a new and enterprising element seems necessary' (1950, 21), and Wace found it difficult to accept the novel features of Shaft-Grave archaeology 'without some fresh stimulus provided by the influx of a further wave of people' (Wace and Stubbings 1962, 348). Stubbings, too, felt that 'there is a case for inferring the arrival in Greece at this time of new rulers from abroad' (in Hayes *et al.* 1962, 74) and has since dealt with the question at some length (Stubbings 1963).
19. Hardly 'the earliest examples of monumental sculpture in Europe' (Lorimer 1950, 17) in view of the statue-menhirs already referred to (p. 62), unless these are all to be dated later than the Shaft-Graves!
20. As pointed out to me by Miss N. K. Sandars.
21. Cf. Piggott 1962c, 115.
22. Sandars 1961.
23. Cf. Hawkes on 'Mycenae as the seat of an essentially European culture' (1940, 351) and evidence of contacts given on p. 134; it was Sir Arthur Evans who originally pointed out the north-easterly influences implicit in the red deer rhyton, the animal-headed and antler shaped pins, and the double spiral gold wire ornaments (A. Evans 1929, 43); cf. here too Piggott 1948a.
24. Forssander 1936; Childe 1957, 127-35 (general); Junghans *et al.* 1960, 43-48 (metallurgy); Neustupný and Neustupný 1961, 87-108 (Czechoslovakia); von Brunn 1959 (Saxo-Thuringia); Billig 1958 (Saxony).
25. Cf. Uenze 1938, von Brunn 1959. Since Ó Ríordáin's pioneer study (1937) it has usually been thought that the halberd was a metal type invented in Ireland and traded thence to the European continent, but within the framework of more recent knowledge it is becoming increasingly probable that this sequence must be reversed, and the halberd seen as of central European origin, (or possibly north Italian; cf. Coghlan and Case 1957) highly developed in Saxo-Thuringia and spreading widely to, e.g. Ireland and Iberia, in the latter case forming one of the central European elements in the Argar culture (J. D. Evans 1958, 65; von Brunn 1959, 25-29).
26. Childe 1958, 172.
27. I use 'Minoan' here to emphasise the elements in Mycenaean culture not shared with other contemporary societies in Europe (e.g. conditional literacy, complex bureaucracy, palace-centred social units, etc.); cf. Finley

1956 for a full discussion; 'the world of Odysseus was not that of the seventh century B.C., neither was it the Mycenaean age five or six or seven hundred years earlier.'

28. Carpenter 1958, 17.
29. Cf. note 8 above.
30. Argar Culture, Childe, 1957, 282-6; J. D. Evans 1958, 64-70; Junghans *et al.* 1960, 50; Breton Tumulus-Graves, Piggott 1938, 64-69, 99; Giot *et al.* 1960, Chapter VIII; the radiocarbon date of the Kervingar tumulus, of the second series, is *c.* 1600 (Vogel and Waterbolk 1963, 187) and dates for a later phase (from the Kervellerin tumulus) are *c.* 1285 and *c.* 1385 B.C. (Giot 1962). Wessex culture, Piggott 1938; ApSimon 1954; Terremare, Säflund 1939, Childe 1957, 246-51; East Europe and Scandinavia, Forssander 1936; Hachmann 1957a; Lomborg 1960.
31. Childe 1957, 200; Behn 1962, Pl. 56.
32. Stukeley 1740, 43.
33. Perşinari, Piggott 1960; Borodino, Gimbutas 1956b.
34. Gimbutas 1961b.
35. Hungarian evidence in Mozsolics 1954, 1960; Monteoru (Rumania), unpublished but cf. Piggott 1960 for summary of sequence.
36. Trialeti, Kuftin 1941; Minns 1943; Schaeffer 1943, 1944, 1948, Figs. 286-92; Lchashen, Lake Sevan, Mnatsakanian 1957, 1960a,b (double-spiral gold beads as in Shaft-Graves, etc.); restored wagons and chariots from Trialeti and Lchashen, Mnatsakanian 1960a, Rumyantsev 1961. Cf. too the Helenendorf tomb in Azerbaijan (Hummel 1933).
37. Piggott 1962c; Telepinus text in Pritchard 1955, 126-8.
38. Gimbutas 1961b and in Munro Lecture, University of Edinburgh, October 1959.
39. For examples of Caucasian (Koban) metalwork, second half of second millennium B.C. and later, Schaeffer 1948, Figs. 300-3; Hančar 1932, 1934; Phillips 1961; Luristan, Frankfort 1954, 207-13; Godard 1931; Luristan, Amlash, etc., Ghirshman 1961. From the Alaca Hüyük Royal tombs one can follow the artistic tradition through rather later Anatolian metalwork as at Amasya, Horoz Tepe and Hasan Oglan (Akurgal and Hirmer 1962, Pls. 12, 27, VIII) and in the treatment of animals of the remarkable low-relief stone carvings of the second half of the second millennium B.C. from the city walls of Alaca Hüyük (*ibid.* 117; Pls. 94-96). Cf. A. Evans 1929, 43 for the animal style as represented in the Shaft-Graves, Piggott 1948a for animal-headed pins in Eurasia, and Mnatsakanian 1960a, 149-50 for animals of twelfth to thirteenth century B.C. from Lchashen. Minns (1913, 1942) derived Scythian art almost exclusively from that of the 'Northern Nomads', ultimately of Mesolithic and sub-Mesolithic origins, but Frankfort (1954, 212) pointed out the likely Luristan connections, and Rice

(1957, 150) and Phillips (1961) would see Hittite influences behind this again. It is interesting that representations of stags in Kurgan 3 at Kostromskaya were considered by the excavator to date the grave as early Scythian, but they have since been compared with the Alaca Hüyük carvings and assigned to the second millennium B.C. (Yessen 1950).

40. Dow 1960, 13 ff.
41. Full documentation in Taylour 1958.
42. Wessex culture and Bush Barrow, Piggott 1938; Stone 1958, 94-120; Powell 1961, 336; the mounts from Grave Iota are unpublished, in the Nat. Museum, Athens; Nienhagen cup, Ebert 1924, Pl. 53a; Beitzsch and other helmets, Hencken 1952; Fritzdorf cup, von Uslar 1955; Rillaton and other amber and shale cups, Stone 1958, frontispiece and Pls. 51-53; Powell 1961, 334-5.
43. The existence and significance of these connections was first pointed out by Childe (1927); objects with Mycenaean-derived ornament, Werner 1952; Hachmann 1957a; general problems, Marinatos 1962; faience and glass beads, Stone and Thomas 1956.
44. Amber and space-plate necklaces, Childe 1948b; Hachmann 1957b; Sandars 1959.
45. Double axes, Piggott 1953; Deshayes 1960, Chapter X; Pelynt, Childe 1951, Benton 1962; Sandars 1963; Stonehenge, Atkinson 1960a; gold earrings, Hawkes 1961.
46. The quotations are from Onians 1954, 3-5.
47. For these and other aspects of early chariotry, Powell 1963.
48. In the Sulgi hymn already referred to above, p. 141.
49. Powell 1963; Hayes 1962a, 18; 1962b, 24; Drioton and Vandier 1952, 300. Buhen horse, Emery 1959, and cf. the later (fifteenth century) horse-burial at Thebes, Chard 1937.
50. *Iliad* IV, 485-7; *Rig-Veda* VII, 32, 20 (cf. Piggott 1950a, 277). I am grateful to Professor A. J. Beattie and Dr A. K. Warder for the translations here given.
51. Cf. the illustrations in Mnatsakanian 1960, Fig 6; Rumyantsev 1961, Fig. 3 (Lake Sevan); Rudenko 1953, Fig. 146 (Pazyryk). The modern ethnography of the single-felloe wheel is briefly discussed in Berg 1935, 121.
52. Swedish rock engravings: Althin 1945 and especially those at Frännarp, Pls. 70-73, and Kivik, Pl. 77, for which also cf. Grinsell 1942. Of the model wheeled vehicles, the famous Trundholm horse-drawn sun-disc (e.g. Powell 1961, 338) is usually assigned to Montelius II, and so perhaps fourteenth century B.C.; the four-wheeled 'cauldrons' (Childe 1949c) are equated with Reinecke Bronze D, dated by Müller-Karpe (1959, 113) to the thirteenth century B.C.; cf. also Forrer 1932.
53. Marathon tomb, Vanderpool 1959; Old Paphos, Karageorghis, 1963a;

Salamis, *ibid* 1962; 1963b. Cf. the two bronze horse-bits from a 'late Mycenaean' tomb at Miletus; Sandars 1963, 136.

54. See below, p. 171, for these situlae.

55. Early Aegean shipping, Barnett 1958; best illustrations of Scandinavian rock-engravings, Althin 1945 (south Sweden); Fett and Fett 1941 (south-west Norway); Marstrander 1963; ship on sword-blade, Mathiassen 1957; Powell 1961, 339; Caergwrle bowl, Piggott and Daniel 1951, nos, 28-29; Corcoran 1961; shields, Coles 1962.

56. This is of necessity a very abbreviated summary of a complex situation. The development of the 'Tumulus Bronze Age' (equivalent to Reinecke's Bronze B and C phases; cf. Holste 1953a; Torbrügge 1959b; Feustel 1958) has in the past usually been attributed to new elements, notably the rite of burial under a tumulus, intruding into the earlier A traditions. I share the views of Dr Gimbutas, that tumulus-burial was already present in Bronze A (as recent Czechoslovakian evidence stresses) and that the B phase is an internal development in cultural traditions. The intrusive bronzes associated with destruction-levels in the Hungarian 'tells', of central European types, are discussed by Mozsolics (1958) but perhaps dated too late. The earlier cremation-cemeteries have been frequently discussed (e.g. in Childe 1948, 1950, suggesting Near Eastern origins for the cremation-rite, not now usually accepted). For Kisapostag, Mozsolics 1942; Cîrna, Dumitrescu 1961. General review of Urnfield situation in Smith 1957; Powell 1963b, and cf. Sandars 1957; chronology in Müller-Karpe 1959.

57. For the earlier development of sword-types, cf. Sprockhoff 1934; Holste 1953b; Müller-Karpe 1961. The flange-hilted swords have been studied in a series of papers by Cowen 1951, 1952, 1955, 1966; for the Aegean swords, Catling 1956, 1961, 1964, in the second paper accepting the central European origin as set out by Cowen. Miss Sandars notes spear-heads of continental European types in the Aegean at this time, and suggests mercenaries armed with swords and spears (Sandars 1963, 142-3).

58. Elp, Waterbolk 1961b; Wasserburg, Reinerth 1929 (plan also in Clark 1952, 157; Childe 1950, 201); Perleberg, Schubart 1958, 215; wall-plaster, Müller 1959.

59. Lough Gur, ÒRíordáin 1954; Gwithian, Thomas 1958; Megaw *et al.* 1961; Thorny Down, Stone 1941; Itford Hill, Burstow and Holleyman 1957. These and similar sites in Wessex and Sussex have in the past been assigned in part to a 'Deverel-Rimbury Culture' and classified as Late Bronze Age. They must now be dated to around the eleventh century B.C., in Hawkes's Middle Bronze Age 2, by general considerations of the Bronze types in their continental relationship, as shown by M. Smith (1959), and (for Gwithian), an imported Urnfield-type pin.

60. Gwithian, Megaw *et al.* 1961; ploughs and ards, Glob 1951.

61. General discussion in Hatt 1949; Megaw *et al.* 1961; Pätzold 1960; van der Poel 1961; other sites in Schubart 1958, Fig. 36; van Giffen 1962. Pätzold and van Giffen have regarded the ploughmarks under barrows as 'ritual', but a more probable explanation is simply that the burial-mound was made on arable land and thenceforward protected the old land-surface from erosion or solution.
62. Discussed in Glob 1951.
63. There has been much discussion on body-armour in the later Bronze Age of barbarian Europe, *vis-à-vis* that of the Aegean world. Not all authorities accept the dating of the Beitzsch helmet to a position roughly contemporary with that from the Knossos Warrior Grave, but Mycenaean helmet-forms (including later examples, such as that from Enkomi Tomb 18, of the late thirteenth century B.C., with a flange-hilted sword: Schaeffer 1952, 341; Catling 1956, 115), could well have initiated the central and eastern European 'Bell Helmet' group to which it typologically belongs (cf. von Merhart 1941, Map 2 for distribution). The Čaka corselet (Točik and Poulík 1960) is unique, and of early Urnfield date; it is, however, significantly similar in basic construction to the *thorax* of the Mycenaean form, as known from the Dendra find (Hood 1961; Vanderpool 1963). The main work on the barbarian European material has been by von Merhart (1941, 1942, 1954, 1956, 1957), and recent summaries have been given by Müller-Karpe (1962a,b) and Kimmig (1964b). In general the likelihood is that we should see an Aegean or Greek derivation for the body-armour in continental Europe, as against the suggestions previously put forward by von Merhart and others that barbarian Europe had priority. The situation may well have been a complex one, for one has always to reckon with mercenaries and deserters in such contexts. And behind the Aegean traditions may again lie Oriental prototypes, such as are perceptible later (p. 212).
64. Here again von Merhart's studies (1952 on bronze vessels, and as above) are fundamental; cf. too Hawkes and Smith 1957; Childe 1949c; Hencken 1958.
65. Piggott 1959a.
66. Taylour 1958; Brea 1957a; Brea and Cavalier 1960, Pt. II; Müller-Karpe 1959.
67. Pittioni 1951; the possible Aegean connections were suggested by Childe (1948, 189).
68. Sardinia, Zervos 1954 (good illustrations); Lilliu 1955, 1959; there is a radiocarbon date of 1470±200 B.C. from the Barumini nuraghe (Tauber 1960, no. K-151: not 1270±200 as in Lilliu 1959); Guido 1963. Corsican sites in Grosjean 1955, 1956, 1958, 1961; radiocarbon dates of *c.* 2300 and 1900 B.C. from the *torri* of Tappa, but *c.* 1190 B.C. from Filitosa (Coursaget *et al.* 1961)!

69. Broholm and Hald 1940; Hald 1950.
70. For north German examples, Piesker 1958, Figs. 4, 5, Pl. 66; Schubart 1958, Fig. 32. Mold (Flintshire) shoulder-cape, Powell 1953.
71. Kličevac has often been illustrated; cf. Behn 1962, Pl. 61; Cîrna in Dumitrescu 1961.
72. The Sea Peoples have attracted a large literature: cf. Drioton and Vandier 1952, 430–9. Among the more recent and significant studies are Wainwright 1939, 1959; Page 1959a; especially on 'Achean' identification (p. 21); Schaeffer 1952, 350–69 discusses Cyprus in this context; Acheans, Gurney 1952, 46–58; Huxley 1960; Mycenaean collapse, Desborough and Hammond 1962; Desborough 1964. Claims have been made for the introduction of a number of central European metal types (other than the swords and spearheads mentioned above) in the context of the Sea Peoples, e.g. Milojčić 1948, 1955b. Some flange-hilted knives of the 'Peschiera' group certainly appear in the two areas (cf. Peroni 1956 for the types), but cf. Sandars 1955 on the Aegean origin of other (single edged) knives and in general Kimmig 1964b.
73. Medinet Habu text from Pritchard 1955, 262.
74. Kohler and Ralph 1961.
75. Cf. Page 1959a,b; Blegen 1961.
76. Nylander 1963.

5

New Techniques and Peoples

IN the last chapter I somewhat anticipated the strict chronological course of events by describing the circumstances of the fall of Mycenaean and Hittite power around 1200 B.C. in order to indicate the part played in these events by barbarian Europe beyond the Alps. For Europe beyond the Aegean the disruption of the ancient seats of power seems long to have been remembered as the beginning of an epoch. Dim folk-memories rumbled down the centuries, muddled now with the legends of Troy, and the New Peoples of the first millennium B.C. liked to date their beginnings to the movements of heroes after the Trojan War. It was not only the Romans; in the first century B.C. the Celtic peoples are recorded as thinking themselves of like origin,[1] and while this might have been merely a quest for respectable ancestors, and a keeping-up with the Aeneases, it could be something more. And even the medieval stories about Trojan, Scythian, or Thracian origins for Britons, Irish, and Picts may be not only learned inventions based on Homer, Virgil, Dictys Cretensis, Dares Phrygius and the rest, but might once again in part strike back to indigenous oral tradition, and a faint memory of a time when peoples were on the move, especially from east to west.[2]

In the western Mediterranean, the Mycenaean contacts established in the sixteenth century continued into the thirteenth and twelfth in Sicily,[3] and then Sub-Mycenaean and even Cypriot and Levantine brooch types appear, and indeed by the eighth or seventh century derivatives of the latter get as far west as France and Spain.[4] The legend of Ausonius seems archaeologically supported by evidence of emigrants from south Italy into the Lipari Island about 1250-1150, after a destruction-level,[5] and in Italy itself about the same time or a little later newcomers with the Urnfield cremation-rite appear. By the tenth century the earliest Rome, the settlement on the Alban Hills, was founded[6]; some archaeologists have turned to the eastern Mediterranean for the motivating force behind this new colonisation,[7] with the anxious wraith of Virgil looking over their shoulder.

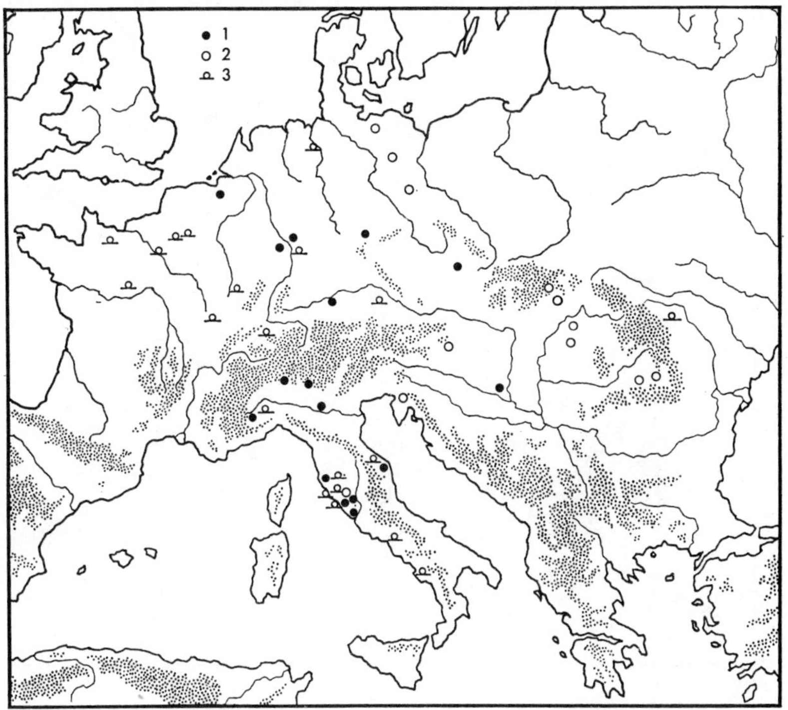

92. *Distribution of Urnfield culture bronze helmets, twelfth-eighth century* B.C.: *1,Cap-helmets; 2,Bell-helmets; 3,Crest-helmets.*

The development of central European beaten metalwork, which as we saw in the last chapter seems associated with an early wine-trade, is certainly to be connected with Aegean contacts in late Mycenaean times, and includes technical tricks, like lathe-working of bowls, not to be generally employed until relatively late in classical times.[8] Central Europe was in fact ahead of the Mediterranean world at this time in bronze-working; most of what were once thought to be the inventions of north Italian, pre-Etruscan ateliers, are now seen to be copies of prototypes imported or introduced to Italy from north of the Alps, laying the foundations of the brilliant schools of metallurgy round the head of the Adriatic, in which as we shall see so much of east and west combined. Bronze helmets, as we have seen, may have been manufactured in central Europe by the fourteenth century B.C. under Mycenaean influence, and certainly in Urnfield times central European types (crested, cap and bell-helmets) are recognisable, reaching Italy from

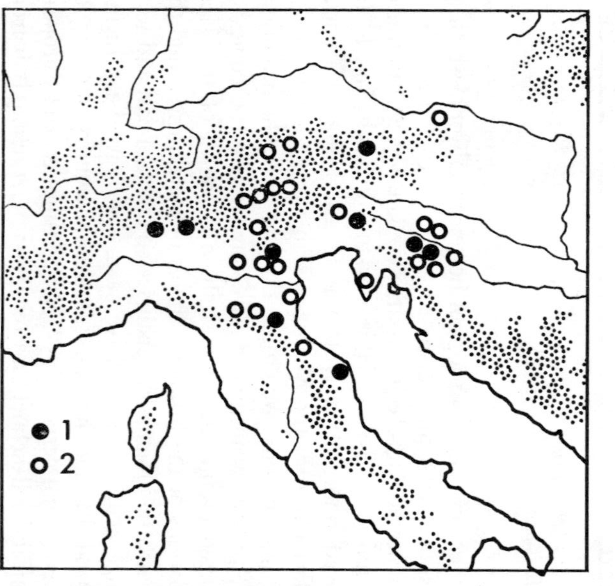

93. *Distribution of decorated bronze-work in the 'Situla' style, sixth–fifth century* B.C.: 1, *earlier*; 2, *later examples.*

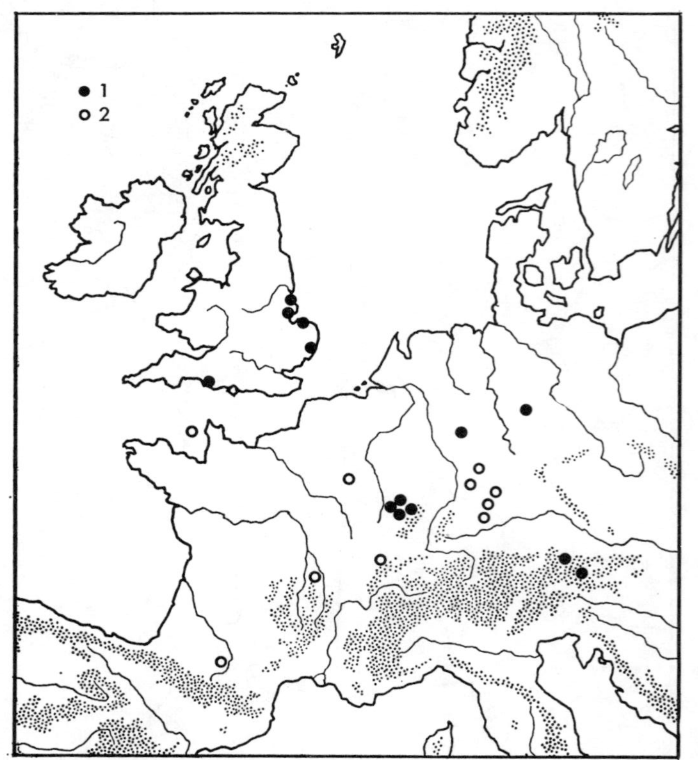

94. *Distribution of sites of Hallstatt salt production, seventh–fifth century* B.C.: 1, *certain*; 2, *probable sites.*

the ninth century B.C.[9] (Fig. 92) The situlae, which I suggested may have been wine-buckets, are again of central European origin, the earlier examples (eighth century B.C.) all coming from that region, whence they were traded and locally copied as far to the north-west as the British Isles, where insular versions were made from early in the seventh century B.C. [10] Similarly, situlae of later types appear in central Italy in Etruscan tombs (as at Vetulonia about 650 B.C.) and in the east Hallstatt world round the head of the Adriatic. Here, from the beginning of the sixth century,[11] a remarkable 'situla art' grew up (Fig. 93), on the buckets and on other contemporary metalwork, with an animal style owing much to Greek orientalising modes of the late Proto-Corinthian phase, but with an even stronger Oriental and non-classical feeling. The situlae have zonal ornament in the manner of some Attic painted wares of the early sixth century, the two main friezes usually depicting the Arts of Peace and of War, again in a markedly oriental, perhaps Phoenician, manner.[12] The lions on the situlae derive from Proto-Corinthian models which have ancestors among those of the Neo-Hittite world,[13] and we shall see how Asia Minor, Syria, and the far-off kingdom of Urartu round Lake Van, contributed to the toreutic arts of prehistoric Europe. (Pl. XXIV)

Meanwhile central Europe, now reasonably enough to be considered an early Celtic world, was building up its economic position on a basis of resources not only of metal, but of that essential commodity, salt. [14] We have already noted the development of actual deep mining for copper in the eastern Alps, and here too salt was soon to be mined as well. Its exploitation goes back to at least the second millennium B.C., and at places where Indo-European names (usually thought Illyrian) survive to denote its existence—Halle in Thuringia, Hallein, and most famous of all, Hallstatt in Austria. (Fig 94.)

By the seventh-fifth centuries there are at least fifteen certain sites of salt-mining in Europe, and a dozen more probably go back to that time, and one must reckon from now on not only with a trade in salt itself, but with the food products made possible by its use, notably salt fish, pork, bacon and ham, for which after all Gaul came to have a high reputation in the Roman world.[15] And, curiously enough, other food products may have been made available in quantities worthy of trade in unexpected ways. The development of the European bronze industry from the second millennium onwards involved the increasing use of the cire-perdue or lost wax process of casting, in which a wax model is melted out from a mould to be replaced by bronze. The commercial need for wax would lead first to increased gathering of wild honey, and then to bee-keeping, and with the production of wax

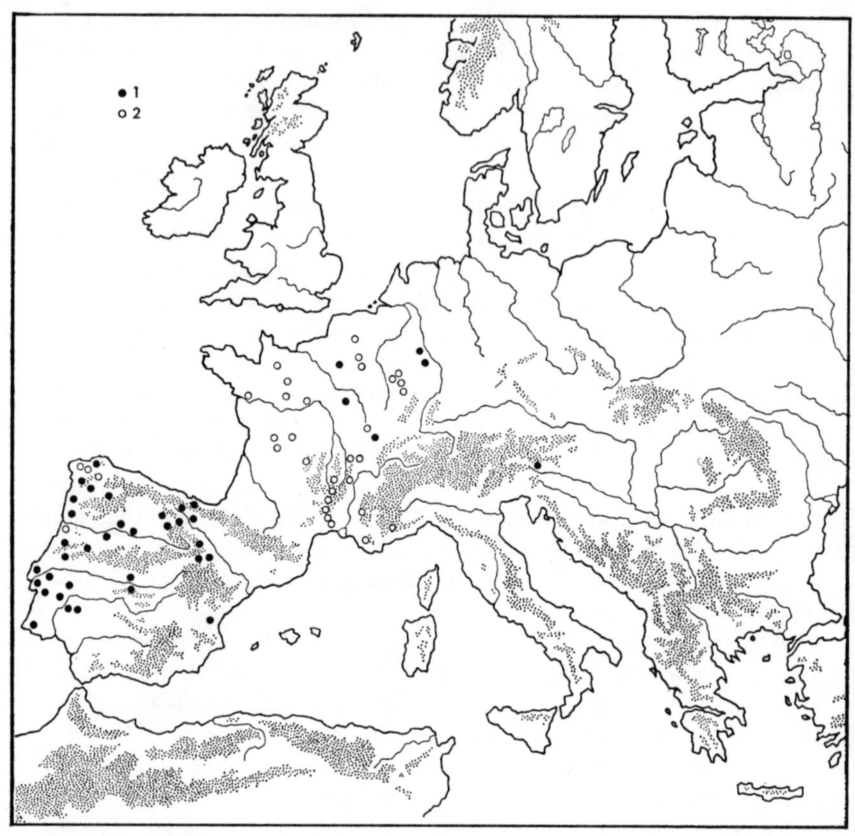

95. *Distribution of Celtic place-names in* -briga*: 1, Classical; 2, post-Classical source.*

would go that of honey on an accelerated scale; so too, one hopes, the brewing of mead.[16] Nor, with the development of higher civilisations in the Mediterranean world, must we forget slaves as an object of trade; slavery is as much a part of the history of civilisation as is warfare.

Expansion of peoples from the original centres of the so-called Urnfield culture soon began taking place. Southwards and eastwards we see, by the eighth and seventh centuries B.C., new types of tools, weapons and ornaments, basically central European, in Italy, the Balkans, and the Aegean; pins for dress-fastening are now being replaced by brooches, still worn in pairs, and those of spiral-wound bronze wire were particularly popular.[17] A few objects of Urnfield origin even reached south Russia—a bronze cup, and a central European or Italic

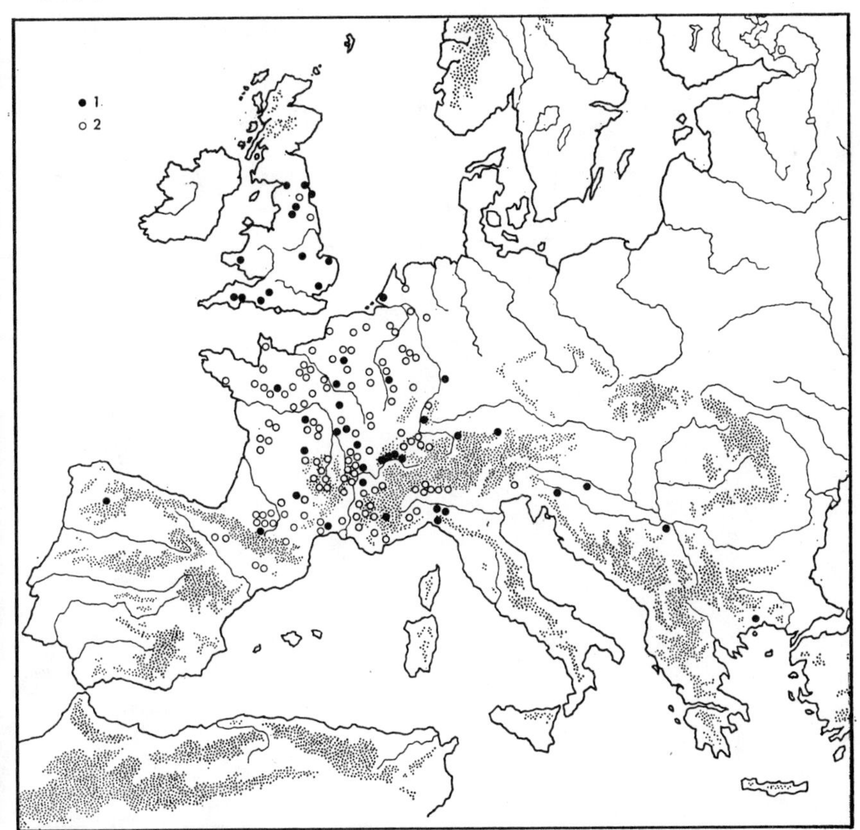

96. *Distribution of Celtic place-names in* -dunum*: 1, Classical; 2, post-Classical source.*

bronze helmet.[18] Helmets, as we saw, had perhaps been made in central Europe ever since the days of Beitzsch in the fifteenth century and certainly were highly developed in Urnfield times. Westwards, France was naturally enough settled first in the east, in the Yonne and the Marne; later there was movement into the Loire region. By 750 or so there is Urnfield colonisation in the south of France,[19] and thence versions of the culture spread naturally enough into Iberia, taking with them, so it seems, the first Celtic to be spoken so far west. A study of three Celtic place-name types—those ending in *-dunum*, *-magus* and *-briga*—has shown that whereas all are common in Gaul (and *-dunum* and *-magus* names are found in Britain as well) *-briga* names alone reach Iberia and so appear to represent an early linguistic stage, before

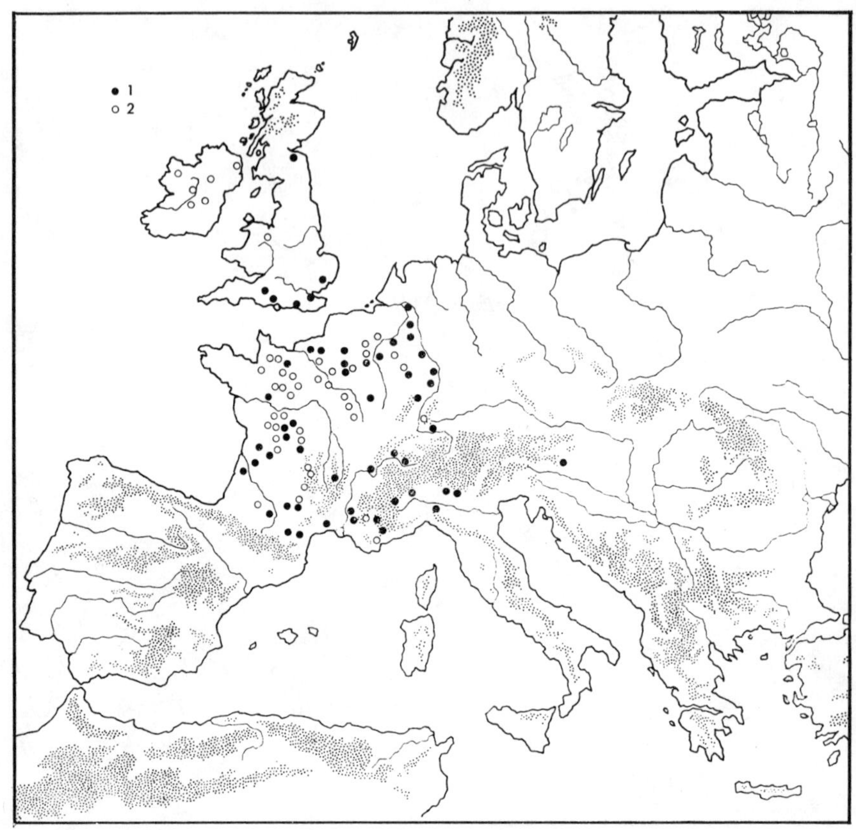

97. *Distribution of Celtic place-names in* -magus *: 1, Classical; 2, post-Classical source.*

contacts with the British Isles, where indeed direct Urnfield influence is not perceptible in archaeological terms.[20] And from the Urnfield cultures we turn to those of Hallstatt. (Figs. 79; 95–97)

In conventional archaeological phraseology—in other words, in terms of the technological-evolutionary model of the past—I should by now have talked about leaving the Late Bronze Age and beginning the Early Iron Age. I have deliberately not yet discussed the question of the adoption of iron for edge-tools in prehistoric Europe, because by and large the continuity in culture during the first millennium B.C. seems to me more important than a division wholly based on a change in metal technology; and where the cultural pattern is in fact modified or changed, the causes appear to be not so much technological but, so far as we may infer, social, and based partly on internal evolution and partly on new ideas or peoples entering the early Celtic world from outside. 'It is not the gradual adoption of iron as the basic cultural material which makes the Hallstatt period the great historical phenomenon it really is . . . the period . . . is the reflection of the dethroned Mycenaean civilisation in new races only now started on the way towards "historization".'[21]

But perhaps we are wrong in using the word 'new'; it is really an old situation, recurring in barbarian central Europe from the eighth century B.C. onwards, that of renewed contact with the regions north of the Black Sea. We must return to the south Russian Steppes and again follow events in this fascinating and formative area of eastern Europe. In my fourth chapter I have said something about the earlier copper- and bronze-using peoples of the second millennium of this area, and especially those of the so-called Timber-Grave culture, mainly centred in the Lower Volga, who appear to be the prehistoric ancestors of the historic Scythians. South-westwards of this cultural area, we can identify another, with close similarities to that of the Timber-Graves (including burial in mortuary houses under barrows) forming a north Pontic culture. Now by the late eighth century, Assyrian records speak of 'a distant people' located west and north of the Euphrates and Lake Urmia, called the Gimmerai; Herodotus relates how the people known to the Greeks as the Kymmerioi had been driven out from their homeland north of the Caucasus, across those mountains, and into what we would now recognise as Phrygian and Urartian territory. It has therefore been suggested that our north Pontic culture represents the Cimmerians before the Scythian aggression of the eighth century B.C. or earlier.[22] The Urartians, to the borders of whose territory the Cimmerians were driven, will concern us again in this chapter in connection with their metal-working skill; their kingdom had been established since the ninth century at least, and was to be destroyed by the Medes in 585 B.C. Westwards in Anatolia were the Phrygians, who had by now founded a state on the débris of the Hittite Empire; the Cimmerian invasions (for another followed in the early seventh century) deprived them of their eastern possessions and made way for the eventual take-over of power by the Lydians. We may recall that the Phrygians themselves had entered Anatolia from the north, probably through Thrace, and buried their royal dead in timber mortuary-houses under barrows in the steppe tradition.[23]

We will shortly return to the contacts between the north Pontic area and central Europe before the expulsion of the Cimmerians by the Scyths, but we should first consider the appearance of these latter masterful people as a portent in east Europe and beyond. The Timber-Grave culture, centred as we have seen on the Lower Volga, has every reason to be regarded as ancestral to that of the Scythians.[24] The use of the timber mortuary-house beneath a barrow is of course a funerary practice later to be known in magnificent form in the Scythian world; so too is the custom of sacrificing horses and burying them with their harness within or adjacent to the tomb chamber: archaeology and Herodotus combine to demonstrate this to us in exciting detail.[25] Historically the Scyths are known as speakers of an Indo-European language and, as we have seen, from at least the eighth century B.C. they followed their Cimmerian onslaught by establishing themselves in what had been Urartian territory, allying themselves with the Assyrians and even raiding into Egypt in 611 B.C.[26] Westwards they moved into the Carpathians, forming local groups of Scythian culture in Transylvania and on the Hungarian plain, and were pursued by Darius about 512 B.C. As we shall see later, there is evidence for Scythian trade and even raiding into north-eastern and western Europe.

But the Scythians have come down in history not merely as a barbarian tribe of the Eurasiatic Steppe-land, but as craftsmen working in a distinctive and moving style of fantastic animal art. Until comparatively recently known almost wholly from metalwork, Scythian art has now been revealed to us in perishable substances such as textiles and felt, wood and leather, preserved in the permafrost conditions of the wooden-chambered cairns of the Altai Mountains.[27] Here we see Scythian art at its height, and we naturally look for its origins. In part, these must lie, as has long been thought, in the surviving traditions of an Eurasiatic animal art among the final hunting and fishing peoples of the northern forest zone, an ultimate relic from Late Glacial times.[28] In part, too, there are influences, at least in the later Scythian phases, from Oriental, including Chinese, sources. But less appreciated is another probable contribution, which may in fact be of great importance. We saw in the last chapter that at the end of the third millennium B.C. a vigorous animal art was represented in metalwork on both sides of the Black Sea, as at Maikop on the north and Alaca Hüyük on the south. We saw too that some Hittite stone sculpture suggests its continuance in Anatolia well into the second millennium, when too a

---

XXV. (*a*) *Wooden cheek-piece of horse-bit, carved in the form of a deer, East Scythian, fourth-third century* B.C., *from Barrow 1, Pazyryk, Altai Mountains.*
XXV. (*b*) *Bridle ornament of carved wood and felt in the form of a fabulous bird, fourth-third century* B.C., *from Barrow 1, Pazyryk, Altai Mountains.*
(Both photos, Hermitage, Leningrad)

XXV (*caption on facing page*)

a

b

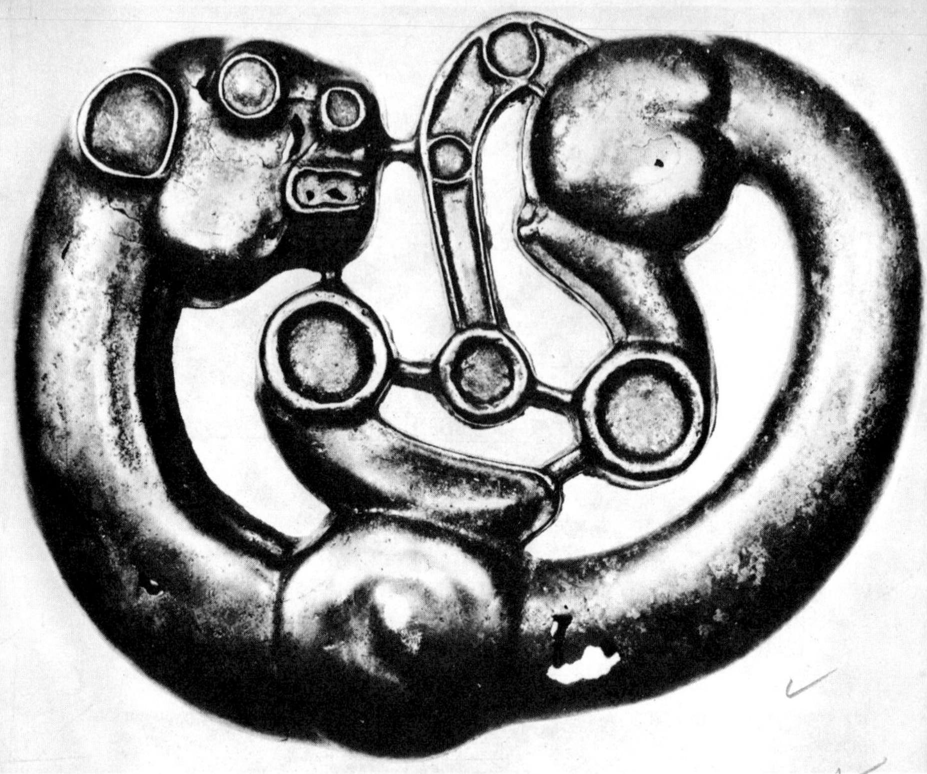

splendid animal style was being developed in the Caucasus and northern Persia by workers in bronze and gold. The Timber-Grave culture lay immediately to the north of the Caucasus, and by the eighth century, as we saw, pushed across the mountains in its now historically Scythian form. The incorporation of the Caucasian metal-working province into that of the Scyths would provide a likely contributory stimulus to the final emergence of Scythian art as we know it. (Pls. XXV; XXVIa)

Let us return now to central Europe and the probably Cimmerian north Pontic peoples. From the eighth century B.C. onwards we begin to perceive, from the Hungarian plain to the Swiss Lakes, Belgium, the south of France, and even Britain and Scandinavia, the appearance of a whole group of novel metal types associated with the bridle-bits and harness of horses. The bronze bits are perhaps the most characteristic, with cheek-pieces or side-bars developed from the basic pattern of those made in antler by the 'tell' peoples of east Europe in the second half of the second millennium; in east Europe they are pre-Scythian.[29] Their distribution stretches eastward to the Caucasus, and it has recently been pointed out that Assyrian horse-bits, constantly depicted on their monumental reliefs, change, late in the eighth century, into versions of this same type, based on a curved antler tine. Actual bits have been found at Deve Hüyük near Carchemish on the Euphrates and in the B Cemetery of Tepe Sialk near Kashan in Persia; finally, by about 500 B.C., we see the type depicted on the reliefs at Persepolis.[30] This oriental phenomenon has been connected with the Cimmerians, and independently the European bits have been attributed to a similar context. The halves of the story seem to fit Cimmerian migrations, taking with them new styles of harness and perhaps also of equitation, spreading under Scythian pressure from Switzerland to Persia. (Figs. 98–99)

The distribution of the characteristic horse-bits and harness-attachments suggests raiding parties moving rapidly from one region to another in the eighth and seventh centuries B.C. In Belgium in the Court-St-Etienne cemetery there are bits with cheek-pieces best paralleled on the one hand in south Bavaria, on the other in the Llyn Fawr find in south Wales; at Mailhac in the south of France, two graves contained similar bits and harness-mounts of Bavarian type.[31] In the Swiss lake-side settlements of this time there occur bone or

XXVI. (*a, above*) *Bronze mounting in the form of a curled feline, Scythian, sixth century* B.C. (Private Collection)

XXVI. (*b, below*) *Bronze ritual vehicle with human and animal figures, Hallstatt culture, sixth century* B.C., *from grave at Strettweg, Graz, Austria.* (Photo. Fürbock, Graz)

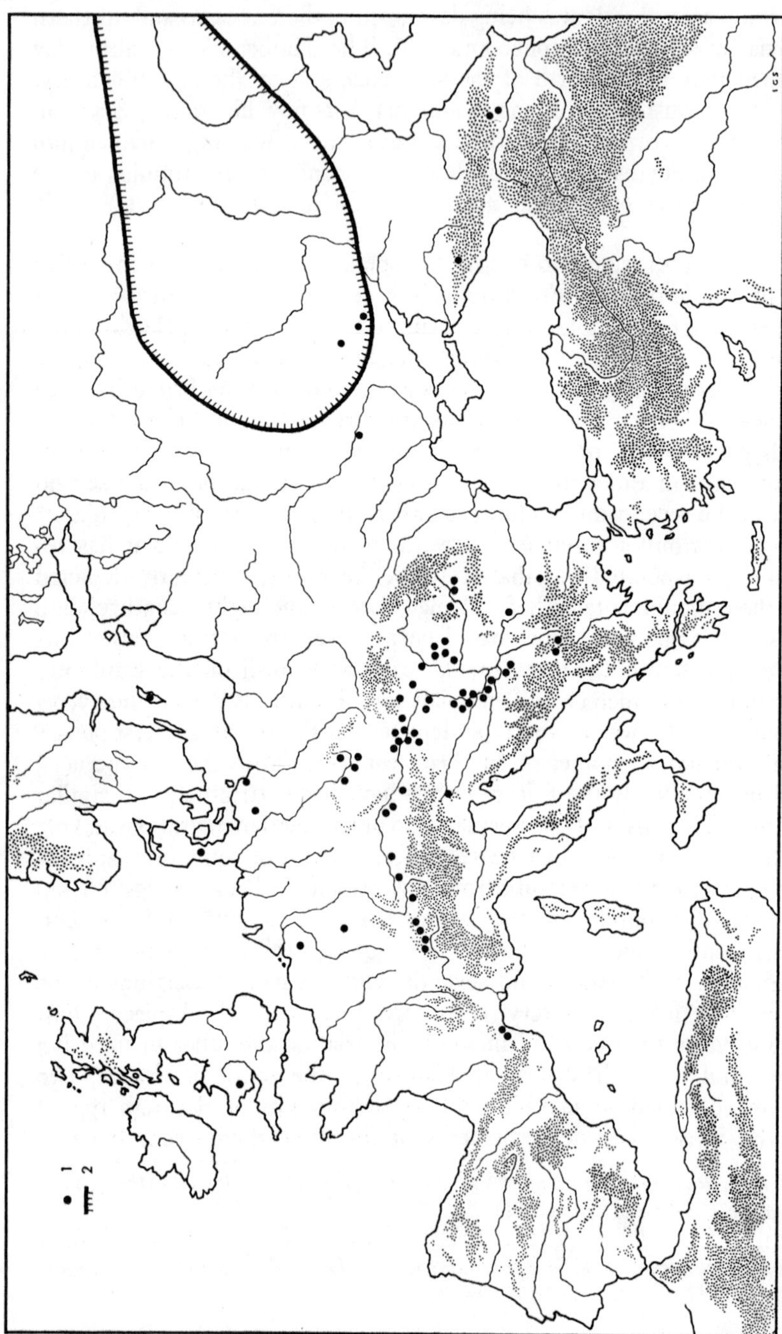

98. *Distribution of* 1, *'Thraco-Cimmerian' horse-bits and harness mountings, eighth–seventh century* B.C.; 2, *Timber-grave cultures.*

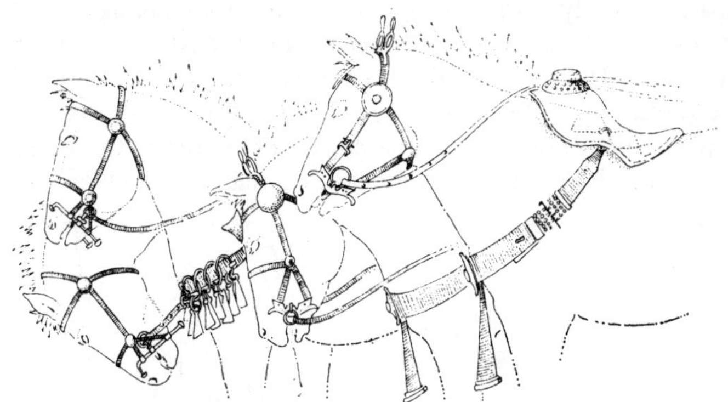

99. *Horse-bits and harness-mountings of 'Thraco-Cimmerian' and derivative types as probably worn, eighth-seventh century* B.C., *from Court-St-Étienne, Belgium.*

antler cheek-pieces ultimately related to Hungarian prototypes we have already noted; so too in Britain at sites such as Heathery Burn in Co. Durham, with a bronze situla of native type, copying continental late Urnfield forms, and the hub-mountings of a wagon, the whole dating from the seventh century B.C.[32] In Gotland the Eskelhem hoard contained bits and horse-trappings of the same general type, but perhaps here of the sixth century.[33] In Switzerland again, from the Urnfield period hill-fort of the Höhensiedlung Burg comes an antler cheek-piece with one end carved into a horse's head in a very Scythian manner,[34] and it has been noted that the actual horse remains of this date from Swiss sites include the steppe pony or tarpan type, as found for instance in the contemporary wagon-graves at Szentes-Vekerzug in Hungary.[35]

From about 700 B.C. onwards we find in Czechoslovakia, and westwards into the Upper Danube region, burials in wooden mortuary houses, often sunk in the ground and frequently under barrows, in which the dead man (or exceptionally woman) is buried with, or on, a spoked four-wheeled vehicle, wagon or hearse or both. The earlier graves belong to the Hallstatt C period, the later to Hallstatt D. The horses are not buried but their harness and yokes are, with bits basically of the Cimmerian type, and frequently there are three of these, two for the paired draught of the wagon (or in one instance at least a two-wheeled cart or chariot) and one for the warrior's charger. We have encountered wagon or cart-burial before, on the Steppe from the beginning of the second millennium B.C.: the wooden mortuary house under the barrow tells the same tale. By the sixth century these chieftains' graves with wagon-burials are found as far west as France. To anticipate, princely burials with a cart or chariot taking the place of the wagon then appear in the Rhineland and the Marne, from the fifth century onwards, and in Yorkshire we have the latest known chariot- or cart-graves, up to the second century B.C. And in the wagon-graves of continental Europe, spanning a couple of centuries from about 700 to 500, we can hardly have anything other than evidence of some kind

100. *Distribution of 1, Hallstatt culture, seventh–fifth century* B.C.*; 2, Wagon-graves of Hallstatt* C*; 3, Wagon-graves of Hallstatt* D*; 4, Wagon-graves,* C *or* D.

of a renewed contact with the Steppe region where wagon-burials and mortuary houses to contain them have a history going back to 2000 B.C. at least; what is most significant is that the earliest of our graves, those of the seventh century, are at the easternmost point of their distribution, mainly in Czechoslovakia, and the Swiss and French examples in the west are up to a hundred years or so later.[36] (Figs. 100–102)

A word on the warrior's charger implied by the third bit in some graves may be apposite. The evidence all suggests that the horse was primarily a traction-animal harnessed to pair draught like an ox, with an unsuitable yoke, not to be replaced by the rigid horse-collar until its invention in China in the first century B.C.[37] Sporadic evidence for ridden horses appears in the Near East from the last three centuries or so of the second millennium; mounted warriors are shown on Syro-Hittite monuments of the eleventh-tenth centuries, in the reliefs depicting Assyrian armies from the early ninth, and at much the same date on Greek geometric vases—the Cimmerians have been invoked as an ultimate agent in the further adoption of cavalry from the seventh century onwards by the contemporary civilisations of antiquity.[38] It seems too as if the barbarians of Europe also learnt new tactics in warfare from this source, from the seventh century B.C. at least. Contemporary representations of both men and women on horseback are found on the situlae already mentioned, on the remarkable vessels from Sopron in the extreme west of Hungary, and the still more extraordinary 'cult-vehicle' from Strettweg near Graz. This elaborate bronze model comprises a wheeled platform on which stands the figure of a woman holding a shallow bowl above her head, surrounded by other, male, figures, including four men on horseback carrying oval shields and spears and wearing conical helmets. The object is unique in itself, though other model wheeled cars of around the same date are known, some (like the earlier Urnfield examples already mentioned) carrying bronze vessels. These ritual objects remind us not only of the wheeled 'lavers' in Solomon's Temple, of the tenth century, but of the ritual wagon carrying a cauldron or situla later venerated at Crannon in Thessaly, and depicted on coins of that city from the third century onwards.[39] (Pl. XXVIb)

This is a point at which we may remark on a passage in Herodotus. He first comments on the Thracians and their warrior-aristocracy, to whom 'to be idle is accounted the most honourable thing, and to be a tiller of the ground the most dishonourable. To live by war and plunder is of all things the most glorious.' We shall encounter this attitude before long in a Celtic context, but Herodotus then goes on to say that northwards, and beyond the Danube, there are reputedly a people called the Sigynnae, who drive horse-drawn chariots, dress like the Medes (which in this context presumably means they wear trousers) and whose territory stretches 'almost to the Eneti upon the Adriatic Sea'.[40] 'Eneti' is usually emended to 'Veneti' and he is describing a situation presumably of the sixth century, if not before. The distribution, from Thrace to the *caput Adriae*, is that of the Thraco-Cimmerian harness-gear; have we in the Sigynnae a tribe or confederacy of tribes who lurk, archaeologically, behind the jejune title of Hallstatt C and D? It has been suggested, alternatively, that the Sigynnae are in fact the Scythians of the Hungarian group of the sixth to fifth centuries B.C., represented for instance by the Szentes-Vekerzug cemetery already mentioned, or the famous gold stag of Zöldshalompuszta.[41] But although, as we shall see, there is evidence of Scythian raids, at least, further into Europe, one could hardly describe their territory as extending to the head of the Adriatic. Perhaps both identifications could be correct, with the Sigynnae representing an earlier 'Cimmerian' culture later overlaid by 'Scythian' traditions on the Hungarian Plain.

The Thracians were not the only barbarians to despise farming; Herodotus of course had also noted that the Scythians were nomadic pastoralists, 'who neither plough nor sow',[42] and we shall find similar comments by later classical writers, such as Strabo and Tacitus, showing a knowledge of comparable situations in barbarian Europe, including Britain. Strabo, writing at the end of the first century B.C., finds the survival of nomads to his day surprising—'In fact even now', he writes, 'there are Wagon-dwellers and Nomads, so-called, who live off their herds, and on milk and cheese . . . they follow the grazing herds, from time to time moving to other places that have grass . . . they turn over their land to any people who wish to till it, and are satisfied if they receive in return for the land the tribute they have assessed.'[43] We have in fact a classic account of the pastoral nomadism which was to continue on the Steppe for centuries, and which must have been ancient in Strabo's day. But how ancient? Recent studies have all emphasised that nomadism is not a simple stage intermediate between food-collecting and agriculture, but is a technology which 'includes a complex of animals . . . balanced in terms of grazing characteristics to utilise all the grass cover of each locality . . . cattle, horses and camels graze well on long grass, sheep and goats crop close'. And to obtain the necessary mobility, the ridden horse is a necessity: 'the invention of riding, as applied to the horse, was the final "tip-over" factor which permitted, for the first time in history, the crystallisation of an Inner Asiatic pastoral nomad way of life' it has been recently said,[44] and this will equally apply to Europe. It is then in just the context of the first horse-riding in central Europe, in the seventh century B.C. that the beginnings of an element of pastoral nomadism in Celtic or Germanic Europe, which is perceptible later, first became possible.

In many nomadic or semi-nomadic peoples of antiquity the use of the bow and arrow by the mounted archer on horseback was a major factor in their success in war—the Scythians are of course a case in point. Mounted archers were known to the Babylonians and Assyrians, at least by repute, from the second half of the second millennium B.C., and are represented as armed centaurs; in the early ninth century the

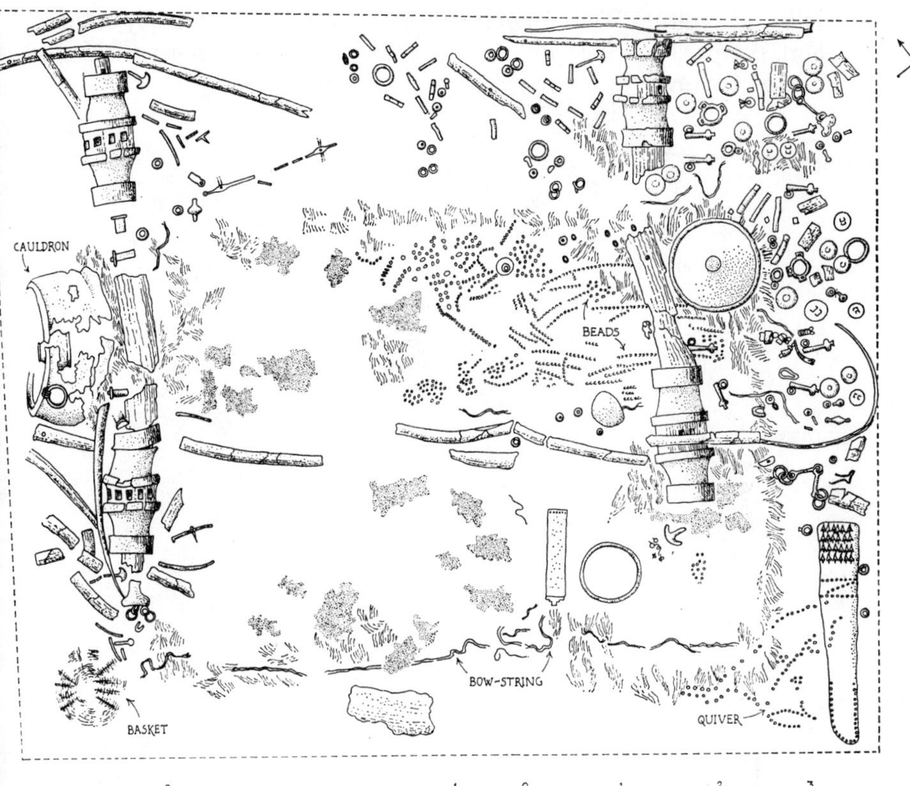

101. *Wagon-grave in plank-built chamber, showing remains of wagon, position of male and female burials, grave-goods, etc., Hallstatt* D *culture, sixth century* B.C., *Grave* VI, *the Hohmichele barrow, Heuneburg, South Germany.*

bow was adopted by the Assyrian cavalry itself.[45] In barbarian Europe after the early second millennium B.C. archaeological evidence for bows and arrows virtually vanishes for a time, though bronze arrowheads sporadically occur from early Urnfield times onwards (e.g. those in the Wollmesheim grave in the Middle Rhineland), and are of types which suggest oriental origins.[46] Later, bronze arrowheads of Scythian types in central and even west Europe seem attributable, as we shall see, either to actual incursions of these peoples around 500 B.C., or (in the west) to their use by Scythian mercenaries among the Greeks; but in the Hohmichele tomb near the Heuneburg, of the sixth century B.C., the iron arrowheads found with the remains of a quiver seem of another Scythian type, but in a context of the local highly developed

Hallstatt D culture. The bow of the steppe horseman was normally of the short, composite or 'Turkish' type, but the Hohmichele archer wielded a long-bow, over 6 feet in length.[47] (Fig. 101)

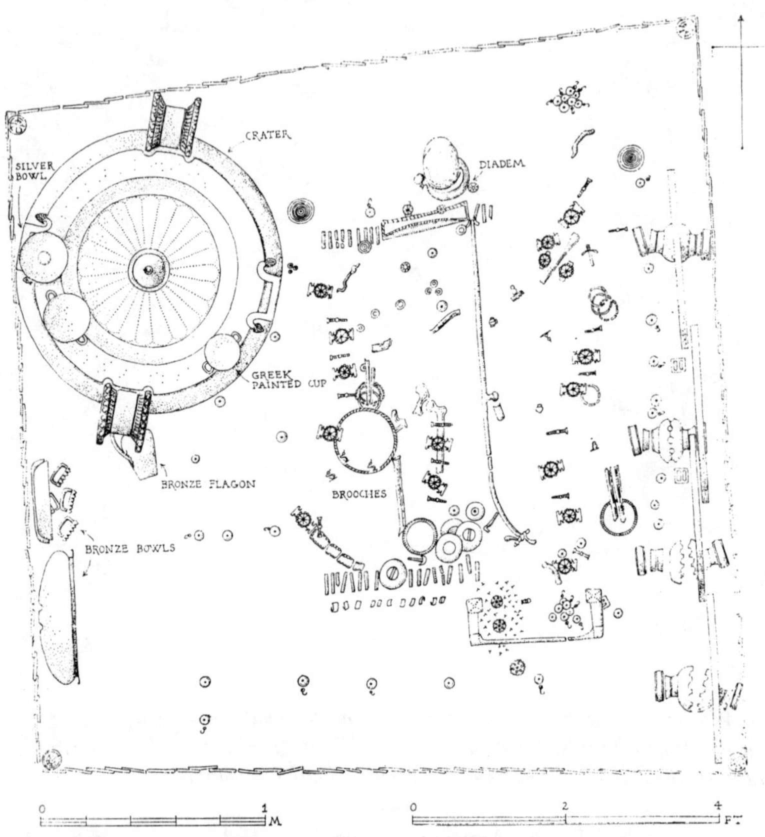

102. *Wagon-grave in plank-built chamber, showing dismantled wagon, female burial, imported Greek bronze crater and other objects, Hallstatt* D *culture, sixth century* B.C., *at Vix, Chatillon-sur-Seine, France.*

The chieftains' graves, with their frequent wooden mortuary houses and wagon burials, and their evident spread during the seventh and sixth centuries B.C. from Czechoslovakia to France, are difficult to interpret. Have we to think of new aristocracies from the Steppe establishing themselves in east-central Europe and then pressing westwards, or have we no more than the adoption of new ideas by the indigenous, presumptively Celtic, ruling houses? There are no demonstrably foreign imports in the earlier tombs that could relate to the eastern world; when imports do appear, in more westerly tombs from the seventh century onwards, they are of Greek or Etruscan origin, traded as we shall see over the Alpine passes or up the Rhône. On the whole, it seems likely that there was a change in burial rite brought about partly by outside stimulus (and indeed, possibly through dynastic marriages) and partly perhaps by the resurgence of a dormant but long established set of customs going back to the second millennium, themselves derived from the Steppe, involving mortuary houses, barrow-burial, and wheeled vehicles to carry the dead (even if they were only bronze models holding a cinerary urn as passenger, which as we have seen were known as early as the twelfth century B.C.) (Figs. 101, 102)

We have deferred discussion of the most important development in metal technology of first millennium barbarian Europe: the working of iron. I mentioned in passing that the technological model of the prehistoric past divides a Bronze Age from an Iron Age, but divides it, so far as most of Europe is concerned, at a rather inconvenient point. Recent work on early iron working in ancient Eurasia has shown it to be a complicated and interesting story. We must remember at the outset that iron metallurgy involves more complex techniques than that of copper and bronze, both in the extraction of the metal from its ore and in its subsequent treatment. In any but wholly modern conditions iron cannot be cast, but has to be forged or wrought into shape, and subsequently, if its full properties as a substance for edge-tools are to be utilised, must be submitted to processes including tempering, quenching, and the addition of carbon to convert it to steel. Against these difficulties—especially great to craftsmen with a long-established tradition in the quite different non-ferrous techniques—can be set the fact that iron ore is abundant, and that therefore, the technical complexities once mastered, iron tools and weapons can be cheap.

Pure metallic iron, in the form of meteorite fragments, was sporadically used from Predynastic Egyptian times; occasional objects of smelted iron are known from the third millennium onwards—an iron dagger from the Alaca Hüyük Tombs is a good example. In the form in which it was then produced, iron was harder, and gave a better cutting edge, than copper, but it was not superior to bronze, so that with the development of bronze-working, iron was relegated to the position of a curious and expensive metal used occasionally for ornaments. But probably by the fifteenth century iron was being produced on a commercial scale by the Hittites, and by the mid-thirteenth century it is being mentioned in diplomatic correspondence (such as the well-known and much-discussed letter from Hattusilis III to a correspondent, probably a king of Assyria) as a recognised commodity of trade.[48] With the break-up of Hittite power, the techniques of iron-working appear spread out beyond Anatolia and the Near East, and this can hardly be coincidence. From the eleventh century onwards iron objects appear in Greece and Crete, as in the Kerameikos and Fortetsa cemeteries and the Athenian Agora grave; in continental Europe some iron objects occur in later Urnfield times (around the eighth century) and in south Italy (as at pre-Greek Cumae) a century earlier, but in general the first use of iron on a comparatively large scale in barbarian Europe is marked by the appearance of the long iron swords in the Czechoslovakian wagon-graves and other Hallstatt tombs of the seventh century B.C.[49]

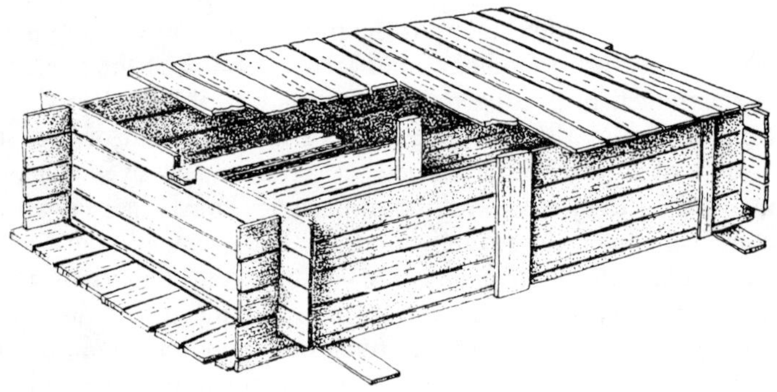

103. *Constructional details of plank-built burial chamber, Hallstatt* D *culture, sixth century* B.C., *central grave of the Hohmichele barrow, Heuneburg, South Germany.*

While investigations are still at an early stage, it appears on the present evidence that iron technology hardly advanced beyond the stage it had reached in Europe of the seventh and sixth centuries B.C., until medieval times. Tools and weapons so far examined show no signs of having been treated by the normal processes of tempering and quenching (though steel was occasionally produced in pre-Roman times). What is even more curious is that Roman techniques were no more advanced, and that even in the early centuries A.D. their untempered tools were technologically not superior to those of the barbarians. A break-through in efficient sword production was indeed made at this time beyond the Imperial frontiers in Scandinavia, by the invention of the pattern-welded blade incorporating steel, but the true Damascene crucible-steel, probably of Indian origin, was not to reach Europe until the eleventh century A.D.[50]

The development of iron tools, however, was rapidly to influence other crafts, such as those of the carpenter and wheelwright. The planks making up the great central mortuary chamber in the Hohmichele barrow (Fig. 103) were nearly 20 feet long and had been sawn out of the tree-trunk, not split and adzed, and the use of a two-man saw seems likely enough, though no such tool has survived.[51] But even when sawn planks were not used, adzes could do remarkable work, particularly in boat-building. In the bed of the River Humber near North Ferriby in Yorkshire extraordinary plank-built boats have been found, the component timbers 'stitched' together with yew withes, and a recent radiocarbon reading places them at *c.* 750 B.C.: here the planks, up to 35 feet long, were adzed.[52] (Fig. 104) It is uncertain whether the lathe was in use in barbarian Europe before late in the first millennium B.C., and the fine turned wooden drinking-cup from a grave of the sixth century B.C. at Uffing in Bavaria is more likely to be an import from the Greek or Etruscan world than a native product.[53]

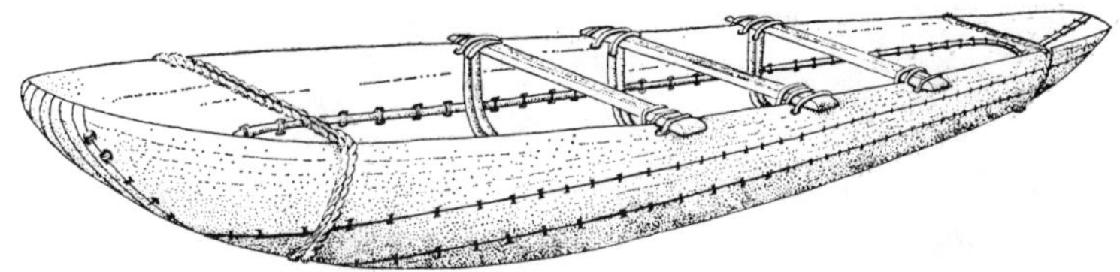

104. *Restoration of boat with 'sewn' planks, eighth century* B.C., *from River Humber at North Ferriby, E.R.Yorks., England.*

In the seventh and sixth centuries B.C. we have then the establishment of iron-using cultures over much of central and western Europe, from Yugoslavia and the eastern Alps to eastern France, and extending northwards to the Middle Rhine and Bohemia, inherently likely to have been Celtic-speaking and in archaeological terms the Hallstatt C and D (or I and II) phases. We can recognise a particularly important and rich area in Burgundy and south Germany with, as we shall see, a notable series of imports resulting from the wine trade up the Rhône from the Graeco-Etruscan world. (Fig. 105) The Mont Lassois hill-fort and adjacent tumulus-burials such as Vix and Ste Colombe must denote one centre of power, with another represented by the Heuneburg fort, with the Hohmichele and other princely graves. (Figs. 101, 102) Over this area too gold finds of the period are abundant. In the east Hallstatt region there is Hallstatt itself, enriched by the salt trade and with its cemetery of some 2,500 graves; to the south-east again

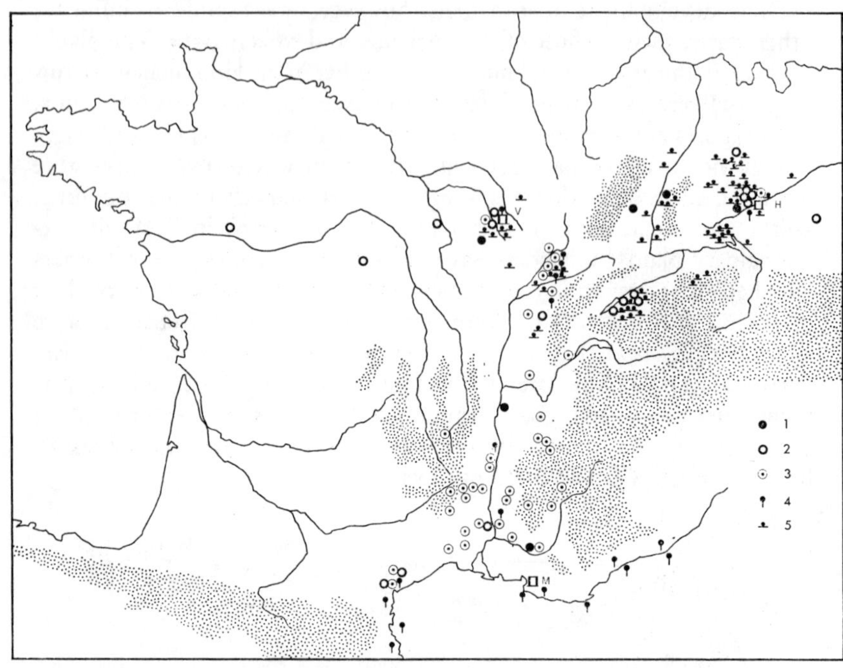

105. *Distribution of Hallstatt imports and luxuries: 1, Imported Greek etc. bronzes, seventh century* B.C.; *2, Imported bronzes and gold, sixth century* B.C.; *3, Imported Greek pottery, seventh–sixth centuries* B.C.; *4, Massaliote amphorae, seventh–sixth centuries* B.C.; *5, Hallstatt* C *and* D *gold objects*; M, *Massalia*; H, *the Heuneburg*; V, *Vix*.

great cemeteries denote the power and influence of the same cultural traditions in Carniola, Croatia and Bosnia towards the end of the period.[54] (Pls. XXVII–XIX) To the east, the iron-using Scythian culture was developing into its classical form. Northwards lay the territories of tribes later to be included in Germania Magna; beyond them again the Scandinavian and Baltic peoples. Here the Urnfield cultures lingered on as a final Bronze Age, often vaguely called Lusatian, though in north Germany iron objects appear from at least the sixth century onwards. In western France and Iberia again versions of 'Atlantic' bronze-using cultures can be identified, with bronze versions of the Hallstatt iron swords being manufactured.[55] We will look at the Mediterranean world in a moment, for here in Greece and Italy momentous developments are taking place by this time. In the British Isles, as we shall see shortly, from 700 B.C. or before, continental metalwork was being imported and influencing local techniques: our earliest long bronze swords had been brought into south-east England at the time of the Mediterranean sea raiders in the eleventh century, and perhaps by their northern counterparts. But from the seventh century, continental contacts may well have introduced our first domesticated horses and spoked-wheel vehicles, and certainly brought us our first knowledge of iron-working from the middle sixth; so too fortification techniques which we will discuss later.[56]

The archaeological evidence suggests that there were not only trading activities between the Hallstatt and Scythian worlds, but actual Scythian inroads into central and north-eastern Europe: we have already noted the distribution of their bronze arrow-heads as suggestive in this respect. In the burnt and destroyed remains of several late Urnfield forts in Poland and adjacent areas such arrow-heads have been found, in one instance in the ribs of a man slain at the hill-fort gateway, and some of the local population seems to have taken refuge in caves during this time of troubles around 500 B.C. The similar arrow-heads stuck in the fort walls at Karmir-Blur, over 2,000 miles away in Russian Armenia, archaeological witnesses of the Scythian attack in the sixth century, are a reminder of the vast distances that could be traversed by the nomadic peoples of antiquity.[57] (Fig. 106)

After the collapse of the Mycenaean and Hittite kingdoms the Aegean and the Near East were re-aligning the balance of power. We have seen how the Phrygians established themselves over much of Asia Minor, with Urartians and Assyrians as eastern neighbours; in the eastern Taurus and north Syria something of the Hittite tradition was carried on in the Syro-Hittite or Neo-Hittite state until its submergence under Assyrian rule in the eighth century. In the late eleventh and early tenth centuries the Hebrews and the Phoenicians were consolidating their power in the Levant under Solomon and Hiram. In Greece, the move of the Dorians south into the Peloponnese, and the Ionian migration into south-west Anatolia had taken place, probably in the eleventh century. We move into the Greek Dark Ages, with civilisation there no higher, and perhaps rather lower, than in contemporary central Europe of the Urnfield periods.

But the beginnings of historical Greece are not far away, with the first Olympiad traditionally in 776, and the foundation of the prototypes of the city-states; and by the mid-eighth century, the planting of colonies in the west—Cumae about 750, Syracuse in 733, and the rest.[58] Writing, in the form of the adaptation of the Phoenician alphabet into a Greek script, may go back to the ninth or even tenth century; Homer and Hesiod to the eighth-seventh centuries.[59] Attic and Corinthian

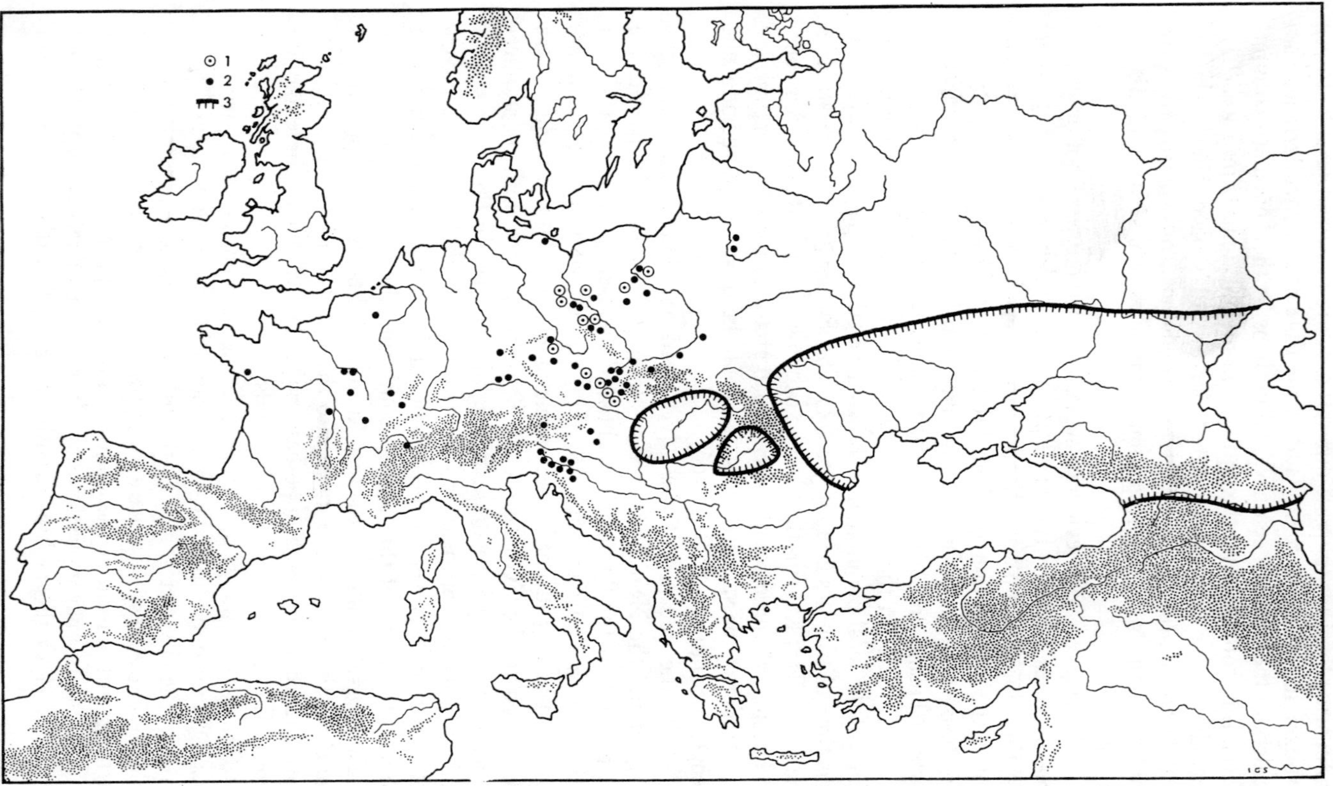

106. *1, Hill-forts with evidence of Scythian attack ; 2, Stray Scythian finds, mainly arrow-heads ; 3, Scythian settlement areas.*

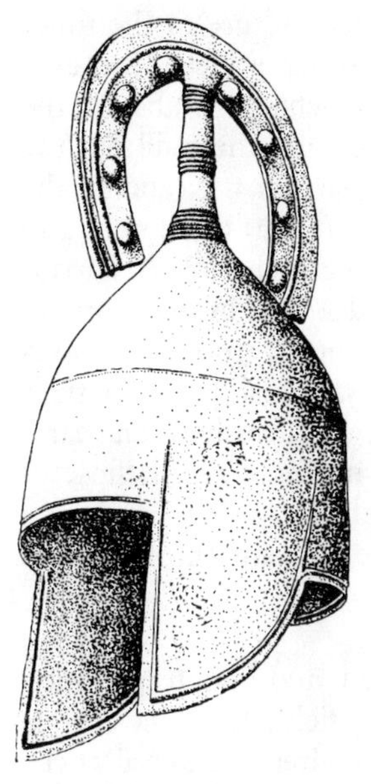

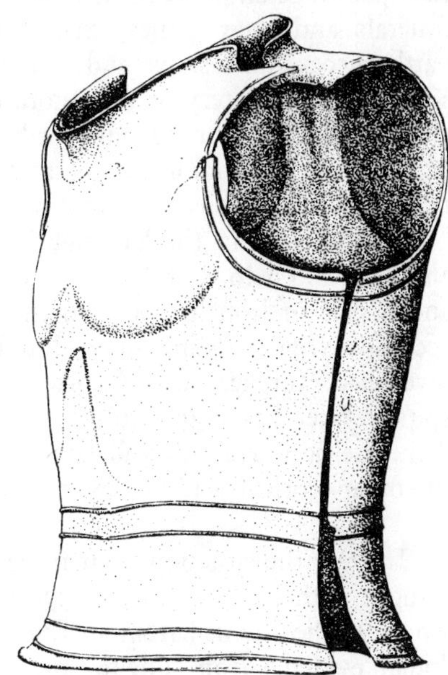

107. *Bronze crested helmet and corselet, Geometric Period, eighth century* B.C., *from male grave at Argos, Greece.*

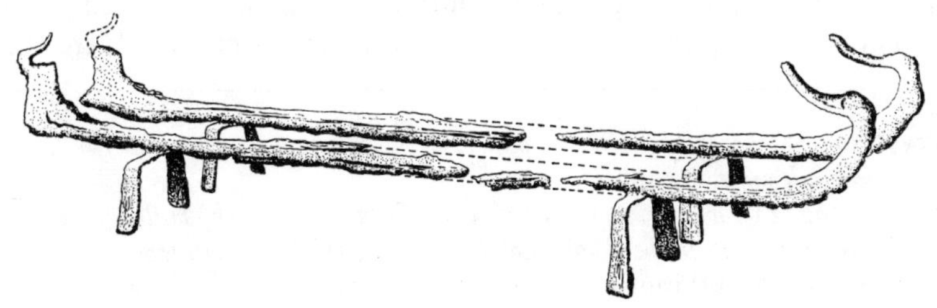

108. *Pair of iron fire-dogs in the form of stylised ships, Geometric Period, eighth century* B.C., *from male grave at Argos, Greece.*

vase-paintings show us something of the material culture of the time; funerals and their games, chariot races and other athletic contests, battle-pieces, and ships and sea-coast engagements. Tombs in the Kerameikos cemetery or the Agora in Athens or elsewhere fill out the archaeological picture. Iron swords and spears are in use, and in the Agora grave of about 900 B.C. (cremated and in an urn) there were also two horse-bits, perhaps symbolically representing a chariot. A warrior buried at Argos in the late eighth century had a fine bronze corselet and a crested helmet of Assyrian derivation, two heavy iron double-axes and a pair of iron fire-dogs in the form of stylised ships, with their accompanying roasting-spits. Similar fire-dogs furnished an early seventh-century grave in Cyprus; such finds not only recall those of spits in later Etruscan tombs, but of these and of fire-dogs in the La Tène Celtic graves we will later consider: the concept throughout is the other-world feast.[60] (Figs. 107–108)

In Italy the situation is far more complicated, and its interpretation fraught with hazards even to specialists in the field, let alone to one whose studies lie in barbarian Europe. We have already glanced at the Italian evidence from time to time and seen the presence there from the twelfth century of some kind of 'Urnfield' population in Umbria; by the ninth, in the earlier Villanova or Tarquinia phase, contacts with the trans-alpine region are shown (as we saw) by imported bronzes such as the crested helmets and situlae. With continued contacts between Italy and central Europe, we can follow the story on into fully iron-using cultures comparable and contemporary with that of Hallstatt, and with the earlier western Greek colonies, in the eighth century B.C.; but by the seventh century the Italian picture is transformed and we are looking, however uneasily, not at prehistoric Villanovans, but historical Etruscans. And here, as is well known, informed opinion is divided today, as it was in antiquity, on the question of Etruscan origins. Were they

---

XXVII. (*a*) *Leather cap, Hallstatt culture, sixth century* B.C., *from the Kilb-werk salt mine, Hallstatt, Austria.*
XXVII. (*b and c*) *Two views of leather, wood-framed, rucksack, Hallstatt culture, sixth century* B.C., *from the Appold-werk salt mine, Hallstatt, Austria.*
(Both photos. Naturhistorisches Museum, Vienna)
XXVIII. (*a, on following page*) *Bronze vessel engraved with animal figures, Hallstatt culture, sixth century* B.C., *from Grave 682, Hallstatt, Austria.*
XXVIII. (*b*) *Bronze bowl with figures of cow and calf, Hallstatt culture, sixth century, from Grave 671, Hallstatt, Austria.*
(Both photos. Naturhistorisches Museum, Vienna)

XXVII (*caption on facing page*)

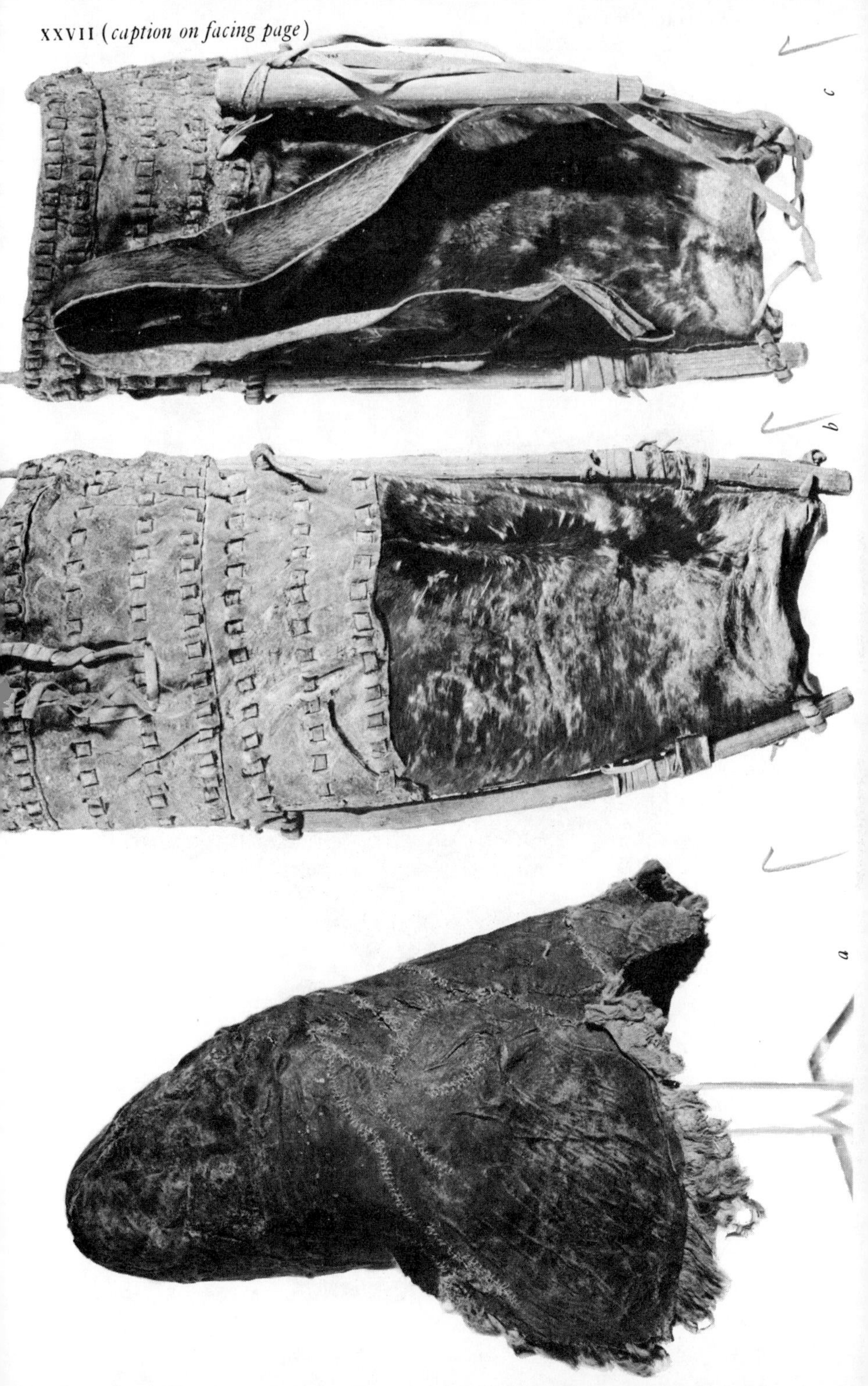

XXVIII (*caption on p. 192*)

a

b

XXIX. (*a*) *Gold bowl, Hallstatt culture, sixth century* B.C., *from wagon-burial at Bad-Cannstadt, South Germany.*
XXIX. (*b*) *Gold neck-ring, Hallstatt culture, sixth century* B.C., *from wagon-burial at Bad-Cannstadt, South Germany.* (Both photos. Württemburgisches Landesmuseum, Stuttgart)

a

b

XXX. (*a*) *Imported bronze cauldron on tripod, Greek, sixth century* B.C., *from grave of Hallstatt culture at Ste Colombe, Côte d'Or, France.*
(Photo. Chambon, Chatillon-sur-Seine)
XXX. (*b*) *Bronze cauldron on tripod, Urartian, eighth century* B.C., *from Altin Tepe, Turkey.* (Photo. R. D. Barnett)

simply Villanovans who had become profoundly orientalised by trade and other contacts, or were they immigrants from the east, perhaps from Lydia as Herodotus thought? These are the two poles in the dispute, but it is not my lack of courage that persuades me to take a position of compromise, and see a complex mixture of indigenous, central and eastern European and oriental elements in the Etruscan people, accumulating over some centuries of trade and other contacts and culminating in a strongly orientalising phase; archaeologically it looks probable and fits more of the evidence than the extreme views.[61] From our immediate viewpoint, however, concerned as we are with the more northerly and from now on, more barbarous world beyond Etruria, it is the fact of Etruscan civilisation and that of the western Greek colonies from the eighth century B.C. onwards that is important. With the foundation of Carthage and the other Punic settlements in North Africa and Spain by about 800 B.C. the Mediterranean had become a civilised lake; after 540 B.C. or so the Carthaginian hold on Iberia meant the effective closing of the Straits of Gibraltar and a diversion of traffic from the Atlantic sea-ways to the routes across France.[62]

Its merchants, however, did not confine their trading activities to its shores. In at least two instances we can perceive evidence of some indirect contact between the Aegean and the Atlantic seaways leading to the British Isles, though more probably by the Narbonne-Carcassonne-Loire route than through the Straits of Gibraltar. Circular shields of a distinctive type, their concentric ribs interrupted by a V-shaped 'notch', were in use in Greece, Crete, Cyprus, and the Aegean Islands in the eighth-seventh centuries; and in the west we first find them carved on a grave-slab near Montpellier in the south of France, and again on tombstones in Iberia between the Guadiana and Tagus rivers, and then versions of the actual shields from Ireland. A variant type in Scandinavia and Germany may be an Irish development or the result of independent contacts via the Adriatic: at all events an Aegean style of shield found its way west and north.[63] (Fig. 109) The other instance may take us ultimately to connections with the kingdom of Urartu in eastern Anatolia, and at least to Syria where accomplished metalsmiths were producing exceptionally fine single-piece bronze cauldrons which were exported to Phrygia, and to Greece from the eighth century B.C., where they were copied. Ritual versions, with griffins' heads and handle attachments in the form of winged humans, were particularly resplendent and reached not only the Etruscan world: one, on its tripod, found its way into a grave of the early sixth century at Ste Colombe near Vix and Mont Lassois in the Côte d'Or. (Pl. xxx) A griffin mount from such a cauldron was found near Angers, and a cauldron deprived of

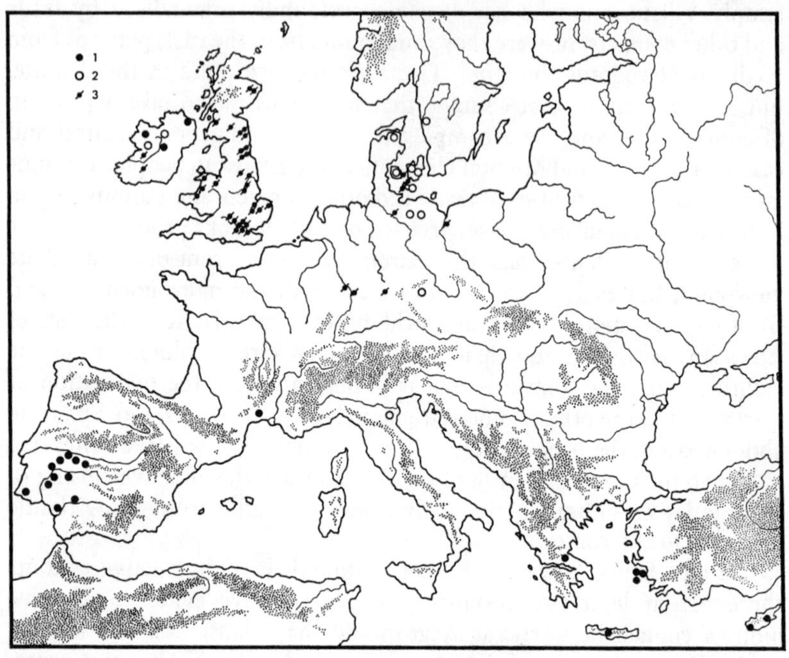

109. *Distribution of circular shields, eighth-seventh century* B.C.*: 1, V-notched; 2, U-notched; 3, British and northern types.*

mountings strayed, with other Hallstatt objects, as far north as near Stockholm; fragments of another tripod were found near Auxerre.[64] The basic cauldron type was copied in the west by Irish and British bronze-smiths and thence exported to France, Spain, and Scandinavia, around 600 B.C.; and we see the trade along the Atlantic seaways at this time reflected in the fragments of a Greek sailing-manual or *Periplus* of the sixth century B.C. contained in the *Ora Maritima* of Avienus. This incidentally tells us that Britain was then known as the 'Island of the Albiones'. It is not until Pytheas in the late third century B.C. that the phrase 'Pretanic Islands', ancestral to our 'Britain',[65] is used.

We may note in passing that shields of types other than the circular forms just mentioned were being developed in the east Hallstatt world, and their evolution can be seen on the decorated situlae touched on early in this chapter. The earlier vessels (obviously under strong Greek influence) show warriors with circular and oval shields and spears; oval shields alone then appear, like those of the warriors on the Strettweg car, and in their latest forms are clearly closely related to those which we encounter in the later Iron Age cultures of La Tène. The development of Hallstatt helmets can likewise be traced on the situlae and the Strettweg figures, and by actual finds, in which an earlier 'Italian' domed and plumed form is replaced by conical casques, themselves leading into one of the early La Tène types, current from the fifth century century B.C. onwards. (Pl. XXXI)

From the seventh century, however, the main trade between the Mediterranean and the Celtic world was that in wine, reflected archaeologically in imported vessels for serving and drinking it, which were then frequently buried with the dead as an expression of the idea already to be seen in the Argive tomb with its fire-dogs and spits and Attic crater—the feast beyond the grave. Apart from their intrinsic interest as trade objects, these imports help us enormously in dating the phases of the barbarian cultures of Hallstatt and La Tène in which they occur. An early import is an Etruscan bronze pyxis of the seventh century B.C. from a grave at Hatten in Alsace, and around 600 B.C. we have a few imported bronze wine-flagons thought by some to be of Rhodian origin but more likely, in such contexts, of Italian manufacture. About a century later come the griffin-cauldron and tripod from Ste Colombe and the fantastic great Greek bronze crater from nearby Vix, in a timber mortuary-house under a tumulus, with a bronze-mounted wagon and riches including the so-called diadem, a piece of gold-work that may be a neck-ornament and of Iberian origin. (Fig. 102; Pl. xxxii b) Other types of bronze vessels were also traded north, and to this time too belongs the import of painted Greek vases, fragments of which turn up in settlements, and also the adoption of Greek techniques of fortification in regions as far from the Mediterranean as the Heuneburg fort on the upper Danube. The trade continues in the fifth century, with Greek painted cups and bronze flagons in the later Celtic graves which now include not wagon, but cart or chariot-burials.[66]

Around 600 the Greek colony of Massalia near the mouth of the Rhône had been founded, and the earlier wine trade seems to have passed up the Rhône, the characteristic micaceous Massaliote wine amphorae being traded as far north as the Heuneburg.[67] Vix and Ste Colombe and other exceptional pieces like the bronze hydria from Grächwil in Switzerland (Pl. XXXII a) suggest that we must reckon with the interchange of rich gifts between civilised authorities and barbarian potentates to obtain concessions and of course (as in the *keimelion* of the early Greek world) the interchange of presents between the Celtic rulers themselves. Much of the later trade, perhaps most of it, must, however, have been in Etruscan hands, and operated over the Alpine passes, especially when the trans-Appenine Etruscan colonies, from Milan to

Bologna, had been founded in the late sixth century. Fragments of garments embroidered in Chinese silk from a princely grave of the early sixth century near the Heuneburg fort show the extent of trade at this time, perhaps via the island of Cos.[68]

We have been looking at aspects of early Celtic society—before about the fifth century B.C.—as represented in the main by evidence from graves. These have shown us a predominantly aristocratic aspect, in which members of a ruling class (and both men and women as Vix and other graves remind us) were given elaborate burial, often in timber mortuary houses and under barrows, sometimes with a four-wheeled wagon which must in some sense have been a status-symbol, as the chariot was in later times or a carriage and pair in a Victorian household, or the Jaguars and Cadillacs of today. Doubtless it is only the advent of Christianity that has deprived us of fascinating vehicle-burials in Europe of a later date except among the gypsies. Here we may appositely turn to an eye-witness account of a recent wagon-burial in such a context. Into the caravan of the lately deceased 'mother' of a clan of 400 were placed her possessions, including the harness worn by the horses but excepting the crockery she had used. It was then burnt, and the two horses were killed, one of the relatives saying that 'the ritual must be observed'. Finally, the pots and pans were smashed, and these, with the iron framework of the caravan surviving from the fire, were buried in a pit. This survival of an archaic rite, which might have been described by Herodotus and not *The Times* reporter, took place at Garsington, within sight of Oxford, that city of lost causes, in 1953.[69]

The salt and copper mines of the Tyrol give us a glimpse of something approaching an industrial aspect of Hallstatt society and for the rest we can see the development of the basic rural arts and crafts already established a millennium and more before. The increased command of carpentry and joinery made possible by new tools, we have already noticed, and it is only the accident of decay that has deprived us of so much here, as with other crafts employing perishable substances. Wagons and their accoutrements obviously gave great scope to fine craftsmanship, combining the skills of wheelwrights, leather-workers, blacksmiths, and bronze-smiths: elaborately bronze-sheathed wooden wheels, at least for ritual cars, go back to late Urnfield times, and later (in Hallstatt C and D) we have bronze or iron hub-mounts and nailed-on iron tyres. From graves in Czechoslovakia and Switzerland come elaborate horse-yokes, padded and leather-covered and decorated with patterns of massed bronze studs.[70] (Pl. XXXIII) Fine pottery vessels were made, still without the wheel, and a polychrome style of painting in red, white, black, and yellow was in vogue in south Germany and Switzerland; in some instances a technique was used, allied to the 'batik' method of dyeing fabrics, in which the pattern was stopped out, probably with wax, to show as a reserved motif after painting and firing.[71]

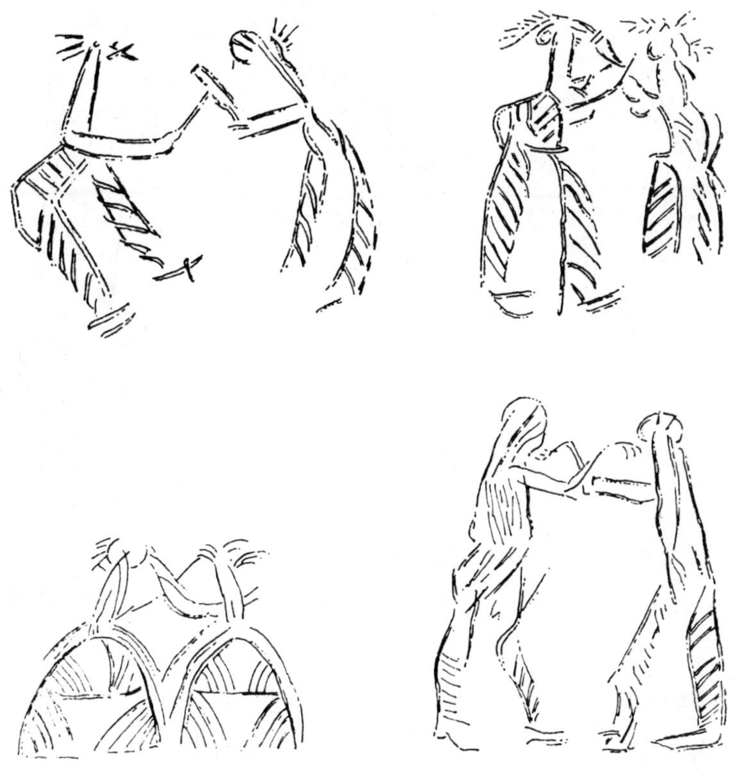

110. *Representations of men and women fighting, Hallstatt culture, sixth century, incised on pottery from Sopron, Hungary.*

We have some fascinating woollen textiles preserved in the salt-mines, as at Durrnberg near Hallein, one with a pattern woven in dark brown, buff and green; and there are other patterned pieces. From the copper- and salt-mines of the Tyrol, we have miners' leather caps and tunics of Urnfield or Hallstatt date.[72] Clothing styles in general are difficult to assess as usual, and the people shown on the decorated situlae, in tunics and huge *petasos*-type hats, must be specifically Venetic or Atestine and

111. *Representations of women, Hallstatt culture, sixth century* B.C., *incised on pottery from Sopron, Hungary: 1, spinning; 2, weaving on upright loom; 3, playing the lyre; 4, dancing; 5, riding on horse-back.*

their fashions not likely to apply north of the Alps. But on the remarkable decorated pots from Sopron, in extreme north-west Hungary, we have a whole series of unsophisticated but vigorous scenes of men and women —the former in long trousers and the latter with slim waists and flared or bell-shaped skirts recalling those of the Cîrna figurines described in Chapter IV. Some of the women may have indications of curls or ringlets on each side of the highly stylised head and neck, and they are shown engaged in spinning, weaving on a big upright loom, dancing to the music of a lyre-player and riding a horse. The men ride horses, or lead horse-drawn wagons, or herd and chase animals; one curious little group of pictures shows pairs of men and women apparently fighting, and pulling at each other's hair. These charming scenes are presumably of about the sixth century B.C., and the representations of trousers about the earliest known in barbarian Europe outside the Scythian world. They were destined, of course, to be the typical Celtic garment, and their adoption can hardly be unrelated to the contemporary development of horsemanship.[73] (Figs. 110, 111)

A fortified settlement of some 12 acres in extent on the Goldberg in south Germany consisted of a group of a dozen or so rectangular timber-built houses, with others presumably barns or byres, basically similar to the Urnfield settlements such as Perleberg; another defended Hallstatt C-D site is the Kyberg in Bavaria.[74] In one corner of the fortifications of the Goldberg a roughly square area was delimited by palisades, and contained two buildings of more massive post-construction which have been interpreted as representing the chieftain's 'palace', but the buildings could of course have served other functions; a somewhat similar problem is posed by the Heath Row site in England, probably of the fourth-third centuries B.C. with a rectangular building interpreted as a temple, among circular houses and discussed further in the next chapter. (Figs. 112, 131)

In Britain, as we have already seen, the circular house was being almost exclusively used from at least the second half of the second millennium —the twelfth-eleventh century settlement on Itford Hill is a good example. By the sixth and fifth centuries, we can see not only small villages, but homesteads with a single large circular house, sometimes with ancillary buildings for storage or cattle-shelter; Staple Howe in East Yorkshire, a palisaded enclosure with imported Hallstatt C bronze razors, is an example. (Fig. 113) This development of single farmstead units must in some way reflect a modification of social tradition, and I do not know of its existence on the Continent at this time; in the British Isles it was to prove not only a persistent, but in some areas a dominant

112. *Settlement with post-holes of timber houses and other buildings, Hallstatt culture, seventh–sixth century* B.C., *at the Goldberg, South Germany.*

XXXI. (*above*) *Bronze figure of mounted warrior with helmet, spear and shield, Hallstatt culture, sixth century* B.C., *from the Strettweg ritual vehicle* (Pl. XXVIb), *Graz, Austria*. (Photo. Landesmuseum Johanneum, Graz)

XXXII. (*a, on following page*) *Upper part of imported bronze hydria, Greek, sixth century* B.C., *from grave of Hallstatt culture at Grächwil, Switzerland*. (Photo. Historisches Museum, Bern)
XXXII. (*b*,) *One of a pair of Pegasus figures on the gold 'diadem' or neck-ring from grave of Hallstatt culture, sixth century* B.C., *at Vix, Côte d'Or, France*. (Photo. Ina Bandy)

XXXIII. (*on following page*) *Neck-pad of wooden yoke for two horses, with decorative bronze studding, Hallstatt culture, seventh century* B.C., *from wagon-grave at Lovosice, Czechoslovakia*. (Photo. Archeologický Ústav, Prague)

XXXII (*caption on previous page*)

a

b

XXXIII (*caption facing p. 200*)

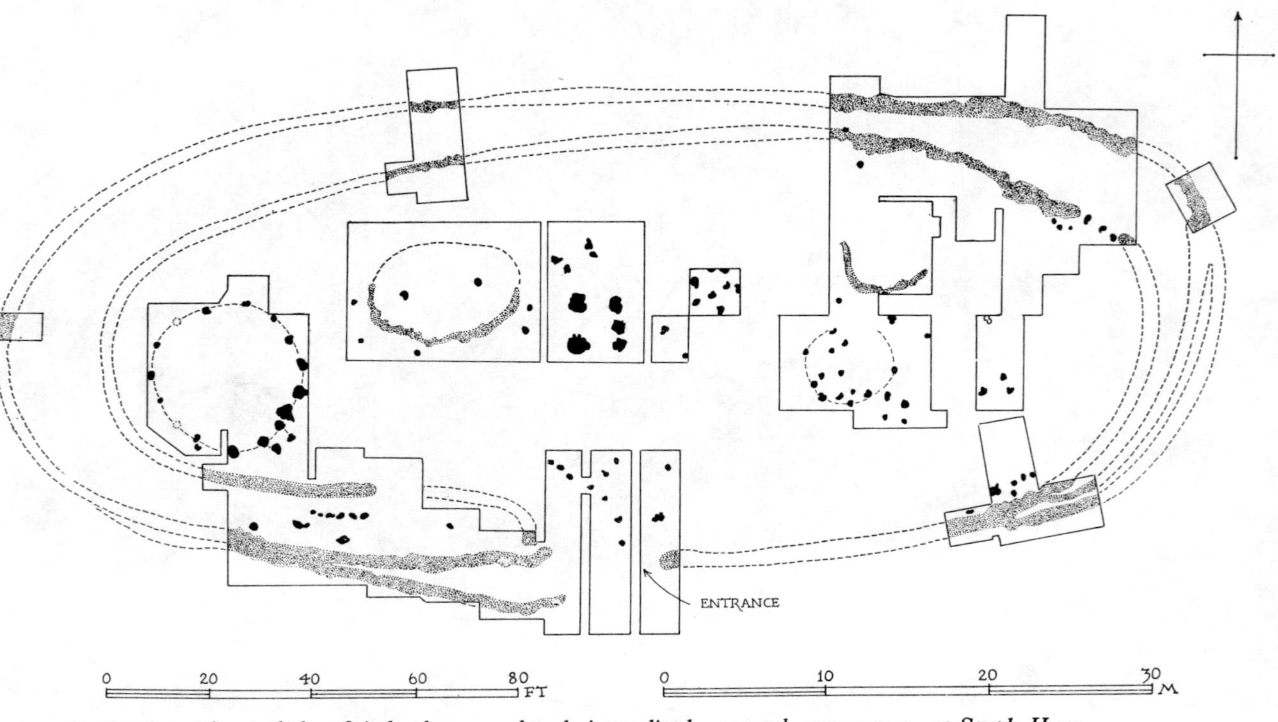

113. *Settlement with post-holes of timber houses and enclosing palisades, seventh century* B.C., *at Staple Howe,* N.R. *Yorks., England.*

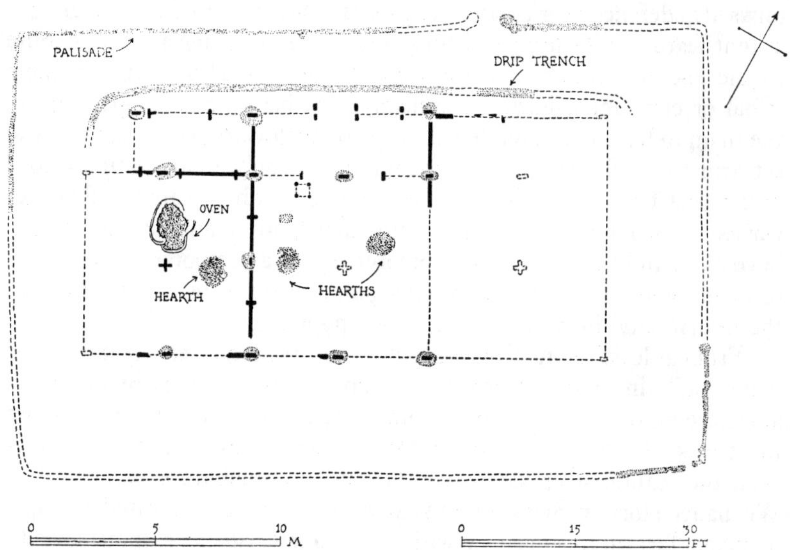

114. *Burnt traces of timber-built house in palisaded enclosure, Hallstatt* D *culture, sixth century* B.C., *below Tumulus* IV, *the Heuneburg, South Germany.*

form of social unit in later prehistoric antiquity.[75] A single building which may be interpreted as a chieftain's house is that of which the burnt traces were found under Tumulus IV near the Heuneburg. There were two phases of construction, of which the later was the better preserved, indicating the plan of a rectangular house of four rooms, about 35 by 80 feet overall, comprising a kitchen with hearth and oven, a main central room with two hearths, and one large and one small room without hearths, the whole suggesting living and sleeping quarters. The building seems to have been of plank construction, and had been burnt down before the placing of the barrow, with its contained timber mortuary chamber, on top of the remains.[76] (Fig. 114) In Spain, the extraordinary Hallstatt settlement of Cortes de Navarra, of the seventh-sixth centuries, is a 'tell' formed of accumulated levels of rectangular mud-brick houses of *megaron* plan, set in rows along regular streets, strongly reminiscent of the layout of a Greek provincial town.[77]

In the last chapter I touched briefly on the subject of fortifications in early first millennium Europe, but suggested it was more apposite to consider the matter as a whole, as we can now do. We have noted occasional fortified settlements in earlier periods, as around 2000 B.C. in central Europe, but from the first half of the first millennium B.C.

onwards, defence works on a large scale became an increasingly insistent feature in Celtic prehistory, and constitute a melancholy tribute to the endemic internecine warfare of these quarrelsome and unstable tribal or clan units. Earlier fortifications in barbarian Europe seem in the main to have been simple palisades, or earthwork banks and ditches, set around a village; now we encounter not only more complex constructional features in the defences, but forts which cannot all be regarded as defended permanent settlements, for many of them must have been built either in some emergency as a temporary stronghold, or conceived of as defended rallying-points offering recurrent refuge to the human, and increasingly the cattle, population.

From at least the tenth century B.C. we have large-scale fortifications being built in central Europe—a couple of dozen sites in Germany alone are known to belong to the ninth-eighth centuries and many more must exist. Frequently a promontory is fortified by defences across its root, the natural steep slopes affording natural defence elsewhere. The Wittnauer Horn in Switzerland is an excellent, fully excavated example of such a fort, in this instance with a permanent village of about seventy rectangular houses (and so a population of about 350) terraced on the two sides of the ridge behind the great defences, which in their first constructional phase consisted of a sloping-faced rampart with horizontal timber lacing, later modified about 700 B.C. to a vertical-faced and timber-braced wall. Ammunition dumps of sling-stones show how the fort was defended, as were so many forts later in time and nearer home, like Maiden Castle in Dorset. Another Swiss hill-fort of this period, the Montlingerberg near Oberreit, has an elaborately constructed rampart, with timber-framed 'boxes' on stone bases, packed with clay and tying the structure together.[78] (Fig. 115) Some other forts of late Urnfield culture in north-east Germany (many on promontories) show this now recurrent feature of the sheer-faced timbered rampart, utilising both vertical and horizontal timbers, and some have internal structures, as at Starzeddel (where the defences may be early medieval), with, however, eight rectangular Late Bronze Age buildings, four with hearths and so presumably houses, almost filling the inner area of only 300 by 200 feet. Further east, at Biskupin in Polish Pomerania, a peninsula jutting out into a lake was used for a defended settlement, with elaborate timber-laced ramparts of 'box' construction. Having three phases, and containing 80 to 100 wooden houses arranged in a strictly regimented plan with a ring-road and cross-streets of corduroy construction, the site is probably of the sixth-fifth centuries B.C.[79] As we saw earlier in this chapter, several forts of this type in Poland seem to have fallen before attacking Scythian raiders about 500 B.C. The appearance in so many areas of Europe of the

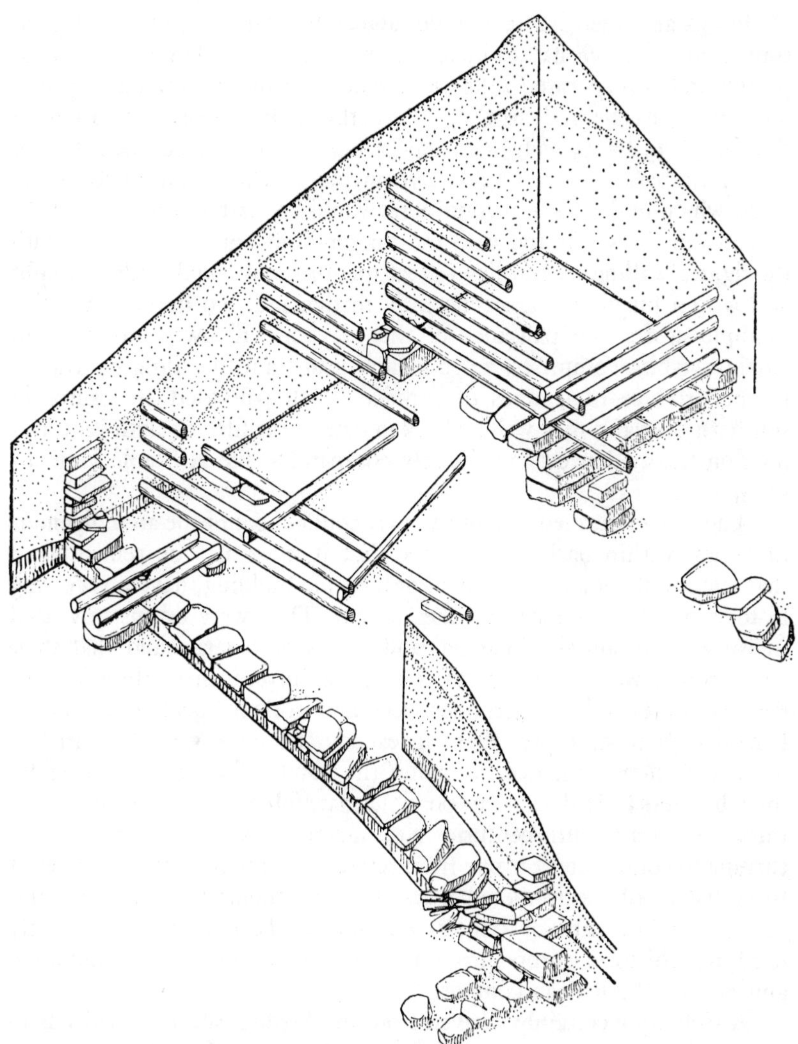

115. *Timber-framed rampart of hill-fort, late Urnfield culture, ninth-eighth century* B.C., *at Montlingerberg, Oberreit, Switzerland.*

timber-laced defensive wall raises interesting problems: in Britain it occurs for instance at Hollingbury in Sussex perhaps as early as the fifth century and, as is well known, is represented by the vitrified and timber-faced stone-wall forts of Scotland, whose origins may well lie in late Urnfield traditions in north Germany.[80] (Pls. XXXIV-XXXV)

It was an expensive technique, demanding large quantities of good timber, all of which had to be felled, cut and trimmed, and then transported and incorporated into the defences on the usually hill-top site. The tiny timber-laced 'fort' at Abernethy in Perthshire, enclosing an area only 135 by 45 feet, demanded a minimum of 3,200 linear feet of 9-inch timbers, which would have involved felling some 640 young trees, which under natural conditions would be scattered through about 60 acres of forest. So too with the timber-built houses, and even with the lighter walling by hurdles—great quantities of felled timber or split and woven hurdling were constantly in demand. To quote a Scottish example again, the palisades of the Hayhope Knowe settlement in Roxburghshire comprised 2,600 8-inch posts, and hurdling equivalent to the produce of 9 acres of coppice. Such palisaded enclosures in southern Scotland may well go back in date to the fifth or sixth centuries B.C., on the evidence of the closely comparable site at Staple How already referred to.[81]

The timber-framed wall or rampart could of course be an indigenous invention within barbarian Europe, but it must also be remembered that such walls, for defence or in peace-time building, have a very long history in the Near East and the Aegean. They were extensively used in early Crete and in Anatolia, and it has been suggested that their construction was a measure to ensure stability in an earthquake; the defences of Troy II were timber-laced and in their burnt condition led Dörpfeld to misinterpret them in exactly the same way that vitrified forts were first explained, as being the result of deliberate firing by their builders.[82] It does seem possible that, following the events of the thirteenth and twelfth centuries B.C., mercenaries and adventurers returning to continental Europe from service in foreign parts remembered the strength of the timbered walls they had themselves attacked, and introduced the technique to their own land. At all events, it was constantly used in prehistoric Europe, from the Carpathians to Inverness, and up to and beyond the Roman conquest.

A technique certainly derived from the Mediterranean world was in fact used at the Heuneburg hill-fort on the Upper Danube, where we saw that Massaliote wine was being imported perhaps via the Rhône and Saône. For its service, Greek black-figure pottery of about 520-470 B.C. was also acquired, and in a reconstruction of the hill-fort defences at this time, a part of the circuit was built of unbaked clay bricks on a stone base and in a series of rectangular bastions. Both plan and construction are characteristically Greek—a brickwork wall of the mid-fourth century B.C. in the Greek colony of Gela in Sicily is a good example—and must indicate the introduction of new techniques in just the

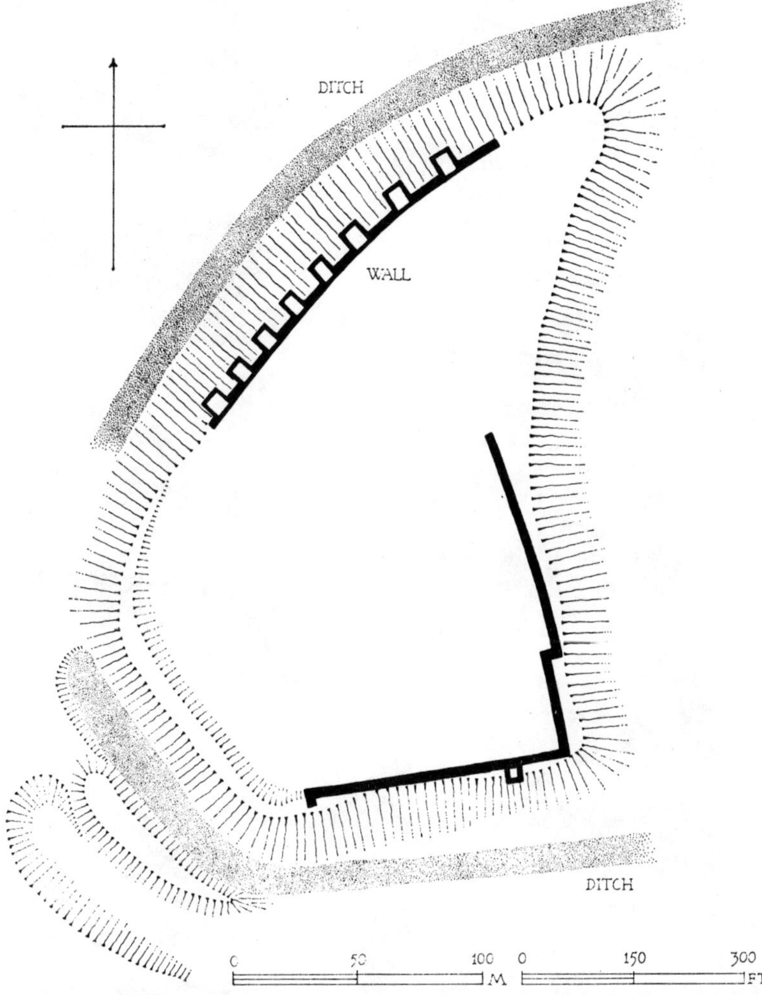

116. *The Heuneburg hill fort, South Germany, with bastioned stone and clay-brick wall, Hallstatt* D *culture, sixth century* B.C.

circumstances I have suggested for the earlier timber-framing. Incidentally, the crowding of the Heuneburg bastions along the north-west side of the forts shows that their defensive purpose was not really understood by the barbaric Celtic chieftain who was dimly apprehending that his stronghold should be fortified in a manner vaguely like a contemporary Greek acropolis. The discovery of the wagon-grave of what

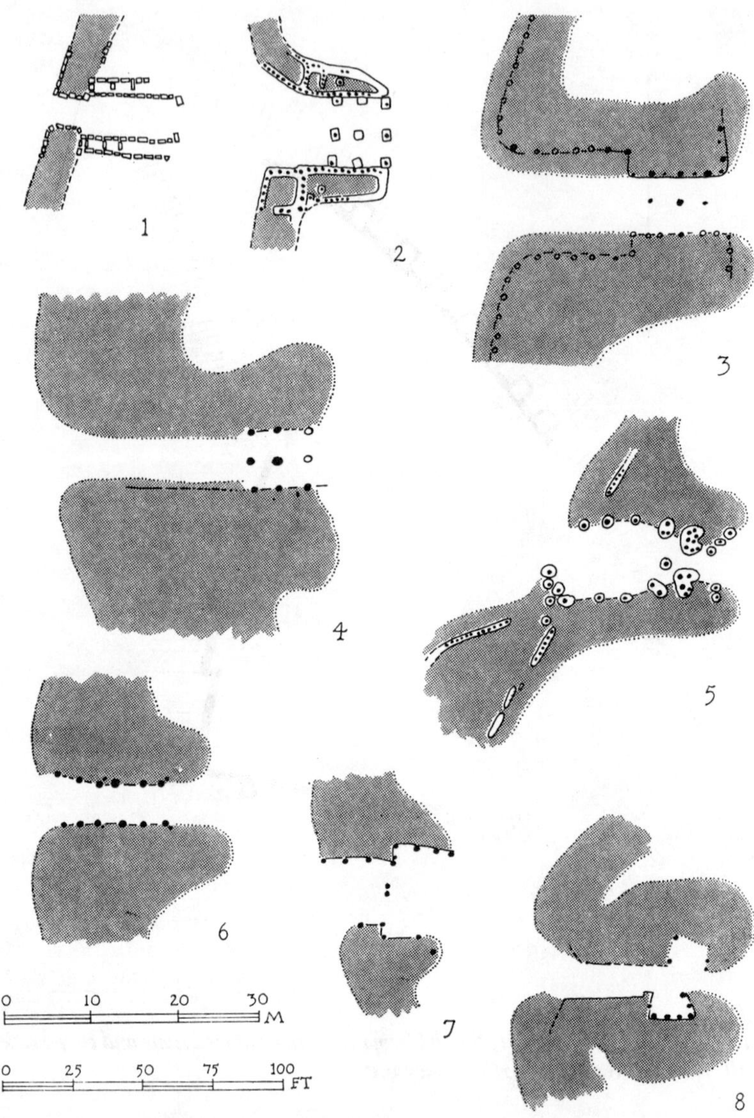

117. *'Inturned' gateways: 1, Stabian Gate, Pompeii, Italy, third century* B.C.; *Hill-forts, third-first century* B.C., *at 2, Nitrianski Hradok, Czechoslovakia; 3, Finsterlohr, Germany; 4, Fécamp, France; 5, Hembury, Devon, England; 6, The Trundle, Sussex, England; 7, St Catherine's Hill, Winchester, England; 8, The Wrekin, Shropshire, England.*

may have been the Captain of the Bowmen, with his quiver-full of arrows, in the Hohmichele barrow outside the Heuneburg, suggests to us how the fort was defended.[83] (Pl. XXXVI; Figs. 101, 116)

The European hill-forts develop in size and complexity in the last four centuries or so B.C., and some of their final developments must be left for the last chapter. Promontory forts are replaced largely by forts with defences following the contours of the hill (like the Heuneburg), and outworks to enclose springs or wells imply that the protection of large herds of cattle is now becoming one of their functions. Ramparts are multiplied, and the defences of the gateway—always the vulnerable point of the defences—take an elaborated form of inturned passage-ways, sometimes with flanking guard-chambers, known from Czecho-slovakia, Austria, Germany, France, and (in great numbers) Britain. Here again Mediterranean prototypes, represented for instance in the third century B.C. Stabian Gate at Pompeii, have been suggested.[84] At all events the hill-fort, in one form or another, becomes the most typical field monument of the Celtic world from about the second century B.C. onwards, from Iberia to Rumania, from the Midi to the Baltic. (Fig. 117)

In the last chapter I will review the mature Celtic achievement in the archaeological phase of La Tène; the Celtic world grew with astonishing rapidity, from the invasion of north Italy in 400 B.C. and the sack of Rome a decade later, to the raid on Delphi and the establishment of the Galatae in Asia Minor in 279, and with Celtic mercenaries operating *in partibus*, as at Syracuse in 368 and in Egypt in 274, where a La Tène shield has been found. And La Tène objects (and even a likely chariot-burial) in south Russia are one aspect of a story represented in another way by the boar-headed *carnyx* or war-trumpet not only from Deskford in Scotland but carved on the Pergamon reliefs in Asia Minor.[85] The Celts had spread themselves widely, but without coherence; no political structure held the scattered tribes together and they had not even the unity of the later barbarian hordes under Attila or the Avar khans. Fragmentation was rapid, and inevitable from the first.

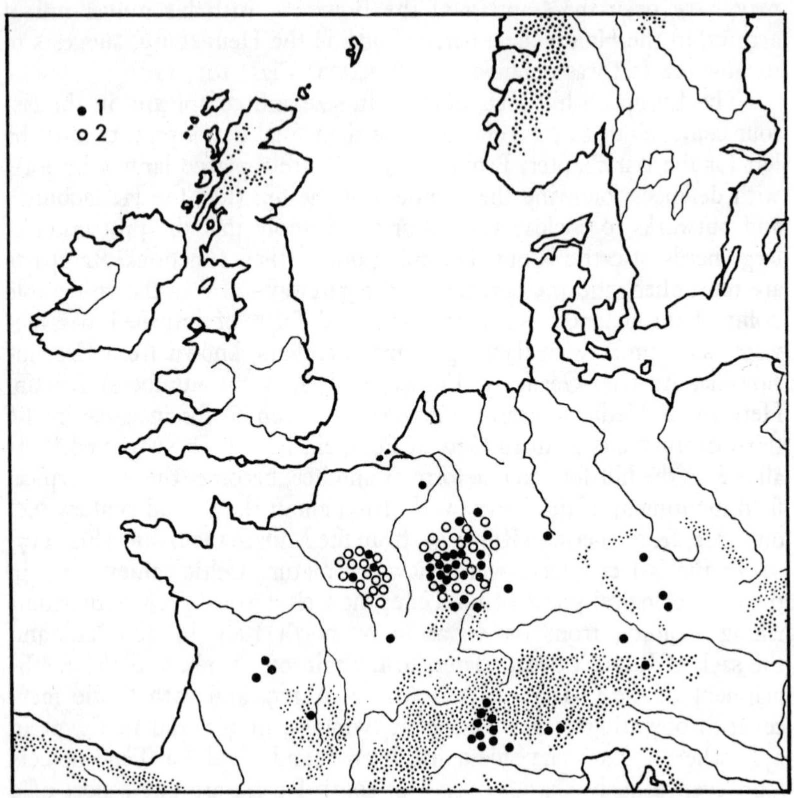

118. *Distribution of early La Tène culture: 1, Imported bronze wine-flagons, fifth century* B.C.; *2, chariot-burials.*

XXXIV. (*on facing page*) *Air view of excavations, showing timber houses, corduroy streets, and timber-framed fortifications, Urnfield culture, sixth century* B.C., *at Biskupin, Poland.* (Photo. Muzeum Archeologiczne, Warsaw)

XXXV. (*on following page*) *Timber-framed defences, corduroy street and houses, Urnfield culture, sixth century* B.C., *at Biskupin, Poland.* (Photo. Muzeum Archeologiczne, Warsaw)

Notes

1. Ammianus Marcellinus XV, 9, 5, quoting Timagenes—'*Aiunt quidam paucos excidium Troiae fugitantes Graecos ubique loca haec occupasse tunc vacua.*'
2. For a discussion of these and other origin-legends, cf. Chadwick 1949, 81-88.
3. Taylour 1958; Brea 1957a, 136-200; Hawkes 1952; Sandars 1963.
4. Hawkes 1952; Maxwell-Hyslop 1956a; Hencken 1956; Almagro 1957; Birmingham 1963.
5. Brea and Cavalier 1960, 80-172; 1959.
6. I follow here the chronology of Müller-Karpe 1959.
7. As Hencken (1958).
8. Piggott 1959a.
9. Merhart 1941; Laur-Belart 1950; Hencken 1958; Müller-Karpe 1959.
10. Merhart 1952; Hawkes and Smith 1957.
11. Kastelic 1956; Pallottino *et al.* 1961; Frey 1962; Lucke and Frey 1962.
12. The famous crater from an Etruscan tomb at Vulci, known as the 'François Vase' and dated to about 570 B.C. is a case in point (convenient illustration in Richter 1959, no. 432). The Peace and War antithesis in oriental art goes back to the 'Standard' of Ur, and the zonal arrangements recalls works such as the Balawat Gates of Shalmaneser III (859-824 B.C.: Frankfort 1954, Pls. 91-92).
13. Frey 1962; cf. Dunbabin 1957, especially p. 47, quoting Payne; Brown 1960. Cf. too the animals on the bronze mountings in the Ny Carlsberg Glyptothek, bought in Italy without provenance; Poulsen 1962, nos. 324-4.
14. For a full study of salt-mining in prehistoric Europe, Nenquin 1961; cf. Clark 1952, 127-8; Kromer 1963.
15. Clark 1952, 128, quoting Strabo III 2, 6 (fish) and IV 3, 2 (pork).
16. Clark 1942; 1952, 128.
17. Childe 1948a, suggesting *inter alia* Greek origins for double-spiral ('spectacle') brooches; Merhart 1952 with map, p. 61, for central European genesis in Urnfield contexts. For the later Balkan brooch types, cf. Alexander 1962.
18. There is a bronze cup of Friederichsrühe type (early Urnfields) from Pavlovka in Bessarabia (Minns 1913, 80, Fig. 23) and a 'Villanovan' helmet from Podoka (Merhart 1941, 20).
19. Kimmig 1954; Sandars 1957.
20. Rix 1954; for Iron Age archaeology and Celtic peoples in Iberia, Schüle 1960; Maluquer 1954a; Powell 1958.
21. Mahr in Mahr *et al.* 1934, 11.
22. Lloyd 1956, 73, 191; Ghirshman 1954, 96; Herodotus I, 103; IV, 12. Dr Gimbutas discussed this theme in an unpublished Munro Lecture, University of Edinburgh, October 1959.

23. Lloyd 1956, *loc. cit.* Cf. the wooden burial chamber with horse-skeletons outside in the burial-pit under Tumulus KY at Gordion (Young 1960).
24. Cf. above, p. 130, and Gimbutas 1961b.
25. The basic English study is still Minns 1913; for later work (with good illustrations), Rice 1957; Phillips 1961; Rudenko 1953, 1960, 1962; Griaznov 1958.
26. For the Scythians in the Near East, Sulimirski 1954.
27. Rudenko 1953, 1960; Griasnov 1958 for illustrations.
28. Cf. Mirns 1942 for a statement of this position.
29. These have been grouped as 'Thraco-Cimmerian'; Gallus and Horvath 1939; Childe 1948, 191; 1950, 228; Kossack 1954.
30. Anderson 1961, 67-69, Pls. 34-35 (Asiatic bits), 38 (Assyrian reliefs), 39 (Persepolis). Tepe Sialk, Ghirshman 1949, II, Graves 15 and 74 (Pls. LVI, LXXV).
31. Court-St-Etienne, Mariën 1958; Bavaria, Kossack 1954; Llyn Fawr, Alcock 1961; Mailhac, Taffanel and Taffanel 1962.
32. Switzerland, Childe 1929, 356; Drack 1959, Pl. 14, 2, 3; Heathery Burn and comparable sites, Hawkes and Smith 1957; cf. too Powell 1950 (Welby); Piggott 1953b (Horsehope).
33. Montelius 1922, nos. 1450-6.
34. Tschumi 1953, 350, Fig. 209; cf. Scythian examples in Ebert 1929, Pl. 39 A.
35. Lundholm 1949; first noted by Childe 1929, 355; Szentes-Vekerzug, Párducz 1952, 1954; Bökönyi 1952, 1954.
36. Dvořak 1938 (Czechoslovakia); Schiek 1954 (Germany and general survey); Drack 1958 (Switzerland and general survey); Joffroy 1958 (France).
37. For horse-harness, des Noëttes 1931; Chinese harness, Needham and Lu 1960.
38. Anderson 1961, *passim*.
39. Strettweg, Schmid 1934; Behn 1962, Pl. 85; Powell 1961, Fig. 28; lavers in Solomon's Temple, Hawkes 1948, 203; Crannon, Forrer 1932, 68. Wheeled stands in Cyprus and Aegean, Catling 1964, 190.
40. Herodotus V, 6; V, 9.
41. Sulimirski 1961.
42. Herodotus IV, 19.
43. Strabo VII, 3, 7; 17, 4, 6.
44. Both quotations from Beardsley 1953.
45. Sulimirski 1952.
46. Illustrated in Cowen 1951, Pl. X. Cf. similar Scythian types in Ebert 1929 Pl. 30A, b.
47. Scythian arrowheads in central and west Europe, Sulimirski 1945, 1961; Kleeman 1954. Hohmichele, Riek and Hundt 1962, with comment on arrows, 156-9, comparing them with Scythian examples in Ebert 1929, Pl. 33C. For Scythian archers as mercenaries in Greece, Vos 1963.

48. I here follow the discussion of early iron technology as set out in Coghlan 1956 and Tylecote 1962. For Hittite iron working and the Hattusilis letter, Gurney 1952, 82-84.
49. For early iron objects in Greece, see Snodgrass 1962, disposing of claims for priority of iron working in the east Hallstatt region made in Foltiny 1961; Müller-Karpe, 1962; Alexander 1962 for Jugoslavia; Müller-Karpe 1959 *passim* for earliest iron in Italy; in Continental Europe, Kimmig 1964b.
50. Coghlan 1956.
51. The planking of the funerary chambers in the Hohmichele is discussed in Riek and Hundt 1962, 44 ff.; massive timber mortuary chambers are recorded in many Hallstatt tombs; cf. that at Villingen, illustrated in Behn 1962, Pl. 78. For early saws, Rieth 1958.
52. The Ferriby boats were at the time of their discovery dated to 'not before the third century B.C. and not after the 1st century A.D.' (Wright and Wright 1947), but without any very conclusive evidence. The radiocarbon reading of 750±150 B.C. (BM-58; Barker and Mackey 1960) gives a permissible range of 900-600 B.C.
53. Clark 1952, 216.
54. For Mont Lassois, Vix, Ste Colombe, etc., Joffroy 1954, 1958, 1960a,bc; for the Heuneburg and its barrows such as the Hohmichele, Dehn 1953, 1957, 1958; Dehn and Sangmeister 1954; Riek and Hundt 1962; Schiek 1959; Kimmig and Hell 1958, 73 ff.; Kimmig and Rest 1954; Kossack 1959; Drack 1960. The Hallstatt cemetery has been fully published in Kromer 1960; short account (with salt-mining), Kromer 1963; general survey for Austria in Pittioni 1954; east Hallstatt provinces, Mahr *et al.* 1934; Benac and Covic 1957; Garašanin 1962; Condurachi 1963.
55. France discussed in Sandars 1957; France and Iberia in Savory 1948, 1949; Hencken 1956; Hawkes 1952; Iberia in Almagro 1957, 1958b; MacWhite 1951.
56. Earliest British bronze swords, Cowen 1951; for early horses and vehicles in Britain, Hawkes and Smith 1957; Powell 1950; Piggott 1953b; earliest iron-using cultures discussed in Hawkes 1945, 1959; Brewster 1963.
57. For Scythian raids and Polish forts, Sulimirski 1954, 1961; Kleeman 1954; Scythians at Karmir-Blur, Piotrovsky 1954, 56; cf. Phillips 1963.
58. For the Near East generally, Delaporte 1948, *passim*; Lloyd 1956, 156 ff.; Urartians, Piotrovsky 1954, 1962; Akurgal 1959; Phillips 1963; Greek Dark Ages and migrations, Desborough and Hammond 1962; Cook 1961; Desborough 1964; Greeks in west and east, Dunbabin 1948, 1957.
59. Diringer 1962, 149; Wace and Stubbings 1962, 159.
60. Agora and Kerameikos graves, Blegen 1952; Kraiker and Kübler 1939; Müller-Karpe 1962; Kimmig 1964b; Müller-Karpe 1962b; Argos grave, Courbin 1957: Dr Snodgrass pointed out the Oriental prototypes of the

helmet in lectures in the University of Edinburgh 1962, citing Barnett and Faulkner 1962, Pl. LXXIII (relief of *c.* 740 B.C.). The Old Paphos grave in Cyprus is published by Karageorghis (1963a). For Etruscan and later fire-dogs, cf. Drost 1954, and below p. 247.

61. The enormous literature is admirably summarised in Pallottino 1955 (for origins, especially Chapter II, stressing autochthonous elements), and an archaeological case for Oriental and east European origins has been put forward by Hencken (1958a, and in Munro Lectures, University of Edinburgh, November 1959).

62. Cf. Harden 1962, 62 ff.; Hawkes 1952, 1963.

63. Hencken 1950; Coles 1962, and since then the shield from Old Paphos (Karageorghis 1963a).

64. There is a considerable literature on these vessels and their decorative attachments, summarised in Hawkes and Smith 1957, 165 ff. Cf. Phillips 1963; Lloyd 1956, 188; Akurgal 1959; Piotrovsky 1962; for Urartian cauldrons such as that from Altin Tepe; Lloyd 1961, 193 and Young 1958 for Phrygian cauldrons at Gordion; Jantzen 1955 for Greece; Mrs Maxwell-Hyslop (1956b) discusses Urartian bronzes in Etruscan contexts but, cf. warning on dates in Hawkes and Smith 1957, 171. Griffins, Bolton 1962, 85-93. A case for a north Syrian rather than an Urartian origin for such cauldrons (or at least the 'siren' attachments) has recently been put forward (Muscarella 1962). For French finds, Ste Colombe in Joffroy 1958, 1960b, c; Angers griffin-protome and Auxerre tripod *ibid.* 1960 c; Rolley 1962. The alleged protome from Sens (cf. Déchelette 1927, 1104; de Navarro 1928, 425) appears to be a medieval piece (Joffroy 1960c). The Hassle (Stockholm) cauldron, found with Hallstatt swords and ribbed buckets, is illustrated in Stenberger 1962, Pl. 38.

65. Cauldrons in Hawkes and Smith 1957; Avienus discussed in Hawkes 1952; Albion in Powell 1958, 25; Jackson 1948. Some philologists consider 'Albion' to contain a pre-Celtic Indo-European root of Krahe's 'Old European' group already referred to (p. 91).

66. The first large-scale discussion of Mediterranean imports north of the Alps in this period was that of Déchelette (1927, 1104 with list and map); further studies in de Navarro 1928 (general); Jacobsthal 1929; Villard 1956; Frey 1963 ('Rhodian' flagons); Jacobsthal and Neuffer 1933 (Massalia and south France); Villard 1960; Frey 1957 (Hatten pyxis); Hencken 1958b (Etruscan bowls); Kimmig 1958 (general study); Lerat 1958 (Conliège amphora); Cahn 1958 (Grächwil hydria); Boardman 1964; Vix, Ste Colombe, Heuneburg, etc., in references already given; possible Iberian context for Vix 'diadem' Schüle 1960. A fully documented summary of the chronological implications of these finds is in Dehn and Frey 1962. For the La Tène imports, see below, p. 216.

67. For the inland distribution of amphorae of micaceous Massaliote fabric (and also of Mediterranean coral, significant in this respect), cf. Benoit 1958.
68. Riek and Hundt 1962, 213 ff. For a good account of the ancient silk trade and its routes in Classical and later times, see Huzayyin 1942; for possible Greek knowledge of central Asia in the seventh century, cf. Bolton 1962.
69. *The Times*, 13 January 1953.
70. Bronze-sheathed wheels on ritual vehicles are discussed in Hawkes and Smith 1957, 153; to references there given add Chapotat 1962 on the Côte-Saint-André car. Horse-yokes and leather girdles with bronze studding, Dvořak 1938; Drack 1958, 14 ff.; Filip 1960, Pl. II.
71. Vogt 1947.
72. Textiles in Vogt 1947; Hundt 1961b; leather garments in Pittioni 1951; Kromer 1963; both discussed by Clark, 1952, 221-2; 236-8.
73. The Sopron (Oedenburg) pots have often been illustrated in part, completely only in Gallus 1934; cf. Clark 1952, Fig. 131; Behn 1962, Pl. 72a. For trousers, see above, p. 111, and Hald 1961.
74. The plan of the Goldberg settlement is in Childe 1950, Fig. 178; the Kyberg (Oberhaching), Pätzold and Schwarz 1961; Pätzold 1963.
75. The homestead with single round house was first identified as a type in the Little Woodbury (Wilts.) excavations (Bersu 1940) and appears to go back to the earliest southern First A cultures of Iron Age Britain as at Longbridge Deverill (S. Chadwick 1961), and to persist (at least in Ireland) into the early Middle Ages (Proudfoot 1961, and below, p. 237). For Staple Howe, Brewster 1963.
76. Schiek 1959.
77. Maluquer 1954b.
78. For the Wittnauer Horn, Bersu 1945, 1946; Montlingerberg, Frei 1955; Drack 1959, Pl. 19, 4.
79. General discussion of 'Lusatian' forts in Tackenburg 1950; earlier excavations in Schuchhardt 1909, 1926; later in Schubart 1961 (Kratzeburg fort now dated to c. 815 B.C.-Bln-78). Biskupin, Kostrewski 1938, 1950. It now appears that some defences formerly considered Late Bronze Age (as the Römerschanze near Potsdam) are in fact early medieval fortifications built on prehistoric sites. (Herrman 1960; Nováki 1964).
80. The problems of the British timber-laced forts have been reviewed in Cotton 1955; a possible late Urnfield ancestry of the Scottish forts would be consonant with the north European contacts perceptible in the local Late Bronze Age (Coles 1960).
81. The figures for timber in Scottish forts were originally calculated by Mr Roy Ritchie, using estimates of natural woodland resources, etc., based on those in the Trelleborg report (Nørlund 1948); the hurdling estimates are

based on figures obtained from Dorset hurdle-makers in the nineteen-forties. For the relevant south Scottish sites, cf. R.C.A.M. (S) 1956.

82. Cf. Lloyd 1956, 102.
83. Heuneburg and Hohmichele references as above; Gela, Adamesteanu 1957, dating the construction there to *c.* 355 B.C.
84. For inturned entrances with guard-chambers in continental Europe, Dehn 1961; British examples in Hawkes 1931; Varley 1950.
85. See below, p. 215. Celtic mercenaries and raids, Powell 1958; later Gauls in North Africa, Leglay 1962. La Tène armlet from the Isthmus of Corinth, Krämer 1961.

XXXVI. (*a*) *Stone footings of bastion, with clay brick walling above, Hallstatt culture, sixth century* B.C., *at the Heuneburg hill-fort, South Germany.*
XXXVI. (*b*) *Excavated footings of bastion in hill-fort rampart, Hallstatt culture, sixth century* B.C., *at the Heuneburg, South Germany.*
(Both photos. Staatliche Amt für Denkmalpflege, Tübingen)

XXXVI (*caption on facing page*)

a

b

XXXVII. *Bronze flagon with paste inlay, one of a pair, early La Tène culture, fourth century* B.C., *from Basse-Yutz, Lorraine, France.*
(Photo. British Museum)

6

The Celtic World and its Aftermath

THE last phase of Celtic culture in Europe, a mature stage of which constituted the Celts as known to the Greek, and soon the Roman world, begins in archaeological terms around 500 B.C. The date is determined by the Etruscan and Greek objects found in graves as in the couple of centuries before; concurrently, in the fifth century, important internal changes take place in material culture, at least among the aristocracy.[1] Political power seems to shift northward from Burgundy and south Germany, and in the middle Rhine, and in France in the Marne region, we suddenly encounter at this time princely graves showing a change in funerary custom, for no longer is a four-wheeled wagon buried with the upper-class dead, but a two-wheeled cart or chariot. This presumably means a change not only in funerary practice, but correspondingly in tactics on the field of battle, and we must shortly consider the question of the likely origins for such a change. However it may have been brought about, the use of the chariot in warfare and parade was to become a characteristically Celtic institution, continuing in Gaul up to the second century B.C., though burial of the vehicle was given up there a century or so earlier; in Britain, apart from a restricted group of third-second century graves, we have evidence of chariot-warfare up to the second century A.D.[2] Outside the main area of the earlier development of the culture, La Tène cart- or chariot-burials occur sporadically throughout the last three centuries or so B.C. in regions such as Hungary, Bulgaria, and even probably south Russia, and the use of the chariot in Galatia is attested by representations on Hellenistic reliefs of native trophies as at Pergamon.[3] The east European area was to become the Roman provinces of Pannonia, Moesia, and Thracia, and here chariot- and wagon-burials of the early centuries A.D. appear to represent the continuance of the Celtic tradition, though Sarmatian contributions or even a long indigenous tradition presumably cannot be excluded.[4] (Fig. 118)

But with the chieftains' chariot-burials and other graves with rich offerings including Etruscan and Greek imports (notably bronze wine-flagons) the archaeological phase of La Tène begins in the Rhineland and almost concurrently in the Marne. Trade now seems to have been across the Alpine passes rather than via Massalia and the Rhône. In the armoury of the warriors distinctive long iron swords in decorated scabbards (usually of bronze) appear. The long or oval shield, continuing the Hallstatt tradition as seen for instance on the Strettweg warriors or the situla scenes, now comes into general use, and, by the middle of the period at least, is buried with the warrior. Above all, as we shall see, these and other luxury objects display in their ornamentation an art style new to Europe; barbarian even as Scythian art is, and indeed with strong affinities to it; exciting and mysterious and wholly alien to the Mediterranean world, early Celtic art is one of the major aesthetic contributions of ancient Europe. (Pls. XXXVII; XLV-XLVII)

We will return to art and warriors' equipment, and we have already looked at the earlier history of Celtic fortification. The timber-framing of ramparts, whereby they were made in effect sheer-faced walls, was further developed. A characteristic middle La Tène type, with uprights along the inner and outer faces of the wall, with transverse cross-ties, is exemplified by the fort at Preist in the Rhineland, and harks back to late Urnfield prototypes, as we saw last in chapter 5. (Fig. 119) In the first century B.C., and in response to Roman siege-tactics, the basic form was modified, and strengthened by fastening the timbers at their intersections by iron nails; a technique probably first evolved in Gaul and thence spread to other Celtic areas on the eve of their attack by the Roman armies. Caesar encountered and described it, naming it the *murus gallicus* or Gaulish wall.[5] (Fig. 120) Some of the forts, of great size, must have had political status as *oppida*, in the sense of a tribal or cantonal centre, commensurate with their magnitude and fortifications. (Figs. 121-122) Manching in Bavaria, an *oppidum* of the Vindelici, started in Middle La Tène times, encloses a roughly circular area of flat land about a mile-and-a-half across with a rampart (in its final form) of *murus gallicus* construction and over four miles in circuit; if one assumes a minimum of ten courses of timber-work this would have involved no less than 300 tons of iron nails. The area enclosed, in terms of London, is a circle with Piccadilly Circus as its centre, running through Euston Station, the Aldwych, Westminster Abbey, Buckingham Palace and the American Embassy in Grosvenor Square. The recent excavations show that a central roughly oval area, about a mile by three-quarters of a mile in extent, was largely built up with timber structures which can be interpreted as houses, barns, stores, and probably rows of shops or 'bazaars' along streets up to 30 feet or so in width. (Fig. 123) The space between

119. *Timber-framed wall of hill-fort, middle La Tène culture, second century* B.C., *at Preist, Trier, Germany.*

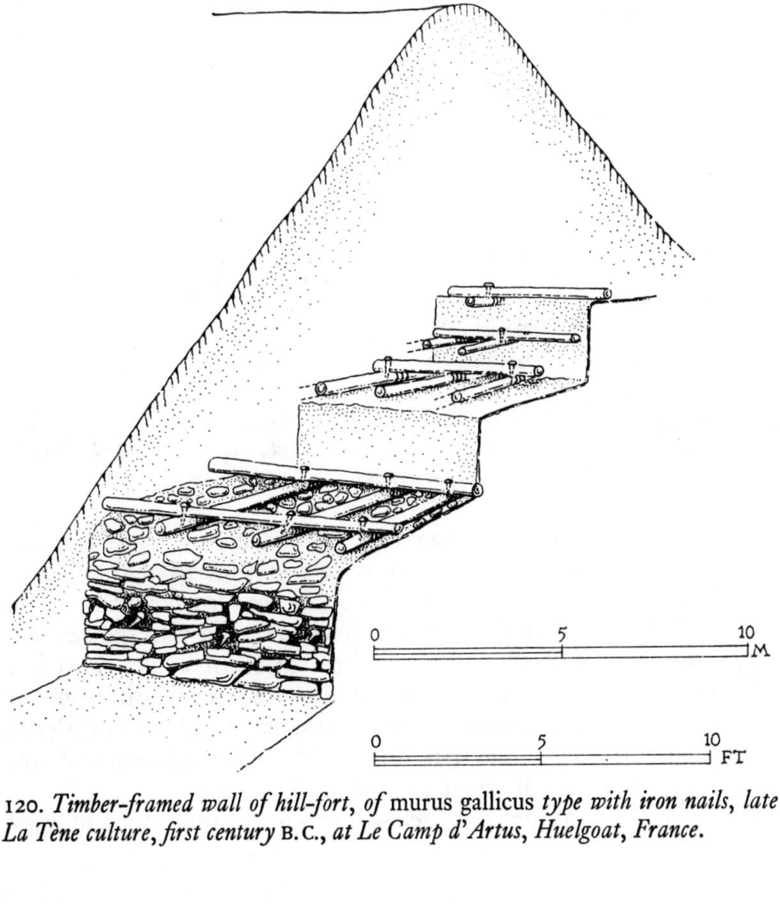

0 5 10 M

0 5 10 FT

120. *Timber-framed wall of hill-fort, of* murus gallicus *type with iron nails, late La Tène culture, first century* B.C., *at Le Camp d'Artus, Huelgoat, France.*

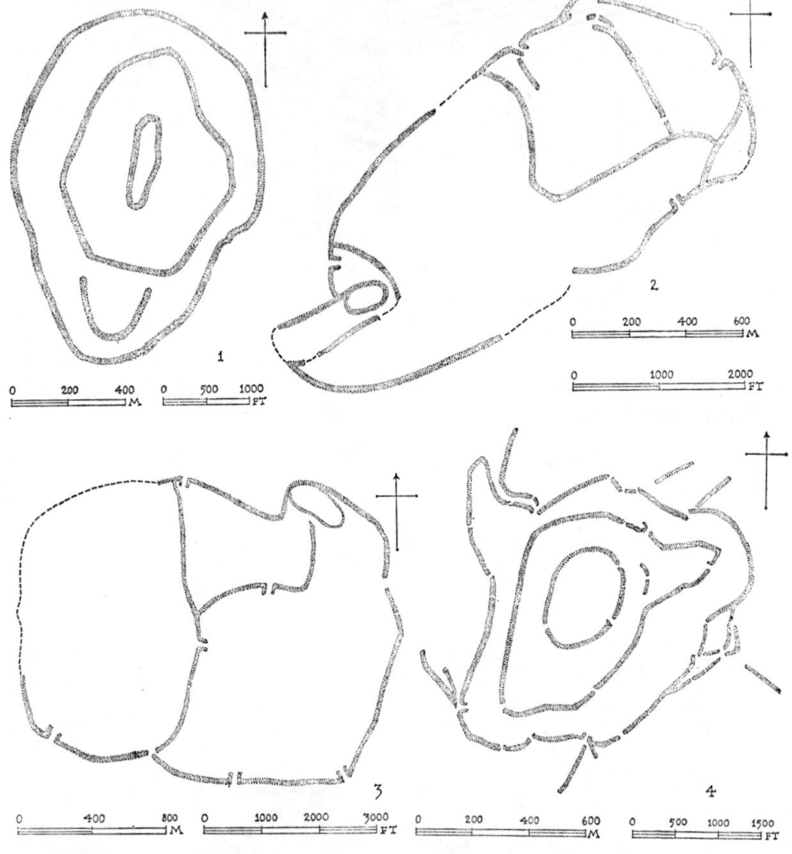

121. *Hill-forts of* oppida *status, late La Tène culture, probably first century* B.C. *in final constructional phase, at 1, Steinburg, Römhild; 2, Heidentränk-Talenge; 3, Donnersberg; 4, Dürnsberg: all Germany.*

this township and the defensive rampart would afford pasture and protection for cattle in times of insecurity or war, with water supplied by the tributary of the Danube that forms the western boundary of the site.[6] If Manching is at all typical, we have to reckon with the development, in late pre-Roman Celtic Europe, of social and architectural units that can only be called towns; similar circumstances in Gaul had indeed led to fortified settlements (as for instance at Bibracte or Alesia), to which Caesar did not hesitate to apply the words *oppidum* and *urbs*, and which we can hardly think of as other than towns.

Bibracte (near Autun) was enclosed with nearly three miles of *murus*

a

b

XXXVIII. (*a, above*) *Bastion of fort wall, middle La Tène culture, second century* B.C., *at Entremont, Aix-en-Provence, France.*
XXXVIII. (*b, below*) *Stone pillar with carvings of severed human heads, re-used as threshold, middle La Tène culture, second century* B.C., *at Entremont, Aix-en-Provence, France.* (Both photos. author)

a

b

XXXIX. *Silver cauldron with decorative panels in relief, middle La Tène culture, first–second century* B.C., *votive deposit in bog at Gundestrup, Jutland, Denmark.* (*a*) *General view;* (*b*) *detail of internal panel.* (Photos. Nationalmuseet, Copenhagen)

0 500 1000 M
0 2000 4000 FT

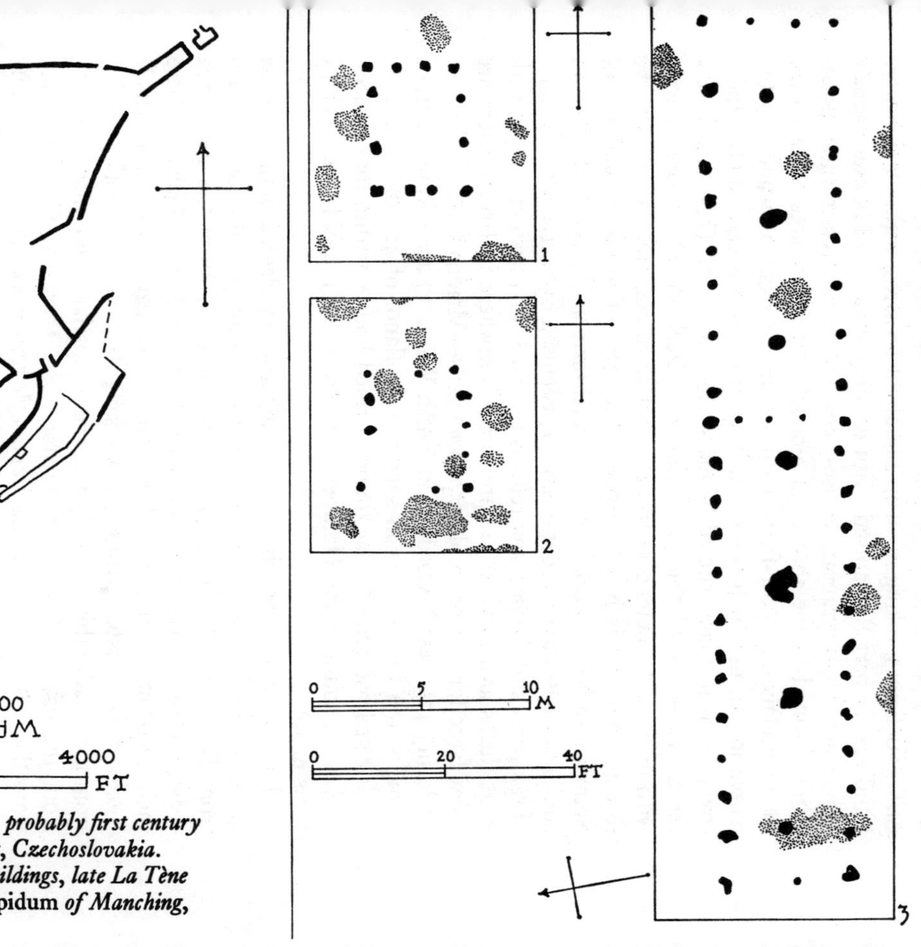

122. (*left*) Oppidum, *late La Tène culture, probably first century* B.C. *in final constructional phase, at Zavist, Czechoslovakia.*
123. (*right*) *Post-holes of timber-framed buildings, late La Tène culture, second–first century* B.C., *in the* oppidum *of Manching, South Germany.*

gallicus defences, taking in an area of about 60 acres, within which were buildings, in part Romanised 'with winding streets and houses vaguely suggesting Mediterranean house-plans but with architectural possibilities limited by the absence of mortar'. But in one area at least were found rectangular post-framed houses and workshops wholly in the native idiom, in which the enamelling of metal was carried out; and a row of similarly constructed 'bazaars' along a street.[7] (Fig. 124) In the eastern Celtic world, the fort of Zavist in Czechoslovakia covers 80 acres with its complex defences (probably not all of one building phase); the fort at Stradonic is half this size.[8] (Fig. 122) The exceptional site of Stanwick in North Yorkshire, in its final form at the eve of the Roman conquest of Brigantia around A.D. 71, enclosed 850 acres with six miles of ramparts and ditches, and reflects the needs of a pastoral people with large flocks and herds to be protected. Elsewhere in Britain there are a few large forts of probable *oppidum* status—Maiden Castle in Dorset, enclosing 45 acres; Y Corddyn in North Wales, 37 acres in its enlarged form; or the Eildon Fort in southern Scotland, of 40 acres and containing at least 300 circular timber-framed houses within its defences. In Britain south of the Humber there are some 150 hill-forts over 15 acres in area.[9]

Large fortifications which can be superficially classed in the *oppidum* group are in fact scattered across the wholly or partially Celtic world from Iberia to the Carpathians, only 300 miles from the Black Sea coast; a classical writer says the Celts built hill-forts in Galatia, where their recognition in the field is still a challenge to archaeologists.[10] Again at their eastern fringes, as we saw, they touched another world; from the middle third century B.C. the Sarmatians were moving slowly from the east into Scythian territory, and there was Celtic pressure from the west. Objects of La Tène style and workmanship, including a sword and scabbard, are distributed beyond the bounds of East Celtic settlement into south Russia as far as the Crimea and the River Dneipr, and even sporadically as far east as the Volga. What may have been a chariot-burial near Melitopol (already referred to) contained a bronze helmet of a type known in two other south Russian finds, and not only characteristic of the Italo-Celtic west, but represented on the Pergamon reliefs of the second century B.C. as a Galatian form; contacts across the Black Sea are by no means improbable.[11] Raiding and service as mercenaries took Celts to distant places, as history and archaeology combine to show. The civilisation of the Mediterranean, in the east aloof and uninterested in the northern barbarians, was nevertheless in the Roman world sharply aware of the Celtic settlement established south of the Alps since the early fourth century, and not subdued until 225

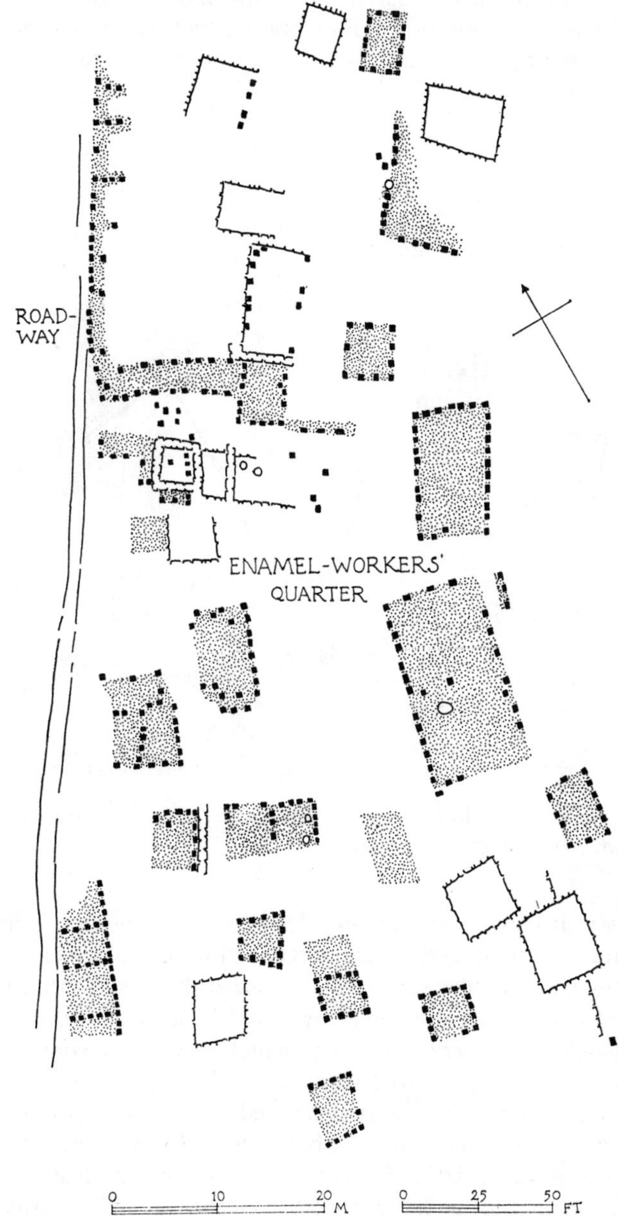

124. *Remains of burnt buildings with squared timbers, late La Tène culture, first century* B.C., *in the* oppidum *of Bibracte (Mont Beuvray), Autun, France.*

B.C. Linguistically this barbarian world was united, however loosely (if at all) it had any sense of social or political coherence beyond the individual tribe, by the mature P-Celtic form of the language.

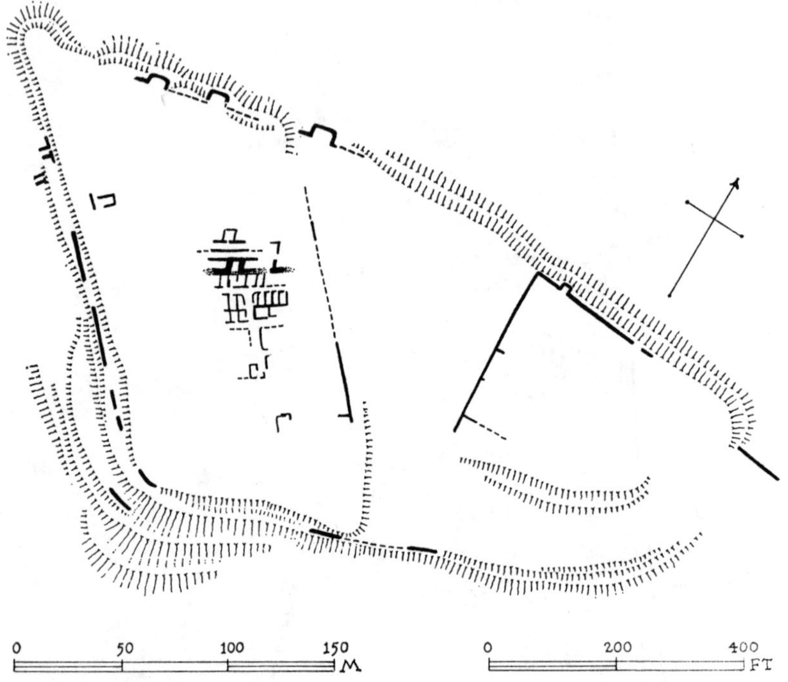

125. *Stone-walled* oppidum, *middle La Tène culture, second century* B.C., *at Entremont, Aix-en-Provence, France.*

As is well known, the British Isles present an anomalous linguistic situation at this time. Ireland alone retained until the present day a Q-Celtic language, philologically probably earlier than the P-form, and elsewhere in Celtic Europe submerged by this with the exception of a very few names (such as *Sequana*, the River Seine). A possible context for the introduction of Q-Celtic to Ireland could be seen in the appearance there in some quantity of Hallstatt-derived bronze swords of the seventh century B.C.; in La Tène times, although with direct continental as well as British contacts, Ireland takes a very peripheral place in Celtic Europe: for instance adopting the characteristic La Tène brooch only in the first century B.C., and then at second hand from southern England. In the Pictish area of eastern Scotland linguistic considerations suggest the mingling of a P-Celtic not identical with Old Brittonic and presumptively earlier, with a local non-Indo-European language: the contacts between north Britain and the surviving late Urnfield cultures of northern Europe in the seventh and sixth centuries B.C. might, as we saw, provide a context for such a situation.[12]

In the south of France, finally incorporated as a Roman province in 121 B.C., Celtic culture developed side by side with that centred on the Greek colony of Massalia. The capital of the Saluvii at Entremont near Aix, ranked as a *polis* by Strabo, and destroyed in 123 B.C., is a hill-fort of some 9 acres with a bastioned stone wall, single-room houses along streets, and a sanctuary of the 'severed-head' cult referred to again below; Ensérune near Béziers is a promontory-fort with stone houses and grain-storage pits; Cayla de Mailhac is a fortified site occupied from the sixth century B.C. into middle La Tène times.[13] (Fig. 125; Pl. XXXVIII)

In Iberia a complex situation developed beyond the southern coastal zone of Greek and Carthaginian colonies, with a Celtic population mainly in the centre and west of the peninsula, Iberians (with a non-Indo-European language) in the south and east, and a mixed Celtiberian element resulting from the mingling of the two. The Celtic hill-forts, with ramparts or stone walls, contain houses sometimes rectangular or oval, but predominantly circular, as in contemporaneous Britain. In the Iberian area, Greek influences led to a lively style of native vase-painting, which includes representations of birds, animals, and scenes depicting human beings; and also to local schools of sculpture, as in the south French sanctuaries we will touch on later.[14] (Figs. 126-127)

In central Europe, the Celtic world marched with another, vaguely grouped as Germanic. Linguistically of course, we are still in an Indo-European world, and at least one school of philological thought sees the Germanic language group as representing a development later than that of the Celtic-Italic-Hittite-Tocharian series, but holds that contact between Germanic and the Italic group must have existed in the middle Danube area, with the Celts established further west; a possible situation in Urnfield times.[15] But quite apart from linguistics, we should be on our guard in attempting to make too sharp a distinction between Celts and Germans. The archaeology involved, it has been remarked, is 'easy to misconstrue because so drab'; nevertheless it does seem impossible to make any meaningful division before the end of the first millennium B.C., and then the whole question is to some extent clouded by the manipulation of facts for personal and political ends in such documents as the *Gallic War* of Julius Caesar. An enemy-image had to be built up and put across, and while tribal differences operated powerfully between the two banks of the Rhine, it was worthwhile to exaggerate them. Added to this, the ever-latent myth of the Noble Savage among Roman intellectuals led to counter-distortions, culminating in the *Germania* of Tacitus; a tract for the times if ever there was one.[16]

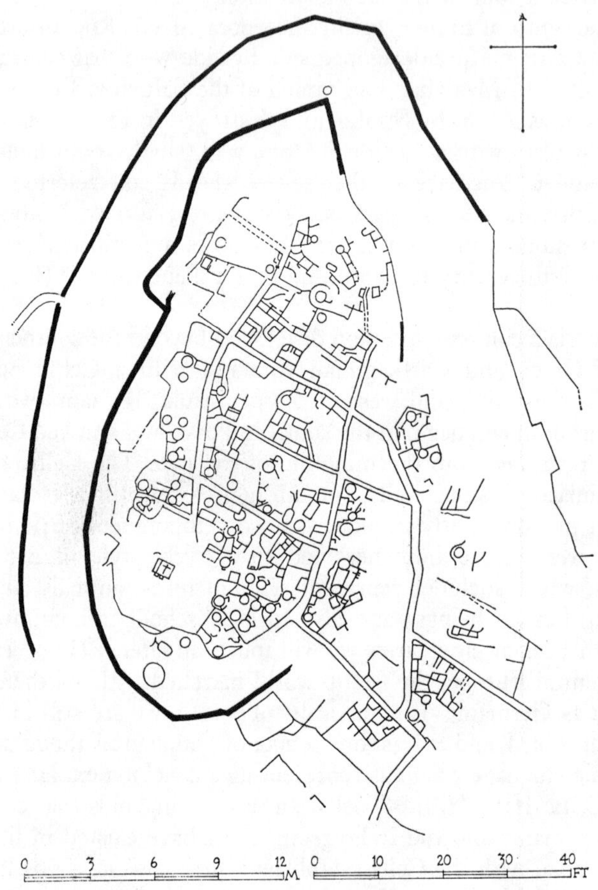

126. *Stone-walled hill-fort and settlement, probably second-first century* B.C., *at Citania, Guimarães, Portugal.*

XL. (*a*) *Gold helmet with relief ornament, Dacian, third-second century* B.C., *from Poiana-Coţofenşti, Rumania.* (Photo. Institutul de Arheologie, Bucharest)
XL. (*b*) *Silver helmet with relief ornament, Dacian, third-second century* B.C. *from River Danube at the Iron Gates, Rumania.* (Photo. Detroit Institute of Arts)

XL (*caption on facing page*)

b

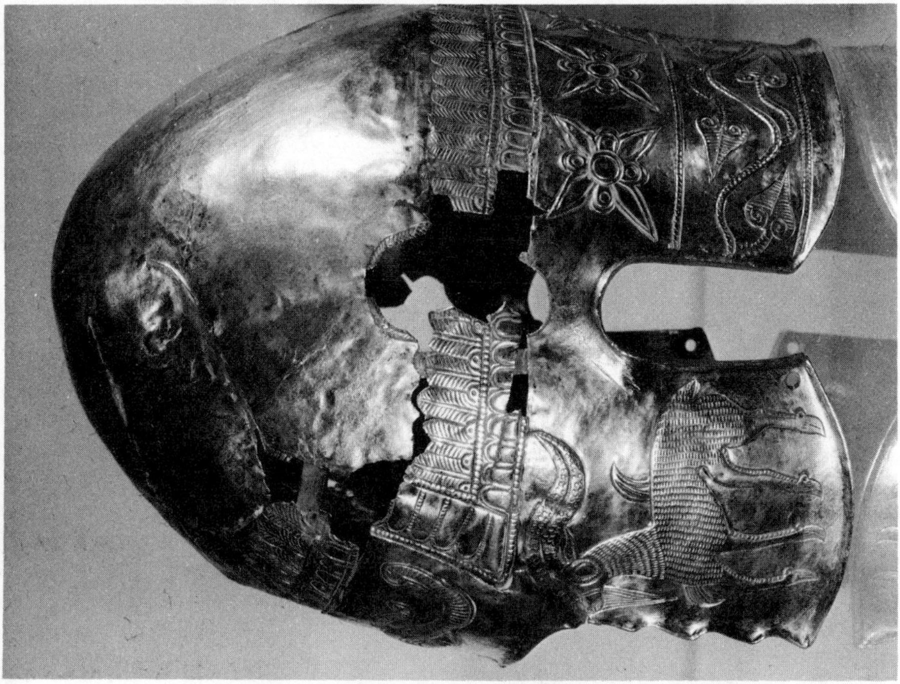

a

a

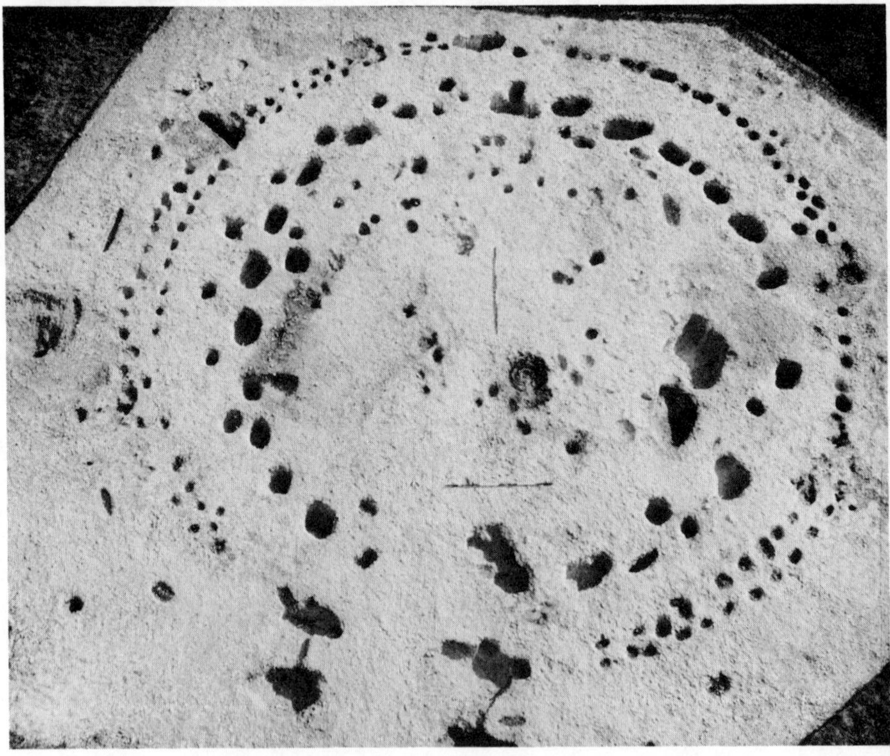

b

XLI. (*a*) *Stone-built circular house during excavation, second century* A.D., *at Sollas, North Uist, Scotland.* (Photo. Malcolm Murray)

XLI. (*b*) *Excavated post-holes of circular timber-framed house, third century* B.C., *at Pimperne, Dorset, England.* (Photo. I. M. Blake & D. W. Harding)

127. *Painted designs on pots, Iberian culture, third century* B.C., *from south-east Spain.*

128. *Painted frieze of warriors on pot, Iberian culture, third century* B.C., *San Miguel de Liria, Spain.*

The degree of Celtic influence in Scandinavia has been much discussed, but the archaeological evidence suggests that it was as strong as in, for instance, north Britain. It includes among its products objects of trade not only from the nearer Celtic peoples of the south, but to my mind also from the remoter south-east, from that Carpathian-north Pontic world along the same route as those contacts of the middle second millennium B.C. The famous Danish ritual silver cauldron from Gundestrup is considered by some to be an imported north Gaulish piece, but it has very strong stylistic links with other silver, silver-gilt, and gold works of art known from tombs and hoards in Dacia and Thrace, such as the helmet, greaves, cups and bowls in silver-gilt from the tomb (with attendant horse-burials) at Hagighiol, or the Poroina rhyton and the massive gold helmet from Poiana-Coțofenești, all in Rumania; or the Lukovit hoard in Bulgaria. A well-known series of decorated silver discs, with a distribution from the Crimea to the Haute Savoie and Holland, emphasises these east-west connections within the Celto-Sarmatian world of the second to first century B.C.,[17] and the story is continued in the evidence for ritual horse-sacrifice, with the veneration of the hide, from south Russia to Scandinavia in the first five centuries A.D.[18] The Viking settlements in south Russia and on the Black Sea from the ninth century A.D. onwards were surely, in some sense, the heirs of a long tradition of contacts. (Pls. XXXIX; XL).

Our sources for a study of the last phase of prehistoric Celtic Europe are threefold: archaeology, the comments of Greek and Roman writers, and the oral vernacular tradition that survived in Ireland long enough to become incorporated in written documents in the Middle Ages, and which in part relates to a pre-Christian, prehistoric order of Celtic society. This last source is, needless to say, the most difficult to use, and is full of potential ambiguities and pitfalls, but it cannot be ignored. The major Celtic scholars—Jackson, Dillon, Binchy—have endorsed its value in such enquiries as ours, as part of the oldest vernacular literature in Europe north of the Alps, and it is on their interpretations that I now rely. There are two major sources: a group of legal documents usually called the Law Tracts, committed to writing in the seventh or sixth century A.D.; and the earlier group of hero-tales, the so-called Ulster Cycle, mainly in twelfth century manuscripts, but preserving linguistic forms of the eighth, and in content referable to events earlier than the fifth century A.D.—in general to the centuries around the beginning of the Christian era.[19]

It should be said straight away that the picture of the structure and nature of Celtic society as given in early Irish literature is consonant with that contained in the classical writers, notably the Stoic philosopher and ethnographer Posidonius, writing in the mid-first century B.C., and upon whose account of Celtic customs Athenaeus, Diodorus, Strabo, and Caesar all draw.[20] It is also in accord with such inferences as we can make from the archaeological evidence. On the other hand, we must remember that it relates to Ireland, and so not necessarily in detail even to Britain, and the archaeological evidence, as we shall see, emphasises that Celtic Britain in the last few centuries B.C. had very distinctive qualities which differentiated it from the contemporary continent. This is just a warning that we should not too closely compare Cú Chulainn with Commius, nor the state of affairs at Manching with that of Emain Macha.

With these reservations, Celtic society in these sources emerges as, in Binchy's words, 'tribal, rural, hierarchical and familiar'. The major territorial unit is the tribe—the *túath*, a version of a recurrent Indo-European word meaning 'the total body of people', present indeed in the tribal name of the Teutones. But the Irish tribal area was small, ruled over by a chieftain or 'king'—*rí*—below whom came the 'grades of nobility'; the warrior aristocracy, the *equites* of Caesar. Between them and the main body of freemen, the Irish lawyers recognised an intermediate class to which they themselves belonged, composed of the craftsmen and the *literati*, the poets and the priests—the 'men of art', including the Druids.[21] The Irish literary evidence suggests that this professional class came nearer to the nobility than to the citizenry in status and esteem, and archaeological confirmation of this might be seen in the contents of a Bavarian grave of about 200 B.C., where a man was provided not only with the sword, shield and spear of a knight, but the retractor, probe and trephining-saw of a surgeon.[22] (Fig. 129) Some unfree serfs seem to have existed, but there is no evidence for the organised slavery of the contemporary civilised world among the Celts, any more than there was among the Germanic tribes.[23] A slave-market existed wherever Roman traders could set up the machinery for such operations, as the Belgic slave-chains from south-east England remind us;[24] but this was an export trade in a commodity which Celtic society did not itself employ, except in so far as women captured in warfare, their familial status lost, became bondwomen. Among the aristocracy a council seems to have existed, and the kingship was within certain limits elective: women were eligible for chieftainship, as Boudicca and Cartimandua in Britain remind us, by reason of their family and dynastic connections.[25]

It is the basic structure of society in Celtic and Germanic communities, with its graded obligations of relationship and service, which has often been miscalled 'feudal'. We have seen its existence in ancient Sumer and Anatolia, and inferred it in the 'tell' type settlements of

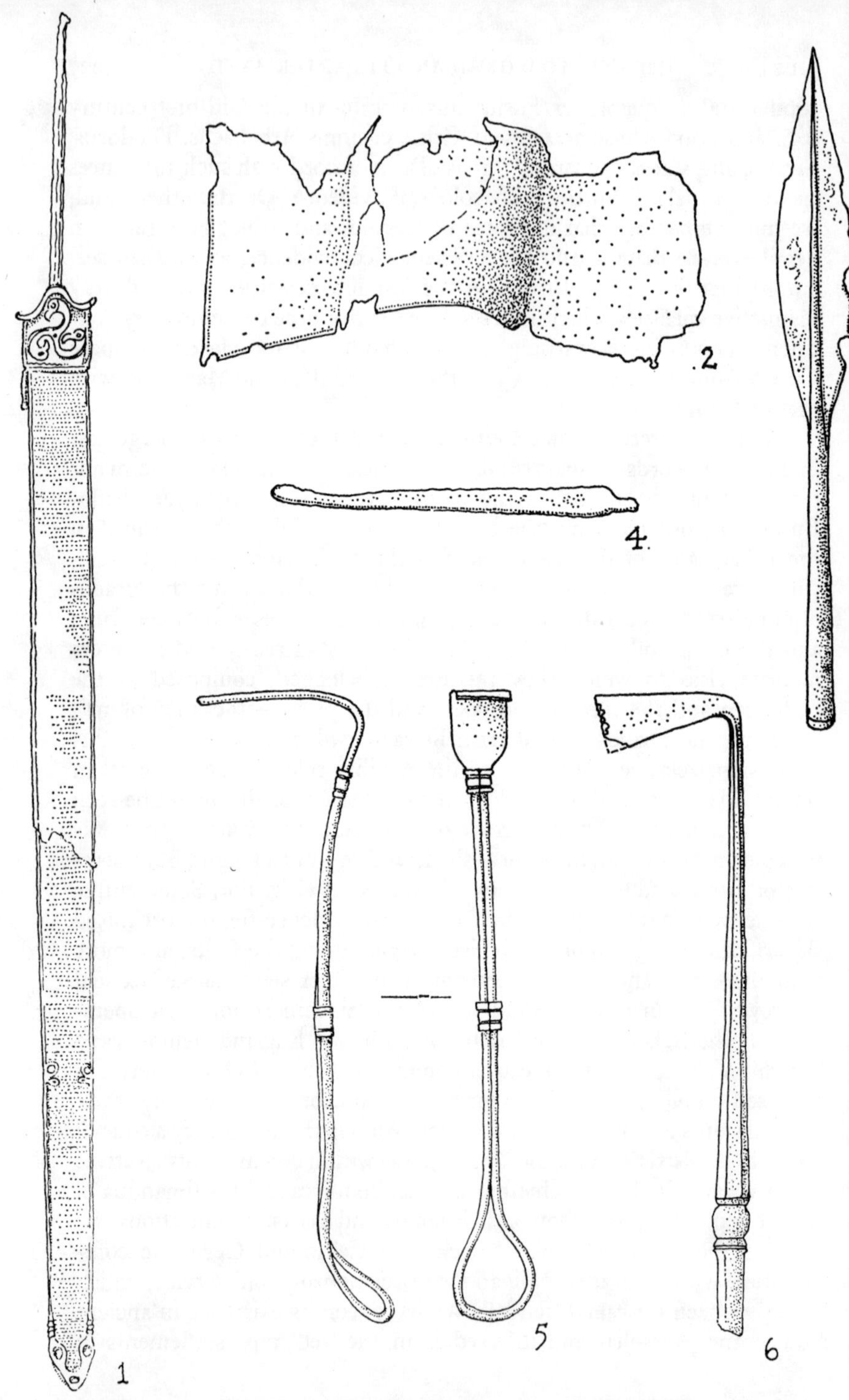

129. *Objects from middle La Tène grave, second century* B.C., *at Obermenzingen, South Germany: 1, sword in scabbard; 2, shield boss; 3, spear-head; 4, surgeon's probe; 5, retractor; 6, trephining saw. (All iron; 4–6, twice scale of weapons.)*

Oriental derivation in east Europe. If it can be construed as other than an example of the parallel evolution of simple social systems in ancient societies, and thought to be specifically Indo-European, the archaeological background of the emergence in the second millennium B.C. of such linguistic groups gives us every opportunity of seeing its genesis in circumstances linked to the general development of barbarian societies at that time. It was certainly characteristic of late prehistoric barbarian Europe, and could, as we shall see, have contributed to what can legitimately be called feudal society in the early Middle Ages. It is a structure appropriate to rural rather than urban, to simple rather than complex societies, with personal loyalties and a rustic code of behaviour suited to the restricted groups of family, clan and petty tribe and to conditions of endemic small-scale warfare; it is not in its primitive form capable of intellectual expansion nor can it easily accommodate more impersonal and so more civilised modes of polity or of organisation, and it was eventually, as we shall see, to show its utter incompatibility with the *mores* of the Mediterranean world.

For the rest, the texts, vernacular and classical, and the archaeological evidence interpreted with their guidance, show us a rudely barbarous society whether in Europa Celtica or Germanica. The Celtic feasts described in Posidonius or the Irish tales, show us swaggering, belching, touchy chieftains and their equally impossible warrior crew, hands twitching to the sword-hilt at the imagined hint of an insult, allotted as in Homer the champion's portion (of boiled pork, in the Celtic world), wiping the greasy moustaches that were a mark of nobility, 'moved by chance remarks to wordy disputes . . . boasters and threateners and given to bombastic self-dramatisation', as Posidonius coldly remarks.[26] Tacitus, while on the one hand lauding for his own purposes the savage virtues of the German tribes, nevertheless noted that 'whenever they are not fighting, they pass much of their time in the chase, and still more in idleness, giving themselves up to sleep and feasting, the bravest and most warlike doing nothing'.[27] It was an archaic way of life and one long to endure. 'The inhabitants stick close to their ancient and idle way of life; retain their barbarous customs and maxims; depend generally on their chiefs as their sovereign lords and masters; and being accustomed to the use of arms, and inured to hard living, are dangerous to the public peace.' This is not Tacitus, nor Posidonius, nor Caesar; it is Duncan Forbes writing of his Scottish contemporary world in A.D. 1745, where the Early Iron Age had perhaps its longest survival.[28]

Little has been said up to this point about barbarian European religion, and this omission has been deliberate, because this is an aspect of society upon which we can be convincingly informed only by literary evidence, in the light of which we may in favourable circumstances be able to interpret the strictly archaeological material. Archaeological evidence alone at best affords grounds for tenuous inferences, and at worst for uncontrolled guesswork. The Druids are the first priesthood, or witch-doctors, or shamans, or seers in prehistoric Europe of which we have direct literary knowledge, but even here the sources are either so vague, or so tainted with wishful idealistic thinking on the part of classical *literati*, that their interpretation is hazardous and can easily be nugatory. We know of human and animal sacrifice, and of divination by ritual murder; presumably too there was Druidic sanction for the head-hunting of the warrior caste attested by classical and vernacular sources.[29] The Scythians too were head-hunters, as were the Huns; wherever you go in the nomad world, as Grousset said, there is the same smell of blood.[30] Archaeological and iconographic evidence show us the tangible expression of the cult of the 'severed head', spread wide across the Celtic world.[31] In the south of France, under Greek influence, we have monumental stone-built sanctuaries with life-size human sculptures, such as those at Roquepertuse and Entremont, with not only carved representations of detached heads, but niches containing actual human skulls, sometimes nailed into place.[32] Such sacred skulls in niches also adorned hill-forts, as at L'Impernal, the *oppidum* of the Cadurci near Cahors, while at the Bredon (Gloucestershire) fort, skulls had evidently decorated the lintel of the gateway, to be brought crashing to the ground when the defences were stormed and burnt in the early first century A.D.[33] When Celtic iconography takes on a sculptural form under Roman influence, as in Gaul and Britain, the severed head motif again recurs, and skulls themselves seem associated with divinities worshipped at springs or wells.[34] (Pl. XXXVIII b)

Iconography and inscriptions, and again the oral tradition, inform us of a barbaric pantheon of shifting shapes, sometimes animals or birds, sometimes men and women, immanent and pervasive, hostile or helpful, the *genii loci* of well and woodland, mountain and ocean, disturbingly elusive to the Roman writers who tried to pigeon-hole them in their own reasonable, accommodating and erastian system.

Apart from the exceptional stone-built sanctuaries of the south of France, and rock-carved areas like the Val Camonica in the Italian Alps,[35] archaeological evidence for cult-sites in transalpine Europe before the Roman Conquest is perhaps not very abundant, but of great interest. Votive deposits of bronze and iron objects in lakes and pools are known from many places—La Tène itself, and also Tiefenau in Switzerland, Kappel in south Germany, Llyn Cerrig Bach in Wales, Santon in

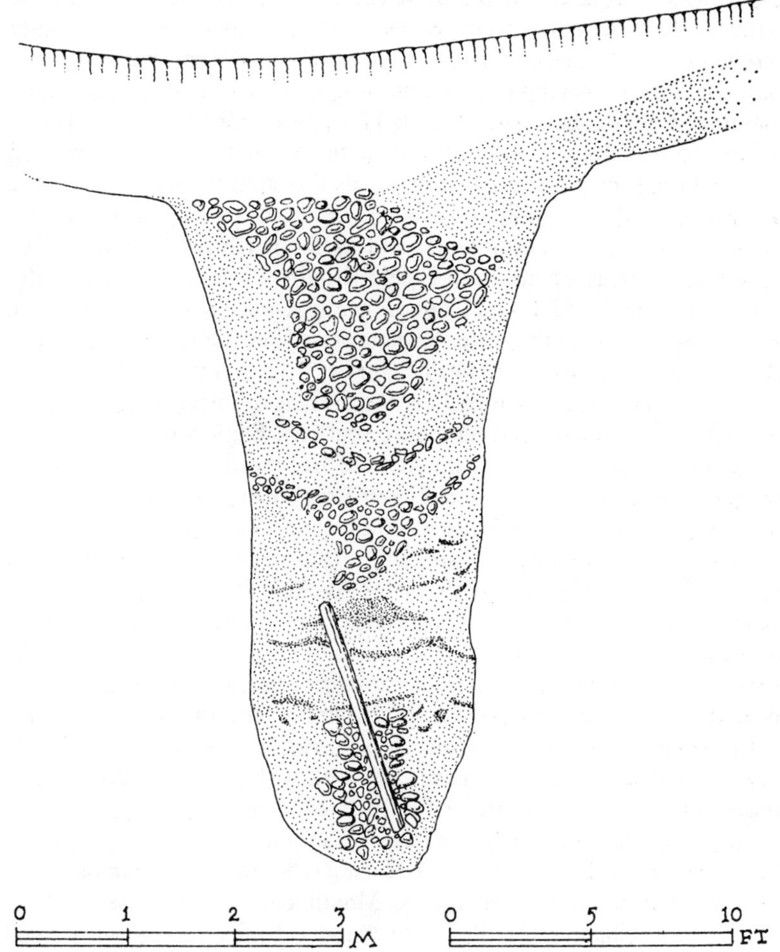

130. *Section of ritual shaft with upright wooden stake; late La Tène culture, first century* B.C., *in the* viereckshanze *at Holzhausen, South Germany.*

Norfolk, Carlingwark in Scotland, Hjortspring and Gundestrup in Denmark are all finds best explicable in this manner, and the gold offerings of Toulouse, the *aurum Tolosanum*, cynically robbed by the conquering Romans, were certainly of this character. Linked with these are the votive offerings at natural springs or wells like the Giants' Springs at Duchcov (Dux) in Czechoslovakia, wit ha bronze cauldron containing 1,200 bronze and iron objects of middle La Tène date.[36]

These lead us to some of the most extraordinary of the cult-sites, the artificial shafts or ritual wells, either as features associated with other ceremonial structures or burials, or in isolation. Recent excavations in Bavaria, within rectangular sanctuary sites of the first century B.C., mentioned below, have revealed (at Holzhausen for instance) shafts of up to 120 feet deep, one containing at the bottom an upright wooden post and the remains of organic materials denoting the former presence of flesh and blood. Similar shafts up to about 40 feet deep are also known as far west as Aquitaine, and as far north as the Oder; they have further representatives in Belgic Britain, all containing ritual deposits of animal and human bones, pottery, etc. What appear to be votive deposits in wells of the Roman period on the Continent and in Britain would be explicable in this context.[37] (Fig. 130)

The rectangular earthwork enclosures again have a distribution from Bavaria to Gaul, and may have southern English representatives; these are in turn connected on the one hand with the double-square temple represented in wood at Heath Row in the third century or so B.C., and on the other with the enclosures, and masonry double-square 'Romano-Celtic' temples, of the later Roman period, some of which may overlie pre-Roman sanctuaries.[38] At Aulnay-aux-Planches in the Marne, and Libenice in Czechoslovakia, long parallel-sided rectilinear or elongated oval enclosures are also only explicable as Celtic cult-sites; in the Marne too are small square enclosures, some containing post-structures, some round La Tène burials, and in their latter form with analogies in the La Tène burials of Yorkshire. Finally, the Goloring near Coblenz is a large circular earthwork with a central setting for a massive timber post, of late Hallstatt date.[39] (Figs. 131, 132)

Not the least interesting feature of all these curious examples of Hallstatt or La Tène cult-sites is their archaism.[40] The Goloring, as its excavator stressed, is a 'Henge Monument' in the sense of those described in Chapter III; the Aulnay and Libenice long parallel-sided enclosures immediately recall the long mortuary enclosures and cursus monuments of the same late third millennium B.C. Even square earthwork enclosures from the same early period can be cited, as at Dorchester-on-Thames. (Fig. 62) The shafts again have early parallels in Britain, as in that of Stanwick in Hampshire (with upright post and blood traces), or more dramatically that on Normanton Down near Wilsford in Wiltshire, over 100 feet deep, and both of about the twelfth century B.C.[41] The Val Camonica was a sacred valley in the early second millennium B.C., and its rock engravings are spread over a couple of thousand years. The antiquity of Druidism, or at least of the components of barbarian Celtic religion in the first few centuries B.C., has been stressed

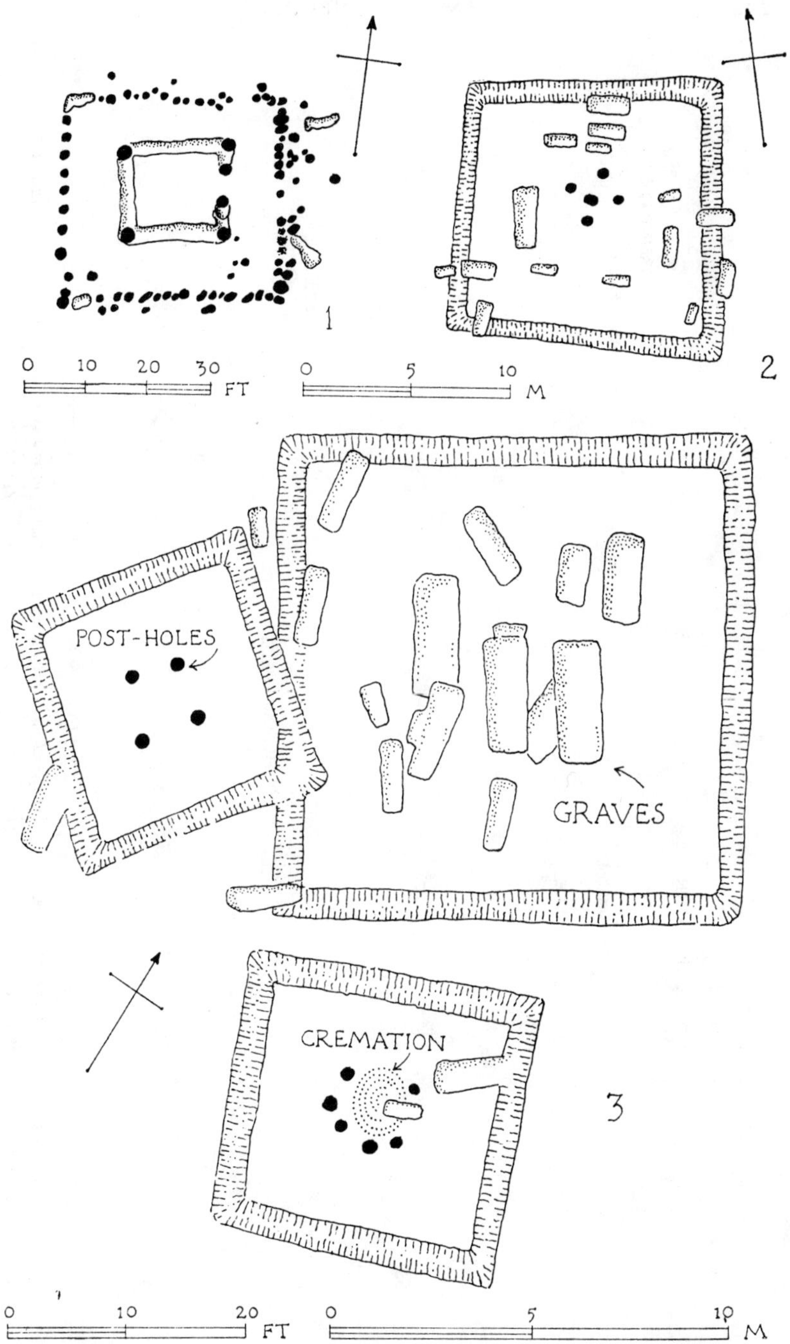

131. *Square sanctuaries and cemeteries, with post-holes of timber structures and enclosing ditches, La Tène culture, third-first century* B.C., *at* 1, *Heath Row (London Airport), England;* 2, *Écury-le-Repos;* 3, *Fin d'Écury; both Marne, France.*

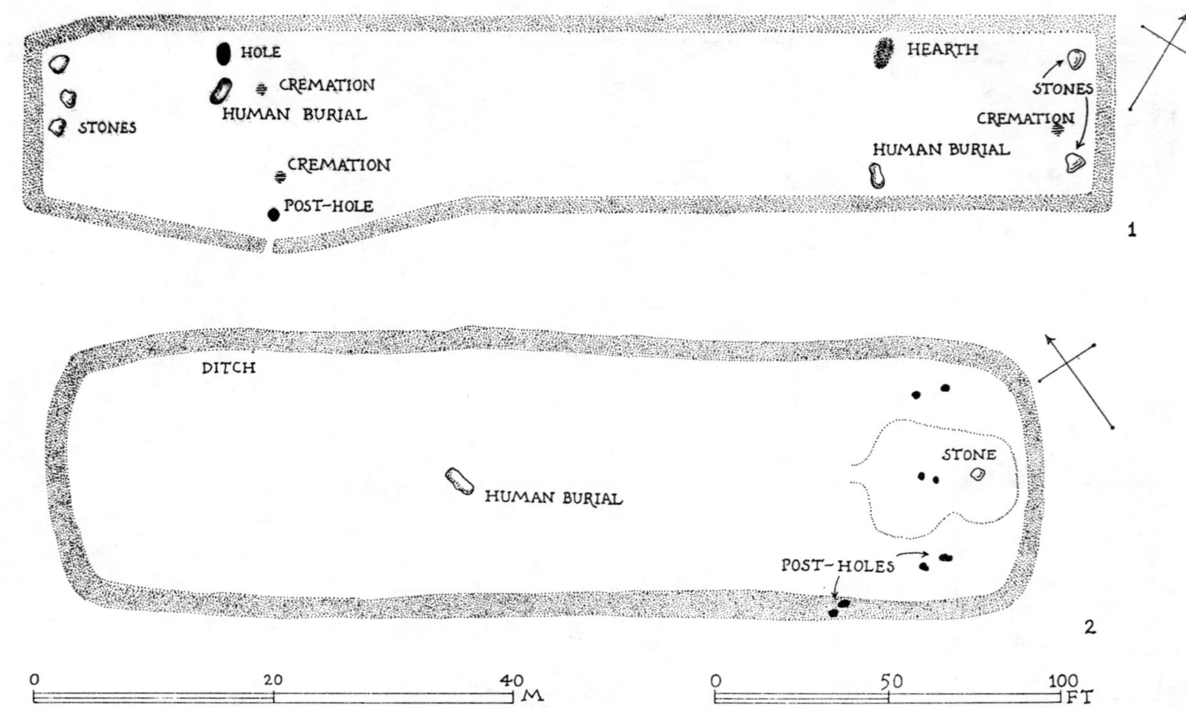

132. *Long ditch-enclosed sanctuary sites:* 1, *Urnfield culture, eleventh-tenth century* B.C., *at Aulnay-aux-Planches, Marne, France;* 2, *final Hallstatt culture, third century* B.C., *at Libenice, Czechoslovakia.*

more than once, and all recent discoveries confirm this thesis. And with the British parallels for henges and long enclosures and ritual shafts long centuries before the Druids, may we not have to reconsider Caesar's statement that their doctrine was in fact of British origin?

Celtic and Germanic society, as we see it in its immediately pre-Roman phase, had in it an element of mobility which the prehistorian recognises as characteristic of an earlier Europe, the historian as familiar in the context of the post-Roman Migration Period. From the second half of the second century B.C. the Roman world had been aware of the movements of the Germanic tribes towards and into north-east Gaul; the Helvetii had moved into Switzerland from south Germany and had decided on another mass migration, which in 58 gave Caesar his opportunity for extending the Roman occupation of Gaul northwards from the Province acquired in 121 B.C. At the beginning of the second century B.C. a Germanic tribe, the Bastarnae, moved eastward to the mouth of the Dneister, bordering on the Sarmatians; at the end of the century the Cimbri, Teutones, and Ambrones moved south into Gaul. Caesar and Strabo both noted the pastoral nomadism of the Germani and the Suebi, and Tacitus was to underline how the Germanic economy was based on herds of cattle in a manner that recalls the similar background of the Irish hero-tales, no less than the modern Masai; in Britain itself, north and west of the Jurassic Ridge, literary and archaeological evidence combine to indicate widespread pastoralism rather than intensive settled agriculture.[42] Similarly, we may reasonably infer a predominantly pastoral economy in Ireland in the early centuries of the Christian era.[43] We took a glance at pastoral nomadism as a phenomenon in an earlier chapter, and in late prehistoric Europe pastoralism with an element of nomadism was certainly present in some areas. We may have, in fact, two contrasted economies co-existing, one based on sedentary agriculture and the other on pastoralism with at times a nomadic aspect, the latter contributing greatly to the general potential mobility of the tribes.

In the earlier Irish hero-tales the wealth of the chieftain was in cattle, flocks and herds, and treasure in metal. In the opening scene of the 'Cattle-Raid of Cooley', Ailill, chieftain of Cruachan, and Medb his wife, boast of their respective riches, and cause their possessions to be brought to them in the reverse order of their value, beginning with cauldrons and other vessels, followed by their gold ornaments and their clothing, and then by flocks of sheep, their horses, their herds of pigs, and finally (and so most important) their cattle. The unit of value for all property (including bondwomen) was a cow: we are back in the Homeric world where Laertes bought Eurycleia for the value of twenty oxen, and 'cattle were the measuring stick of worth, in that respect, and only in that sense, cattle were money . . . the measure of value, cattle, did not itself function as a medium of exchange'. So, too, with the Germani: their cattle were poor, Tacitus records, but 'it is number that is chiefly valued; they are in fact the most highly prized, indeed the only riches of the people'.[44]

We have noted the developments in fortification techniques that culminated in the *murus gallicus*, and seen that the abundant hill-forts pose problems of function—were they temporary refuges, or permanent defended settlements of an almost urban type? Here unfortunately only very large-scale excavation is going to yield the required evidence, but on present showing it seems likely that the forts represent almost every gradation of use, from a town to a chieftain's castle; from a tribal cattle compound to a sheep-pen.

Within the obvious diversity of social and economic structure the British Isles stand out as having a peculiar and insular quality. The general European pattern of settlement, from Neolithic to late La Tène, was the village or agglomerated settlement of several households in rectangular buildings. In the British Isles, as we saw, the circular house-plan was firmly established in the second millennium, and it persisted to the time of the Roman Conquest despite the repeated immigrant drafts from the Continent representing various aspects of the Hallstatt and La Tène cultures, in their homeland presumptively builders of rectangular houses, byres and barns, unless Gaul (as a phrase in Posidonius suggests) retained in part the tradition of the circular plan. This in itself must mean that Celtic Britain retained an archaism of tradition in that fundamental element of human culture, the home, and this is not all. From the earliest settlements reflecting continental Hallstatt traditions in Britain—in other words, from the beginning of the Iron Age in these islands—the typical settlement-unit is not the village, but the isolated farmstead, based on a large circular house. The hamlet or village tradition (as seen for instance in the twelfth century B.C. at Itford Hill) continues (as at Glastonbury or Meare) and perhaps more strongly in north Britain than elsewhere, where it may itself be a local archaism, but the settlements of the type of West Harling or Woodbury, the Irish rath and the Scottish crannog or wheelhouse, dominate the scene. Now these isolated farmsteads seem virtually unknown in Hallstatt or La Tène Europe; nor do they occur marginally, for northern Europe and Scandinavia show us villages of rectangular houses at this time, ancestral to those of the post-Roman Migration Period, of the Anglo-Saxons, and of medieval Europe at large.[45] It is this provincial and exceptional nature of the British Early Iron Age that makes one cautious in extra-

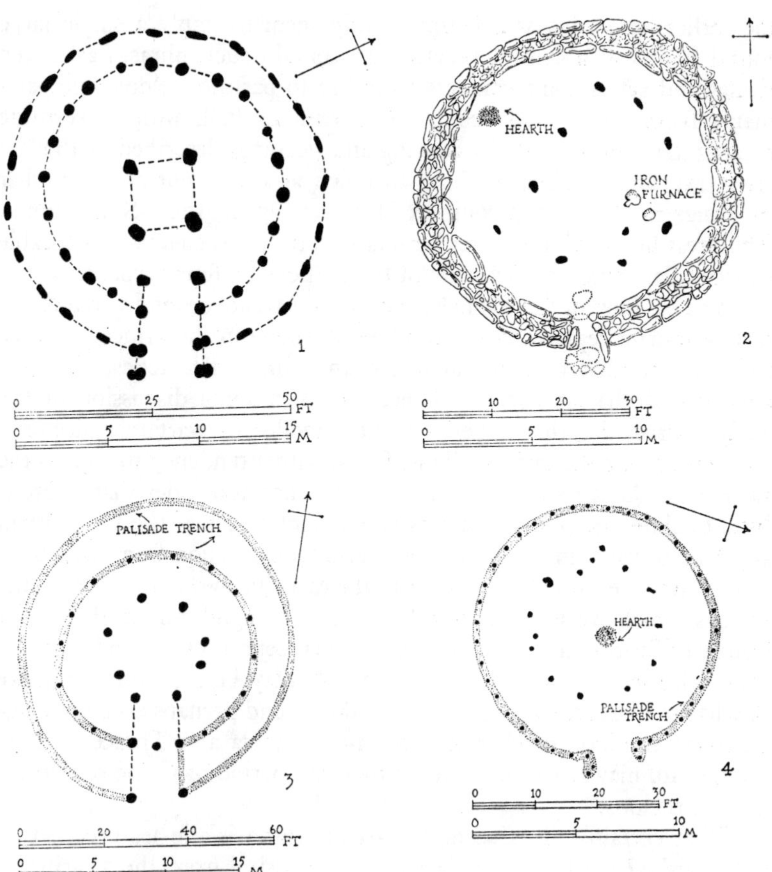

133. *Circular house plans in Britain, timber and timber-and-stone, third century* B.C. *to first century* A.D., *at 1, Little Woodbury, Wilts.; 2, Kestor, Devon; 3, Scotstarvit, Fife; 4, West Plean, Stirlingshire.*

polating too readily from the Irish vernacular sources, set in circular rath or farmstead or rustic palace, to the Europe of the nucleated villages and defended townships of rectangular cottages and outbuildings. (Fig. 133; Pl. XLI).

The Irish literary evidence for the early centuries A.D. contains references to houses which in the legal texts are graded in terms of a single dimension, suggesting the diameter of a circular structure. It has, however, been argued that rectangular houses or halls are implied; but this hardly seems consonant with the total weight of evidence today, and indeed with the admittedly imprecise and romanticised descriptions in the earlier hero-tales, which consistently seem to imply a single large round house with central hearth, and contain such phrases as 'seven circles and seven compartments from fire to partition', 'nine compartments from fire to wall', contrasting with the hall, with its separate rectangular outbuildings for cooking and sleeping, described in a rather later text, and recalling nothing so much as the layout of the timber buildings in the palatial complex of Yeavering in Anglo-Saxon times. The great house of the Ulster hero tales certainly seems best explicable as a circular structure, basically of the Little Woodbury type.[46]

We saw how in the Rhineland and the Marne, around 500 B.C. the cart or chariot replaces the four-wheeled wagon in the princely graves, and inferred that this indicated a change in actual tactics, with the adoption of chariot warfare. There has been some discussion of the likely sources for this impetus to new modes of warfare and burial customs among the early La Tène Celts, with a tendency to look to the Etruscans. But a recent review of the evidence concludes that 'there is little to show, despite statements to the contrary, that the Celts learnt anything of value in the subject of chariot construction from the Etruscans',[47] and we should look rather to the east European and west Asiatic regions which we have seen to have been so significant in the earlier history of European wheeled vehicles. The recent discovery in Cyprus of chariot-burials of the seventh century B.C. may be significant, and we should not forget the Sigynnae of Herodotus, and perhaps even the long-surviving tradition of chariot-burial in Pannonia and Thrace, already referred to, may have roots deeper than the period of Celtic settlement in those regions.[48]

What certainly does seem of eastern origin is the feature that so distinguished the Celts and Germans in classical eyes, the wearing of trousers. Representations of men in trousers go back, as we saw, to the seventh to fifth centuries B.C. in central Europe, and seem likely to be associated with horse-riding and the Steppe tradition, as seen for instance among the Scythians and the Medes; Herodotus said the Sigynnae wore Median dress. At the period of the Warring States the Chinese army adopted trousers from their nomadic enemies who were to be known as Huns; 307 B.C. is the traditional date.[49]

Fighting from the chariot or on foot was with sword and spear and sling; as we saw, bows and arrows seem rarely to have been used in barbarian Europe after the early second millennium, and were only to return in force with the invasions from the Steppe early in the Christian era. Swords, apparently mainly of untempered iron, though steel was used on occasion, were now long and narrow, and certainly from the second century B.C. recognisably the products of local schools of

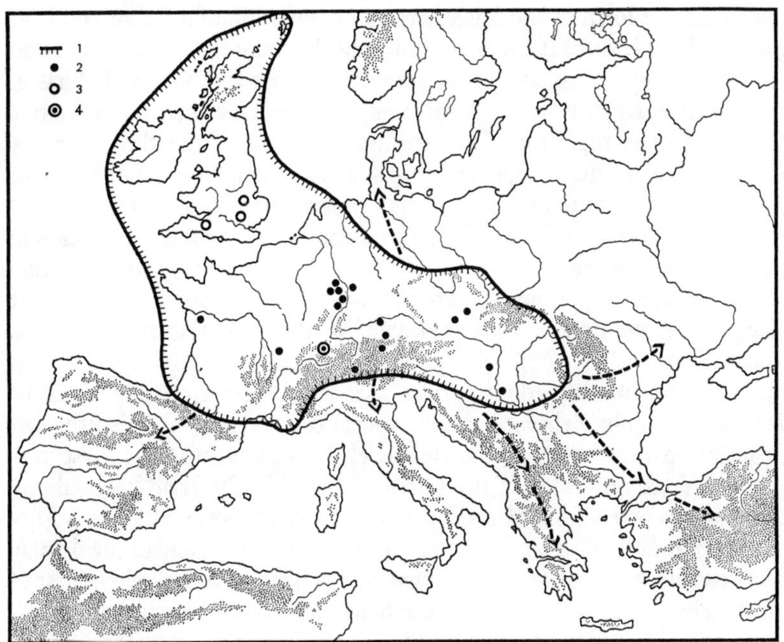

134. *Distribution of mature La Tène culture ; 1, La Tène culture and influences ; 2, Sword scabbards in Swiss style ; 3, British derivatives ; 4, Many scabbards.*

armourers, notably those centred in Switzerland.[50] There is evidence for the ritual nakedness of the Celtic warrior in battle or at festivals; painting or tattooing the body is well documented, a custom shared in Britain with the Picts, and also with the eastern tribes such as Thracians, Dacians, Sarmatians, and Scythians. Even naked prisoners of war could transmit an art-style.[51] (Pl. XLII)

Early La Tène helmets belong to at least two types, both widely distributed, one a pointed or conical form, seemingly wholly Celtic and perhaps derived from Hallstatt types such as those shown on the situlae or the Strettweg warriors, and the other 'Italo-Celtic', reflecting Etruscan modes but also basically similar to the late Urnfield 'bell helmets' already mentioned.[52] The long oval shield, again seen on the situlae or the Strettweg figures, is shown on a well-known engraved sword scabbard of early La Tène date from Hallstatt, and by the remains of rather later examples in graves, by rare finds such as that from the Fayum sands or those from La Tène and the Hjortspring peatbog in Denmark, and representations in sculpture in Gaul and Pergamon; metal mountings of such shields are known from Britain. It was the characteristic form in the Irish hero-tales; mention of a fall of snow 'as high as the shields of the men and the wheels of the chariot' show us that we are dealing with such shields, some 3 feet long.[53] The use of shirts of mail, of iron rings as in medieval times, is shown by such purely native Celtic finds as that from Hjortspring, probably of the third century B.C., and sculptured representations as at Pergamon in Galatia or Vachères in the south of France. The Romans attributed the invention of mail to the Gauls, and its early appearance in Celtic contexts appears to owe nothing to classical sources, but rather to the Scytho-Sarmatian world, where similar mail shirts are known; one from Zharovka near Kiev in a grave dated by a Greek kylix of the fifth century B.C.[54] (Pls. XLIII–XLIV).

The Roman army adopted from barbarian sources, mainly Celtic or Iberian, not only elaborate cavalry sports or exercises, but also the appropriate parade armour, and tight Celtic trousers, worn at these displays. We are reminded of the warriors' 'feats' in the Irish hero-tales—the 'twenty-seven feats of skill' proper to a chariot-warrior, 'the apple-feat, and thunder-feat, and the blade-feat...' and so on, and of the display of virtuosity given by the Belgic charioteers before Caesar, when 'first of all the charioteers drive all over the field, the warriors hurling missiles', with the drivers ready to check and turn the horses in an instant, and to 'run along the pole, stand on the yoke, and step backwards again to the chariot with the greatest nimbleness'. And in another barbarian setting, there is the similar display given before the Roman army by the Gothic chieftain Totila, in the fourth century A.D., when on horseback he began to 'perform the dance under arms skillfully between the armies', and carried out elaborate 'feats' in the saddle 'like one who has been instructed with precision in the art of dancing from childhood'.[55]

The chariot with its driver and warrior was the object of a recurrent formulaic description in the hero-tales, in which the gorgeousness of the vehicle, the clothing, and the equipment, can be exaggerated to legendary improbability, yet with a strain of underlying truth. We hear of 'a chariot of fine wood with wicker-work, moving on wheels of white bronze. A pole of white silver, with a mounting of white bronze. Its frame very high, of creaking copper, rounded and firm. A strong curved yoke of gold; two firm-plaited yellow reins. . . .' This may sound improbably magnificent, but when in a Roman triumph of 121 B.C. Bituitus, ruler of the Arverni, was displayed, the sober historian of the occasion records that 'no one in the triumph was more conspicuous than King Bituitus himself, in vari-coloured battle array and in a silver chariot, exactly as he had fought'. We are not far from Cú Chulainn, nor indeed from a gold-plated Cadillac.[56]

XLII. *Tattooed design on right arm of East Scythian man, fourth–third century B.C., from Barrow 2, Pazyryk, Altai Mountains.* (Photo. Hermitage, Leningrad)

XLIII. *Shields, La Tène culture, third century* B.C. – *early first century* A.D. (*a*) *Stone sculpture, Augustan, from Mondragon, Vaucluse, France;* (*b*) *Wood, from the Fayum, Egypt;* (*c*) *Bronze, from River Witham, Lincs., England;* (Photos. Musée Calvet, Avignon; Services des Antiquités, Cairo) British Museum

XLIV. *Replica of bronze flagon with engraved ornament, La Tène culture, early fourth century* B.C., *from a woman's grave at Reinheim, Saarbrücken, Germany.* (Photo. Römisch-Germanische Zentralmuseum, Mainz)

Parade and acrobatic feats, the contest between individual champions, and wars that were no more than cattle-raids, form the background to the La Tène military equipment of helmet and shield, spear and chariot. The very use of chariots demanded a formal engagement on carefully selected terrain: 'It must be borne in mind that the battle-ground was a chosen level area on which opposing sides could array themselves. There was no question of operations on an extended front over unprepared ground. . . . This was the phase for display and intimidation.'[57] And in the Greek and Irish traditions there is little to distinguish Cú Chulainn's boast

'Three things countless on the Cattle-Raid
Which have fallen by my hand:
Hosts of cattle, men and steeds,
I have slaughtered on all sides'—

from Nestor's reminiscent enumeration—'exceedingly abundant was then the booty we drove out of the plain together, fifty herds of cattle, as many droves of swine, as many herds of goats, and a hundred and fifty bays, all mares'. The raid for booty or private vengeance was ever the mainspring of the heroic world.[58]

To this warrior-aristocracy, the knights or barons of the Celtic world, and to the 'men of art' in the social sphere only just below them, we owe the genesis and development of early Celtic art from the fifth century B.C. It is one of the great unclassical arts of early Europe. The art of the Scythians was another of these, based I have suggested partly on the Eurasiatic animal-styles, which hark back to Mesolithic traditions, partly on the other animal style that developed around the Caucasus from the late third millennium. Scythian or Sarmatian art in fact affected Celtic art to some extent, but most points of apparent similarity seem due rather to shared traditions or origins. Celtic art is unclassical in that, like that of the Scyths, it does not share the Mediterranean preoccupation with the naturalistic portrayal of the human form, which goes back through Etruscan and Greek to Egyptian and Mesopotamian sources—perhaps ultimately to the modelled skulls of Jericho. Its origins lie partly in the archaic Hallstatt and Urnfield traditions, partly in Oriental sources which may ultimately hark back to the Cimmerian world, but mainly in the free adaptation of non-representational motifs in Greek

---

XLV. (*a, above*) *Gilt bronze helmet, La Tène culture, fourth–third century* B.C., *from Amfreville, Eure, France.* (Photo. Musée des antiquités nationales, St Germain-en-Laye)

XLV. (*b, below*) *Bronze mounting in the form of a fantastic bird, La Tène culture, third century* B.C., *from Malomerice, Czechoslovakia.* (Photo. Kleibl)

135. *Engraved decoration on bronze wine-flagon, early La Tène culture, end of fourth century* B.C., *from near Besançon, France.*

136. *Decorated pots, early La Tène culture, fourth century* B.C.: 1, *incised, from St Pol-de-Léon, Brittany*; 2, *painted, from Prunay, Marne, France.*

art—palmettes, tendrils, leaf-forms—introduced into the early fifth-century Celtic world of the Rhineland by the wine trade. In Celtic art, 'man is a stranger' and even the animals that inhabit its strange world are apt to shift shape and become a pattern. It was an art, as Jacobsthal said, 'with a future and a European mission . . . it is attractive and repellent; it is far from primitiveness and simplicity, is refined in thought and technique; elaborate and clever; full of paradoxes, restless, puzzlingly ambiguous; rational and irrational; dark and uncanny, far from the lovable humanity and the transparence of Greek art. Yet it is a real style, the first great contribution by the barbarians to European arts, the first great chapter in the everlasting mutual stocktaking of Northern, Southern and Eastern forces in the life of Europe.'[59] (Pls. XXXVII; XXXIX; XLII–XLVII; Figs. 135, 136).

It was essentially an art of aristocratic patronage, devoted to the adornment of the warriors and their equipment, their courts and their women. It could only exist in the ambience of an heroic society, and with the destruction of that society by Roman conquest, Celtic art likewise withered. Its eclipse by 'the common vulgar ugliness of the Roman empire' was surely not so much (as Collingwood thought for this country) the shrinking of the sensitive Celtic artist from the 'uniform and sordid ugliness of drab Romano-British daylight,' as the removal by Roman civilisation of the aristocratic patronage of a barbaric and flamboyant martial tradition. The panoply and equipment of the battle-drunk, screaming tribal chieftain in his chariot hung with the decapitated heads of his foes, the air raucous with the sound of the *baritus* and the *carnyx*, was hardly appropriate for the new Romano-British world with the chieftain now a Celtic country gentleman in reduced circumstances taking a quiet stroll round the forum of his market town.[60] In the south of France and in Iberia, as we saw, Celtic and classical art combined, to form local styles of monumental stone sculpture which included some notable and moving works of art; it is however characteristic of the Celtic world that some of the best pieces adorned the shrine at Roquepertuse, the niches in the pillars of which held severed human skulls.

Late prehistoric Europe, on the eve of Roman conquest, seems then to have included a diversity of economies. On the one hand we have a group ranging from the true pastoral nomadism of the Sarmatians on the Steppes to modified forms of pastoralism among the Germanic tribes, and perhaps in parts of the British Isles, to yet other versions in which agriculture plays some part; but cattle-ranching and herding form the major content: the early Irish hero-tales have such a background. Elsewhere we have a second range, of sedentary agricultural economies based in central Europe and in Gaul on social units which may attain the status of towns, and certainly of villages; in the British Isles at least the single farmstead plays an important role. Generally, at any rate in Celtic Europe westwards from Transylvania, we have a fairly uniform achievement in technology at no mean level of competence; a mastery of the rural crafts which apart from the harnessing of wind and water power is hardly inferior to that of much of Europe in the early Middle Ages.

Through Celtic chariotry we can see how a high degree of proficiency in the wheelwrights' and coachbuilders' crafts was gained from the fifth century B.C. onwards, with the chariot as the aristocratic status-symbol up to the time of the Roman Conquest of Britain and the Irish hero-tales. The spoked wheels had single-piece bent felloes as in the *Iliad* and the *Rig-Veda*, and the iron tyres, nailed on in all the Hallstatt wagons, are now themselves single-piece and shrunk on to the wheel by being forced on while red-hot and expanded. In wheelwright's language, the Hallstatt wheels had nailed-on strakes, the La Tène wheels had hoop-tyres. Wheels with single-piece felloes and hoop tyres seem to have been intermittently used in the Middle Ages and beyond for aristocratic vehicles, but the hoop-tyre was unknown to the Roman world, and strakes were almost universal in Europe up to the nineteenth century A.D. In England the hoop-tyre was re-invented; it had still not quite superseded strakes for farm carts and wagons in George Sturt's wheelwright's shop in Surrey in 1884. Chariots are but upper-class carts, and the use of the aristocratic vehicle presupposes the existence of the utilitarian country cousin on the farm or in the village, and we may therefore see La Tène origins for the inclusion of Britain and much of Gaul within the 'cart zone' of modern ethnography, the farm wagon having been introduced to England from the Low Countries in the sixteenth century A.D.[61]

Four-wheeled vehicles of elegant design were however made in the Celtic world, as the votive wagons from a peat-bog at Dejbjerg in Denmark remind us. These were ornamented with bronze fittings in a manner recalling Hallstatt wagons such as that at Vix, their twelve-spoked wheels with oak hubs, hornbeam spokes, and single-piece ash felloes turning on unexpectedly sophisticated wooden roller-bearings. The style and technique of wheel construction, down to the details of the complex morticing of the spokes to the hub, recur in other finds as widely scattered as Newstead and Bar Hill in south Scotland, Glastonbury in Somerset, and the Saalburg Roman fort in Germany.[62] This argues a 'Common Celtic' tradition in the wheelwright's craft no less real than one that might be postulated for language, and we shall note another instance shortly. What has become the 'standard' gauge between wheels of 4 foot $8\frac{1}{2}$ inches

XLVI. *Engraved back of bronze mirror, early first century* A.D., *from a woman's grave at Birdlip, Glos., England.* (Photo. Gloucester Museum)

a

b

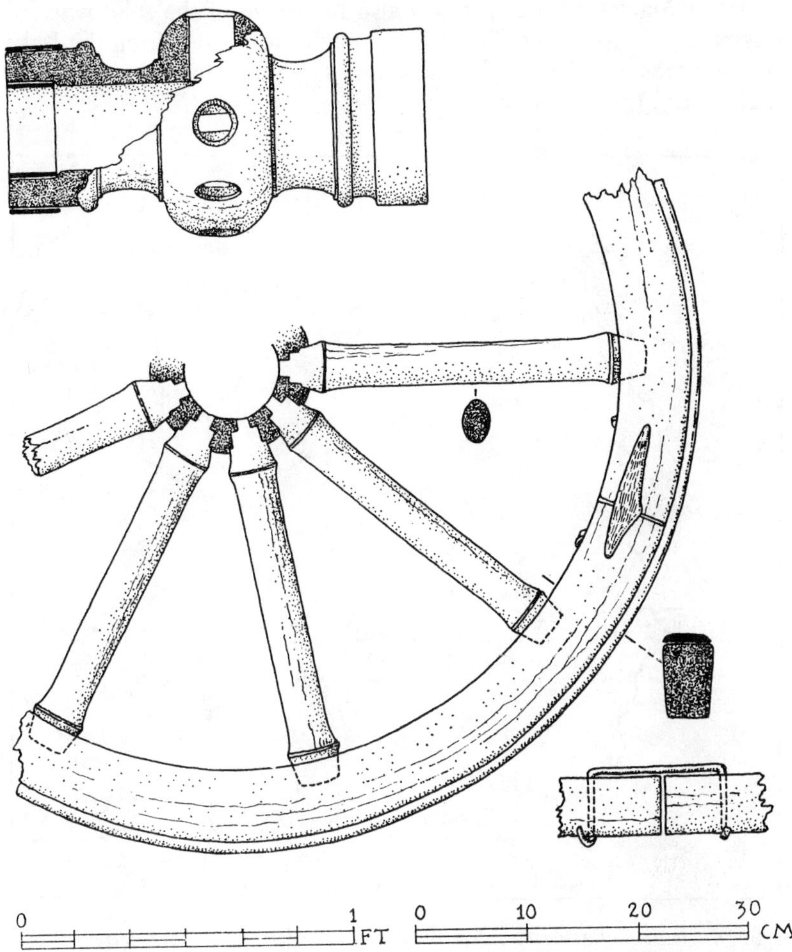

137. *Constructional details of wooden chariot-wheel with single-piece felloe, iron tyre and nave-bushes, first century* A.D., *from Newstead, Scotland.*

was established by La Tène chariots, carts, and wagons, as the chariot-burials, and wheel-ruts at for instance Alesia, Verulamium, and Maiden Castle show. The Hallstatt wagons had a narrower gauge—about 3 feet 6 inches to 3 feet 9 inches—and wheel-ruts of this interval were also

---

XLVII. *Bronze mountings from cauldron, La Tène culture, third century* B.C., *from Brå, Jutland, Denmark.* (*a*) *Owl-head handle-attachment;* (*b*) *bull-head ornament.* (Photos. Jysk Archaeologisk Selskab)

found at Maiden Castle[63]; it was also the gauge of the solid-wheeled wagons in the Royal Tombs of Ur, though the wagons from the Lake Sevan tombs of the second millennium B.C. approximated to 5 feet or slightly less. (Fig. 137)

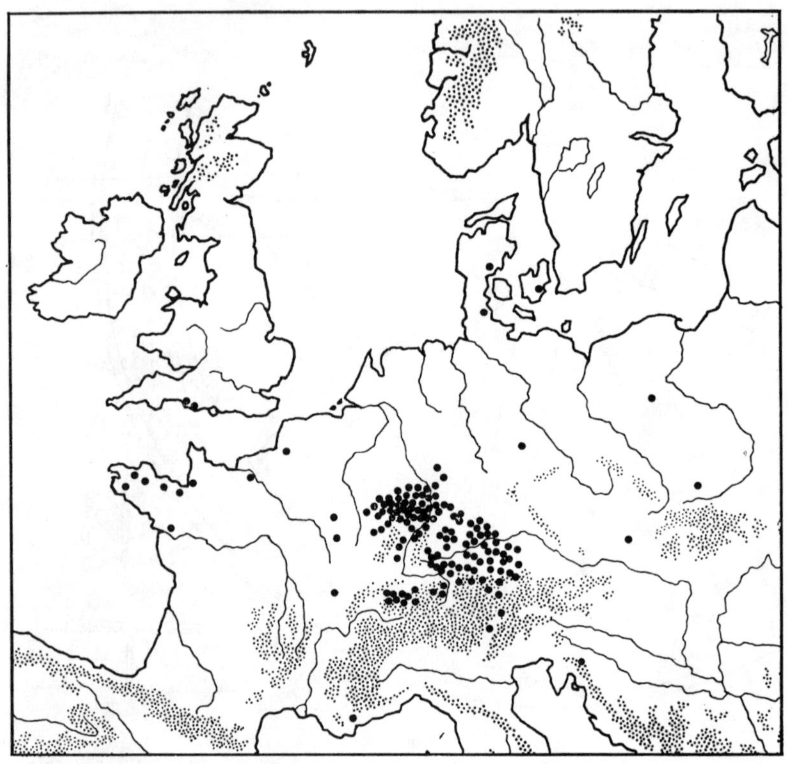

138. *Distribution of double-pointed iron ingots, late La Tène culture, second-first century* B.C.

The blacksmith worked hand-in-hand with the carpenter and wheelwright in making vehicles, and again with the military engineer in fortifications of *murus gallicus* type; we saw how at Manching each single stage of timbering would have used 30 tons of nails. Iron production must have been on a relatively formidable scale: in the La Tène world it was worked into characteristic double-pointed ingots of from 9 to 44 lb. in weight, and in Britain, as we shall see, used in the form of rough-out sword blades for currency. The distribution of the continental double-pointed ingots (of which over 700 are known) shows us a concentration south of the Roman *limes* in southern Germany and Switzerland, and scattered finds elsewhere, but something of a secondary concentration in Brittany. This we may equate with the Veneti and their need for iron not only in the construction of *murus gallicus* defences like most of the rest of the Gaulish tribes, but for their shipping, built as Caesar noted with iron-bolted timbers, and with iron anchors and chains. The two British ingots of this type, from Portland in Dorset, fit with the evidence for cross-channel contacts with the Veneti, and indeed with the iron anchor and chain from the hill-fort of Belbury, not far away.[64] In the Irish hero-tales the metal worker and smith could hold a social position in which he could invite a powerful chieftain to a feast held in his house within its defensive earthworks. He had flocks and herds, but 'neither land nor domain had he, but only the product of his hammer, his anvil, and his tongs'. He was a 'man of art' with an assured position in his community.[65] (Fig. 138)

We saw that in the technical processing of wrought iron, the barbarian peoples were roughly at a level with the Roman world, but here mass-production of the raw metal and of finished tools gave an economic advantage. Steel was occasionally produced, perhaps half-accidentally, the chariot tyres of Llyn Cerrig Bach winning the technical approval of a modern firm of ironmasters.[66] It is remarkable how workshop practice and patterns remained constant right across the Celtic world up to and beyond the initial impact of Romanisation. A map of the often noble ox-headed iron fire-dogs, (Fig. 139; Pl. XLVIII) or of a standardised type of jointed rod-and-chain hanger for a cauldron over an open hearth for instance, shows a Common Market area from Britain to Czechoslovakia and Austria; many other items of domestic metalwork would show the same pattern, which must be that of common workshop traditions and no more than local trade. This is in fact a parallel for the 'Common Celtic' wheelwright's practice mentioned above, and the same could be said of many other contemporary crafts. In Britain, fire-dogs mainly come from Belgic graves of the first century A.D., furnished like those of the Etruscans, or of eighth-century Argos and seventh-century Cyprus, with the symbol of the hospitable hearth for the feast beyond the grave, together with other provisions, such as amphorae of imported wine. The fire-dogs, in their alternative name of andiron, or the French *landier*, seem to preserve through late Latin forms a Common Celtic root meaning a bull-calf or a heifer, which can only be in reference to their original zoomorphic form.[67]

In other crafts production was improved and intensified. Pottery becomes increasingly a wheel-turned and professionalised product,[68] and from the fourth century B.C. bronze-work begins to be adorned with enamel, initially in red alone. This technique, still regarded as worthy of

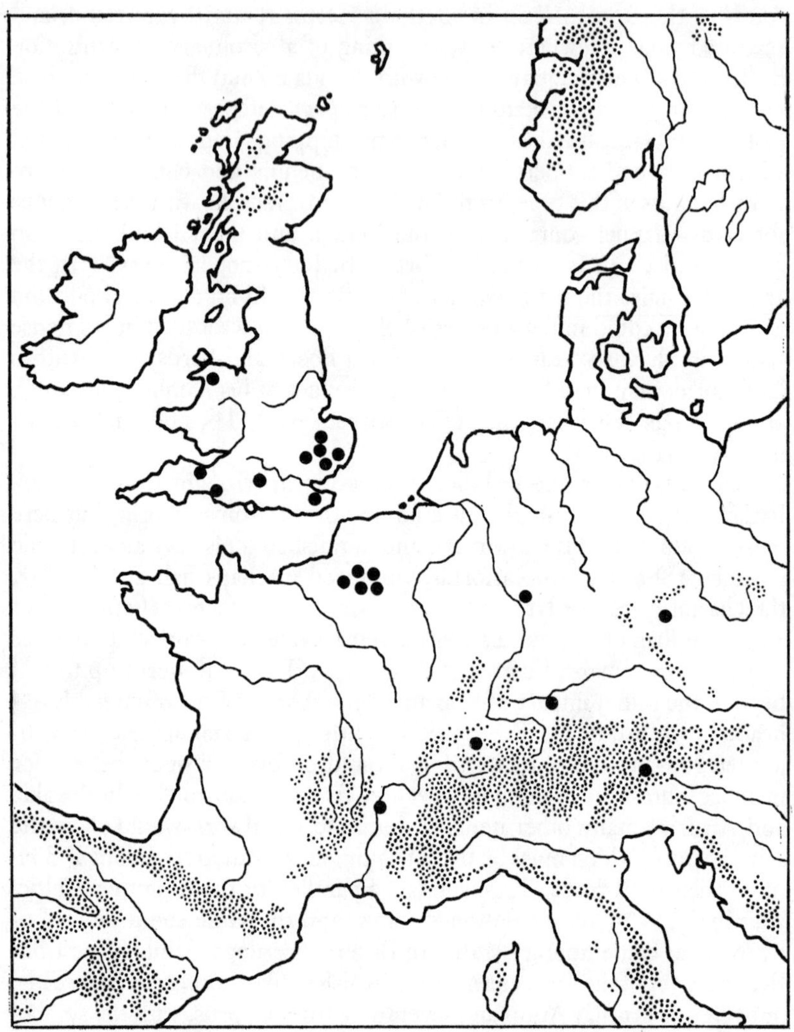

139. *Distribution of iron fire-dogs, late La Tène culture, first century* B.C.

note as a barbarian achievement in the Roman world of the third century A.D., has been considered to be Oriental, and more specifically Caucasian, in origin, and affords another Celtic contact with the eastern world.[69] Salt continued to be won in the old inland mines and wells, but the coastal exploitation of sea-salt by panning was increased; on the Atlantic shores of France, in the Low Countries, and along the English coast from

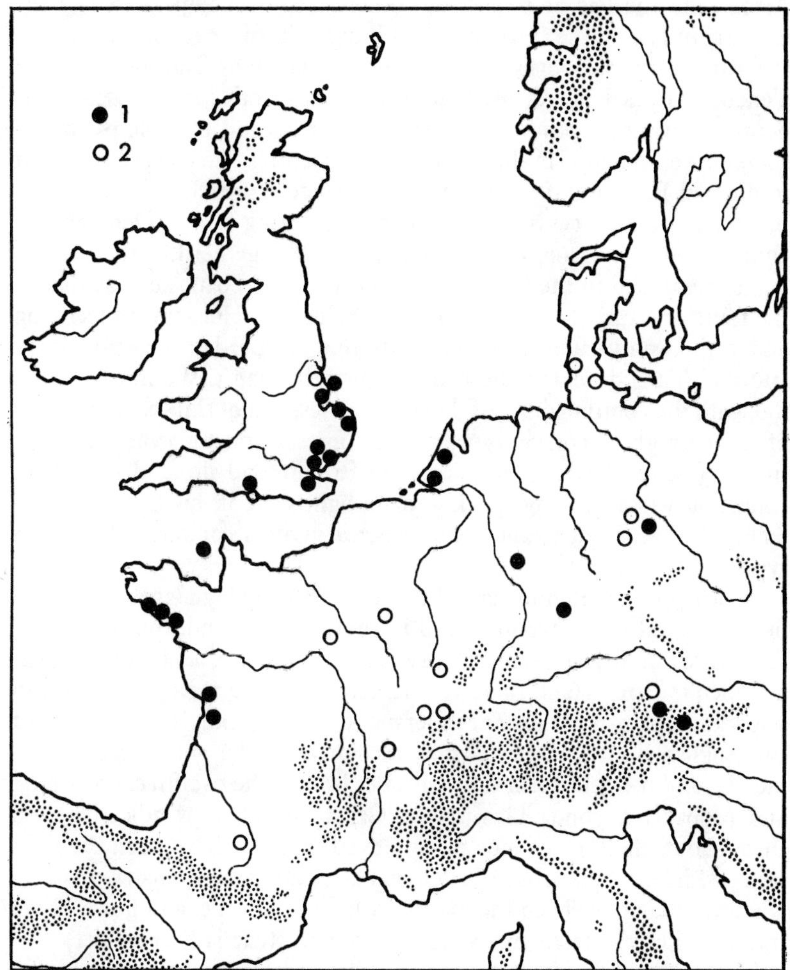

140. *Distribution of sites of La Tène salt production, fifth–first century* B.C.: *1, certain; 2, probable sites.*

the Solent to the Humber; a pattern further developed under Roman rule.[70] (Fig. 140) Strabo notes the trade from Gaul to Italy of salted meat, and of blankets, a tribute to sheep-breeding and textile manufacture. Gaulish and British woollen cloaks became famous and highly taxed in Roman times, and their renown went on into the eighth century A.D. at least,[71] while Pliny notes the production of sail-cloth by a number of Gaulish tribes, some coastal, like the Morini and Caleti in Picardy,

Artois, and the Pas-de-Calais, but others inland but up-river, like the Cadurci in Lot on the Garonne, the Bituriges in Indre on the Loire, and the Ruteni on the Tarn, not far from the coast by Narbonne.[72] The Veneti, as Caesar noted, used leather and not cloth for their sails, evidently drawing on pastoral resources of cattle; and their ships, which some have thought to have embodied features surviving in recent traditional Breton craft, show us the competence reached by the boat-builder in the first century B.C.[73] The Hjortspring find in Denmark included a boat or canoe, 58 feet long, 'stitched' together like the Ferriby boats mentioned in the last chapter, and the later boats, such as that of the fourth century A.D. from Nydam in Schleswig-Holstein, 77 feet long and with twenty-eight oars, help to bridge the gap between prehistory and the Viking development of the shipwright's craft. We must reckon, too, with the continued use of dug-out canoes, and of skin-covered boats of the curragh or coracle type, the one for sea and the other for river traffic; Caesar observed the former in Britain, and profited by his recollection when needing quickly-made light craft in his Spanish campaigns five years later, and other classical writers commented on both types.[74]

Corn-production must have been at a relatively high level over much of continental Celtic territory and in southern England. Surviving surface traces of field-systems of pre-Roman date are, as is well known, confined to Britain (and there very largely to southern England), and to a few examples in for instance Denmark and Holland. The problem of the English 'Celtic Fields' is now recognised to be one of great complexity, and the field-form certainly goes back to the twelfth century B.C., and probably beyond. This makes 'Celtic' an unhappy adjective, and throughout, the type of plough employed seems to have been the light 'ard', with heavy ploughs in Britain not antedating the Roman Conquest, whatever may have been the case elsewhere in Europe, and however we interpret Pliny's statements about ploughs in Rhaetia.[75] (Fig. 141)

It has recently become apparent that a momentous innovation in corn-grinding, the use of the rotary flour-mill or quern, is almost certainly a barbarian contribution to the ancient world, Celtic or Celtiberian, and only adopted in Roman Italy in the second century B.C. The Greek and Roman world up to this time had used saddle-querns, of remote Neolithic ancestry, or at best the improved oscillatory 'Olynthian' type; gearing and water-mills soon followed in the classical world, though evidence for windmills in Europe does not appear until perhaps the seventh, or more surely the twelfth century A.D.[76] Barbarian technological innovations of this kind may probably be perceived in other directions in classical times: the reaping machine used on the large

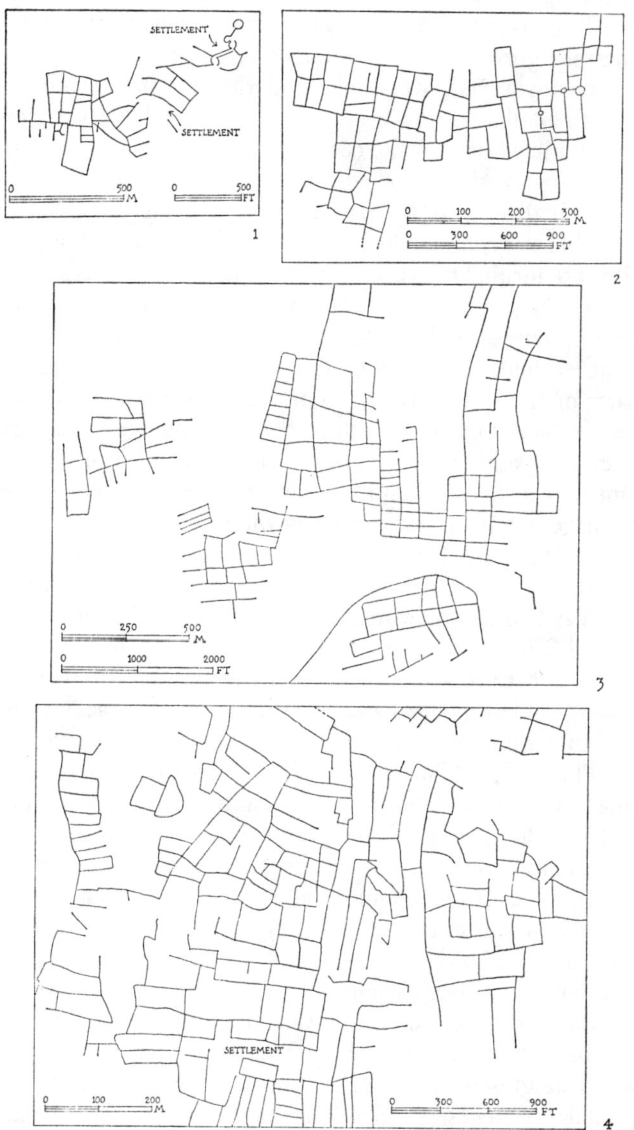

141. *Ancient field-systems at 1, Plumpton Plain, Sussex, England, twelfth century* B.C.; *2, Nordse Veld, Zeyen, Netherlands; 3, Figheldean Down, Wilts., England; Skøbaek Hede, Jutland, Denmark; all probably second-first century* B.C. *to first century* A.D.

Gaulish cornfields and known from sculptures as well as literary references may be a case in point, as may the regular shoeing of horses.[77]

Using the figures for grain production and consumption with which we have already toyed, we would find that for provisioning his two legions, with auxiliaries and headquarters staff, in Kent for a fortnight, Caesar would have needed the consumption-crop of some 70,000 acres. It has been suggested that the consumption-yield from the cornfields of a southern English Iron Age farmstead was about 50 bushels, so that Caesar would have commandeered the annual harvest of about 1400 such farms, if these formed the social economic unit of south-east England at this time, which is by no means certain. Whatever the detailed validity of these figures, there is no doubt that corn in some quantity was available.

By the second century B.C. local coins were being produced in most parts of the Celtic world; implying that in some transactions at least a move had been made into a money economy, though exchange and barter and payment in kind must have continued to play the most important part in the mercantile life of craftsmen, traders and farmers. Celtic coinage, while almost wholly in the idiom of the native art, was stylistically ultimately derived from old gold and silver coins, most of Macedonian origin, circulating in the Roman Empire as currency alternative to that from Roman mints. 'They like the old and well-known money', said Tacitus of the Germani, 'coins milled, or showing a two-horse chariot'.[78] Europe was broadly divided into two currency areas, mainly using gold in the west and silver in the east; a great group of gold coins in Gaul (and thence Britain) derive (via the Danube) from the gold staters of Philip II of Macedon (with its two-horse chariot), while from the Rhine to Czechoslovakia it was Alexander of Macedon's stater that formed the prototype. In Hungary and the Carpathians Philip's silver stater, and a silver tetradrachm of Alexander the Great were copied in silver, and in the Lower Danube there was more silver coinage but a little gold, derived from Byzantine types; the north Pontic silver coinage was based on a tetradrachm of Thasos. Coinage was introduced into Britain with the first Belgic colonisation of the end of the second century B.C. and was then widely used in a variety of forms in Belgic and para-Belgic territory, side-by-side with the west English use of iron ingot-bars of standard weights in the form of rough-out swords. Mints existed in tribal capitals—Colchester, Silchester, Bagendon—using techniques and moulds identical with those from comparable continental sites such as Manching.[79]

The wine trade between the Mediterranean world and that north of the Alps, going back as we have seen to Hallstatt, and perhaps even Urnfield times, was not unnaturally continued as Roman contacts were

XLVIII. *Iron fire-dogs, late La Tène culture, first century* B.C. *– first century* A.D. (*a*) *Firedog from Niederurssel, Mainz, Germany* (Photo. Stadtmuseum, Frankfurt-am-Main); (*b*) *Detail of fire-dog, Capel Garmon, Wales* (Photo. National Museum of Wales)

XLIX. *Stone relief showing captive Dacians, Roman, first century* A.D., *on Trajan's Trophy at Adamklissi, Rumania.* (Photo. Institutul de Arheologie, Bucharest)

strengthened through the pacific alliance of client peoples or by conquest, notably that of southern Gaul in 121 B.C. Wine production in Italy (rather than importation from Greece and the Greek islands) began late in the third century B.C., and a couple of centuries later home consumption has been estimated at 660 million gallons a year. Celtic wine imports can be traced by the standard amphorae used for its trans-shipment or overland trade, and found for instance by underwater archaeology in offshore wrecks such as that at Grand Conglué off Marseilles. By the end of the second century characteristic amphorae show wine reaching Bibracte near Autun, Switzerland and the Rhineland; fifty years or so later we similarly detect it as far as Alesia and Manching; by the early first century A.D. the Belgic chieftains of south-east England are importing their wine in amphorae, each holding the equivalent of rather over two dozen modern bottles apiece.[80] An allocation of three amphorae apiece for the lord and his guest was provided in the Belgic tombs furnished for the otherworld feast we have already noted. The occasional bronze flagons and shallow handled bowls of Italian manufacture from such British graves and many continental sites represent in the same way the north-westerly extent of this same wine trade, which continued beyond the Roman frontiers at a later date into northern Germany and Scandinavia.[81] (Figs. 142, 143)

It was of course an expensive and aristocratic drink, and the Celts were scorned by their classical contemporaries for their intemperance and their habit (very reasonable it would seem to us) of drinking their wine undiluted with water. 'It is a race greedy for wine', Ammianus Marcellinus remarked, 'devising numerous drinks similar to wine, and among them some people of the baser sort, with wits dulled by continual drunkenness, . . . rush about in aimless revels.' Indigenous drinks were mead (favoured it seems by the Celtiberians) and beer, either *cerevisia* or *xythus*, brewed from barley, or *celia* or *ceria* brewed from wheat.[82]

From at least the second century B.C. inscriptions copied from the Greek prototype coins, and later, independent inscriptions in Greek or Roman characters, are found on continental Celtic coinage, and from about 50 B.C. there is a British inscribed coinage, normally giving the name of the tribal ruler and his mint in abbreviated form. This shows at least conditional literacy among a learned class, in which orthographic innovations were introduced to represent Celtic sounds not included in the normal Roman alphabet, such as the crossed 'D' (Đ) to indicate the aspirated form in the name ADĐEDOMAROS. Caesar refers to the occasional use of Greek letters by the Druids, and a late La Tène sword from Switzerland has not only the swordsmith's stamp on it, but his name KORISIOS in Greek characters. Some graffiti scratched on sherds

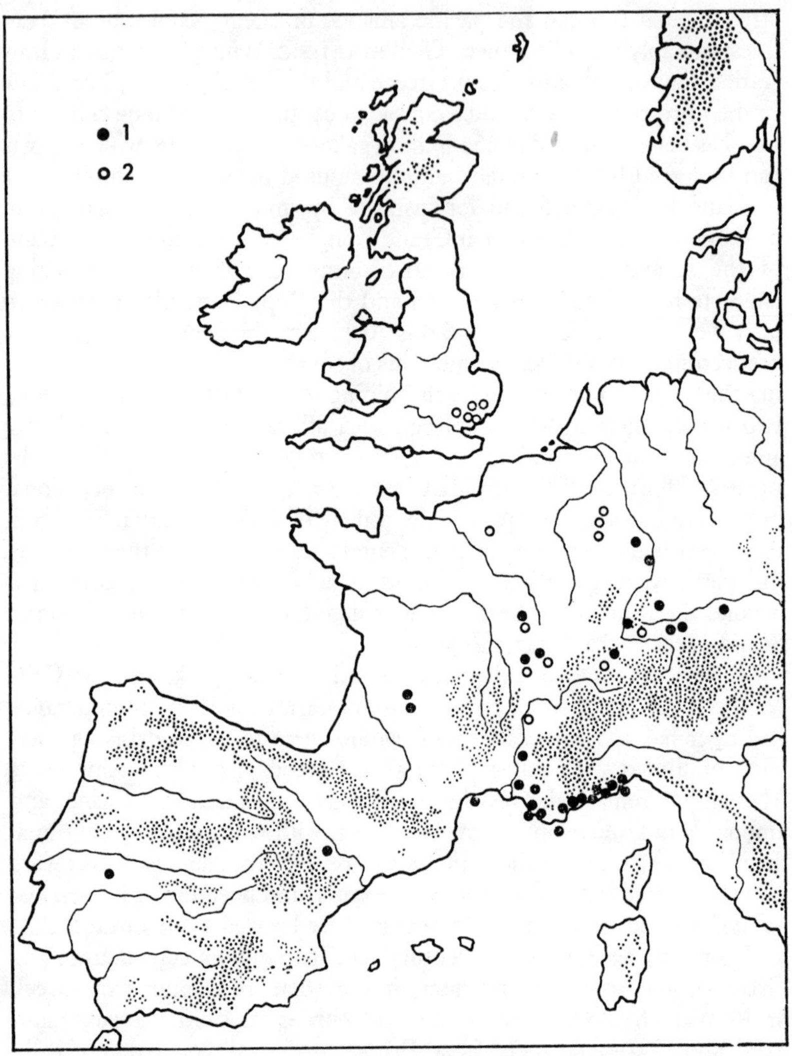

142. *Distribution of Roman wine amphorae imported into the late La Tène world. 1, Pre-Caesarian; 2, Caesarian-Augustan.*

from the Magdalenensburg in Austria may represent a Celtic use of a debased Etruscan alphabet in the first century B.C., and in Camulodunum (Colchester) graffiti on pots in Roman letters go back to the pre-Roman period. But by and large writing was not a Celtic accomplishment, nor need it have been in a society where song and story, law and genealogy,

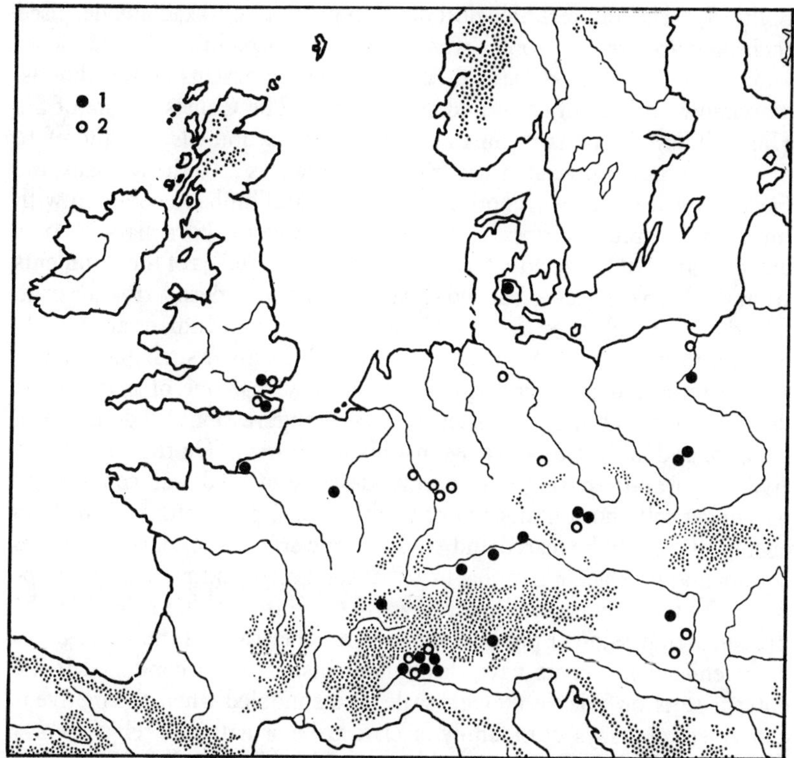

143. *Distribution of Roman bronze wine-flagons and pans imported into the late la Tène world, first century* B.C.*-first century* A.D.*: 1, flagons; 2, pans.*

were safely transmitted by an active and effective oral tradition, and political or mercantile affairs were not so complex as to need the written record.[83] Whatever superficial accomplishments Celts or Germans or others outside the Mediterranean world may have acquired, there would be no doubt of their classification in the minds of Greeks and Romans—they were barbarians.

We have in fact reached a crisis of antithesis in Europe which we have already seen recurring in other contexts of the remoter past. It is the theme I indicated in my first chapter, that of the developed and under-developed peoples, the innovators and the conservators, presented in its acute form as the division between the civilised and the barbarian worlds of ancient Europe. Each of the major civilisations of antiquity had found their frontiers marching with those of communities at a differing level of political, social and technological development. The Akkadians despised their neighbours as people 'who knew not kingship' and 'had never known a city'; the Assyrians described the Cimmerians as 'vagabonds, who know nothing of oaths and agreements'. The Chinese wrote of the Huns, 'These barbarians must be looked upon as animals, and therefore one should not appreciate their friendly utterances'. To the Romans, the Germani were 'men with nothing but voices and limbs in common with humanity', 'arch-deceivers of the utmost savagery, born liars'.[84] It is unfortunate that the accident of illiteracy has deprived us of the comments from the barbarian side, but the situation has too modern a ring for us to find them difficult to envisage; after all Palefaces and Indians are a comparable antithesis known since our childhood. In my first chapter, again, I have indicated my sympathy with the view that one of man's most deeply seated and most cherished needs is for aggression and dominance, violence and killing, directed against his fellow-men. On the frontiers of civilisation and barbarism a continuous state of cold war could exist, psychologically not unsatisfactory to either side, providing both with an enemy that could be feared and envied while still despised, conducive to comforting feelings of national or tribal solidarity, and providing an opportunity for cathartic outbursts of warlike zeal from either side when the pressures of passion or policy demanded it. The ethics of the street gangs of juvenile delinquents have throughout history been condoned if the enterprise is on a large enough scale, and ennobled when the motive is conceived of as loyalty to family or clan, tribe or nation, a religious or a political faith. Much of human history and prehistory has no grander theme than that of the Jets and Sharks in *West Side Story*.

In the world of Roman and barbarian in Europe, there was, as Alföldi[85] put it, a 'moral barrier on Rhine and Danube'. To some extent, we have conditions of technological disparity between innovating and conserving traditions, but this had been narrowed down to restricted limits, with literacy as the greatest single factor of differentiation. Celtic and Roman iron-working or salt-winning for instance, had virtual technological parity; where the classical world excelled that of the barbarians was in the social contexts of organisation of labour, and the use of slaves, making higher productivity possible without actual improvement of techniques, and in the mechanics of distribution and trade within a politically stable Empire with accepted mercantile laws and efficient methods of recording business transactions. The moral barrier existed in terms of incompatible patterns of culture, in narrowed intellectual horizons on either side, unable to contain loyalties or concepts of parity beyond the limits of the political, tribal or familial units of the protagonists. But while treachery and atrocities were committed by both parties,

1. *Defeated Britons: stone relief on distance-slab from Bridgeness on the Antonine Wall, Scotland, mid second century* A.D. (Photo. National Museum of Antiquities of Scotland)

LI. *Part of silver dish, Byzantine, representing barbarian members of the Imperial Bodyguard of Theodosius* I, *388* A.D., *from Almendralejo, Spain*
(Photo. Römisch-Germanische Zentralmuseum, Mainz)

as between European settlers and Indians in North America a century or so ago, one cannot take up a wholly neutral standpoint. 'The conduct of the barbarians was rendered worse by the incalculable changes of their moods; they were not guided by logical and reasoned thinking but rather by sudden emotion.' Their habits involved an archaic, incoherent and impermanent world of raid and counter-raid, feud and vendetta; nomads were particularly impossible to fit into any scheme of settled and durable government. At a later date, when Christendom was becoming the seat of moral authority in the Empire, Alföldi has quoted the nomad's objection (in the fourth century) to living even an approximately Christian life—'If we do not plunder and rob the goods of others any more, on what shall innumerable masses as we are, live? . . . We shall no more be able to mount our horses as is the tradition and custom of our tribe.' A later nomad ruler, in 1246, put the matter succinctly when replying to a Papal reprimand: 'It is said in your letter that the slaughter of men . . . puzzled and embarrassed you. We can simply reply that we are not able to understand this.'[86]

One does not have to be an uncritical optimist, wedded to an unthinking belief in inevitable progress and mankind's perfectibility, to recognise civilisation for what it is, even if as its heirs we are inevitably conditioned to accepting it as the desirable norm. With all their faults, the successive civilised communities of antiquity achieved an organisation of man's powers, and a control of his frailties, immensely superior to anything brought about by the barbarians. To laud the barbaric virtues is to fall a victim of the myth of the Noble Savage: Duncan Forbes was surely right to deplore those who 'stick close to their ancient and idle way of life . . . dangerous to the public peace'. The Roman Conquest of parts of Celtic Europe may perhaps have prevented the ultimate emergence there of an indigenous civilisation of a sort, but it was hardly a disaster. If Gallia Comata, shaggy Gaul, had achieved something of coherent political and economic entity on its own, it could hardly have been more than a provincial imitation of what had been established further south by Roman conquest in the second century B.C. The northern world, always beyond the Imperial frontiers, made no steps towards civilisation until the Middle Ages.

But medieval Europe, and our own, was not wholly the product of the Roman tradition. What I have attempted to show in this book is that the prehistoric, non-literate, peoples must not be ignored in any examination of European origins. Their existence has never been in doubt, but it is only in recent years that the techniques of archaeology have begun to give them substance. I would repeat again, however, what I hope I made clear at the outset, that archaeological evidence does not, in its very nature, afford us the material from which we can write history, in the usually accepted sense of the word. Where my tedious enumeration of archaeological records of tombs and settlements, pits or post-holes, flints or pottery or bronzes, has momentarily acquired something of the character of historical narrative, it has been when historical evidence could in fact be used to illuminate the catalogue of traits of material culture. Again, to return to a point already made, I have chosen themes and aspects within prehistory which I personally regard as important and significant: the selection and arrangement, the emphasis and the organisation of the evidence I have put before you is my own. Continuity of tradition, technological development, the interaction of East and West, have been some of these themes, but while personal, as all study of the human past must be, I do not feel that my interpretation is so wildly idiosyncratic as not to be in general agreement with those of other scholars.

What I think we have been able to see is that the essential rural economy of what was to become historical Europe has roots which strike very deep in prehistoric antiquity. Mixed farming—the growing of a cereal crop and the concurrent breeding of stock for meat and milk, fleece and hide—began in Europe probably in the sixth, certainly in the fifth millennium B.C. Just as we are ourselves the personal descendants of these and earlier peoples, so are our chops and steaks taken from the ultimate heirs of the first domesticated animals of Karanovo or Windmill Hill. From grain first scattered in Jarmo or Jericho descends that which makes our blanched and etiolated modern loaves—for the fishes, we look back still further, to those skin-clad stalwarts with net or line who first practised their craft at Maglemose or Star Carr.

The village settlement of temperate Europe, with its rectangular cottages and cow-sheds, barns and granaries, in a loosely-planned unit of individual holdings, we saw in the sixth millennium in the 'tell' settlements of the Balkans; saw, too, how the layout with separated houses differentiated it from the closely packed villages and towns of the Near East, before long to be transmitted to the Aegean and so today to persist in the Mediterranean world. The crafts of building in wood and clay-daubed wattle have their beginnings in this remote Neolithic past, and the Olde Half-Timbered Tea Shoppe has behind it a tradition very Olde indeed. In Central and Eastern Europe at least the timber-framed ramparts of the medieval period have a direct ancestry in those of the late Bronze and Iron Ages. So too with the rural industries of blacksmith and wheelwright (and in the earlier Middle Ages the still rural crafts of the local bronzesmith and potter): these were a commonplace in Hallstatt and La Tène, and in Britain at least, as well as the village and its craftsmen, the independent farm or croft. And not only the utilitarian skills of the village and farmstead, for some elements of pre-Roman Celtic art were transmitted to enrich the metalwork and manuscripts of post-Roman Britain and Ireland.

The conservatism of barbarian Europe, as in other comparable groups of societies, led to the retention and transmission of tradition, either orally, or by the handing on of skills by the direct precept of master to apprentice, or from priest to pupil. Archaeological evidence is favourable to the study of ancient technology, and we have seen how much continuity links the craftsmen in stone and metal, wood or textile, from the beginnings of agriculture to the dawn of the Christian era; seen too that in general, once certain not very ambitious demands have been adequately met, innovation and radical change were exceptional, and accustomed modes preserved and transmitted intact down the generations.

Throughout prehistory we have also encountered the phenomenon of barbarian European art, on the whole not concerned with the accurate reproduction of natural forms or the portrayal of the human figure, and as such in aesthetic contrast to the man-centred representational and narrative arts of the civilisations of the ancient Near East, or their classical successors in the Mediterranean. In the later and most exciting phases, when we can speak of Celtic art, we see how it combines ancient barbarian traditions stretching to Siberia and the borders of China, with those of eastern and western Europe beyond the bounds of the world of Greece and Rome.

What we can infer of religion, or rather of the practices that found tangible expression in places of cult or burial, shows again remarkable continuity. The sanctuary open to the sky, the pits or shafts dug deep down into the earth, the cult of head and skull, the ritual enclosures of late Celtic Europe, all have their prototypes in the second millenium B.C. at least, if not earlier; the tradition of burial in a wheeled vehicle runs almost unbroken in time from before 2000 to the last centuries B.C., and in space from south Russia to the Yorkshire Wolds. A similar territory, from Anatolia and the steppe to Scandinavia, shared the cult of hide- or fleece-burial from the late third millennium B.C. to the Middle Ages and beyond. The coming and going of people and ideas between eastern and western Europe has been an inevitably recurrent theme, and set the stage for the continuance of such circumstances after the fall of the western Roman Empire.

Finally, if our inferences from archaeological and philological evidence are not too far off the mark, and our interpretation of the Celtic evidence sound, it does look as though some of the germs of the social structure of early medieval Europe may have been present not only in immediately pre-Roman times, but in far earlier periods. Searching for the origins of medieval feudalism, Marc Bloch found the evidence demanded the existence of 'rural chiefdoms in primitive Europe' with hereditary chiefs or *principes*, 'odd little potentates' of a society linked by obligations imposed by gift and custom. He quoted Tacitus on the Germani—'it is the custom that each tribesman shall give the chieftain presents either of cattle or of part of his harvest. These free gifts are marks of respect, but they also supply the needs of those who receive them.' He also saw in the ludicrous practices associated with some medieval tenancies or serjeanties a survival from a prehistoric antiquity in which the chieftain presided over ritual ceremonies. 'We catch glimpses', Bloch wrote of the early historical evidence, 'of peasant communities under their chiefs, to whom various families (in the wide sense) that made up the group owed ritual gifts, and no doubt assistance in a general way, which would be sure to take the form of certain services. The existence of these village chieftains is clearly attested in Gaul before Caesar and in Germany before the invasions: it may be traced in the society of Armorica; it appears more distinctly in that of Wales.' 'We may assume', he added 'something of the sort in ancient Europe more or less everywhere.'[87] In this book I have tried to indicate that there is evidence to suggest that the pattern of society demanded by Bloch could in fact be very ancient, and characteristic of barbarian Europe for millennia.

'The raw material of prehistory is not men, but things.' I quoted this dictum of Professor Atkinson's with approval in my first chapter, and do so again. As men, the barbarians elude us, early and late; we have tried to glimpse something of their workmanship, their art, their movement and settlement, even of their social order. To the Romans, they were the wild men of the woods, to be crudely caricatured in humiliating defeat, whether in Britain, Gaul or Dacia (Pls. XLIX, L). But there is one most moving work of art from the ancient world into which one could read an epitome of the final situation, the great silver birthday-present dish of Theodosius I, of 388 A.D. (PL. LI) The emperor sits flanked by the youths of his barbarian guard, the *Germani corpore custodes*, whose institution went back to Claudian times; bewildered boys whose anxious eyes look out, away from the Byzantine world, beyond the barbarian Europe that was theirs, and into that of the Middle Ages, and of our own time.

Notes

1. General account of Celtic Europe, Powell 1958; Filip 1962; Hawkes 1963; imports and chronology in Dehn and Frey 1962; late situlae, Kimmig 1964a.
2. Chariot-graves in middle Rhine listed and mapped by Schiek 1954; in Marne by Joffroy and Bretz-Mahler 1959; cf. pottery distribution in Dehn 1950; in Low Countries, de Laet 1958, 164, 178; Mariën 1961, 173-8. Earlier literature and later La Tène chariotry, Déchelette 1927, 686-708; in Britain, Fox 1946, 1958; Belgic chariotry, Frere 1961. British chariot (or cart) graves, Fox 1946; Stead 1961. The latest reference to British chariots is among the Caledonii in the Severan campaigns of A.D. 207 (Dio LXXVI, 12).
3. Hungary, Márton 1934, 158, 161; Bulgaria, Jacobsthal 1944, 151 (Mezek); south Russia, Yakounina-Ivanova 1927 (no chariot remains but a pair of bits); Pergamon, Powell 1958, Pl. 49.
4. Hungarian burials listed in Alföldi 1935; Bulgarian burials, Seure 1901, 1904; Welkow 1943; Botuscharova 1950.
5. Timber-laced, *muri gallici* and other forts, Cotton 1955, 1957; Wheeler and Richardson 1957; Dehn 1960, 1962.
6. Interim reports on the Manching excavations, Krämer 1960, 1962; Krämer *et al.* 1961.
7. Alesia and Bibracte, Cotton 1957, 190-8; quotation from Stevens 1957.
8. Závist and Stradonic, Filip 1962, 104-6.
9. There has been no general study of British hill-forts since that of Hawkes 1931, except in terms of their overall typology and distribution in Rivet 1962. Stanwick, Wheeler 1954a; Maiden Castle; *ibid.* 1943; Y Corddyn and other North Welsh forts, Gardner 1926; Eildon, R.C.A.M. (S), 1956, no. 597.
10. Rivet 1962, 13, quoting Livy XXXVIII. xix: '*fossam quoque et alia munimento verticibus iis quos insederant circumiecere*'.
11. For East Celtic settlement, cf. maps in Filip 1956, 1962, 57. Russian distributions, Kucharenko 1959; Rosen-Pshchevskaya 1963; La Tène sword, Bodyanskiy 1962; helmets in Reinecke 1948: they belong to Jacobsthal's Group B (1944, 116). Pergamon helmet, Powell 1958, Pl. 49.
12. General linguistic considerations in Jackson 1953; Pictish language, Jackson 1955; Irish continental and British connections, Rynne 1961; Jope 1962.
13. Entremont, Benoit 1955, 1957; Eydoux 1958, Chapter 2; Ensérune, Jannoray 1955; Mailhac, Louis and Taffanel 1955-60.
14. For Iberia, Powell 1958; Maluquer 1954a,b,c; 1958; Schüle 1960; Harden 1962; Sandars 1913; Cabrè *et al.* 1950; Arribas 1963.
15. Crossland 1957.

16. Cf. Hawkes 1957a, 14.
17. Discussion of outside influences in Denmark at this time in Klindt-Jensen 1950, 1953a; for Gundestrup, *idem.* 1959, 1960, 1961. Hagighiol, Andriescu 1937 and much unpublished in National Museum, Bucharest; Poroina rhyton, Durnăreanu-Vulpe in Oprescu *et al.* 1958; Poiana-Coţofeneşti helmet, Andriescu 1937; Sulimirksi 1963, 284. Lukovit, National Museum, Sofia; silver discs, Klindt-Jensen 1952, 1961, with map, Fig. 57 (add new disc from Roman fort of Oberaden, Westphalia). A silver beaker was allegedly found with a helmet at 'the Danube downstream from the Iron Gates' and both are very close to Hagighiol in style: beaker in Jacobsthal 1944, 36; Pls. 226, 227 and now in Metropolitan Museum, New York; helmet now in Institute of Arts, Detroit. (*Bull. Detroit. Inst. Arts* XLII: 4 (1963), 63).
18. Piggott 1962c.
19. There is no single modern study of any length dealing with the archaeological and social content of early Irish literature. O'Curry 1873 still remains a basic source, but most subsequent work is linguistic, Thurneysen 1921 remaining a fundamental study. Short treatments of the Law Tracts in Binchy 1943; secular institutions in *ibid.* 1954; cf. Dillon *et al.* 1954, 1959; tradition and literature, Dillon 1947, 1948; Binchy 1961. Translations of texts conveniently in Cross and Slover 1936.
20. Critical study with text and translation in Tierney 1960.
21. Binchy 1954.
22. De Navarro 1955.
23. Cf. Thompson in Finley *et al.* 1960.
24. For slave chains, Fox 1946, 37; 1948, 66.
25. Cf. comments in Richmond 1954.
26. All quotations from Posidonius are from the translation in Tierney 1960.
27. Germ. XV.
28. D. Forbes 1746, 298.
29. The best study of the Druids is still Kendrick 1928; since this, cf. Powell 1958; Sjoestedt 1949; Lambrechts 1942, 1954; Hawkes 1957a; de Vries 1963.
30. Grousset 1960, 58.
31. Lambrechts 1954; Ross 1958.
32. Benoit 1955, 1957.
33. The L'Impernal fort is described in Benoit 1957, 22-23; Cotton 1957, 186-7. For the Bredon excavations, T. C. Hencken 1938.
34. Discussed (with recent Celtic survivals) in Ross 1962.
35. Cf. Anati 1964 for representative illustrations.
36. There has been discussion of the status of some of these finds—secular hoards or votive deposits?—but the latter explanation seems plausible in most instances. La Tène, Vouga 1923; Tiefenau, Tschumi 1929; Kappel,

Fischer 1959; Llyn Cerrig Bach, Fox 1946; Scotland and England, Piggott 1953c; Hjortspring, Rosenberg 1937; Gundestrup, Klindt-Jensen 1961; *aurum Tolosanum*, Posidonius in Strabo IV. i. 13; Justin XXXII, 3, quoted with comment by I. A. Richmond in Fox 1946, 69. The Duchcov (Dux) site, Filip 1956, 342.

37. Ritual shafts and wells in Germany and France, Schwarz 1960, 1962; for a British example, cf. Burchell 1949. Deposits in Roman wells, comments in Piggott 1953c; Ross 1962.
38. For these rectangular earthworks (*viereckschanzen*), Schwarz 1958, 1960, 1962; Decker and Scollar 1962; Stead 1962; Stead 1961; possible comparable sites in Britain, Hood and Walton 1948; Cotton 1961. Heath Row temple, Grimes 1961; Romano-Celtic temples, Wheeler 1928; Wheeler and Wheeler 1936; Wheeler 1943; the map in Schwarz 1962; Beilage 5, 2, is out-of-date for Britain. For native shrines associated with or beneath these temples, cf. Bradford and Goodchild 1939 (Frilford, Worth, with model shields and sword as votive deposits) and Wheeler 1943, 76 for continuity at Maiden Castle; later pagan temples, Pettazoni 1946.
39. Aulnay-aux-Planches, Schwarz 1962, 55; Libenice, Rybova and Soudsky 1962; Marne sites, Schwarz 1962, 54-55; Stead 1961; Goloring, Röder 1948.
40. As stressed by Kendrick (1928) and Hawkes (1957a).
41. Dorchester and cursus monuments, Atkinson *et al.* 1951; Swanwick shaft, C. F. Fox 1930; Wilsford, Ashbee 1963.
42. General discussion in Piggott 1958.
43. Archaeological demonstration in Proudfoot 1961.
44. Cattle-Raid of Cooley (*Táin Bó Cúailnge*); translated text in Cross and Slover 1936, 281-327; Dunn 1914; Laertes and Eurycleia (*Od.* I, 430), Finley 1956, 71; cattle among Germani, Tacitus Germ. V.
45. The earlier (upper Palaeolithic to late Neolithic) house-types in Europe have been assembled by Schlette (1958); later (Bronze Age to Hallstatt D) examples of rectangular houses have been given elsewhere in this book; good La Tène plans in Bersu 1930. In western Europe, the circular house-type appears early, as in the Apulian Neolithic, and continues into the second and first millennia (e.g. in nuraghic sites) and into the Iberian Iron Age (above, pp. 150-155). Gaulish circular houses, Posidonius in Strabo IV, iv, 3 (Tierney 1960, 268). West Harling, Clark and Fell 1953 (the reconstruction is open to criticism); Little Woodbury, Bersu 1940; Glastonbury, Bulleid and Gray 1911-17; Scottish sites, Feachem 1963; raths, Proudfoot 1961. The Scandinavian and north European excavated sites are numerous: discussions with plans in Klindt-Jensen 1953b (general); Stenberger *et al.* 1955, 100-254; 977-1048 (Vallhagar, Migration Period, and affinities); Hatt. 1957 (Nørre Fjand, second century B.C. to second century A.D., with discussion of early medieval survivals of the house-types).

46. The thesis of the rectangular plan of the houses in the Irish hero-tales was put forward by Richmond (1932). Some raths certainly contained rectangular structures, but these sites range in date from perhaps the third century B.C. to the Middle Ages; Proudfoot (1961), quoting the relevant legal text (*Críth Gablach*) is cautious here. The quotations are from 'Bricriu's Feast' (*Fled Bricrend*: Cross and Slover 1936, 254, 267), while the description of rectangular hall and outbuildings are in 'The Intoxication of the Ulstermen' (*Mesca Ulad*: Cross and Slover 1936, 220).
47. Powell 1963, 164.
48. See above, p. 215.
49. Representations on for instance the Sopron vessels; for trousers, cf. Hald 1961; Chinese evidence, Grousset 1960, 54.
50. Iron and steel swords, Coghlan 1956, 185-6; Tylecote 1962, 211-13. Continental styles, Jacobsthal 1944, 95-97, 114-15; de Navarro 1955: 1959b; British swords and daggers, Piggott 1950b; Jope 1961b.
51. There are numerous references in the classical writers to the painting or tattooing of the body by barbarians: F. T. Wainwright, 1955, 2, for British and Pictish evidence, with sources and comment; Strabo VII. 3. 15 (Illyrians, Thracians, etc.); Rice 1957, 115-16; Rudenko 1953, 136-42; Griaznov 1958, Pl. 43 (Scythian).
52. Déchelette 1927, 661-73; Jacobsthal, 1944, 116-18.
53. La Tène scabbard from Hallstatt, Jacobsthal 1944, no. 96; Fayum shield, Kimmig 1940; La Tène, Vouga 1923, Pls. XV-XVIII; Hjortspring, Rosenberg 1937; shields in sculpture, Powell 1958, Pls. 48-49 (Pergamon); Pls. 50, 51 (Orange); Déchelette 1927, 673-81; Eydoux 1962, Figs. 72-74 (Narbonne, Montdragon, Nîmes); British shields, Fox 1958. The Irish quotation is from the *Táin*: Henderson 1899, 183 ff.; cf. Livy XXXVIII, xxi, on 3-foot high Galatian shields.
54. For Celtic mail, cf. Piggott 1953c, 38-40; Hjortspring, Rosenberg 1937; Pergamon, Powell 1958, Pl. 48; Vachères, Déchelette 1927, 661; Eydoux 1962, Fig. 74. Wheeler suggested Asiatic origins for Celtic and Germanic mail (1954b, 59), and the south Russian finds support this view (Minns 1913, 175-6).
55. The authority here is Arrian, writing in 136 A.D. (*Tactics*, XXXII ff.), commented on in this connection by Curle (1911, 173) and Toynbee (Toynbee and Clarke 1948, 24). Arrian's passage on tight trousers is almost identical with one in Tacitus, *Germania* XVII (written A.D. 98), and may be derived from this or both share a common source. The Irish 'Feats' recur in the tales of the Ulster Cycle; for Belgic charioteers, Caesar, Bell. Gall. IV, 33; Totila, Procopius, Gothic War VIII, 32.
56. Irish quotation from 'The Wooing of Emer' (*Tochmarc Emire*); Cross and Slover 1936, 156; Bituitus, Florus I. 37. 5.

57. Powell 1963, 165-6.
58. Irish quotation from the *Táin* (Cross and Slover 1936, 326); for Nestor (*Iliad* XI, 670-84), Finley 1956, 49.
59. The fundamental work is that of Jacobsthal 1944; cf. his short essay (1941). Subsequent studies of importance include Klindt-Jensen 1953a; Frey 1955; de Navarro 1959a; Megaw 1962 1963; (Europe); Fox 1958; Jope 1961a; Atkinson and Piggott 1955; MacGregor 1962; Megaw 1963 (British Isles). Quotation from Jacobsthal 1944, 163.
60. Quotation from Collingwood 1936, 249-50. For the *baritus* battle-song—'not so much an articulate sound, as a general cry of valour'—Tacitus, *Germania* III; for the carnyx animal-headed trumpet, Piggott 1959b.
61. Chariot references as on p. 261. For tyres and smith's work, Fox 1946; Jope 1956a; general wheelwright's craft, Sturt 1934; Jenkins 1961; Sandars 1962.
62. Djebjerg, Klindt-Jensen 1950, 87-100; wheels, Piggott 1949.
63. Verulamium, Wheeler and Wheeler 1936, 43; Maiden Castle, Wheeler 1943, 47, 77, 109, 115, 121; Alesia, Cotton 1957, 197.
64. Iron ingots, Kleeman 1961; Rädeker and Naumann 1961 (general European and metallurgical); Giot and Mazéas 1962 (Brittany); Tylecote 1962, 206-11 (currency bars); Venetic ships, Caesar Bell. Gall. III, 13; Portland ingots and Belbury anchor, Grinsell 1958, 137, 158.
65. The smith Culann, in the *Táin*, is so described; Cross and Slover 1936, 139.
66. Fox 1946, 74-76; cf. the tribute to the strength of the Llyn Cerrig gang chains, used at the time of their discovery 'by tractor drivers to draw lorries out of the mud' (*ibid.* 38).
67. Incomplete list of La Tène firedogs in Drost 1954; for additions, cf. Déchelette 1911, 47; Gaudron 1955a,b, 1956 (France), Fischer 1959 (Germany); Piggott 1948b (Britain); Cauldron chains, Piggott 1953c. Etymology, Drost 1954, 126-8; cf. entries s.v. *landier* in *Franz. Etym. Wörterbuch* (1928) and s.v. *ander* in Vendryes, *Lex. Etym. d'Irlandais Anc. A* (1959), 76. I am grateful to Professor Kenneth Jackson for advice here.
68. Dehn (1963) draws attention to the earliest wheel-turned pottery north of the Alps at Mont Lassois (Hallstatt D) and later (early La Tène) at the Heuneburg, etc., and relates this to the trade in grey, wheel-turned, 'Phocean' ware northwards from Massalia from the late sixth century B.C.
69. Jacobsthal 1944, 133-4; Henry 1963.
70. Nenquin 1961.
71. Strabo IV. 4. 3; for woollen cloaks, cf. Carus-Wilson 1952, 355-67; Brogan 1953, 158; Piggott 1958; Wild 1963.
72. Pliny *Nat. Hist.* XIX. ii.
73. Caesar Bell. Gall. III. 13; Posidonius in Tierney 1960, 267; Creston 1961.
74. Hjortspring, Rosenberg 1937; Nydam, Shetelig 1930; dug-out canoes, Clark, 1952, 282-92; curraghs and coracles, Hornell 1938.

75. For earlier fields, see above, p. 150. Among studies of later prehistoric agriculture, cf. Hatt 1949; Glob 1951; van Giffen 1950; Bowen 1962; Rivet 1956; Piggott 1958.
76. Detailed survey of the whole problem, Moritz 1958.
77. For reaping-machines, Jope 1956b, 96; shoeing of horses, Heichelheim 1956, 325; Hell 1963.
78. *Germania* V.
79. There is no general up-to-date treatment of Celtic coinage: Pink 1960 deals with Central and East Europe; P. La Baume 1960 gives a useful short summary of types and their antecedents, with bibliography. For the Gaulish (and thence British) Philippus coinage, Allen 1961, with derivation via the Danube from Macedonia rather than through Massaliote trade: detailed mapping in Rivet 1962. Later British inscribed coinage, Allen 1944; coin types in Mack 1953. The division of Celtic Europe into provinces favouring gold or silver respectively was stressed by Milne (1940) and is apposite in connection with the problems raised by Gundestrup and related pieces already referred to. Currency bars, Tylecote 1962, 206-11.
80. Roman wine production, Forbes 1956, 133-9; amphorae in late La Tène contexts, Uenze 1958.
81. Bronze wine-vessels, Werner 1954; Fischer 1959, 16-19; Roman trade conveniently summarised in Wheeler 1954, 72-94.
82. Ammianus XV. 12. 4; Cider and beer, Forbes 1956, 139-41; Pliny XXII. 25 (Gaulish beer); Tacitus, *Germania* XXIII (beer among the Germani); Diodorus V. 2 (Celtiberian mead); Posidonius in Tierney 1960, 247 (*corma* or wheat beer flavoured with honey in Gaul); Pytheas, in Strabo IV. v. 5, (drink of corn and honey in Britain); *cerevisia*, *ceria*, etc., Du Cange, *Gloss. med. et inf. Lat.*, s.v.; *xythus*, Ammianus *loc. cit.*
83. Inscribed coinage, Allen 1944; Addedomaros, Jackson 1953, 530; Gauls and Greek, Caesar Bell. Gall. I. 29; VI. 14; Korisios sword, Wyss 1956; Magdalenensburg inscriptions, Mossler 1961; Colchester graffiti, Hawkes and Hull 1947, 284-6.
84. Quotations from Alföldi 1952; cf. comments in Lattimore 1962, *passim.*
85. *Loc. cit.*
86. Alföldi *loc. cit.* 13; a rather different translation from the original Persian of the last quotation is given in Dawson 1955, 85.
87. Bloch 1941; cf. Hawkes 1957a.

A

ADAMESTEANU, D. 1957
'Nouvelles fouilles a Géla . . .', *Rev. Arch.* XLIX (1957), 20–46.

AKURGAL, E. 1959
'Urartäische Kunst', *Anatolia* IV (1959), 77–114.

AKURGAL, E., & HIRMER, M. 1962
The Art of the Hittites (1962).

ALCOCK, L. 1961
'The Winged Objects in the Llyn Fawr Hoard', *Antiq.* XXXV (1961), 149–51.

ALEXANDER, J. 1962
'Greeks, Italians and the Earliest Balkan Iron Age', *Antiq.* XXXVI (1962), 123–30.

ALFÖLDI, A. 1935
'Die wichterigen Wagenfunde bzw. Wagenbegräbnisse aus Nordost-pannonien', *Arch. Ertesitö* XLVIII (1935), 269–70.

1952
'The Moral Barrier on Rhine and Danube', *Congress of Roman Frontier Studies 1949* (ed. E. Birley, 1952), 1–16.

ALLEN, D. 1944
'The Belgic Dynasties of Britain and their Dynasties', *Arch.* XC (1944), 1–46.

1961
'The Origins of Coinage in Britain: a Reappraisal', in Frere (1961), 97–308.

ALMAGRO, M. 1957
'Las Fibulas de Codo de la Ria de Huelva . . .', *Cuad. Escuela Espan. de Hist. y Arch en Roma* IX (1957), 7–46.

1958a,b
Origen y Formacion del Pueblo Hispano (1958).
Deposito de la Ria de Huelva (1958). (Invent. Arch. España Fasc. 1–4).

ALMAGRO, M., & ARRIBAS, A. 1963
El Poblado y la Necrópolis Megalíticos de los Millares (1963).

ALTHIN, C. A. 1945
Studien zu den bronzezeitlichen Felszeichnungen von Skåne (1945).

1951
'The Scanian Flint Mines', *Medded. Lunds Univ. Hist. Mus.* (1951), 139–58.

ANATI, E. 1964
Camonica Valley (1964).

ANDERSON, J. 1961
Ancient Greek Horsemanship (1961).

ANDRIESCU, I. 1937
Revista de Preistorie si Antichitati Naţionale I, no. 1 (1937).

ARDREY, R. 1961
African Genesis (1961).

ARNAL, J. & BURNEZ, C. 1957
'Die Struktur des französischen Neolithikums auf Grund neuester stratigraphischer Beobachtungen' *Bericht. R. G. Komm.* XXXVII–XXXVIII (1956–57), 1–90.

ARNAL, J., & MARTIN-GRANEL, H. 1961
'Le château préhistorique du Lébous', *Bull. Soc. Préhist. Français* LVIII (1961), 571–82.

ARNAL, J., & SANGMEISTER, E. 1963
'Lébous, eine frühbronzezeitliche Befestigung in Südfrankreich', *Germania* XLI (1963), 229–43.

ARNAL, J. *et al.* 1960
'Les Styles céramiques du Neolithique français', *Préhist.* XIV (1960), 1–200.

ARRIBAS, A. 1959
'El urbanismo peninsular durante el bronce primitivo', *Zephyrus* X (1959), 81–128.

ARRIBAS, A. 1960
'Megalitismo peninsular',
Prim. Sympos. Prehist. Peninsula Iberica 1959 (1960), 69–102.

1963
The Iberians (1963).

ASHBEE, P. 1958
'The Fussell's Lodge Long Barrow',
Antiq. XXXII (1958), 106–11.

1963
'The Wilsford Shaft',
Antiq. XXXVII (1963), 116–20.

APSIMON, A. M. 1954
'Dagger Graves in the "Wessex" Bronze Age',
Univ. Lond. Inst. Arch. Ann. Reports X (1954), 37–62.

ATKINSON, R. J. C. 1955
'The Dorset Cursus',
Antiq. XXIX (1955), 4–9.
Stonehenge (1960).

1961a,b
Archaeology, History and Science (1960).

ATKINSON, R. J. C., & PIGGOTT, S. 1955
'The Torrs Chamfrein',
Arch. XCVI (1955), 197–235

ATKINSON, R. J. C., *et al.* 1951
Excavations at Dorchester, Oxon. (1951).

B

BANNER, J. 1930
'Beiträge zur Wohnungsfrage der Theisskultur',
Prähist. Zeitschr. XXI (1930), 184–193

BANNER, J. *et al.* 1957
'Die Ausgrabungen von L. Marton in Tószeg',
Acta Arch. Hung. X (1957), 1–140.

BARKER, H., & MACKEY, C. J. 1960
'British Museum Natural Radiocarbon Measurements II',
in Flint & Deevy (1960), 26–30.

BARNETT, R. D. 1958
'Early Shipping in the Near East',
Antiq. XXXII (1958), 220–30.

BARNETT, R. D., & FAULKNER, 1962
Sculptures of Tiglath-Pileser III (1962).

BARRIÈRE, C. 1954
Les Civilisations Tardenoisiennes en Europe Occidentale (1954).

BASTIAN, W., & SCHULDT, E. 1961
'Das jungsteinzeitliche Flächgräberfeld von Ostorf, Kr. Schwerin',
Bodendenkmalpflege im Mecklenburg (1961), 7–178.

LA BAUME, P. 1960
Keltische Münzen: Ein Brevier (1960)

LA BAUME, W. 1961
Frühgeschichte der europäischen Kulturpflanzen (1961).

BEARDSLEY, R. K. 1953
'Hypotheses on Inner Asian Pastoral Nomadism and its Culture Area',
Mem. Soc. Amer. Arch. No. 9 (1953), 24–28.

BECKER, C. J. 1948
'Mosefundne Lerkar fra Yngre Stenalder',
Aarbøger (1948), 5–318.

1951
'Late-Neolithic Flint Mines at Aalborg',
Acta Arch. XXII (1951), 135–52.

1954
'Stenalderbebyggelsen ved Store Valby . . .',
Aarbøger (1954), 127–97.

1955a,b
'The Introduction of Farming into Northern Europe',
Journ. World Hist. II, 4 (1955), 749–66.
'Die Mittel-Neolithischen Kulturen in Südskandinavien',
Acta Arch. XXV (1955), 49–150

BECKER, C. J. 1958
'4000-aarig minedrift i Thy',
Nationalmus. Arbejdsmark (1958), 73–82.

1959
'Flint Mining in Neolithic Denmark',
Antiq. XXXIII (1959), 87–92.

BEHN, F. 1962
Vorgeschichtliche Welt (1962).

BEHRENS, H. 1952
'Ein neolithisches Bechergrab aus Mitteldeutschland . . .',
Jahrb. f. Mitteldeutsch. Vorgesch. XXXII (1952), 52–69.

1962
'Quellenkritische Bemerkungen zu einigen neolithitisch-frühmetallzeitlichen Pferdeskelettfunden in Europa',
Zeitsch. f. Tierzücht. u. Züchtungsbiol. LXXVI (1962), 186–9.

BENAC, A., & COVIC, B. 1957
Glasinac I–II (1956–57).

BENEDICT, R. 1959
Patterns of Culture (1959).

BENOIT, F. 1955
L'Art Primitif Méditerranéen de la Vallée du Rhône (1955).

1957
Entremont: Capitale celto-ligure des Salyens de Provence (1957).

1958
'Observations sur les Routes du Commerce Gréco-Étrusque',
Actes du Coll. sur les Influences Hell. en Gaule (1958), 15–20.

BENTON, S. 1952
'The Pelynt Sword-hilt',
Proc. Prehist. Soc. XVIII (1952), 237–8.

BERCIU, D. 1961
Contribuții la problemele Neoliticului în Romînia în lumina noilor cercetări (n.d., 1961).

BERG, G. 1935
Sledges and Wheeled Vehicles (1935).

BERG, G. *et al.* 1950
Finds of Skis from Prehistoric Time in Swedish Bogs and Marshes (1950).

BERSU, G. 1930
'Fünf Mittel-La-Tène-Häuser vom Goldberg . . .',
Schumacher Festschrift (1930), 156–9.

1940
'Excavations at Little Woodbury, Wiltshire',
Proc. Prehist. Soc. VI (1940), 30–111.

1945
Das Wittnauer Horn (1945).

1946
'A Hill-fort in Switzerland',
Antiq. XX (1946), 4–8.

BEVERIDGE, W. I. B. 1961
The Art of Scientific Investigation (1961).

BIBBY, G. 1957
The Testimony of the Spade (1957).

BILLIG, G. 1958
Die Aunjetitzer Kultur in Sachsen (1958).

BINCHY, D. A. 1943
'The Linguistic and Historical Value of the Irish Law Tracts',
Proc. Brit. Acad. XXIX (1943), 195–227.

'Secular Institutions', 1954
in Dillon *et al.* 1954, Chap. IV.

1961
'The Background of Early Irish Literature',
Studia Hibernica I (1961), 1–18.

BIRMINGHAM, J. 1963
'The Development of the Fibula in Cyprus and the Levant',
Pal. Exp. Quarterly (July-December 1963), 80–112.

BISHOP, A. H. 1914
'An Oransay Shell-Mound: A Scottish Pre-Neolithic Site',
Proc. Soc. Ant. Scot. XLVIII (1913–14), 52–108.

BLANCE, B. 1961
'Early Bronze Age Colonists in Iberia',
Antiq. XXXV (1961), 192–202.

BLEGEN, C. W. 1952
'Two Athenian Grave Groups of about 900 B.C.',
Hesperia XXI (1952), 279–94.

1961
'Troy',
Camb. Anc. Hist. (rev. ed.), I, Chaps. XVIII, XXIV; II, Chaps. XV, XXI (1961).

BLOCH, M. 1941
'The Rise of Dependent Cultivation and Seignorial Institutions',
Camb. Econ. Hist. I (1941), Chap. VI.

BOARDMAN, J. 1964
The Greeks Overseas (1964).

BODMER-GESSNER, V. 1950
'Provisorische Mitteilungen über die Ausgrabung einer mesolithischen Siedlung in Schotz ("Fischerhäusern") . . .',
Jahrb. Schweiz. Gesellsch. Urgesch. XL (1950), 108–26.

BODYANSKIY, A. V. 1962
'Scythian Burials with a La Tène Sword on the Central Dneipr' (in Russian),
Sov. Arkh. (1962), I, 272–6.

BÖHM, J., & DE LAET, S. (ed). 1961
Europe à la Fin de l'Âge de la Pierre (1961).

BÖKÖNYI, S. 1952
'Les chevaux Scythiques du Cimitière de Szentes-Vekerzug',
Acta Arch. Hung. II (1952), 173–82.

1954
'Les chevaux Scythiques de Szentes-Vekerzug',
Acta Arch. Hung. IV (1954), 93–113.

BOLTON, J. D. P. 1962
Aristeas of Proconnesus (1962).

BONA, I. 1960
'Clay Models of Bronze Age Wagons and Wheels in the Middle Danube Basin',
Acta Arch. Hung. XII (1960), 83–111.

BOTUSHAROVA, L. 1950
'A Thracian Tumulus-burial with a Chariot' (in Bulgarian),
Ann. Nat. Mus. Arch. Plovdiv II (1950), 101–35.

BOWEN, H. C. 1962
Ancient Fields (1962).

BRADFORD, J. 1949
'"Buried Landscapes" in Southern Italy',
Antiq. XXIII (1949), 58–72.

1957
Ancient Landscapes: Studies in Field Archaeology (1957).

BRADFORD, J., & WILLIAMS-HUNT, P. R. 1946
'Siticulosa Apulia',
Antiq. XX (1946), 191–200.

BRADFORD, J. S. P., & GOODCHILD, R. G. 1939
'Excavations at Frilford, Berks., 1937–38',
Oxoniensia IV (1939), 1–70.

BRAIDWOOD, R. J. 1960
'Seeking the World's First Farmers in Persian Kurdistan . . .',
Illus. London News (22 October 1960), 695–7.

BRAIDWOOD, R. J., HOWE, B., *et al.* 1960
Prehistoric Investigations in Iraqi Kurdistan (1960).

BRAIDWOOD, R. J., & REED, C. A. 1957
'The Achievement and Early Consequences of Food-Production . . .',
Cold Spring Harbor Symposia on Quantitative Biology XXII (1957), 19–31.

BRAIDWOOD, R. J., & WILLEY, G. R. (ed.) 1962
Courses towards Urban Life (1962).

BRAIDWOOD, R. J. *et al.* 1953
'Did Man once live by Beer alone?', *Amer. Anthrop.* LV (1953), 515–26.

BRANDTNER, F. J. *et al.* 1961
'More on Upper Palaeolithic Archaeology', *Current Anthrop.* II (1961), 427–54.

BREA, L. B. 1950
'The Prehistoric Culture Sequence in Sicily', *Univ. Lond. Inst. Arch. Ann. Reports* VI (1950), 13–29.

1952
'Civiltá preistoriche delle Isole Eolie', *Arch. Prehist. Levantina* III (1952), 69–93.

1955
'A Bronze Age house at Poliokhni, (Lemnos)', *Proc. Prehist. Soc.* XXI (1955), 144–55.

1957a,b
Sicily Before the Greeks (1957).
'Recenti scavi a Poliochni nell'Isola di Lemnos', *Bolletino d'Arte* III/IV (1957), 193–217.

BREA, L. B., & CAVALIER, M. 1956
'Civiltá Preistoriche delle Isole Eolie e del Territorio di Milazzo', *Bull. Paletnol. Ital.* LXV (1956), 3–94.

1957
'Stazioni preistoriche delle Isole Eolie', *Bull. Paletnol. Ital.* LVI (1957), 5–59.

1958
Il Castello di Lipari e il Museo Archeologico Eoliano (1958).

1959
Mylai (1959).

1960
Meligunìs-Lipára, I (1960).

BREWSTER, T. C. M. 1963
The Excavation of Staple Howe (1963).

BRIUSSOV, A. 1962
Le problème Indoeuropéen et la civilisation des Haches de Combat, (Reports and Communications by Archaeologists of the U.S.S.R. to VI Internat. Cong. of Prehist. & Protohist. Sciences, 1962).

BROGAN, O. 1953
Roman Gaul (1953).

BROHOLM, H. C., & HALD, M. 1940
Costumes of the Bronze Age in Denmark (1940).

BROTHWELL, D., & HIGGS, E. 1963
Science in Archaeology (ed.) (1963).

BROWN, W. Ll. 1960
The Etruscan Lion (1960).

BRUNN, W. A. VON 1959
Bronzezeitliche Hortfunde (1959).

BULLEID, A., & GRAY, ST. G. 1911–17
The Glastonbury Lake Village (1911–17).

BURCHELL, J. P. T. 1949
'Romano-Belgic "Ritual Pit" ', *Arch. News Letter* No. 9 (January 1949), 13.

BURKART, W. 1946
Crestaulta, eine bronzezeitliche Hügelsiedlung . . . (1946).

BURSTOW, G. P., & HOLLEYMAN, G. A. 1957
'Late Bronze Age Settlement on Itford Hill, Sussex', *Proc. Prehist. Soc.* XXIII (1957), 167–212.

BUTTLER, W. 1938
Der Donauländische und der Westische Kulturkreis der jüngeren Steinzeit (1938).

C

CABRÉ AGUILÓ, J. *et al.* 1950
El Castro y la Necropolis del Hierro Celtico de Chamartin de la Sierra (Avila) (1950).

CAHN, H. A. 1958
'Le Vase de Bronze de Graechwil . .',
Actes du Coll. sur les Influences Hell. en Gaule (1958) 21–29.

CARPENTER, RHYS 1958
Folk Tale, Fiction and Saga in the Homeric Epics (1958).

CARR, E. H. 1961
What is History? (1961).

CARUS-WILSON, E. 1952
'The Woollen Industry',
Camb. Econ. Hist. II (1952), Chap. VI.

CASE, H. 1962
'Long Barrows, Chronology and Causewayed Camps',
Antiq. XXXVI (1962), 212–16.

CASKEY, J. L. 1955
'Excavations at Lerna, 1954',
Hesperia XXIV (1955), 25–49.

1956
'Excavations at Lerna, 1955',
Hesperia XXV (1956), 147–73.

1957
'Excavations at Lerna 1956',
Hesperia XXVI (1957), 142–62.

1960
'The Early Helladic Period in the Argolid',
Hesperia XXIX (1960), 285–303.

CASTILLO, A. DEL 1928
La Cultura del Vaso Campaniforme (1928).

CATLING, H. W. 1956
'Bronze Cut-and-Thrust Swords in the Eastern Mediterranean',
Proc. Prehist. Soc. XXII (1956), 102–25.

1961
'A New Bronze Sword from Cyprus',
Antiq. XXXV (1961), 115–22.

1964
Cypriot Bronzework in the Mycenaean World (1964).

CHADWICK, H. M. 1949
Early Scotland (1949).

CHADWICK, J. 1963
'The Prehistory of the Greek Language',
Camb. Anc. Hist. (rev. edn.), II, Chap. XXXIX (1963).

CHADWICK, S. 1961
'Early Iron Age Enclosures on Longbridge Deverill Cow Down, Wiltshire',
in Frere, S.S. (ed.), *Problems of the Iron Age in Southern Britain* 1961, 18–20.

CHAPOTAT, G. 1962
'Le Char Processionel de la Côte-Saint-André',
Gallia XX (1962), 33–78.

CHARD, T. 1937
'An Early Horse Skeleton',
Journ. Heredity XXVIII (1937), 317–19.

CHERNYCH, E. 1962
Territoire orientale des tribus de la céramique linéaire,
(Reports and Communications by Archaeologists of the U.S.S.R. to IV Internat. Cong. of Prehist. and Protohist. Sciences, 1962).

CHILDE, V. G. 1926
The Aryans: A Study of Indo-European Origins (1926).

1927
'The Minoan Influence on the Danubian Bronze Age',
Essays in Aegean Arch. pres. to Sir Arthur Evans (1927), 1–4.

1929
The Danube in Prehistory (1929).

1936
Man Makes Himself (1936).

1939
'The Orient and Europe',
Amer. Journ. Arch. XLIV (1939), 10–26.

1948a,b
'The Final Bronze Age in the Near East and in Temperate Europe',
Proc. Prehist. Soc. XIV (1948), 177–95.

CHILDE, V. G.
'Cross Dating in the European Bronze Age',
in *Festschrift für Otto Tschumi* (1948), 70–76.

1949a,b,c
'The Origin of Neolithic Culture in Northern Europe',
Antiq. XXIII (1949), 129–35.
'Neolithic House-Types in Temperate Europe',
Proc. Prehist. Soc. XV (1949), 77–86.
'The First Bronze Vases to be made in Central Europe',
Acta Arch. XX (1949), 257–64.

1950a,b
'Cave Men's Buildings',
Antiq. XXIV (1950), 4–11.
Prehistoric Migrations in Europe (1950).

1951a,b
'The First Waggons and Carts—from the Tigris to the Severn',
Proc. Prehist. Soc. XVII (1951), 177–94.
'A Bronze Dagger of Mycenaean Type from Pelynt, Cornwall',
Proc. Prehist. Soc. XVII (1951), 95.

1954
'The Diffusion of Wheeled Vehicles',
Ethnog.-Arch. Forschungen II (1954), 1–17.

1957
The Dawn of European Civilization (1957).

1958
The Prehistory of European Society (1958).

CHMIELEWSKI, W. 1952
Le problème des sépultures de Cuyavie dans la lumière de récentes études (1952).

CLARK, J. G. D. 1936
The Mesolithic Settlement of Northern Europe (1936).

1938
'The Reindeer Hunting Tribes of Northern Europe',
Antiq. XII (1938), 154–71.

1939
Archaeology and Society (1st edn. 1939).

1942
'Bees in Antiquity',
Antiq. XVI (1942), 208–15.

1943
'Education and the Study of Man',
Antiq. XVII (1943), 113–121.

1948
'Fishing in Prehistoric Europe',
Antiq. Journ. XXVIII (1948), 45–85.

1950
'The Earliest Settlement of the West Baltic Area . . .',
Proc. Prehist. Soc. XVI (1950), 87–100.

1952
Prehistoric Europe: The Economic Basis (1952).

1954
Star Carr (1954).

1958
'Blade and Trapeze Industries in the European Stone Age',
Proc. Prehist. Soc. XXIV (1958), 24–42.

1960
Archaeology and Society (Revised paperback edn. 1960).

1961
World Prehistory: An Outline (1961).

1962a,b
'Prehistoric Ancestors of the Weapons which brought England Victory at Crecy . . .',
Illus. Lond. News Arch. Section no. 2079 (10 February, 1962).
'A Survey of the Mesolithic Phase in the Prehistory of Europe and South-West Asia',
Atti VI Cong. Internat. Scienze Preist. e Protost. I (1962), 97–111.

CLARK, J. G. D. 1963
'Neolithic Bows from Somerset, England, and the Prehistory of Archery in North-West Europe', *Proc. Prehist. Soc.* XXIX (1963), 50–98.

CLARK, J. G. D., & FELL, C. I. 1953
'The Early Iron Age Site at Micklemoor Hill, West Harling, Norfolk . . .', *Proc. Prehist. Soc.* XIX (1953), 1–40.

CLARK, J. G. D., & GODWIN, H. 1962
'The Neolithic in the Cambridgeshire Fens', *Antiq.* XXXVI (1962), 10–23.

CLARK, J. G. D., & PIGGOTT, S. 1933
'The Age of the British Flint Mines', *Antiq.* VII (1933), 166–83.

CLARK, J. G. D., & RANKINE, W. F. 1939
'Excavations at Farnham, Surrey (1937–38): The Horsham Culture and the question of Mesolithic Dwellings', *Proc. Prehist. Soc.* V (1939), 61–118.

CLARK, J. G. D. *et al.* 1960
'Excavations at the Neolithic Site at Hurst Fen, Mildenhall, Suffolk . . .', *Proc. Prehist. Soc.* XXVI (1960), 202–45.

CLUTTON-BROCK, J. 1962
'Near Eastern Canids and the Affinities of the Natufian Dogs', *Zeitschr. für Tierzücht. u. Züchtungsbiol.* LXXVI (1962), 326–33.

1963
'The Origins of the Dog', in Brothwell & Higgs 1963, 269–74.

COGHLAN, H. H. 1951
Notes on the Prehistoric Metallurgy of Copper and Bronze in the Old World (1951).

1954
'Metal Implements and Weapons', in Singer *et al.* 1954, 600–22.

1956
Notes on Prehistoric and Early Iron in the Old World (1956).

COGHLAN, H. H., & CASE, H. 1957
'Early Metallurgy of Copper in Ireland and Britain', *Proc. Prehist. Soc.* XXIII (1957), 91–123.

COLE, S. 1959
The Neolithic Revolution (1959).

COLES, J. M. 1960
'Scottish Late Bronze Age Metalwork . . .', *Proc. Soc. Ant. Scot.* XCIII (1959–60), 16–134.

1962
'European Bronze Age Shields', *Proc. Prehist. Soc.* XXVIII (1962), 156–90.

COLLINGWOOD, R. G. 1936
'Roman Britain', in Collingwood, R. G. and Myres, J. N. L., *Roman Britain and the English Settlement* (1936).

1936
An Autobiography (1939).

1946
The Idea of History (1946).

CONDURACHI, E. 1963
'Influences grecques et romaines dans les Balkans, en Hongroie et en Pologne', *Rapp. et Comm. VIIIe. Cong. Internat. d'Arch. Class.* (1963), 111–36.

COOK, J. M. 1961
'Greek Settlement in the Eastern Aegean and Asia Minor', *Camb. Anc. Hist.* (rev. ed.), II, Chap. XXXVIII (1961).

CORCORAN, J. X. W. P. 1960
'The Carlingford Culture',
Proc. Prehist. Soc. XXVI (1960), 98–148.

1961
'The Caergwrle Bowl: a contribution to the study of the Bronze Age',
Ber. V Internat. Kong. Vor- und Frühegesch. 1958 (1961), 200–3.

COTTON, M. A. 1955
'British Camps with Timber-laced Ramparts',
Arch. Journ. CXI (1955), 26–105.

1957
'*Muri Gallici*',
in Wheeler and Richardson 1957, 159–225.

1961
'Robin Hood's Arbour: and rectilinear enclosures in Berkshire',
Berks. Arch. Journ. LIX (1961), 1–35.

COURBIN, P. 1957
'Une Tombe Géometrique d'Argos',
Bull. Corres Hell. LXXXI (1957), 322–86.

COURSAGET, J. *et al.* 1960
'C-14 Neolithic Dates from France',
Antiq. XXXIV (1960), 147–8.

1961
'New Radiocarbon Dates from France',
Antiq. XXXV (1961), 147–8.

COWEN, J. D. 1951
'The Earliest Bronze Swords in Britain and their Origins on the Continent of Europe',
Proc. Prehist. Soc. XVII (1951), 195–213.

1952
'Bronze Swords in Northern Europe: a reconsideration of Sprockhoff's *Griffzungenschwerter*',
Proc. Prehist. Soc. XVIII (1952), 129–47.

1955
'Eine Einführung in die Geschichte der bronzenen Griffzungenschwerter in Süddeutschland und den angrenzenden Gebieten',
Ber. Rom. Germ. Komm. XXXVI (1955), 52–155.

1966
'The Origins of the Flange-hilted Sword of Bronze in Continental Europe',
Proc. Prehist. Soc. XXXII (1966), 262–312.

CRAWFORD, O. G. S. 1957
The Eye Goddess (1957).

CRESTON, R. Y. 1961
'Les Navires des Vénètes',
Actes IIe. Cong. Internat. d'Arch. Sous-marine 1958 (1961), 369–80.

CROSS, T. P., & SLOVER, C. H. 1936
Ancient Irish Tales (n.d., but 1936).

CROSSLAND, R. A. 1957
'Indo-European Origins: the Linguistic Evidence',
Past & Present XII (1957), 16–46.

CSALOG, J., MOZSOLICS, A. *et al.* 1952
'Die Ausgrabung in Tószeg im Jahre 1948',
Acta Arch. Hung. II (1952), 19–142.

CURLE, J. 1911
A Roman Frontier Post and its People (1911).

D

DANIEL, G. E. 1943
The Three Ages; An Essay on Archaeological Method (1943).

1950a,b
A Hundred Years of Archaeology (1950).
The Prehistoric Chamber Tombs of England and Wales (1950).

1958
The Megalith Builders of Western Europe (1958).

DANIEL, G. E. 1960
The Prehistoric Chamber Tombs of France (1960).
1962
The Idea of Prehistory (1962).

DARBY, H. C. (ed). 1936
An Historical Geography of England before 1800 (1936).

DAWSON, C. 1955
The Mongol Mission (1955).

DÉCHELETTE, J. 1911
'Les Origines de la Drachme et de l'Obole',
Rév. Numis. XV (1911), 1–59.
1927
Manuel d'Archéologie . . . IV (1927).

DECKER, K. V., & SCOLLAR, I. 1962
'Iron Age Square Enclosures in the Rhineland',
Antiq. XXXVI (1962), 175–8.

DEEVY, E. S. *et al.* 1963
Radiocarbon 5 (1963).

DEGERBØL, M. 1961
'On a find of a Preboreal domestic dog . . .',
Proc. Prehist. Soc. XXVII (1961), 35–55.

DEHN, W. 1950
'Älter-laténezeitliche Marnekeramik im Rheingebiet',
Reinecke Festschrift (1950), 33–50.
1953
'A prehistoric wall of sun-dried brick',
Antiq. XXVII (1953), 164.
1958
'Die Heuneburg an der oberen Donau und ihre Wehranlagen',
Neue Ausgrab. in Deutschland (1958), 127–45.
1960
'Einige Bemerkungen zum "Murus Gallicus"',
Germania XXXVIII (1960), 43–55.
1961
'Zangentore an Spätkeltischen Oppida',
Památky Arch. LII (1961), 390–6.
1962
'Aperçu sur les Oppida d'Allemagne de la fin de l'époque celtique',
Celticum III (1962), 329–86.
1963
'Frühe Drehscheibenkeramik nördlich der Alpen',
Alt-Thüringen VI (1962–63), 372–82.

DEHN, W., & FREY, O. H. 1962
'Die absolute Chronologie der Hallstatt-und Frühlatènezeit Mitteleuropas auf Grund des Südimports',
Atti VI° Cong. Internat. Scienze Preist. e Protost. I (Relazioni generali) (1962), 197–208.

DEHN, W., & SANGMEISTER, E. 1954
'Die Heuneburg bei Tallhof',
Germania XXXII (1954), 22–59

DELAPORTE, L. 1948
Les Peuples de l'Orient Méditerranéen : Le Proche-Orient Asiatique (1948).

DESBOROUGH, V. R. d'A. 1964
The Last Mycenaeans and their Successors (1964).

DESBOROUGH, V. R. d'A., & HAMMOND, N. G. L. 1962
'The End of Mycenaean Civilization and the Dark Age',
Camb. Anc. Hist. (rev. ed.) II, Chap. XXXVI.

DESHAYES, J. 1960
Les Outils de Bronze, de l'Indus au Danube, IV-II Millénaire (1960).

DETEV, P. 1959
'Matériaux de la préhistoire de Plovdiv',
Ann. Mus. Nat. Arch. Plovdiv III (1959), 3–80 (Bulgarian; French résumé).

DIKAIOS, P. 1953
Khirokitia (1953).

DILLON, M. 1947
'The Archaism of Irish Tradition', *Proc. Brit. Acad.* XXXIII (1947), 245–64.
1948
Early Irish Literature (1948).
DILLON, M. *et al.* 1954
Early Irish Society (1954).
1959
Irish Sagas (1959).
DIRINGER, D. 1962
Writing (1962).
DOW, S. 1960
'The Greeks in the Bronze Age', *Rapports XIe Cong. Internat. Sciences Hist.* (*Stockholm*) (1960), 1–34.
DRACK, W. 1958
'Wagengräber und Wagenbestandteile aus Hallstattgrabhügeln der Schweiz', *Zeitschr. Schweiz. Arch. u. Kunstgesch.* XVIII (1958), 1–67.
1959
L'Âge du Bronze en Suisse (1959).
1960
L'Âge du Fer en Suisse (1960).
DRIEHAUS, J. 1955
'Zur Datierung und Herkunft donauländischer Axttypen der frühen Kupferzeit', *Arch. Geog.* II (1952–55), 1–8.
1960
Die Altheimer Gruppe und das Jungneolithikum in Mitteleuropa (1960).
DRIOTON, E., & VANDIER, J. 1952
Les Peuples de l'Orient Méditerranéen: II, L'Égypte (1952).
DRIVER, H. E., & MASSEY, W. C. 1957
'Comparative Studies of North American Indians', *Trans. Amer. Phil. Soc.* n.s. XLVII (1957), 167–456.
DROST, D. 1954
'Zur Gliederung und Herkunft der metallen FeuerböckeMitteleuropas', *Ethnog.-Arch. Forschungen* II (1954), 100–58.
DUMITRESCU, V. 1945
'La station préhistorique de Traian', *Dacia* IX–X (1941–44), 11–114.
1961
Necropolada de Incinerație din Epoca Bronzului de la Cîrna (1961).
DUMITRESCU, V., *et al.* 1954
Hăbășești, monografie arheologica (1954).
DUNBABIN, T. J. 1948
The Western Greeks (1948).
1957
The Greeks and their Eastern Neighbours (Soc. Prom. Hell. Studies Supp. Paper 8, ed. J. Boardman, 1957).
DUNN, J. 1914
The Ancient Irish Epic Tale Táin Bó Cúalnge . . . (1914).
DVOŘAK, F. 1938
Wagengräber der älteren Eisenzeit in Böhmen (Praehistorica I, 1938). (Czech and German text).

E

EBERT, M. (Ed.) 1924–29
Reallexikon der Vorgeschichte I–XIV (1924–29).
'Südrussland: D. Skytho-sarmatische Periode' In Ebert 1924–29 XIII, 53–114.
EMERY, W. B. 1959
'A Master-Work of Egyptian Military Architecture of 3,900 Years ago . . .', *Illus. London News* 12 Sept. 1959, 250.
ESCALON DE FONTON, M. 1956
'Préhistoire de la Basse-Provence', *Préhist.* XII (1956).
EVANS, A. 1929
The Shaft Graves and Bee Hive Tombs of Mycenae (1929 = *Palace of Minos* III, Supplementary Section).

EVANS, J. D. 1958
'Two Phases of Prehistoric Settlement in the Western Mediterranean',
Univ. Lond. Inst. Arch. Ann. Reports XIII (1958), 49–70.

1959
Malta (1959).

EVENS, E. D. *et al.* 1962
'Fourth Report of the Sub-Committee of the South-Western group of Museums . . . on the Petrological Identification of Stone Axes',
Proc. Prehist. Soc. XXVIII (1962), 209–66.

EYDOUX, H. P. 1958
Monuments et Trésors de la Gaule (1958).

1962
La France Antique (1962).

F

FEACHEM, R. 1963
A Guide to Prehistoric Scotland (1963).

FERRARA, G., *et al.* 1961
'Carbon-14 Dating in Pisa: II',
In Flint & Deevy (ed.), 1961.

FETT, E., & FETT, P. 1941
Sydvestnorske Helleristninger (1941).

FEUSTEL, R. 1958
Bronzezeitliche Hügelgräberkultur im Gebiet von Schwarza (Südthüringen), 1958.

FILIP, J. 1956
Keltové ve středni Evropě (1956).

1962
Celtic Civilization and its Heritage (1962).

FINLEY, M. I. 1956
The World of Odysseus (1956).

1957
'The Mycenaean Tablets and Economic History',
Econ. Hist. Rev. 2nd series, X (1957), 128–41.

FINLEY, M. I. *et al.* 1960
Slavery in Classical Antiquity (1960)

FISCHER, F. 1959
Der spätlatènezeitliche Depot-Fund von Kappel (Kreis Salgau) (1959).

FLINT, R. F., & DEEVY, E. S. 1960
American Journ. Science Radiocarbon Supplement 2 (1960).

1961
Radiocarbon 3 (1961).

FOLTINY, S. 1961
'Athens and the East Hallstatt Region: Cultural Interrelations at the Dawn of the Iron Age',
Amer. Journ. Arch. LXV (1961), 283–97.

FORBES, D. 1746
'Some Thoughts concerning the State of the Highlands of Scotland' (1746),
in *Culloden Papers* . . . (1815), 297–300.

FORBES, R. J. 1950
Metallurgy in Antiquity (1950).

1954a,b
'Chemical, Culinary and Cosmetic Arts',
in Singer *et al.* 1954, 238–98.
'Extracting, Smelting and Alloying',
in Singer *et al.* 1954, 572–99.

1956
'Food and Drink',
in Singer *et al.* 1956, 103–46.

FORRER, R. 1932
'Les Chars Cultuels préhistoriques . . .',
Préhistoire I 1932, 19–123.

FORSSANDER, J. E. 1936
Der Ostskandinavische Norden während der ältesten Metallzeit Europas (1936).
(Skrift. Kungl. Humanist. Vetenskaps. Lund XXII).

FOSTER, I. Ll., & ALCOCK, L. (ed.) 1963
Culture and Environment: Essays in Honour of Sir Cyril Fox (1963).

FOX, C. 1946
A Find of the Early Iron Age from Llyn Cerrig Bach, Anglesey (1946).

1958
Pattern and Purpose: A Survey of Early Celtic Art in Britain (1958).

FOX, C. F. 1930
'The Bronze Age Pit at Swanwick, Hants . . .',
Antiq. Journ. X (1930), 30–33.

FRANKFORT, H. 1951
The Birth of Civilization in the Near East (1951).

1954
The Art and Architecture of the Ancient Orient (1954).

FRANKFORT, H. *et al.* 1949
Before Philosophy (1949).

FREI, B. 1955
[Die Grabung auf dem Montlingerberg]
Jahrb. Schweiz. Gesell. Urgesch. XLIV (1954–55), 146–51.

FRENCH, D. H. 1962
'Excavations at Can Hasan: First Preliminary Report, 1961',
Anat. Stud. XII (1962), 27–40.

FRERE, S. S. 1961
Problems of the Iron Age in Southern Britain (n.d. but 1961).

FREY, O. H. 1955
'Eine Etruskische Bronzeschnabelkanne', *Ann. Litt. Univ. Dijon* 2e Série, II, fasc. i. (1955).

1957
'Die Zeitstellung des Fürstengrabes von Hatten im Elsass',
Germania XXXV (1957), 229–249.

1962
'Der Beginn der Situlakunst im Ostalpenraum',
Germania XL (1962), 56–72.

1963
'Zu den 'Rhodischen' Bronzekannen aus Hallstattgräbern',
Marburger Winckelmann-Programm 1963, 18–26.

G

GABEL, W. C. 1957
'The Campignian Tradition and European Flint Mining',
Antiq. XXXI (1957), 90–92.

1958
'European Secondary Neolithic Cultures',
Journ. Roy. Anthrop. Inst. LXVIII (1958), 90–107

GADD, C. J. 1963
'The Dynasty of Agade and the Gutian Invasion',
Camb. Anc. Hist. (rev. ed.), I, Chap. XIX (1963).

GALLUS, S. 1934
Die figuralverzierten Urnen vom Soproner Burgstall (Arch. Hung. XIII, 1934).

GALLUS, S., & HORVATH, T. 1939
Un Peuple cavalier préscythique en Hongrie (Diss. Pann. 2, I, 1939)

GARAŠANIN, M. V. 1958
'Neolithikum und Bronzezeit in Serbien und Makedonien',
Bericht R. G. Komm. XXXIX (1958), 1–130.

1961
'The Neolithic in Anatolia and the Balkans',
Antiq. XXXV (1961), 276–80.

1962
'Chronologische und Ethnische Probleme der Eisenzeit auf dem Balkan',
Atti VI° Cong. Internat. Scienze Preist. e Protost. I (Relazioni generali) (1962), 179–95.

GARDNER, W. 1926
'The Native Hill-Forts in North Wales and their Defences', *Arch. Camb.* (1926), 221–82.

GARROD, D. A. E. 1957
'The Natufian Culture: The Life and Economy of a Mesolithic People in the Near East', *Proc. Brit. Acad.* XLIII (1957), 211–27.

GARSTANG, J. 1953
Prehistoric Mersin (1953).

GAUDRON, G. 1955a,b
'Landiers gaulois en fer forgé . . .', *Bull. Soc. Préhist. Français* LII (1955), 275–7.
'Landiers gaulois . . .', *Bull. Soc. Préhist. Français* LII (1955), 542–3.

1956
'Chenets gaulois en fer . . .', *Bull. Soc. Préhist. Français* LIII (1956), 119.

GEORGIEV, G. I. 1961
'Kulturgruppen der Jungstein- und der Kupferzeit in der Ebene von Thrazien (Südbulgarien)', In Böhm & De Laet 1961, 45–100.

GFELLER, C. *et al.* 1961
'Bern Radiocarbon Dates ii', in Flint & Deevy 1961, 15–25.

GHIRSHMAN, R. 1939
Fouilles de Sialk (two vols. 1939).

1954
Iran: from the earliest times to the Islamic Conquest (1954).

1961
Sept Mille Ans d'Art en Iran (Catalogue of Exhibition, 1961).

VAN GIFFEN, A. E. 1950
'De nederzettingsoverblijfselen in het Bolleveen en de versterking . . .', *Nieuwe Drentsche Volksalmanak* (1950), 89–123.

1962
'Grafheuvels uit de Midden-Bronstijd . . . bei Oostwoud', *West-Frieslands Oud & Nieuw* XXIX (1962), 197–209.

GIMBUTAS, M. 1956a,b
The Prehistory of Eastern Europe: Part I (1956).
'Borodino, Seima and their Contemporaries', *Proc. Prehist. Soc.* XXII (1956), 143–72.

1960
'Culture Change in Europe at the start of the Second Millennium B.C.: a contribution to the Indo-European Problem', *Papers V Internat. Cong. Anthrop. & Ethnog. Sciences, Philadelphia 1956* (1960), 540–51.

1961a,b
'Notes on the Chronology and Expansion of the Pit-Grave Kurgan Culture', In Böhm & de Laet 1961, 193–200.
' "Timber-Graves" in Southern Russia', *Expedition* (Bull. Univ. Mus. Pennsylvania) III (1961), 14–20.

1963
'The Indo-Europeans: Archeological Problems', *Amer. Anthrop.* LXV (1963), 815–36

GIOT, P. R. 1960
Brittany (1960).

1962
'Chronique des Datations Radiocarbone Armoricaines', *Ann. de Bretagne* LXIX (1962), 29–35.

GIOT, P. R., & MAZÉAS, G. 1962
'Observations sur les lingots de fer de Belle-Etoile . . .', *Mém. Soc. d'Émulation des Cotes-du-Nord* (1962), 1–7.

GIOT, P. R. *et al.* 1960
'Une station du néolithique primaire Armoricain: Le Curnic . . .', *Bull. Soc. Préhist. Franc.* LVII (1960), 38–50.

GJESSING, G. 1944
'Circumpolar Stone Age',
Acta Arctica Fasc. II (1944), 1–70.
'The Circumpolar Stone Age', 1953
Antiq. XXVII (1953), 131–6.

GLOB, P. V. 1949
'Barkaer: Danmarks Aeldeste Landsby',
Fra Nationalmus. Arbejdsmark (1949), 5–16.

1957
Ard og Plov (1951).

1952
Danske Oldsager: II, Yngre Stenalder (1952).

GLORY, A. 1948
'Les Peintures de l'Âge du Métal en France Méridionale',
Préhistoire X (1948), 7–135.

GODARD, A. 1931
Les bronzes du Luristan (1931).

GODWIN, H. 1960
'Prehistoric wooden trackways of the Somerset Levels . . .',
Proc. Prehist. Soc. XXVI (1960), 1–36.

GONZENBACH, V. VON 1949
Die Cortaillodkultur in der Schweiz (1949).

GRAZIOSI, P. 1960
Palaeolithic Art (1960).

GRIAZNOV, M. 1958
L'Art ancient de l'Altai (1958), (Russian and French text).

GRIMES, W. F. 1961
'Settlements at Draughton . . . and Heathrow, Middlesex',
in Frere 1961, 21–28.

GRINSELL, L. V. 1942
'The Kivik Cairn, Scania',
Antiq. XVI (1942), 160–74.

1958
The Archaeology of Wessex (1958).

GROSJEAN, R. 1955
'Les Statues-Menhirs de la Corse',
Études Corses (1955), 1–36 of reprint.

1956
'Les Statues-Menhirs de la Corse',
Études Corses 1956, 1–19 of reprint.

1958
'Balestra et Foce: Monuments circulaires megalithiques de la moyenne vallée du Taravo',
Études Corses, n.s. XVIII (1958), 30–73.

1961
Filitosa et son contexte archéologique (Monuments Piot, LII, Fasc. 1, 1961).

GROUSSET, R. 1960
L'Empire des Steppes (1960).

GUIDO, M. 1963
Sardinia (1963).

GURNEY, O. 1952
The Hittites (1952).

GUYAN, W. U. 1950
'Beitrag zur Datierung einer jungsteinzeitliche Gräbergruppe im Kanton Schaffhausen',
Jahrb. Schweiz. Gesellsch. Urgesch. XL (1950), 1963–92.

GUYAN, W. U. *et al.* 1955
Das Pfahlbauproblem (1955).

H

HACHMANN, R. 1957a,b
Die frühe Bronzezeit im westlichen Ostseegebiet und ihre mittel- und südosteuropäischen Bezeihungen (1957).
'Bronzezeitliche Bernsteinschieber',
Bayer. Vorgeschichtsbl. XXII (1957), 1–36.

HÁJEK, L. 1957
'Die Knöpfe der Mitteleuropäischen Glockenbecherkultur',
Památky Arch. XLVIII (1957), 389–424.

1961
'Zur relativen Chronologie des Äneolithikums und der Bronzezeit in der Ostslowakei',
Komm. Äneo. und ält. Bronzezeit, Nitra 1958 (1961), 59–76.

HÁJEK, L. 1962
Die Glockenbecherkultur in Böhmen und Mähren
(Invent. Arch. Československo 2, 1962).

HALD, M. 1950
Olddanske Tekstiler (1950).

1961
'Dragtstudier',
Aarbøger (1961), 37–88.

HANČAR, F. 1932
'Die Nadelformen des prähistorisches Kaukasusgebietes',
Eur. Sept. Antiq. VII (1932), 113–82.

1934
'Kaukasus-Luristan',
Eur. Sept. Antiq. IX (1934), 47–112.

1956
Das Pferd in prähistorischer und früher historischer Zeit (1956).

HARDEN, D. 1962
The Phoenicians (1962).

HARTNETT, P. J. 1957
'Excavation of a Passage Grave at Fourknocks, Co. Meath',
Proc. Roy. Irish Acad. LVIII (C), no. 5 (1957), 197–277.

HATT, G. 1949
Oldtidsagre (1949).

1957
Nørre Fjand: An Early Iron-Age Village Site in West Jutland (1957).

HÄUSLER, A. 1960
'Neue Funde steinzeitlicher Musikinstrumente in Osteuropa',
Wiss. Zeitschr. Martin Luther Univ. Halle-Wittenberg IX (1960), 321–32.

1962
'Die Grabsitten des mesolithischen und neolithischen Jäger- und Fischergruppen auf dem Gebiet der UdSSR',
Wiss. Zeitschr. Martin Luther Univ. Halle-Wittenberg XI/10 (1962), 1141–83.

1963a,b
'Ockergrabkultur und Schnurkeramik',
Jahreschr. Mitteldeutsch. Vorgesch. XLVII (1963), 157–79.

'Ist eine Ableitung des Schnurkeramik von der Ockergrabkultur möglich?',
Forschungen und Forschritte XXXVII, 12 (1963), 363–8.

HAWKES, C. F. C. 1931
'Hill-Forts',
Antiq., V. (1931), 60–97.

1940
The Prehistoric Foundations of Europe (1940).

1945
'The Early Iron Age Settlement at Fengate, Peterborough',
Arch. Journ. C. (1945), 188–223.

1948
'From Bronze Age to Iron Age: Middle Europe, Italy and the North and West',
Proc. Prehist. Soc. XIV (1948), 196–218.

1951
'British Prehistory half-way through the Century',
Proc. Prehist. Soc. XVII (1951), 1–15.

1952
'Las relaciones en el bronce final, entre la Península Ibérica y las Islas Británicas . . .',
Ampurias XIV (1952), 81–116.

1954
'Archaeological Theory and Method: Some Suggestions from the Old World',
Amer. Anthrop. LVI (1954), 155–68.

1957a,b
'Prehistory and the Gaulish Peoples',
in J. M. Wallace-Hadrill & J. McManners,
France: Government and Society (1957), 1–18.

HAWKES, C. F. C.
'Archaeology as Science: Purposes and Pitfalls',
Advancement of Science LIV (1957), 1–11.

1959
'The ABC of the British Iron Age',
Antiq. XXXIII (1959), 170–82.

1961
'Gold Ear-rings of the Bronze Age, East and West',
Folklore LXXII (1961), 438–74.

1963
'The Celts: Report on the study of their culture and their Mediterranean relations, 1942–1962',
Rapp. et Comm. VIIIe. Cong. Internat. d'Arch. Class. (1963), 3–23.

HAWKES, C. F. C., & HULL, M. R. 1947
Camulodunum (1947).

HAWKES, C. F. C., & SMITH, M. A. 1957
'On some Buckets and Cauldrons of the Bronze and Early Iron Ages ...',
Antiq. Journ. XXXVII (1957), 131–98.

HAYES, W. C. 1962a,b
'Egypt from the Death of Ammenemes III to Seqenenre II',
Camb. Anc. Hist. (rev. ed.), II, Chap. II (1962).

'Egypt: Internal affairs from Tuthmosis I to the death of Amenhophis III',
Camb. Anc. Hist. (rev. ed.), II, Chap. IX. (1962).

HAYES, W. C. *et al.* 1962
'Chronology: Egypt, Western Asia, Aegean Bronze Age',
Camb. Anc. Hist. (rev. ed.), I, chap. VI (1962).

HEICHELHEIM, F. M. 1956
'Man's Rôle in changing the face of the Earth in Classical Antiquity',
Kyklos IX (1956), 318–59.

1958
An Ancient Economic History I (1958).

HELBAEK, H. 1952a,b
'Early Crops in Southern Britain',
Proc. Prehist. Soc. XVIII (1952), 194–233.

'Preserved Apples and Panicum in the Prehistoric site at Nørre Sandegaard in Bornholm',
Acta Arch. XXIII (1952), 107–15.

1956
'Vegetables in the Funeral Meals of Pre-Urban Rome',
in Gjerstad, E., *Early Rome* II (1956), 287–94.

1959
'Notes on the evolution and history of *Linum*,'
Kuml (1959), 103–29.

1960
'The Palaeoethnobotany of the Near East and Europe', in Braidwood, Howe *et al.*, (1960).

1963a,b,c
'Textiles from Çatal Hüyük',
Archaeology XVI (1963), 39–46.

'Late Cypriote Vegetable Diet at Apliki',
Opuscula Atheniensia IV (1963), 171–86.

'Palaeo-Ethnobotany',
in Brothwell & Higgs 1963, 177–85.

HELL, M. 1963
'Weitere Funde zum Problem der keltischen Hufeisen aus Salzburg',
Arch. Austriaca XXXIV (1963), 22–31.

HENCKEN, H. 1950
'Herzsprung Shields and Greek Trade',
Amer. Journ. Arch. LIV (1950), 295–309.

1952
'Beitzsch and Knossos',
Proc. Prehist. Soc. XVIII (1952), 36–46.

HENCKEN, H. 1955
Indo-European Languages and Archaeology, (Amer. Anthrop. Ass. Memoir 84, 1955).

1956
'Carp's Tongue Swords in Spain, France and Italy', *Zephyrus* VII (1956), 125–78.

1958a,b
'Archaeological Evidence for the origin of the Etruscans', in *CIBA Sympos. Medical Biology & Etruscan Origins* (1958), 29–47.

'Syracuse, Etruria and the North: Some Comparisons', *Amer. Journ. Arch.* LXII (1958), 259–72.

HENCKEN, T. C. 1938
'The Excavation of the Iron Age Camp on Bredon Hill . . .', *Arch. Journ.* XCV (1938), 1–111.

HENDERSON, G. 1899
Fled Bricrend, (Irish Text Soc. II, 1899).

HENRY, F. 1933
'Émailleurs d'Occident', *Préhist.* II (1933), 65–146.

HENSEL, W., & GIEYSZTOR, A. 1958
Archaeological Research in Poland (1958).

HENSHALL, A. S. 1963
The Chambered Tombs of Scotland, vol. I (1963).

HERRE, W. 1963
'The Science and History of Domestic Animals', in Brothwell & Higgs (1963), 235–49.

HERRMAN, J. 1960
'Die vor- und frühgeschichte Burgwälle Gross-Berlins und des Bezirkes Potsdam', *Deutsch. Akad. Wiss. Berlin, Schrifter Sektion Vor- und Frühgeschichte* IX (1960), 41.

HEYBROEK, H. M. 1963
'Diseases and Lopping for Fodder as possible causes of a prehistoric decline of Ulmus', *Acta Botanica Neerlandica* XII (1963), 1–11.

HIGGS, E. 1959
'Excavations at a Mesolithic Site at Downton, near Salisbury, Wiltshire', *Proc. Prehist. Soc.* XXV (1959), 209–32.

HILL, W. C. O. 1957
Man as an Animal (1957).

HINSCH, E. 1953
'Tragtbegerkultur-Megalithkultur', *Univ. Oslo Oldsaksamling Arbok* (1951–53), 10–177

HOLSTE, F. 1953a
Die Bronzezeit in Süd- und Westdeutschland (1953).

Die bronzezeitlichen Vollgriffschwerter Bayerns (1953).

HOOD, M. S. F. 1960
'*Tholos* Tombs of the Aegean', *Antiq.* XXXIV (1960), 166–76.

1961
'Archaeology in Greece', *Arch. Reports 1960–61* (Brit. School Athens, 1961), 9–10.

HOOD, M. S. F., & WALTON, H. 1948
'A Romano-British Cremating Place on Roden Down, Berkshire', *Trans. Newbury Dist. Field Club* IX (1948), 10–62.

HORNELL, J. 1938
British Coracles and Irish Curraghs (1938).

HUMMEL, J. 1933
'Zur Archäologie Azerbeidžans', *Eur. Sept. Antiq.* VIII (1933), 211–34.

HUNDT, H. J. 1958
Katalog Straubing: I, Die Funde der Glockenbecherkultur und der Straubinger Kultur (1958).

HUNDT, H. J. 1961a,b
'Beziehungen der "Straubinger" Kultur zu den Frühbronzezeitkulturen der östlich benachbarten Räume',
Komm. Äneo. und. ält. Bronzezeit, Nitra 1958 (1961), 145–76.
'Neunzehn Textilreste aus den Durrnberg in Hallein',
Jahrb. R. G. Zentralmus. Mainz VIII (1961), 7–25.

HUTCHINSON, R. W. 1962
Prehistoric Crete (1962).

HUXLEY, G. L. 1960
Achaeans and Hittites (1960).

HUZAYYIN, S. A. 1942
Arabia and the Far East: Their Commercial and Cultural Relations in Graeco-Roman and Indo-Arabian Times (1942).

I

IVERSEN, J. 1941
Land Occupation in Denmark's Stone Age,
(Danmarks Geol. Undersøgelse II Series no. 66, 1941).

1949
The Influence of Prehistoric Man on Vegetation,
(Danmarks Geol. Undersøgelse IV Series, vol. 3, no. 6, 1949).

1960
Problems of the Early Post-Glacial Forest Development in Denmark,
(Danmarks Geol. Undersøgelse IV Series vol. 4, no. 3, 1960)

J

JACKSON, K. H. 1948
'On some Romano-British Place-Names',
Journ. Rom. Stud. XXXVIII (1948), 54–58.

1953
Language and History in Early Britain (1953).

1955
'The Pictish Language',
in *The Problem of the Picts*, ed. F. T. Wainwright (1955), Chap. VI.

JACOBSEN, T. 1943
'Primitive Democracy in Ancient Mesopotamia',
Journ. Near Eastern Stud. II (1943), 159–172

JACOBSTHAL, P. 1929
'Rhodische Bronzekannen aus Hallstattgräben',
Jahrb. Deutsch. Arch. Inst. XLIV (1929), 198–223.

1941
'Imagery in Early Celtic Art',
Proc. Brit. Acad. XXVII (1941).

1944
Early Celtic Art (1944).

1956
Greek Pins and their Connexions with Europe and Asia (1956).

JACOBSTHAL, P., & NEUFFER, E. 1933
'Gallia Graeca—Récherches sur l'Hellénisation de la Provence',
Préhistoire II (1933), 1–64.

JANNORAY, J. 1955
Ensérune: Contribution a l'étude des civilisations préromaines de la Gaule méridionale (1955).

JANTZEN, U. 1955
Griechische Greifenkessel (1955).

JAŻDŻWESKI, K. 1961
'The Funnel Beaker Culture . . .',
Prace i Materiały Mus. Arch. i Ethnog. w Łódżi Ser. Arch. no. 6 (1961), 91–100.

JENKINS, J. G. 1961
The English Farm Wagon: Origins and Structure (1961).

JESSEN, K., & HELBAEK, H. 1944
Cereals in Great Britain and Ireland in Prehistoric and Early Historic Times (1944).

JOFFROY, R. 1954
Le Trésor de Vix (1954).
(Mon. et Mém. Piot XLVIII–1).
1958
Les Sépultures à Char du Premier Age du Fer en France (1958).
1960a,b
L'Oppidum de Vix et la Civilisation Hallstattienne finale dans l'est de la France (1960).
'Le Bassin et le Trépied de Sainte-Colombe',
Monuments Piot LI (1960), 1–23.

JOFFROY, R., & BRETZ-MAHLER, D. 1959
'Les Tombes à Char de la Tène dans l'Est de la France',
Gallia XVII (1959), 5–35.

JOPE, E. M. 1956a,b
'Vehicles and Harness',
in Singer *et al.* 1956, 537–62.
'Agricultural Implements',
in Singer *et al.* 1956, 81–102.
1961a,b
'The Beginnings of La Tène Ornamental Style in the British Isles',
in Frere 1961, 69–83.
'Daggers of the Early Iron Age in Britain',
Proc. Prehist. Soc. XXVII (1961), 307–43.
1962
'Iron Age Brooches in Ireland: a Summary',
Ulster Journ. Arch. XXIV/XXV (1961–62), 25–38.

JUNGHANS, S. *et al.* 1954
'Untersuchungen zur Kupfer- und Frühbronzezeit Süddeutschlands',
Bericht R. G. Komm. XXXIV (1954), 77–114.
1960
Metallanalysen kupferzeitliche und frühbronzezeitliche Bodenfunde aus Europa
(Studien zu den Anfängen der Metallurgie I, 1960).

K

KAELAS, L. 1955
'Wann sind die ersten Megalithgräber in Holland enstanden?',
Palaeohist. IV (1955), 47–79.
1962
'Stenkammargravar i Sverige och deras Europeiska bakgrund',
Proxima Thule (1962), 26–36.

KAHLKE, D. 1954
Die Bestattungssitten des Donauländischen Kulturkreises der jüngeren Steinzeit: I, Linienbandkeramik (1954).

KAMMENHÜBER, A. 1961
Hippologia Hethitica (1961).

KARAGEORGHIS, V. 1962
'A "Homeric" Burial discovered in a Royal Tomb of the 7th Century B.C. . . .',
Illus. London News (2 June 1962) 894.
1963a,b
'Une Tombe de Guerrier à Palaepaphos',
Bull. Corr. Hell. LXXXVII (1963), 265–300.
'Une rombe "Royale" à Salamine',
Bull. Corr. Hell. LXXXVII (1963), 373–80.

KASTELIC, J. 1956
The Situla of Vače (1956).

KEHOE, T. F. 1961
'Stone Tipi Rings',
Antiq. XXXV (1961), 145–7.

KENDRICK, T. D. 1928
The Druids (1928).

KENDRICK, T. D., & HAWKES, C. F. C. 1932
Archaeology in England and Wales 1914–1931 (1932).

KENYON, K. M. 1956
'Jericho and its Setting in Near Eastern History',
Antiq. XXX (1956), 184–97.

KENYON, K. M. 1960
Archaeology in the Holy Land (1960).

KERND'L, A. 1963
'Gebaute dauerhafte Behausungen bereits im Mousterien zu sowjetischen Grabungsergebnissen', *Berliner Blätt. Vor- und Frühgesch.* x (1963), 41–45.

KERSTEN, K. 1938
Zur älteren nordischen Bronzezeit (1938).

KIMMIG, W. 1940
'Ein Keltenschild aus Ägypten', *Germania* XXIV (1940), 106–11.

1954
'Zur Urnenfelderkultur in Südwesteuropa', *Festschrift für Peter Goessler* (1954), 41–98.

1958
'Kulturbeziehungen zwischen der nordwestalpinen Hallstattkultur und der Mediterranen Welt', *Actes du Coll. sur les Influences Hell. en Gaule* (1958), 75–87

1964a,b
'Bronzesitulen aus dem Rheinischen Gebirge, Hunsrück-Eifel-Westerwald', *Ber. Röm. Germ. Komm.* XLIII-XLIV (1964), 31–106.

'Seevölkerbewegung und Urnenfelderkultur', *Studien aus Alteuropa* I (ed. von Uslar and Narr) (1964), 220–83.

KIMMIG, W., & HELL, H. 1958
Vorzeit an Rhein und Donau (1958).

KIMMIG, W., & REST, W. 1954
'Ein Fürstengrab der späten Hallsttzeit von Kappel am Rhein', *Jahrb. Röm. Germ. Komm. Zentralmus. Mainz* I (1954), 179–216.

KJAERUM, P. 1955
'Templelhus fra Stenalder', *Kuml* (1955), 7–35.

KLEEMAN, O. 1954
'Die dreiflügeligen Pfeilspitzen in Frankreich', *Abhandl. Geist. u. Sozialwiss. Klasse Akad. Wiss. u. Lit. Mainz* (1954), no. 4, 89–142.

1961
'Stand der archäologischen Forschung über die eisernen Doppelpyramiden-(Spitz)-Barren', *Archiv f.d. Eisenhüttenwesen* XXXII (1961), 581–5.

KLIMA, B. 1954
'Palaeolithic Huts at Dolní Věstonice', *Ant.* XXVIII (1954), 4–14.

1962
'The First Ground-Plan of an Upper Palaeolithic Loess Settlement in Middle Europe . . .', in Braidwood, R. J. and Willey, G. R. 1962, 193–210.

KLINDT-JENSEN, O. 1950
Foreign Influences in Denmark's Early Iron Age (1950)

1952
'Keltisk Tradition i Romersk Jernalder', *Aarbøger* (1952), 195–228.

1953a,b
Bronzekedelen fra Brå (1953).
'Byggeskik i Danmark i Forhistorisk Tid', *Nordisk Kultur* XVII (1953), 71–107.

1959
'The Gundestrup Bowl: a Reassessment', *Antiq.* XXXIII (1959), 161–9.

1960
'Le Chaudron de Gundestrup', *Analect. Rom. Inst. Danici* I (1960), 45–66.

1961
Gundestrup Kedelen (1961).

KOHLER, E., & RALPH, E. K. 1961
'C-14 Dates for Sites in the Mediterranean Area', *Amer. Journ. Arch.* LXV (1961), 357–67.

KOSSACK, G. 1954
'Pferdegeschirr aus Gräbern der älteren Hallstattzeit Bayerns', *Jahrb. Röm. Germ. Zentralmus. Mainz.* I (1954), 111–78.

1959
Südbayern während der Hallstattzeit (1959).

KOSTREWSKI, J. 1938
'Biskupin: an Early Iron Age village in Western Poland', *Antiq.* XII (1938), 33–17.

1950
Compte-rendu des fouilles de Biskupin en 1938–39 et 1946–48 (1950) (Polish with French resumé).

KRAHE, H. 1954
Sprache und Vorzeit: Europäische Vorgeschichte nach dem Zeugnis der Sprache (1954).

KRAIKER, W., & KÜBLER, K. 1939
Kerameikos I: Die Nekropolen des 12 bis 10 Jahrhunderts (1939).

KRÄMER, W. 1960
'The *Oppidum* of Manching', *Antiq.* XXXIV (1960), 191–200.

1961
'Keltische Hohlbuckelringe von Isthmus von Korinth', *Germania* XXXIX (1961), 32–42.

1962
'Manching II: Zu den Ausgrabungen in den Jahren 1957 bis 1961', *Germania* XL (1962), 293–317.

KRÄMER, W. *et al.* 1961
'Neue Funde aus dem Oppidum von Manching', *Germania* XXXIX (1961), 299–383.

KROMER, K. 1960, 1963
Das Gräberfeld von Hallstatt (1960).

1963
Hallstatt: Die Salzhandelsmetropole des ersten Jährtausends vor Christus in den Alpen (1963).

KUCHARENKO, YU. V. 1959
The Distribution of La Tène Material in Eastern Europe' (in Russian), *Sov. Arkh.* (1959), 1, 31–51.

KUFTIN, B. A. 1941
Archaeological Excavations in Trialeti (1941: Georgian with English summary).

KÜHN, H. 1952
Die Felsbilder Europas (1952).

KUPPER, J. R. 1963
'Northern Mesopotamia and Syria', *Camb. Anc. Hist.* (rev. ed.) II, Chap. I (1963).

KUTZIAN, I. B. 1958, 1963
'Über südliche Bezeihungen der Ungarischen Hochkupferzeit', *Acta Arch. Hung.* IX (1958), 155–90

1963
The Copper Age Cemetery of Tiszapolgár Basatanya (1963).

L

DE LAET, S. 1958
The Low Countries (1958).

DE LAET, S. J., & GLASBERGEN, W. 1959
De Voorgeschiedenis der Lage Landen (1959).

LAMB, W. 1936
Excavations at Thermi in Lesbos (1936).

LAMBRECHTS, P. 1942
Contributions à l'étude des Divinités Celtiques (1942).

1954
L'Exaltation de la Tête dans la pensée et dans l'art des Celtes (1954).

LAMING, A. 1959
Lascaux: Paintings and Engravings (1959).

LARSEN, H. 1960
'The Circumpolar Conference in Copenhagen 1958',
Acta Arctica Fasc. XII (1960), 1–92.

LATTIMORE, O. 1962
Inner Asian Frontiers of China (1962).

LAUR-BELART, R. 1950
'Ein Helm der Urnenfelderzeit aus Basels Umgebung',
Jahrb. Schweiz. Gesellsch. Urgesch. XL (1950), 202–8.

LEGLAY, M. 1962
Les Gaulois en Afrique (1962).

LEISNER, G., & LEISNER, V. 1943
Die Megalithgräber der Ibersichen Halbinsel: I. Der Suden. (1943).

1951
Antas do Concelho de Reguengos de Monsaraz (1951).

1956
Die Megalithgräber der Iberischen Halbinsel: II. Der Westen, Bd. I. (1956).

1959
Die Megalithgräber der Iberischen Halbinsel: II Der Westen, Bd.II. (1959).

LEISNER, V. *et al.* 1961
Les Grottes artificielles de Casal do Pardo (Palmela) . . . (1961).

LERAT, L. 1958
'L'Amphore de bronze de Conliège (Jura)',
Actes du Coll. sur les influences Hell. en Gaule (1958), 91–98

LEROI-GOURHAN, A. 1960
'Flores et Climats du Paléolithique Récent',
Compte Rendu du Congrès préhistorique de France, Monaco 1959 (1960).

1961
'Les Fouilles d'Arcy-sur-Cure (Yonne)',
Gallia-Préhist. IV (1961), 3–16.

LILLIU, G. 1955
Il Nuraghe di Barumini e la Stratigrafia Nuragica (1955).

1959
'The Nuraghi of Sardinia',
Antiq. XXXIII (1959), 32–38.

LLOYD, S. 1956
Early Anatolia (1956).

1961
'Melting Pot of Peoples: the early settlement of Anatolia',
In Piggott 1961 c, 161–94.

LOMBORG, E. 1960
'Donauländische Kulturbezeihungen und die relative Chronologie der frühen nordischen Bronzezeit',
Acta Arch. XXX (1960), 51–146.

LORIMER, H. L. 1950
Homer and the Monuments (1950).

LOUIS, M., & TAFFANEL, O. & J. 1955–60
Le Premier Âge du Fer Languedocien I (1955); II (1958); III (1960).

LUCKE, W., & FREY, O. H. 1962
Die Situla in Providence (Rhode Island) (1962).

LUNDHOLM, B. 1949
'Abstammung und Domestikation des Hauspferdes',
Zoolog. Bidrag fran Uppsala XXVII (1949), 1–293.

M

MCBURNEY, C. B. M. 1960
The Stone Age of Northern Africa (1960).

1961
'Aspects of Palaeolithic Art',
Antiq. XXXV (1961), 107–14.

MACGREGOR, M. 1962
'The Early Iron Age Metalwork Hoard from Stanwick, N.R. Yorks',
Proc. Prehist. Soc. XXVIII (1962), 17–57.

MACK, R. P. 1953
The Coinage of Ancient Britain (1953).

MACWHITE, E. 1951
Estudios sobre las Relaciones Atlanticas de la Peninsula Hispanica en la Edad del Bronce (1951).

MAHR, A. *et al.* 1934
The Mecklenburg Collection: Prehistoric Grave Material from Carniola (1934).

MAIER, R. A. 1961
'Neolithische Tierknochen-Idole und Tierknochen-Anhänger Europas', *Bericht R.-G. Komm.* XLII (1961), 171–305.

1962
'Fragen zu Neolithischen Erdwerken Südbayerns', *Jahresber. bayerisch. Bodendenkmal-pflege* (1962), 5–21.

MALMER, M. P. 1962
Jungneolithische Studien (Acta Arch. Lund. 8° S., no. 2, 1962).

MALUQUER DE MOTES, J. 1954a,b,c
'Pueblas Celtas', (in Pidal, ed. *Historia de España*, I, Pt. 3a, 5–194).
El Yacimiento Hallstáttico de Cortes de Navarra I (1954).
'Pueblos Ibéricos', (in Pidal, ed. *Historia de Espana*, I, Pt. 3a, 305–70.)

1958
El Yaciemento Hallstáttico de Cortes de Nararra II (1958).

MARIEN, M. E. 1958
Trouvailles du Champ d'Urnes et des Tombelles hallstattiennes de Court-Saint-Etienne (1958).

1961
La période de La Tène en Belgique: Le Groupe de la Haine (1961).

MARINATOS, S. 1962
'The Minoan and Mycenaean Civilization and its Influence on the Mediterranean and on Europe', *Atti VI° Cong. Internat. Scienze Preist. e Protost. I (Relazioni generali)* (1962), 161–76.

MARINGER, J., & BANDI, H. G. 1953
Art in the Ice Age (1953).

MARSEEN, O. 1960
'Ferslev-huset', *Kuml* (1960), 36–55.

MARSTRANDER, S. 1963
Østfolds Jordbruksristninger (1963).

MÁRTON, F. 1934
'Das Fundinventar der Frühlatène-gräber', *Dolgozatok Szeged* IX/X (1933–34).

MARYON, H. 1954
'Fine Metal-Work', in Singer *et al.* 1954, 623–62.

MASSON, V. M. 1961
'The First Farmers in Turkmenia', *Ant.* XXXV (1961), 203–13.

1962
The Neolithic Farmers of Central Asia (Reports and Communications by Archaeologists of the U.S.S.R. to VI Internat. Cong. of Prehist. and Protohist. Sciences, 1962).

MATHIASSEN, T. 1943
Stenalderbopladser i Aamosen (1943).
'Endnu et Krumsvaerd', 1957
Aarbøger, (1957), 38–55.

MAXWELL-HYSLOP, K. R. 1956a,b
'Notes on some distinctive types of Bronzes from Populonia, Etruria', *Proc. Prehist. Soc.* XXII (1956), 126–42.
'Urartian Bronzes in Etruscan Tombs', *Iraq* XVIII (1956), 150–67.

MEGAW, J. V. S. 1960
'Penny Whistles and Prehistory', *Antiq.* XXIV (1960), 6–13.

1961a,b
'Penny Whistles and Prehistory: Further Notes', *Antiq.* XXXV (1961), 55–57.
'The Neerharen Silver Vase', *Helinium* I (1961), 233–41.

MEGAW, J. V. S. 1962
'A Bronze Mount from Mâcon . . .',
Antiq. Journ. XLII (1962), 24–29.
1963a,b
'A British Bronze Bowl of the Belgic Iron Age from Poland',
Antiq. Journ. XLIII (1963), 27–37.
'A Medieval Bone Pipe from White Castle, Monmouthshire',
Galpin Soc. Journ. XVI (1963), 85–94.

MEGAW, J. V. S. *et al.* 1961
'The Bronze Age Settlement at Gwithian, Cornwall: Preliminary Report on the evidence for early agriculture',
Proc. West Cornwall Field Club II (1961).

MELLAART, J. 1958
'The End of the Early Bronze Age in Anatolia and the Aegean',
Amer. Journ. Arch. LXII (1958), 9–33.
1959
'Architectural Remains of Troy I and II',
Anat. Stud. IX (1959), 131–162.
1960a,b,c
'Anatolia and the Balkans',
Antiq. XXXIV (1960), 270–84.
'Excavations at Hacilar',
Anat. Stud. X (1960), 83–104.
'Excavations at Hacilar: Fourth Preliminary Report, 1960',
Anat. Stud. XI (1961), 39–75. 1961
'Anatolia, c. 4000–2300 B.C.',
Camb. Anc. Hist. (rev. ed.), I, 1962
Chap. XVIII, (1962).

MERHART, G. VON 1941
'Zur den ersten Metallhelmen Europas',
Ber. Röm. Germ. Komm. XXX (1940–41), 4–42.
1942
'Donauländische Bezeihungen der früheisenzeitlichen Kulturen Mittelitaliens',
Bonner Jahrb. CXLVII (1942), 1–90.
1952
'Studien über einige Gattungen von Bronzegefässen',
Festschrift Röm. Germ. Zentralmus. Mainz II (1952), 1–71.
1954
'Panzer-Studien',
Origines: Raccolta di Scritti in onore di Mons. Giovanni Baserga (1954), 33–61.
1956
'Über blecherne Zierbuckel (Faleren)',
Jarhb. Röm. Germ. Zentralmus. Mainz III (1956), 28–104.
1957
'Geschnürte Schienen',
Ber. Röm. Germ. Komm. XXXVII/XXXVIII (1957), 91–147.

MERPERT, N. YA. 1961
'L'Énéolithique de la zone steppique de la partie européene de l'U.R.S.S.',
in Böhm & de Laet 1961, 176–92.

MICHAEL, H. N. 1958
'The Neolithic Age in Eastern Siberia',
Trans. American Phil. Soc. n.s. XLVIII, Pt. 2 (1958), 1–108.

MIKOV, V. 1959
'The Prehistoric Mound of Karanovo',
Archaeology XII (1959), 88–97.

MILNE, J. G. 1940
'The 'Philippus' Coin at Rome',
Journ. Rom. Stud. XXX (1940), 11–15.

MILOJČIĆ, V. 1948
'Die Dorische Wanderung im Lichte der Vorgeschichtlichen Funde',
Arch. Anz. (1948), 12–36.
1951
'Die Siedlungsgrenzen und Zeitstellung der Bandkeramik im Osten und Südosten Europas',
Bericht R.G. Komm. XXXIII (1943–50: (1951)), 110–24.

MILOJČIĆ, V 1954
'Vorbericht über die Versuchsgrabung an der Otzaki-Magula bei Larisa',
Arch. Anzeiger (1954), 1–27.

1955a,b
'Zur Zeitstellung der Hammerknopfnadeln',
Germania XXXIII (1955), 240–2.
'Einige "Mitteleuropäische" Fremdlinge auf Kreta',
Jahrb. Röm. Germ. Zentralmus. Mainz II (1955), 153–69.

1959
'Ergebnisse der Deutschen Ausgrabungen in Thessalien',
Jahrb. R. G. Zentralmus. Mainz VI (1959), 1–56.

MILOJČIĆ, V. *et al.* 1962
Argissa-Magula I (1962).

MINNS, E. H. 1913
Scythians and Greeks (1913).

1942
'The Art of the Northern Nomads',
Proc. Brit. Acad. XXVIII (1942).

1943
'Trialeti',
Antiq. XVII (1943), 129–35.

MNATSAKANIAN, A. O. 1957
'Excavations in the Kurgans on the shore of Lake Sevan, 1956' (in Russian),
Sov. Arkh. (1957), no. 2, 146–53.

1960a,b
'Chariots from Bronze Age tumuli on the shores of Lake Sevan' (in Russian),
Sov. Arkh. (1960), no. 2, 139–52.
Bronze Age Culture on Lake Sevan Coast in Armenia (Papers pres. by USSR Deleg. to XXV Int. Cong. Orientalists, 1960).

MODDERMAN, P. J. R. *et al.*

1959
Twelve papers on Bandkeramik settlements in the Netherlands,
Palaeohist. VI-VII (1958–59).

MONTELIUS, O. 1922
Swedish Antiquities I: The Stone and Bronze Age (1922).

MORGAN, F. 1959
'The Excavation of a Long Barrow at Nutbane, Hants.',
Proc. Prehist. Soc. XXV (1959), 15–51.

MORITZ, L. A. 1958
Grain-Mills and Flour in Classical Antiquity (1958).

MOSSLER, G. M. 1961
'Sinnzeichen auf einheimischer Keramik',
Bericht V Internat. Kong. Vor- u. Frühgeschichte Hamburg 1958 (1961), 557–61.

MOVIUS, H. L. 1950
'A Wooden Spear of Third Interglacial Age from Lower Saxony',
Southwestern Journ. Anthrop. VI (1950), 139–42.

1960
'Radiocarbon Dates and Upper Palaeolithic Archaeology in Central and Western Europe',
Current Anthrop. I (1960), 355–91.

MOZSOLICS, A. 1942
Der Frühbronzezeitliche Urnenfriedhof von Kisapostag (1942).

1954
'Mors en Bois de Cerf sur le Territoire du Bassin des Carpathes',
Acta Arch. Hung. III (1954), 69–109.

1958
'Archäologische Beiträge zur Geschichte der grossen Wanderung',
Acta Arch. Hung. VIII (1958), 119–56.

1960
'Die Herkunftsfrage der ältesten Hirschgeweihtrensen',
Acta Arch. Hung. XII (1960), 125–35.

MÜLLER, H. H. 1959
'Bemalter Wandverputz aus einer Siedlungsgrube der späten Bronzezeit von Rottelsdorf . . .', *Ausgrab. und Funde* IV (1959), 15–18.

MÜLLER-KARPE, H. 1959
Beiträge zur Chronologie der Urnenfelderzeit nördlich un südlich der Alpen (1959).

1961
Die Vollgriffschwerter der Urnenfelderzeit aus Bayern (1961).

1962a,b
'Zur spätbronzezeitlichen Bewaffnung in Mitteleuropa und Griechenland', *Germania* XL (1962), 255–87.
'Die Metallbeigaben der früheisenzeitlichen Kerameikos-Gräber', *Jahrb. Deutsch. Arch. Inst.* LXXVII (1962), 59–129.

MUSCARELLA, O. W. 1962
'The Oriental Origin of Siren Cauldron Attachments', *Hesperia* XXXI (1962), 317–29.

N

NAVARRO, J. M. DE 1925
'Prehistoric Routes between Northern Europe and Italy defined by the Amber Trade', *Geog. Journ.* LXVI (1925), 481–507.

1928
'Massilia and Early Celtic Culture', *Antiq.* II (1928), 423–42.

1955
'A Doctor's Grave of the Middle La Tène Period from Bavaria', *Proc. Prehist. Soc.* XXI (1955), 231–48.

1959a,b
'A Bronze Mount of the La Tène Period from Kelheim, Lower Bavaria', *Germania* XXXVII (1959), 131–40.
'Zu einigen Schwertscheiden aus La Tène', *Bericht Röm. Germ. Komm.* XL (1959), 79–119.

NEEDHAM, J., & LU, G. 1960
'Efficient Equine Harness: the Chinese Inventions', *Physis* II (1960), 121–62.

NENQUIN, J. 1961
Salt: A study in economic prehistory (Diss. Arch. Gandenses VI, 1961).

NEUSTUPNÝ, E., & NEUSTUPNÝ, J. 1961
Czechoslovakia Before the Slavs (1961).

NEUSTUPNÝ, J. 1950
'Fortifications appartenant a la civilisation Danubienne néolithique', *Archiv Orientální* XVIII (1950), 131–58.

NICOLAISEN, W. 1957
'Die Alteuropäischen Gewässernamen der Britischen Hauptinsel', *Beiträge zur Namenforschung* VIII (1957), 209–68.

NOETTES, L. DES 1931
L'Âttelage: Le Cheval de Selle à travers les Ages (1931).

NØRLUND, P. 1948
Trelleborg (Nord. Fortidsmind. IV-I, 1948).

NOVÁKI, GY. 1964
'Zur Frage der sogenannten "Brandwälle" in Ungarn', *Acta Arch. Hung.* XVI (1964), 99–149.

NYLANDER, C. 1963
'The Fall of Troy', *Antiq.* XXXVII (1963), 6–11.

O

OAKLEY, K. P. 1950
Man the Tool-Maker (1950).

OCTOBON, E. 1931
'Statues-menhirs, Stèles gravées, Dalles sculptées', *Rev. Anthrop.* XLI (1931), 299–579.

O'CURRY, E. 1873
On the Manners and Customs of the Ancient Irish (1873).

OKLADNIKOV, A. P. 1959
Ancient Population of Siberia and its Cultures (1959).

ONIANS, R. B. 1954
The Origins of European Thought (1954).

OPRESCU, G. *et al.* 1958
Studii asupra Tezaurului restituit de URSS (1958).

ÖSTLUND, H. G., & ENGSTRAND, L. G. 1960
'Stockholm Natural Radiocarbon Measurements III',
in Flint & Deevy 1960, 186–96.

OZOLS, J. 1962
Ursprung und Herkunft der Zentralrussischen Fatyanovo Kultur (1962).

P

PAÇO, A. DO, & SANGMEISTER, E. 1956
'Vila Nova de S. Pedro: eine befestige Siedlung der Kupferzeit in Portugal',
Germania XXXIV (1956), 211–30.

PAGE, D. L. 1959a,b
History and the Homeric Iliad (1959).
'The Historical Sack of Troy',
Antiq. XXXIII (1959), 25–31.

PALLOTTINO, M. 1955
The Etruscans (1955).

PALLOTINO, M. *et al.* 1961
Mostra dell'Arte delle Situle dal Po al Danubia (1961).

PALMER, L. R. 1955
Achaeans and Indo-Europeans (1955).

PÁRDUCZ, M. 1952
'Le Cimitiére Hallstattien de Szentes-Vekerzug',
Acta Arch. Hung. II (1952), 143–69.

1954
'Le Cimitiere Hallstattien de Szentes-Vekerzug',
Acta Arch. Hung. IV (1954), 25–89.

PASSEK, T. 1962
Relations entre l'Europe occidentale et l'Europe orientale a l'époque néolithique (Reports and Communications of the Archaeologists of the U.S.S.R. to VI Internat. Cong. of Prehist. & Protohist. Sciences, 1962).

PATAY, P. 1938
Frühbronzezeitliche Kulturen in Ungarn (1938).

1958a,b
'Kupferzeitliche Goldfunde',
Arch. Értesitő (1958), 37–46.
'Beiträge zur Metallverarbeitung in der Küpferzeit auf dem Gebiet der Slowakei',
Slovenská Arch. VI (1958), 301–13.

PÄTZOLD, J. 1960
'Rituelles Pflügen beim vorgeschichtlichen Totenkult',
Prähist. Zeitsch. XXXVIII (1960), 189–239.

1963
'Ein späthallstatzeitlicher Herrensitz im Alpenvorland bei München',
Germania XLI (1963), 101–3.

PÄTZOLD, J., & SCHWARZ, K. 1961
'Ein späthallstattzeitlicher Herrensitz am Kyberg . . .',
Jahresb. Bayer. Bodendenkmalpflege, (1961), 1–15.

PÉQUART, M., & ST J., & LE ROUZIC 1927
Corpus des Signes Gravés des Monuments Mégalithiques du Morbihan (1927).

PERICOT, L. 1950
Los sepulcros megaliticos Catalanes y la Cultura Pirenaica (1950).

PERONI, R. 1956
'Zur Gruppierung mitteleuropäischer Griffzungendolche der späten Bronzezeit',
Badisch. Fundber. XX (1956), 69–92.

PERROT, J. 1957
'Le Mésolithique de Palestine et les récentes découvertes à 'Eynan ('Ain Mallaha)',
Antiq. & Survival II, 2/3 (1957): The Holy Land, 91–110.

1960
'Excavations at 'Eynan ('Ein Mallaha): Preliminary Report on the 1959 Season',
Israel Explor. Journ. X (1960), 14–22.

PETRESCU-DIMBOVIȚA, M. 1957
'Les principaux résultats des fouilles de Trușesti . . .',
Analele Științifice Univ. din Iași, n.s. Sect. ii, III (1957), Fasc. 1–2.

PETTAZONI, R. 1946
'Pagan Origins of the Three-Headed Representation of the Christian Trinity',
Journ. Warburg & Courtauld Insts. IX (1946), 135–51.

PHILLIPS, E. D. 1961
'The Royal Hordes: The Nomad peoples of the Steppes',
in Piggott 1961 c, 303–28.

1963
'The Peoples of the Highlands: the vanished cultures of Luristan, Mannai and Urartu',
in *Vanished Civilizations* (ed. E. Bacon, 1963), 221–150.

PIESKER, H. 1958
Untersuchungen zur älteren Lüneburgischen Bronzezeit (1958).

PIGGOTT, S. 1938
'The Early Bronze Age in Wessex',
Proc. Prehist. Soc. IV (1938), 52–106.

1940
'Timber Circles: a Re-examination',
Arch. Journ. XCVI (1940), 193–222.

1948a,b
'Notes on certain Metal Pins and a Mace-head in the Harappa Culture',
Anc. India IV (1947–48), 26–40.

'Fire-dogs Again',
Antiq. XXII (1948), 21–28.

1949
'A Wheel of Iron Age Type from Co. Durham',
Proc. Prehist. Soc. XV (1949), 191.

1950a,b
Prehistoric India (1950).

'Swords and Scabbards of the British Early Iron Age',
Proc. Prehist. Soc. XVI (1950), 1–28.

1953a,b,c
'Bronze Double-Axes in the British Isles',
Proc. Prehist. Soc. XIX (1953), 224–26.

'A Late Bronze Age Hoard from Peebleshire',
Proc. Soc. Ant. Scot. LXXXVII (1952–53), 175–86.

'Three Metal-Work Hoards of the Roman period from Southern Scotland',
Proc. Soc. Ant. Scot. LXXXVII (1952–53), 1–50.

1953–4
'Le Néolithique occidentale et le Chalcolithique en France: Esquisse préliminaire',
L'Anthrop. LVII (1953), 401–43; LVIII (1954), 1–28.

1954
The Neolithic Cultures of the British Isles (1954).

1955
'Windmill Hill—East or West?'
Proc. Prehist. Soc. XXI (1955), 96–101.

1958
'Native Economies and the Roman Occupation of North Britain',
in Richmond 1958, 1–27.

PIGGOTT, S. 1959a,b,c
'A Late Bronze Age Wine Trade?', *Antiq.* XXXIII (1959), 122–3.
'The *Carnyx* in Early Iron Age Britain', *Antiq. Journ.* XXXIX (1959), 19–32.
Approach to Archaeology (1959).

1960
'Neolithic and Bronze Age in East Europe', *Antiq.* XXXIV (1960), 285–94.

1961a,b,c
'The British Neolithic Cultures in their Continental Setting', in Böhm & de Laet 1961, 557–4.
Review of Deshayes 1960, *Antiq.* XXXV (1961), 330–1.
The Dawn of Civilization (ed.) (1961).

1962a,b,c
The West Kennet Long Barrow: Excavations 1955–56 (1962).
'From Salisbury Plain to South Siberia', *Wilts. Arch. Mag.* LVIII (1962), 93–97.
'Heads and Hoofs', *Antiq.* XXXVI (1962), 110–18.
The Prehistoric Peoples of Scotland (ed. and Chap. III, 1962).

1963
'Abercromby and After: the British Beaker Cultures re-examined', in Foster & Alcock 1963, 53–91.

PIGGOTT, S., & DANIEL, G. E. 1951
A Picture Book of Ancient British Art (1951).

PIJOAN, J. 1953
El Arte Prehistórico Europeo (Summa Artis, vol. VI, 1953).

PINK, K. 1960
Einführung in die keltische Münzkunde mit besonderer Berücksichtigung des österreichischen Raumes (1960).

PIOTROVSKIY, B. B. 1954
Ourartou (1954) L'Orient Ancien Illustré (ed. Virolleaud), no. 8.

1962
Urartian Art (1962) (in Russian).

PITTIONI, R. 1951
'Prehistoric Copper Mining in Austria: Problems and Facts', *Univ. Lond. Inst. Arch. Report* VII (1951), 16–45.

1954
Urgeschichte des Österreichischen Raumes (1954).

POEL, J. M. G. VAN DER 1961
'De Landbouw in het verste verleden', *Ber. R.O.B. Nederland* X/XI (1960–61), 125–94.

POULSEN, V. 1962
'Sculpture and Engraving', in *Etruscan Culture: Land and People* (Swedish Institute in Rome, 1962).

POWELL, T. G. E. 1950
'A Late Bronze Age Hoard from Welby, Leicestershire', *Arch. Journ.* CV (1950), 27–40.

1953
'The Gold Ornament from Mold, Flintshire, North Wales', *Proc. Prehist. Soc.* XIX (1953), 161–79.

1960
'Megalithic and other Art: Centre and West', *Antiq.* XXXIV (1960), 180–90.

1961
'Barbarian Europe: From the first farmers to the Celts', in Piggott 1961 c, 330–57.

1963a,b
'Some Implications of Chariotry', in Foster & Alcock 1963, 153–69.
'The Inception of the Final Bronze Age in Middle Europe', *Proc. Prehist. Soc.* XXIX (1963), 214–34.

POWELL, T. G. E., & DANIEL, G. E. 1956
Barclodiad y Gawres (1956).

PRITCHARD, J. B. (ed.) 1955
Ancient Near Eastern Texts relating to the Bible (1955).

PROUDFOOT, V. B. 1961
'The Economy of the Irish Rath', *Medieval Arch.* V (1961), 94–122.

Q

QUITTA, H. 1957
'Neue Hüttengrundrisse aus dem Ukrainischen Jungpaläolithikum', *Ausgrab. und Funde* (1957), 312–22.

1960
'Zur Frage der ältesten Banderkamik in Mitteleuropa', *Prähist. Zeitschr.* XXXVIII (1960) 153–188

R

RADEKER, W., & NAUMANN, F. K. 1961
'Untersuchung vor- oder frühgeschichtlicher Spitzbarren', *Archiv f.d. Eisenhüttenwesen* XXXII (1961), 587–95.

RADULESCO, C., & SAMSON, P. 1962
'Sur un centre de domestication du Mouton dans le Mésolithique de la grotte "La Adam" en Dobrogea', *Zeitschr. für Tierzücht. u. Züchtsungsbiol.* LXXVI (1962), 282–320.

R.C.A.M. (S). 1956
Royal Commission on Ancient Monuments (Scotland), *Roxburghshire Inventory* (1956).

REDLICH, C. 1935
'Die Knochennadel von Werla', *Die Kunde* III (1935), 57–65.

REED, C. A. 1960
'A Review of the Archaeological Evidence on Animal Domestication in the Prehistoric Near East', in Braidwood, Howe *et al.* 1960, Chap. IX.

1961
'Osteological evidences for prehistoric domestication in southwestern Asia', *Zeitschr. für Tierzücht. u. Züchtungsbiol.* LXXVI (1961), 31–38.

REINECKE, P. 1948
'Ein neuer Bronzehelm italischer form aus der Ukraine', in *Festschrift für Otto Tschumi* (1948), 91–96.

REINERTH, H. 1929
Das Federseemoor als Siedlungsland des Vorzeitmenschen (1929).

RICE, T. T. 1957
The Scythians (1957).

RICHMOND, I. A. 1932
'The Irish analogies for the Romano-British barn dwelling', *Journ. Rom. Stud.* XXII (1932), 96–106.

1950
Archaeology, and the After-life in Pagan and Christian Imagery (1950).

1954
'Queen Cartimandua', *Journ. Rom. Studies* XLIV (1954), 43–52.

1958
Roman and Native in North Britain (ed. & contrib.), 1958.

RICHTER, G. M. A. 1959
A Handbook of Greek Art (1959).

RIEK, G., & HUNDT, H. J. 1962
Der Hohmichele: ein Fürstengräbhugel der späten Hallstattzeit bei der Heuneburg (1962).

RIETH, A. 1958
'Werkzeuge der Holzbearbeitung: Sägen aus vier Jahrtausend', *Saalburg-Jahrbuch* XVII (1958), 47–60.

Ó RÍORDÁIN, S. P. 1937
'The Halberd in Bronze Age Europe',
Arch. LXXXVI (1937), 195–321.
1954
'Lough Gur Excavations: Neolithic and Bronze Age Houses on Knockadoon',
Proc. Roy. Irish Acad. LVI (C), (1954), 297–459.

RIVET, A. L. F. 1956
Map of Roman Britain: Third Edition (Ordnance Survey, 1956).
1962
Map of Southern Britain in the Iron Age (Ordnance Survey 1962).

RIX, H. 1954
'Zur Verbreitung und Chronologie einiger keltischer Ortsnamentypen',
Festschrift für Peter Goessler (1954), 99–107.

ROCHE, J. 1960
Le Gisement mésolithique de Moita do Sebastião (1960).

RODDEN, R. J. 1962
'Excavations at the Early Neolithic site of Nea Nikomedeia, Greek Macedonia',
Proc. Prehist. Soc. XXVIII (1962), 267–88.

RÖDER, J. 1948
'Der Goloring: Ein eisenzeitliches Heiligtum vom Henge-charakter im Koberner Wald',
Bonner Jahrb. 148 (1948), 81–132.

ROGACHEV, A. N. 1956
'Études des Vestiges de la Colonie Paléolithique . . . d'Avdeevo',
Paléolithique et Néolithique de l'URSS (1956), 114–67 (=*Materialy* XXXIX, 1953).

ROLLEY, C. 1962
'Trouvailles Méditerranéennes en Basse-Bourgogne',
Bull. Corres. Hell. LXXXVI (ii) (1962), 476–93.

ROSENBERG, G. 1937
Hjortspringfundet (1937).

ROSEN-PSHCHEVSKAYA, YA. 1963
'The Question of Celto-Scythian Relations' (in Russian),
Sov. Arkh. (1963), 3, 67–78.

ROSS, A. 1958
'The Human Head in Insular Celtic Religion',
Proc. Soc. Ant. Scot. XCI (1957–58), 10–43.
1962
'Severed Heads in Wells: an aspect of the Well Cult',
Scottish Studies VI (1962), 31–48.

RUDENKO, S. I. 1953
The Culture of the Population of the Upper Altai in Scythian times (1953: in Russian).
1960
The Culture of the Population of the Central Altai in Scythian times (1960: in Russian).
1961
The Ancient Culture of the Bering Sea and the Eskimo Problem (1961).
1962
The Siberian Collection of Peter I (1962: in Russian).

RUMYANTSEV, E. A. 1961
'Restoration and conservation of early wooden carts from Transcaucasia and Altai' (in Russian),
Sov. Arkh. (1961), no. 1, 236–42.

RUST, A. 1937
Das altsteinzeitliche Renntierjägerlager Meiendorf (1937).
1943
Die alt- und mittelsteinzeitlichen Funde von Stellmoor (1943).
1951
'Über de Kulturentwicklung des endglazialen Jungpalaeolithikums',
Schwantes Festschrift (1951), 48.
1958a,b
Die Funde von Pinnberg (1958).
Die Jungpaläolithischen Zeltanlagen von Ahrensburg . . . (1958).

RYBOVÁ, A., & SOUDSKÝ, B. 1962
Libenice: Sanctuaire celtique en Bohême centrale (1962).

RYNNE, E. 1961
'The Introduction of La Tène into Ireland',
Bericht V Internat. Kong. Vor- und Frühgesch. Hamburg 1958 (1961), 705–9.

S

SÄFLUND, G. 1939
Le Terremare (1939).

SALOMONSSON, B. 1960
'Fouilles à Belloy-sur-Somme en 1952 et 1953',
Medd. frå Lunds Univ. Hist. Mus. 1959 (1960), 5–109.

SALONEN, A. 1950
'Notes on Wagons and Chariots in Ancient Mesopotamia',
Stud. Orient. XIV (1950), 1–8.

1951
Die Landfahrzeuge des alten Mesopotamien (Ann. Acad. Scient. Fennicae B, Vol. 72, 1951).

1956
Hippologica Accadica (Ann. Acad. Scient. Fennicae B, Vol. 100, 1956).

SANDARS, H. 1913
'The Weapons of the Iberians',
Arch. LXIV (1913), 205–94.

SANDARS, N. K. 1955
'The Antiquity of the One-edged Bronze Knife in the Aegean',
Proc. Prehist. Soc. XXI (1955), 174–97.

1957
Bronze Age Cultures in France (1957).

1959
'Amber Spacer-Beads Again',
Antiq. XXXIII (1959), 292–5.

1961
'The First Aegean Swords and Their Ancestry',
Amer. Journ. Arch. LXV (1961), 17–29.

1962
'Wheelwrights and Smiths',
Celticum III (1962), 403–8.

1963
'Later Aegean Bronze Swords',
Amer. Journ. Arch. LXVII (1963), 117–53.

SANGMEISTER, E. 1957
'Ein geschlossener Glockenbecherfund im Museum Cordova',
Zephyrus VIII (1957), 257–67.

1963
'La Civilisation du Vase Campaniforme',
Les Civilisations Atlantique: Actes du 1er Colloque Atlantique, Brest 1961 (1963), 25–56.

SAUTER, M. R. 1959
'Quelques réflections a propos du problème des Palafittes',
Genava n.s. VII (1959), 35–56.

SAVORY, H. N. 1948
' "The Sword-Bearers": a reinterpretation',
Proc. Prehist. Soc. XIV (1948), 155–76.

1949
'The Atlantic Bronze Age in South-West Europe',
Proc. Prehist. Soc. XV (1949), 128–55.

SCHAEFFER, C. F. A. 1943
'La date des kourganes de Trialeti',
Antiq. XVII (1943), 183–7.

1944a,b
'Archaeological Discoveries in Trialeti-Caucasus',
Journ. Royal Asiatic Soc. (1944), 25–29.
'In the Wake of the Argo',
Man (1944), no. 30.

1948
Stratigraphie Comparée et Chronologie de l'Asie Occidentale (IIIe et IIe. millénaires) (1948).

SCHAEFFER, C. F. A. 1949
'Porteurs de Torques',
Ugaritica II (1949), 49–120.

1952
Enkomi-Alasia I (1952).

SCHIEK, S. 1954
'Das Hallstattgrab von Vilsingen',
Festschrift für Peter Goessler (1954), 150–67.

1959
'Vorbericht über die Ausgrabungen des vierten Fürstengrabhügels bei der Heuneburg',
Germania XXXVII (1959), 117–31.

SCHLETTE, F. 1958
'Die ältesten Haus- und Siedlungsformen des Menschen',
Ethnog.-Arch. Forschungen V (1958), 1–185.

SCHLIZ, A 1901
Das steinzeitliche Dorf Grossgartach (1901).

SCHMID, W. 1934
Der Kultwagen von Strettweg (1934).

SCHMIDT, R. R. 1945
Die Burg Vučedol (1945).

SCHUBART, H. 1958
'Nordische Bronzezeit in der DDR',
Ausgrab. und Funde III (1958), 210–21.

1961
'Jungbronzezeitliche Burgwälle in Mecklenburg',
Prähist. Zeitsch. XXXIX (1961), 143–75.

SCHUCHHARDT, C. 1909
'Die Römerschanze bei Potsdam',
Prähist. Zeitsch. I (1909), 209–38.

1926
'Witzen und Starzeddel, zwei Burgen der Lausitzer Kultur',
Prähist. Zeitsch. XVII (1926), 184–201.

SCHULDT, W. 1961
Hohen Viecheln (1961).

SCHÜLE, W. 1960
'Probleme der Eisenzeit auf der Iberischen Halbinsel',
Jahrb. Röm. Germ. Zentralsmus. Mainz VII (1960), 59–125.

SCHWABEDISSEN, H. 1944
Die mittlere Steinzeit im westlichen Nordwestdeutschland (1944).

SCHWARZ, K. 1958
'Spätlatènezeitliche Viereckschanzen Keltische Kultplätze',
Neue Ausgrab. in Deutschland (1958), 205–14.

1960
'Spätkeltische Viereckschanzen ...',
Jahresb. Bayer. Bodendenkmalpflege (1960), 7–41.

1962
'Zum Stand der Ausgrabungen in der spätkeltischen Viereckschanze von Holzhausen',
Jahresb. Bayer. Bodendenkmalpflege (1962), 22–77.

SCOLLAR, I. 1959
'Regional Groups in the Michelsberg Culture',
Proc. Prehist. Soc. XXV (1959), 52–134.

SEURE, G. 1901
'Voyage en Thrace I',
Bull. Corr. Hell. XXV (1901), 168–220.

1904
'Un char Thraco-Macédonien',
Bull. Corr. Hell. XXVIII (1904), 210–37.

SHETELIG, H. 1930
'Das Nydamschiff',
Acta Arch. I (1930), 1–30.

SINGER, C. *et al.* 1954
A History of Technology I (1954).

1956
A History of Technology II (1956).

SJOESTEDT, M. L. 1949
Gods and Heroes of the Celts (1949).

SLOTKIN, J. S. 1948
'Reflections on Collingwood's *Idea of History*',
Antiq. XXII (1948), 98–102.

SMITH, I. 1959
'Excavations at Windmill Hill, Avebury, Wilts, 1957–58', *Wilts. Arch. & N.H.Mag.* LVII (1959), 149–62.

1960
'Radio-Carbon Dates from Windmill Hill', *Antiq.* XXXIV (1960), 212–13.

SMITH, M. A. 1953
'Iberian Beakers', *Proc. Prehist. Soc.* XIX (1953), 95–107.

1958
'The Limitations of Inference in Archaeology', *Arch. News Letter* VI (1955), 1–5.

1957
'A Study in Urnfield Interpretations in Middle Europe', *Zephyrus* VIII (1957), 195–240.

1959
'Some Somerset hoards and their place in the Bronze Age of Southern Britain', *Proc. Prehist. Soc.* XXV (1959), 144–87.

SNODGRASS, A. M. 1962
'Iron Age Greece and Central Europe', *Amer. Journ. Arch.* LXVI (1962), 408–10.

SOLECKI, R. S. 1963a,b
'Prehistory in Shanidar Valley, Northern Iraq', *Science* CXXXIX (1963), 179–93.
'Two Bone Hafts from Northern Iraq', *Antiq.* XXXVII (1963), 58–60.

SOUDSKÝ, B. 1953
'Únětická Osada v Postoloprtech', *Arch. Rozhledy* V (1953), 308–18.

1962
'The Neolithic Site of Bylany', *Antiq.* XXXVI (1962), 190–200.

SPROCKHOFF, E. 1934
Die germanischen Vollgriffschwerter (1934).

1938
Die nordische Megalithkultur (1938).

STEAD, I. M. 1961
'A Distinctive Form of La Tène Barrow in Eastern Yorkshire and on The Continent', *Antiq. Journ.* XLI (1961), 44–62.

STEKELIS, M., & YIZRAELY, T. 1963
'Excavations at Naḥal Oren: Preliminary Report', *Israel Explor. Journ.* XIII (1963), 1–12.

STENBERGER, M. 1962
Sweden (1962).

STENBERGER, M. *et al.* 1955
Vallhagar: A Migration Period Settlement on Gotland, Sweden (1955).

STEVENS, C. E. 1957
'Roman Gaul', in J. M. Wallace-Hadrill and J. MacManners, *France: Government and Society* (1957), 19–34.

STIEREN, A. 1950
'Bandkeramische Grossbauten bei Bochum und ihre Parallelen in Mitteleuropa', *Bericht R. G. Komm.* XXXIII (1943–50), 61–88.

STONE, J. F. S. 1941
'The Deverel-Rimbury Settlement on Thorny Down, Winterbourne Gunner, S. Wilts.', *Proc. Prehist. Soc.* VII (1941), 114–33.

1948
'The Stonehenge Cursus and its Affinities', *Arch. Journ.* CIV (1948)), 7–19.

1958
Wessex Before the Celts (1958).

STONE, J. F. S., & THOMAS, L. C. 1956
'The Use and Distribution of Faience in the Ancient East and Prehistoric Europe', *Proc. Prehist. Soc.* XXII (1956), 37–84.

STRONACH, D. 1959
'An Early Metal Hoard at Beycesultan',
Anat. Stud. IX (1959), 47–50.

STUBBINGS, F. H. 1963
'The Rise of Mycenaean Civilization',
Camb. Anc. Hist. (rev. ed.), II, Chap. XIV (1963).

STUKELEY, W. 1740
Stonehenge: a Temple restor'd to the British Druids (1740).

STURT, G. 1934
The Wheelwright's Shop (1934).

SULIMIRSKI, T. 1945
'Scythian Antiquities in Central Europe',
Antiq. Journ. XXV (1945), 1–11.

1952
'Les archers à cheval; cavalerie légère des anciens',
Rev. Internat. Hist. Militaire III (1952), 447–61.

1954
'Scythian Antiquities in Western Asia',
Artibus Asiae XVII (1954), 282–318.

1961
'Die Skythen in Mittel- und Westeuropa',
Bericht V Internat. Kong. Vor- und Frühgesch. Hamburg 1958 (1961), 793–9.

1963
'The Forgotten Sarmatians',
in E. Bacon (ed.), *Vanished Civilizations* (1963), 279–98.

SYLVEST, B., & SYLVEST, I. 1960
'Årupgårdfundet',
Kuml, (1960), 9–25.

T

TACKENBURG, K. 1950
'Die Burgen der Lausitzer Kultur',
Prähist. Zeitsch. XXXIV/V (1949–50), 18–32.

TAFFANEL, O., & TAFFANEL, J. 1962
'Deux Tombes de Cavaliers du 1e Age du Fer à Mailhac',
Gallia XX (1962), 3–32.

TAUBER, H. 1960
'Copenhagen Natural Radiocarbon Measurements III . . .',
in Flint & Deevy (1960), 5–11.

TAYLOUR, LORD WILLIAM 1958
Mycenaean Pottery in Italy and Adjacent Areas (1958).

THIEME, P. 1954
Die Heimat der indogermanischen Gemeinsprache (1954).

THOMAS, A. C. 1958
Gwithian: Ten Years' Work (1949–1958) (1958).

THOMPSON, E. A. 1948
A History of Attila and the Huns (1948).

THOMPSON, M. 1954
'Azilian Harpoons',
Proc. Prehist. Soc. XX (1954), 193–211.

THURNEYSEN, R. 1921
Das Irische Helden- und Königsage . . . (1921).

TIERNEY, J. J. 1960
'The Celtic Ethnography of Posidonius',
Proc. Royal Irish Acad. LX (C) (1960), 189–275.

TOČIK, A., & POULÍK, J. 1960
'Výskum mohyly v Čake v rockoch 1950–51',
Slov. Arch. VIII (1960), 59–124.

TORBRUGGE, W. 1959a,b
'Die Bronzezeit in Bayern: Stand der Forschungen zur relativen Chronologie',
Bericht R. G. Komm. XL (1959), 1–78.
Die Bronzezeit in der Oberpfalz (1959).

TOYNBEE, J. M. C., & CLARKE, R. R. 1948
'A Roman Decorated Helmet and other objects from Norfolk', *Journ. Rom. Stud.* XXXVIII (1948), 20–27.

TROELS-SMITH, J. 1953
'Ertebøllekultur-Bondekultur', *Aarbøger* (1953), 5–62.

1959
'En Elmetraes-bue fra Aamosen . . .', *Aarbøger* (1959), 91–145.

1960
Ivy, Mistletoe and Elm: Climate Indicators—Fodder Plants (Danmarks Geolog. Undersøgelse IV Series, Vol. 4, no. 4, 1960).

TRUMP, D. H. 1961
'Skorba, Malta and the Mediterranean', *Antiq.* XXXV (1961), 300–3.

1963
'Carbon, Malta and the Mediterranean', *Antiq.* XXXVII (1963), **302**–3.

TSCHUMI, O. 1929
'Der Massenfund von der Tiefenau . . .', *Jahresb. Schweiz. Gesellsch. f. Urgesch.* XXI (1929), 1–18.

1953
Urgeschichte des Kantons Bern (1953).

TYLECOTE, R. F. 1962
Metallurgy in Archaeology (1962).

U

UCKO, P. J. 1962
'The Interpretation of Prehistoric Anthropomorphic Figurines', *Journ. Royal Anthrop. Inst.* XCII (1962), 38–54.

UENZE, O. 1938
Die frühbronzezeitlichen triangulären Vollgriffdolche (1938).

1958
Frührömische Amphoren als Zeitmarken im Spätlatène (1958).

USLAR, R. VON 1955
'Der Goldbecher von Fritzdorf bei Bonn', *Germania* XXXIII (1955), 319–23.

V

DE VALERA, R. 1960
'The Court Cairns of Ireland', *Proc. Roy. Irish Acad.* LX (C), no. 2 (1960), 9–140.

VALMIN, M. N. 1938
The Swedish Messenia Expedition (1938).

VANDERPOOL, E. 1959
'News Letter from Greece', *Amer. Journ. Arch.* LXIII (1959), 279–83.

1963
'News Letter from Greece', *Amer. Journ. Arch.* XLVII (1963), 280–1.

VARLEY, W. J. 1950
'The Hill-Forts of the Welsh Marches', *Arch. Journ.* CV (1950), 41–66.

VATCHER, F. 1959
'The Radio-Carbon dating of the Nutbane Long Barrow', *Antiq.* XXXIII (1959), 289.

VILLARD, F. 1956
'Vases de bronze Grecs dans un tombe Étrusque du VII e siécle', *Monuments Piot* XLVIII (ii) (1956), 25–53.

1960
La Céramique Grecque de Marseille (1960).

VOGEL, J. C., & WATERBOLK, H. T. 1963
'Groningen Radiocarbon Dates IV', in Deevy *et al.* 1963, 163–202.

VOGT, E. 1937
Geflechte und Gewebe der Steinzeit (1937).

VOGT, E. 1947
'Basketry and Woven Fabrics of the European Stone and Bronze Ages', *CIBA Review* LIV (1947), 1938–70.
1948
'Die Gliederung der Schweizerischen Frühbronzezeit', *Festschrift für Otto Tschumi* (1948), 53–69.
1951
'Das steinzeitliche Uferdorf Egolzwil (Kr. Luzern)', *Zeitschr. Schweiz. Arch. u. Kunstgesch.* XII (1951), 193–215.

VOS, M. F. 1963
Scythian Archers in Archaic Attic Greek Vase-Painting (Arch. Traiectina VI, 1963).

VOUGA, P. 1923
La Tène (1923).

DE VRIES, J. 1963
La Religion des Celtes (1963).

VULPE, R. 1957
Izvoare: Săpăturile din 1936–1948.

W

VAN DER WAALS, J. D., & GLASBERGEN, W. 1955
'Beaker Types and their Distribution in the Netherlands', *Palaeohist.* IV (1955), 5–46.

WACE, A. J. B., & STUBBINGS, F. H. 1962
A Companion to Homer (1962).

WACE, A. J. B., & THOMPSON, M. S. 1912
Prehistoric Thessaly (1912).

WAINWRIGHT, F. T. 1955
The Problem of the Picts (ed. and contrib. 1955).

WAINWRIGHT, G. A. 1939
'Some Sea-Peoples and others in the Hittite Archives', *Journ. Egypt. Arch.* XXV (1939), 148–53.
1944
'Early Tin in the Aegean', *Antiq.* XVIII (1944), 57–64.
1959
'The Teresh, the Etruscans and Asia Minor', *Anat. Stud.* IX (1959), 197–213.
1962
'The Meshwesh', *Journ. Egypt. Arch.* XLVIII (1962), 89–99.

WATERBOLK, H. T. 1959
'Die prehistorie van Nederland in absolute getallen', *Hondeed Eeuwen Nederland* (Antiq. & Survival II, 5–6, 1959), 12–26.
1960
'The 1959 Carbon-14 Symposium at Groningen', *Antiq.* XXXIV (1960), 14–18.
1961a,b
'Preliminary Report on the Excavations at Anlo in 1957 and 1958', *Palaeohist.* VIII (1961), 59–90.
'Bronzezeitliche dreischiffige Hallenhäuser von Elp (Drenthe)', *Helinium* I (1961), 126–32.

WATTS, W. A. 1960
'C-14 Dating and the Neolithic in Ireland', *Antiq.* XXXIV (1960), 111–16.

WEINBERG, S. S. 1962
'Excavations at Prehistoric Elateia 1959', *Hesperia* XXXI (1962), 158–209.

WELKOW, I. 1943
'Chariot Burials' (in Bulgarian), *Bull. Inst. Arch. Bulgare* XIV (1943), 189–207.

WERNER, J. 1952
'Mykenae-Siebenbürgen-Skandinavien', *Atti 1º Cong. Internat. Preist. e Protost. Mediterranea 1950* (1952), 293–308.

WERNER, J. 1954
'Die Bronzekanne von Kelheim',
Bayer. Vorgeschichtsbl. XX (1954), 43–73.

WHEELER, R. E. M. 1928
'A "Romano-Celtic" Temple near Harlow, Essex. and a note on the type',
Antiq. Journ. VIII (1928), 300–26.

1943
Maiden Castle Dorset (1943).

1954a,b
The Stanwick Fortifications: North Riding of Yorkshire (1954).
Rome beyond the Imperial Frontiers (1954).

WHEELER, R. E. M., & RICHARDSON, K. M. 1957
Hill Forts of Northern France (1957).

WHEELER, R. E. M., & WHEELER, T. V. 1936
Verulamium: a Belgic and two Roman cities (1936).

WHYTE, R. O. 1961
'Evolution of Land Use in South-Western Asia',
UNESCO Arid Zone Research XVII,
A History of Land Use in the Arid Regions (1961), 57–118.

WILD, J. P. 1963
'The *Byrrus Britannicus*',
Antiq. XXXVII 1963, 193–202.

WILLIS, E. H. 1963
'Radiocarbon Dating',
in Brothwell & Higgs 1963, 35–46.

WRIGHT, E. V., & WRIGHT, C. W 1947
'Prehistoric Boats from North Ferriby, East Yorkshire',
Proc. Prehist. Soc. XIII (1947), 114–38.

WYSS, R. 1956
'The Sword of Korisios',
Antiq. XXX (1956), 27–28.

Y

YAKOUNINA-IVANOVA, L. 1927
'Une trouvaille de l'âge de La Tène dans la Russie méridionale',
Eur. Sept. Antiq. I (1927), 100–9.

YESSEN, A. A. 1950
'Chronology of the Great Kuban Barrows' (in Russian),
Sov. Arkh. XII (1950), 157–200.

YOUNG, R. S. 1958
'The Gordion Campaign of 1957: Preliminary Report',
Amer. Journ. Arch. LXII (1958), 139–54.

1960
'The Campaign of 1955 at Gordion: Preliminary Report',
Amer. Journ. Arch. LX (1960), 249–66.

Z

ZERVOS, C. 1954
La Civilisation de la Sardaigne (1954).

ZEUNER, F. E. 1954
'Cultivation of Plants',
in Singer *et al.* 1954, 353–75.

1956
Dating the Past (1958).

1963
A History of Domesticated Animals (1963).

Index

Italicised figures denote the nearest page reference for illustrations; those followed by an asterisk refer to the plates

A

Abercromby, Lord, 100
Abernethy, fort at, 204
Achaeans, 159
Acton, Lord, 4, 8
Adamklissi, stone relief at, 253*
Advanced Palaeolithic cultures
  chronology of, 27-28
  clothing of, 104
  duration of, 27
  hunting communities of, 27-28
  naturalistic art of, 27, 176
  tool-making techniques of, 27, 28
  traditions of, 25
adze
  copper, *82*
  use of, in carpentry, 187
Aegean, The
  as a centre of higher civilisation, 107
  bastioned walled towns of, 76
  beginnings of metallurgy in, 64
  copper-working in, 73, 107-8, 113
  Dark Ages in, 158-60
  fighting tactics in, 145
  glass beads from, 136-7
  Homer's, 140
  influence at Stonehenge, 116, 138-9, 140
  links with Iberian copper colonies, 74, 76-77, *77*
  shields, 194
Aeolian Islands
  excavated settlement in, *145**
  faience beads from, 136
  Lipari settlement in, 97, *152*, 155, 168
  Mycenaean colonies in, 134
Agamemnon, 140
Agora, iron objects from grave at, 186, 192
agriculturalists
  and models of the past, 25
  and the domestication of animals, 35
  as distinctive of the Neolithic period, 25
  Bell-Beaker people as, 102
  central and north-western European, 50-52
  coexistence of nomadic pastoralism and, 235-6
  coexistence with hunting and fishing communities, 27, 64, 97, 113
  copper-using, of South Russia, 81-82
  'cyclic' movement of semi-migratory, 52
  distribution of, in east Europe, *43*
  east European, 40-49, 56
  generalised distribution of, *57*, *59*
  making of pottery among, 26
  spread of, to western Europe, 56-60, 62-64
  temporal overlap of hunting communities and, 27
  the earliest, 24-64
agriculture
  as a feature of the undivided Indo-European homeland, 80, 91
  beginnings of, 24-64
  botanical evidence on the beginnings of, 8-9
  Celtic system of, 250, 252
  conditions of transition from hunting and gathering to, 26, 35-39
  in Europe in 2000 B.C., 113
  in Scandinavia, 62-63
  invention of, 21, 258
  mixed farming, 36, 258
  Near Eastern origins of, 39-41, 49, 56, 67
  necessary background for origins of, 26-35
  ploughing, *145**, 150
  pre-pottery Neolithic, in Europe, 40-41
  shifting, 113
  technological competence in, 16-17
  use of stone edge-tools in, 113
  zoological evidence on the beginnings of, 9
Ahhiyawa, King of, 159
Ahrensburg, tent-stance at, 30
Aichbühl
  megaron-plan houses at, 121
  village site at, 89
Akawasha, 158
Akhenaton, 158
Akkadians
  background of, 44

Akkadians *contd*
  break-up of kingdom of, 77-78, 116, 118
  political status of, 113
  views on their neighbours, 256
  words for carts and wagons, 92
alabaster
  figurines, *114*
  mace-head, 130, *131*
Alaca Hüyük Royal Tombs
  art styles from, 130, 133
  copper figures from, *71**, 72
  iron dagger from, 185
  link with Greek shaft-graves, 123
  link with Kurgan culture graves, 81, 84
Alalakh, decorated bone and antler objects from, *135*
Alasiya, 158, 159
Alesia, fortified settlement at, 218, 245
Alföldi, A., 16, 256 257
Almendralejo, silver dish from, *257**, 260
Altai Mountains, Scythian art from, 176, *176**, *240**
Altamira, art work from, 28
'altar', anthropomorphic, of Tripolye culture, 56, *56*
Amazons, horse sacrifices of, 130
amber
  cups, 129;
  main routes of trade and exchange in, 137 *138*, 161
  ornaments in Greek shaft-grave, 123
  space-plate beads, 137, *137*
  trade in, 120, 137-8, 161
Ambrones, 235
Amenophis I, 142
Amfreville, gilt bronze helmet from, *241**
Amlash, art styles from, 130
Amorites, invasions of the, 78, 103-4
amphora(ae)
  buried in graves, 247
  distribution of Roman, 253, *254*
  Massaliote, *188*, 195, 204
amulets, oriental stamp-seals as, 49
Anatolia
  Assyrian trading colonies in, 79, 141-2
  as the home of the war-chariot, 141-2
  cold-hammering of copper in, 71, 72, 107
  copper working in, 73, 107
  destruction of towns in, 78, 79
  Hatti in, 79
  Hittites in, 79, 116, 118
  Homer's, 140
  Indo-European speakers in, 79
  megaron-type houses in, 89, 121
  pre-pottery Neolithic culture in, 40
  rise of Mycenae and, 134
  social organisation of peasant communities in, 44, 81
  timber-laced structures in, 204
  urban cultures in, 113
Anau, excavations at, 25
anchors iron, 247
andiron, 247
animal(s)
  art, 130, 132, 176-7, *192**, 241
  bones, determination of type of economy from, 24
  distribution of, under modern climatic conditions, 35-36, *37*
  domestication of, *see* domestication
  ecological research on bones of, 25
  establishment of relationships between man and, 36
  generalised distribution of, *37*
  husbandry, transition from hunting to, 26
Anlo, palisaded cattle-kraal at, 85, *87*
anthropomorphic
  'altar', 56, *56*
  pot of Tisza culture, *49*
antler
  cheek-pieces, 130, *132*, 177, 179
  decorated bone and, objects, *135*, 136
  from Stone Age, 24
  Magdalenian spear-point, 28
  Mesolithic technology in, 25
apples, initial cultivation of, 39, 60, 66
Apulian sites, ditch-enclosed, 59
Arbor Low, henge monument at, *112**
archaeology
  and prehistory, 13
  dates in, 11, 12
  dynamic character of, 2
  evidence for prehistoric Celtic Europe, 226-7, 229
  inter-disciplinary approach to, 9-10, 24-25
  prehistory and classical, 21
archer's wrist-guard, Bell-Beaker, *99*, 100
  archers, mounted, 182-4
Arcy-sur-Cure, tent-stances at, 29, *30*
Ares, Island of, 130
Argar culture, trade relations with, 129, 163
Argissa, pre-pottery Neolithic site at, 40-41
Argonauts, world of the, 140
Argos
  finds from, *191*, 192
  fire-dogs from, 247
armaments
  beginnings of competitive, 106-7
  Bronze Age, 134

Arminghall, rings of stones at, 115
armlet, gold, *129**
Arnuwandas IV, 159
arrow(s)
  buried with warriors, 102, 129
  depicted in cave-paintings, 33
  used in hunting, 29, 65, 66
  used in warfare, 182-3, 238
  with flint tips, 129
arrow-head(s)
  Bell-Beaker, *99*, 100, *101*
  bronze, 183, 189
  flint, *99*, *101*, 129
  iron, 183-4
art
  animal, 130, 132, 176-7, *192**, 241
  barbarian European, 259
  Celtic, 216, 241-3
  Chinese, 133, 176
  Cimmerian, 241
  early Celtic, 216
  naturalistic, of Advanced Palaeolithic cultures, 27, 176
  of Magdalenian culture, 28
  Sarmatian, 241
  Scythian, 133, 176-7, *176**, *177**, *240**, 241
  South Russian Timber-Grave, 130, 133, 176
  toreutic, 171
art-history and archaeology, 25
Aruișd, clay-rendered gable-end of house from, *55*, 56
Asenkofen, dress-pins from, *105*
Asia Minor, contribution of, to toreutic arts, 171
Asine, decorated object from, *135*
Assyria
  horse-bits, from 177
  kingdom of, 189
  mounted archers, 182-3
  records of the Gimmerai, 175
  trading colonies in Anatolia, 79, 141-2
  view of the Cimmerians, 256
Athenaeus, 227
Athens, beginnings of heroic age of, 123
Atkinson, R. J. C., 7, 260
Attic vase-paintings, 189, 192
Aulney-aux-Planches, sanctuary site at, 232, *234*
aurum Tolosanum, 231
Ausinius, 168
Ausonian II culture, settlement of, *152*
Australian aborigines, 28
Auxerre, tripod from, 194
Avdeevo, tent-stance at, 30, *31*
Avienus, 194
awl, copper, *84*
axe(s)
  buried with south-central European warriors, 102
  copper shaft-hole, 73, *74*, 74
  distribution of shaft-hole double-, *139*
  hafted stone, *115*
  iron double-, 192
  Mycenaean double bronze, 138, *139*
  south-central European use of, 104
  trade in stone, 64
axe-adzes:
  copper, 73-74, *74*, *82*
  distribution of, *75*
axe-blades:
  bronze, *128*, 129
  copper, 74;
  distribution of shaft-hole, *75*
  flint, 24, 63
  grinding of, 24
  making of, 63
  of pre-pottery Neolithic cultures, 26
  polishing of, 24
  representation of stylised stone, *70**
  stone, 39
axe-head, used in cultivation, 150

B

Baden culture
  advent of, 92
  evidence of domestication of the horse in, 95
  pottery model from, *97**
Bagendon, mint at, 252
Balestra, *torri* at, *157*
Balkans
  early cultures as homeland of the Indo-European languages, 80-81
  peasant communities in, 41, 44, 113
Balto-Slav language groups, 81
Bantu building in Southern Rhodesia, 140
barbarism
  and civilisation in prehistory, 3-4, 126
  civilisation as a development from, 18-19
  disparity between civilisation and, 16-17, 256-7
  of man, 14-15, 257
  relation to classical Europe, 21-22
  skills and inventions of, 35, 257-60
  technological parity between civilisation and, 16-19, 256-7
  value-judgments on, 19-20
Barca, houses at, 118, 126
Bar Hill, wheel, from, 244
Barkaer, Neolithic site at, 63

barley
  distribution of, 36, *38*
  growing, among Bell-Beaker people, 102
  initial cultivation in Europe, 40-41, 60
  varieties of, 39
basketry, development of, in Europe, 60, 69
Basse-Yutz, bronze flagon from, *215**
Bastarnae, 235
Battle-Axe people
  dispersion of, 84, 85
  house—types of, 89, 121
battle-axes
  jadeite, 130, *131*
  shaft-hole stone, 84, 89
  silver, 129
  stone, 92
battle-cars, 92, 141-2
Baudelaire, 14
bazaars, 216, 220
beads
  amber space-plate, 137, *137*
  distribution of faience, *136*
  distribution of space-plate, *138*
  glass, 136-7
  gold, from Mycenaean shaft-grave, *124*
  gold, from Únětice culture, *129**
  oriental faience, 129, *135*,* 136
  shale, *135**
  south-central European copper, *103*
beaker
  bell, *99*, *101*
  British, 100
  corded, from Bleckendorf, *84*
beans, initial cultivation of, 39, 60
bedding trenches, *50*, *53*
Beitzsch, bronze helmet from, 134, 154, 173
Belbury, anchor and chain from, 247
Belgium, finds from, 177, 179
Bell-Beaker culture
  burial rites of, 100
  clothing of, 105
  Eastern and central groups, *101*
  exploitation of gold and copper, 98, 100
  generalised distribution of, *101*
  hybrid pottery, 100
  'maritime groups', *101*
  mixing with indigenous cultures, 100
  movements of, 100-2, *101*, 118
  objects from graves, *99*, *101*
  origin of name, 7
  physical features of, 100, 102
  pottery of, 100, *112**
  Reflux movement, 100, *101*, 111, 129
  supersession of, 104
  survey of, 110-11
belt-hook, gold, *128*
benches, clay models of, 47
Benedict, Ruth, 18
Besançon, La Tène flagon from, *242*
Beveridge, W. I. B., 5
Bibracte, fortified settlement at, 218, 220, *221*
Binchy, D. A., 226, 227
Birdlip, bronze mirror from, *244**
Biskupin, fort at, 202, *208**, 209*
bits (horse), earliest appearance of, 95
Bituitus, 240
Bleckendorf, object from burial at, *84*
Bloch, Marc, 80, 260
Blučina, bone mounting from, *135**
boats
  carvings and diagrams of, 144-5, *144*, *144**
  Celtic, 249-50
  in use in second millenium, 144-5, 165
  invention of, 35, 66, 144
  plank-built, 187, *187*
  rowing, 144-5
  sails of, 250
body armour, development of, 134, 145-6, 166
Boian culture, distribution of, *59*
bone
  cheek-pieces, 95, *96*, 130, 136, 177
  distribution of decorated, objects, *136*
  flint-bladed tools, *42*
  from Stone Age, 24
  hammer-headed pin, *84*
  human comprehension and working in, 71
  Magdalenian barbed, 28
  Mesolithic technology in, 25
  mountings of sceptre, *128*
  objects of antler and, *135*, *135**, 136
Borodino, hoard at, 129-30, *131*
Bosnia, cemeteries in, 188
botanical climax, after Last Glacial Period, 31
botany
  and prehistory, 8-9, 64
  beginnings of agriculture and the natural factors of, 26, 27
Boudicca, 227
bowls
  bronze, *192**
  gold, *193**
  shallow handled, 253
  silver-gilt, 226
  stone, 40
  wooden, *144**, 145

bows
buried with warriors, 102
depicted in cave paintings, 33, *34*
long, 184
short, 184
used in hunting, 29, 65, 66
use in warfare, 182-4, 238
Brå, bronze mounting from, *245**
bracer, 100
Bredon, skulls from fort at, 230
Bridgeness, stone relief from, *256**
bridles
earliest appearance of, 95
ornaments, *176**
Britain
amber beads from, *137*
as a peninsula of Europe, 30
as the Island of the Albiones, 194
as the Pretanic Islands, 194
beginning of agriculture in, 63-64, 70
beginning of cremation in, 145
Bell-Beaker culture in, 100, *112**
bronze industries of, 120
bronze objects from, 138, 189, 194
burial sites, 63
Celtic houses in, 236-8
Celtic language in, 222-3
Celtic place-names in, 173
conservative use of the button, 105-6
contacts with Urnfield culture, 223
copper metallurgy in, 100
distinctive quality of Celtic, 227
domesticated horses in, 189
fortification techniques, 189, 216-21
henge monuments in, *112**, 115-16, *117*, 161, 232
house-plans in second millenium, 147
iron-working in, 189
jet buttons from, *104*
likely population about 7500 B.C., 32
metal resources of, 120
Mycenaean objects from, 136, *137*, 138
Mycenaean trade with, 137-8
Neolithic houses in, 63-64
red-deer hunting communities in, 31-32
ritual enclosures, 115-16
settlement pattern in 2000 B.C., 113
spoked-wheeled vehicles in, 189
stone-chambered tombs, 60-63, *62*
trade in Bronze Age, 129
trade routes in, 120
votive deposits, 230-1
wagon graves in, 180
Wessex culture burial objects, *128*
British Columbia
communal houses in, 52
Indians of, 35, 97
Brittany
metal resources of, 120
standing stones in, 115-16
trade routes in, 120
warrior graves in, 129
bronze
annealing of, 154
appreciation of the potentialities of, 72
arrowheads, 183, 189
axe-blades, *128*, 129
beaten vessels, 154-5
beginnings of metallurgy, 107
bowl, *192**
buckets, *see* situlae
cauldrons, *193*, 193-4, 195, 231
cire-perdue method of working, 171
corselet, 154, *191*, 192
crater, *184*, 195
cult vehicle, *177**, 181 ,194-5, 216, 239
cup, 172
dagger and halberd, *125*
daggers, *128*, 129, *129**
development of metallurgy, 44
distribution of beaten vessels, *154*
distribution of decorated 'situla' type, *170*
distribution of flange-hilted swords, *148*
distribution of Late Mycenaean, *139*
distribution of pans and wine flagons, *255*
distribution of Urnfield culture helmets, *169*
Eastern technology in, 64
enamelled, 247-8
establishment of workings in European localities, 78
Etruscan pyxis, 195
figures, 155, *155**, *200**
flagon, *215**, *241**
gold-hilted dagger, 129, *129**
Greek crater, 195
Hallstatt vessel, *192**
helmets, 134, 154, 169, 171, 173, 220, *241**
horse-bits, 177
hydria, 195, *200**
imported by Hallstatt cultures, *188*
industries of Britain and Brittany, 120
long swords, 189
mirror, *244**
mountings, *177**, *241**, *245**
objects from Russia, 172-3;
objects from 2000-1500 B.C., 118
Persian workers in, 177
prototypes of objects in, 102
rarity of components of, 72
razors, 199
rivets, *128*
-sheathed wheels, 196
shield, 154, *240**
situlae, *161**, 179

bronze *contd*
spiral-wound wire brooches, 172
sword, engraving of, boat on, 144, *144*
swords and rapiers, 123, 222
technology and the invention of the spoked wheel, 141
trade and the development of metallurgy in, 106
trade in, 118, 120, 192
transalpine trade in, 192, 216
Unětice culture objects, 123, *125*, 126
use in Timber Grave cultures, 175
use in 2000 B.C., 118
version of iron swords, 188
votive deposits, 230
wine flagons, 195, *215**, 216 *241**
working as a feature of an undivided Indo-European homeland, 80
working in central Europe, 89, 91, 169
working in north Italy, 155
working in Scandinavia, 155-6
Bronze Age
as a model of the past, 6
Early European, 111, 118
Early Iron and Late, 174-5, 185
end of, 188-9
flint-bladed bone tools from, *42*
Homer and, 126
Middle, 118
brooch(es)
La Tène, 222
spiral-wound wire, 172
sub-Mycenaean, Cypriot and Levantine types, 168
Budakalász, pottery models of wagons from, *93*, *97**
Buhen, horse burial at, 142
Bulgaria
conserving peasant communities in, 44
Karanovo site, *42*, 44, *45*, *47*, *47**, 89, 91, *97**, *112**, 121
'tell' settlements in 46-47, 49, 91, 258
burial(s)
and warfare, 238-41
Asiatic steppe, 84, 89, 185
at Vix, 89, *184*, 187, 188, 195, *200**, 244
Bell-Beaker, 100
cart, 178-9, 195, 215, 238
Celtic, 196, 207, 215-6, 232, *233*, *234*, 235
chariot, 179-80, *208*, 215, 220, 238-41, 261
Cimmerian, 179-80, 184-5
Corded Ware and allied cultures, 89
cremation, 145, 168
gypsy, 196
Kurgan culture, 81-82, 84, 130
La Tène, 215-16, 232, *233*, *234*, 235, 238-41
Near Eastern, 102
Northern European, 115-16, *116*
North Pontic culture, 175
of fleeces and hides, 130, 226, 259
of women, showing position of dress-pins, *105*
Phrygian, 159
Scythian, 89, 176
south-central European, 102
South Russian Timber Grave, 130, 175, 176
Viking, 89
see also graves, stone chambered tombs
burnous, 104-6
Buryet, tent-stance at, 30
Bush Barrow, objects from, *128*, 134
Butterwick, jet buttons from, *104*
buttons
clothing fastened with, 102, 104-5
jet, *104*
use in Britain, 105-6
Byblos, copper objects from, 102
Bylany, Linear Pottery houses at, *50**, 52

C

Cadmus, 123
Caergwrle, wooden bowl from, *144**, 145
Caesar, 216, 218, 223, 227, 235, 247, 250, 252, 253
Capel Garmon, fire-dog from, *252**
Capo Graziano culture, settlement of, *145**, *152*
Caribou Eskimos, 28
Carlingwark, votive deposits from, 231
Carnac, stone alignments at, *62**
carnelian, from Kurgan culture graves, 82
Carniola, cemeteries in, 188
carnyx, boar-headed, 207
Carpathians
bronze industry in, 118
contacts with Scandinavia, 226
distribution of Mycenaean objects in, 136
'factories' in, 106
peasant communities in, 113
Carpenter, Rhys, 21, 126
carpentry, use of iron tools, in, 187
Carpini, 89
Carr, E. H., 5
cart(s)
as vehicles with two wheels, 92
burials, 178-80, 195, 215, 238
Celtic, 244-6
distinction between wagons and, in Akkadian and Sumerian languages, 92
evidence of early existence in Europe, 92, 95

cart(s) *contd*
horse-drawn, 141-2
Indo-European languages and the dispersal of, 95
models of, 95
modern distribution of, in Europe, 95
rock-carvings of, 142-4, *143*
solid-wheeled wooden, 82, 109, 141-2
wheels, in burials, *83*
zone, 95, 244
Carthaginians, 193
Cartimandua, 227
carving(s)
first representational stone, 123
of Advanced Palaeolithic hunting communities, 27
of boat, on sword-blade, 144, *144*
of boats, on rock, 144-5, *144**
of chariots and carts, 142-4, *143*
of dagger at Stonehenge, 139
relief, at Courjeonnet, *115*
rock, 142-5, *143*, *144**, 150
spiral relief at Tarxien, 98, *112**
stone monuments in Corsica, 155
casques, conical, 195
castles, Sardinian, *see nuraghi*
Çatal Hüyük
cold-hammered copper at, 72, 107
extent of, 17
woollen textiles, at 36
cattle
as wealth, 235-6
distribution of, *37*
domestication as a feature of an undivided Indo-European homeland, 80, 81
domestication by Bell-Beaker people, 102
grazing and slash-and-burn cultivation, 51-52
initial domestication of, in Europe, 41, 60
kraal at Anlo, 85, *87*
kraal, Bell Beaker, 102
Cattle-Raid of Cooley, 235
cauldrons
as objects of wealth, 235
bronze, *193**, 193-4, 195, 231
copies, of 194
Danish ritual silver, 226
hanger for, 247
mountings, *245**
ritual, 193, 195, 226
silver, *219**, 226
tripods of, *193**, 193, 194, 195
cavalry sport, 240-1
cave-paintings, 33, *33*, *34*
cave shelters
naturalistic art on walls of, 27, 28
of Magdalenian culture, 28
of Natufian culture, 40
Cayla de Mailhac, fortified site at, 223
Celtic
agriculture, 250, 252
art, 216, 241-3
beginning of the last phase of, culture, 215
boats, 249-50
burial customs, 196, 207, 215-16, 232, *233*, *234*, 235
chariot warfare, 215
clothing, 240, 249
coinage, 252, 253
common culture, 244, 247
conditional literacy, 253-5
crafts, 244-7
economy, 236-8
field systems, 250, *251*
fortifications, 216-21
houses, 236-8, *237*
iconography, 230
influence in central Europe, 223
influence in France, 223
influence in Iberia, 223
influence in Ireland, 222
influence in Scandinavia, 226
influence in Scotland, 222-3
languages, 79, 81, 173-4, 222-3
movement of peoples, 235
pastoral nomadism and agriculture, 243-4
peoples, antecedents of, 107, 168
place-names, distribution of, *172*, *173*, 173-4, *174*
religion, 229-35
Roman view of, 223-4, 226-7, 229, 256, 260
society, structure of, 196, 207, 226-7, 229, 255-6
-speaking Hallstatt cultures, 187-8
use of chariots, 142
warfare, 215, 216, 238-41
world and its aftermath, 215-60
see also La Tène
cemeteries
Celtic, 232, *233*, *234*, 235
in Hungary, Transylvania and the Balkans, 145, 188
of copper 'colonies', in Iberia, 74, *76*, 77
of Hallstatt cultures, 187-8, *234*
of hunting and fishing communities, 35
of Urnfield culture, *234*
open, 145
cereals
distribution of, 36, *38*, 39
evidence from Near East for initial cultivation of, 40
initial cultivation of, 36, 39, 40
secondary, 39

Cernavoda, pottery figures from, *51**
Cevazy, decorated bone object from, *135*
chains, iron, 247
chairs, clay models of, 47
Chalandriani, bastioned defences of, 76, *77*
chambered tombs, *see* stone-chambered tombs
change, climax and, 113-60
chariot(s)
  burials, 179-80, *208*, 215, 220, 238-41, 261
  buried with warriors, 144, 179-80, 195
  Celtic, 244-6
  representation on situlae, 144
  rock carvings of, 142-4, *143*
  spoked-wheeled, 130, 142
  use in warfare, 142, 215, 240-1
Chassey-Cortaillod cultures, distribution of main sites of, *58*
cheek-pieces
  antler, 130, *132*, 177, 179
  bone, 95, *96*, 130
  decorated antler and bone, 136, 177
  metal, 177
  wooden, *178**
chieftain(s)
  burials, 215-61
  houses, 199, 201
  in Celtic society, 227
    see also warrior
Childe, Gordon, 6, 7, 13, 25, 126
China
  animal art of, 133, 176
  invention of the horse-collar in, 181
  use of trousers in, 238
  view of Huns, 256
chiton, 104-6
chronology
  methods used in dating, 11-12
  of Advanced Palaeolithic cultures, 27-28
  of Glacial Period, 27
Cicero, 21-22
Cimbri, 235
Cimmerians
  adoption of cavalry, 181
  art of, 241
  Assyrians' view of, 256
  forebears of, 118
  identity of, 175
  metal horse-bits and harness-mountings, 177-9, *179*
  migration of, 177
  war tactics, 181
Circumpolar Zone
  influence on Skara Brae planning, 64
  survival of hunting communities in, 27, 35
Cirna
  cemetery at, 145
  figurines from, 157, *158*, 199
Citania, hill-fort at, *224*
cities
  rise of, in Mediterranean, 141
  size of ancient, 121-2
city-state, rise of the, 141, 189
civilisation
  and barbarism in prehistory, 3-4, 126
  as an abnormal event, 20
  technological advances among literate, 64
  technological parity between barbarism and, 16-19, 256-7
  value-judgments on, 19-20
  viewed as a normal development from barbarism, 18-19
Clacton, spear-tip from, 29
Clark, Grahame, 9, 13, 21, 28
clay models, 47, 114
Clegyr Boia, rectangular houses at, 63
climate
  beginnings of modern conditions of, 27, 30-31
  distribution, of animals under modern conditions of, 35-36, *37*
  modification of architecture in response to changed, 44, 46
  Stone Age, 24
climax and change, 112-60
clothing
  basic types of, 104-6, 111
  Celtic, 240, 249
  fastening of, 102, 104-6, 172
  gold plate from, *128*
  in second millennium, 156-7
  of Hallstatt cultures, 197, 198, 199
  woollen, 156-7, *160**
coachbuilding, 244-6
coalitions in the second millennium, 140-1
coinage, 252, 253
Colchester
  mint at, 252
  pots from, 254
Colchis
  expedition to, 140
  Golden Fleece in Pontic, 130
Collingwood, R. G., 11, 19, 243
Commius, 227
communities
  aggression and the formation of, 14-15
  means of acquiring knowledge of, 2, 10-11

communities *contd*
  readjustment to natural conditions, 27
  types of, 2
confederacies in the second millenium, 140-1
conserving societies
  Celts as, 255, 256-7, 259
  coexistence of literate innovating and, 21-22
  crafts and inventions of, 35, 258-9
  distinction between innovating and, 17-18, 73
  Neolithic agricultural peasantry as, 44
  of hunting communities, 27
  of hunting-fishing communities in the Circumpolar Zone, 35
  use of wheeled vehicles in, 92
consolidation, trade, metal-working and, 71-107
copper
  adze, *82*
  Aegean industry, 73, 74, 76-77, 107-8, 113
  awl, *84*
  axe-adzes, 73-74, *74*, *82*
  axe-blades, 74
  beads, *103*
  beginnings of metallurgy, 107
  casting of, 72, 98
  cire perdue method of casting, 72
  cold-hammering of, 71-72, 107
  'colonies' in Iberia, *see* Copper 'colonies' in Iberia
  daggers, *84*, *99*, *128*
  deep-mining of, 155, 171
  development of metallurgy, 44
  distribution of earliest Transylvanian industry, 75, 113
  Eastern technology in, 64
  establishment of trading centres in Europe, 78
  establishment of workings in European localities, 78
  figures, *71**, 72
  ingot-torcs, 102, *103*
  knives, riveted, *103*
  metallurgy and the development of trade, 106
  metallurgy in Bell-Beaker culture, *99*, 100
  metallurgy in Britain, 100
  Mycenaean sources of, 134, 137
  objects from Karanova, 46
  objects from Maikop grave, 82
  occurrence of, in Old World, 71, 72
  open-mould casting, 98
  ore, sources of, *75*, 102-3, 118, 120, 134, 137
  ornaments, 74, 102, *103*, 104
  pin, Bell-Beaker, *99*
  pin, dress, 74
  pins, south-central European, 102, *103*
  pins with double-spiral head, 74, *75*
  pin-types common to Iberia and the Aegean, 76
  rings, *103*
  shaft-hole axes, 73, *74*, 74
  smelting of, 72
  south-central European cultures' use of, 102-3, *103*
  spread of centres and the Indo-European languages, 78
  tanged knife-dagger, *99*
  tools, 64, 74, 102, 104
  trade in, 73-74, 91
  use of, in 2000 B.C., 118
  —using agriculturalists of South Russia, 81-82
  weapons, 102
  working, *see* copper-working
copper 'colonies' in Iberia
  bastioned defences of settlements 76-77, *77*, 98
  distribution of objects, *76*
  links with the Aegean, 74, 76-77, *77*
  origin of, 74, 76, 97, 106, 113, 120
  pin-types common to the Aegean and, 76
  smelting and working in, 77
copper-working
  as a feature of an undivided Indo-European homeland, 80
  in Anatolia, 73, 107
  in Britain, 100, 120
  in Brittany, 120
  in central Europe, 89, 91
  in Crete, 73
  in Europe, 118
  in Hungary, Rumania, and Slovakia, 73-74, 97, 113
  in Iberia, 77
  in Ireland, 120
  in Sardinia, 155
  in South Russia, 74, 175
  in the Aegean, 73, 107-8, 113
  in the Tyrol, 155, 196
  of Bell-Beaker culture, 98
Corded Ware culture
  and indigenous cultures, 91
  beaker of, *84*
  clothing of, 105
  dispersion of peoples, 84, 85
  finds of horse bones from sites, 96
  generalised distribution of, *86*
  house—types of, 89, *90*
  impact of Bell-Beaker people on, 100, 102

Corded Ware culture *contd*
mortuary houses of, *87*, *88*
pottery of, *84*, 84, 85, 100
supercession of, 104
Corinthian vase-painting, 189, 192
corn, grinding of, 250
Cornford, F. M., 1, 22
corselet
beaten bronze, 154
bronze, *191*, 192
Corsica
carved stone monuments of, 155
torri of, 155, *157*
Cortes de Navarra, settlement at, 201
Cos, 196
couches, clay models of, 47
Courjeonnet, relief carvings at, *115*
Court-St-Etienne, finds in cemetery at, 177, *179*
crafts
barbarian, 35, 258-9
Celtic, 244-7
crannog, 236
Crannon, situla at, 181
crater, Greek bronze, 195
Crawford Moor, jet buttons from, *104*
cremation
as an alternative to inhumation, 145
Urnfield rites of, 168
Crestaulta, houses at, 118, *119*
Crete
copper-working in, 73
iron objects in, 186
Minoan period, 120-3, 134
Mycenaean assumption of power in, 134
timber-laced structures in, 204
Croatia, cemeteries in, 188
crop-growing
among Kurgan culture, 81-82
as a feature of an undivided Indo-European homeland, 80
beginnings of, in Scandinavia, 62-63
Celtic, 250, 252
conditions for transition from food-gathering to, 26
initial stages of, 36, 39, 40, 258
in Mesolithic Palestine, 40
slash-and-burn cultivation and, 51-52, 62-63
crops
generalised distribution of wild, *38*
implements for cutting, 40
manuring of, 39
yields and consumption, 47, 49, 252
Cú Chulainn, 227, 240, 241
Cueva Remegia, cave paintings at, 33, *33*, *34*
cult figures, 114, 115
cultivation, slash-and-burn, 51-52, 62-63
see also, agriculture, crop-growing
cult-sites, 230-4
culture
barbarism of man and material, 14-15
patterns, incompatibility of, 256-7
patterns, introduced by Steppe peoples, 89, 91
traits, 19
traits, borrowing of, 35
unequal development of material, 15-16
cultures
common vocabulary of, and Indo-European languages, 79, 80
definition of, 7
identity of, 18
in Europe in 2000 B.C., 113-18
naming, of 7
urban, of East Europe and Near East, 113
'cult vehicle', *177**, 181, 194-5, 216, 239
Cumae
colony at, 189
iron objects from, 186
cup(s)
amber, 129
bronze drinking, 154-5, 172
distribution of beaten bronze, *154*
gold, 129, 134, *134**
Greek painted, 195
pottery, 134
silver-gilt, 226
Vapheiro, 134
wooden drinking, 187
currency, 246, 252
cursus
at Dorchester-on-Thames, *117*, 232
enclosures, 115, 232
Cyprus
brooch-types, 168
chariot-burials in, 238
fire-dogs, 192, 247
pre-pottery Neolithic culture in, 40
twisted ear-rings, 138
Czechoslovakia
Bell-Beaker peoples in, 100
decorative antler and bone objects from, *135*, 136
tin deposits of, 118
Únetice culture in, 123
wagon-graves in, 180, 186

D

Dacia
  silver and gold objects from, *224**, 226
Dacians
  stone relief depicting, *253**
  tattooing practice among, 239
dagger(s)
  blade, riveted into haft, 102
  bronze, *128*, 129, *129**
  buried with warriors, 102
  carving at Stonehenge, 139
  copper, *84*, *99*, *128*
  gold-hilted bronze, 129, *129**
  iron, 185
  of Perşinari, 129, *129**
  replaced by other weapons, 145
  south-central European peoples' use of, 104
  Únětice bronze, 123, *125*, 126
  used in fighting, *147*
Danaus, 123
Daniel, G. E., 19
Danubian culture
  absence of evidence of religious cults, 114
  as the undivided homeland of Indo-European languages, 80-81
  impact of steppe peoples on, 91-92
  long houses of, *50**, 52, 84, 85, 89, 113, 118, 150
  settlement pattern of, 113, 147
  see also Linear Pottery culture
Danuna, 159
Dares Phrygius, 168
Darius, 176
Dawson, Christopher, 13
de Chardin, Teilhard, 6
De Eese, wooden wheel from, *96**
Dejbjerg, votive wagon from, 244
Denmark
  copper tools in Neolithic, 64, 74
  excavation of kitchen-middens in, 25
  flint-bladed bone tools from, *42*
  influences in, 262
  link with Kurgan culture, 84
  number of stone-chambered tombs in, 60
  temples in, 115, *116*
  trade with rest of Europe, 120
  votive deposits from, 230-1
Deskford, war trumpet from, 207
despotism, development of Oriental, 44
Deve Hüyük, horse-bits from, 177
Deverel-Rimbury culture, settlements of, *152*, *153*, 165
Dhlo-Dhlo, 140
Dictys Cretensis, 168
Dillon, M., 226
Dimini, *megara* at, 121, *122*, 161
Diodorus, 227
discs
  bone and antler, 136
  distribution of decorated silver, 226
dish, silver, of Theodosius I, *257**, 260
ditch-enclosed settlements in Italy, 59
dog, domestication of the
  for hunting, 26, 33, 35, 65
  for pastoralism, 35, 36
  initial, in Europe, 41
dolls, 114
Dolni Vĕstonice, tent-stance at, 30
domestic animals
  excavation of remains of, 24-25
  of pre-pottery Neolithic cultures, 26
domestication of animals
  among Kurgan cultures, 81-82
  and the economic bases of communities, 25
  as a feature of an undivided Indo-European homeland, 80
  conditions necessary for, 26, 35-36
  dating of earliest, 40, 41
  earliest, 25, 66
  factors limiting area of initial, 36
  for agriculture, 35-36, *37*
  for transport, 36
  herding as first, 36, 39-40
  origin of, in Near East, 39-40, 41
  see also cattle, dog, goat, horse, sheep
Donnersberg, hill-fort at, *218*
Dorchester-on-Thames, henge monument at, *112**, *117*, 232
Dorians, migration of, 189
Dorset, excavation of domestic animal remains in, 25
Downton, post-glacial settlement, at 33
dress-pin, copper, with double-spiral head, 74
drinks, fermented, 39, 66
Druids
  place in society, 227
  religion of, 230, 232, 234
Duchcov, votive offerings from, 231
Dullenried
  house-plans, at, *90*
  settlement at, 89
Dürnsberg, hill-fort at, 218
Durrnberg, textiles from, 197

E

Early Neolithic, use of term, 26
Early Pit-Grave culture, generalised distribution of, *86*
ear-ring
  Bell-Beaker gold, *101*
  Bell-Beaker silver, *99*
  Cypriot style twisted, 138
  gold, *101*, *129**
  silver, *99*
East European
  agricultural communities, 40-49, 56, 113
  communities, absence of evidence of religious cults, 113-14
ecology, and prehistory, 24-25
Écury-le-Repos, sanctuary at, *233*
edge-tools
  flint and stone as criterion of Stone Age, 24
  iron, 185
Egolzwil, Swiss lake-dwellings at, 57-58
Egypt
  advances in metallurgy, 64
  break up of central authority in, 78, 116, 118
  copper smelting and casting in, 72-73, 113
  glass beads from, 136-7
  kingdom of, 113
  Neolithic reaping-knife from, *42*
  rise of Mycenae to power and, 134
  social organisation in, 113
  warfare in, 142
Eildon Fort, 220
elk, advent of the, 31
Elp, settlement at, 147
Elsloo, Linear Pottery house at, *50**
Emain Macha, 227
enamelling of metal, 220, 221, 247-8
enclosures, 115-16
England
  estimated population of Late Glacial, 28
  post-glacial settlement in, 33
  see also Britain
Ensérune, promontory fort at, 223
Entremont
  oppidum at, *218**, *222*, 223
  sanctuary at, *218*, 230
Eskelhem, hoard at, 179
Eskimos:
  clothing of, 104
  cold-hammering of meteoric iron, 71
  habitation and food supply, 28
Essé, megalithic chambered tomb at *62**
Etruscan(s)
  bronze manufacture, 154, 195
  bronze, pyxis, 195
  chariot construction, 238
  objects in Hallstatt graves, 185
  origins of, 192-3
  situlae from tombs, 171
  trade with, 195
evidence
  and models of the past, 5-7
  botanical, 8-9
  handling of, 2, 10-11
  interpretation of, 5-8
  nature of archaeological, 4-5, 7-8
  reliance on other disciplines, 9-10
  zoological, 9
excavation
  chronology and, 11-12
  problems of, 10-11
'Eynan, houses at, 40, *41*

F

fabrics, woven, 82
facts, interpretations of, 5-6, 7
faience
  beads, 129, *135**, 136
  distribution of beads, *136*
  ornaments, 136
farmstead units, 199, 201, 236, *237*, 244
Farnham, post-glacial settlement at, 33
fashion
  as a factor linking Eurasia, 74
  see also clothing
Fayum, shield from, 239, *240**
feast
  Celtic, 229
  concept of the other-world, 192, 195, 247, 253
feats, 240-1
Fécamp, hill-fort at, *206*
Fertile Crescent, basis of peasant economies of, 40
feudal
  land-tenure in prehistory, 80-81
  obligations, 129, 140-1, 227, 229
fibre, from Stone Age, 24
field
  cross-ploughed, *145**
  systems, 250, *251*
Figheldean Down, field system at, *251*
figurines and figures
  alabaster, *114*
  bronze, Hallstatt, *200*
  bronze, Sardinian, 155, *155**
  clay, from Near East, 114
  copper, *71*, 72

figurines and figures *contd*
  evidence of clothing from, 157, *158*
  limestone, *114*
  Near Eastern and East European, 49
  Neolithic pottery, *48*
  pottery from Rumania and Jugoslavia, 157, *158*, 199
  Tisza culture, *50*, *51**
  Tripolye culture, 54
Final Mesolithic culture, 25
Fin d'Ecury, sanctuary at, *233*
Finley, Moses, 20
Finsterlohr, hill-fort at, *206*
fire-dogs
  Greek Geometric period, 192
  distribution of La Tène, *248*
  iron, from Argos, *191*
  La Tène culture, 192, 247, *252**, 265
  ox-headed iron, 247
fishing communities
  adoption of agriculture in Scandinavia, 62-63
  art of, 113, 133, 176
  coexistence with agricultural communities, 64, 97
  continuation of traditions, 35
  crafts and inventions of, 35, 258-9
  economic basis of, 25
  in Mesolithic cultures, 25, 66
  permanent settlements of, 35
  post-glacial settlement of, 33
flagons, bronze wine-
  distribution of imported, *208*
  distribution of Roman, *255*
  engraved decoration on, *242*
  imported by Hallstatt cultures, 195
  imported by La Tène culture, *215**, 216, *241**, 253
flax
  growing by Bell-Beaker peoples, 102
  initial cultivation of, 39, 60, 66
fleeces
  burial in graves, 130, 259
  Golden Fleece in Pontic Colchis, 130
Fleure, *Corridors of Time*, 13
flint
  arrow-heads, *99*, *101*, 129
  axe-blades, grinding and polishing of, 24
  Bell-Beaker arrow-heads, *99*, *101*
  -bladed bone tools, *42*
  -bladed reaping knives, 40, *42*
  domestication of animals and Mesolithic equipment, 26
  equipment at Argissa, 41
  human comprehenson and working in, 71
  implements of pre-pottery Neolithic cultures, 40
  mining of, in western Europe, 64
  new techniques for manufacturing instruments, 27
  trade in, 72
  use of, for edge-tools as criterion of Stone Age, 24
Foce, *torri* at, *157*
Font-de-Gaume, art at, 28
food
  consumption and crop yields, 47, 49, 252
  efficiency of acquiring, 27-28
  estimated availability of, 32
  introduction of salted, 171
  modification of gear to requirements for, 27-28
  readjustment of societies and 27
  red deer as main source of, 31-32
  reindeer as main source of, 28-29, 31
food-gathering communities
  conditions for transition to agricultural economy, 26, 35-39
  definition between food-producing and, 26
  economic basis of, 25
  general characteristics of final, 26-35
  in the leanest season, 28
food-producing communities
  conditions for transition from food-gathering to, 26, 35-39
  definition between food-gathering and, 26
  economic basis of, 25
Forbes, Duncan, 229, 257
forest clearance and agriculture, 51-52, 62-63
Fortetsa, iron objects from, 186
fortifications
  Aegean, 76-77, *77*
  brick-work, 204-5, *205*
  Celtic, 216-21
  copper 'colonies' in Iberia, 76-77, *77*, 98
  development of, 201-7
  Greek techniques of, 195
  La Tène, 216-21, 236, 246-7
  murus gallicus, 216, *217*, 218, 220, 236, 246, 247
  techniques in Britain, 189, 216-21
  timber-framed ramparts, 202, *203*, 204, *208**, *209**, 216
forts
  as emergency strongholds, 202
  defence of, 202, 207
  promontory, 202, 207, 223
  see also hill-forts
France
  bronze-using cultures in, 188
  Celtic culture in, 223
  Celtic place-names in, 173

France *contd*
first agricultural settlements in, 57
hill-forts in, 223
Mycenaean objects in, 136
salt-production in, 248
stone-chambered tombs in, 60, 61, 62, *62**, *63**, *70**
stone sanctuaries in, 230, 232, *233*, *234*, 243
wagon graves in, 180
Frankfort, Henri, 6, 19
Frånnap, rock-carvings at, *143*
French archaeologists'
definition of prehistory, 3
ecological approach, 24-25, 27
L'Âge du Renne, 27
Fritzdorf, gold cup from, 134, *134**
fruits, initial cultivation of, 39
furniture, clay models of, 47
furs, trade in, 120
Füszesabony culture, finds from, *132*

G

Gagarino, tent-stance at, 30
gallery graves, 61
gateways, 'inturned', *206*, 207
Gav'r Inis, chambered tomb at, 61, 62, *70**
Gela, fortifications at, 204
Geleen, houses of Linear Pottery at, 50*
geography
as limiting the area of initial domestication, 36
of the Last Glacial Period, 30-31
Stone Age, 24
geology, time scale and archaeology, 24
Germanic
language groups, 81, 223
peoples, antecedents of, 107
society, movement of, 227, 229, 235-6
Germany
arrival of Bell-Beaker people in, 100
post-glacial settlements in, 33
reindeer-hunters of, 28-29
tent-stances in, 30
Urnfield culture in, *149*, *151*
votive offerings in, 230
Ggantija, temple at, 97, *98*
Giant's Springs, votive offerings from, 231
Gimmerai, 175
glaciation
dating of Würm, 27
end of late glacial period, 27
population in late glacial period, 28
glass beads, distribution of, 135-7
Glastonbury
Iron Age settlement at, 122, 236
wheel from, 244
Globular Amphorae culture
arrival in Europe, 84
generalised distribution of, *86*
house-types of, 89
goats
distribution of, 36, *37*
domestication of, by Kurgan culture people, 81
domestication of, in Palestine, 40
herding of, 39-40
initial domestication of, 36, 39-40
gold
acquisition of, by Mycenaeans, 133-4, 137
armlet, *129**
bead, 124, *129**
Bell-Beaker people's exploitation of, 100, *101*
belt-hook, *128*
bowl, *193**
bulls, *82*
coins, *252*
cups, 129, 134, *134**
Dacian objects in, **226**
dagger, *129**, 129
ear-rings, 101, *129**
Eastern technology in, 64
finds in Hallstatt graves, **187**, *188*
finds in Maikop grave, 82
finds in Mycenaean shaft-graves, 123, *124*
helmet, *224**, 226
-hilted bronze dagger, 129, *129**
jewellery, Irish, 138
lion appliqué, *82*
maces, 129
mask of Mycenaean culture, *113**
neck-ring, *193**
objects, distribution of, 91
offerings of Toulouse, 230
ornaments, 123, 124, 129, *131*
pendant, *124*
Persian workers in, 177
pins, *124*, *129**
plate from clothing, 128
prospecting for, 73
resources of Britain, Brittany and Ireland, 120
ring, *147*
shoulder-cape, 157
spear-head, *131*
stag of Zoldshalompuszta, 182
trade and development of, metallurgy, 106
work of Wessex culture, 134

Goldberg
  house-plans at, 90, *199*
  village site at, 89, *200*
Goloring, sanctuary site at, 232
Gordion, tumuli at, 159
Grächwil, bronze hydria from, 195, *200**
grain
  -growing by pre-pottery Neolithic cultures, 26
  -growing, and classification of cultures, 25
  storage pits, 228
  see also crops
Grand Congluè, wreck off, 253
grasslands
  and the domestication of animals, 36
  beginnings of, 31
graves
  barrow, 81-82, 83, 89, 175
  barrow, earthen unchambered long, 63
  barrow, of ochre-grave type, 84
  Bell-Beaker, 100
  cart, 179-80, 195, 215, 238
  Celtic, 195, 196, 207, 215-16, 232, *233*, *234*, 235
  chariot, 179-80, *208*, 215, 220, 238-41, 261
  Early Pit culture, *84*, 115
  evidence from, in 2000-1500 B.C., 118-40
  gallery, 61
  hut, 123
  Kurgan, 81-82, 84, 130
  La Tène, *208*, 227, 228, 232, *233*, *234*, 235, 238-41
  mortuary enclosures, *117*
  mortuary houses, 82, 84, *87*, *88*, 89, *127*, 159, 175, 176, 179-80, 184-5, 195, 196, 201
  Mycenaean shaft-, 81, *113**, 123, *124*, 133-4, 137, *137*, 162
  ochre, 84
  passage, 61
  plank-built chambered, 183, *184*, *186*, 187
  rock-cut, 197, *112**
  Scandinavian, 63
  Scythian, 89
  steppe, 84, 89, 185
  stone-chambered, 60-62, *61*, *62*, *62**, 63, *63**, 77, 114-15
  stone cists, 63
  Timber, 123, 130, 175
  tree-trunk coffins, *88*
  tumulus, 129, 145
  Únětice culture, *127*
  Urnfield culture, 145, 168, 232, *234*
  Viking, 89
  wagon, 179-80, *180*, 184-5, *183*, *184*, *186* 205, 207, 215, 238
  warrior, of heroic world, 126-33
  see also burial
Graz, bronze figure from, *200**
greaves, from Dacian tomb, 226
Greece
  beginning of, 107
  beginning of historical, 189, 192
  Dark Ages of, 189
  decorated antler and bone objects from, *135*
  destruction of townships, 78, 118, 121
  development of the *megaron*, 89, 121, *122*
  Early Helladic II period, 121
  fortified settlements in, 121
  Geometric period finds, *191*
  import of amber, 137, *137*
  import of copper, 73
  iron objects from, 186
  Middle Helladic period, 121, 123
  Mycenaean *see* Mycenae
  palaces, 121
  peasant communities of northern, 113
  pre-pottery Neolithic culture in, 40-41, 44
  relation of barbarian Europe to, 21-22
  slavery in, 20
  south-central European cultures and, 106
Greek
  art, 243
  black-figure pottery, 204
  bronze crater, *184*, 195
  colony at Massalia, 188, 195, 223
  development of the language, 79
  document in Linear B relating to land-tenure, 80
  geometric vases, 181
  objects in Hallstatt graves, 185, *188*
  painted cups, 195
  painted vases, 195
  palace bureaucracies, 81
  script, 189
  three main dialects, of, 79
  writers on the Celts, 226-7, 229
Grossgartach, coloured wall-plaster from, 46-47
Grotte de Renne
  post-holes, 29, *30*
  tent-stances at, 29, *30*
Grousset, R., 230
Grünhof-Tesperheide, mortuary-house at, *88*
Gumelniţa culture, houses of, *97**
Gundestrup
  silver cauldron from, *219**, 226
  votive deposits from, 231
Guti, 78
Gwithian, houses at, *145**, 150
gypsy burial rites, 196

H

Habaşeşti, Tripolye culture site at, *54*
Hagar Qim, figures and models from, 114
Hagighiol, tomb at, 226
hair
  styles, 199
  use of false, 156
hair-nets, 156
hair-rings, Egyptian penannular, 138
halberd, bronze metal-shafted, *125*, 126, 162
Haldon, rectangular houses at, 63
Hallstatt culture
  art, 241
  background of, 174-5
  bowl, *193**
  bronze razor, 199
  clothing, *192**, 197, 198, 199
  dating of, 195
  distribution of, imports and luxuries, *188*
  distribution of sites of salt production, *170*
  fortifications, 205, *205*
  helmets, 195, 239
  houses, 201, *201*, 236
  imports of, 187-8, *188*, 195
  industrial aspect of society, 196
  iron swords, 186, 188
  Mycenae and, 175
  origin of name, 7
  plank-built burial chamber, *186*
  pottery, 196-7, *197*, *198*, 199
  sanctuary sites, 232, *234*
  salt production, *170*, 171, 187
  Scythian trade contacts with, 189
  settlements, 199, *200*, 201
  vessel, *192**
  wagons, 244, 245
  wagon graves, 179, *180*, *183*, *184*
Hal Saflieni
  figurines and models from, *114*
  rock-cut temple at, *112**
harness-mountings
  Bavarian type, 177
  distribution of, 177, *178*, 181
  metal, 177, *179*
Hattusilis III, 186
Hatten, pyxis from, 195
Hatti
  commercial association with Anatolia, 79
  social organisation of, 81
Hawkes, Christopher, 13
Hayhope Knowe, fort at, 204
head-hunting, 230
Heathery Burn, finds at, 179
Heath Row
  site at, 199
  temple at, 232, *233*
Hebrews, 189
Heichelheim, F. M., 15
Heidentränk-Talenge, hill-fort at, *218*
helmet(s)
  beaten bronze, 154
  bell, 169, 171, 239
  Beitzsch, 134, 154, 173
  bronze, 134, 154, 169-71, 220, *241**
  cap, 169, 171
  conical, 181, 239
  crested, 169, 191, *191*, 192
  distribution of bell, *169*
  distribution of cap, *169*
  distribution of crested, *169*
  distribution of Urnfield, 169, *169*, 171, 172-3
  from Dacian tombs, *224**, 226
  gold, *224**, 226
  Hallstatt, 195, 239
  La Tène, 239, 241
  Mycenaean model of, 134
  pointed, 239
  silver, *224**
Helmsdorf, warrior grave at, 129
Helvetii, 235
Hembury, hill-fort at, *206*
henge monuments in Britain, *112**, 115-16, *117*, 161, 232
herding
  as the first animal domestication, 36, 39-40
  Celtic, 243
Herodotus, 175, 176, 181, 182, 193, 238
Hesiod, 106, 189
Heuneburg
  finds at, 195, 196
  fortification at, 195
  hill-fort at, 187, 188, 204, 205, *205*, *214**
  timber-built houses at, 201, *201*
hides, burial of, in graves, 130, 226, 259
High Barbarian phase
  beginning of, 107, 118
  contacts with Mycenae, 134
  spheres of Mycenaean influence in, 137-8
hill-fort(s)
  at Hohensiedlung Burg, 179
  at Mont Lassois, 187, 193
  Celtic, 236
  development of, 207
  in France, 223
  in Iberia, 223, *224*
  inturned gateways of, *206*, 207
  murus gallicus, 216, *217*, 218, 220, 236, 246, 247

hill-fort(s) *contd*
 number of, 220
 of *oppidum* status, 216, *218*, 218, *219*, 220, *221*, *222*
 Scythian attacks on, 189, *190*
 sites of, 207
 size of, 218, 220
 stone-walled, *214**, *218**, *222*, 223, *224*
 timber-framed ramparts of, 202, *203*, 204, 216, *217*
 vitrified, 203
Hinton, R. W. K., 6
Hiram, 189
historiography, attitude of Western, to barbarism, 18-19, 20
history
 and prehistory, 3-4, 11, 13
 as concerned with literate societies, 3
 coexistence of prehistory and, 17-18
 dates in, 11, 12
 estimates of population in, 28
 pattern of progress in, 20
 prehistory and ancient, 21
Hittites
 conquest of Anatolia, 79
 end of empire, 159-60, 168
 iron-working among, 185-6
 language of, 91, 116, 118, 160, 223
 monuments of, 181
 Osmankayasi cemetery finds, 130
 social organisation of, 81
 stone sculpture of, 133, 176
 warfare tactics, 142
Hjortspring, votive deposits at, 230, 239, 240, 250
Hohensiedlung Burg, hill-fort at, 179
Hohmichele
 archer, 183, 184
 finds from, *193*, 207
 plank-built burial chamber, *186*, 187
Hollingbury, fort at, 203
Holocene period, 24
Holzhausen, ritual shaft at, *231*, 232
Homer, 106, 126, 130, 140, 142, 168, 189, 229, 235-6
Homolka, village site at, 89
honey
 as the basis of fermented drinks, 39
 gathering of, for wax, 171-2
 paintings depicting collection of wild, 33
horse(s)
 bones, evidence from, 110, 130
 burial in Egypt, 142
 buried with warriors, 144, 159, 179
 collar, invention of, 181
 domestication of, 36, 95-97, 130
 domestication of, in Britain, 189
 -drawn chariots, 123, 141-2
 forest type, 95, 96
 Indo-European languages and domestication of the, 96-97
 knowledge of, as a feature of an undivided Indo-European homeland, 80, 81
 main groups of wild, 95
 Mycenaean use of, 142
 Przewalski's, 95, 96
 riding of, 180-1, 182, 238-41
 rock-carvings of, *143*
 sacrifice of, 130, 176, 226
 steppe type, 95, 141, 179
 Tarpan, 95, 96, 179
 traction, 141, 180-1
 warfare and domestication of the, 141-2, 238-41
 yokes, 196
horse-bits
 Assyrian, 177
 bronze, 177
 distribution of, 177, *178*
 earliest appearance of, 95
 from Greece, 192
 metal, 177-9, *179*
Hörste, post-glacial settlement at, 33
houses
 architectural modification with climatic change, 44, 46
 Bronze Age, 118, *119*
 Celtic, 236-8, *237*
 chieftain's, 199, 201
 circular, 40, 59, 147, 150, *154**, 199, 220, 223, *225**, 236, *237*, 238
 communal, of North American Indians, 52
 construction in Neolithic Europe, 44-46
 construction in Turkmenia, 41, 44, *45*
 contiguous, 44
 Corded Ware and allied cultures, 89, *90*
 Danubian long, *50**, 52, 84, 85, 89, 113, 118, 150
 detached, 44, 46, 59
 Deverel-Rimsbury culture, *152*, *153*
 external decoration of, 89, *90*
 Kurgan culture, 81
 La Tène, 216, *219*, 220, *221*, 236
 Linear Pottery culture, 49, *50**, 52, 53, 84, 85
 log-built, *46*
 long, 49, *50**, 52-56, *55*, 113, 118, 150
 many-roomed, 40, 44, *45*
 megaron type, 49, 89, 121, *122*, 147, 201
 Mesolithic, 40, 41, *41*
 mud and wattle, 46, 47, *47**, *97**, *112**
 mud-brick, 40, 41, 44, 49
 mud-walled, 40, 41, 44, *45*
 Natufian, 40, *41*

houses *contd*
- Neolithic in Britain, 63-64
- oblong with porch, 46, 49, 58
- oval, 40, 59, *145**, 223
- palisaded timber-built, 199, 201, *201*
- plans and social structure, 56
- plans in European 'tell' settlement, 44
- plans in second millennium, 147
- pottery model of, *46*
- rectangular, 40, 44, 63-64, 81, *97**, *112**, 118, *119*, 147, 150, 199, 201, 202, 220, 223, 236, 237
- rectangular many-roomed, 40, 44
- settlement planning on oval or circular, 59
- single-roomed, 40, 44, *45*, 46, 89, *90*
- Skara Brae type, 64
- square one-roomed, 44, 46, *47**
- stone-built, *145**, *152*, *154**, 223
- sub-rectangular, 147, 150
- Swiss Lake, 57-58
- timber-built, 52, 53, 81, *149*, *152*, *153*, 155, 199, *200*, 201, 216, *219*, 220, *221*, *237*
- timber-framed, 118, *119*, *208**, *209**
- timber-framed and mud-walled, 41
- Tripolye culture, 54, *55*, 56
- two-roomed, 58
- Urnfield culture, *149*, 151, 199
- wattle and mud, 44, 46, 47, *47**, *97**, *112**
- with framework of poles, 44
- with painted wall-plaster, 40, 46-47, 147

Hradenin, Celtic burial at, 89

Hundersingen-Weidenhang, amber beads from, *137*

Hungary
- Bronze Age houses in, 118
- copper metallurgy in, 73-74
- pottery figurines from, *48*
- supercession of tell culture in, 145

hunting
- arrows used in, 29, 65, 66
- -bands, size of, 28, 32
- changing modes of, 27
- communities, *see* hunting communities
- domestication of the dog for, 26, 33, 35, 65
- efficiency of methods of, 27-28
- gazelle, 40
- in the leanest season, 28
- mammoth, 29-30
- red deer, 31-32
- reindeer, 28-29, 31
- scenes depicting, *33*
- spears used in, 29
- techniques and changing fauna, 27

hunting communities
- adoption of agriculture in Scandinavia, 62-63
- Advanced Palaeolithic, 27-28
- art of, 27, *33*, 133, 176
- coexistence of agriculture and, 27, 64, 97, 113
- conditions for transition to agricultural community, 26, 35-39
- continuation of traditions of, 33
- crafts and inventions of, 35, 258-9
- economic basis of, 25
- general characteristics of final, 26-35
- in Mesolithic period, 25
- magic, 28
- mammal bones and classification, 24
- movements of, 30-31
- population of Late Glacial Europe, 28
- post-glacial settlement of, 33
- readjustment to natural conditions, 27-28
- survival of, 27, 35
- tool-making techniques, 27
- use of bows and arrows, 29
- *see also* food-gathering communities

hut(s)
- circular in Neolithic Britain, 63-64
- earliest humanly-constructed, 29-30
- grave, 123
- later representations of, 29, 65
- mud-brick oval single-roomed, at Jericho 40
- of early Near East agriculturalists, 39
- of post-glacial settlements, 33

Huxley, Sir Julian, 14, 15

hydria, bronze, 195, *200**

Hyksos dynasty in Egypt, 142

I

Iberia
- Bell-Beaker peoples from, 98, 118
- bronze-using cultures in, 188
- Celtic culture in, 223
- Celtic place-names in, 173
- copper colonies in, 74, 76-77, 106, 120
- copper working in, 73, 97, 98, 113
- first agricultural communities in, 56-57
- hill-forts in, 223, 224
- houses in, 223
- pots from, *225*
- representation of shields from, 193
- vase-painting, 223, 225

iconography, 230

Iliad
- warrior aristocracy in, 106
- wheels mentioned in, 244
- world of, 126, 140, 142

Impressed Pottery culture
- and Bell-Beaker culture, 98
- distribution of main sites of, *58*
- generalised distribution of, *57*

India, Aryan invasion of, 108
Indians of British Columbia, 35, 97
Indo-European languages
  affinities of Baden culture, 92
  area of origin, 78, 80
  case for the early Balkan or Danubian Neolithic cultures, 80-81
  correlation of linguistic groups and archaeological evidence, 81-91
  date of assumed linguistic unity, 79
  dispersal of speakers, 106
  evidence of common institutional patterns and, 80-81
  Hittites in Anatolia and, 79, 116, 118
  homeland as site between Caucasus and Carpathians, 82, 84, 85, 89, 91
  identification of linguistic groups through archaeology, 79
  in Mesopotamia, 81
  land-tenure and allocation as characteristic, 80
  movement of peoples in the third millennium and, 78
  place-names and salt-production, 171
  Scythians and, 176
  speakers in Anatolia, 79
  three-caste system of society and, 80-81
  transmission of by Bell-Beaker peoples, 102
  vehicles and, 95-97
  warrior aristocracy and, 118
ingot-torcs
  copper, 102, *103*
  distribution of double-pointed iron, *246*
  double-pointed iron, 246-7
  of Near East and south-central European cultures, 102
  used as coins, 252
innovating societies
  and the Celtic world, 255-6
  assumptions and beliefs of, 18
  distinction between conserving and, 17-18, 73
  literate, 21-22
  metallurgy in, 72-73
  use of copper, 72
  use of wheeled vehicles, 92
  Western historiographers' views on, 18-19, 20
institutions, common pattern of, and the homeland of the Indo-European languages, 80-81, 91
Ionian migration, 189
Iran
  cold-hammering of copper in, 71
  Neolithic houses in, *45*
  Neolithic reaping-knives from, *42*
Iraq: pre-pottery Neolithic culture in, 40
Ireland
  bronze cauldron from, 194
  chambered tombs in, 61, 62
  Celtic languages in, 222
  Celtic pastoral economy in, 235
  copper and gold resources of, 120
  gold jewellery from, 138
  Mycenaean bronze double axe from, 138
  rectangular houses in, 63
  shields from, 193
  tales of the Ulster Cycle, 140, 226, 238
  vernacular tradition, 226-7, 229, 235, 237-8, 243-4, 247
Iron Age
  as a model of the past, 6
  beginnings of, 174-5, 185-6
  Homer and, 126
iron
  anchors and chains, 247
  arrowheads, 183-4
  carpentry and working in, 187
  Celtic-speaking peoples' use of, 187
  dagger, 185
  Damascene steel, 186
  distribution of double-pointed ingots, *246*
  edge-tools, 185
  Eskimo's technique of cold-hammering of, 71
  fire-dogs, *191*, 192, 247, *248*, *252**
  Hittite production of, 185-6
  ingots, 246-7, *246*
  long swords, 216
  nails, 216
  objects, export of, 186
  objects from La Tène grave, 227, *228*
  production of, 246-7
  Roman techniques in, 186
  Scandinavian working of, 186
  smelting of, 185
  spear, 192
  swords, 186, 188, 192, 216, 227, *228*, 238
  tools, 185, 186, 187
  votive deposits of objects of, 230
  weapons, 185, 186
  working, beginnings of, 185-6
  working in Britain, 189
  working in south-central Europe, 106
  wrought, 247
Iroquois, long houses of, 52
Ischia, Mycenaean trading-post at, 134
Italic language groups, 81, 223
Italy
  beginnings of historical, 192-3
  ditch-enclosed settlements of, 59
  first agricultural settlements in, 56-57
  Terremare settlement, 129

Itford Hill
  circular houses at, 150, 199, 236
  settlement at, *152*
ivory
  from Stone Age, 24
  human comprehension and working in, 71

J

Jackson, K. H., 226
Jacobsthal, P., 243
jadeite, battle-axes of, 130, *131*
Jarmo, pre-pottery Neolithic culture at, 40, 258
Jeitun
  settlement pattern of, 44
  single-roomed houses at, *45*
Jericho
  cultivation at, 258
  description of site, 40
  extent of, 17, 40
  human portraiture at, 40, *46**, 241
  mud-brick oval single-roomed houses at, 40
  rectangular many-roomed houses at, 40
jet, buttons, *104*
  maces of, 129
jewellery, Irish gold, 138

K

Kakovatos
  amber beads from, *137*
  decorated antler and bone objects from, *135*
Kamose, King, 142
Kanesh, documents relating to chamber of commerce at, 79
Kappel, votive deposits from, 230
Karanovo
  animal domestication at, 258
  end of settlement, 91
  flint-bladed bone tools from, *42*
  house construction in, 44, *45*, 46-47, *47*, *47**, 89, *97**, *112**
  megaron-plan houses at, 121
  section through tell, *47**
Karmir-Blur fort, 189
Kerameikos, iron objects from, 186, 192
Kercado, chambered tomb at, 61
Kestor, house-plan at, *237*
kingdom(s)
  Celtic, 227
  in the second millennium, 140-1
  of Near East, 113
  of Salisbury Plain, 120
Kisapostag group of cemeteries, 145
kitchen-middens, technique of excavating, 25
Kličevac figure, 157, *158*
knights in second millennium, 141
knives
  copper riveted, *103*
  dagger, copper tanged, *84*
  dagger of Bell-Beaker culture, *99*
  flint-bladed bone, *42*
  reaping, 40, *42*
Knossos
  helmet from, 134
  size of, 122
Köln-Lindenthal, Linear Pottery long houses at, 52
Kökenydomb, decoration of houses at, 89, *90*
Kolomiishchina, Tripolye culture settlement at, *55*, 56
Komarovka, bone cheek-pieces from, *96*
Korakou, *megara* at, 121, *122*
Korostarcsa, cheek-pieces from, *132*
Kostienki, tent-stance at, 30
Krahe, H., 91, 102
kurgan, 81-82
Kurgan culture
  agriculture of, 81-82
  disc-wheeled carts, 109
  fortified settlements of, 84
  graves of, 81-82, 84, 130
  houses of, 81
  impressed pottery of, 84
Kwakiutl, communal houses of, 52
Kyberg, settlement at, 199
Kymmerioi, 175

L

La Adam cave, evidence from, 40, 66
Lachish, extent of, 17
L'Âge du Renne, *see* Reindeer Age
Lake, amber beads from, *137*
Lake Baikal
  flint-bladed bone tools from, *42*
  tent-stances at, 30
'lake dwellings', technique of excavation, 25
  see also Swiss Lake Dwellings
Lake Sevan
  fleeces and hides from graves, 130
  grave finds at, 130, *133*
  use of wheeled chariots, 142
  wheel gauge measured at, 246
Lake Van, 171
La Madeleine, cave shelter of, 28

landier, 247
land-tenure, Indo-European, 80-81
Lancaster, Osbert, 5
Lapps, domestication of the reindeer by, 35
Lascaux, art work at, 28
La Tène culture
  art of, 216
  beginnings of, 216
  bronze wine-flagons, *208*, *241**
  brooch, 222
  burials, 215-16, 232, *233*, *234*, 235, 238-41
  casques, 195
  chariot burials, *208*
  crafts, 244-7
  dating of, 195
  distribution of objects, *207*, 220, 222, *239*
  fire-dogs, 192, 247, *248*, *252**
  fortifications, 216-21, 236, 246-7
  helmets, 239, 241
  houses, 216, *219*, 220, *221*, 236
  inscribed sword, 253
  iron objects from grave, 227, *228*
  pottery, *242*, 243, 247
  salt production, 247-9, *249*
  shields, 194-5, 216, 227, *228*, 239, *240**, 241
  social organisation, 207
  trade, 216
  votive deposits, 230-1
  warfare, 215, 216, 238-41
lathe-working, invention of, 169, 187
Latin, development of the language, 79
Lattimore, Owen, 16, 18
'lavers', wheeled, 181
Law Tracts, 226
Lébous, copper 'colony' at, 76
Le Camp d'Artus, fort at, *217*
leguminous plants, initial cultivation of, 39
Lehringen, wooden spear from, 29
lentils, initial cultivation of, 39, 60
Lerna, *megarą* at, 121
Leubingen, Únětice culture grave at, 127, 129, *129**
Levant
  barbarian raids in, 116, 118
  brooch types from, 168
  rise of Mycenae to power and, 134
  urban cultures in, 113
Libanius, 16
Libenice, sanctuary site at, 232, *234*
limestone figurines, *114*
L'Impernal, sacred skulls from, 230
Linear Pottery culture
  agricultural techniques of, 50-52
  cyclic occupation of houses, 52
  distribution of settlements, *51*
  excavation area of settlement, *53*
  generalised distribution of, *57*
  houses of, 49, *50**, 52, 53, 84, 85
  origin of, 52
  population of settlements, 52
  slash-and-burn cultivation, 51-52
  social organisation of, 52
  spread into north-western Europe, 50
  village plans of, 52, 147
linguistics, 222-3
Lipari Islands
  legend of Ausonius and, 168
  Mycenaean contacts with, 155
  obsidian trade in, 97
  settlement at, *152*
literacy
  achievement of, 113
  and non-literate societies, 3-4, 8
  barbarism, civilisation and, 16-17, 21-22, 256
  conditional, of the Celts, 253-5
  Mycenae before, 126
Little Woodbury, settlement at, 236, *237*, 238
Llyn Cerrig Bach
  chariot tyres from, 247
  votive deposits at, 230
Llyn Fawr, horse-bits from, 177
Los Millares
  bastioned defences of, 76, *77*
  cemetery at, 77
  copper 'colony' at, 76
Lough Gur
  circular huts at, 150
  rectangular houses at, 63
Lovosice, neck-pad from, *201**
Lubbock, 24, 26
Luka, 158, 160
Lukovit hoard, 226
Luristan art styles, 130
Lusatian culture, 188, 213
Lustenitz, bronze weapons from, *125*
Lycians, 158
Lydians, 175

M

Macedonia, Nea Nikomedeia site in, 41, 44
mace-head
  alabaster, 130, *131*
  stone, *128*
maces, 129
Maes Howe, chambered tomb at, 61
Magdalenian culture
  art of, 28
  distribution of, 65

Magdalenian culture *contd*
  origin of name, 28
  weapons and tools, 28
Maglemose, 258
Maiden Castle
  fortification of, 202, 220
  wheel ruts at, 245, 246
Maikop
  objects from, *82*, 82, 95, 176
  wooden mortuary-house at, 81-82
Mailhac, horse-bits from, 177
mail shirts, 240
Mallia, palace at, 122
Malomerice, bronze mounting from, *241**
Malta
  figures and models from, *114*
  rock-cut tombs in, 97
  temples in 97, *98*, *112**, 114-15
  tent-stances in, 30
Malthi, fortified settlement at, 121
mammoth
  bones in tent-stances, 29, *29*, 30
  hunters, camping-sites of, 30
Mammoth Age, as a classification, 24-25
man
  barbarism of, 14-15, 257
  establishment of relationship between animals and, 36
Manching
  mint at, 252
  oppidum of, 216, 218, *219*, 227, 246
manure, initial use of, 39
Manyes, 158
Mapungubwe, 140
Marathon, Mycenaean tomb at, 144
Marcellinus, Ammianus, 253
Marne chalk-cut tombs, 62, *63**
Massalia, colony at, 188, 195, 223
Massaliote amphorae, distribution of, *188*, 195, 204
Maturabilla, chambered tomb at, 61
mead, brewing of, 172, 253
Meare hamlet, 236
Medes, 175, 238
Medinet Habu, inscription at, 159
Mediterranean, rise of cities, 141
  trade with Europe, 193-6
megalithic chambered tombs, 60-62, *61*, *62*, *62**, *63**, 114-15
megaron
  construction of, 121
  plans of, *122*
  type houses, 49, 89, 121, *122*, 147, 201
  use as a public hall, 121
Megiddo, extent of, 17
Mehrstetten, amber beads from, *137*
Meiendorf
  camping-sites of reindeer-hunters at, 28-29
  wooden arrows from, 29
Melitopol, chariot burial near, 220
merchant class, rise of the, 141
Merenptah, 158
Meshwesh, 158
Mesolithic cultures
  as early Neolithic, 26
  cave-paintings of, *33*, *34*
  crafts and inventions of, 35
  definition between Neolithic and, 26
  domestication of animals among, 35
  flint and stone equipment of, 26
  flint-bladed bone tools, *42*
  garments of, 104
  houses of Natufian culture, 40, 41
  settlement at Moita do Sebastião, *32*
  technologies of, 25
  use of term, 26
Mesopotamia
  as the home of the war chariot, 141-2
  beginnings of metallurgy in, 64
  origin of the wheel in, 92
  urban cultures in, 113
metal-working
  control of resources, 145
  distribution of Mycenaean, *136*
  in Greece, 121
  Minoan, 134
  origin of non-ferrous, 72-73
  pottery-making and, 71
  resources of south-central European cultures, 103-4
  resources tapped by the Mycenaeans, 133-4
  significance of the beginnings of, 71-72
  skill of the Urartians, 175, 193
  trade, consolidation and, 71-107
  workers, dispersion of at end of second millennium, 103-4
metallurgy
  advances in Near East by 2500 B.C., 64
  beginnings of copper and bronze, 107
  Bell-Beaker peoples' knowledge of, 100
  foundation of Adriatic schools of, 169
Mezin, tent-stance at, 30
Middle Palaeolithic period
  as a classification, 24-25
  tent-stances of, 29, *29*, 30
Mikhailovka, settlement at, 81
millet
  initial cultivation of, 39
  cultivation in Europe, 41
Ministry of Agriculture and Fisheries, 35

Minoan period
  art of, 123
  growth of power, 120
  metal-working in, 134
  Middle, 120-1
  palace-building in, 121, 122
  practice of shaving in, 123
  weapons of, 123
mints, 252
mirror, bronze, *244**
Mitchell, Sir Arthur, 9
models of the past
  and Neolithic and Palaeolithic periods, 24
  combination of technological and subsistence-economic, 24-25, 26
  cyclical, 19
  difficulties of the conceptual, 26
  economic, 6, 8, 24-25, 26
  evidence and, 5-6, 7-8
  Late Bronze and Early Iron Ages and, 174-5, 185
  new conceptual, 8
  subsistence-economic, 25, 26
  technological, 6, 7, 24, 26, 174-5, 185
  types of, 6
Moita do Sebastião, Mesolithic settlement at, *32*, 33
Molodova, tent-stance at, 29, *29*, 30
Monteoru, settlement at, 118, 130
Mont Lassois hill-fort, 187, 193
Montlingerberg, fort at, 202, *203*
Montpellier, representation of shield from, 193
monuments
  Corsican carved stone, 155
  henge, *see* henge monuments
  Hittite, 181
Morison, R. S., 20
Mousterian phase, tent-stances of, 29, *29*, 30
mud-brick houses, 40, 41, 44, 49
mud-walled and wattled houses, 46, *47*, *47**, *97**, *112**
Muhltal, dress pins from, *105*
Munro, Robert, 4, 5, 8, 12, 21
Murartu, *nuraghi* at, *157*
murus gallicus, 216, *217*, 218, 220, 236, 246, 247
Mycenae
  assumption of power in Crete, 134
  before literacy, 126
  break up of, 145-6, 158-60, 168
  bronze double axes, 138, *139*
  bronzes, distribution of Late, *139*
  culture and Hallstatt, 175
  culture and Stonehenge, 138-9
  distribution of objects from, 136-7, *136*
  dynasties of, 123, 133
  engraved gold ring from, *147*
  gold mask, *113**
  growth of power, 120
  megara in, 121
  metal resources, 133-4, 136
  palaces in, 121
  pottery, evidence of, 155, 159
  products, distribution of, 134
  relief carving from, *128**
  shaft-graves, 81, *113**, 123, *124*, 133-4, *137*, 137, 162
  trade in amber, 137, *138*
  trade with High Barbarian Europe, 134, 137-8
  trading-posts, 134, 137
  wheeled chariots from, 142

N

Naḥal Oren, houses at, 40
nails, used in *murus gallicus*, 216, *217*
Natufian people
  cave shelters of, 40
  cultivation of crops, 40
  houses of, 40, *41*
  huts of, 40
  reaping-knives, 40, *42*
natural sciences and the classification of cultures, 24-25
Nea Nikomedeia
  date of site, 41
  house-plans at, 44
Near East
  and East European cultures, 49
  contact with south-central European cultures, 102-3
  domestication of wolves in, 35
  evidence for local domestication of animals and crops in, 39-40
  fashion in, 102
  peasant economies of, 113
  technique of excavation in, 25
necklaces
  amber, 137
  faience, *135**
neck-pad, *210**
neck-ring, *193**, *200**
Neolithic cultures
  as agricultural cultures, 25
  creation of, 24
  criterion of, 24
  definition between Mesolithic and, 26
  distinction between Palaeolithic and, 24, 25
  flint-bladed bone tools, *42*

Neolithic cultures *contd*
  in geological time, 24
  making of pottery as criterion of, 24
  pre-pottery, 26
  origin of agricultural communities in, 25
  Revolution, 25
  Russian use of the term, 26
  use of term, 26
Netherlands, Bell-Beaker people in, 100, *101*, 102
New Grange, chambered tomb at, 61, 62
Newstead, wheel from, 244, *245*
New Stone Age, 24
Niederursseĺ, fire-dog from, *252**
Nienhagen, pottery cup from, 134
Nieuw Dordrecht, corduroy roadway at, *96**
Nitrianski Hradok
  hill-fort at, *206*
  decorated antler and bone objects from, *135*
Noble Savage, myth of the, 224, 257
nomadism, pastoral, 182, 235-6, 243-4
Nootka, communal houses of the, 52
Nordse Veld, field system at, *251*
Normanton Down, ritual shaft at, 232
North American Indians
  cold-hammering of copper, 71
  long houses of, 52
  population density of, 32
  ritual of, 115
  slash-and-burn cultivation of, 52
  'tipi rings' of, 33
Northern Europe, evidence of ritual in, 115, *116*
North Ferriby, plank-built boat from, 187, *187*, 250
North Pontic area
  coinage, 252
  contact with central Europe, 175
  contact with Scandinavia, 226
  metal horse-bits and harness-mountings of, 177-9
nuraghi, development of, in Sardinia, 155, *157*
Nuraghic culture
  figures of, *155**
  settlement of, *154**, *156*
Nydam, boat from, 250

O

oats, initial cultivation of, 39
Obermanzingen, objects from grave at, 227, *228*
observational data, 5
obsidian
  equipment at Argissa, 41
  in Lipari Islands, 97
  trade in, 72, 97
Odyssey, world of the, 126, 140
Old Paphos, grave finds at, 144
Old Stone Age, 24
oppida status, forts of, 216, 218, *218*, *219*, 220, *221*, *222*
Oransay, post-glacial settlement at, 33
ornaments
  amber, 123
  copper, 74, 102, *103*, 104
  distribution of Mycenaean, 136
  gold, 123, 124, 129, *131*
  silver, 123, 129
  spread of Urnfield culture, 172-3
Osmankayasi, cemetery at, 130
Ostfold, carvings at, *144**
Otzaki-Magula, house-plans at, 44, *45*
oxen
  distribution of, *37*
  domestication of, 35

P

Pádozdvár, cheek-pieces from, *132*
palace-buildings
  ashlar, 140
  complex in Mediterranean, 141
  of Minoan period, 121, 122
  of Mycenaean period, 121
  size of, 121-2
Palaeolithic cultures
  crafts and inventions of, 35
  creation of, 24
  criterion of, 24
  distinction between Neolithic and, 24, 25
  grinding and polishing of stone in, 26
  in geological time, 24
  use of term, 26
Palestine
  crop-growing in, 40
  destruction of townships of, 78
  domestication of goats in, 40
palisades, 199, 201, *201*, 202
pan-pipes, possible invention of, 35, 66
pans, distribution of Roman bronze, *255*
passage graves, 61
pastoralism
  among Bell-Beaker people, 102
  domestication of dogs and, 35, 36
  nomadic, 182, 235-6, 243-4
  of Corded Ware people, 84, 89, 97
  theoretical basis for, 36

pastoralists, technology and the steppe, 17-18
Peake, H. J. E., 13
peas, initial cultivation of, 39, 60
peasant communities
  coexistence with literate cultures, 44
  conserving character of, 44
  houses of, 41
  Neolithic, in Scandinavia, 62-63
  of Near East and Eastern Europe, 113
  social organisation of, 44
  towns and villages of, 41
Peleset, 159
pendants
  gold, *124*
  spiral wire, 102
peploi, 105
Pergamon, reliefs at, 207, 215, 220, 239, 240
Perleberg, settlement at, 147, 150, *151*, 199
Persepolis, reliefs at, 177
Perşinari, golden dagger of, 129, *129**
Philistines, 159
phillimore, 104-6
philology, and the homeland of the Indo-European languages, 79, 80, 81, 82, 84
Phoenician(s)
  alphabet, 189
  consolidation of power, 189
Phrygians, settlements in Anatolia, 159, 175, 189
pigs
  as scavengers, 36
  distribution of, 35-36
  domestication by Bell-Beaker people, 102
  domestication of, as a feature of an undivided Indo-European homeland, 80, 81, 108-9
  initial domestication of, 35-36, 41
Pimperne, house at, *225**
pin(s)
  arrangement of, 111
  Bell-Beaker copper, *99*
  bone hammer-headed, *84*
  clothing fastened with, 102, 104-5, 172
  distribution of hammer-headed, *85*
  gold animal-headed, *124*
  gold, of Únětice culture, *129**
  Near Eastern, 102
  silver, *131*
  south-central European copper, 102, *103*, 104-5, *105*
  trade in hammer-headed, 84
  types common in Iberia and the Aegean, 76
  with double spiral heads, distribution of, 74, *75*
piracy, 140, 146, 158
pits in ritual enclosures, 115
Pitt-Rivers, 25
place-names, distribution of Celtic, *172*, *173*, 173-4, *174*
plant(s)
  cereal, initial cultivation of, 36, *38*, 39
  conditions necessary for cultivation of, 26
  crops and the domestication of animals, 36
  domestication of, 35, *38*, 39
  evidence from Near East for initial domestication of, 39-40, 66
  leguminous, initial cultivation of, 39
  post-glacial botanical climax, 31
  remains, ecological research on, 25
plaster
  painted wall, 46-47, 147
  polished red-painted, 40
plate, gold, *128*
platters, from Jericho, 40
Pleistocene period, 24, 35, 40, 95
Pliny, 249, 250
plough
  ard type, 150, 250
  rock-engravings of, 150
Plumpton Plain, field system at, 251
Poiana-Coţofeneşti, helmet from, 226
Poliochni, *megara* at, 121
pollen grains, and archaeological evidence, 8-9, 51, 62-63
polychrome technique
  Hallstatt, 196-7
  Magdalenian, 28
Pompeii, Stabian Gate, *206*, 207
population(s)
  at 2000 B.C., 106
  estimates of, in antiquity and history, 28
  of Britain about 7500 B.C., 32
  of Late Glacial England, 28
  of peasant villages, 47
  of Swiss lake villages, 58-59
  of 'tell' settlements, 58-59
Poroina rhyton, 226
Portland, ingots from, 247
portraiture, earliest individual human, 40, *46**, 241
Portugal, Mesolithic settlements in, *32*, 33
Posidonius, 227, 229
post-holes
  in Bronze Age houses, *119*
  in Deverel-Rimbury culture houses, *152*, *153*
  in La Tène houses, *219*

post-holes *contd*
in La Tène sanctuary sites, *233*, *234*
in Linear Pottery houses, *50**, *53*
in Mesolithic settlement, *32*, 33
in tent-stances, 29, 30
in Urnfield culture houses, *151*
Postoloprty, houses at, 118, *119*
pot(s)
anthropomorphic, *49*
graffiti on, 253-4
Iberian painted, *225*
La Tène decorated, *242*
pottery
absence of, in agriculturalist Mesolithic cultures, 40-41
Bell-Beaker hybrid, 100
Bell-Beaker standardised, 100, *112**
Corded Ware, *84*, 84, 85, 100
cup, 134
distribution of Mycenaean, *136*, 155, 159
evidence for sites of Mycenaean trading-posts, 134
figures from Cernavoda, *51**
figurines from Rumania and Jugoslavia, 157, *158*
Greek black-figure, 204
impressed ware, 84
La Tène, painted, *242*, 243, 247
making of, as criterion for the Neolithic period, 24, 26
Middle Helladic, 134
models of vehicles, *93*, *97**
Near Eastern and Eastern European style, 49
Neolithic, *48*
polychrome, 28, 196-7
relationship between metal-smelting and making of, 71
representations on Hallstatt, *197*, *198*, 199
Tisza culture figurines, *50*
transmission of traditions to Western Europe, 56-57
types common to Iberia and the Aegean, 76
wheel-turned, 247
Prague, Bell-Beaker objects from, *99*
prehistoric
and historic, coexistence of, 17-18, 21-22
the meaning of, 2, 3
prehistory
and ancient history, 21
archaeology and, 13
as the study of non-literate peoples, 3-4
contribution to the present, 20-21
definitions of, 3-4
history and, 3-4, 11, 13
means of acquiring knowledge of, 2, 6-7
problems of, 1-12
reconstruction of, 4-5
recovery of, 12
under-development in, 16, 20
Preist, fort at, 216, *217*
pre-pottery Neolithic culture
features of, 26
in Near East and Eastern Europe, 40-41, 258
origin of name, 26
probe, iron, 227, *228*
prospectors for metals, 72, 73, 106
Proto-Corinthian art, 171
Pumpelly, 25
Pylos
destruction of, 159
megara at, 121
size of palace, 121
pyxis, Etruscan bronze, 195

Q

querns
Celtic, 250
stone, from Jericho, 40

R

radiocarbon dating
of objects from cultures, 8, 27-28, 41, 60, 85, 97, 100, 115
technique of, 11-12
Radley, Bell-Beaker objects from, *101*
raiding
and the break up of Mycenaean power, 146, 158-60
Celtic, 220
Cimmerian, 177
Scythian, 176, 189, *190*
Ramesses III, 159
rapiers
as weapons of attack, 145
from Mycenaean shaft-graves, 145
rath, 236
razors, Hallstatt culture bronze, 199
reaping-knives
flint-bladed, 40
flint-bladed bone, *42*
Natufian, 40
Recent period, 24
red deer
advent of, 31
communities of hunters, 31-32
population of, 32
Reflux Movement
Argar culture and, 129
as colonisation of Bell-Beaker peoples, 100
concept of, 111
generalised distribution of, *101*

reindeer
  as the main quarry, 27
  distribution of, and hunting cultures, 65
  domestication of, 35, 66
  end of hunting of, 31
  -hunters in the Franco-Cantabrian area, 28
  of northern Germany, 28-29
  sacrifices of, 28
Reindeer Age, as a classification, 24-25, 27
Reinheim, bronze wine-flagon from, *241**
religion
  absence of, evidence of in East European and Danubian cultures, 113-14
  barbarian, 229-35, 259
  cult sites, 230-4
  evidence of, in Mediterranean and Western Europe, 114-15
  evidence of ritual in Northern Europe, 115-16, *116*
  figurines, 49, 114
  ritual shafts, *231*, 231-2
  sanctuary sites, 230, 232, *233*, *234*, 235
  stone-chambered tombs and, 60, 114-15
retractor, 227, *228*
rhyton, Poroina, 226
Richmond, Ian, 13
Riedschachen, village site at, 89
Rig-Veda
  use of wheeled chariots in, 142, 244
  warrior aristocracy in, 106
Rillaton, gold cup from, 134, *134**
ring(s)
  from Mycenaean shaft-grave, *147*
  of standing stones, 115-16
rivets, bronze, *128*
roadway, corduroy, *98**, 202, *208**, *209**
Roman Empire
  relation of barbarian Europe to, 21
  south-central European culture and, 106
Romans
  iron technology of, 186
  myths concerning the origin of, 168
  views on the Celts, 223-4, 226-7, 229, 256, 260
Rome, settlement of the earliest, 168
Romeral, chambered tomb at, 61
roofs of houses, 44, *46*
Roquepertuse, sculpture at, 230, 243
Rørby, engraved sword-blade from, 144, *144*
Roundway, Bell-Beaker objects from, *99*
routes
  bronze-working and trade, 118, 120
  of trade and exchange in amber, 137, *138*, 161
  Scandinavian-Carpathian, 226
  trade and the development of, 106
Rudstone, jet buttons, from, *104*
Rumania
  barrow burials in, 84
  copper metallurgy in, 73-74
  evidence of domestication of animals from, 40
  gold and silver objects from, 226
Russia
  copper working in South, 74, 175
  evidence of carts and wagons from graves in South, 95
  Kurgan culture of South, 81-82, *82*, *83*
  Viking settlements in South, 226
Russian
  archaeologists' use of technological models, 26
  Timber Grave culture, *see* South Russian Timber Grave culture
rye, initial cultivation of, 39, 41

S

Saalburg, Roman fort at, 244
Sa Coà Filigosa, *nuraghi* at, *157*
sacrifices of animals, 28, 130, 176, 226
Sagas, warrior aristocracy in, 106
Salamis, grave finds at, 144
Salisbury Plain
  bronze industries of, 120
  graves in, 129
salted food, 171, 248
salt production
  distribution of sites of Hallstatt, *170*
  evidence of Indo-European place-names, 171
  in the Tyrol, 196, 197
  La Tène sites, 247-9, *249*
  trade in, 171, 187
Saluvii, 223
San Miguel de Liria, painted vase from, *225*
Sanskrit, development of the language, 79
Santon, votive deposits from, 230
Sardinia
  bronze figures from, 155, *155**
  copper resources of, 155
  nuraghi in, *154**, 155, 157
  raiding parties from, 159, 160
  stone-built settlement in, *156*
Sarmatians
  art of, 241
  contacts with Celts, 226
  migration of, 220
  pastoral nomadism of, 243
  practice of tattooing, 239

Sarmenstorf, Corded Ware culture mortuary-house at, *87*
scabbards
  British, *239*
  distribution of, 238-9, *239*
  La Tène, 220
  Swiss, *239*
Scandinavia
  beginnings of agriculture in, 62-63
  bronze-working in, 155-6
  burial sites in, 63
  Celtic influence in, 226
  house-plans in, 236
  hunting communities in, 31
  lack of metal resources in, 120
  Neolithic peasant settlements in, 63
  shields from, 193
  sword-making in, 186
sceptres
  bone mounting of, *128*
  from Bush Barrow, 134
  in graves, 129
Schöltz, post-glacial settlement at, 33
Scotstarvit, house-plan at, *237*
sculpture
  Celtic stone, 230, 243
  earliest examples of, 115, *115*
  Hittite stone, 133, 176
Scythian(s)
  art, 176-7, *176**, *177**, *240**, 241
  forebears of, 118
  head-hunting among, 230
  horse-riding, 238
  horse-sacrifices of, 130, 176
  language of, 176
  raids in Europe, 176, 189, *190*
  settlement areas of, *190*
  Timber Grave folks as ancestors of, 130, 175, 176-7
  tombs and Celtic burials, 89
  trade of, 176, 189
  use of wheeled chariot, 142
Sea Peoples, 158-9, 167
Secondary Neolithic, 65
seed remains, ecological research on, 25
Seifartsdorf, mortuary-house at, *88*
Sequana, 222
Sesklo, *megara* at, 121
settlement(s)
  and house planning on circular or oval units, 59
  at Capo Graziano, *143**, *152*
  at Lipari, *152*
  at Malthi, 121
  Danubian, size of, 147, 150
  ditch-enclosed, of south Italy, 59
  fortified, 84, 97, 118, 121, 126, 147, 150, 199, 201-2, 218
  Hallstatt C-D, 199, *200*, 201
  Iberian, 74, 76-77, *77*, 98, *224*
  Kurgan culture, 84
  lack of sites from 2000-1500 B.C., 118, 126
  Mesolithic, *32*
  of Corded Ware and allied cultures, 89
  of Danubian culture, 113, 147
  of Deverel-Rimsbury culture, *152*, *153*
  of first agriculturalists, 39
  of Nuraghic culture, *154**, *156*
  of post-glacial hunting and fishing groups, 33
  of Urnfield culture, 147, *149*, 150, *151*, 199
  permanent, of hunting and fishing communities, 35
  permanent, of pre-pottery Neolithic cultures, 26
  seasonal, 32
  semi-permanent, 39
  size of Danubian, 147, 150
  size of, in Neolithic Scandinavia, 63
  size of, in 2000 B.C., 118
  size of, in second millennium, 147, 150
  'tell', *see* 'tell' settlements
  tent-stances, 29-31
  with earthwork enclosures, 97, 150
  Upper Palaeolithic, 31
severed-head cult, *218**, 223, 230, 243
shaft-graves
  amber beads from, 137, *137*
  construction of, 123
  contents of, 123, *124*
  dynasties of, 123, 162
  engraved gold ring from, *147*
  link with British graves, 129
  Mycenaean B shaft, 134
  objects from Mycenaean, 133-4
  weapons from, 123
Shechem, extent of, 17
sheep
  distribution of, 36, *37*
  domestication as a feature of an undivided Indo-European homeland, 80
  domestication of, 36, 39-40
  domestication of, by Bell-Beaker people, 102
  domestication of fleeces, 36
  evidence from La Adam cave, 40
  herding of, 39-40
  initial domestication in Europe, 40, 41
  predominance of remains over those of goats, 40
Sheklesh, 158, 159

shells
- *Columbella rustica*, 103
- for ornaments among Linear Pottery people, 52, 68
- for ornaments in south-central European culture, 103

shelters, earliest humanly-constructed, 29-30
Sherden, 158, 159
shield(s)
- as a weapon of defence, 145
- beaten bronze, 154
- British and northern types, 194
- circular, 193
- distribution of circular, 193, *194*
- from Bavarian grave, 227, *228*
- La Tène, 194-5, 216, 227, *228*, 239, *240**, 241
- long, 216
- oval, 194-5, 216, 239
- representations of, 193, 194
- U-notched, 194
- V-notched, 193, 194
- variants of Aegean type, 193

Sicily
- ditch-enclosed settlement in, 59
- first agricultural settlement in, 56-57
- Mycenaean objects from, 136, 155, 168
- Mycenaean trading-post in, 134
- raiding parties from, 158, 160

sickles, 40, *42*
Sidonius, 16
Sigynnae, 181-2, 238
Silchester, mint at, 252
silver
- acquisition of, by Mycenaeans, 133-4
- Bell-Beaker ear-ring, *99*
- battle-axes, 129
- coins, 252
- Danish ritual cauldron, *219**, 226
- demand for, 134
- discs, 226
- dish, *257**, 260
- Eastern technology in, 64
- helmet, *224**
- objects from Greek shaft-graves, 123, *124*
- objects from Maikop, *82*
- ornaments from graves, 129
- pin, *131*
- prospecting for, 73
- spears, 129
- vase from Maikop, 95
- vessel from Maikop, *82*

silver-gilt objects from central Europe, 226
Single-Grave folk
- advent of, in Europe, 84
- Bell-Beaker culture and, 100, 102
- generalised distribution of, *86*
- house-types of, 89, 121
- indigenous cultures and, 91
- pastoralism of, 85, *87*

Sittard, Linear Pottery settlement at, *53*
situlae
- bronze, *161**, 179
- decoration of, 171
- distribution of, *154*
- Hallstatt, 171
- representations on, 144, 181, 194, 216, 239
- 'situla' style bronze work, distribution of, *170*
- trade in, 171
- use of, 154-5

Skara Brae, circumpolar influence on planning of, 64
skins, trade in, 120
skis, invention of, 35, 66
Skøbaek Hede, field system at, *251*
slash-and-burn cultivation, 51-52, 62-63
slave(s)
- absence of, in Celtic society, 227
- trade in, 172
- use of, 20, 256

Slavs, antecedents of, 107
sledges, invention of, 35, 66
sling, 238
Slovakia
- Bronze Age house sites in, 118, 126
- bronze corselet from, 154
- copper metallurgy in, 73-74, *74*

Snow, Lord, 10
social comprehension, enlargement of, 72
social organisation
- among barbarian peoples, 17
- and house-plans, 56
- and the building of Stonehenge, 139-40
- common, and the homeland of the Indo-European languages, 80-81
- evidence from graves, 129
- in Bronze Age, 129-30
- in Mediterranean, 140-1
- in northern Europe in second millennium, 140-1
- land-tenure and, 80
- of Danubian and allied cultures, 113
- of earliest peasant communities, 44
- of elected ruler, council of elders, and assembly of freemen, 80-81, 91, 106, 107, 227
- of Linear Pottery culture, 52
- of south-central European culture, 106-7
- of Tripolye culture, 54
- palace bureaucracies, 81
- single farmstead units, 199, 201
- skilled craftsmen and, 126

social organisation *contd*
stratified, in 2000 B.C., 118
teuta, 80
three-caste system, 80-81, 106-7, 140
warrior caste, 80-81, 106-7, 118, 227
society
aggression and the formation of, 14-15, 256
class-conscious, 118, 140-1
conserving, 17-18, 21-22, 27, 35, 44, 73, 92, 256-7
innovating, 17-18, 21-22, 72-73, 92, 255-6
pattern of Mycenaean, 126
readjustment to natural conditions, 27-28
stratified, 118, 126, 140-1
structure of barbaric and civilised, 16-17
structure of Celtic, 196, 207, 226-7, 229, 255-6
underdeveloped, 15-16, 20, 255
Sollas, 9
Solomon, 189
Somerset Fens, cart tracks in, 95
Sopron
pottery from, *197*, *198*, 199
vessels from, 181
South-central European culture
copper objects of, 102, *103*, 106
copper ores of, 102-3
distribution of copper objects, 103
fashions of, 102, 104-6
social structure of, 106-7
trade with Europe, 106
trade with Syria, 102-4
weapons of, 102, 104
South Italian-Sicilian cultures, generalised distribution of, *59*
South Russian Timber Grave culture
absence of princely graves, 130
art of, 130, 133, 176
as ancestors of the Scythians, 130, 132, 175, 176-7
as Homer's 'proud mare milkers', 130
burial of fleeces and hides, 130
cheek-pieces from, 95, *96*, 130
continuation of tradition, 130
evidence of domestication of the horse, 95, 130
graves and Mycenaean shaft-graves, 123
origin of name, 7
use of copper and bronze, 175
Spain
first agricultural settlements in, 56-57
painted pottery from, *225*
spear(s)
from Bavarian grave, 227, *228*
iron, 192
silver, 129
use in Celtic warfare, 238, 241
use in second millennium, 145, *147*
wooden, 29
spear-heads
from Bavarian grave, *228*
with gold ornament, *131*
spear-points
from Clacton, 29
Magdalenian, 28
Spencer, Herbert, 18-19
staffs, ferrules of, 136
'stamp seals'
Neolithic, *48*
used as amulets, 49
standing stones in Britain and Brittany, 115-16
Stanwick, site at, 220, 232
Staple Howe, 199, 204
Star Carr, hunting community site at, 32, 258
Starčevo-Körös culture
and allied cultures, generalised distribution of, *57*
distribution of, *43*
pottery figurines from, *48*
square wattle-and-mud-walled houses of, *47**
Starzeddel, fort at, 202
statue-menhirs, 62, 115
St Catherine's Hill, fort at, *206*
Ste Colombe
finds from, 193, *193*, 195
tumulus burials at, 187
steel
Damascene, 186
swords, 186, 238
use of, 247
Steinberg, hill-fort at, *218*
Stellmoor
camping-site of reindeer hunters at, 28-29
wooden arrows from, 29
Stentinello, ditch-enclosed settlement at, 59
stone
axe, hafted, *115*
axe-blades, 24, 39, *70**
axes, trade in, 64
bowls, 40
-built settlements of Nuraghic culture, *156*
-built towers, *157*
carvings, *128**
chambered tombs, *see* stone-chambered tombs
domestication of animals and Mesolithic equipment, 26

stone *contd*
dressing at Stonehenge, 138-9
edge tools, 113
grinding and polishing of, as criterion for classification, 26
human comprehension and working in, 71
implements of pre-pottery Neolithic people, 26, 40, 41
mace-heads, *128*
maces, 129
Mesolithic technology in, 25
monuments, Corsican carved, 155
relief, *253**, *256**
use of, for edge tools as criterion of Stone Age, 24
vessels of pre-pottery Neolithic cultures, 26
Stone Age
as a model of the past, 6
criteria of, 24
splitting of, 24
stone-chambered tombs
age of, 60
'Atlantic' type, 63
corbelled burial chambers, 60
decoration of, 61-62, *63**, *70**, 115
distribution of, 60
East Mediterranean origin of, 77
gallery grave, 61
generalised distribution of, *61*
in Britain, 63
in Scandinavia, 63
Marne chalk-cut, 62; 63*
notable examples of, 61, *62**
numbers of, 60
of Iberian copper 'colonies', 77
origin of, 60-61
passage graves, 61
religious significance of, 60, 114-15
variety of plans of, 60-61
West Kennet, 61, *62*
Stonehenge
Aegean influence at, 116, 138-9, 140
final phase of, 116
first phase of, 115
social organisation and the building of, 139-40
St Pol-de-Leon, La Tène pottery from, *242*
Strabo, 182, 223, 227, 235, 249
Stradonic, fort at, 220
strainers
distribution of beaten bronze, *154*
use of, 155
Straubing, copper objects from, *103*
Strelice, pottery model of house at, *46*
Strettweg, 'cult' vehicle from, *177**, 181, 194-5, 216, 239
Stukeley, William, 129
Sturt, George, 244
subsistence economies as models of the past, 6, 8
Sumer
background of civilisation, 44
battle-car from, 141-2
break up of central authority in, 77-78, 116, 118
copper smelting and casting in, 72
development of copper and bronze metallurgy in, 44
invention of writing and the emergence of, 44, 113
kingdom of, 113
social organisation of, 17, 81
words for carts and wagons in language of, 92
written records from, 44
Su Nuraxi, stone-built settlement at, *154**, *156*
Surčin, decorated antler and bone objects from, *135*
Sweden
rock-carvings of chariot wheels from, 142, *143*
rock-carvings of ploughing scenes from, 150
Swiss Lake Dwellings
horse-bits from, 177
houses with porches, 58
house-plans of, 57-58
populations of, 58-59
siting of, 57
village plans of, 58
Switzerland
Bronze Age houses in, 118, *119*
description of 'lake dwellings', 57-59
excavation of 'lake dwellings', 25
first agricultural settlements in, 57
hill-fort in, 179
post-glacial settlement in, 33
votive offerings from, 230
wagon graves in, 180
sword(s)
blade, engraving of boat on, 144, *144*
bronze flange-hilted, *148*
bronze from Britain, 189
bronze La Tène, 222
distribution of square-shouldered short, *139*
in Celtic warfare, 238
iron, 186, 188, 192, 216, 227, *228*, 238
La Tène, 216, 220, 222, 253
long, 145, 189, 216, 239
Mycenaean shaft-grave, 123
'Naue II type', distribution of, *148*
replacing daggers, 145-6, 147, 165

sword(s) *contd*
scabbards, distribution of, *239*, 239-40
short, 138, 145
slashing, 146, 159-60
steel, 186, 238
Syria
as the home of the war chariot, 141-2
contribution to toreutic arts, 171
burial customs of, 102
ingot-torcs from, 102
metalsmiths and merchants from, 102, 193
specific pin forms, 102
trade between south-central European cultures and, 102-4
Szentes-Vekerzug, wagon grave at, 179, 182

T

Tacitus, 182, 224, 229, 235, 236, 252, 260
Tain Bó Cuailnge, warrior aristocracy in, 106
Tal-i-Bakun, houses at, *45*
Tannstock, post-glacial settlement at, 33
Taranto, Mycenaean trading-post at, 134
Tarquinia phase of culture, 192
Tarxien, spiral relief carvings at, 98, *112**
tattooing, 239, *240**
techniques, problems of excavation, 10-11
technology
advances in Near East, 64
barbarism, civilisation and, 16-19
competence in agriculture, 16-17
disparities in, 26, 256-7
innovating societies, 17-18
innovations of writing and metallurgy, 44
new, for manufacturing flint tools and weapons, 27
of Mesolithic cultures, 25
precocity of innovation, 72-73
under-development and, 15-16, 20
westward movement of copper and bronze, 78
Telepinus myth, 130
tell
evidence from formations, 44
formation of, 49
section through, *47**
Tell Agrab, copper model from, 72, 107
'tell' settlements
houses of, 44
in Bulgaria, 46-47, 49, 91, 258
in Eastern Europe, 91-92, 113, 118
in Europe, 92, 113, 118
population of, 58-59
social structure of, 52, 56
supersession of culture, 145
temples
absence of evidence of, in Danubian culture, 114
absence of evidence of, in East Europe, 113-14
in Denmark, 115, *116*
in West Mediterranean, 114-15
plans of Malta, *98*
rock-cut, 97, *112**
stone-built, 97
trefoil-plan, 97
with spiral-relief carvings, 98, *112**
tent-stances
as the earliest humanly-constructed shelters, 29-30
circular, 30
construction of, 29-30
in central and East Europe, 30
Middle Palaeolithic Mousterian phase, 29, *29*, 30
of post-glacial period, 33
plans of, 33
Upper Palaeolithic, 29, *30*, *31*
Tepe Sialk, horse-bits from, 177
Terremare settlements, 129
teuta, 80
Teutones, 235
textiles
development of, in Europe, 60, 69
woven, 104-5
Theodosius, I, silver dish of, *257**, 260
theology and models of the past, 6, 7, 8
Thermi, *megaron* at, 121
Thompson, E. A., 16
Thomsen, Christian, 6, 24
Thorny Down, sub-rectangular houses at, 150, *153*
Thracians
chariot burials of, 238
Herodotus on, 181
hoards of, 226
tattooing practice among, 239
'Thraco-Cimmerian' horse-bit and harness-mountings, *178*, *179*, 1181
Thucydides, 140
Tiefenau, votive deposits from, 230
Timber Grave culture, *see* South Russian Timber Grave culture
tin
and copper for bronze-making, 72, 118
Cornwall mines, 120
Czechoslovakian deposits, 118
demand for, in 2000-1500 B.C., 134
Mycenaean sources of, 137
occurrence of, in Old World, 72
resources of Britain and Brittany, 120

'tipi rings', 33
Tisza culture
  anthropomorphic pot of, *49*
  end of, 91-92
  house decoration of, 89, *90*
  pottery figures of, *50*, *51**
Tiszafüred, decorated antler and bone object from, *135*
Tocharian language group, 91, 223
toga, 104-6
toggles for fastening clothes, 104
tombs
  megalithic, 114
  rock-cut in Malta, 97, 114-15
  stone-chambered, *see* stone-chambered tombs
tool(s)
  bronze, 129
  copper, 64, 102, 104
  distribution of, 106
  flint-bladed bone, *42*
  forms common to Iberia and the Aegean, 76
  harpoon-headed, *42*
  in non-metallic substances, 71
  iron, 185, 186, 187
  spread of Urnfield culture, 172-3
  stone for edge-, 113
tool-making
  Advanced Palaeolithic techniques, 27, 28
  Magdalenian, 28
torri, 155, *157*
Tószeg
  cheek-pieces from, 130, *132*
  houses at, 118
Totila, 240
Toulouse, gold offerings of, 231
towers, *see nuraghi*, *torri*
towns
  bastioned, of Iberia and the Aegean, 76-77, *77*
  Celtic, 218, 220, 244
  destruction of, 78, 79, 118, 121
  of peasant communities in Europe, 41
  wall-grit, of Homer's world, 140
Toynbee, Arnold, 6, 19
toys, 114
trade
  arrangements and skilled craftsmen, 126
  as a factor linking Eurasia, 74
  beginnings of, and the demand for metal, 72
  between south-central European culture and Syria, 102-4
  development of metallurgy and, 106, 118, 120
  in amber, 120, 137, *138*, 161
  in Bell-Beaker age, 100
  in copper products, 74
  in flint, obsidian, and other stones, 72, 97
  in raw materials and finished products, 118
  international in 2000-1500 B.C., 129
  La Tène, 216
  metal-working, consolidation and, 71-107
  Scythian, 176
  setting up of 'factories', 106
  trading-posts of the Mycenaeans, 133-4
  trans-alpine, 192, 216
  Transylvanian, 120, 136
transport
  development of trade and, 106
  domestication of animals for, 36
Transylvania
  control of metal resources, 145
  copper-working in, 73, 97, 113
  distribution of earliest copper industry, *75*
  pottery models of wagons from, *93*
  'tell' settlements in, 118, 145
  trade with rest of Europe, 120, 136
TRB cultures
  generalised distribution of, *59*
  generalised distribution of earliest finds, *63*
trephining saw, 227, *228*
Trialeti, grave finds at, 130
tribe, 227
Tri Brata barrows, finds from, *83*
Tripolye culture
  anthropomorphic 'altars' from, 56, *56*
  clay-rendered gable-end of house, *55*, 56
  defended promontory settlement of, *54*, 54, 56
  destruction of settlements, 84
  figures of, 54
  generalised distribution of, *59*
  generalised distribution of sites, *63*
  impact of steppe peoples on, 91
  long houses of, 54, 56
  social organisation of, 54
  village plan of, 54, *54*, *55*, 56
  villages, size of, 54
trousers, 104, 199, 238, 240
Troy
  destruction of second city, 78
  myths concerning the war of, 168
  II, *megara* at, 121
  II, size of, 122
  II, timber-lacing at, 204
  II, 'treasures' of, 130
  VI, date of siege, 159
  VI, size of, 122

Troy *contd*
  VIIa, date of siege, 159
  VIIb, as the city of the siege, 159
The Trundle, hill-fort at, *206*
Truşeşti
  anthropomorphic altar from, *56*
Tsangli, house-plans at, 44, *45*
Tudhaliyas IV, 159
Turkmenia
  cities of, 17
  conserving peasant communities in, 44
  excavations at Anau, 25
  houses in, 41, 44, *45*
  peasant communities in, 41, 44
  towns in, 41
  villages in, 41, 44
turquoise from Kurgan culture graves, 82
Tursha, 158
Tüsköves
  anthropomorphic pot from, *49*
  pottery figures from, *50*
Tustrup, temple at, *116*
Tyrol
  copper resources from, 118, 155, 196, 197
  'factories' in, 106
  salt-mines of, 196, 197
Tyrrhenians, 159, 160

U

Uffing, wooden drinking-cup from, 187
Ugarit, copper objects from, 102
Ukraine
  settlement patterns in, 113
  tent-stances in, 30
  Tripolye culture in, 54, *55*, 56
Ulster cycle, 140, 226, 238
under-development
  explanations of, 15
  in prehistory, 16, 255
  reasons for, 15
  technology and, 15-16, 20
Únětice culture
  bronze metallurgy of, 123, 126
  daggers, 123, *125*, 126
  grave, *127*, 129, *129**
Upper Palaeolithic
  period as a classification, 24
  settlement of, *31*
  tent-stances, 29, *30*
Upton Lovel
  amber beads from, *137*
  faience necklace from, *135**
Ur, wagons from, 246
Urartians
  and the Cimmerians, 175
  contribution to the toreutic arts, 171
  metal-working skill of, 175, 193
  Scythians and, 176, 189
  single-piece bronze cauldrons, 193
urbanisation
  among non-literate peoples, 17
  in Near East and Eastern Europe, 113
  in the Mediterranean, 141
Urnfield culture
  art of, 241
  burial rites of, 145, 168, 232, *234*
  contact with Britain, 223
  distribution of beaten bronze vessels of, *154*
  distribution of bronze helmets, *169*
  distribution of swords of Naue II type, *148*
  end of, 188-9
  fortifications, *208**, *209**, *216**
  forts of, 179, 202, *203*
  generalised map of expansion of, *146*
  helmets of, 169, 171, 239
  houses of, *149*, 151, 199
  settlement of, 147, *149*, 150, *151*, 199
  spread of, 172-4

V

Vače, situla from, *161**
Vachères, sculpture from, 240
Val Camonica
  cult site at, 230, 232
  rock-carvings from, 150
value-judgments on civilisation and barbarism, 19-20
Vapheio cup, 134
vase
  Greek Geometric, 181
  Greek painted, 195
  -painting, Attic and Corinthian, 189, 192
  -painting, Iberian, 223, *225*
  silver, from Maikop, 95
Vattina, decorated antler and bone objects from, *135*
vehicles
  and the Indo-European languages, 96-97
  basic forms of wheeled, 92
  communities which use, 92
  distribution of models of, *94*
  distribution of solid-wheeled, *94*
  four-wheeled, 92
  in burials, *94*
  solid-wheeled wooden, 82, *94*, 109, 141-2
  spoked-wheeled in Britain, 189

vehicles *contd*
story of wheeled draught, 92-95
three-wheeled, 92
two-wheeled, 92
wheeled, as a feature of an undivided Indo-European homeland, 80, 109
Verulamium, wheel-ruts at, 245
vessel(s)
distribution of beaten bronze, *154*
Hallstatt bronze, *192**
silver, from Maikop, *82*
silver, from Mycenaean shaft-grave, *124*
types of beaten bronze, 154
vetches, initial cultivation of, 39
Vĕteřov, decorated antler and bone objects from, *135*
Vetulonia, situla from, 171
Viking
barrow burials, 89
settlements in South Russia, 226
ships, shields on, 145
Vila Nova de São Pedro, copper 'colony' settlement at, 76, 98
village(s)
'collective' in Indo-European society, 80-81
in Britain, 236-8
of Celtic Europe, 244
of Kurgan culture, 81
of peasant communities in Europe, 41
of Urnfield culture, 147
palisaded timber-built, 140
plan of Celtic, 258-9
plan of Linear Pottery culture, 52, 147
plan of scattered houses in, 46
plan of Swiss Lake, 58
plan of Tripolye culture, 54, *54*, *55*, 56
population of Linear Pottery culture, 52
population of peasant, 47
settlement pattern of, in Turkmenia, 44
size of Corded Ware, 89
size of Linear Pottery culture, 52, 86, 89
size of Tripolye culture, 54
Villanova, 192
Vinča, decorated antler and bone objects from, *135*
Virgil, 168
viticulture, 155
Vix, Celtic burial at, 89, *184*, 187, 188, 195, *200**, 244
votive deposits, 230-1, 239, 240, 250

W

wagon(s)
as vehicles with four wheels, 92, 238, 245
dispersal of, and Indo-European languages, 95
evidence for early existence in Europe 92, 95
farm, 245
graves, *see* wagon-graves
Hallstatt, 244, 245
hub-mounting of, 179
La Tène, 245-6
models of, *93*, 95, *97**
modern distribution of, in Europe, 95
solid-wheeled wooden, 82, *97**, 130, 133, 141-2, 196
spoked four-wheeled, 179
Sumerian and Akkadian words for, 92
warfare and, 141-2
zone, 95, 244
wagon-graves
at Heuneburg, 205, 207
Czechoslovakian, 180, 186
distribution of Hallstatt C and D, *180*
finds from Hallstatt D, *183*, 183-4, *184*
history of, 179-80
spread of, 184-5
supersession of, 215, 238
Wales
horse-bits from, 177
metal resources of, 120
rectangular houses in, 63
trade routes through, 120
votive offerings from, 230
war-chariots
Celtic, 215, 238-41
Greek, 123
light carts as, 92
origin of, 141-42
warfare
burials and, 238-41
Celtic chariot, 215, 238-41
chariot, in Egypt, 142,
Cimmerian, 181
depicted on engraved gold ring, *147*
development of the art of, 141-5
domestication of the horse and, 141-2, 238-41
fighting tactics, 145-6
improvement in the art of, 157-8
invention of the spoked wheel and, 141
representations of, 142
the break up of Mycenaean power and, 145-6
the wheel and, 141-2
warrior caste
aristocracy, 181, 215, 227
Aryan, 142
equipment of south-central European culture, 102, 104
graves of, 126-33
in literature, 106
in Northern Europe in the second millennium, 140-1

warrior caste *contd*
  in the structure of Indo-European society, 80-81, 89, 92, 118
  mounted, 180-1
  rise of the, 106-7
  weapons buried with, 84, 89, 102, 104, 129-30
Wasserberg, settlement at, 147, *149*
wattle-and-mud houses, 44, 46, *47*, *47**, *97**, *112**
wax, trade in, 171-2
weapon(s)
  Advanced Palaeolithic techniques in the making of, 27
  bronze, *125*, 129
  buried with warriors, 84, 89, 102, 104, 129-30
  copper, 102
  distribution of, 106
  from Mycenaean shaft-graves, 123
  increasing use of, 118
  iron, 185, 186
  Magdalenian, 28
  new style of, 104
  of south-central European culture, 102, 104
  spread of Urnfield culture, 172-3
Wessex culture
  metal industries of, 120
  objects from graves of, *128*, 129, 134
  trade of, 129
Western Europe
  folk-movement at the end of the third millennium, 97-102
  settlement patterns in 2000 B.C., 113
'Western' European cultures, generalised distribution of, *59*
West Harling, settlement at, 236
West Kennet
  Bell-Beaker pottery from, *112**
  chambered tomb at, 61, 62, *62*
West Plean, house-plan at, *237*
West Side Story, 256
wheat
  distribution of, 36, *38*
  initial cultivation of, 40-41, 60
  varieties of, 38, 39
wheel(s)
  as a feature of an undivided Indo-European homeland, 80
  bronze-sheathed wooden, 196
  common words for axles, hubs and yokes, 80
  distribution of models of, *94*
  distribution of wooden, *94*
  hoop-tyres on, 244
  hub-mountings of, 179, 196
  iron-tyred, 244, *245*
  La Tène, 244-6, *245*
  -making and the development of iron tools, 187
  models of spoked, 142
  of carts in burials, *83*
  rock-carvings of, *143*
  single-felloe, 142, 244, *245*
  solid, 82, 92, *96**, 130, *133*, 141-2
  spoked, 80, 92, 130, 141-2, *143*, 189, 244
  standard gauge, 244-5
  story of the, 92-95
  straked, 244
wheelhouse, 236
wheelwrights, 244-7, 258
whetstones, ceremonial, 129
whistles, possible invention of, 35
William of Rubruck, 89
Wilson, Daniel, 3
Windmill Hill culture
  distribution of main sites of, *58*
  domestication of animals by, 258
wine, trade in, 155, 168, 187, 195, 242, 252-3
wine-flagons
  distribution of Roman, *255*
  in Europe, 195, *208*, 215*, 216, *241**, *242*, 253
Wittnauer Horn, fort at, 202
Wixhausen, dress-pins from, *105*
Wölfflin, 7
Wollmesheim grave, finds from, 183
wolves, domestication of, 35
wood
  arrows of, 29
  bowls of, *144**, 145
  cheek-pieces of, *178**
  drinking-cup of, 187
  from Stone Age, 24
  human comprehension and working in, 71
  spears of, 29
Woodchester, Roman villa at, 122
woodlands, beginning of, 31
woollen textiles
  at Çatal Hüyük, 36
  Celtic, 249
  fine clothing, 156-7, *160**
  from barrow burials, 156
  Hallstatt, 197
Wrekin, The, hill-fort at, *206*
wrist-guard, Bell-Beaker archer's, *99*, 100
writing, the invention of, 44

Y

Y Corddyn, hill-fort at, 220
Yeavering, site at, 238

Z

Zavist, *oppidum* of, *219*, 220
Zawi Chemi Shanidar, 39-40
Zharovka, mail from, 240
Zimbabwe, 140
Zoldshalompuszta, gold stag of, 182
zoology
 and classification of cultures, 24-25
 and prehistory, 8, 9, 64
 classification of discarded food bones, 24-25
 limiting the likely area of initial domestication, 36
 natural factors of, and the beginnings of agriculture, 26, 27